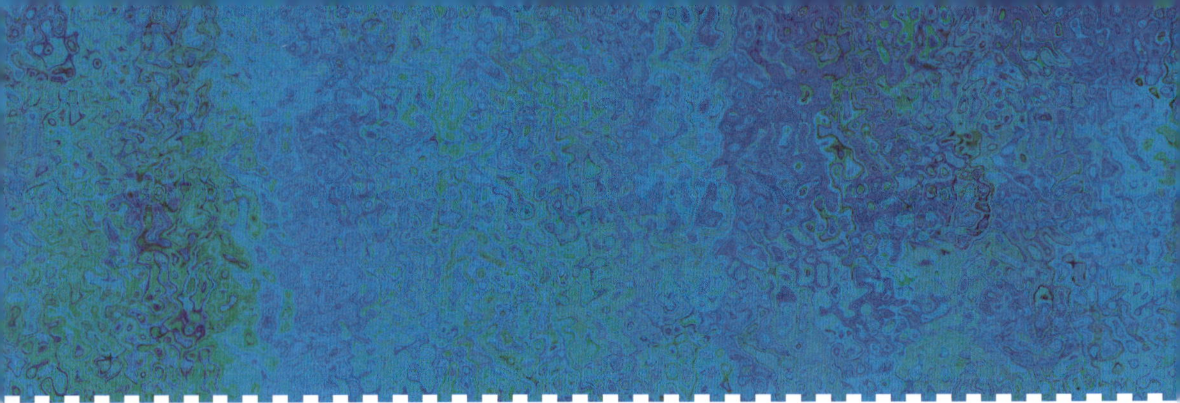

PHILANTHROPY

IN THE BAY AREA FOR BETTER LIFE

THE FOURTH WORLD PHILANTHROPY FORUM

慈善湾区 美好生活

第四届世界公益慈善论坛

（上册）

汉英对照

本书编写组 编

第四届世界公益慈善论坛部分与会人员合影

Photo of Participants of the Fourth World Philanthropy Forum (WPF)

第四届世界公益慈善论坛部分与会人员闭幕式合影

Photo of Participants of the Fourth World Philanthropy Forum at the Closing Ceremony

中国第十三届全国政协副主席李斌发言

Speech by Li Bin, Vice-Chairperson of the 13th National Committee of the Chinese People's Political Consultative Conference

第四届世界公益慈善论坛会见（左起：卡洛斯·列朗、彼得·麦杰西、李斌、李小林）

Meetings of Leaders (From Left: Carles Llorens, Péter Medgyessy, Li Bin, Li Xiaolin)

论坛联合主席、中国人民对外友好协会会长李小林主持
Host of Officiating Speech, Li Xiaolin, Co-chair of the World Philanthropy Forum, President of the Chinese People's Association for Friendship with Foreign Countries

论坛联合主席、清华大学校务委员会主任陈旭致辞
Speech by Chen Xu, Co-chair of the World Philanthropy Forum, Chairperson of Tsinghua University Council

论坛联合主席、香港中文大学校长段崇智致辞

Speech by Rocky S. Tuan, Co-chair of the World Philanthropy Forum,
Vice-Chancellor and President of the Chinese University of Hong Kong

香港大学副校长区洁芳致辞

（论坛联合主席、香港大学校长张翔视频致辞，香港大学副校长区洁芳代为现场致辞）

Speech by Terry Au, Vice-President and Pro-Vice-Chancellor of The University of Hong Kong
(On behalf of Professor Zhang Xiang, Co-Chair of the World Philanthropy Forum,
President and Vice-Chancellor of University of Hong Kong. Professor Zhang Xiang gave a speech via video.)

彼得·麦杰西

匈牙利前总理

论坛顾问、匈牙利前总理彼得·麦杰西发言

Speech by Péter Medgyessy, WPF Advisor, Former Prime Minister of Hungary

论坛顾问、意大利前总理马西莫·达莱马致辞

Speech by Massimo D' Alema, WPF Advisor, Former Prime Minister of Hungary

第四届世界公益慈善论坛开幕式会议现场

Meeting Venue of the Fourth World Philanthropy Forum Opening Ceremony

第四届世界公益慈善论坛联合主办方代表、深圳市副市长艾学峰致辞

Speech by Ai Xuefeng, Representative of co-host of the Fourth World Philanthropy Forum, Vice Mayer of Shenzhen Municipal People's Government

论坛顾问、中国民政部副部长王爱文演讲

Speech by Wang Aiwen, WPF Advisor, Vice Minister of Ministry of Civil Affairs of the People's Republic of China,

中国中央人民政府驻香港特别行政区联络办公室副主任谭铁牛致辞

Speech by Tan Tieniu, Deputy Director of the Liaison Office of the Central People's Government in the Hong Kong S.A.R

香港赛马会主席周永健演讲

Speech by Dr. Chow Wing-kin, Anthony, Chairman of the Hong Kong Jockey Club

联合国儿童基金会私人筹款和伙伴关系部总监加里·斯塔尔演讲

Speech by Gary Stahl, Director of Division of Private Fundraising and Partnerships of UNICEF

慈善湾区与人才培养专题（左起：张亮、王淑英、肖海鹏、楚明伟）
Philanthropy in the Greater Bay Area and Talent Nurturing
(From Left: Cheung Leong, Wong Suk-ying, Xiao Haipeng, Christopher Tremewan)

21世纪公共健康与慈善专题
（左起：阿尼尔·卡普尔、加斯普·布兰德佳德、刘斯奇、罗乐宣、林大庆）
Public Health and Philanthropy in the 21st Century
(From Left: Anil Kapur, Jesper Brandgaard, Liu Siqi, Luo Lexuan, Lam Tai-hing)

青年与湾区社会创新和社会企业专题（左起：何永昌、查尔斯·埃斯利、吴学明）
Youths, Community Innovation & Social Enterprise in the Greater Bay Area
(From Left: Ho Wing-cheong, Charles Eesley, Wu Xueming)

体育人慈善路专题（左起：莫滕·汉森、李娜、李希奎、胡里奥·冈萨雷斯·隆科、张强强）
Sports and Philanthropy
(From Left: Morten Mølholm Hansen, Li Na, Li Xikui, Julio Ronco Gonzalez, Zhang Qiangqiang)

高等教育社会捐赠的探索与实践——中国案例专题
（左起：涂蓉辉、赵文莉、梁晖、房涛、刘迅、沈黎勇、袁桅、王振民）
Philanthropy & Fundraising in Higher Education – China's Practice
(From Left: Tu Ronghui, Zhao Wenli, Liang Hui, Fang Tao, Liu Xun, Shen Liyong, Yuan Wei, Wang Zhenmin)

善财传承专题
Wealth and Philanthropy

赠与亚洲理事长薛希璞（左上）主持善财传承圆桌专题
珀杜家族与喜来登家族代表米齐·珀杜（右上）、清华大学华商研究中心主任龙登高（左下）
与中欧商学院教授及中欧家族传承研究中心联合主任芮萌（右下）进行专题演讲

Moderator: George SyCip, Board Chairman of Give2Asia (Upper Left)
Speakers: Mitzi Perdue, on behalf of Perdue & Sheraton Family (Upper Right).
Long Denggao, Director of Center for Chinese Entrepreneur Studies, Tsinghua University (Lower Left).
Rui Meng, Professor of China Europe International Business School,
Co-Director of CEIBS Centre for Family Heritage (Lower Right)

湾区未来，儿童福利专题——儿童健康与福祉

（左起：刘庆龙、郭朋、黄文锋、魏巍、侯春艳、塞巴斯蒂安·库斯特、霍泰辉、王林）

Future Visions for Children's Wellbeing: Children's health and welfare

(From Left: Liu Qinglong, Guo Peng, Huang Wenfeng, Wei Wei, Hou Chunyan, Sebastien Kuster, Fok Tai-fai, Wang Lin)

湾区未来，儿童福利专题——为所有儿童提供教育的机会

（左起：郑道、彼得·威廉姆斯、萧凯恩、李红艳、塞巴斯蒂安·库斯特、吕德雄）

Future Visions for Children's Wellbeing: Providing All Children with a chance of education

(From Left: Douglas Noble, Peter Williams, Siu Hoi Yan, Li Hongyan, Sebastien Kuster, Lyu Dexiong)

善学明辨专题

Education and Philanthropy

“一带一路”公益慈善合作专题（左起：卡洛斯·列朗、梁星心、林碧玉、凌冲、陈勇）

Philanthropic Cooperation with Countries along the “Belt and Road Initiative”
(From Left: Carles Llorens, Liang Xingxin, Lin Biyu, Ling Chong, Chan Yung)

全国工商联原副主席、天津市人大常委会原副主任，中华红丝带基金理事长张元龙演讲

Speech by Zhang Yuanlong, Former Vice Chairman of All-China Federation of Industry and Commerce, Former Deputy Director of the Standing Committee of Tianjin Municipal People's Congress, and Chairman of the China Red Ribbon Foundation

湾区发展，善商之道专题（左起：张俊勇、索尔坦・玛姆玛多夫、黄学思、张元龙、陈家乐）

How to Develop a Good Business Path in the Greater Bay Area

(From Left: Thomas Cheung Tsun-Yung, Soltan Mammadov, Wong H. Henry, Zhang Yuanlong, Kalok Chan)

腾讯集团主要创始人、腾讯公益慈善基金会发起人兼荣誉理事长陈一丹演讲

Speech by Chen Yidan, Co-Founder of Tencent Group, Initiator and Honorary Chairman of Tencent Charity Foundation

论坛联合主席、中国人民对外友好协会会长李小林为匈牙利前总理彼得・麦杰西颁发第四届世界公益慈善论坛顾问证书

WPF Advisor Certificate Presentation（From Left: Li Xiaolin, Péter Medgyessy）

论坛联合主席、中国人民对外友好协会会长李小林与意大利前总理马西莫・达莱马
举行会见并颁发第四届世界公益慈善论坛顾问证书
Meetings of Leaders and WPF Advisor Certificate Presentation
（From Left: Massimo D' Alema , Li Xiaolin）

慈善湾区 美好生活
Philanthropy in the Bay Area for Better Life
2019.9.5-6

论坛联合主席、中国人民对外友好协会会长李小林为
第四届世界公益慈善论坛合作伙伴颁发证书
WPF Partner Certificate Presentation

战略合作伙伴及合作伙伴
Strategic Partners and Partners
深圳市基金会发展促进会 Shenzhen Commonweal Fund Federation
创行
TCL公益基金会
赠与亚洲

论坛顾问、匈牙利前总理彼得·麦杰西
为第四届世界公益慈善论坛战略合作伙伴及合作伙伴颁发证书
WPF Strategic Partners and Partners Certificate Presentation

世界公益慈善论坛
WORLD PHILANTHROPY FORUM
支持单位
Supporting Units
山西省公益事业促进会
Shanxi Welfare Work Promotion Association
上海市华侨事业发展基金会
Shanghai Overseas Chinese Foundation
浙江省社会组织总会

论坛顾问、意大利前总理马西莫·达莱马为第四届世界公益慈善论坛支持单位颁发证书
WPF Supporting Units Certificate Presentation

世界公益慈善论坛·地方政府慈善促进合作计划启动
（左起：卡洛斯·列朗、阿尼尔·卡普尔、邓岚）
Launch of Regional and Local Governments Philanthropy Promotion Cooperation Plan
(From Left: Carles Llorens, Anil Kapur, Deng Lan)

世界公益慈善论坛·善财传承计划启动
（左起：曾宪章、薛希璞、马洁芝、比格尔·斯坦德伯格）
Launch of Philanthropy and Wealth Inheritance Plan
(From Left: Carter Tseng, George SyCip, Jennifer Ma, Birger Stamperdahl)

世界公益慈善论坛 · 社会服务领军人才培养计划发布

（左起：倪锡钦、刘庆龙）

Announcement of Social Services Leading Talents Training Plan

(From Left: Ngai Sek-yum, Liu Qinglong)

世界公益慈善论坛 · 基金会国际友好合作计划启动

（左起：黄真平、陈行甲）

Launch of Foundation's International Friendship and Cooperation Program

(From Left: Huang Zhenping, Chen Xingjia)

国际公益人才培养计划代表团在泰国参加联合国开发计划署（UNDP）
社会组织国际合作培训工作坊

International Philanthropic Talent Development Plan Delegation attended the UNDP's training workshop on the international cooperation of social organizations in Thailand

国际公益人才培养计划代表团在越南与越南友好组织联合会主席阮芳娥女士（中）合影

International Philanthropic Talent Development Plan Delegation with Ms. Nguyen Phuong Nga (Center), President of Vietnam Union of Friendship Organizations in Vietnam

国际公益人才培养计划代表团在菲律宾出席“中菲气候变化研讨会”
International Philanthropic Talent Development Plan Delegation attended the "China-Philippines Seminar on Climate Change" in the Philippines

国际公益人才培养计划代表团在中国香港参加香港中文大学国际慈善项目管理培训工作坊
International Philanthropic Talent Development Plan Delegation attended the training workshop of The Chinese University of Hong Kong on the Management of International Philanthropic Projects

世界公益慈善论坛2019年华人社会工作协同合作年会会议现场

Meeting Venue of the WPF 2019 Annual Meeting of Collaboration Mechanism for Chinese Social Work

世界公益慈善论坛2019年华人社会工作协同合作年会部分与会嘉宾合影

Group Photo of WPF 2019 Annual Meeting of Collaboration Mechanism for Chinese Social Work

世界公益慈善论坛2018年华人社会工作协同合作年会部分与会嘉宾合影

Group Photo of the WPF 2018 Annual Meeting of Collaboration Mechanism for Chinese Social Work

世界公益慈善论坛2018年华人社会工作协同合作年会部分与会嘉宾于会场合影

Group Photo of the WPF 2018 Annual Meeting of Collaboration Mechanism for Chinese Social Work of at the Meeting Venue

目 录

第一部分 主旨演讲

一 主旨发言 003

主持人：中国人民对外友好协会会长、论坛联合主席 / 李小林

主旨发言：**续写公益慈善事业新篇章**

中国第十三届全国政协副主席 / 李斌

善用金融力量促成美好社会——匈牙利经济模式经验谈

匈牙利前总理 / 彼得·麦杰西

二 嘉宾致辞 010

主持人：中国人民对外友好协会秘书长、中国友好和平发展基金会理事长 / 李希奎

中国中央人民政府驻香港特别行政区联络办公室副主任 / 谭铁牛 致辞

清华大学党委书记、校务委员会主任、论坛联合主席 / 陈旭 致辞

香港大学副校长 / 区洁芳 致辞

香港大学校长、论坛联合主席 / 张翔 视频致辞

香港中文大学校长、论坛联合主席 / 段崇智 致辞

深圳市副市长 / 艾学峰 致辞

三 主题演讲 018

聚慈善之力助推湾区发展，扬慈善精神共建美好世界

中国民政部副部长 / 王爱文

慈善共创 建设更美好社会——香港赛马会经验浅谈

香港赛马会主席 / 周永健

公益促进发展 携手为儿童

联合国儿基会私人筹款和伙伴关系部总监 / 加里·斯塔尔

第二部分 专题对话

四 慈善湾区与人才培养 031

主持人：环太平洋大学联盟秘书长 / 楚明伟

对话嘉宾：中山大学副校长 / 肖海鹏

香港中文大学协理副校长、社会学系教授 / 王淑英

香港赛马会慈善及社区事务执行总监 / 张亮

五 21 世纪公共健康与慈善 040

主持人：香港大学李嘉诚医学院罗旭龢基金教授（公共卫生学）、社会医学讲座教授 / 林大庆

对话嘉宾：世界糖尿病基金会主席 / 阿尼尔·卡普尔
诺和诺德血友病基金会委员会主席 / 加斯普·布兰德佳德
华大集团联合创始人、监事长，深圳猛犸公益基金会理事长 / 刘斯奇
深圳市卫生健康委员会主任 / 罗乐宣

六 青年与湾区社会创新和社会企业 052
主持人：粤港澳大湾区青年总会主席兼执行主席 / 吴学明
对话嘉宾：斯坦福大学管理科学与工程系学者 / 查尔斯·埃斯利
香港青年协会总干事 / 何永昌

七 体育人慈善路 062
主持人：北京体育大学产业管理集团总经理 / 张强强
对话嘉宾：皇家马德里基金会总经理 / 胡里奥·冈萨雷斯·隆科
中国网球运动员、亚洲首位大满贯单打冠军得主 / 李娜
中国人民对外友好协会秘书长、中国友好和平发展基金会理事长 / 李希奎
丹麦国家奥林匹克委员会首席执行官兼秘书长 / 莫滕·汉森

八 善财传承 074
主持人：赠与亚洲理事长 / 薛希璞
赠与亚洲理事 / 曾宪章
对话嘉宾：论坛学术委员会委员、中欧国际工商学院教授及中欧家族传承研究中心联合主任 / 芮萌

珀杜家族、喜来登家族代表 / 米奇·珀杜
亚洲艺术品金融商学院院长 / 范勇
赠与亚洲总裁兼首席执行官 / 比格尔·斯坦普德尔
福特基金会北京代表处首席代表 / 高倩倩
纽约梅隆银行财富规划师 / 贾斯汀·米勒
纽约梅隆银行高级总监 / 琼·克雷恩
香港科技大学陈江和亚洲家族企业与创业研究中心主任 / 彭倩
连氏基金会主席、亚洲慈善圈创始人 / 连宗诚
联合国驻纽约业务伙伴关系司前司长 / 萨卡·科佩拉
芝加哥白沙集团投资基金合伙人 / 埃利奥特·唐纳利
香港荣信远东集团有限公司董事长 / 彭敏
论坛学术委员会委员、清华大学华商研究中心主任 / 龙登高

九　高等教育社会捐赠的探索与实践：中国案例　124
主持人：香港浸会大学协理副校长 / 黄煜
清华大学法学院教授、清华大学教育基金会理事 / 王振民
嘉宾演讲：**教育兴邦，百年树人**
广东省国强公益基金会理事长 / 陈翀
捐赠高等教育心得分享
张荣发基金会总执行长 / 钟德美
中国高等教育慈善捐赠的若干思考
香港中文大学国学中心主任 / 邓立光
对话嘉宾：广州市东浦混凝土有限公司总经理 / 梁晖
深圳市政协常委、深圳市慈善会执行副会长兼秘书长 / 房涛

深圳市新同方投资管理有限公司董事长 / 刘迅

浙江大学教育基金会秘书长 / 沈黎勇

清华大学教育基金会秘书长 / 袁桅

南方科技大学教育基金会秘书长 / 涂蓉辉

北京大学教育基金会副秘书长 / 赵文莉

十 湾区未来，儿童福利 151

主持人：论坛学术委员会委员，清华大学公共管理学院教授 / 刘庆龙

联合国儿童基金会驻华办事处副代表 / 郑道

嘉宾演讲：**儿童大病救助的探索之路**

中华少年儿童慈善救助基金会理事长 / 王林

全民教育的中国之路与国际努力——从一个教育家的宏愿说起

中国陶行知研究会常务副会长兼秘书长 / 吕德雄

对话嘉宾：北京一路阳光慈善基金会创始人、理事 / 郭朋

凤凰网副总编辑 / 侯春艳

香港中文大学副校长 / 霍泰辉

深圳市妇女儿童发展基金会秘书长 / 黄文锋

救助儿童会北京代表处首席运营官 / 塞巴斯蒂安·库斯特

鼎昆教育集团董事长 / 魏巍

联合国教科文组织教育顾问 / 李红艳

菲律宾国际乡村建设学院主席 / 彼得·威廉

著名钢琴家，融合教育倡议者 / 萧凯恩

十一 善学明辨 189

主持人：北京师范大学法学院宪法与行政法教研中心主任 / 刘培峰

嘉宾演讲：**中国民间社会发展指数报告**

清华大学公益慈善研究院副院长 / 贾西津

好公益指数：亚洲慈善事业发展趋势

亚洲慈善与社会中心首席执行官 / 夏露萍

中国慈善行业调研报告

亚洲公益创投网络首席战略官 / 艾莉森·霍洛韦尔

善经济的思想与实践

善经济倡导者、慈济人文志业发展处主任 / 何日生

中国公益慈善人才的培养机制和项目探索

论坛学术委员会委员、香港中文大学社会工作学系教授及系主任 / 倪锡钦

国际公益人才培养计划：中国香港及泰国参访汇报

深圳市企业评价协会常务副会长兼秘书长 / 李亚平

国际公益人才培养计划：菲律宾及越南参访汇报

深圳市恒晖儿童公益基金会创始人 / 陈行甲

对话嘉宾：清华大学公益慈善研究院副院长 / 贾西津

亚洲慈善与社会中心首席执行官 / 夏露萍

亚洲公益创投网络首席战略官 / 艾莉森·霍洛韦尔

善经济倡导者、慈济人文志业发展处主任 / 何日生

论坛学术委员会委员、香港中文大学社会工作学系教授及系主任 / 倪锡钦

深圳市企业评价协会常务副会长兼秘书长 / 李亚平

深圳市恒晖儿童公益基金会创始人 / 陈行甲
点评嘉宾：亚洲理工学院尤努斯社会事业中心发展管理主任、塔玛萨特大学创新学院客座教授 / 法伊兹·沙阿
越南农村可持续发展中心常务主任 / 阮金恩

十二 “一带一路”公益慈善合作 228
主持人：中国第十三届全国人大代表、香港新界社团联会理事长、香港民主建港协进联盟副主席 / 陈勇
对话嘉宾：世界大区联合组织秘书长 / 卡洛斯·列朗
中国浙江省社会组织总会会长 / 梁星心
慈济基金会副总执行长 / 林碧玉
中国深圳市社会组织管理局局长 / 凌冲

十三 湾区发展，善商之道 235
主持人：论坛学术委员会委员、香港中文大学工商管理学院院长 / 陈家乐
对话嘉宾：华钻创投董事长 / 黄学思
盖达尔·阿利耶夫基金会国际关系部负责人 / 索尔坦·玛姆玛多夫
中国第十三届全国人大代表、国际潮青联合会执行会长 / 张俊勇
嘉宾演讲：**善心改变世界**
全国工商联原副主席、天津市人大常委会原副主任、中华红丝带基金理事长 / 张元龙

十四 闭幕式 251

主持人：中国人民对外友好协会秘书长、中国友好和平发展基金会理事长 / 李希奎

嘉宾演讲：**公益无国界，以理性精神推动全球公益可持续发展**

腾讯集团主要创始人、腾讯公益慈善基金会发起人兼荣誉理事长 / 陈一丹

闭幕致辞

意大利前总理 / 马西莫·达莱马

第三部分

十五 成果发布、证书颁发 263

第一部分

主旨演讲

一　主旨发言

主　　持　　人：中国人民对外友好协会会长、论坛联合主席　李小林

主旨发言嘉宾：中国第十三届全国政协副主席　李斌

匈牙利前总理　彼得·麦杰西

续写公益慈善事业新篇章

中国第十三届全国政协副主席　李　斌

尊敬的彼得·麦杰西先生，各位来宾，女士们，先生们，大家上午好，很高兴来到美丽、开放、富饶的深圳，和各位嘉宾共同出席第四届世界公益慈善论坛。今天是一年一度的“国际慈善日”及“中华慈善日”，来自各行各业致力于慈善发展的中外嘉宾齐聚一堂、共迎盛会，具有特殊的意义，首先请允许我对远道而来的各位嘉宾，表示热烈的欢迎。

当今世界正处于大发展、大变革、大调整时期，国际形势正发生着深刻复杂的变化，世界多极化、经济全球化深入发展，科技革命取得新的突破，社会信息化影响越来越大。国际社会相互联系、相互依存更加紧密，和平、发展、合作、共赢已经成为世界潮流，中国人民历来重友谊，重责任，讲信义，讲和平，对和平和睦的追求深深植根于中华民族的精神世界。中国始终是世界和平的建设者，全球发展的贡献者，国际秩序的维护者。我们将继续坚定不移走和平发展道路，推动构建人类命运共同体。我们将继续秉持共商、共建、共享原则，加强和世界各国的互融互建，将自身的

发展和机遇与世界各国分享，为实现共同发展贡献中国智慧、中国方案和中国力量。

在新的历史背景下，公益慈善发挥着重要的作用，习近平总书记多次强调，要树立慈善意识，发展慈善事业，慈善代表了仁慈、富裕、善良，集合了人类最朴素的情感，慈善事业是这些内涵的具体化和实现化，是人类爱心的表现，对改善民生具有重要的作用。慈善事业的不断发展是社会文明进步的重要标准之一，我们要用切实有效的方法尊重、增进各国人民之间的情谊，让地球村更加和睦，让人类文明永不止步。

近年来，中国慈善事业蓬勃发展，截止到 2018 年底，中国社会捐赠总额达到 1128 亿元，中国社会组织总的数量超过了 80.6 万个，志愿者服务的时间为 21.97 亿小时，贡献价值达到 823 亿元。慈善事业法制建设不断健全，社会组织管理办法、慈善组织公开办法等一系列政策法规出台，完善了《慈善法》的配套体系。伴随着公益事业的不断发展，世界公益慈善论坛莅临中国，面向世界，甚至于促进公益慈善组织的学术交流、政策探讨、经验分享和人才培养，推动更多的公益慈善组织参与社会建设，为各国公益慈善机构资源共享提供了重要的平台，有力地促进了世界慈善事业的发展。本届论坛在粤港澳大湾区重要城市——深圳召开，以“慈善湾区 美好生活”为主题，旨在以公益慈善为抓手，以湾区发展为基点，以改善民生为目标，围绕人才交流、青年创新、健康卫生、教育、“一带一路”建设等领域，分享发展的经验，实现互利合作。我们期待以论坛为平台，为世界公益事业的发展贡献力量。

女士们，先生们，朋友们，中国有一句古话——“上善若水”，公益慈善的力量会像水一样，润物无声，希望公益慈善人不忘初心，持之以恒，不断推动论坛迈上新高度，实现新突破，立足论坛展望未来。

我也提出三点建议。（1）加强平台建设，深化合作。世界公益慈善论坛作为交流的重要平台，旨在为公益慈善组织构建信任与支持，共享资源与信息，我们要开展公益慈善与社会服务成果经验的分享和探讨。建议社会服务组织与企业对接常态化，提高平台的影响力，为慈善事业锦上添花。积极推动国内外慈善活动，在医疗保健和儿童保护等公共服务领域加强合作。推动国际公益项目在各地落地，让慈善造福各国人民。（2）加强领域研究，促进学术交流。世界公益慈善论坛自成立以来，吸引了诸多知名慈善家、慈善组织、社会服务机构和慈善工作服务者。论坛开展至今，已成立了学术委员会，发起成立了公益慈善组织，我们应继续完善学术委员会的建设，持续发挥论坛学术平台的作用，吸引公益慈善领域的知名学者、专家和专业的从业人员加入相关的学术研究队伍，培养公益慈善领域的人才，打造公益慈善的智库，进一步加强对公益慈善指数的研究，为公益慈善事业的发展提供参考，促进公益慈善领域的专业化发展。（3）倡导同舟共济，共创美好世界。慈善事业体现了人类社会真挚的情感表达，是缓解人道主义危机、惠及全人类的崇高事业。慈善跨越国际、种族和文化，世界各国都有扶贫、济贫的慈善团体。慈善事业的发达反映了社会文明的进步，人人皆可为舜尧，慈善事业不仅需要每一位公民参与，更需要社会企业支持。我们呼吁更多的企业参与到公益慈善活动中，为世界公益慈善事业增光添彩，推动慈善影响世界；构建人类命运共同体，打造共同繁荣、开放包容、清洁美丽的世界。

女士们，先生们，朋友们，慈善是传递爱心最真诚、最直接的方法，大道至简，让我们不忘初心，共同谱写公益慈善事业新的篇章，携手共创更加美好的未来。

在这里预祝论坛圆满成功，谢谢大家！

善用金融力量促成美好社会

——匈牙利经济模式经验谈

匈牙利前总理 彼得·麦杰西

早上好，李斌女士，李小林女士，女士们，先生们。首先，我想要感谢你们的邀请，让我来此参加非常重要的论坛，感谢你们所付出的辛劳，也十分感谢你们在接下来几天将会付出的努力。接下来我说一下关于慈善方面的话题，我今天要讲的主题挺复杂的，就是匈牙利如何利用金融的力量促进社会包容和共同繁荣。我想要提及三点：（1）匈牙利的模式；（2）世界金融慈善的新形式；（3）世界最大的问题之一，就是移民。

第一，李斌女士说到了人道主义危机，这是目前世界上十分严重的危机，也是我们所面临的大问题。匈牙利一直都处在整个区域的变革中心，即使是在冷战时期，匈牙利也是非常开放的，加入国际金融组织，比如IMF、世界银行、OECD、WTO，还有其他的经济和金融组织，我们尝试让改革在社会主义的框架和思维中不断地前行。这些改革是为了让我们实现市场经济，所以我们希望可以使用一些市场经济元素，但并不是完全使用，而是有选择性地使用。匈牙利是中欧和东欧地区第一个对中国开放的市场，那时候是2002年，当时我们踏出了第一步，我也非常高兴，当时做了先行试验。

尽管匈牙利进行了改革，但还是受到了2008~2009年金融危机的消极影响，故我们又开始了非常重要的经济改革。在2009年的时候，我们做出了决定，是非常困难却坚定的决定，那就是要向金融平衡迈出非常重要的一步。自2002年以来，我们开始了新的财政和货币政策，它使得我们可以保持经济的平衡。从 2015 年开始，匈牙利的经济增长率是 4%~5%，而对于欧洲国家来说，这个数据很重要，代表着长足的进展，因为在 2019 年，经济增长率为 4%~5%，意味着匈牙利应该是欧盟地区经济增长最快的国家之一，而我们的财政赤字率大概是 2%，是相对较低的。通胀率是 2%~3%，是可以接受的。我们的失业率为 3%~4%，这是非常棒的，我们都以此为荣。尽管我们存在一些不足，关于劳动力方面的不足，在特定劳务活动中存在一定的不足。匈牙利于 2004 年加入欧盟，我也参与签署了加入欧盟的协议。我们有着非常多的来自欧盟的支持，我们每年得到 50 亿 ~70 亿欧元的支持，然而我们并不只是专注于欧盟内部，我们与中国亦有非常良好的关系，从 2002 年开始，每一年与中国的外交关系都在不断加强，我很荣幸地说，这也是匈牙利的政界达成的共识，不过民主很难达成共识，因为存在争论，有不同的问题。但是我们有一个非常重要的政界的共识，就是要与中国建立友好的关系，并且不断深化这种友好的关系。我们与美国、印度、俄罗斯都有非常良好的关系，因为我们的外交政策是从实用主义出发的，而我们的方式也是非常好的，我们在发展中迎接来自国外的直接投资，外国公司对证券交易所的投资总额大概是 1000 亿美元，这对于匈牙利这样的小国家来说是非常可观的数字。同时我们不会掩盖自己面临的问题，这些问题涉及不同社会团体之间不断拉大的差距，贫困在匈牙利仍然存在，为了进一步促进匈牙利的稳定和平发展，贫富差距要缩小。大家也知道，目前政权要创造出中产阶级，这是需要时间的，这也是我们为什么需要慈善事业，如果中产阶级发展的话，整个匈牙利的社会问题也会得到解决。匈牙利目前的教育体系也存在问题，尽管我们取得了长足的进步，我们有非常知名的高校，但这是不够的，我们需要进一步努力。同时我们的医疗体系也存在一定的问题，我觉得全球很多国家都面临这样的问题，对我以及国家的领导人来说，我们必须对自己的国家负责，我们必须要去改善和优化我们的医疗体系，必须促进医改。为了使这一切成为可能，或者为了支持我的第一个观点，我们的公益项目开展得非常成功、非常良好，而且有这样的机会让慈善得以存身。匈牙利的 GDP 是慈善的基础，匈牙利必须要有稳健发展的经济，并且有这样一群人愿意积极投身慈善事业，只有这样，才能使慈善事业取得成功。慈善是一种理念，也是投入其中的资金。在匈牙利，慈善事业以基金会的形式存在和运作，我们有非常重要的儿童基金会等，并且基金会的数量还在不断增加，我们还有其他非常重要的私人筹建的基金会，以及帮助弱势群体保持健康的基金会，我们也有支持艺术和文体事业发展的基金会。总的来说，我们还是取得了长足的进步和巨大的成功，我们也需要慈善获得越来越大的发展，我们也需要越来越多的人有慈善的意识，履行自然的责任和义务。我对现状并不是十分满意，但我认为这是良好的开端。

第二，2016 年的第一届世界公益慈善论坛，以及过去的这些年，已经见证了经济、文化、全球化的发展，以及慈善事业在全球的进展，这是一个非常重要的陈述，也反映了经济的现状。这样的一个宣言，也意味着慈善体系在金融体系中的发展和进步，因此我希望给大家举两个例子来表达我对这一发展的看法。其一，联合国非常重视慈善事业，专门设有顾问促进慈善事业的创新和发展，而且其是直接向秘书长汇报的，这样一种任命必须要更多地专注于慈善事业的发展。当时的副秘书长直接负责倡议的实施。法国的前财长也为慈善事业、思想的发展做出了很多贡献，提出了多项的机制，从政府政策到公私合营机制，再到赞助机制，提出了涵盖多个领域（包括和公众相关）的问题，比如环境问题。一些机构和组织，大力促进了慈善事业的发展，比如 AMC 和市场促进协会，它们创新解决方案，大力促进了医药业和慈善业的发展，尤其是针对比较贫困的国家。这个清单是很长的，我们也看到了活动的进展，看到了全球慈善事业的发展 ，我们希望多方共同努力，进一步推动慈善事业意识和思维的进步。其二，海地前首相发起鼓励公私合营企业支持政府创新融资的倡议，目的是支持政府创新融资，这并不是很容易的。为了支持教育事业的发展，目前已经有相当多的资金流入了教育和慈善事业。在全球，筹集了很多的资金支持教育事业的发展，这是在海地执行的政策。我觉得这是很好的想法，我会建议大家思考这样的模式，并且在其他国家进行推广。慈善融资的模式正在不断变化和改善，有新的组织和个人响应了这样的倡议，不断完善这个体系，投入更多的资金。我们也深深认识到慈善需要意识和资金才能实现。

第三，我想要说一个非常特殊而巨大的问题，就是移民。关于移民的慈善学，对于我来说，就是要热爱人类，而移民是全球人口的移动，也意味着全国人口的移动。所以有些时候，在全世界的国家和人民的做法之间是有冲突的，政府必须解决这样的争议和争端。自 2000 年开始，我们看到了世界上非常大的移民潮。我可以接受政府的反应，它想要关闭边境，或者是建立起大墙反对非法移民，这是有必要的吗？我们必须要为移民过度输出找到长期的解决方案。移民和环境变化有很大的关系，意味着某些国家可能正在遭遇缺乏水资源、缺乏食物和干旱的问题。移民和难民可能和当地的教育也有关系，如果我们不重视移民和难民问题的话，怎么才算是慈善？所以我认为，出于人道主义和慈善的考虑，我们要做出深刻的分析。分析难民和移民形成的深刻原因，找出长久的解决方案。长久的解决方案和教育、水供应有关，我们也要看一下是否可以帮助他们实现更好的发展，以及帮助他们在某些区域创造更多工作岗位。但是我们首先要解决的是地区冲突问题，去加强冲突地区对于和平的渴望，创造出更多的条件来达成这一目标，让人们可以在这些地区安居乐业。关闭边境是有必要的，但这一举措不足以解决现有问题。

女士们，先生们，我已经解释了慈善的宽泛范围，但是慈善需要我们负起责任，并且有更广泛的思考，我所说的这样的一些方式对于论坛来说是不够的。因为我们同在世界当中，我们是命运共同体。再一次感谢你们的耐心倾听。我希望在接下来的几天，会议可以圆满地举行，谢谢。

二 嘉宾致辞

主 持 人：中国人民对外友好协会秘书长、中国友好和平发展基金会理事长 李希奎

致辞嘉宾：中国中央人民政府驻香港特别行政区联络办公室副主任 谭铁牛

清华大学党委书记、校务委员会主任，论坛联合主席 陈旭

香港大学副校长 区洁芳

香港大学校长、论坛联合主席 张翔

香港中文大学校长、论坛联合主席 段崇智

深圳市副市长 艾学峰

谭铁牛致辞

中国中央人民政府驻香港特别行政区联络办公室副主任 谭铁牛

尊敬的全国政协李斌副主席，尊敬的彼得·麦杰西前总理，王爱文副部长，李小林会长，陈旭书记，段崇智校长，区洁芳副校长。在今天这个特殊的日子，我非常荣幸，在深圳参加一年一度的世界公益慈善论坛。感谢全国政协副主席李斌女士、彼得·麦杰西先生以及其他尊贵的来宾出席论坛，体现了这一论坛广泛的号召力和影响力，在此请允许我代表中央人民政府驻

香港特别行政区联络办公室对会议的召开表示衷心的祝贺，对远道而来的国内外朋友表示热烈的欢迎，对中国人民对外友好协会、清华大学、香港大学、香港中文大学，以及深圳市人民政府致以诚挚的敬意。

2016 年，为推动世界公益慈善的发展、加强国内外交流与合作，中国人民对外友好协会、清华大学等联手发起并举办了世界公益慈善论坛，吸引了来自全球各国的朋友参与，形成了越来越大的影响。让我倍受鼓舞的是，从 2018 年开始，香港大学、香港中文大学成为这一重要论坛的共同举办单位，我觉得这对推动香港和内地公益慈善的合作、推动两地教育科研的合作、促进两地的交流和信任具有非常重要的意义。特别是 2019 年，在大湾区的深圳召开，意义非同一般。大家知道，粤港澳大湾区是中国政府推出的一项重大战略举措，对于丰富“一国两制”、升华改革开放具有重大意义。我也知道这个论坛每年都有一个鲜明的主题，今年的主题叫“慈善湾区　美好生活”，也是粤港澳大湾区建设中的应有之义，美好生活离不开高等教育和科技创新的支撑。因此今天的论坛在这里召开，特别是香港一流的大学联合清华大学和中国人民对外友好协会共同举办，可谓珠联璧合、相得益彰。大家听说我来自香港，一定很关心香港的局势，当下世界各地的朋友都很关心香港的局势，香港正在经历风雨，也在面临自 1997 年回归以来最严峻的局面。但是我们有理由相信，行政长官和特区政府有能力带领社会各界走出当前的困境，我们也会坚定地支持行政长官和特区政府依法有效施政，坚定地支持香港警察执法，我们相信未来会更加美好，东方之珠的风采不会褪色。香港在公益慈善方面有悠久的历史、优良的传统，我可以提及很多香港公益慈善组织和机构，比如东华三院，成立于 1870 年，是香港规模最大、影响力很大的公益慈善机构，也有很多成功人士、爱心人士慷慨解囊，为推动慈善事业做出巨大的贡献，所以大家看到很多大学的教学科研楼，包括内地的教学科研设施，是以香港的一些人的名字命名的。

我衷心希望我们能够以世界公益慈善为纽带，以世界公益慈善论坛为平台，加强内地和香港的交流合作，加强我们伟大的祖国和国际社会的合作，共同努力，创造美好生活，建设美好家园，为构建人类命运共同体携手同行。我真诚希望，在不远的将来，这个论坛在香港召开，也预祝本次论坛取得圆满成功，谢谢大家。

陈旭致辞

清华大学党委书记、校务委员会主任，论坛联合主席 陈 旭

尊敬的全国政协李斌副主席，尊敬的彼得·麦杰西先生，尊敬的李小林会长、王爱文副部长，尊敬的段崇智校长，各位嘉宾，女士们，先生们，大家上午好。很高兴在第四个“中华慈善日”到来之际，与大家相聚在深圳，共同出席第四届世界公益慈善论坛。我谨代表清华大学，对各位嘉宾的到来表示热烈的欢迎和衷心的感谢!

世界公益慈善论坛创立四年来，一直致力于推动全球公益慈善事业的健康发展。从北京到上海再到深圳，论坛视野逐渐开阔，视角更加多元，朋友圈日益壮大，号召力和影响力不断提升。在各界同人的共同努力下，世界公益慈善论坛已逐渐成为公益慈善领域跨界型、研究型、行动倡导型的综合性国际交流平台，对推动构建人类命运共同体、促进世界和平与发展发挥着越来越重要的作用。

2019 年是中华人民共和国成立 70 周年、澳门回归 20 周年。在这个重要的历史节点上，党中央、国务院先后发布了《粤港澳大湾区发展规划纲要》和《关于支持深圳建设中国特色社会主义先行示范区的意见》，充分彰显了新时代党和国家推动形成全面开放新格局、推动“一国两制”事业实现新发

展、奋力实现中华民族伟大复兴中国梦的坚定信心和强大决心。习近平主席在会见香港澳门各界庆祝国家改革开放 40 周年访问团时，充分肯定了港澳同胞和社会各界人士在改革开放历程中所发挥的投资兴业的龙头作用、市场经济的示范作用、体制改革的助推作用、双向开放的桥梁作用、先行先试的试点作用和城市管理的借鉴作用，对港澳同胞热心捐助内地教育慈善事业、扶贫济困公益事业给予了高度赞赏。长期以来，一批爱国重教的港澳企业家在内地捐资兴学，支持教育事业发展，清华大学也是其中的受益者。今天矗立在清华园里的许多教学科研建筑、发挥了重要作用的许多教育科研基金，都来自港澳同胞的慷慨捐助。这些善款为清华大学的改革与发展提供了宝贵的支持，从中我们深切感受到了血浓于水的同胞之情。

在当前国家全面开放的新格局下，在粤港澳大湾区建设的重要战略中，深圳作为我国改革开放的重要窗口和中国特色社会主义先行示范区，将在其中发挥更加显著的重要作用。深圳不仅是撬动粤港澳大湾区发展活力的重要支点，也是推进新时代改革开放的更高起点，是中国走向世界、联通全球的关键节点。

清华大学与深圳市有着深厚的合作渊源和丰硕的合作成果。在 20 多年的长期合作中，我们见证了深圳生机勃勃的飞速发展，感受到了特区敢为天下先的创新精神。本届论坛在深圳举办并以“慈善湾区　美好生活”为主题，寓意是十分深远的。慈善事业作为中国特色社会主义事业的重要组成部分，是具有广泛群众性的道德实践活动，涉及领域宽广、形式多样、参与主体多元，在促进经济社会发展、保障和改善民生、弘扬社会主义核心价值观等方面发挥着重要作用。我们希望以本届论坛为契机，进一步弘扬中华民族崇德向善的传统美德，进一步凝聚最广泛的公益慈善力量，进一步增进同世界先进经验的交流互鉴，直面挑战，坚定信心，共同推动粤港澳大湾区和中国特色社会主义先行示范区的发展建设，让祖国的繁荣富强和湾区的美好未来为人民所世代共享，让民族复兴的历史责任和慈善精神的弘扬传承成为社会各界的共同担当。

“青年是国家的未来，也是世界的未来。”清华大学秉承“自强不息，厚德载物”的校训，注重引导青年学生树立公益意识、增强社会责任感、厚植家国情怀、增进人类关怀，做可堪大任的时代新人。同时，清华大学也积极开展公益慈善研究，成立了国家级智库——清华大学公益慈善研究院，通过高水平研究为公益慈善事业发展提供对策建议和学术支持。教育承载了国家和人民最深厚的期望，得到了社会各界最多的关怀，培养更多具有担当精神、奉献精神的优秀人才是教育对国家和人民的最好回馈。面向未来，清华大学将继续坚持立德树人，积极推动公益慈善教育和研究，与各方携手一道共创美好湾区，共同为国家发展、人民幸福、人类文明进步做出应有的贡献。

感谢中国人民对外友好协会、香港大学、香港中文大学、深圳市政府以及各方朋友给予论坛的大力支持！相信本届论坛将会为粤港澳大湾区的发展建设汇集更多的公益智慧、凝聚更强的慈善力量，为大湾区更加美好的明天写下精彩的一笔！

预祝论坛取得圆满成功！

谢谢大家！

区洁芳致辞

香港大学副校长　区洁芳

尊敬的来宾，各位朋友，大家好，能代表香港大学参与这个论坛，我感到十分有意义。四年来，这个论坛非常积极地推动公益慈善和社会工作在全球的发展。香港大学作为四家主办方之一，有幸参与其中，我们深感任重而道远。香港大学校长张翔教授很重视这次论坛，但他不能出席，为此他特意拍摄了一段视频，祝愿这次论坛取得圆满成功，让我们大家一起来看一看，谢谢大家。

张翔视频致辞

香港大学校长、论坛联合主席　张　翔

尊敬的各位来宾，女士们，先生们：

欢迎来到第四届世界公益慈善论坛。很抱歉由于时间的安排，我无法到深圳与大家相见，见证论坛的开幕，非常遗憾。在这里我衷心感谢所有为此次论坛倾情付出的同道伙伴，并感谢各位来宾的积极参与令论坛顺利召开，祝愿此次论坛取得圆满成功。

过去三年，世界公益慈善论坛得到了各方的支持与信赖，目前已发展成为会聚海内外学者、专家、从业人员的重要交流平台，全球各界得以共同探讨公益慈善的未来发展。今年，论坛在深圳举办，我认为其意义、影响更加深远。自《粤港澳大湾区发展规划纲要》发布以来，大湾区内经贸合作、跨界交流日益增多，在经济飞速发展的同时，民众对教育、医疗等公共服务的需求也不断增加。这给大湾区内的公益慈善事业带来了新的机遇与挑战，需要我们凝聚各界的经验、力量和智慧，共同探索、实践。

作为香港历史最悠久的高等教育学府，香港大学致力于培养未来领袖和人才，鼓励学生在探索知识之余，学以致用。通过服务学习，回馈社会，我们也一直致力于倡导慈善事业和加强非营利部门的能力。

展望未来，我们将继续通过知识交流，结合政府和公众的力量，携手合作，运用知识为人类社会、文化和环境谋取更大的福祉。我们期待通过这次论坛能与各位新老朋友共同探讨、分享经验，为大湾区公益慈善的未来发展出谋献策。大学应当成为创新的引擎，让大湾区不仅成为全球的科技创新中心，也成为全球的社会创新中心。群策群力，众志成城，我深信，本次论坛会带来丰硕的成果。谢谢！

段崇智致辞

香港中文大学校长、论坛联合主席　段崇智

尊敬的各位领导、各位嘉宾、各位同人：

首先热烈欢迎各位出席2019年世界公益慈善论坛。香港中文大学非常荣幸，从上一届开始与中国人民对外友好协会、清华大学及香港大学共同主办这个论坛。作为主办单位之一，我们今年能与各位在深圳聚首一堂，实在非常难得。

世界公益慈善论坛于2016年成立，一直团结各领域的领导人、翘楚，汇聚专业知识和慈善经验，推动全球公益慈善和社会服务实践、学术交流及人才培养。香港中文大学自创校以来，致力于维系多元文化的环境，以发掘、丰富及应用知识为谋，以改善人类生活、应付世界挑战为任，前瞻社会所急所需，达成造福香港、国家以至全球社群的目的。

我谨向此次论坛的其他主办单位、论坛的联合主办单位深圳市人民政府、给予论坛支持的各个部委，以及积极参与论坛的各位演讲嘉宾、友校和机构致以由衷的感谢。我们将在这两天就湾区慈善未来发展的重要课题，交换意见和心得。在此祝愿此次论坛取得丰硕成果，谢谢各位！

艾学峰致辞

深圳市副市长　艾学峰

尊敬的麦杰西先生，尊敬的李斌副主席、李小林会长，各位来宾，女士们，先生们：

大家上午好！

值此第四个“中华慈善日”到来之际，很高兴和大家欢聚在美丽的鹏城，举行第四届世界公益慈善论坛。在此，我谨代表深圳市政府，向远道而来的各位领导和嘉宾表示热烈欢迎，向长期以来关心和支持深圳慈善事业发展的国内外社会各界人士表示衷心感谢！

深圳作为中国改革开放的重要窗口，各项事业取得显著成绩，已成为一座充满魅力、活力、创新力的国际化创新型城市。在国家民政部、广东省委和省政府的关心支持下，深圳市委、市政府着力打造民生幸福城市，培育涉及公益慈善的城市文化，不断优化政策环境，初步建立起制度完善、依法治理、作用明显、管理规范、健康有序的现代慈善生态体系。近年来，深圳探索出多项中国公益慈善领域的新成果，创新社区基金会制度化模式，成立了第一家由民间发起的公募基金会；创立全国最大的全民互联网公益日“99公益日”，成功备案国内首个慈善信托计划；连续7届参与主办中国公益慈善项目交流展示会。在“中国城市公益慈善指数”排名中，深圳综合指数连续多届位居全国前列。

在喜迎新中国成立70周年之际，第四届世界公益慈善论坛在深圳举办，与会嘉宾将围绕“慈善湾区　美好生活”主题开展广泛研讨，共享思想盛宴。在此，我衷心希望大家能为深圳的公益慈善事业和社会建设多提宝贵意见和建议。我相信，本次论坛取得的丰硕成果，必将对我国尤其是粤港澳大湾区的公益慈善事业发展产生重要影响。

经过 40 余年的发展，站在开启建设中国特色社会主义先行示范区的关键节点，深圳将落实“城市文明典范”“民生幸福标杆”的战略定位，以特区担当努力交出新时代慈善事业的特区答卷，为推动中国和国际公益慈善事业的创新发展，做出更大的贡献。

最后，预祝本次论坛获得圆满成功!

三 主题演讲

主题演讲嘉宾： 中国民政部副部长 王爱文

香港赛马会主席 周永健

联合国儿基会私人筹款和伙伴关系部总监 加里·斯塔尔

聚慈善之力助推湾区发展，扬慈善精神共建美好世界

中国民政部副部长 王爱文

尊敬的各位来宾，女士们，先生们:

很高兴参加第四届世界公益慈善论坛，我谨代表中华人民共和国民政部，对论坛的召开表示热烈的祝贺!

今天是第四个“中华慈善日”，2016 年颁布的《慈善法》将每年的 9 月 5 日设立为“中华慈善日”，目的就是传播慈善文化、宣传慈善理念、弘扬慈善精神。前不久，民政部还专门公布了“中华慈善日”标志，旨在促进慈善意识更加深入人心。在国家支持粤港澳大湾区发展、支持深圳建设中国特色

社会主义先行示范区的战略决策相继出台之际，中国人民对外友好协会联合清华大学、香港大学、香港中文大学举办这次论坛，对于总结国内外慈善事业发展经验，推动大湾区慈善事业加快发展，引导慈善力量在建设中国特色社会主义现代化强国、构建人类命运共同体的历史进程中贡献力量，都将起到促进作用。

推进粤港澳大湾区建设，是以习近平同志为核心的党中央做出的重大决策。从 2017 年 7 月 1 日《深化粤港澳合作 推进大湾区建设框架协议》的签署，到粤港澳大湾区建设被写入党的十九大报告，从2019年2月中共中央、国务院发布《粤港澳大湾区发展规划纲要》，到 8 月中共中央、国务院发布《关于支持深圳建设中国特色社会主义先行示范区的意见》，这一系列重要举措不仅为大湾区的经济社会建设描绘了新蓝图，更为大湾区的慈善事业发展提出了新目标。

改革开放以来，中国慈善事业取得了可喜成绩，粤港澳地区做出了突出贡献。

随着中国改革开放的全面深入推进，中国慈善事业已经进入发展的快车道，展现出巨大的发展潜力和广阔的作为空间。从《公益事业捐赠法》《基金会管理条例》的出台到《慈善法》的颁布，慈善事业的法制体系日趋完善。互联网慈善方兴未艾、迅速发展，获得社会广泛关注和参与。从狮子山下到三江源头，慈善活动遍地开花，给困难群体送去温暖，在城乡社区传递关爱，使社会更加美好，让人与人之间更加和睦。

粤港澳大湾区作为改革开放的先行区，不仅是中国经济活力最足、开放程度最高的区域，也在社会发展、文化培育方面开风气之先，为本地区慈善事业发展提供了物质和精神基础，成为改革开放以来孕育中国现代慈善的沃土。广东有 900 多个慈善组织，数量和净资产总额在全国排名第二，除了服务广东本地、深耕基层社区，也积极参与国内其他地区的脱贫攻坚、乡村振兴、科教文卫体事业发展，有的还走出国门、走到海外。广东已经成为输出慈善人才和理念的高地。香港、澳门有着深厚的慈善传统，“人人慈善”的生活习惯、“行善有道”的专业素养有力推动着港澳地区的慈善文化建设和慈善事业发展。长期以来，港澳地区的慈善组织在养老、慈幼、助残等方面提供了大量的民生服务，成为当地社会福利的重要供给者。港澳地区的慈善力量也长期积极支持内地发展，在历次的重大自然灾害中都给予了无私的援助，2008 年的汶川大地震，香港政府拨付和社会捐赠的赈灾款物超过 230 亿港元，港澳同胞捐建的中小学校遍及内地的城市、乡村，这血浓于水的情谊，内地人民都铭记在心。

开启全面建设社会主义现代化国家的新征程，为慈善事业发展带来重大历史机遇，粤港澳地区要乘势而上。

开启全面建设社会主义现代化国家的新征程，将为慈善事业开辟出更大、更光辉的发展空间；实现中华民族伟大复兴的中国梦需要慈善力量更大力度、更广范围的推动和支持。虽然不同文化背景的人对慈善的理解有些许差异，但慈善的力量可以跨越国家和地区，跨越制度和文化，甚至能穿越历史、联通未来。不同的法律制度下慈善的领域有大有小，但是慈善反映的是人类普遍的伦理道德，是构建现代社会的重要基石。从物质形态看，慈善吸纳社会捐赠、组织志愿者参与，再转化为服务，满足社会需求，解决社会问题，是对社会资源的重新分配。从价值形态看，慈善是运用伦理道德对社会进行再造，让人们通过相互联结而相互扶持，是爱的力量的传递和升华。构建人类命运共同体，慈善是桥梁纽带，也是重要基础。

大湾区是中国经济社会最发达的区域之一，是中国向世界开放的重要窗口，在经济建设、科技创新上领先，也必须在社会建设、慈善事业发展上走在前列。我们高兴地看到，广东包括深圳近年来非常重视对慈善组织、慈善力量的培育，有效地激发了慈善所蕴含的社会创新力，体现了慈善消弭差异、融合多元的柔韧力道，展示了慈善对于社会和谐、文明进步的重要作用。将慈善的这种力量、作用进一步发挥出来，推进粤港澳大湾区的融合发展，将是助力改革开放的重要社会实践，也是建设中国特色社会主义先行示范区的重要举措。

中国的慈善事业还处于上升阶段，未来大有可为。在满足人民的美好生活需要的过程中，还有很大的空间有待开发；在动员社会力量广泛参与方面，还有很多的路径有待尝试；在加大慈善服务供给力度方面，还有很多的方法有待探索；在道德引领、价值观培育上，还有更大的能量有待释放；在推进社会和谐文明进步中，还有更多的作用有待发挥。相比于国内其他地区，粤港澳地区的慈善发展水平已经处于领先地位，随着深圳先行示范区和大湾区建设的推进，大湾区的慈善事业会具有更加美好的前景。希望粤港澳大湾区积极探索培育慈善力量、积累慈善方面的有效经验，将中国优秀慈善文化和现代慈善理念有机融合，先行走出一条新时代中国特色慈善之路，为其他地区的慈善事业发展提供借鉴参考。

下一步，建议粤港澳大湾区在五个方面加快推进慈善事业发展。一是发挥先行示范优势，引导慈善力量开展育幼、办学、养老、医疗、助残服务，促进民生服务优质均衡；通过鼓励开展慈善活动、提供志愿服务来解决差异化、多元化的需求问题，增加老百姓的幸福感、获得感。二是发挥科技创新优势，大力发展“互联网＋”慈善、智慧慈善，让科技为慈善插上腾飞的翅膀。三是发挥综合领先优势，有效引导慈善人才、理念等向贫困地区流动，为脱贫攻坚、东西部地区协作贡献更多力量，实现互惠共赢。四是发挥区域合作优势，推进粤港澳大湾区慈善事业的融合发展，在慈善领域探索“一国两制”的新实践。五是发挥国际化优势，让粤港澳大湾区成为融汇中西，培育中国特色社会主义慈善模式、慈善文化、慈善理论的前沿阵地。

女士们，先生们：

作为主管慈善工作的职能部门，民政部非常关注和支持世界公益慈善论坛的举办，每年都到会参与。近年来，中国慈善事业在助力脱贫攻坚、推进民生发展和社会进步中积累了丰富经验，发挥了重要作用。希望通过持续举办这一高级别论坛，不断分享我们在扶贫和其他方面的经验做法，贡献更多的中国智慧和中国方案。也希望与会的各位嘉宾畅所欲言、凝聚共识，让论坛不断结出丰硕成果。我们愿意支持世界公益慈善论坛进一步扩大影响、发挥作用，成为慈善领域国际交流的亮丽名片和重要平台。让我们共同用慈善联通民心、用慈善凝聚共识，让慈善的源泉充分涌流，让慈善的光芒照亮八方。

最后，祝本届论坛圆满成功！祝论坛越办越好！谢谢大家！

慈善共创　建设更美好社会

——香港赛马会经验浅谈

香港赛马会主席　周永健

尊敬的李斌副主席、彼得·麦杰西先生、各位领导、各位嘉宾，早上好。我的广东话比普通话好得多，但为了公益慈善，我愿意挑战用普通话发言。

首先，我很荣幸能代表香港赛马会在这里和大家分享马会通过自身独特的运营模式，为香港创造经济和社会价值、建设更美好社会的经验。在座的某些朋友可能对香港赛马会不是很了解，请允许我向大家简单介绍马会的基本情况，然后和大家分享马会的主要内容和模式。

马会成立于 1884 年，当时是以推广赛马和马事运动为宗旨的会员制会所，截止到今日，马会发展成为世界级的赛马机构，是香港唯一授权举办赛马博彩的机构。我们推行有机制的博彩措施，配合政府打击非法赌博行动，在满足人们博彩需求的同时，我们把博彩的收益转化为支持香港社会发展和慈善事业的经济来源。马会对香港社会的贡献主要体现在两个方面，第一个方面是纳税。马会是香港最大的单一纳税机构，我们于 2019 年 8 月底公布了财务业绩，在 2018 年、2019 年，我们给香港特区政府纳税 233 亿港元，占香港税务局收入的 6.8%。第二个方面是马会的捐赠。2018 年度审批专款为 43 亿港元，支持 294 个社会项目，创下历史新高。马会于 1915 年开始接触社会公益，公益慈善的内容也可反映社会变化，在 20 世纪四五十年代，香港开始战后重建，大量的移民和人口是问题，我们主要支持社会建设，包括教育、医疗设施等。但是到 70 年代，公众对康体娱乐的需求增加，我们就兴建康体设施，比如海洋公园等。马会也专注于专项教育，包括兴建香港科技大学。2019 年马会积极回应社会议题，在革新慈善上，我们转变审批专款的模式，联系不同的社会力量，积极寻求解决方法。

我在这里跟大家分享一下马会运营策略的两个重点。第一，马会在满足社会需要的同时，通过投放资金推动青年、长者和艺术等的发展。我们的资金主要用于深入了解社会问题的根源，并透过借助别的平台，联系政府、非政府组织及商业机构等合作伙伴，共同回应社会的需要，制定解决方案，展开创造幸福的计划。马会也鼓励创新服务模式和善用课题，如香港面临人口老龄化的问题，预计 2020 年，1/3 的人口年龄将为 65 岁以上，为了应对人口老龄化带来的问题，马会展开了一系列的项目。其中自 2015 年开始，我们配合香港特区政府，分阶段在 18 个地区推动实施“赛马会灵活城市计划”，采取由下至上、以地区为本的模式，与本地研究“老龄学”的单位合作。在社会上弘扬尊敬长者及友善的风气，提升长者幸福指数，建构共荣社会。第二，要提升业界的水准，借助社会服务单位以及非政府组织。马会大部分的慈善捐赠项目，除了向首次申请的机构和非政府组织进行捐赠，也提供专业培训，主要涉及教师、社工等。赛马会教师、社工计划，致力于培养相关人才。多年来，马会透过赛马会信托基金，一直为建设更美好的社会做贡献。我们的业务表现近年来大幅改善，大力加强对慈善社区的捐助。我们现在更是全球十大捐助机构之一。马会之所以能够一直支持社会服务、推动社会发展，离不开马会的运营模式，透过赛马等有节制的体育博彩，为社会创造价值。

我们坚信任何问题都不是单一力量可以解决的，公益慈善在城市发展进程中担当着重要的角色。近年来，随着社会的发展和《慈善法》的颁布，内地慈善事业蓬勃发展。由于全球化进程的加快等，公益慈善有了更多新的模式，一个新的公益时代已经到来。

我们期待和内地及世界各国的同人交流，共同探讨及应对社会问题。马会在 2016 年举办了“慈善共创 · 都市聚焦”国际慈善论坛，邀请大中华地区的慈善家和企业家，以及非政府组织，交流和分享我们的经验，促进多方的协作，建立长远的伙伴关系，共建美好城市。第二届论坛在 2018 年成功举办，有超过 1400 个地区的业界代表参与，下一届论坛定于 2020 年 9 月举办，我们欢迎大家参加。2019 年 2 月，中共中央、国务院发布了《粤港澳大湾区发展规划纲要》，其中专门提及了港澳要与内地加强合作，作为大湾区的一分子，我们也非常期待未来和大家加强交流与合作。

最后我衷心感谢中央人民政府、深圳市政府和主办单位——中国人民对外友好协会、清华大学、香港大学、香港中文大学的安排，为大家提供交流的机会。我祝愿论坛取得圆满成功，谢谢各位！

公益促进发展　携手为儿童

联合国儿基会私人筹款和伙伴关系部总监　加里·斯塔尔

尊敬的李斌副主席、李小林会长、彼得·麦杰西先生、王副部长、艾学峰副市长，以及本次论坛的主办方、协办方，各位早上好。今天能代表联合国儿童基金会执行主任亨丽埃塔·福尔（Henrietta H. Fore）在这里发言，我感到非常荣幸和开心。我的上司让我向大家致以她诚挚的问候。在她一年半的任期中，她曾三次到访中国，践行与中国建立合作伙伴关系的承诺，这不仅是为了支持中国政府应对国内与儿童相关的困难和挑战，还是为了与中国合作改善世界儿童的生活。

联合国儿基会致力于加强双方的合作，在卫生、营养、健康、儿童保护、教育和社会政策方面面向中国2.71亿名儿童提供帮助。我们在中国筹划新的项目时，参考了政府的意见，继续开展2021~2025年的活动。我们正继续实施已经建立的项目，也在发展新的项目。新项目聚焦于青少年、性别反应、城市儿童未满足的需要、贫困地区儿童和残疾儿童。联合国儿基会执行主任与中国国家发展和改革委员会在前不久的“一带一路”论坛上签署了合约，认可了中方与联合国儿基会旨在为儿童、年轻人和家庭提供中央服务和公共服务的合作。这为联合国儿基会和中国政府在中国和全球的合作铺设了道路。

截至目前，我们双方合作开展了黎巴嫩的叙利亚国际难民项目、索马里营养项目等，并即将开展南非的飓风救济项目和非洲健康项目。国际社会要实现可持续发展目标，面临的挑战是十分巨大的，而中国将会起到非常重要的作用。2030年联合国可持续发展目标包括17项，将解决可持续发展在社会、经济和环境上遇到的问题。联合国儿基会正和190多个国家合作，一起达成联合国可持续发展目标。在全球范围内，联合国儿基会平均每年处理了300件突发事故。我们募集了超过39亿美元资金，为59个国家中的4.1亿名儿童提供人道主义援助。目前，鉴于我们面对的发展情况非常复杂、紧急挑战很大，慈善家很难做出最为有效的贡献。

比尔·盖茨经常说，他的基金会中的资源仅仅是九牛一毛。根据数据估算，我们每年需要2.5万亿美元才能达成发展目标。十分明显，单靠慈善的力量无法填补这一巨大的资金缺口。我们必须要有创新的方式，将慈善机构、联合国、政府和企业联合起来，去推动持续的改变。我举两个例子告诉大家联合国如何通过慈善的路径以持续的活动达成发展目标。

第一个例子，在印度，联合国儿基会与一个慈善家族合作发起了第一个印度家庭营养分析全面计划，提供国家数据，研究儿童和青少年患病的微量营养元素量、寄生虫和营养风险因素。多亏了初始慈善投资，政府和当地行动者如今拥有所需数据开展项目以提高儿童的营养水平。

第二个例子，在南非，我们得到了长久的慈善伙伴的资助，正致力于青少年权利获取。这包括一个基于社区的儿童关爱模型，在模型中，经过挑选、训练和监督的儿童和青少年关爱工人在饱受艾滋病困扰的赤贫地区提供基本的支持和关爱服务。这种支持包括陪伴儿童前往学校、诊所或是医院，帮助他们获取重要文件和服务，和他们一起洗衣服、做饭，帮助他们了解如何照顾自己。我们取得的成果有两方面，一是年轻人得到了重要的支持，二是社区成员得到收入和发展的经济基础。四年的实验非常成功，这一模型将由南非政府在全国推广。

这些例子展现了慈善家进行投资、与联合国儿基会合作带来长久变革的不同方式。这种行动让基金会、富裕个人和慈善群体的支持从2012年每年的 1.5 亿美元增长至 2017 年的 4 亿美元。并且，现在全球有 500 万人每年给予我们支持。我们在 2017 年的时候会集了 4 亿人，2018 年惠泽了 5 亿人，我们希望有更多的人可以加入。

在中国，联合国儿基会与私营部门和慈善家建立了成功的合作伙伴关系。比如，我们和腾讯合作了互联网儿童保护项目，和强生合作建立了怀孕妇女健康家庭程序。我们也和其他伙伴进行合作，比如和海尔合作支持学校儿童的社会情感研究。我们的儿童冠军项目让慈善家能够和我们合作进行赤足社工项目。

我想这些项目也得到了在座一些人的支持。我们感谢你们为提高儿童的生活水平所做出的努力。现在有许多合作和建立合作伙伴关系的机会。我希望你们考虑与我们合作，为中国和世界儿童的福祉做出努力。如果你和我们一样，希望世界的儿童都可以有光明的未来，可以在安全的环境中健康成长、受到教育，那么请不要不好意思，我们可以谈一下怎样为中国的儿童和世界的儿童带来更多的福祉。再一次感谢各位。

第二部分

专题对话

四　慈善湾区与人才培养

主 持 人： 环太平洋大学联盟秘书长　楚明伟

对话嘉宾： 中山大学副校长　肖海鹏

香港中文大学协理副校长、社会学系教授　王淑英

香港赛马会慈善及社区事务执行总监　张亮

楚明伟： 欢迎来到议题一“慈善湾区与人才培养”板块。大家好！我是环太平洋大学联盟秘书长楚明伟。环太平洋大学联盟（APRU）成立于1997年，是由环太平洋地区顶尖研究型大学组成的联盟组织。我们现在拥有50个成员，其中有11所是中国内地顶尖的大学，有3所是来自香港特区的大学。目前，我们的国际秘书处设立在香港。我们非常希望可以加强大湾区的研究创新生态圈建设。我们的现任主席是加州大学洛杉矶分校校长，有3名中国大学校长是我们的主席团成员，分别是香港中文大学校长段崇智、香港科技大学校长史维与复旦大学校长许宁生。我们希望加强大湾区的合作研究，提高应对国际政策变化和挑战的教育和创新能力。我们也致力于实现联合国的可持续发展目标、应对气候变化、推进全球健康等，为此，我们与非营利的民间组织、政府机构和企业进行合作，所以今天下午成为本次分论坛的主持人，对我来说是莫大的荣幸。现在，我介绍一下第一位对话嘉宾——肖海鹏先生，他将介绍大湾区高等教育和健康科学方面的合作潜力与机会。肖海鹏是中山大学药学教授和中山大学附属第一医院内分泌科资深专家，中山大学附属第一医院是广东省非常有名的医院。他也是中央政府的医保咨询师和多个医学教育联盟和医学院联盟的主席。他现在是中山大学的副校长。欢迎肖

海鹏给我们致辞。

肖海鹏：谢谢主持人的介绍。尊敬的王副校长，女士们，先生们，今天我非常荣幸受到邀请，在世界公益慈善论坛上发表致辞。我非常感谢主办方，感谢你们提供这个机会把新湾区介绍给世界。我想借此机会分享这个地区在健康科学方面的高等教育。2019 年 2 月 18 日，中央政府发布了《粤港澳大湾区发展规划纲要》，这标志着世界第四湾区的建立。粤港澳大湾区联合了香港、澳门与包括广州、深圳在内的珠三角地区九座城市。作为中国最开放、经济最活跃的地区，大湾区将会成为一个世界轴心，它致力于科技创新与发展，而且展示了内地与香港、澳门之间的三体合作。其也是中国科技创新与发展、“一带一路”倡议的代表。大湾区有着非常著名的学校和高等教育，我要给大家说一下 4 个大湾区里关于高等教育的数据。

粤港澳大湾区一共有 5.6 万平方千米，大约 7000 万的人口。就高等教育而言，大湾区是中国最强劲、最有活力的地区之一。大湾区有着 4 所来自香港的世界排名前 100 的大学，1 所来自澳门的世界排名前 500 的大学，还有 1 所来自广东省的世界排名前 300 的大学——中山大学。但是若将粤港澳大湾区和其他三个湾区相比，我们的高等教育水平不够。我们的博士生数量也比世界其他国家少。这意味着我们在健康卫生、高等教育领域可以有很多发展的空间。为了推动大湾区高等教育合作，我们在 2016 年成立了粤港澳大学联盟，以在此地区积聚力量、集聚资源。作为联盟创办学校和主席学校之一，中山大学的目标是实现大湾区的发展目标。中山大学由“中华民国之父”孙中山先生在 1924 年成立，现在是中国排名前 10 的高校。其现在共有 5 个校区，分布在广州、珠海和深圳这些大湾区非常重要的城市。广州校区的专业有医学、艺术、科学和工程，珠海校区主要做大海、宇宙、土壤的深入研究与原子弹工程，深圳校区马上就要开了，其将涵盖医学院和新的科学院。我们有超过 5.6 万名全日制学生和 1.7 万多名教职员工。中山大学共有 63 个院系与 10 所附属医院，其中 19 个学科排名在全球前 1%（ESI），在数量上位居中国第二。除此之外，我们还与全球 230 个学校建立了伙伴关系。医学是中山大学的基石。1866 年，孙中山先生成立了中山医学院，中国前领导人邓小平为学校刻上了名字。校训“除了治疗疾病，也要治愈灵魂与身体”凸显了医学院的精神。在过去 100 年间，中山医学院产生了非常多的知名医学专家，这些专家如今影响了中国的医学界。很多中国医学界的“第一次”是在这里发生的，比如第一个胆结石的移除和麻醉手术的案例都发生于中山大学。医学是中山大学的拳头专业之一，基础医学和临床医学也是中国的“双一流”学科，中国共有 4 所大学的基础医学和临床医学被列为“双一流”学科。在过去的 8 年里，中山大学医学毕业生的国家医学从业考试通过率在中国位居前三。2011~2014 年，中山医学院的毕业生在教育部和卫生部（卫计委）举办的全国医学技术临床技能大赛中荣获奖项。今天，中山医学院拥有全国第二大且强的医疗健康系统，我们拥有 10 所附属医院，其中有 7 所在广州、1 所在珠海、2 所在深圳，其中中山大学附属第一医院规模最大、技术最强。中山大学附属第一医院的总部设在广州，同时在惠州设立分院。南沙区的南沙国际医院坐落于大湾区的中心，其中包含教育部认可的 5 个国家学科和卫健委认可的技术资格。医院正努力加强对患者的关爱，并推动医学的发展。

医院目前也取得了多项成就，包括肝移植、人类脱细胞神经移植、最大的腹膜透析系统。我们一直关注于科技研究，推动中国医学发展，精准医学也获得了世界的关注。现在，为了推动科技研究，我们在医院中成立了精准医学机构，其中包含五大紧密相关的元素，即基础研究、测试、临床医疗、大数据、生物库等。这是精准医学的方向，我们在肿瘤学当中有使用这些医疗知识和技能。比如肿瘤学、糖尿病、肠胃科、神经科、公共健康等。我们期望在大湾区应用精准医疗技术。我们也从世界获得资源，我们同世界上其他的医疗机构建立了合作伙伴关系，其中包括加林糖尿病中心、布朗大学、伯明翰大学、墨尔本大学等，它们也是我们在医学联盟计划当中的合作伙伴。接下来三年，我们将会继续完成医学计划。我们现在在南沙区建立了国际医院，这所医院位于大湾区的中心，将会比中山大学附属第一医院总部大两倍。其距离香港、澳门半小时车程。南沙区是我们的先导试验区，推动着粤港澳地区的深度研究。而且南沙是我们的自由贸易港，和香港、澳门有非常紧密的自由贸易关系，南沙国际医院将于 2021 年竣工，其面积为 2 万平方米，将会是中国最大的医院。医院正和伯明翰大学探讨在南沙区共办医学院的可能，其他英国的知名大学也在寻找契机，它们将会在中国建立医学院。大湾区中有着许多机会和无限可能。我们有政府政策的支持，还有对高等教育的无限希望。我想借此机会邀请各位为大湾区发展出谋划策，将大湾区建设得更好。谢谢大家！

楚明伟：非常感谢肖海鹏博士，您的演讲非常精彩。我们的第二位演讲者是来自香港中文大学的王淑英博士。她在环太平洋大学联盟中也是非常活跃的成员，还是香港中文大学社会学系教授、协理副校长。她在斯坦福大学读博士时曾在北京师范大学及南开大学做访问讲师。1997 年，她加入香港中文大学，在此之前，她曾在美国和日本都有教学经历，并且获得了多个奖项。我们有请王淑英博士。

王淑英：尊敬的领导，女士们，先生们，大家下午好！对于我来说，这是一份非常困难的工作，因为我是一名候补选手。我们的校长——香港中文大学段崇智有一些非常紧急的事情要处理，必须马上回到香港，我是填补他的空缺，为大家展示。香港有一份非常容易做的工作就是替工，但是这份工作有时难度也比较高。我尽量做好，希望大家见谅。

我今天讲的是粤港澳大湾区，2019 年 2 月份，中央政府出台了《粤港澳大湾区发展规划纲要》。该规划纲要非常重要，而且我花很多时间看了，觉得有非常重要的聚焦点，我们应该首先去理解一下。我们看看高等教育能否在机遇和挑战之间，在产业部分、学研部分，抓住机遇。我介绍一下粤港澳大湾区的战略、地位、发展目标，根据它的发展目标，我们看看整个时间表，我们怎么发展，希望对香港、对全世界的人类有一个贡献。

粤港澳大湾区涵盖的范围非常广，从这个表中可以看到，世界上有 4 个湾区，粤港澳大湾区和纽约湾区是最大的，粤港澳大湾区的 GDP 已经超过旧金山湾区。讲到大湾区，我请来了一位教授会给我们再详细介绍旧金山发展独特的地方。总的来说，粤港澳大湾区的 GDP 已经超过旧金山湾区，已经跟纽约湾区非常靠近。

《粤港澳大湾区发展规划纲要》非常详细，而且非常精锐，我把 5 种战略定位介绍一下。1. 首先是发展成为世界级的城市群。2. 具有全球影响力的国际科研创新中心。3. 国家发展非常重要的战略就是“一带一路”的建设。粤港澳大湾区的发展会成为“一带一路”建设非常重要的支撑。4. 内地与港澳深度合作示范区。粤港澳大湾区通过深度合作成为示范区，会对世界发展有非常重大的影响。5. 宜居宜业宜游的优质生活圈，也是我们慈善论坛的主题。这是粤港澳大湾区战略性的定位。

2022 年，我们应该有一个框架基本要形成，目标是 2035 年，宜居宜业宜游国际一流湾区全面建成，所以 16 年以后，我们会看到整个湾区充分和全面的发展。

它的战略定位也有分工，首先是中心城市，大湾区是“9+2”，“9+2”里面有 4 个城市被定为中心城市，就是香港、深圳、广州、澳门。它也把 7 个重要的节点城市——珠海、中山、佛山、江门、惠州、肇庆、东莞列出来。

整个纲要里有 6 个方向，这 6 个方向很重要，也体现了它的系统化。1. 加强科技的创新合作。科技创新成为大湾区的发展方向。2. 加强产学研融合。3. 深化大湾区创新体系改革。硬件比较容易建设起来，经济的改革我们都看得很清楚，中央政府希望在现有的机制里进行透彻的改革。4. 促进科技成果的转化。这种转化非常重要，也是提供机会给湾区的年轻人，希望随着转化，机遇也增多。5. 推动教育的合作发展，有一些已经在合作当中。6. 指导性的方向，就是培育壮大新兴产业，包括信息技术、生物技术、高端装备制造、新材料。香港特区政府在大湾区的政策范畴里，我们抓住了几个范畴，比如教育、医疗产业、金融服务、环保和可持续发展、青年发展等。

我们的特首林郑月娥，她上一个施政报告用 400 亿港币鼓励香港，希望大学在各个方面发展，给香港的研究基金注资。

香港未来的工作重点，一边发展，一边抓住机遇，聚焦工作重点，建设国际科技的创新平台是一个。特别是推动科研要素的流动，因为这一方面我们还需要探讨和发展。人才培训方面，高端人才的流动性很强，但是在大湾区，技术耕耘很重要。科研的基建配套，总的来说，要在 4 个方面通过产学研不同的方向发展。

香港中文大学在大湾区已经有发展基地，比如香港大学（深圳）。

大湾区主要的挑战是人才不足，此外文化和系统上的差异、发展条件和配套、持份者的看法等，这些都是很大的挑战。

校长说一定要说这句话：近邻就是我们的挚友，我们和其他的城市应该更深入地合作。我的报告到这里，谢谢！

楚明伟：非常感谢王淑英博士的发言。第三位演讲嘉宾是张亮先生，他是香港赛马会慈善及社区事务执行总监。2014 年的时候加入香港赛马会，也参与了香港联合国可持续发展解决方案网络。在加入赛马会之前，他曾经是贝恩资本的合伙人、溢达集团全球采购及供应链管理董事总经理、教育互联网新创企业创办人及行政总裁、波士顿咨询公司高级顾问。他也是香港多个社会企业的CEO以及咨询顾问。他现在是香港特别行政区政府安老事务委员会和关爱基金专责小组成员，并担任香港按揭证券有限公司董事。张亮先生同时是香港中文大学客座教授，他获得了哈佛大学工商管理硕士学位与香港中文大学的学士学位。再一次邀请张亮先生给我们致辞。

张亮：尊敬的各位领导，各位老师，各位朋友，非常荣幸今天在这里和大家分享我们作为慈善信托基金的经验，香港作为大湾区的一分子，从慈善基金的角度讲人才的机遇。

早上主席可能跟大家讲过赛马会经营的模式，赛马会在香港是非营利的机构，没有股东，所有的钱取之于赌民，取之于市民。香港赛马会是香港最大的单一交税库，占香港政府税收的6%~7%，这是什么概念？今天有很多高校朋友在场，香港有一个UGC（大学教育资助委员会），一年资助180亿港币左右，我们赛马会可以缴200多亿港币的税，所以对香港来讲是非常重要的税收来源。除了缴税，我们有一个慈善信托基金，这个信托基金每年的捐款能够达到40亿港币，2009年只有十几亿港币的捐款，现在达到了40多亿港币的捐款。

几年前，整个董事会商量了一次，就是对于整个慈善怎样做？我们从慈善的角度来说，希望有4个重点，希望我们能够主动把挑战看清楚，看一下有什么方法可以解决，包括人口老龄化、青少年、体育、艺术文化、保育。有一点和人才培育很有关切性，不单纯是从高等教育的角度思考，而是思考整个慈善公益界发展需要什么样的人才；我们如何领导在慈善公益方面的参与者，包括社会工作者，也包括操作基金的人；我们怎么提高自己的能力，扩散自己的网络。这一方面就不多讲了。

我讲一讲对教育的看法，对于高等教育有3件事情是我们很多年都在做的。首先是基础的建设。香港赛马会规模比较大的时候，就是20世纪90年代，香港大学创建时收到香港赛马会捐款，大约20亿港币。演艺学院也是我们捐赠建造的。利用高校本身的研究能力和对社会政策的影响能力，把它们和社会服务机构结合起来，在不同的议题上进行创新、相互合作，可以为我们的政策提供一些更有效率的参考。

在知识转移方面，我们做得比较多。对于人才发展措施，包括设立奖学金等，我们有不少的想法，令得奖者不单纯是拿到钱完成学业，而是日后成为有同理心的人，这是非常重要的。

在基础教育方面，我们相信教育创新是很重要的方向，一个地方的市民或者一个国家的国民要想跟上时代就要不断创新自己。下面的几点是我们这几年做得比较多的东西。1. 鼓励、交流、讨论。大家在一些平台上互相交流。2. 培育创新的能力。有不同的计划项目，有些支持个人，有些支持机构，我们希望创新的精神在教育界也有。3. 另类的教学理念。中小学教育中有很多的条条框框，我们把正向心理学引导到学校，帮助学生减轻压力。4. 编制新的课程。一个是在科技方面的，比如编码教育，是和香港理工大学一起做的，效果非常好。5. 支援共融教育。总的来讲，教育创新是需要摸索的，利用科技、教育，帮助我们减少鸿沟，这是我们的重点。

我最后举一个例子，就是“喜伴同行”计划，是涉及自闭症小朋友的。香港有8000多名“喜伴同行”儿童，如何帮助他们融入课堂教育和深入学校？如何帮助他们的家长减轻压力？我们做了4年，现在有超过500个学校在这个计划里，60%有自闭症的学生在学校里，希望帮助到更多的人。这个项目的成果非常有效，所以香港特区政府也在思考是不是把整个项目变成政策。变成一个政策，不代表我们就不做了，如果能够把有验证的方法变成政策，我们可以将资金用于支持其他的创新项目。谢谢。

楚明伟：非常感谢张亮先生。我们今天听了三位的精彩演讲，关于高等教育、医疗卫生、粤港澳大湾区面临的机遇和挑战等。在粤港澳大湾区，有很多的模式、很多的战略定位需要更新，需要用更创新的方式建立一个生态系统。我们讨论的时间比较少了，因为讲者们都有非常多的干货分享给我们。我还是想问三位一个相同的问题，我所在的机构非常清楚环太平洋地区的挑战不是局限于某一个国家和地区，也就是说应对这些挑战需要不同的国家和地区找到新的合作方式，不仅是跨国界，还是跨学科、跨机构。粤港澳大湾区的建设会引出许多挑战，我们可以从三个层面进行总结，第一个便是合作。什么样的合作模式应该提倡？不仅是高校之间，还有高校和慈善组织，或者是非政府组织与政府之间，大家觉得用什么样的合作模式，能够推动大湾区这个概念与现实的蓬勃发展？我们的最高目标是增进社会的福祉，我们需要定下衡量成功的方式。我们可以从合作、福祉与何为成功可以帮助我们创造新型合作模式出发进行探讨。现在我想有请大家讨论一下大湾区的新型合作模式。我们先请肖海鹏先生回答。

肖海鹏：我们如今都在期待新型合作模式的出现，但是我认为，有了慈善机构的支持，我们的人才培育、人才发展、师资培训、学生交换项目都得到了支持。此外，我们可以在医院建立实验室，这个实验室是向整个湾区开放的，大家可以用这个设施。

楚明伟：请王淑英教授发言。

王淑英：从大学的角度来说，我们肯定需要政府、行业与研究机构之间更紧密的合作。比如，我们现在对于如何收集初创公司的启动资金非常迷惑，或许我们可以寻找天使资金。我认为在可见的未来，这可以靠公司、行业与高校之间的合作解决。这可能有两个解决途径。一方面，就像日本一样，参照东京湾区的发展，我们需要在产学研之间建立非常好的对接机制。

目前我们可能过多依赖于个人网络和经验。另一方面，我们需要中小型企业的积极合作与参与。在 2017 年，大湾区只有 1% 的中小企业具备达到国际标准规定的技术实力，所以我觉得这一方面也是极具发展潜力的。

楚明伟： 请张亮先生回答。

张亮： “合作”是一个非常棒的词，其中包含了冲突和共识。你刚刚提到的最高目标听起来非常好。我们希望产生社会影响，但是“社会影响”这样的词并不总是能够说服人们和你合作。对我来说，激励也是很重要的。我们共同负责联合国可持续发展解决方案网络，所以现在我们提出了一项计划，即将所有香港高校联合在一起并考虑在校园内开展计划。而且赛马会也愿意拿一部分钱支持这样好的倡议或者机制。这看起来非常诱人，但是需要花很长的时间才能让几所大学共同建立这样的机制。所以对于我来说，合作是非常好的事情，但合作取决于激励和使合作行之有效的投入。

楚明伟： 非常感谢，您说的这些我也非常赞成，确实需要花一些时间和资金才能找到共同利益所在。今天第一个分论坛硕果累累，谢谢诸位。

五 21 世纪公共健康与慈善

主 持 人： 香港大学李嘉诚医学院罗旭龢基金教授（公共卫生学）、社会医学讲座教授 林大庆

对话嘉宾： 世界糖尿病基金会主席 阿尼尔·卡普尔

诺和诺德血友病基金会委员会主席 加斯普·布兰德佳德

华大集团联合创始人、监事长，深圳猛犸公益基金会理事长 / 刘斯奇

深圳市卫生健康委员会主任 / 罗乐宣

林大庆：大家下午好！我们现在开始第二个分论坛。我是香港大学的林大庆。这一次分论坛的主题是“21 世纪公共健康与慈善”。我们有请第一位演讲嘉宾上台。我们共有 4 位嘉宾，每位有 10 分钟的发言时间。希望大家接下来会有一些讨论的时间。我们首先欢迎世界糖尿病基金会主席阿尼尔·卡普尔先生演讲。

阿尼尔·卡普尔：女士们、先生们。首先感谢主办方邀请我来到论坛。我们知道健康是人类发展的基石，但我们有些时候对健康的关注远远不够。并且健康与环境、教育、经济之间的联系是十分密切的，所以在 21 世纪，人类可持续发展与社会发展面临的最大挑战就是健康问题。我们现在面临的主要挑战是一些非传染病，所以我们成立了世界糖尿病基金会。世界糖尿病基金会成立于 2002 年，目标是预防和治疗发展中国家的糖尿病。总的来说，我们关注于缓解患有糖尿病及其并发症人群的痛苦，并且满足发展中国家亟须帮助人群的需要。糖尿病是现在非常大的挑战，很多人不知道这是一个非常大的挑战。在未来的 20 年里，它会使地球上近 10 亿人饱受痛苦，会有 6.29 亿名糖尿病患者，5.32 亿人会因为糖尿病一直待在医院里。它基本会影响到地球上一半人口的生命和健康安全，但是很多人对此束手无策。

未经治疗的糖尿病会引起严重的并发症，甚至导致英年早逝。接下来我给大家介绍一些细节。但我想说，糖尿病为我们建立 21 世纪整合的医疗体系提供了最大的机会，因为糖尿病引发了很多现代人面临的其他疾病。世界糖尿病基金会在 2002 年成立，当时获得了诺和诺德公司一笔慷慨的捐助，成立的原因是解决南非的艾滋病问题。本议题下一位发言人就是诺和诺德公司的前任首席财务官加斯普·布兰德佳德，他现在是诺和诺德血友病基金会委员会主席，他现在决定把关注点放在发展中国家的糖尿病问题上。世界糖尿病基金会的管理人员是糖尿病领域内的专家。作为世界糖尿病基金会的主席，我感到十分荣幸。

世界糖尿病基金会在 100 多个国家拥有合作伙伴，他们分布在基层、地区、国家和全球。我们支持需求驱动的项目，项目在地方产生，融合到已经建立的项目中。我们一直尊重自己的合作伙伴和受惠者，并与他们在当地定期会面，这样我们就能有更多的对话机会，更明白他们的需求。世界糖尿病基金会是一个催化剂，基金会投入项目中的每一分钱都可以翻倍使用。尽管在过去许多年里，我们得到的捐赠很少，但我们贡献了 1.5 亿美元。相比我们得到的捐赠我们的影响要大很多。我们的目标是通过我们的项目，让当地社区在世界糖尿病基金会的资助结束后依然受益。我们允许合作伙伴寻求其他资助资源以扩展活动规模。我们重视一些可能被遗忘的联系，比如我们是第一个提及糖尿病和肺结核关系的机构，我们也关注到了母亲健康和慢性非传染性疾病之间的关系，在未来我们也会看到糖尿病和慢性非传染性疾病之间的关系。我们今天如果有时间的话可以讲一下这方面的知识。目前我们资助了 558 个项目，资助资金总数近 1.5 亿美元。除此之外，我们还对发展中国家一些有关糖尿病的项目给予支持。我们有以下两个聚焦点。一、让很多人可以获得免费的医护服务，比如传授病人及其家属非传染病的知识、创建诊所并提升诊所的专业水平、建立指导系统。二、强化对糖尿病的预防。我们会开设健康防护课；将项目与母婴健康联系在一起；在婴儿降生时就开始糖尿病防护，甚至在婴儿降生之前就开始防护以保证母亲是健康的，可以生下健康的孩子，比如在中国，1/5 的妇女在生孩子时可能会患妊娠糖尿病，这会影响母婴在妊娠期间与未来的健康。这些便是我们想和机构、组织合作解决的问题。提到给予支持，我们会召开峰会、研究会和利益相关方会议，播下长期变化的种子。在基金会成立的 17 年里，我们的项目帮助了 840 万名患者，帮助检查了 1140 万名患者，训练了 41.2 万名专业人士，培育并强化了

13858座诊所疾病治疗的能力，这里的疾病治疗并不仅限于糖尿病，还有高血压等疾病。

在过去的17年里，我们学到了什么呢？确保项目的所有权完全集中在当地，我们要解决的是当地的问题，故要由项目的申请方确定当地的需求；确保项目从小开始，先建立信任，再扩大规模；鼓励创新型与可行、可复制的解决方案；确保项目可以解决大家的需求问题、满足供给；我们要牢记维护当地的环境和健康系统，不开展难以维系的行动；我们小心改变自己的观点，适应当地的环境；我们确保整个项目可以支持国家的健康标准和目标及行动计划；我们强化了已经存在的项目，并将新项目与之结合，完善健康系统，增强水平建设；我们也要确保项目的目标是针对非常弱势的人群；我们在技术支持、交互学习、建设当地网络上会给我们的合作伙伴以更多的支持；我们和更多的利益相关方和决策者一起合作，确保我们可以去捕捉、推广和分享项目的成功方案。我们所做的一件事是加强南南合作，尼日利亚有人明白若是他们能在印度做一件事，他们也可以在尼日利亚实施，而非将设备和人力带到欧洲去实施。所以构建南南交流网络对于我们来说是非常重要的，这意味着我们能把自己所学跨国传递给邻居。我可以谈论很多关于基金会所做的事，但是时间已经到了。非常感谢大家，这就是我的演讲。

林大庆： 接下来让我们邀请诺和诺德血友病基金会委员会主席加斯普·布兰德佳德先生演讲。

加斯普·布兰德佳德： 谢谢大家！今天非常荣幸能够代表诺和诺德血友病基金会来到深圳参加世界公益慈善论坛。诺和诺德血友病基金会致力于预防治疗血友病、糖尿病。今天我作为诺和诺德血友病基金会委员会的主席，接下来将介绍一下基金会的具体情况，我想给大家举两个实际例子。我们的原则和刚刚卡普尔博士讲述的世界糖尿病基金会的原则是十分相似的。诺和诺德血友病基金会于 2005 年在瑞士成立，我们意识到，诺和诺德公司不仅可以是一个生产药物的公司，还可以积极为世界做出贡献。成立这个基金会的目的是希望为世界带来更多的关爱，这就是为什么我们有了世界糖尿病基金会，3 年之后，我们又成立了诺和诺德血友病基金会。我们希望和全球的专家以及当地的人一起去提升专业能力，做更多的诊断和登记、教育和赋能。我们已经在 73 个国家做了 274 个项目，这和阿尼尔・卡普尔先生讲的糖尿病项目相比，可能只是小份额。我们在中国做了哪些事情？血友病是中国少有人认识的病症。我们开始在中国工作的时候是 10 年前，那时只有 7000 名血友病患者确诊，现在已经有 3 万名血友病患者得到了治疗，中国可能有几十万名血友病患者。我们在中国开展了 10 个有关血友病的项目，通过这些项目，我们诊断出了 4000 多名血友病患者，提升了实验室的建设水平。在中国，强化了 113 个实验室，而且我们有一些基于网页的患者注册渠道。我们培训了 1500 名医保从业者，在中国建设了科技中心，我们和病人、社区之间建立了非常紧密的联系。在过去 10 年，我们一直做这方面的工作。我想讨论的第一个项目在巴拿马展开，这是我们的经典项目之一，有关通过科技中心建设强化人们的健康意识。此项目和我们目前在山东省进行的项目有许多相似性，这个计划运行得非常良好，也是我们在 2018 年最成功的计划之一。

我想讨论一下我们在巴拿马的项目。在 2007 年，巴拿马的医护资源非常有限，全城仅有一个基本护理中心。我们在一所医院了解到了当地的需求，即建立基本护理中心。我们发现当地许多血友病患者住在乡下，处于非常糟糕的状态，无法前往城里得到治疗。所以进行这个项目的第一步是找到合作伙伴，共建护理中心。我们找到了一位有名的医生，共同加强中心建设，不仅是训练医护人员，还要传授给患者及其家庭成员相关知识。第二步，我们建立了 6 家中心，我们对 6 位医生、6 位护理、6 位社工进行了深度培训，向经济困难的血友病患者提供援助。通过这种方式，我们减少了患者 76% 接受治疗的路途花费。这是一项非常大的成就。这个经典示例展现了我们如何在发展中国家培育可持续的医疗能力。

第二个例子在乌干达。2015 年，3600 人当中只有 42 人被确诊为血友病，首都坎帕拉的医疗资源十分有限，没有基础设施可以诊断血友病。我们开展项目的第一步是在乌干达开展了一个增强公共意识的活动。我们建立了实验室，并且培训当地的技术人员。有一些培训师志愿去乌干达，又诊断出 49 名血友病患者，140 人参与了这个项目。我们希望把这个举措扩展到全国，无论是增强预防血友病意识还是培训方面，以及早发现患者。项目进行两年后，我们又确诊了 200 名患者。最后，我们和医疗机构合作，提出了一项议会同意的政策，有关如何在乌干达治疗血友病。作为慈善机构，和医疗机构合作是非常重要的，因为这是获取当地政府疾病治疗政策信息的渠道。

以上的两个项目是我们在全球做的案例，非常感谢。

林大庆：接下来邀请刘斯奇先生——华大集团联合创始人，请他上台演讲。

刘斯奇：感谢刚刚对我的介绍。尊敬的各位嘉宾，女士们，先生们，大家下午好，我非常高兴来到这里展示我在公共卫生领域的工作经验。

华大基因是深圳当地的一家非典型的企业，在过去 20 年中，我们试图把产业、教育、研究放在一起。之所以称非典型，是因为在华大过去 20 年中，我们始终把公共健康作为研究的重点。感谢中国改革开放的大好时机，虽然走得很困难，但是到今天，我们依然能够成为世界最大的基因组研究中心，也成为世界上最大基因组的产业基地。

今天我和大家分享华大基因在公共卫生方面的想法，这个想法主要考虑了出生健康的问题。中国有 7000 种遗传性疾病，每年大概有 3000 万个家庭要接受出生时有缺陷的孩子，支出 300 亿元。作为医生，我们最关心的问题是能够找到一种方法预防出生缺陷，一定是找一些发生频率很高，而且可以做的事情。我们把主要的注意力放在唐氏综合征上，其于 150 年前在西方被发现，1959 年的时候知道是染色体导致的，而且确定了基本的临床症状。除了智力发育非常慢，最终就是七八岁的智力，还有两个基本的特征，其一是两眼的距离是宽的，从分子上讲就是有三条染色体。这样的工作持续 150 年了，大家在预防上没有太多的办法，尽管生物学的标识很清楚。传统上讲有三种方法：1. 抽血检查，但是出现的时间特别晚，而且假阳性率特别高；2. 超生，晚期才能看到；3. 羊水穿刺，这种方法非常精准，但是没有普及，而且假阳性率很高，有可能引发流产和其他意外。所有的事情让唐氏综合征的研究变得非常缓慢，1997 年的时候，香港中文大学有一个很重要的发现，怀孕的母体可能有微量的 DNA，当时使用 PCR 的办法可以检测到一部分，这极大地鼓励了早期对唐氏综合征特征的检测。但是没有基因组序列的信号，极有可能引起假阳性，而且操作的过程比较缓慢，不适合大规模的临床检验，所以临床检验都是找熟悉的人群，比如高龄的妇女。总之，老百姓日常能够普遍接受的检测技术还没有出现。

华大在 1999 年注意到这个技术，我们有三方面的考虑。1. 从技术的敏感度来讲，有没有办法变成大规模的检测？2. 和健康中国的大目标一致，和政府合作，找到造福于中国人民，乃至造福于世界人民的方法。在这个过程中，华大做了很多的工作。2007 年的时候，华大使用了当时最先进的技术，叫作第二代测序技术，这决定了未来基因组技术能够用于临床的测定，这个技术最大的特点是不管是测序的规模、速度还是费用均超过了一般人接受的摩尔定律。因为这个技术的出现，我们才有可能在这个时候，把准确率、普及率提高，把实验的费用降低。2006 年开始，我们引进高通量测序技术，2010 年成果发表，然后发表一系列的文章。抽检大概 2000 万人，400 人在华大做完了，我们的检测发现了 1.8 万个唐氏综合征患者，对深圳有很大的贡献。在所有的工作中可以看到，从 2009 年开始到 2017 年，在政府的推动下，我们把所有的费用降到 800 元，现在还会进一步降低。我们有两个很大的贡献，在深圳，将近 70% 的妇女可以检测唐氏综合征。在 8 年的历史中，由 1 万个人里的 3.49，现在降到 0.8，降低患有唐氏综合征胎儿的出生率。最重要的是，深圳模式的推广能不能惠及全中国的老百姓？所以我们进一步推广到长沙，长沙受到深圳的影响，把它变成全体长沙市民受惠的项目。2019 年到河北石家庄，全市的孕妇可以做这个项目。我们在全国 18 个省市做了这个项目。我们也会做病人的感染、肿瘤等项目，利用现在基因组的技术解决国计民生问题，谢谢各位。

林大庆：下面请深圳市卫生健康委员会主任罗乐宣演讲。

罗乐宣：尊敬的各位来宾，各位专家，女士们，先生们，大家下午好，感谢论坛邀请我围绕健康主题做演讲，前面三位的演讲离不开健康的话题，我借这个话题介绍一下健康深圳的情况。

“健康中国”已经是国家的战略了，在全民奔小康的征程中，党和国家非常重视健康问题。习近平总书记在卫生健康大会上强调，没有全民健康，就没有全面小康，经济要发展，健康要上去。人民群众的获得感、幸福感、安全感都离不开健康，所以健康事业已经成为国家的战略部署，也是民族昌盛和国家富强的重要标志。在这样的定位下，国家采取一系列的战略措施。

2009年启动了医改，新的医改主要目标是建立基本医疗卫生制度，让人民群众公平享有、公平获得，提高便携性。我们围绕建立基本医疗卫生制度，有四个保障体系——全民卫生医保体系、医疗服务体系、公共卫生服务体系、药品供应保障体系，在这四个体系下有八项重点工作需要推进。随着医改的推进，"十三五"期间，在这个基础上，我们有了整体的设计。建造基本医疗卫生智库，主要的问题是完善、推进几项制度：一个是加快推进分级诊疗制度，一个是巩固深化公立医院综合改革，一个是完善全民基本医保制度，一个是药品保证，一个是改革开放以后加强监管。

2016年，中国卫生健康大会明确提出"健康中国"战略，发布了规划纲要；在发布规划纲要的同时，出台了医改规划和专项规划纲要。在这样的基础上，到了2019年，把规划纲要变成了"健康中国行动计划"，这个行动计划有15项内容，一个是全方位干预影响健康的因素，维护全生命周期健康，在这个基础上抓好五大重大疾病的防治。全方位干预包括六个方面，最基础的是普及健康教育，提升健康素养是最关键的。我们的世界卫生组织指南强调四大基石，从合理的膳食到全民的健身运动，到健康计划，到心理卫生。全生命周期维护健康，有四个阶段，妇幼保健阶段只是其中一个，然后是中小学青少年，到成年解决职业健康问题，然后是长者健康，四个阶段是全生命周期，从怀孕开始到临终是一个全生命周期。五大重大疾病，即心脑血管疾病、糖尿病、慢性病等。

深圳围绕国家部署也在推进，我们的工作主线是补短板、强基层、建高地、促健康。第一，深圳发展40年，40年的医疗卫生基础和2000万人的需求水平还是有差距的，我们最大的问题是资源不足，我们的医生数在全国全省所占比例很低。第二，形成分级诊疗体系。第三，提高医疗水平。第四，按照"健康中国"战略促健康，所有工作要围绕提升人民健康水平进行推进。四个方面我们都有具体的工作，比如加强医院的建设。2020年，我们需要 603000 张床位，千人床位数达 4.3 张，千人医生数达到 3.8 名。我们通过实施医疗卫生“三名”工程，引进国内外优势资源，如名院、名医。除了在建医院，建好的医院都交给名校运营管理，包括港大深圳医院，其定位是深圳市的公立医院，只不过交给港大运营管理，但是日常的所有维护按照公立医院的补助标准。我们引进国家团队，让国家的肿瘤医院、医学科来深圳落地，包括深圳市第三人民医院获批国家感染性疾病临床研究中心。促健康方面，我们全面推进健康深圳建设，比如公共卫生强化行动及市民健康素养提升、医疗服务提升行动等，我们围绕这些方面开展工作。

我们也承担了国家 17 项医改卫生任务，比如食品安全，资源配置效率也有明显的提升，个人卫生支出降到 20% 以下。

《中共中央 国务院关于支持深圳建设中国特色社会主义先行示范区的意见》颁布后，我们有十项工作，一个方面是人大要立法，三个方面要先行示范，六个方面需重点突破，有三个阶段目标，最终打造国际一流的医疗中心，谢谢大家！

林大庆：感谢所有的演讲者注意时间的限制，你们的演讲也是干货满满，我们只有几分钟的时间可以提问，我想问一下观众有没有问题想要问在座的各位嘉宾，我们可以把时间留给观众。我先代表大家问一个问题。我们深圳发展得这么好，但是我们也谈大湾区，深圳怎样助力大湾区发展？

罗乐宣：谢谢主持人。粤港澳大湾区建设也是国家的战略布局，粤港澳大湾区涵盖了“9+2”，即香港、澳门加广东的 9 个市，粤港澳大湾区的发展，国家定位目标有 5 项，最核心的是打造国际科技创新中心。现在是以广州、深圳、香港为核心引擎，特别是注重香港的国际创新地位，我觉得推进这方面目标的实现，核心引擎城市要实现规则的衔接、制度的相通，特别是人流、物流、信息流的融通，这是粤港澳大湾区发展的重点。大家一起比肩前行，大家一起发展。

林大庆：我觉得深圳的工作做得非常好。

罗乐宣：人大立法是最早的，但是我们在强化执法上，还有很多问题，而全民的意识，我觉得在明显增强。特别是国家提出了 15 项行动内容，我们要把这份工作做得更好。

林大庆：我问一下刘斯奇博士，您刚才提到基因，请讲一讲这方面的工作和公益慈善的关系是怎样的?

刘斯奇：我们的基金会的初衷是希望用科技的力量助力慈善，我们从两个方面着手，利用我们的技术力量为贫困地区提供帮助。另外，我们希望使基因组的理念更加科普化，因为这些知识看上去非常深奥，但是通过其他的科普知识，老百姓更容易接受，这有很大的建设性作用。回顾 20 年前的中国，现在有很大的变化，我们以前想做基因组研究，主流的科学家是反对的。绝大多数科学家不认同华大基因的理念，但是到现在，我们创造的 1% 计划已经写进了小学课本，所以科学普及的力量是很大的，科学发展的速度也是很快的。

林大庆：基因组研究的成果一般是有钱人可以享受到，但是你们让老百姓也可以享受到，我非常感动。我想问两位嘉宾，两位都来自基金会，为什么要更多地强调建立可持续的模式，而不是直接为当地的人们提供经济资助?

加斯普·布兰德佳德：不管是糖尿病基金会还是血友病基金会，如果我们只是向患者提供药物治疗服务，那我们就陷入了道德困境中。我们的目的是帮助病人，帮助他们诊断这种疾病是伴随他们一生的。如果直接提供帮助，只是管用一时。若是我们同当地政府建立联系、建立能力中心，就能长远地帮助这些人。我们现在正和中国一些比较贫穷的省份合作，我们可以关注这个项目，从这个地方，然后扩展到另外一个地方，推动政策进步，建立可持续的、长期的体系。

阿尼尔·卡普尔：我完全同意，可持续非常重要，尤其是预防，预防比治疗更具前瞻性。我们认为糖尿病的治疗是不昂贵的，而不预防、不治疗糖尿病的代价是非常昂贵的，所以我们在做的事是帮助当地加强能力建设、解决诊所供应不足等问题。我们提供教育和培训的机会，让人们可以均等地获取服务。这是可持续的做法。如果直接把药物分配给病人，那么当地的环境不会改变。我们作为基金会不可能独自解决糖尿病问题，我们要和地方进行合作，建立合作伙伴关系，优化当地的体系。治疗糖尿病、提供药物，这在世界上所有区域都不需要花费太多，重要的是让人们关注到糖尿病问题，加强人们对糖尿病的理解，增强能力建设。我说一个有关糖尿病预防治疗的例子。我想说的是改变。基金会的一个创意是跟中国疾控中心和中国糖尿病防治中心合作的，在六个我们开展项目的城市中，有一个是深圳，还有厦门、西安、上海、北京、青岛，我们一开始跟当地的社区健康中心进行联动和合作。那时候，我们并没有过分注重糖尿病的社区，遵照组织的规范，并没有得到当地的支持。后来到青岛，我们和青岛卫健委合作开展了大规模的活动，超过120万人接受了糖尿病的筛查，我们和地方建立合作关系，才使得筛查成为可能。如果我们直接提供药物，则没有办法建立可持续的体系。

林大庆：每个城市让120万人接受筛查，几年后可以让很多人受惠。

刘斯奇：关于我们讲的疾病治疗的问题，减少成本、让更多的人享受到科技带来的红利是非常好的。但是在中国并没有那么多的数据，甚至某些疾病的病发率在上升，我们需要更多的教育和培训，让人们增强疾病防治的意识。

加斯普·布兰德佳德：以我之前作为首席财务官的经验来说，治疗疾病最基本的是改变行为、减肥和更多的锻炼。

阿尼尔·卡普尔：我觉得这是消灭糖尿病和其他疾病的基础疗法。这个项目是从欧洲开始的。中国的相关数据包括20世纪60年代的饥荒显示，那时出生的孩子很容易患上糖尿病和心血管疾病。为什么我们要迅速发展经济呢？我们要吸取经验和教训。教育从长远来看会解决健康问题，但是意识到这一点的人很少。我也提到了结核病这种疾病，在中国结核病的发病率还是很高的，此外，现在中国比较关注艾滋病，但是受艾滋病影响的人只是很少一部分，而结核病和糖尿病影响到的人的基数是非常大的，糖尿病是结核病的主要威胁因素。我们的项目在中国和印度都取得成功，我们都进行了筛查，让糖尿病患者知道其可能也患了肺结核，然后改变他们的生活习惯。

林大庆：现在现场的听众没有其他的提问，因为时间关系，我们的分论坛二到此结束。我们希望湾区能够成为健康湾区，能够成为最快乐的一个湾区，能够成为全球的健康湾区。感谢我们嘉宾的展示和讨论，谢谢！同时感谢诸位的参与。

六 青年与湾区社会创新和社会企业

主 持 人：粤港澳大湾区青年总会主席兼执行主席 吴学明

对话嘉宾：斯坦福大学管理科学与工程系学者 查尔斯·埃斯利

香港青年协会总干事 何永昌

吴学明：大家好，我是粤港澳大湾区青年总会主席兼执行主席，这个论坛由我来担任主持人，接下来有请斯坦福大学管理科学与工程系学者查尔斯·埃斯利先生演讲。

查尔斯·埃斯利：我非常感谢主办方的邀请。今天我非常高兴可以有机会和那么多的人在深圳一起去讨论很有意义的话题。

在我的职业生涯中，我一半投身科研，一半关注初创企业。若是提及科研与教育，我的关注点是企业家精神——发展中经济体的企业家精神。

斯坦福是一所世界知名的大学，在创业和创新方面做得非常好，很多校友在经营营利性的企业，但鲜为人知的是我们学校的学生、校友和教师也非常积极地创建非营利性企业和社会企业。除了 PPT 上这些知名的营利性公司，我们有很多校友也创建了非营利性公司，如睿智基金（Acumen Fund）。

PPT 中图片右侧是我的一名学生。她当时谈论的是我们教授的知识框架，这些知识可用于营利性企业，也可用于非营利性企业。她上了我的课——“科技企业家精神”，曾在课上做项目。毕业后，她的来自巴基斯坦的童年伙伴来找她，最终她们两个决定在巴基斯坦推动女性教育。她拒绝了伦敦一家咨询公司的高薪工作，和伙伴一起创立了一个基金会。该基金会为巴基斯坦和印度促进女性受教育的项目提供资金支持。现在她也创建了一家风投基金公司，致力于培育中东女性企业家精神。这名女生是我所教过的最令我感到骄傲的学生之一，因为她对世界产生了很大的影响。

另一个例子。斯坦福大学有一家名叫“拥抱”（Embrace）的公司，为新生儿提供孵化器。这家公司产生自一门课程——“可支付的极限设计”。让我讲一下这门课是做什么的。在发展中经济体如非洲的经济体中，孵化器是必不可少的。在美国，孵化器用于医院，价格很高，一件要 2 万美元。学生想在这个项目里为贫困地区解决这个问题，他们做了比较便宜的孵化器，只需要 25 美元，可以保暖，也可以防水，这是工程上的技术创新。

再讲另外一个例子。明天下午三点的时候，我的一位同事，来自硅谷的黄学思，会具体地谈一下这个项目，所以我不会过多地讲这个项目。明天下午你们会听到一手汇报，他会介绍这个项目。这个项目主要针对非洲国家的村庄，在那些地方，有些儿童因使用煤油灯而被灼伤。这个项目为这部分在晚上使用煤油灯照明的人群提供太阳能照明，为南非 5 亿个无法得到电力供应的人提供安全便宜的夜间照明。

多年来，这些有关社会企业精神的项目和活动已经有了确定的模式，并且有了教育下一代、发展非营利性机构的特殊组织。斯坦福 King 国际发展中心是由 King 家族资助成立的，该中心这个暑期资助了一些学生，让他们前往泰国工作，促进泰国培育社会企业家精神和发展经济。斯坦福 Seed 是另一个项目，专注于创新减贫、促进经济发展。

我主要负责收集创业公司的数据，我们做了针对斯坦福大学校友的调研，这个调研针对 14 万名左右在 20 世纪 30 年代到 2011 年间从 7 个院系毕业的校友，跨度非常广。我们获得了 2.7 万份答卷。王教授分享了湾区的 GDP 数据，我们收集了斯坦福大学初创企业的数据，将它们的营收转化为 GDP。若斯坦福大学校友组成一座城市，以 GDP 衡量，它将会是世界上第十大经济体。如果研究斯坦福大学对硅谷的贡献，我们会发现其中重要的一点是斯坦福大学吸引了很多人才，有很多学生来自加州，可以看到有很高比例的人才毕业后决定留在加州，并且致力于为旧金山湾区的经济发展做贡献，要么是自己创业，要么是在高新技术公司工作。所以大学是人才的磁石，为硅谷和旧金山湾区输送了很多人才，这是一个重要的例子。我们问了一位校友，你来斯坦福大学读书是因为其在社会企业精神方面的声誉还是其他？我们看到，越来越多的校友选择来斯坦福大学读书，这是因为其创业方面的声誉。

我刚刚也提到了，不仅有校友创建营利性的公司，也有校友创建非营利性的公司。大家可以看一下数据分布。有的校友创立了天使基金，有的校友成为早期的雇员，有的校友成为董事会的成员。可以看到，建立营利性公司和建立非营利性公司之间是存在联系的，他们通过营利性机构创造经济价值，同时通过非营利性机构分布价值。我们也调研了非营利性组织所在的行业，其中包括教育、经济发展、全球健康与消费者权益等。我们还可以看到创建非营利性机构的校友来自的院系，大部分校友来自法学院，然后是教育学院和商学院。我想要强调的是，我们可以收集这些社会企业精神和非营利性组织的数据来做科研，来发现到底是什么促进了创业的成功？何种技术、何种教育经历可以让学生变得更具影响力、更加成功地建立社会机构？可以做这样的研究。

早年间，毕业生创建非营利性机构的趋势一直在上升，有越来越多的毕业生投入其中。但在最近 10 年，这个趋势有所下降，因为他们需要人生阅历让自己判断是否能创建一个非营利性的机构且拥有足够的资源。其中让我感到非常振奋的一点是，2000~2017 年的毕业生越来越感兴趣于创建营利性机构，包括刚刚从斯坦福大学毕业的学生。

很多创建了营利性机构的校友后续又创建了非营利性机构，这体现了其在创造经济价值和财富积累过程中的心态转变。他们在创立营利性机构之后，有了资金支持非营利性机构的运转，从而回馈社会，创造自己的财富。

最后我想提一下支持学生创业活动的斯坦福创新中心，其中一个已经有一些年份的中心叫作斯坦福社企中心。自 20 世纪 90 年代起，该中心帮助学生在非营利性机构寻求职业发展。Taproot 基金会是另外一个机构，由商学院成立。这个机构为其他非营利性机构提供顾问咨询服务，可以帮助其他非营利性机构解决在信息技术、人力资源方面遇到的问题。还有一个机构是成立于 20 世纪 80 年代的汉斯公共服务中心，支持学生在非营利性机构中获得实习的机会，并提供教育资料。Fusion 是将未来社会创新人士和企业家聚在一起的机构。慈善和市民社会中心是最近成立的机构，专注于教学和社会企业家精神等偏科研的方向，也就是说让这些学生分析数据、趋势或者寻找成功因子等。所以说这个中心可能需要基于证据做研究。

以上就是我想要展示的全部内容，非常感谢诸位的倾听，非常期待稍后的问答环节，谢谢。

吴学明：谢谢查尔斯·埃斯利教授的精彩展示。下面请香港青年协会总干事何永昌先生上台演讲，谢谢。

何永昌：非常感谢，大家下午好，今天我非常高兴有这个机会和你们分享香港青协的经验，我先用英文介绍今天的想法。另外一部分，可以和大家用普通话交流。刚才听了查尔斯·埃斯利在大学的经验，今天我想从青年服务的角度谈一谈。

先谈关于年轻人作为变革的实施者。为什么年轻人参与了社会创新的进程？我分享一下自己的见解。年轻人在四个方面具有优势。第一，年轻人更有动力，他们愿意追逐自己的梦想和目标，而不只是以财富为出发点。第二，他们更具有创新的能力，不必受传统模式的束缚。第三，这个时代的年轻人已经习惯于同时做多项工作，他们享受从事有意义的工作，也非常重视生活和工作的平衡。第四，社会创新就是年轻人的教练，它能够教会年轻人如何更好地实现社会创新。没有比社会创新更好的教练了，通过社会创新，年轻人可以培养自己的技能，更清楚地理解一些社会问题。

我想分享一下为什么专注于这个领域。在2005年，很多人知道这样一个消息，当时联合国和国际劳工组织提出了四项核心战略，主要是为了解决年轻人的失业问题，这四项核心战略是设立工作岗位、弘扬创业精神、增强可就业性、给予公平机会。我们需要在这些方面有更多的考量，同时我们开启了新的项目——香港青年商业计划，这是一个微型金融计划，旨在培养青年的创业技能，让他们有更好的发展。

这是一个非常重要的项目，在这里我和大家分享一下香港青年商业计划的路线图及我们对这一计划的实施。2002 年，我们第一次涉足支持青年创业的计划，为他们提供的是创业培训，而且培养他们的创业思维，这和原先的就业服务所提供的内容是不一样的。2005 年，我们提出了香港年轻人创业计划，用来支持年轻人商业国际计划，这是我们为香港本地青年创业家提供的首次“一站式”服务，填补了青年初创企业领域的空缺。2014 年，我们有了前海深港青年梦工场，这是在 2014 年 12 月份开启的项目，它坐落于深圳前海。青年梦工场由前海管理局、深圳青联、香港青协三方发起成立，与香港青协和深圳青联有着战略合作关系。自青年梦工场成功引进了几十家青年企业之后，我们建立了新项目，有了香港青协赛马会社会创新中心 SIC，这是 2015 年设置的，支持年轻人去创造以及执行自己的创业计划与创造可持续发展计划。

我们积累了 17 年的经验与智慧，我们在青年创业中有更长足的发展，我们创造出更多有用的服务模式、多种服务项目，可以让年轻人很快、有效地创立企业，并且更快地融入社会创新项目。2020 年，我们将有一个新的项目在四川成都设立，这对于我们来说是一个重大的举措，可以将自己的经验广泛传播给内地的合作伙伴。

我们给年轻人的支持是什么？我们为他们提供创新企业的服务，包括初创培训。作为一个初创企业的企业家，我们可以为他们提供更多的初创知识，他们会获得更多的市场拓展和营销知识。我们也可以提供 2 万 ~20 万元不等的初始创业基金，让年轻人在我们联盟的指导下创建自己的企业。我们也会安排不同的活动支持他们，包括全球创业家联盟论坛等。在我们的经验当中，有几点希望和大家分享。

首先，社会影响和可持续发展。大多数香港青年创业家很有创意，他们有很好的创业思维，让他们更好地去利用技术解决问题。但是有些时候，他们没有办法思考项目的可持续性，所以他们只想到方案，却没有想过这个方案要怎样可持续地进行下去。

我给大家讲一个成功的例子——一个年轻人创立绿行侠的项目，我们把它叫作生态绿色项目，该项目提供了环保解决方案。他对残余咖啡渣进行处理，把食物废物回收这样的意识反馈到社区中。这样的意识其实是可以进入市场的，并且可以超越市场，创造出产品。所以他能持续开展自己的项目。

其次，科技不是必要的东西，但是一定要有经验和热情。我们在和年轻人玩的时候会问他们，为什么要开启这个公司，他们说这很简单，因为他们可以用一些人工智能的技术。这个问题的焦点，并不是他们有这个问题，只是说使用了人工智能技术，他们并没有依靠此技术发展相关的智能，所以我们支持年轻人的时候会问他们这些问题。我也问过一个室内设计师，他说他的父亲几年前去世了，他唯一的遗憾是，他的父亲在生前没有享受过舒适的家居，所以他成立了一个室内设计小团队，这个团队有 15 人，并在不停地扩张。这是非常好的创业家的精神。此外，成为企业家不容易，成为创业家更困难。

最后，我想要和大家分享我们在社会创新生态系统上的差距，或者是我们的缺口，这是我们需要支持的方面。第一，我们播下的公司的种子还不够多，因为培养企业家精神并不是容易的事情。我们一定要早早开始，对青年人进行这方面的教育。第二，缺少跨界联合。在香港，其实对于企业家精神的支持已经有很多了，但是大多数支持者是单独作战。所以年轻人有一个巨大的问题，他们加入了一个项目，必须因为要得到资金的支持而不断开展重复的内容。第三，社会企业家没有得到定制化的支持。在未来的香港或者内地，应该有协同的力量一起去定制，为社会企业家定制支持，我觉得这会是年轻人非常需要的。这是我今天想和大家分享的，也希望和大家有更多的交流，谢谢。

吴学明：我们接下来开始进入对答环节，我先用一分钟介绍一下自己。我从哈佛大学毕业，对 EMS 的市场非常熟悉。我在麻省理工读了研究生，现在做粤港澳大湾区青年总会的主席。现在谈到香港问题，大家有一个共同的概念，不想要暴力，和平就好了，大家有诉求可以和平地说。我想先请教一下查尔斯·埃斯利先生，您也知道，全球有四个大湾区，有两个在美国——旧金山湾区和纽约湾区，还有一个在日本——东京湾区，我们今天探讨的是中国的粤港澳大湾区。您觉得其他几个湾区有哪些经验？或者斯坦福大学为大湾区提供了什么？中国有没有潜力追赶上旧金山湾区成为第二个硅谷？在深圳有没有这样的可能？

查尔斯·埃斯利：这个问题很有意思，我来到这里之前也听过关于粤港澳大湾区的倡议，我当时没有想到湾区能够促进初创企业和科技的发展。认真地来说，我认为粤港澳大湾区正在迎头赶上，但是还存在一些差距，我前不久看到了一些数据。尤其是最近，我们知道北京有最多数量的风投机构和初创企业，接下来就是上海、杭州，大湾区处在第三的位置。从风投的增长率来说，中国是占据高位的，可能是世界第一，尤其是过去一年，中国风投基金总额首次超过美国，好像是 930 亿美元：910 亿美元。不同的经济体有上升期和下降期，我们在考虑估值和资金流动的情况下，下一个起伏还未可知。

吴学明：谢谢您。接下来，我想请教何永昌教授，前海有非常成功的创业项目，我自己也做科技，你们有什么建议？在孵化器方面，我们怎么做到可持续性维持？怎么能持续投成功的创业项目？在这方面如何避免同质化？因为在深圳南山区已经有 700 多个孵化器，有这么多人创业吗？您怎么看？

何永昌：青年梦工场的经验是一个很好的开始，香港和前海，给了我们非常好的经验。但是怎么样可以让这个项目做到更好？因为在大湾区，不单单去前海创业，我相信青年创业最大的困难是去到不同的地方，他们可能面对不了解的情况，然后就不能进行他们的工作。这一方面，我相信可以在不同的地区，让青年对当地的认识多一点，让他们发展好一点。您刚才说孵化器的问题，我相信在大湾区也有很多的孵化器，有同质化的情况出现。每一个孵化器有各自的特点，现在很多不同的孵化器其实是让不同的青年对不同的重点有多一点的兴趣。比如在华强路，青年在那边发展有好处，其他地方也有其他地方的好处，我相信这不是同质化的问题。其他的地方有它们的优势，让它们的优势在青年创业的时候发挥作用，是一种很重要的分工，让不同的孵化器效果好一点。

吴学明：非常感谢何总干事。我再问一下查尔斯·埃斯利博士，您刚刚给了我们很多启迪，就是关于如何发展大湾区。我们对于非营利性机构和慈善事业非常感兴趣，除了金融上的支持，您觉得还有什么因素能够吸引人才，保持人才？因为很多人才是做志愿者工作，没有薪酬。比如我们的总会，我们有 200 名成员，他们是做志愿者工作，只有 2 名是有薪酬的，怎么样让这部分志愿者有这样的使命感和动力免费做志愿者工作？他们都是研究生毕业，毕业之后就要开始做全职的工作，我也在考虑这样的问题。您能不能提供一些参考？肯定许多年轻人会面对这样的问题。

查尔斯·埃斯利：这是一个很重要的问题，因为人才是最重要的方面，哪怕是对于营利性机构而言也已经很难保留人才，对于非营利性机构而言则更难留住人才了，所以存在挑战。社会变得越来越富有了，我们在硅谷看到一个现象，最有才能的人，希望从事的不仅是能够赚钱的工作，在有了资金的积累之后，他们希望从事一些为这个世界带来改变的工作。哪怕是那些在硅谷的公司，如果不能让工程师和经理觉得他们所从事的工作，将为数千万的人带来福祉，能够改变世界，也是会在招聘上吃苦头的。我有一位朋友曾被塔利班枪击头部，但是她奇迹地恢复了健康，她有没有放弃开展鼓励巴基斯坦女性创业的活动，有没有不再有勇气进行公众演讲？她没有。她觉得女性需要受更多教育，尤其是年轻的女性，也希望激励更多人推动这个计划。然后她开始讲述这个故事，这都是很好的案例。

吴学明：谢谢您。您分享了非常棒的经验。我想问何永昌先生，社会创业和青年息息相关，怎么样让年轻人到大湾区创业？第二个问题，很多人愿意为斯坦福大学提供捐赠，但是对于非营利性机构，大家如何融资呢？我们如何说服人们捐赠呢？我们除了向自己的亲人或者是家族筹款，还有什么途径可以融资呢？

何永昌：我们也做了调查，香港青年不回内地创业发展，最重要的原因是他们不了解，没有接触过内地，所以就没有兴趣。所以让香港的青年回内地发展、创业，最重要的是让他们先有一种感觉。我们做青年创业工作，很重要的是同理心的概念，我们让青年到一个地方发展、创业，要让他们建立对那个地方的同理心。

吴学明：关于第二个问题，我们从查尔斯·埃斯利博士开始，这个问题是问两位的。非营利性机构如何筹资的问题，哪怕非营利性机构有非常高尚的目标，但是如何说服捐赠人呢？

查尔斯·埃斯利：从我个人的经历来看，无论是为斯坦福大学融资还是为慈善基金会融资，还有我的妻子为美国糖尿病基金会筹款，她有很多融资的工作经历，我们一开始都比较恐惧，但这是技能，我们必须掌握和不断地练习。我们倾向于和一些想要投身慈善的人一起，所以我们必须要克服这样的恐惧，渐渐就能够建立起非常紧密的关系。

何永昌：我给一个简单的答案，如果我们可以让人们去思考这个项目的社会影响力的话，我们就可以得到更多的支持。所以我觉得，社会创新是个问题，让他们考虑这样的业务是可以解决社会问题的，这是一个很好的方向，可以让我们得到很好的支持。

吴学明： 感谢两位嘉宾给我们分享的经验，也给我们展示了如此具有启发性的对话，非常感谢，我们的分论坛就此结束。

七 体育人慈善路

主 持 人： 北京体育大学产业管理集团总经理 张强强

对话嘉宾： 皇家马德里基金会总经理 胡里奥·冈萨雷斯·隆科

中国网球运动员、亚洲首位大满贯单打冠军得主 李娜

中国人民对外友好协会秘书长、中国友好和平发展基金会理事长 李希奎

丹麦国家奥林匹克委员会首席执行官兼秘书长 莫滕·汉森

张强强： 各位朋友，到了今天的最后一个板块，经过了一天的会议，大家特别累，甚至有些同志饥肠辘辘了。既然是体育板块，我们来一个比赛，比赛很简单，看谁的声音大。

作为大会，能够把体育板块加进来，我觉得特别好，因为体育对现代人来讲，已经被赋予了特殊的含义。我们的伟大领袖毛主席说过，“文明其精神，野蛮其体魄”。习近平总书记也说，体育承载着国家强盛、民族振兴的梦想，体育强则中国强。在当今社会，体育已经成为国家发展的战略，今天我们体育板块也请到了体育界重量级的选手。首先有请皇家马德里基金会总经理胡里奥·冈萨雷斯·隆科先生。

胡里奥·冈萨雷斯·隆科：大家下午好，非常感谢主办方给我这一次机会说一下皇家马德里基金会在慈善方面的活动。

曼德拉说过体育具有改变世界的力量，这种力量给人以凝聚力，可以创造希望，拯救人们于绝望之中。这个想法和另外一个人的说法相呼应，他说过体育是国之常在，体育不仅仅是体育，而且具有教育价值，是非常具有合作精神的运动。我们可以看到，实际上皇家马德里基金会有非常多不同的活动，其成立于 1997 年，是一个非营利性组织。2008 年的时候，我们被西班牙国际合作发展署认定为发展机构，工作框架以联合国《儿童权利公约》为基础，所以这就是为什么我们有很多皇家马德里的球员和儿童一起参与培训项目。因为体育有助于儿童身体的成长，以及智力和情感方面的成长。体育也是一种工具，可以帮助我们促进和平，它是社会凝聚的要素，可以帮助我们更好地度过休闲时光。

我们在不同地方开展体育项目，主要是为皇家马德里足球俱乐部塑造更好的形象，实现人文宗旨。我们的一个目标就是要去做人文，并不是让他们做最强的队伍，我们在国内是针对 6~17 岁的青少年，我们也会进驻收容中心、医院等，帮助残疾人和老年人。在国际层面，我们针对 6~17 岁的青少年开设社会体育学院，也会涉及不同的大洲，逐渐遍布各个国家，各国会有非常多的体育活动。

我介绍一下我们的活动，其可以非常灵活地根据每个国家的具体情况进行调整，主要是足球或者篮球。学生不会遭到任何的歧视，最重要的是，与皇家马德里足球俱乐部没有任何关系，形成的是一个社会足球学校，并不是为皇家马德里足球俱乐部招收学生。我们的优良品格是尊重、平等、友好、自主、忍让。因为我们需要一起踢足球，所以忍让非常重要，平等、友好、自主是每个国家都倡导的优良品格，这在印度和俄罗斯都有展现。我们现在的目标是在开展体育活动的同时，支持文化课的学习，进行职业培训，希望可以做到自重、消除社会壁垒，希望可以实现在体育上的平等。做体育展示的时候会发现这是一个小社会，两队的人需要一些合作，共同迎接挑战。皇家马德里基金会是项目的支点，但需要机构建立合作伙伴关系，我们和当地政府或者赞助商一起合作，我们的目标是让公共和民营的领域集结起来，在一个框架下进行合作。

我们对社会有所贡献。我们有专项的培训，我们告诉教练，可以利用什么方法改善学员们的学习方式，因为我们不仅仅是培育他们的职业技能，更多的是给他们品格上的教育，让他们成为社会的良好公民，所以我们需要个性化的协调、项目媒体宣传等。对于皇家马德里基金会而言，社会体育是一生的承诺，我们会秉持专业性和保证效率，最重要的是鼓励孩子把受教育作为迈向更光明未来的重要途径。

我们所做的计划和整理的材料，都是针对不同的运动，比如足球或者篮球，但我们会融入很基本的学科知识。而且我们集结了非常好的人才编纂这些教材，我们认为真正的教育是培育自己的品格和提升自己的素质。真正的教育应该是品格的培养和体育一起发展，是个人身体发展和体育训练相辅相成，而且我们会确保每一个培训师专员跟进大家的培训，确保他们享有一致性。

在世界上一个地方，我们会培训某一个项目，在另外一个地方可能会提供另外一种项目的支持，无论是在哪里，我们都会帮助学校运行和发展，为它们提供更多的监督教练，而且我们会为它们的工作提供更多的支持。

我们有一些国际项目，比如球星，他们对于慈善基金会来说是非常重要的。

我的演讲到这里，谢谢诸位，希望在未来能够与非营利性机构合作，我们认为非营利性机构像爱情故事一样，我们都是为了让这个世界变得更好，为了让自己的社区变得更好。我认为这是我们根本的使命，谢谢大家。

张强强：谢谢胡里奥·冈萨雷斯·隆科先生的演讲，先生在演讲时谈到曼德拉先生，他说体育具有改变世界的力量，他也说过多建一座球场，就可以少建一座监狱。体育在青少年成长过程中起到的作用，是其他东西无法替代的。下面有请中国网球运动员、亚洲首位大满贯单打冠军得主李娜女士。

李娜：尊敬的嘉宾朋友们，大家好，我是李娜，很高兴今天可以来到深圳分享我个人对于慈善公益的体会。作为一名曾经的职业运动员，我从小的梦想就是成为世界冠军，这应该和所有从事体育的运动员是一样的。在这条道路上，虽然面临很多的困难和挑战，但是我有家人和朋友作为坚实的后盾，还有专业的教练和团队的支持，最终梦想得以实现。我觉得自己非常幸运，因为一路上得到了关心、支持和爱护，才有了今天的我。但是看到世界上许许多多的人因为艰苦的生活条件，或者各种天灾人祸不得不放弃自己的梦想，对此我觉得自己有责任帮助他们，这大概是我投身公益的初心。

这些年，我在全国各地公益机构见到了很多孩子，有经历过玉树地震的、有武汉儿童福利院的，也见到了为流浪儿童提供教育的关爱学校，以及盲人学校和云南大山深处的幼儿园。可能他们生活和学习的环境远不如大部分同龄人，又或者小小年纪需要背负沉重的负担，但是和他们一起做运动和游戏的时候，他们的笑脸让我感触很深，尤其是自己成为两个孩子的妈妈以后，更是在母婴和慈善领域投入了更多关注和热情。

没有人比我更清楚运动的力量，运动真的可以改变世界，也可以改变一个人的命运。运动不仅可以强身健体，更可以健全人格，帮助人获得坚强的意志力，培养合作精神，为人生发掘更多的可能性。在这么多年的运动生涯中，我很享受运动带给我的快乐、自信，以及不惧挑战的勇气。这些不像我拿了奖杯一样是有形的，却是伴随我一生的宝藏。所以在退役后，我找到了自己的新起点，我希望将从职业运动生涯中得到的收获分享给更多人，尤其是女性和孩子们，让更多人受到体育精神的鼓舞，可以勇敢追逐自己的梦想，征服更多的不可能。

2019 年 6 月份，我去到云南大理的乡村幼儿园，那里正开展儿童学前教育和保育项目，之前，幼儿园有一片长满了杂草的土地。当我去到幼儿园的时候，场地已经建好了，有秋千、水池等娱乐设施，孩子们可以在那里尽情地奔跑，玩各种球类运动和玩具，用自己的方式探索未知、挑战自我、学习成长。幼儿园的老师告诉我，园里很多孩子是大山里的留守儿童，有的来自单亲家庭，生活上面临很多的困难。项目实施以后，孩子们的变化非常大，在运动、社交、学习、创造等各方面，表现越来越好。当孩子们拉着我一起玩的时候，我非常幸福，更加坚信自己是在做正确的事情。

当下对于中国运动员和中国公益人员而言都是很好的时代，每一名运动员在赛场上都会希望拿到更好的成绩，我们有了更丰富的资源，还能通过社交媒体和大家保持积极的沟通和互动，影响更多的人。此外，如同第四届世界公益慈善论坛展现的那样，中国的公益慈善事业在快速发展，社会上参与和支持公益的人不断增多，优质的项目和专业的公益纷纷涌现。公益的跨界合作更是成为一种潮流。因此我希望多一些运动员加入公益行业，把我们对于体育精神的理解传递给更多人，特别是帮助儿童和女性实现健康发展，也希望能够有更多的人参与进来。慈善不应该属于某个行业，慈善是大家共同的使命，谢谢大家。

张强强：非常感谢李娜的发言，用我们的一句话来讲，我们的冠军是民族的英雄、国家的力量，他们用自己顽强拼搏的良好形象，塑造国家在世界上的地位，每当国旗升起的时候，我们相信每个人都会心潮澎湃。下面请中国人民对外友好协会秘书长、中国友好和平发展基金会理事长李希奎先生。

李希奎：大家下午好，刚才在会前准备的时候，我和主持人讲，今天对话的四个人中，他们三位是体育专业人士，我是体育非专业人士，所以今天讲一下我作为非专业人士的体会。

我一直觉得体育的力量是巨大的，体育人的影响力和号召力也是巨大的，体育精神是无限的。而且我觉得体育作为人类社会活动，外在的表现是竞技、对抗，我觉得真正的内核，或者真正的内在是一种合作和交流，大家看体育比赛都能感觉到这种合作和交流。体育超越国界、超越语言、超越种族。我们这个论坛设立这样的板块，考虑把体育和慈善很好地结合起来，而我们的对外友协和中国友好和平发展基金会，长期以来做了这方面的尝试，也设计了这方面的项目。比如 2019 年 8 月，和姚明基金会在国内开展了一些公益活动，包括基金会项目有很多涉及体育的，比如篮球的、足球的，2019 年 3 月还观看了特殊运动员的项目和活动。所以我觉得体育有特殊的魅力，慈善有特殊的影响，如果把体育和慈善很好地结合起来，我觉得能够起到巨大的作用。刚才皇家马德里基金会的总经理也讲过，曼德拉说过，体育有改变世界的力量。在中国，我们也有非常好的例子，就是在 40 多年前，大家都了解和熟悉的中美乒乓外交，就是小小的乒乓球推动了地球的前进，促成了中美之间的握手。所以我们这样的机构，怎么样把体育和慈善结合起来？1. 要有很好的整合手段。就是怎么样把慈善和体育很好地整合。2. 我们要有高超的设计本领，要设计体育活动、体育项目、体育比赛。2019 年 8 月，我们基金会曾经在河北组织了友好城市青少年足球邀请赛，我看到孩子们在体育场上超越国界、超越语言、超越种族。一下就能融合起来，所以作为这样机构的人，设计更好的项目和活动是很重要的。3. 传播体育文化和体育精神。刚才我和李娜讲，现在正在进行美国网球公开赛，中国几位运动员也参与了比赛，我觉得很多运动员和李娜比，除了技术，很重要的是缺少李娜的精神。所以我们在开展项目的过程中、组织活动的过程中，要传播体育文化和体育精神，这种文化和精神不是职业人具有的文化和精神，是所有人都具有的文化和精神。所以我们设立这样一个专题，就是要弘扬体育精神、弘扬慈善精神，特别是要把体育精神和慈善精神很好地结合起来，谢谢大家！

张强强：中国人民对外友好协会组织了很多以体育为载体促进国际交流的活动，我们感谢李希奎秘书长的辛勤付出。下面有请丹麦国家奥林匹克委员会首席执行官兼秘书长莫滕·汉森先生。

莫滕·汉森：谢谢，今天我非常荣幸有机会可以和大家说一下丹麦的体育和体育赛事方面的进展。作为一个足球和网球球迷，我非常开心可以和顶级足球俱乐部的负责人及网球球员坐在一起。

首先，我们是谁？National Olympic Committee 是丹麦的国家奥林匹克委员会，我们有 62 个国家体育联盟，有 200 万名活跃会员，有 47 万名志愿者，我相信这和中国相比非常少，但是丹麦的总人口是 500 多万人，所以体育在丹麦有很长足的进展。我们想要在奥林匹克运动会上赢得一块奖牌，所以我们非常希望促进丹麦人在这方面有更多的行动，希望让整个活动变得更加包容和开放，让这个世界更加开放和包容。

在丹麦，要想成为体育俱乐部的一名成员，意味着你不仅要会踢足球，还要会打板球，虽然和体育相关，但是更重要的是它可以让你利用这个契机认识到来自不同社会背景的人。

我们在体育上有额外的想法，我们希望丹麦可以在 2025 年成为最活跃的国家。2025 年的时候，丹麦至少 50% 的人口应该成为体育俱乐部的成员，2025 年的时候，至少 75% 的丹麦人应该是非常活跃的，所以我们就需要带动一部分丹麦人，让他们从不运动变得活跃。虽然令这些不运动的人运动起来不是简单的事情，但这是丹麦政府的决议。因为我们发现抽烟会导致很多人死亡，活动可以让更多的人更加健康。

我们在丹麦也有非常多的合作伙伴，比如体育活动促进局及政府和官员等。我们想要成功的话，必须重新审视自己和创新我们的体育赛事。以前，家庭成员不是一起运动的，他们可能是没有太多的时间做运动。所以我们必须聚焦社交体育，我们希望人在其整个寿命周期当中有不同的活动可以参加，而且让我们的体育活动变得更加易于接近。比如在小场地可以打软式足球，接下来的视频可以让大家看一下这个活动是怎样的。

（视频播放）

我们的项目包括如何和学校的奥林匹克赛事一起合作？学校的奥林匹克比赛不是为了选拔种子选手，而是让学生一起参与，在课堂上进行。

（视频播放）

我们如何让一些不太活跃的人活动起来？我们在丹麦有一个皇家跑步活动，这是由丹麦的皇室发起的，每年都会在国家电视台直播。2019 年的时候有 8 万人参加，我们希望每一个人都可以成为这个赛事的参与者。我们也可以为大家提供培训，告诉大家可以从短距离跑起。

谢谢你们的耐心倾听。

张强强：我们知道丹麦有美人鱼，听过介绍以后，丹麦真的是美丽富强的国度，他们在全民健身上投入了大量的精力。接下来我们进入自由讨论环节。

我们都知道西班牙虽然只有 5000 万人口，却是公认的世界体育强国，在篮球、足球、网球、自行车运动中取得了辉煌的成绩。体育的发展除了国家的支持，社会的体育产业也是非常重要的支撑手段。我把接下来的问题交给胡里奥·冈萨雷斯·隆科先生，请介绍一下皇家马德里足球俱乐部在运营方面是如何做的?

胡里奥·冈萨雷斯·隆科：我觉得在马德里的话，主要是因为我们有非常优良的传统，而且足球是西班牙很强劲的赛事。多年以来，对于西班牙来说，有非常多的体育赛事，它们和足球相对抗。这也是非常好的一点，但是足球仍然是很好的治疗方式，因为我们是一起战斗去赢得尊重、赢得价值、赢得团结。想要赢得赛事就必须一起合作，必须要有这种团结精神。我们在西班牙还有另外的组织，在公共管理和赞助商之间有非常多的协作关系。2018 年我们和各个机构一起合作，创造出协同能力，它可以让足球或者说体育有很好的发展。而且大家已经认识到足球是教育未来一代很好的工具。

张强强：非常感谢，皇家马德里足球俱乐部的足球水平非常高，我们也希望中国足球继续努力，吸取国外优秀俱乐部的经验，让足球为我们国人增光。下面请问李希奎秘书长，刚才您对协会体育方面的布局做了阐述，站在体育外交的角度上，也谈到了 1971 年的中美乒乓外交，在未来的时间，您作为负责人有什么项目可以推广?

李希奎：还是刚才我讲到的，第一，通过体育的特殊项目，开展国际交流，超越国界、超越语言、超越种族，这样很容易拉近彼此的距离，这是我们下一步要推动的。第二，我们更多或者更加注重体育文化的推广。我觉得更重要的是让更多的人具有体育的基本文化。刚才讲到足球，中国友好和平发展基金会有一个项目，邓小平讲到足球要从娃娃抓起，所以我们做了一个幼儿足球基金，从幼儿园抓起，我们希望通过这样的项目培养这些孩子的体育文化意识，让他们从小在这种文化的熏陶之下成长。第三，把体育和慈善更好地结合起来，这是下一步我们要着力实现的，也是要下大功夫的。

张强强：谢谢。我有一个案例和您分享一下，我们北京体育大学为西藏培养了第一个藏族的世界摔跤冠军。通过体育的方式，我们可以改变他的人生，甚至改变他家人的命运，让他融入社会，并成为世界的楷模、社会的顶梁之柱。下面的问题问李娜，我曾经有机会跟您的启蒙教练交流过，我让他像训练您那样训练我，我练了 15 分钟就放弃了，他谈及了当年您顽强拼搏的精神。

李娜：那是被迫的，没有办法。

张强强：我想问一下，什么是冠军的气质和冠军的品质?

李娜：在职业生涯最后两年，我非常幸运，遇到了阿根廷教练，在和他合作之前，我们每一场比赛结束之后都会聊。有一次他问我，他说你觉得 Winner 和 Champion 之间有什么区别? 我用了一晚上时间，第二天给他的答案是：Winner 是场上的，Champion 是场上场下都要像冠军一样生活。之前我在场上有不好的举动，比如摔拍子，有一天我突然领悟，如果我对我的球拍不好，它们也会对我不好，而且我会很愤怒地发泄自己的情绪，可是我并没有意识到现场有 1 万名观众，还不包括看电视的观众。如果把这种不好的习惯传递给看球的人，不光对自己不好，对这项运动也不好。所以我不会让团队以外的人碰我的球拍。球拍对于运动员来说相当于武器，我们需要用它战胜对手，这也是自己成熟以后领悟出来的。我有这样的责任和义务去朝 Champion 的方向发展，不光是在场上。

张强强：谢谢李娜。我们中国的近代史是屈辱史，我们作为泱泱大国被称为“东亚病夫”，身体上的羸弱和精神上的贫瘠是近代中国人受西方列强欺负的重要原因。我非常希望在青少年中弘扬她冠军的品质和气质，让我们的青少年更强大，再次感谢李娜。我们都知道丹麦只有 4 万多平方千米，

500 多万人口，但是丹麦在世界体坛取得了无比辉煌的成绩，也被世界的媒体评为“世界八大体育强大神奇小国”之一。我想问一下莫滕・汉森先生，您国家在推广体育竞赛和全民健身两者结合方面有哪些成功的经验值得我们借鉴?

莫滕・汉森：我觉得我们成功的其中一个原因是我们有一个体系，我们有来自俱乐部的选手，他们会把这种文化传递给父母和身边的其他人，所以 90% 的儿童都会受到这种文化的熏陶，从事某种运动。其实有些儿童有体育上的天赋，我们有后续的体系支持他们赛场上的发展。丹麦的儿童是自愿的、非常积极活跃地参与体育运动，国家有超过 1 万个体育俱乐部，真的是有全民参与体育的文化，这是非常重要的。

张强强：谢谢。我们记住了“1 万”这个数据，丹麦这么小的国家有这么好的社会组织，值得我们学习。这是论坛最后一个环节，在座的各位朋友有没有问题想问一下嘉宾?

观众：各位嘉宾你们好，我来自香港，我和朋友在几年前创办了一个机构，叫灵动香港体育基金，目的是提升香港青年人的抗疫能力，帮助他们借助体育实现更好的成长，特别是来自低收入家庭的学生。我们服务了超过 1000 个小孩，但是 30% 是女生，70% 是男生。我们积极找家长参与我们的活动，很多家长说不要做运动，找女生做运动很困难。所以我想问李娜女士，您是我们的骄傲，我想知道您会怎么样鼓励女生参与运动，比如踢足球。

李娜：谢谢您的提问，这个问题在我们家不可能出现，我会鼓励我的儿子和女儿参与体育项目。我觉得体育是特别好的社交方式，而且通过体育可以学会团队合作。体育不是为了成为冠军，体育是为了明天的你比今天的你强大一些，这是体育的精髓所在。为什么全世界那么多人参与体育? 原因也在于此。可能因为东方和西方文化不一样，其实在西方，80% 以上的家庭，很多是父母带着孩子一起锻炼的。我们还是需要一定的时间，才可以慢慢转变，因为思想的转变是最困难的。我打一个比方，有的女生特别喜欢运动，但是在发育期的时候，她们为了合群，抹杀了自己的梦想，为了合群，没有做自己想做的事情。可能很多女生是因为外界的因素放弃自己的梦想。我想告诉更多的女性朋友，一定要坚持自己的梦想，最后可能没有实现，但是至少尝试过。

张强强：最后一个问题。

观众：我想问胡里奥·冈萨雷斯·隆科，我是来自基金会的，你们做了很多事情，在学校中发展了很多项目，我们想和学校一起做相关的培训。我们在一个国家已经有一个学校了，我们想说以后可不可以从您这边引进一些项目？

胡里奥·冈萨雷斯·隆科：我觉得实现孩子各个方面的发展，不仅需要社会，还要家长和学校配合。体育是好的，因为它可以帮助我们找到一种方式，去认识到孩子是需要很多的锻炼的，它不仅仅是要让孩子去参加一些体育赛事。

观众：所以我说两个基金会一起合作是不是有机会？比如学校的计划，我们有机会可以一起合作。

胡里奥·冈萨雷斯·隆科：我们之后可以聊一下。我们和很多的组织有签协议，我们希望可以为学校提供很多的项目。我们也有很多的项目是和非营利性组织一起做的，它们也可以针对学校做一些类似的项目。我们必须要确保合作的项目一定是可持续的，有一些组织是非营利性的，但是非营利性并不是问题，问题是我们还是需要一些资金上的支持，需要资源，需要帮助，需要让这个项目可以持续地发展下去，让它可以长期运营下去。就像我们说的，体育不仅仅是改善一个人，更多的是改善一个社区，改善未来。

张强强：主办方之所以举办这样的论坛，是希望通过这种方式，让世界各国、各个组织携手共同做好慈善事业。体育可以改变人生，体育可以让世界更美好。今天的论坛到此结束，谢谢各位。

八　善财传承

主 持 人：赠与亚洲理事长　薛希璞

赠与亚洲理事　曾宪章

对话嘉宾：论坛学术委员会委员、中欧国际工商学院教授及中欧家族传承研究中心联合主任　芮萌

珀杜家族、喜来登家族代表　米奇·珀杜

亚洲艺术品金融商学院院长　范勇

赠与亚洲总裁兼首席执行官　比格尔·斯坦普德尔

福特基金会北京代表处首席代表　高倩倩

纽约梅隆银行财富规划师　贾斯汀·米勒

纽约梅隆银行高级总监　琼·克雷恩

香港科技大学陈江和亚洲家族企业与创业研究中心主任　彭倩

连氏基金会主席、亚洲慈善圈创始人　连宗诚

联合国驻纽约业务伙伴关系司前司长　萨卡·科佩拉

芝加哥白沙集团投资基金合伙人　埃利奥特·唐纳利

香港荣信远东集团有限公司董事长　彭敏

论坛学术委员会委员、清华大学华商研究中心主任　龙登高

薛希璞：女士们，先生们，大家下午好！

我们很感谢大家能够参加今天下午的会议，我也很高兴看到来自这么多元背景机构的代表，有来自政府的代表，有来自业界的代表，还有来自大学、科研机构、家族办公室的代表，以及财富传承的顾问、银行家、律师。我们今天在座的各位，每一个都是来自独特的行业，大家的背景非常多元。

首先，我会简单地说一下开场白。

我没有办法讲中文，我想讲讲对于我而言，我怎么样去查“慈善”这个词的中英文意思。我做了一些研究，论坛的英文名字是“World Philanthropy Forum”，我把这几个英文词放到谷歌翻译里面，谷歌上跳出来的是“World Charity Forum”，但是我想，慈善和公益这两个词还是非常不一样的，所以我把我们今天的大会定名为“世界公益慈善论坛”。

大家知道，慈善和公益之间是有区别的，我还是希望大家能够特别注意一下。我想和大家探讨一下慈善和公益到底是什么意思。

慈善是短期的，跟情绪上的触动有关系。而公益是具有战略性的，是长久性的，当然慈善也很不错，有解决问题的慈善，也有解决问题的公益。

有的人说，慈善是为了解决短期的需求，而公益是为了解决长远的需求。所以，给一个缺水的村庄挖井，是慈善；帮助这个村庄自给自足寻找解决的措施，才是公益。

在公益和慈善两个词之间，我还想区分一下，它们在关注个体上有不同：一般情况下做公益是给予，不是索取；而做慈善的话，会关注更多个体的需求。

接下来，我们再想一想，在西方世界，公益到底是怎么发展的?

我又做了一些调研，我发现，公益这个词最早在西方出现是在16世纪，它的词源是拉丁语，这个词的意思是“爱人，对人有利”。在16世纪20年代的时候，我们的移民开始在文献里面使用这个词。慈善或者是公益，它实际上和东方的助人思维不谋而合。

在中文里面我们讲善，那么善和公益又有什么区别呢？在座的一位嘉宾提到了“善”的概念，一会儿也会谈，“善”更具深远意义。

我们再来看 Philanthropy 的另一方面。

在西方，Philanthropy 有两个词源：一个是爱，关爱和关注；一个是人，人类。所以，如果把这两个词的部分加在一起就是爱人、助人。

随着人类历史发展，Philanthropy 也在演进，我们看到这个词不光指代人，也指代动物和植物，以及我们生活的土壤和周围的水源。现在大家能够看到我们新一代，当讲到公益和慈善的时候，它们的意义更丰富了，这是因为人们认识到土壤是我们赖以生存的基础，所以做慈善、做公益，又开始关注环境方面。

Philanthropy 这个词，是一个来自西方的词，但是实际上，它跟东方的风水又不谋而合，尤其是中国的《易经》提到了“五行”或者是“1”的法则。最近关于量子物理学的研究也指出，世界上所有的东西都是粒子和波。它们在同时进行碰撞和交织，在时空的概念里面进行碰撞。西方有很多书是关于量子物理学和量子力学的。

今天我只是指出来，在西方，在东方，今天看到“公益慈善”主题的时候，在善的背后有不同个体的解读。

在今天下午的讨论里面，我们希望能够把今天的主题定为“善财传承”。

这是什么意思呢？大家在谷歌上查“善财”这个词，它的翻译是 Good fortune，对我一个讲英文的人而言，这种翻译讲不通，它的官方翻译应该是怎么样去进行家族财富的传承和供应，也就是善财传承。

善到底是什么意思呢？善和传承都是关于财务传承和处理的方法，善为什么又和公益、慈善联系在一起？在公元前 771 年，人们做了一个关于善的讨论。在 2500 多年前，又做了关于人性本恶还是本善的讨论。其中诸子百家中的儒家认为人性是善的，法家认为人性是恶的。今天，我们不去讲人性善恶的问题，因为我们强调的是把人性的善激发出来。

善到底是什么意思呢？是贤、慈、忠、孝等。对于儒家思想的传承者来讲，善是操作层面具体的做法，比如说行善事、举善思。从哲学的角度来看，做善事、为善人，这样的概念被儒家当作黄金法则。

孔子曾经说：“已欲立而立人，已欲达而达人。”什么意思呢？如果你想自己站起来，你必须帮助别人站起来，如果你想实现什么东西，你必须首先帮助别人去实现他们的梦想。在2000多年之后，孔子思想也成为中国文化的黄金法则，而西方也讲“己所不欲，勿施于人”，这也是《圣经》里面提到的。

我为什么讲这个故事呢？因为我想告诉大家，这是我做慈善的起源。

昨天我们也讲到了这个概念，我的祖父坚信这个黄金法则，我六七岁的时候，他给了我一张卡片，这张卡片上面就写了这个黄金法则。有12个宗教，这12个宗教都是一样的，那个时候我还很小，我不知道它们讲的是什么。我问我的父母，为什么爷爷会给我看这个卡片和黄金法则呢？当时是1957年3月，我的父母告诉我说，在二战的时候，我的祖父曾经被关在监狱里，他必须要进行自我反省。当时他是被日军关押起来，把他一个人关起来，他是要死亡的，但是他后来坚强地存活下来。他战前雇佣过日本司机和管家，他和来自日本的下人处得很好。珍珠港被炸的时候，他的园丁和他的管家是当时日本人的间谍，但是当他被抓以后，日本人对他非常好，因为他在工作之余做了很多的善事。这种善行也最终救了他一命。你想别人怎么对你，你就要怎么对别人。

在20世纪50年代，他发起了自由洁净运动。出于卫生和营养方面的考虑，为不能获得良好水源的地区，尤其是菲律宾地区，提供洁净的水源。菲律宾为了纪念这项运动，50年代也发行了一些邮票。当时，他遇到了一个来自四川的博士，他们一起发起运动，他们也继续着自己的慈善事业，这些运动其实是比较具有变革性的。最后，我们可以看到菲律宾政府为了纪念这些运动，也发行了一些纪念币。我们可以看到，其他的一些人，都是像爱因斯坦一样具有变革思想的人，包括迪士尼的创始人。

他们发起的这项运动可以帮助农民扫盲，他们知道如何去阅读和如何去写字。那位一起发起运动的博士来自四川一个比较偏远的地方，可能我们在座的也有他的老乡。在 60 年代他们又一起发起了国际农村重建运动。大家可以看一下相关的史料，大概是持续了 60 年。

这项运动对于当地甚至全球产生了巨大的影响，并且它会持续地发光发热。

现在我来介绍今天下午的活动安排，我们一共有三个议题，最终会有一个总结，第一个议题是关于如何通过财富管理来回馈社会的，第二个议题是关于我们的慈善机构如何获得最大效益的，第三个议题是关于在慈善管理中的创新以及相关的趋势的，每一个议题大约有一个小时的时间。在最后，大家会进行总结，而每一个议题，我们都会设置问答环节，在最后，我们还是会留出更多的总结和问答的时间。

我们先看第一个议题。我们会有三位讲者，我先介绍第一位讲者的背景，芮萌是会计和财务专业的博士，他现在担任的是论坛学术委员会委员、中欧国际工商学院教授，他也在港交所等金融机构担任要职，他负责中国移动、中国建设银行等的一些内部的培训。同时，他发表了很多高质量的论文，其中有一篇文章，对今天的讨论会大有助益，就是《家族政府的影响和效用》。他在里面提到了“三圈”的管理模式，而不是传统的非家族企业的“两圈”管理模式，大家等会儿可以提出更多的问题。

芮萌也是长期从事中国的慈善事业。接下来，我们一起欢迎芮萌博士来和我们分享他对于如何更好地管理多代财富从而回馈社会的经验。

芮萌：感谢理事长先生的介绍，非常高兴参加今天的会议，和大家分享我对公益和慈善的见解，尤其是我对中国方面的见解。我们的组织是五年前成立的，主要是研究家庭传承和财务规划。当然也包含了慈善和公益，我们也做了这方面的报告，尤其是中国上市家族的财富管理和慈善事业方面，将在 2019 年 11 月份发表。

我们也有关于“家族办公室”的课程，是在四年前开设的。接下来我就跟大家分享一下，我给我学生讲的第一堂课，因为我的幻灯片是中文的，接下来，我就讲中文。

第一个观点，那就是让财富改变世界。

因为我们今天是处在非常关键的时刻，主要是全球人口的增长所带来的对全人类可持续发展的一个思考。

全球人口首次达到 10 亿人是在 1804 年，过了 123 年，全球有了第二个 10 亿人，之后的每十几年，全球就会增长 10 亿人。根据全球人口学家的预测，到 2048 年，全球将有近 90 亿的人口。这 90 亿的人，我们的地球能否负荷？这是我们这一代人需要考虑的问题。

我借此引导我们的同学开始思考这个问题，他们创造财富的最终目的是什么？

《折叠社会》这本书，揭示了过去人类文明取得了重大的进步，比如过去 25 年当中，15 亿人脱离了贫困线，但是还有很多不完美的地方。比如今天 70 亿的人口当中，有 50% 是没有银行账户的，有 40 亿人每天还生活在低于 3.5 美元的贫困线下，还有 14 亿人没有电用。

虽然我们所处城市的人民生活得非常好，但是还有很多人口处于贫困状态。联合国制定了《2030 年可持续发展议程》，大家要实现 17 个目标，根据联合国专家的预测，每一年需要的投资差不多为 4 万亿美元，今天用于投资的不到 1.5 万亿美元，还有 2.5 万亿美元的缺口。那么这 2.5 万亿美元的缺口从哪里来？

我们就要看全球财富的分配。在财富金字塔的最底端，差不多有 33 亿人口，这占成年人的 71%，这 71% 的人口拥有多少财富呢？不到 4%。

但是在财富金字塔的最顶端，0.7% 的人口拥有 40% 多的财富。如果把金字塔最顶尖的加起来，差不多是 8% 的人口，8% 的人口拥有 85% 的财富。所以，要解决全球的问题，应率先解决金字塔最顶尖的问题。

家族企业和非家族企业的最大不同点在于它们的目标是多重性的。对家庭来讲，除了创造财富以外，还有其他的目标，包括社会影响力，包括家庭的幸福，还有基业的长青。家族企业要实现多重目标的平衡。这需要一个工具帮助它们实现，最好的工具就是慈善和公益。

我给我的同学们讲，家族企业不仅是积累财富和追求个人享受的载体，也是精神、价值观、爱和责任的载体。

接下来，我就要分析为什么。

学者发现了家族企业和非家族企业之间的不同，因为它们有社会情感因素。可以用五个英文字母来表示：第一个是 F，家族的影响力；第二个是 I，家族成员身份的认同；第三个是 B，它们跟社会的关系；第四个是 E，它们与家族成员之间的依附关系；第五个是 R，它们的纽带。

这是家族企业和非家族企业最大的不同，除了追求物质财富以外，还追求精神财富，这种精神财富就是社会情感因素。

所以，我的很多学生听完了之后，觉得他是有这方面的诉求和追求的。

接下来，我就和他们分享，因为中国是新钱，国外是旧钱，通过这些旧钱的经验可以告诉他们，慈善和公益是家族传承最重要的密码。中欧国际工商学院做了大量的研究，其中研究了亚洲。其访谈了从事慈善事业的 200 多个亚洲的家族，其中的一个问题是说，是什么样的推动力，让家族积极做慈善来回馈社会和来帮助有需要的人。有一半以上被访谈到的家族的回答是：希望通过家族慈善来形成一种长久的家族传承。所以，这是最好的工具。

传承，不只是我们讲的财富上的传承，还有家族的价值观的传承。这样可以让它的下一代明白财富真正的意义在哪里，而且可以通过一个平台来凝聚家族成员、来培养它的下一代。

长期坚持不懈的、系统性的家族慈善投入，体现出财富家族的社会责任感，回馈社会也会为家族赢得社会的认同和尊重，获得社会归属感和社会资本。最近几年学术界非常流行的一个词就是信任。

今天中国的企业家，普遍缺乏的是一种安全感，或者是社会对他们的认同感。所以，慈善可以帮助他们，形成一种代代相传的从事慈善的家风。所以我给他们的结论是，一个家族的荣耀不取决于，或者是长期不取决于财富的多少，而是在于每一个家族成员对财富的态度。

我让他们看的是，全世界主要的公益基金会都是来自家族。从个人层面也给他们一些激励，中文叫作正能量，现在有大量心理学、医学的研究发现，这种正能量可以让人更加幸福和长寿。这是耶鲁大学和加利福尼亚大学洛杉矶分校做的长达 9 年的、有 7000 多个样本的研究，就是看社会关系如何影响人的死亡率和寿命。

9 年的跟踪调查得出一个结果：乐于帮助别人的人，他们的健康状况和预期的寿命明显优于那些不愿意帮助别人的人。而且，两所学校观察了不同的种族、阶层及其生活习惯，得出了同样的结论。其实，行善或者是弘扬正能量，对个人来讲也是意义非凡。

到底它的价值在什么地方呢？“富不过三代”是家族企业的魔咒。你所打下来的事业，用不了五代，它就没有了。后人在这个基础上发展成今天的“富不过三代”，“道德传家，十代以上，耕读传家次之，诗书传家又次之，富贵传家，不过三代”。如果是价值观、精神财富，那可以传得很久。

最后，我给他们的结论是，你们到中欧来上课，成立家族办公室，主要目的是让财富能够发挥它的应有作用，让财富改变这个世界。

我们既不是财富的奴隶，也不是财富的主人。

我给他们介绍爱马仕家族的成员时讲过，家族企业不是从父母受力面集成的，而是从子女手里借来的。我改了一下，你今天的财富也是从社会借来的，你只是临时的管家而已，你要把这些财富用好，让这些财富可以解决我在第三张 PPT 中讲到的，今天人类社会所面临的共同的可持续发展问题。

这就是我给我们中欧家族办公室讲的第一课，我希望同学们有正确的价值观。用好这些财富，使得这些财富发挥作用，能够真正造福个人、家庭以至于社会，这不光是家族需要做的，学校和在座的专业人士，都可以发挥作用。

谢谢大家!

薛希璞：由刚刚芮萌教授的演讲，大家可以看到，他曾经是我们的教授。经过他的演讲之后，我又想回到大学去听他上课了。

接下来的嘉宾是米奇·珀杜女士，她今天代表两个家族的办公室。她的丈夫写过一本法语的书，曾经在亚马逊的商业评论里面排名第五，希望大家都去读一下这本书。她在她的丈夫去世之后，一直传承家族的事业。

在嫁给珀杜先生之前，她就说过，大米和鸡翅很配，所以她就嫁给了她的先生。她的父亲协办了喜来登酒店集团，当时是在大萧条时期，即 20 世纪 30 年代。到了 20 世纪 40 年代，喜来登成为第一家在纽交所上市的五星级酒店，在全世界开了 100 多家酒店。1985 年，对中国而言，喜来登也是第一家海外的酒店集团在中国开设的新的酒店。这家酒店叫北京喜来登长城酒店，酒店的业务已经被转让出去了，家族成员当时住在加州。

讲到大米，他们家族的企业体量也很大，当时美国妇女协会，在那边有很多的会员，会员中大部分的女性所从事的工作都与大米的生产以及销售相关。

她本人毕业于哈佛大学，酷爱阅读，对很多话题非常熟悉，她今天要和我们分享的是相关的主题。她也是专栏的作家，目前给《妇女健康》杂志写专栏，她过去还写过生物技术以及基因测序方面的专栏。她写过多篇文章，是世界著名的电视剧编剧，还主持过 100 多集的电视节目和访谈。很高兴能够邀请到您来分享您家族的历史。

米奇·珀杜：谢谢您刚刚的介绍。刚刚芮萌教授的分享非常好。我的想法和他不谋而合。我接触过两个家族的业务，我们做的家族的财富传承和刚刚您讲的一模一样，所以您讲的时候，我一直点头。

我今天想和大家分享一个从事鸡腿生产的家族，那就是珀杜家族。珀杜家族在 99 年前开始营业。能在近 100 年里长盛不衰的家族可谓千里挑一。在美国甚至全球，仅仅有 30% 的家族能够完成下一代传承。但家族企业并不都是由家族成员运营的，我们涉及的领域包括房地产，在德国有轮胎业务，以及一些其他的业务。

我的父亲和我的叔父都做过这些业务，但是什么让家族持续至今的呢？我很同意芮萌教授的观点，但是我也想和大家讲一下美国一位教授做的研究。

这位教授一直研究过去 100 年间出现的家族企业。他说实现传承的家族与未能实现传承的家族之间的差别在于慈善。在第三代和第四代的时候，如果这个家族还没有发现慈善和回馈的重要性，那么财富就不会传承下去。我认为这些研究者的实验结果和我们现实的情况是不谋而合的。

我再和大家分享一下珀杜家族和亨德森家族的经验。因为我们经济上的体量很大，并且都传承了很长时间。这两个家族为什么能够长久传承？首先就是因为慈善。慈善把家族成员凝聚在一起，让我们获得认同感，也给了我们骄傲和尊严。

珀杜家族和喜来登家族做慈善的方式有所不同。我想分享两个有效的方法。

在珀杜家族，我的丈夫在设立基金会时有很多考量。我们知道在家禽养殖行业，农民都是因养殖家禽获益的，他们主要是在农村地区，那些地方的人口不太稠密，他们也不富裕。之前我接触到一个案例，其中一个社区的人找到我们说，他们现在非常需要热成像相机，通过这种相机可以看到一个女人抱着一只狗的影像。当时小镇里的一个人找到我们说，大城市居民可以轻而易举买下这种热成像相机，但对于他们来说，两万美金太贵，他们买不起。

当时珀杜的基金会帮助他们买了这种相机。几个月之后，那个地区出现了火灾，烟火缭绕。人们可以呼吸，但是视野是不清楚的，这会影响救援。但是有了热成像相机，就可以看到浓烟中的人，对他们施以援手。知道自己捐助的东西可以造福人民，这种感觉是非常好的。

除了经济上的援助，我们还会为珀杜家族工人及其家属提供一些项目。大家看不清 PPT 上这张照片是什么，现在大家看到的是生蚝或者是牡蛎壳。这里是一个很大的牡蛎产区，很多牡蛎会在这些壳里面生产新的牡蛎。我们把这些壳重新放回海里。我们的雇员大概有 2.2 万人，他们都参与其中。曾经有一场很大的风暴，所有员工及其家属都互相帮助，重建房屋。

而亨德森家族的做法有所不同。珀杜家族是和几个基金会合作，由社区给予支持。亨德森家族则大不相同。亨德森家族有五个分支，分别选择自己支持的基金会。大家看赠与亚洲这个小单子的背面，这个其实是捐赠比例，这个捐赠比例和亨德森家族非常类似，有的人选择医疗、教育、救灾，可能每一方面，它会受到100多次捐助，可能每次受到的捐助的金额会比较小。在这方面，我们做的事情有所不同。

接下来给大家解释一下。

在这五大支里面，我的这一支非常关注慈善和公益。四个月前，也就是2019年4月11日，我在开曼群岛听到了一个演讲，关于联合国会在2030年消除人口贩卖现象，尤其是性走私。美国有许多人不了解这方面的情况。据联合国统计，现在有4000多万人是人口走私的受害者，大部分的受害者是女孩子，而其中有800万人最终都是沦为性奴，年龄是4~12岁，一晚上会被侵犯八九次，她们之后的寿命只有7年，会由于过量吸毒而被谋杀，或者是自杀，或者是死于其他的疾病。

我在听到这样的演讲的时候非常受触动。我觉得这太令人发指了，我想竭尽全力去帮助她们。

如果我开出一张数额巨大的支票帮助这些人脱离苦难，这就说明我要削减支持其他基金会的资金。但是如果我这样做，一些我任职为董事的基金会就不能得到足够的支持，那我怎么选择、怎么做取舍呢？突然我灵机一动，我拥有一些很值钱的东西，其中有一个藏宝箱，可能有四五百年的历史，是我家族的传家宝。我知道这是历史文物，非常值钱，我也非常喜欢它。如果我把它拿去拍卖，肯定会引起广泛重视。

我突然就想到，也许我可以变物为资金。然后我就到处去问别人，后来我们成立了全球反贩卖拍卖会。这个拍卖会一方面是在线上运行的，另一方面是在美国的拍卖所，我希望未来中国也会有拍卖所。主要思路就是你把一些东西拿出来拍卖，把拍卖的钱用来援助那些被贩卖的人，来完成联合国可持续发展目标。

PPT中展示的是1825年亚历山大二世的所有物。我们是希望能够在2021年的1月对其进行全球拍卖。除了帮助我们融资以外，我们希望这场拍卖会能够增强人们的意识，进行慈善宣传。

上述这些就是我所在的亨德森家族的一支下面的慈善机构所做的事情。刚才芮萌博士讲的那些，在我的家族之中都是有所体现的。谢谢大家！

薛希璞：非常感谢米奇·珀杜女士。今天上午李斌副主席在讲话时提到了儿童和妇女保护的问题，这让我感到十分欣慰。因为对儿童和妇女的保护力度确实需要加强。我也从您的演讲中看到了贵基金会在这方面做出的努力。

下一位讲者和您刚刚讲到的事件紧密相关。他是范勇教授，亚洲艺术品金融商学院的创始人和院长，复旦大学商学院名誉院长和上海大学商学院名誉院长，新加坡南洋理工大学中国文化继承方面的一位访问学者。他是一位投资银行家，对文化和艺术也非常感兴趣。今天非常有幸，他跟珀杜家族相关人员在同一个会场上。

与艺术相关的事业一直是由慈善支持的，而艺术是否可以支持慈善的发展呢？我们来看一下家族慈善和艺术到底如何互相支持，有请范勇教授。

范勇：非常感谢您的介绍，也感谢大会的邀请。非常荣幸和各位学者、专家以及业内的人士来做一个分享。我研究的更多是细分领域，就是艺术品在社会发展过程中起到什么样的作用。

今天，我们分享的是更具体的，谈一谈艺术品在中国的未来家族传承事业当中，怎么样变成新的发展趋势。

这个趋势，我从两个方面来分析：第一，从东西方的家族传承过程来看，艺术品在这里面扮演什么样的角色；第二，从中国的历史发展沿革来看，上到帝王，下到普通百姓，如何用艺术品传递他们的价值。

首先，我觉得在谈艺术品在家族传承当中的作用的时候，我们有四个关键词，我希望大家可以有一个了解。第一，我觉得任何一个家族都需要荣耀，他们奋斗的目标就是荣耀。第二，每一个家族都希望我们的传承中有良好的教育，这种教育不仅是在学校里，而且是在我们的家庭里。第三，我们都希望财富是永恒的和保值的。第四，税务是调节社会财富分配的非常重要的工具，在这个方面，如何能够推动我们在慈善和公益当中非常良好地为社会服务，让我们的财富得到更有效的分配？

我们也看到，在西方，尤其是近现代历史当中，更多的家族或者是社会普遍对历史文化的保护和传承非常重视。不少的富裕家族在收藏一些文物，重视文物的价值。

我通过几个著名的家族和大家做分享。

我相信美第奇家族，大家是不陌生的。如果没有美第奇家族，文艺复兴就不见得像我们现在了解的文艺复兴一样。美第奇公爵做的贡献是非常大的，文艺复兴时期一些人著名的作品，是在他的家族和他本人的资助下完成的。我们也看到世界十大美术馆之一，我们看到非常著名的艺术品，在这里，我们更熟悉它们是因为我们在博物馆经常见到。我们也看到美国有一个非常有意思的人，就是保罗盖蒂，他在临终前，做了一个伟大的决定，他是非常热爱艺术的，他虽然富甲天下，但是一生非常吝啬，他成立了信托基金，投入文化艺术，他对文化艺术却一点都不吝啬，他已经成为全世界闻名的对文化艺术传承和保护做出非常巨大贡献的机构的创始人。我们看到的都是对社会有巨大贡献，对我们有榜样作用的。

美国还有非常多的家族，我们旁边还有一位非常杰出的家族代表，刚才有幸听到她分享的关于她的家族的贡献。

以上是西方杰出家族做的贡献，我们再来看看中国，中国怎么来对待文化艺术呢？

文化艺术在整个社会发展过程中，如何在家族里得到保护和发展？

中国是我们研究的一个重点，中国历史上一共发生了五次收藏热，收藏在良性的意义上是指我们以私人财富的形式保管了社会财富，为社会尽义务和担责任。中国在宋代就有一个高潮，在这个时期，主要是以皇家为带头人。宋代出了一位皇帝，他非常喜欢艺术，而且是大艺术家，大家看到的画面就是他的绘画和书法，在皇帝的引领下，士大夫和贵族们纷纷进入收藏领域，形成了人们对社会财富和文化艺术的追求。

到了明代，更多的士大夫扮演越来越重要的角色，他们中的大部分人选择做官，他们又喜欢文化和艺术，而且他们自己能创作艺术品，这个时候他们的地位和经济能力，以及价值传承，就会变成社会的榜样。明代也是中国资本主义萌芽产生的时代，出现了非常系统的关于文化艺术品怎么收藏的理论知识，出了两本著名的书，帮助我们去研究艺术品的收藏，其有分类、有系统、有历史传承，让我们更加了解艺术所代表的社会价值和对人类社会有哪些积极的作用，而且能提升我们的情操。

清代也出了一个伟大的皇帝，他做了一件非常重要的事情。他特别喜欢收藏艺术品，同时他以自己收藏的历朝历代的非常珍贵的文化艺术品为基础编纂了一本书，就像我们在文化艺术传承方面的百科辞典。到了今天，我们要了解历史上有哪些非常重要的文化艺术品，一定要查这本书。我们看到很多大家族在收藏文化艺术品的时候，往往以它作为指南和手册。

到了民国，中国进入了动荡的时期，出了非常著名的四大公子，他们都是有政治背景或者是有家族背景的。中间有一位非常杰出的人，叫张伯驹。当时八国联军来了以后，秦朝文物遗落民间，他为了保护文物，把自己所有的家产卖了，把一幅图保存了下来，并且捐给了故宫。

有位叫王世襄的人，在经济匮乏的年代，凭自己的喜好和毅力去收藏了很多中国珍贵的文物，把这些文物一部分捐给了故宫，还有一部分，通过社会的拍卖，做了一些慈善。

从帝王到普通人，大家都喜欢文化艺术，它的核心是什么？它的核心就是对信仰、价值观的认同。艺术变成了人人都可以去接触的东西，自然也就成为家族关注的重要载体。

在这里面，这个家族延续了三代，我们刚才讲“富不过三代”，我们的文化传承在这方面，是不是有一些特例？清代的时候，有一名学者，他既是史学家也是收藏家，叫吴大澂，他传到第二代的时候，出现了一位大文豪，叫吴湖帆，他是大艺术家和鉴定家，不仅把家族的财富传承下来，更重要的是把家族的文脉也传承了下来，一直到现在，他们传到了“90后”的后辈，第三代人叫吴亦深，不仅继承了家族的物质财富，还继承了文化上的财富。

我们看了西方，看了中国古代和近代，再来看当下。改革开放以来，我们注重的是经济建设和物质消费，现在我们要转到精神消费，理所当然，我们关注艺术品。我们未来的一代，他们越来越多地富有一种责任感和使命感，因为他们都受过非常良好的教育，我们希望未来的一代，他们的兴趣是在历史和文化里面找到自己的定位。

我们看到香港的家族，它们到了第三代，也是开创了非常好的艺术产业。第三代，在国外学的是英美文学，是有人文情怀的企业家，他在继承家族产业的时候，提出如何用文化艺术去做这方面的改良，让家族的事业能长青。

我分享的核心在于如何让我们的物质财富和精神财富都得以良好地传承，而艺术是非常好的载体，谢谢大家，请大家多多支持！

薛希璞：谢谢您，您的演讲也做得相当精彩。我们虽然可以马上开始问答，但是我们应该先开启第二个议题，在第二个议题结束之后，我们再问答。

如果大家有问题，先把问题保留，我们先开始第二个环节，第二个环节和第一个环节的最后一个演讲紧密相关，关于财富参与慈善公益的选择。

在第二个环节中，我们的第一位嘉宾是赠与亚洲总裁兼首席执行官比格尔·斯坦普德尔。他一直在推动赠与亚洲组织的进步，也引领着亚洲慈善。赠与亚洲在 25 个国家推动慈善事业的进步，其中包括中国。赠与亚洲为家族、公司和基金会提供服务，帮助那些急需帮助的群体和社区。赠与亚洲一直和 2000 多家的非政府组织进行合作，他们的会员来自社会各个领域。赠与亚洲为他们提供经济援助、健康支持，帮助儿童和妇女，帮助贫困地区摆脱贫苦。有请比格尔·斯坦普德尔来和大家分享。

比格尔·斯坦普德尔：感谢大家，首先感谢中国人民对外友好协会和清华大学等共同举办这次论坛。我今天只是想简单和大家分享我自己的经验，以及赠与亚洲过去这些年做的事情。

前面的一些嘉宾讲到了在个人层面上的家族慈善和家族财富传承，也提到了家族财富传承方面的个性化决策。接下来我想和大家分享赠与亚洲做的工作和我们的视角及观点。

首先和大家介绍我们的背景。赠与亚洲希望帮助家族会员制定更好的决策，支持他们的项目，同时能够指导项目的执行。我们做的工作是很实际的。我们还关注这些家族项目带来的影响，同境外家族进行合作。我们认为慈善家族处于一个位置，而家族项目在其他地方进行。

我们还会有一些对于慈善项目资金的支持，包括教育项目、健康项目、灾难项目和环境项目。中国是我们最为关注的地区之一。接下来，我想向大家介绍一下在慈善方面的全球格局。

我们主要关注的是有国际视野的家族。在不同的地区，我们都可以看到赠与亚洲的身影，在美国、澳大利亚、加拿大，以及欧洲，都有赠与亚洲的身影。当前，我们也是侧重于立足亚洲、关注亚洲。我们也会考虑一些跨界的项目，我们希望慈善事业是可持续的、长久的。我们会立足亚洲，从而充分考虑我们的捐赠家族，以及项目本身所关注的问题。

我们考虑国际项目的时候，也非常关注当地的合作伙伴，这点非常重要。那些可持续、长久的项目，通常都是立足于当地社区，非常了解当地社区的项目。

另外，我们也要考虑融资情况，当地的合作伙伴可以搭建起当地的捐赠网络。他们更加了解当地，我们觉得在慈善融资方面也要考虑当地伙伴，这是我们在中国、新加坡、澳大利亚、英国的情况，我们的落脚点还是亚太地区，要让慈善家族参与不同的项目。

接下来，我想谈一下我们所接洽的这些家族，它们为什么会参与慈善呢？它们选择项目的动机与考量是什么？我也想谈一下基金的国际流动。

有时候，家族成员是想把钱投到特定的地区。比如说我们合作的一些美国华裔人士，他们希望捐给自己的故土，或者是对某一个问题特别关注，比如说环境、教育和医疗健康，或者是关注特殊的群体，比如说人口贩卖的受害者。总的来说，我们希望社会更加繁荣和更加富强。

在这个过程中，除了获得基金，我们还要充分利用这些捐赠家族的网络，去解决它们所关切的问题。我们要考虑家族的优先关切点是什么，我们接洽了各种各样的家族，不是说哪一种好，哪一种不好，而是说我们接触的家族，有的是一次性地捐赠一个项目，它们的兴趣是集中在一个地区和一个项目上，有的家族则喜欢协同捐赠，它们想和其他捐赠者一起合作，它们会和营利性的企业合作，获得更广泛的社会影响，包括和政府一起合作。

我想说的是，我们赠与亚洲所接触的项目是非常多元化的。这些项目的影响有的是地区性的，有的是国际性的。我们要考虑捐赠家族本身的兴趣和它们的动机，它们是想做本地项目、全国项目、区域项目还是国际项目呢？有时候，它们可能更青睐于本地项目，有时候又希望具有国际视野，接下来讲三个具体的案例。其中两个案例，我已经获得了捐赠人的许可，可以把他们的名字说出来。

第一个案例是大型的国际项目。第一个项目是慈善家玛格丽特发起的，其是美国一个很大的慈善家族的成员，其家族第一个慈善领域是救灾减灾。玛格丽特在设立基金会的目标时，非常关注救灾减灾，而且关注地区主要局限于美国。但现在其家族的下一代成员也参与了基金会的管理，他们关注新环境，也知道在救灾减灾方面哪些是可以动用的资源，以及如何帮助人们提高备灾能力。他们开展了备灾活动，因为他们认识到预防灾害十分重要。他们和其他的一些捐赠者一起合作，他们也希望有更多的捐赠者可以加入其中支持这个项目。当地社区和机构可能更多地关注本地区状况，落脚点是地区性的，在尼泊尔、缅甸或者是东南亚其他地区，慈善的形式就是这样的。这些基金会还会选择和政府进行合作，扩大它们的项目规模，我们会和国际的NGO、IRRR 合作，也会和当地的政府合作。这便是一个多代家族的例子，不断调整自己家族基金的定位和初衷。

另外一个例子是一个位于硅谷的基金会，其也是最早捐助赠与亚洲的组织之一。这个基金会关注的范围很广泛，并非像上一个一样仅仅聚焦于中国等少数地区。该基金会特别关注中国，尤其是奖学金项目，它现在是由第二代家族成员管理，家族成员在整个项目的不同职能部门里面担任不同的角色。比如说有人关注我们的金融财务，也有一些人是关注项目的其他方面。每一年，他们都会去访问这些奖学金项目的受益人，因为他们希望能和这些受益人建立个人层面的纽带。现在他们每年会为中国提供 100 多个奖学金名额，所有因家庭贫困付不起学费的大学生都可以获得他们的奖学金，现在他们向 5 所学校提供奖学金。这个项目也让家族多代人参与其中。

最后一个项目是一个匿名项目，是一位美国华裔人士参与的项目。这个人没有地理上的关注和偏爱，但是他非常关注培养当地的领导力，并通过一些方式培养当地的领导力。每一个他所捐赠的项目，他都会去到现场近距离观察。另外，他非常愿意分享自己的人生经验和自己所学到的东西，这也是慈善多代传承的特点，将经验传给下一代家族成员或家族之外的慈善家，从而扩大整个活动的影响力。

我相信我介绍的三个案例呼应了刚刚几位讲者讲的内容，不同的家族如何在同一个主题下团结起来？比如说救灾减灾就是一个主题，基金会可以团结一致，共同面对这个问题。

最后我想分享鼓励跨代慈善的方式。我们觉得慈善家族成员都想要看到自己的作用、自己所做的慈善真的有效果。他们想要看到这些效果，所以他们会亲自到项目开展现场。有时候他们想看一下家族或整个项目的目标是什么，项目现在是否已经取得了一些成功，或当前还有哪些不足。如果说家族的这些慈善家十分了解项目的成败和进展，他们会更加热情地参与其中。

所以我们在决策过程中，会多与家族成员接洽。某一代人做了慈善可能会影响下一代人作为咨询人员参与其中。让下一代成员加入项目会带来很多好处。

最后一点是慈善在前行中面临障碍，那就是信任缺失。

说到慈善，人们很多时候想知道，我们的基金是否流到了应该去到的地方，资金花费是否透明，这方面存在信任缺失的问题。与人们建立信任，让他们相信我们将资金用到了实处，这一点十分重要。我们要让所有人都相信，我们是在朝着同一个目标前进。

在增强信任方面，我们还需要有更多的举措。作为一个机构，我们要考虑如何在慈善领域提升人们的信任度。对于非政府组织来说，它可能会收到一些基金，可以借此提升捐赠者的信心和信任度。

我希望我刚刚举的这些例子可以给大家一些启示，让大家知道如何让跨代的慈善工作更好地开展下去。

薛希璞：谢谢比格尔·斯坦普德尔的介绍。接下来，我想呼应一下刚刚说到的案例。赠与亚洲本身就是一个案例。今天我们非常有幸邀请到了来自福特基金会的高倩倩。赠与亚洲成立于2001年，与其相比，福特基金会像是一个大姐姐。我们一直合作得非常好，在其他国家我们也有非常好的合作，非常感谢福特基金会。我知道今天高倩倩将会较早离开，我想在这给她一个发言的机会。

今天上午，香港赛马会代表提到，他们的基金会按私人捐赠数量计算已经是全球第五大基金会，赠与亚洲与香港赛马会相比规模小一些，但是其案例也非常有价值。

我知道高倩倩一会儿会有事先走，现在我就先把话筒交给高倩倩。

高倩倩：感谢论坛主办方邀请我来参加今天的公益慈善论坛。

我要讲的是一些比较有趣的例子。福特基金会早先也是家族基金会，但是现在不再是纯家族基金会，我和大家分享一下这一变化背后的过程并回答一些前面提到的问题。

大家都知道亨利·福特创办了福特公司，他的儿子用仅仅2万美金在1936年创办了福特基金会。亨利·福特的儿子去世前，把自己在福特公司的股票放到了福特基金会。福特基金会早期就是一个家族基金会，主要由福特家族的资源支持运转。当时福特公司总部位于美国密歇根州，福特基金会也就位于那里。当时基金会的项目也主要是在密歇根州，其关注当地的社区、员工和项目，尤其是跟福特公司、福特家族相关的产业和社区。

后来在20世纪40年代末期，福特基金会成为世界上最大的慈善组织，但现在不是了。当时亨利·福特先生的第二代认为，既然福特基金会现在已经是最大的基金会了，那是不是应该考虑一下，作为龙头需要扮演什么样的角色，是依然关注密歇根州的事，还是去关注世界呢？所以他们就雇用了一些顾问来给他们做报告。

报告规划了福特基金会未来的发展，它建议将福特基金会变成国际性基金会，把关注点从过去只关注对福特家族成员有利的领域，转移至关注对全世界有利的行业。当时恰好是二战的结束。报告建议基金会去关注与民主、减贫、人类尊严相关的领域。

后来福特基金会就做了转型，变成了更大、更国际化的基金会。我们开始在美国以外的地方发展，1952 年我们在印度设立了第二个办公室，1953 年在埃及设立了第三个办公室，现在它们仍然在运作。最终我们在全球有 20 多个办公室，今天我们又做了缩减，差不多有 10 个办公室。我们依然是关注国际的基金会，第二代的福特先生一直担任我们的信托和董事局主席，后来他在 1976 年退休，从那时起，福特家族成员中就再也没有人担任福特基金会董事会成员，或者是决策基金的使用。

福特基金会变成了专门、独立的基金会，我们有自己的董事会，由其选择成员和主席，主席管理整个基金会，并向董事会做报告。另外，董事会成员都有赠予的责任，原本我们已经不再和原来的福特家族有任何的联系，但是 2019 年我们的主席去了底特律和福特家族的人见面，并确认亨利·福特第三代会成为我们的董事会成员。现在福特家族的人重回福特基金会，但这不是因为他是福特家族的人，而是因为他自己也对底特律和密歇根的公益和慈善事业感兴趣。他作为专业人士加入了基金会。

福特基金会从家族基金会转型成为非家族型的基金会，这一点很有意思。但是我们依然要铭记自己的根源。现在我们也关注密歇根和底特律的慈善事业。这便是我们讲过的家族转型，我想和大家分享的就是这一点。

米奇·珀杜的报告做得非常好。我们跟您一样，也在想怎样更好地利用艺术品，让其成为慈善公益重要的载体。我们福特基金会的主席提出了一个项目，为社会公平而做的艺术。他说，希望像您一样收藏艺术品的人可以出售、拍卖艺术品，我们也希望能够帮助您在美国去做慈善。

我们希望拍卖艺术品的钱，可以为慈善所用，解决像大规模监禁这样的问题。我们希望和您这样的人合作，发掘艺术品的慈善价值，关注美国人口贩卖或大规模监禁这种问题。这些艺术品本身具有价值，也能被发掘出其他价值。我们希望把这些艺术品的价值变成其他我们感兴趣的慈善项目，所以我想和米奇·珀杜说，我们跟您想的是一样的。我觉得这是一个创新方式，可以充分调动、利用资源和资金，让它们能够真正帮助我们解决所关注的社会问题。

此外我认为，今天在座的各位都会同意，人口贩卖、大规模监禁、教育问题、健康问题这些挑战不是一个基金会、一个企业家通过自己的、企业的公益行为就能够应对的。这些挑战需要我们各位共同去应对。

就像第一位嘉宾讲到的，一个基金会或政府没有办法实现联合国的可持续发展目标。我们是世界上最大的基金会之一，但是从自己的角度来讲，我们没有办法应对这么多的挑战。我们愿意跟各位及你们的组织一起合作。

为善收藏和售卖，这是大家未来可以去探索的领域。我就讲这么多，谢谢大家！

薛希璞：大家都有这方面的兴趣，那我们就请贾斯汀·米勒和琼·克雷恩来分享经验。

我们先请贾斯汀·米勒来讲话，你们现在对于艺术品、财富的传承，包括慈善，是怎么做的？尤其是代代相传的财富传承，包括您的子孙后代，第二代、第三代的财富规划。

贾斯汀·米勒是来自纽约梅隆银行的财富规划师，他今天和我们讲的包括税收、家族治理。他是一名法学教授，曾经也在很多的行业会议上讲话。他也是纽约律师协会的会员，他刚从加利福尼亚大学伯克利分校拿到了他的博士学位，也从纽约大学法学院拿到了学位。国家需要规划，而家族的财富需要管理。对于企业的高管和家族的所有者来讲，他们怎么样去做自己的遗产规划、遗嘱规划、财富规划、税务筹划？这些是世界上首富家族所面临的共同的问题。因为税收首先就是一个很重要的话题，其次他今天讲的东西是大多数的家族办公室管理成员非常感兴趣的话题，所以我就把话筒移交给贾斯汀·米勒。

贾斯汀·米勒：一个家族财富传承的秘密，人们总是想知道，为什么有的家族总是能够有办法把自己的财富传承给第二代、第三代、第四代？为什么这些家族可以做到家族传承？纽约梅隆银行拥有很好的员工团队、项目开展经历和学校，但我们会向客户学习。纽约梅隆银行是历史最为悠久的私有银行，是在纽约证券交易所上市的第一个银行集团，也是第一个信托机构。今天纽约梅隆银行也是世界上最大的投资银行之一，同时我们的历史最为悠久，哪怕过了七代，我们有些客户还在。我想谈一下这些客户共同具有的四个特点。当你提及一个成功的家族，它至少会具有这四个特点中的一个。

首先，我给大家介绍一些背景知识。当我们讲到财富传承的时候，它到底指什么？财富的传承是一代一代的传承，很多人听到财富的时候，就觉得它是金融资本，是金钱，所以他们觉得财富传承首先是金钱的传承。金钱固然重要，它近乎相当于地球上的氧气，但有人说，金钱不是人生最重要的东西。我们知道金钱是十分重要的，但成功的家族不仅仅积累金融资本，它们还试图传承其他四种不同的资产。

从各个学科上讲，我们还会有人力资本、社会资本以及其他的资本。以下我所讲的四类财富就是我们的客户想在资金之外传承的东西。

第一，个体资本，他们希望每位家族成员都能够取得成功，受到良好的教育，能够独立生活。第二，集体资本，希望家族成员能够聚集到一起，这样家庭才是一个集体。第三，他们希望能够保留社区基金。不是真空中的家族，而是家族实际为社区带来的扶持，慈善便来源于此。第四，精神财富。不管是什么宗教或信仰，家族成员都会给予尊重，一个成功的家族所传承的物质财富与精神财富之间是有关系的。有什么关系呢？对于成功的家族来讲，它们的钱是帮助其增加其他类型的财富。这也是成功的家族的经验。

如果您要打造一个成功的家族，您一般会遇到什么问题呢？很多人说“富不过三代”，在中国和美国都有类似的看法，为什么呢？因为第一代主要是赚钱，第二代花钱，第三代的时候钱就用尽了。有趣的是，所有的国家，无论文化情况、经济状况、宗教信仰、税收政策如何，它们都有相似的谚语用来表达“富不过三代”这一概念。这是关乎人性的，无论哪一个国家，都有这种现象。

在美国，许多相关研究发现，大家族到了第三代，失败率会达到 70%。我们看一下，在 1983 年的时候麻省理工学院的一位教授就开始了相关的研究，1987 年另一位教授又有进一步的分析。这些类似的研究分析出大家族在第四代时的失败率达到了 90%。

第一代人打江山，他们就是我们的客户，他们积累了财富，他们可能是 CEO、开发商，或者是企业家，第一代人都做得很好。第二代人，他们很多是专业人士，比如说医生、律师等。上一代的财富传承给他们，他们接受了很好的教育。第三代人一般从事什么职业呢？他们是演员、艺术家、音乐家，甚至是冲浪的教练等。很多家族积累下来几代的财富让后代可以随心所欲做任何事情，不需要受到金钱的奴役。这些后代有些是演员、音乐家、教师和社工，我没有说这些职业不好，我只是说我们希望这些人拥有一份工作，不要沉迷于毒品、赌博等。这一点是家族想要避免的事情。

现在我们来看一下，如何实现未来财富的保值？

第一，我们发现对于成功的家族来说，它们并不会自己来做传承，它们会外包给专业的团队，里面有投资银行家、会计师、律师以及管理人员帮助它们一起做计划。它们会关注一些法律文件、税法等，也会关注家族自身。PPT 上左侧的人关注将金钱提供给家族成员，而右侧的人关注让家族成员赚取金钱。这个团队不只关注税法、金融，我们当然知道经济上的成功和避税是非常重要的，但是也要关注家族团结，比如说如何让家族保持团结的状态。

第二，成功的家族都要做一些什么呢？首先它们要思考家族的钱应该投到哪些方面？现在它们还是主管自己的企业吗？还是把企业卖出去了？此外，可以雇佣非常好的投资经理。这个地方面临一个挑战，人们从心理学上来说是不擅长投资的，假如你是家族企业成员或者房地产开发商，你会更倾向做股票、债券这种被动投资。

在 2018 年，标普首次出现了下滑，人们很恐慌，为什么数据会下滑呢？因为整个市场不会一直发生线性变化。2018 年到底发生了什么事情？世界上有各大新闻和头条，每天都说出现了什么情况，它们很少谈论积极的事情，更多的是谈论一些负面的消息，因为负面消息更能抓人眼球。如果天天看这些新闻，会非常沮丧。若你远离这些噪声，仅仅看向股票市场的动态，你会发现它就像心脏病患者的心电图，但这不仅仅是关于投资。

第三，我们要关注我们的税务。我们如何更好地避税呢？你肯定要雇佣一个税务顾问，我本人是税务律师。在美国，我们有各种各样的税，也有各种合法的对策去避税。对于跨国企业而言，你人在亚洲，你的孩子在美国，你要考虑这些跨国架构，这个过程中慈善可能会发挥作用。这也是做慈善最有税务效益的方式。

第四，成功的家族会看到失败现象。很多家族它们有很好的顾问，它们投资做得非常好，税务也做得很好，它们的第四个法宝是什么呢？那就是关注家族本身，关注家族管理、家族活力和家族关系。这是一个很困难的问题。比如说我需要给我的孩子留多少钱呢？留多少钱会留多了呢？有时候我们需要思考留多少钱是够的，留多少钱是多的。这是巴菲特在接受《财富》杂志采访时说过的。所有的这些银行，它们也做了各种的研究，告诉我们说，到底要留多少钱才合适。但是，我们看一下这种跨代的财富传承，你的孩子可能一直非常好，你给他留了 600 万美元，慢慢地这个钱越来越少，我们经过研究最后发现，确实是有一个答案，这个答案不是留多少美元，这个答案也是一个问题，我们是用一个问题在回答另外一个问题。我在学校给学生上课的时候，经常说不能用一个问题去回答一个问题，但是这个地方是非常恰当的。那就是你为孩子做了哪些准备？他们准备好了吗？可能有些孩子 20 多岁就拥有几十万美元，但这可能会毁了他们，他们不工作，甚至是吸毒、离婚。这就说明留给他们的钱太多了。有些家族给孩子留了很多钱，却产生了很好的效果，孩子们会去做慈善等。如何让孩子做好准备呢？我们发现了五点措施。

第一，要让家族成员接受良好的教育。

第二，沟通交流。

第三，要有正确的价值观。

第四，参与慈善工作。很多时候，富二代要到第一代去世之后才接触慈善，这是不对的。

第五，优化家族领导力的过渡过程。不是说富二代要直接接手，而是说要有一个很好的接班计划。

这就是关于家族管理。是谁负责？在哪里做？什么时候？怎么做？这就是我们需要回答的问题。如果你的家族可以很好地回答这几大问题，那你的家族的事业就可以长青。

慈善对家族有多大的影响和作用呢？家族慈善起作用的原因有三个：第一个是减税，在美国，就是因为减税，所以美国拥有很好的 GDP；第二个是社会认同感，人们是非常在乎社会认同感的；第三个是心理学上的原因，就是参与慈善可以提升人们的幸福感，慈善和幸福感是正相关的，就是你的给予和捐赠会让你有幸福感。

那怎么样实现这一点呢？请让我的同事琼·克雷恩讲述她的观点。

谢谢大家。

薛希璞：谢谢贾斯汀·米勒刚刚的介绍，大家可能听说过百老汇的一个音乐剧，这个音乐剧是关于美国一位国务卿的，其也是纽约银行的创始人。我不知道这之间有没有联系，但是我们下一位讲者也是音乐系的高才生，或许她也帮助造就了这个音乐剧的成功。琼·克雷恩是纽约梅隆银行的一位高管，在过去 25 年间，她与多个跨代家族打过交道，专注于家族治理与成功、跨国规划等。感谢琼·克雷恩团队所做的工作。

我们知道梅隆银行公司曾被《财富》杂志评为在家族财富管理方面的优秀团队，今天琼会为我们介绍一些慈善家族的创新和发展趋势，以及如何做到有效的家族财富管理。

琼·克雷恩：我要说一点离题的话，刚刚我的同事提到了让家族成员一起做慈善。很多时候，家族客户找我们说不知道如何起步，不知道如何让孩子参与和接手他的工作，所以我觉得在一开始，我想谈一些具体的东西，关于家族和家族中的不同年龄的孩子，以及如何让家族发展壮大。

关于第一个问题，在何时让我的孩子参与家族治理呢？有人问巴菲特为何要让孩子们做好准备呢？他说，你看这棵树之所以能长这么大是因为有人提前让它做好了准备。家族需要在孩子幼时就让他们做好准备。

我们也调查过一些集团和客户，什么时候开始做慈善？当然是越早越好。那越早越好意味着什么呢？是在高中、大学、大学毕业之后？有的人说干脆等他们准备好了再去做。有的人说那你要一直等着他们准备好，那可能要等一辈子，因为他们永远都准备不好，你必须得推他们一把。

所以最重要的是，孩子们最宝贵的学习时间是在其3岁、4岁、5岁的时候，他们把父母当成榜样来学习，这是让孩子们做好准备的最佳方式。我觉得卡特和他的女儿做得就很好，他是世界上最伟大的慈善家之一，他的孩子对慈善事业耳濡目染。但是孩子仅学习榜样是完全不够的，我们还要有一些其他的准备。

这也是我们的客户教给我们的，如果别人给孩子一些钱，压岁钱或者是其他的一些零花钱，孩子可能会马上花掉，因为他觉得这是他挣来的，他就得花掉，可以采取一种方式，即在他花钱之前，准备三个罐子，请他把一些钱装在第一个罐子里面存起来，然后把同等数量的钱放进第二个罐子里，捐给有需要的机构或者是其他需要这笔钱的人，第三个罐子里才是他在省钱和捐钱之后能花的钱。

另外一个方法是利用假期。最好的机会就是将好处回馈给他人的感恩节，感恩节在周四，我们那儿99%的人周五不去上班，我们可以借感恩节的机会和孩子们谈如何做一些项目。当我们的孩子长大的时候，可能到初中和高中，他们也可以参与一些项目，做小的投资和捐赠。

我们有的客户已经开始第四代、第五代的传承，他们觉得慈善对他们来说非常重要。孩子也是董事会的成员，每一个孩子可以做没有投票权的董事会成员一年到两年，两年之后董事会又把这个名额给更年幼的孩子。这个过程是很重要的，有的时候有些家长还让他们的孩子有投票权，以这样的方式使孩子们感受到做慈善的快乐，并且拥有做决定的自主权，同时发现孩子们中哪一个具有领导力。就像前面福特家族的那个例子，第三代、第四代总是有一个孩子，他特别想成为慈善家，所以大的家族能够通过小活动发现最好的接班人。

我们还有一种情况叫作“橱柜里的大象”，“橱柜里的大象”是我们潜在的风险。当我们谈到家族慈善的时候，我们总是会看配偶的角色。有一天，家族里的孩子会结婚，可能会找一个并不属于这个家族的配偶，我们会不会把他的配偶也纳入我们的家族董事会呢？我可以跟大家说会，也可以说不会，但是这是基于具体的情况。

有一个家族，之前我们和其成员谈论过，前面已经有人做了很好的规划，但是在我出发之前，有一位客户给我打电话，他有五个孩子，他说他兄弟的配偶也要来参加董事会议，我说他之前没有告诉我，他说他哥哥的太太来了他就不去了。当然他的另外一个妹妹也不愿意家族成员携配偶来参加家族的活动。

我给家族成员的建议一般是，也许你们并不想让你们家族成员的配偶参与信托财富传承的决策，但如果是做慈善的话，最好还是让他们也加入，既然你们的孩子决定和这个人共度一生，那你们最好也接纳他，让他参与其中的慈善项目，而且越多越好。

还有卡片游戏。这个例子米奇也讲过，有人在卡片上写上自己认为最重要的事。其中有一张卡片写的是赠予，有一张卡片写的是健康。我们也放很多这样的卡片，并会对这些卡片按照重要性排序。父母也会让孩子做这个游戏，还说孩子都是不一样的。但是，每一次跟我的客户做实验的时候，我会发现，对于很多家族来讲，有三四张卡片上的内容都是一样的。如果您在家族成员里面发现孩子对某些问题，比如气候变化、海平面上升这些问题非常感兴趣，那您就可以设立和这些内容相关的项目，这样孩子们可能会对这些项目更感兴趣。

沟通交流也很重要，这有助于共同决策。假设家族成员没有住在一起，怎么办呢？今天有了现代技术，我们就有更多机会。在我们服务的一个家族中，有一个小男孩，14 岁，他对参加慈善会议根本不感兴趣，我们就告诉他，创建一个在线的让家族成员沟通的平台，这个小男孩做得很好，他做了一个在线的平台，这样家族成员无论分散在世界的什么地方，都可以每周在线上进行讨论，但也要保证每一年能进行一次面对面交流，不是在手机上通过视频见面，而是整个家族找一个时间一起吃顿饭，谈工作，这非常重要。

对于一个成功的家族来讲，假设家族成员的沟通非常顺畅，做慈善项目其实并不难。对于有些慈善家族、财富家族来讲，其成员可能并不想成为一个财富家族的后代，而是想成为他们孩子财富的创造者和慈善项目的创造者。新的技术，可以帮助我们实现更好的沟通。

有些家族成员不仅想做家族的传承者，也想成为后代的先人。大家都知道，科技有助于慈善事业发展，还可以帮助儿童进行赠予。其中一个例子是腾讯公益。腾讯公益的“99 公益日”就是很重要的计划，很多人可以从手机上或者是电脑上为公益事业捐款。如果担心这些项目的透明度，还可以去做追踪，腾讯公益已经做了这样的工作，它有一个在线的平台。支付宝和微信支付也有类似的项目，帮助中国的贫苦地区，比如说要在一些地带植树造林。就支付宝而言，如果去用支付宝的话，就会收到绿色能量，可以去浇水、种树等。这些都是技术上的创新。

包括讲到全球的慈善也有很多的问题，我们通过研究惊奇地发现，慈善事业关注的要点在全球都是一样的，但是每个国家的做法不一样。如何利用美国、英国的基金会更好地去处理一些税务？不光是美国的、英国的，还包括加拿大的。如果你想把自己的财富给予或者是赠予他人，在新加坡是不可以的，因为那里不允许外籍赠予。假设有一两个人，想把家族财富当作赠予来进行传承，如何能做到这一点呢？还是要去做很好的架构，比如说要建立一个私人的基金会，我们会选一个最大的捐赠人，对他来讲，这个税收属地是最有利的，这样我们会更好地帮助这个基金会的创办人。

我们可以在基金会下面做一个子公司，可以设在别的国家，其他的人因此享受到一些减税的待遇。我们还要在成立基金会的时候，考虑家族的主要业务在什么地方，这两个地点之间是什么样的关系。可以直接捐助，也可以间接捐助，亚洲的慈善一般是通过项目直接赠予。当我们做希望项目时，比如说办学校或者是提供资金支持，我们希望给柬埔寨做可携带的饮水。通过这样的项目，我们可以给予当地或国外的慈善机构一些直接的基金支持。大家若想知道项目的细节可以问我。

我也想和大家谈我们的信托和医嘱承诺，我们可以通过这些善行去积累财富。当您做慈善的时候，您觉得最好的建议是什么呢？

比如说在这个过程中，结了多少税，对整个企业来讲获得了多少积极的评价？我的建议是希望大家做简单的架构。另外，家族基金会是代代传承的，新一代的人总是想迅速看到影响，比如说想看项目的量化目标。做慈善公益，最重要的是信任、透明度，因为人们想看到慈善引发的积极变化。他们也对投资和融资渠道非常感兴趣，所有的这些是其他嘉宾要讲到的，影响力和环境投资都非常重要。

我也是社区基金会委员会的成员，也想知道如何通过投资更好地促进社会管制和环境优化，我们希望更重要的是授人以渔。如果做一件事情，一开始就太焦虑，就没有办法开头，可能是因为信息太多了。伏尔泰之前说过一句话，“最佳是良好的敌人”，如果一开始就想做到完美，就很难踏出第一步。所以我们要先开头，而不要一开始就追求完美。

薛希璞：现在是几分钟的问答环节，今天我们分享了很多精彩的内容，大家有什么问题吗？

彭倩：感谢刚刚讲者非常精彩的经验分享。我想向米奇·珀杜提出一个问题。我是香港科技大学的一名教授，我的研究领域是家族基金和家族慈善。我在课堂上经常将家族慈善分为两种：第一种是传统慈善，第二种是战略性慈善。根据我个人的观察以及案例研究，我发现香港很多的家族在关注战略性慈善，战略性慈善就像一种黏合剂，让家族成员更加紧密团结在一起。因为传统慈善就是写支票，是一次性的，而战略性慈善需要家族成员更多地参与其中。所以，我想问一下珀杜家族，因为刚刚的 PPT 也提到了，慈善可以让家族成员联系起来，那究竟如何选择战略性慈善项目？家族成员如何一起做决策？

米奇·珀杜：我们会收到一些建议，可能有二三十个需求，我可以找时间和你细谈。我们有一个捐赠俱乐部，捐赠俱乐部里面是一些 12 岁到 18 岁的孩子。他们共有 2 万美元，并且要共同决定如何花这笔钱，他们要达成一致。这个捐赠俱乐部让孩子们成为决策的一环，其中包括配偶，非血亲成员也会参与其中。这个俱乐部的运作是非常有效的，通过这样的方式，我们可以让配偶更有参与感和归属感。

我的一些朋友，以及其他熟识的人，他们都有这种经验，年轻人很有创新精神，年轻人对于慈善会有新的点子。我们觉得慈善不仅仅是短期的公益，我希望学生可以去思考，可以利用那些创新型技术为慈善带来一些新的想法和点子，谢谢。

贾斯汀·米勒：我做一个补充，开支票不是家族慈善，只是捐钱。家族慈善会让兄弟姐妹、表兄表妹都参与其中，家族成员里面一个 12 岁的孩子可以和 60 岁的人有同等的投票权，这是一个博弈和协商的过程。这是一个有效的方式，可以帮助我们选择想要支持的项目，决定投入多少钱。

为什么这种方式非常有效呢？我给大家分析一下其中的组织理论，因为我们知道，家族管理其实是涉及组织理论的，家族慈善之所以成功是因为水平的运作方式，那就是在同一代中，兄弟姐妹、表兄表妹都会参与其中，同一代的人做决策。如果在一个家族中，父亲说让孩子做什么，这是一种垂直管理方式，通常被证明是不太好的，而水平的方式是更好的。因为我们知道，水平管理是同一代人做决定，他们是同龄人，年轻人在 12 岁到 18 岁的时候已经参与了慈善决策，这是非常有意义的经验。

薛希璞：刚刚提到的 12 岁到 18 岁俱乐部成员非常有意思，还有其他的问题吗？如果没有其他的问题，我们现在休息 5 分钟，再回来参与最后两个环节。

薛希璞：下一个环节，我们会讨论未来的一些创新和发展趋势，尤其是跟家族慈善相关的。首先为我们带来演讲的是连宗诚先生，他是新加坡非营利组织领域的支持者和领头人物，是连氏家族的第三代也是第一代家族成员。他是连氏基金会的主席、全国志愿服务和慈善中心总裁、新加坡社区基金会主席、新加坡国际明爱会副主席、非营利领袖中心副主席和亚洲慈善圈创始人，他也曾是新加坡官委议员，主要关注民间社会问题。连宗诚先生主要关注非营利领域，他也在新加坡担任了一些公职，他获得了多所学校的学位，包括新加坡国立大学、牛津大学和哈佛大学肯尼迪政府学院，并于 2010 年获颁艾森豪奖学金。连氏基金会是连宗诚的祖父连瀛洲成立的，这个基金会主要会用创新的想法来解决社会面临的问题，比如说儿童教育、老年护理、环境可持续发展等。接下来，请大家和我一起来欢迎连宗诚介绍在家族慈善方面有哪些创新和发展趋势。

连宗诚：谢谢主持人刚刚对我的介绍，刚刚的介绍有些已经过时了，有些职位我现在已经不再担任。我现在是连氏基金会主席、亚洲慈善圈创始人，我已经从全国志愿服务和慈善中心离职。

我在慈善方面的经验最早是脱离家族的。我其实在新加坡政府工作了 14

年，但后来我意识到我可以在民间社会发挥作用，打造慈善生态系统，因为当时没有多少人从事这方面的工作。我个人的慈善经验是离不开连氏基金会的，我的祖父不太擅长沟通、展望、制订接班计划，我进入基金会董事会，那是在 2002 年，他 96 岁的时候。两年后他就过世了。那时没有一个战略计划可以让我们按部就班发展基金会。

我们是想用一些创新的方式来做慈善，接下来，我们就发现，其实还是需要一些时间让人们慢慢接受。我们研究了慈善基金可以起到哪些作用，发现它可以提升影响力、募资、解决社会问题。我想这不仅是连氏基金会的发展足迹，也是世界公益慈善的整体趋势。

我们做了更长久的考虑，想建立 10 年、20 年的资助关系，因为我们有很多合作伙伴，他们可以提供很多好且新的解决方案。他们会利用我们的捐助做很多事。连氏基金会和这个领域的领先人物一起合作，他们在这方面已经有了很多的见解和经验。

我们希望慈善越来越有战略性，将我们的捐赠涵盖尽可能广泛的范围，当然其中我们也会聚焦一些特殊的项目。它既有细节，也有广泛的方面。当然决策过程也需要有所改变，需要从“一言堂”“大家长做决定”的方式，变得更民主、更广泛。这应该是水平的结构，而非垂直的，我们现在也在摸索。

我们还关注了传统领域的慈善项目，比如说水、卫生和环境等，这些项目在世界上其他的地方也是受欢迎的，我们还有一些探索式、高风险的项目。

我刚刚分享的是当前慈善界的趋势，它可能还不是慈善的主流，因为主流慈善还是由第一代家族成员创造、管控的，这是比较传统的方式。传统慈善是与个人、遗产、个体的兴趣相关的，而现在我们更多的是需要一种民主、智慧的方式。

我们现在看到，有些人做的慈善远超于基金会的范畴。我想提及我在亚洲慈善圈的一位同事，他本来是应该来到今天的会场进行演讲的，不幸的是他的父亲刚刚过世，他没有办法出差。他在香港出生，在新加坡定居，他有自己的基金会，他的基金会非同寻常。他希望能够探索出养老和老人护理的新模式。

这是一个比较新颖的领域。20 多年前，新加坡还没有出现严重老龄化问题，他和合作伙伴为养老做出了一个新的方案。首先是初级养老的护理，然后是个性化的养老。我们的政府总是能在那边学到经验，并将其融入政府的项目。他们在老年人护理方面做得非常好，甚至可以说他们的基金会是新加坡整个养老护理行业培训领域里最重要的组织。他们一直战斗在养老的最前线，他们做了大量的工作。他们是以家族慈善基金会的基金投入撬动政府资源和公共资源。

我们看到亚洲慈善圈的一些人，他们过去一直将企业的钱作为家族慈善的启动基金，这样做有几个出发点。第一，过去是由大家长负责全权事务，因为他本身是家族慈善的造血人，但是到了第二代、第三代，越来越多的家族成员参与进来，公司就没有办法再去全权负责家族慈善的运营和管理。这个家族觉得公司做的基金会，基本上和公司业务，包括公司的社会责任感相关。基金会的成员没有很强的自主性，难以决定做很大的项目，所以他们做了另外一个家族基金会，他们就从过去的企业基金会的模式转型到家族慈善。他们和市政府，包括卫生部、健康部一起合作，关注儿童健康、女童教育。在菲律宾，他们也会在公共领域推动项目合作。他们完全实现了转型，而且他们现在在妇女、儿童健康方面做得非常好，他们不再像过去一样由一个人来主导，而是每一个人都去做影响力投资，这是战略性业务合作。

为了让大家可以互相学习、借鉴彼此的经验，我们创建了亚洲慈善圈。如果能够推广应用一些非常有效的模式，那就很好了。同时，希望我们的会员能够联合起来，以“1+1 ＞ 2”的形式解决任何单独的机构没有办法解决的巨大问题，比如环境问题。我们最近还有一个基金会专门去做和平倡议，这也是世界上饱受战乱地区比较渴求的。

希望我们的慈善事业能够更富有战略性、更协同，这也是我在亚洲慈善圈看到的变化，这一定是未来的方向。

薛希璞：谢谢连宗诚为我们带来的精彩介绍。接下来我想介绍这个环节的第二位讲者，她是萨卡・科佩拉，来自芬兰，之前在德国工作。在油气领域工作多年后，她加入了联合国，专注于南美地区的联合国开发计划署项目。后来又去了纽约担任联合国驻纽约业务伙伴关系司司长。她也是哥伦比亚大学国际和公共事务学院的助理教授，担任国际乡村建设学院的受托人。她现在帮助孩子照顾孙子和孙女，也和自己的孩子一起学习汉语。她在北京居住了 4 年，也会为 CCTV 提供分析报告。今天我想她会和我们谈论公私合作。

萨卡・科佩拉：谢谢主办方对我的邀请，也谢谢赠与亚洲。我很高兴能够再回到亚洲，回到中国。

今天大家谈论的话题让我感觉热情满满。慈善对我来说意味着用热情的心采取行动。现在的创新以及慈善事业的发展趋势让我思考伙伴关系在其中的作用。我想这涉及如何增加我们的成果，以及扩大影响力和规模，尤其是更好地推进慈善活动和获得慈善效果。

几周前在美国商业圆桌会议上，大家说现在股东的财富积累已经不是企业追求的唯一目标。我想这意味着公司也要关注其他利益相关者。在慈善事业中，我觉得每一个利益相关方都扮演着重要的角色，推动慈善事业发展的其中一个方式就是采取合作伙伴模式。大家应该和谁合作，才能升级自己的慈善事业，使其扎根于慈善领域呢？

我想最好是和其他的基金会结盟。如果和这些基金会结盟，你们可以合作、互动、交流，分享或是推广经验，并且协同双方的资源。这样，项目的启动基金也会更充裕。

大家也可以和非政府组织合作，甚至是和基于项目实践的小型非政府组织合作，比如说跟世界自然基金会（WWF）合作。所有这些都会成为你们项目推进过程中的重要环节。这些小型非政府组织也是很重要的，如果想让你的慈善项目产生持久的影响力，与它们的合作就至关重要。

另外，还可以和谁去合作呢？当你去实施具体项目或者是开展活动的时候，假设项目变得越来越大、越来越复杂，那就必须引入更多的合作伙伴，这些人可能会成为你的助推者。也许大家的背景都不同，文化也迥异，基金会的掌权人个性差异也很大。那么就要有一个中间者把所有的人聚到一起，让他们一起去探讨工作、相互理解、相互协同。

我们也需要一些很重要的合作伙伴，那就是政府机构。我们甚至要引入高层政府。如果大家想让你的项目产生最大的影响力，那就一定要在项目规划、项目策略制定期间就引入政府，这样你的项目才能真正被引入政府的政策范围。

其他的合作伙伴包括联合国机构。我自己原本是在联合国开发计划署和联合国驻纽约业务伙伴关系司工作，很多的联合国机构也作为助推机构和中间机构，帮助我们与更多的非政府组织、企业、政府、基金会进行对话和协作。我们也在地区层面上推进项目，也和其他的机构合作。

在达成合作伙伴关系之后，大家怎么去管理合作伙伴关系呢？具体管理的方式要视项目的性质和范围而定。有的时候，大家追求的目标比较类似。我们前面讲到，你需要找一个非常合适的市场推广者。几年前，一个叫作RED的机构做了很好的推广，其主要是做抗击艾滋病的项目，大家可以相互签订协议，确定各自的权责，优化我们专业的知识。我想在对抗疟疾和面对全球挑战时，我们的联盟可以比较松散，但我们也可以基于具体的合同形成伙伴关系。

各方可以团结起来制定一些可清晰衡量的目标，定下非常清晰的时间节点。为什么要形成伙伴关系呢？主要原因是我们可以集合各方的力量，可以汇集大家的智慧，产生更大的影响，扩大项目规模。另外，我们可以有更强的预见性。

项目有各方参与，可以彼此进行交流，质量会得到监控与保障。有时候面临的问题越困难、越复杂，越需要有不同的资源参与其中。所以，这个考虑还是基于汇聚各方力量。而与政府合作有哪些优势呢？首先，我们可以将一些内在的解决方案与捐助和政府政策融合在一起。然后我们要考虑工作风格，还要考虑官僚主义、选举期以及政客工作年限这些方面的影响。美国非常鼓励公私合作。美国政府在不断削减预算，感觉把更多的压力推到了私营部门，但是我们要想到，跟政府合作会产生非常复杂的影响。此外，我们还要考虑地方政府，这一点也很重要。

我们都是心怀热情的人，我们要与其他人一起合作，真正把热情落到实处。谢谢大家！

薛希璞：谢谢萨卡·科佩拉的精彩分享。我们下一位讲者是埃利奥特·唐纳利。他的履历很长，也许是因为他是这个屋子里个头最高的人。他是芝加哥白沙集团投资基金合伙人，也是芝加哥唐纳利家族第五代成员。他也在硅谷和其他区域创办了一些公司。他曾于 1889~1991 年在北京工作，在学校任职。他今天会和大家分享影响力投资与慈善方面的最佳实践。他是斯坦福大学国际项目中心的理事会成员，主要研究世界基础设施项目。另外，他也是慈善工作坊的信托人，是世界教育网络的主要资助人，这个网络最初是由洛克菲勒基金会创办的。这个网络在 46 个国家拥有 450 个成员。他也是 LGT 风险慈善的董事会成员。他经常发表关于战略性慈善、家族基金、遗产方面的创新型论文。埃利奥特·唐纳利也是一位非常好的舞者，他之前还是位舞蹈老师。感谢您的出席。

埃利奥特·唐纳利：感谢主持人的介绍，也感谢主办方给我们这样的机会。感谢中国人民对外友好协会、清华大学、香港大学、香港中文大学和深圳市政府搭建平台让我们共聚一堂。今天我想谈一谈慈善领域的创新和发展趋势。

我先讲一个故事，关于爱、战争、舞蹈课堂，等等。我的曾曾祖父是爱尔兰移民，他爱上了加拿大一个最富有家族的女儿。他去求婚，那个父亲不同意把自己的女儿嫁给穷小子，他说动女孩和他私奔。为了向他的岳父证明自己，他在 1864 年到芝加哥成立了一家印刷公司。在过去 150 年间，这家公司成为全球最大的印刷公司。在这个过程中，他践行之前讲者提到的家族管理理念。

我的父亲和我的母亲的爱情故事也很感人。我的父亲被送到越南去打仗，而我的母亲在芝加哥和其他家族成员住在一起。她发现公司的价值观发生了改变，下一代人有些迷失了。在我父亲回到家乡之后，我的母亲说想让他留在加利福尼亚，说如果他去往芝加哥可能会拥有很好的前程，但还是想让他留在加利福尼亚，这样会对孩子比较好。我的父亲同意了这个决定，他在 1969 年到了伯克利，成为企业家，也受到很好的教育。那时候我周围的朋友并非来自非常有钱的家庭，但他们的父母大多是大学教授和工程师等。后来我在 13 岁时发现唐纳利家族和我的姓氏一样，我的父亲才告诉我家族的历史。我不在家族里长大，但这也让我成为“第一代”成员。

我当时去了耶鲁大学参加划船队。那个时候，我开始学习中文。1981 年，我去了北京，在北京航空航天大学担任航空学教师。我的祖母在离世以前希望将家族成员集合到一起，所以家族中的人从世界各地聚集到了一起。我慢慢开始参与家族的慈善事业，也学习了金融、财务知识。那个时候我受到了家族事业的启发。我在耶鲁大学学到很多，在家族事业中也学到很多。我决定沿着金融、财富、慈善这条路走下去。关于刚刚说的跳舞，我也会找机会再细谈。

2003 年，我在中国遇到一位男士，他提到了一个慈善工作坊项目。我决定加入其中。后来我也参加了洛克菲勒基金会的项目，更深入地参与到了慈善工作中，一直走到了今天。我现在对慈善非常有热情，我相信我们可以通过慈善和金融创造出一些非常有意义的方案，来改变我们的世界。

我接下来想谈几点。第一点关于影响力投资，第二点关于慈善中的影响力投资，第三点关于人类潜力与金融增长和技术之间的联系，谈谈这些如何重新塑造人类社会与未来。2007 年，洛克菲勒中心提出了“影响力投资”这一说法，人们意识到艺术对于慈善的影响，意识到艺术在投资和慈善过程中所起到的作用。这源于演员给予美国慈善事业的大力支持。类似于洛克菲勒基金会的这些组织是很有影响力的，但是大多时候这些基金会仅仅捐赠大约 5% 的资产，那剩下的 95% 都干什么了？我想这个问题值得我们去探索。

我们的一些同人做出了很多承诺，我们做出了这些美好的承诺，还要考虑如何去践行这些承诺。人们听到投资就非常激动，但很多时候他们并不知道其背后的意义与影响。我们看到慈善对投资有很大的影响，但是很多人并未真正了解这些影响到底是什么。

市场会有利于或者不利于人性事业，其本身是要让利益相关方获益，这是其存在的唯一目的。影响力投资则是要考虑那些不会发生的事情。影响力投资的定义是，在获得经济利益的同时，也要产生有益的社会影响、生态影响与环境影响。但是影响力投资也会受到市场制约，因为要获取经济利益，所以组织也要和市场内的其他机构竞争，与此同时保证产生有益的影响。我们还要讨论市场回报率。

我之前在南非一所金融大学给学生上课，我所做的事就是提供了慈善补贴，我要思考的是我能否用具有更高价值的方式解决问题。很多人对影响力投资感到困惑。说到影响力投资，大家听到的时候可能非常高兴。保险公司、家族基金、私有基金的影响力投资总量可达数万亿美元。

在慈善领域，美国方面的资金总量是 740 亿美元，全球的话是上万亿美元。人们想，如果这些资金都能被用去做好事，那肯定很好。但是人们没有注意到的一点是，这些资金真的可以起到最初的作用吗？当前，我们的企业结构，只是将 5% 的盈利用在慈善事业当中，所以我们要考虑新方式和新结构来实现影响力投资。我们还要考虑税务，如果只是做影响力投资拿税务优惠的话，这个优惠是行善还是作恶呢？此外，还有我们的补助，作为影响力投资，每一个家族要投入一些资金。我们如何去解决真正需要解决的问题？答案是创新。

家族决定拿出 10% 的资金投入具体的项目，资金分配很重要。首先要考虑关注的问题，即最想要创造出来的影响力。比如说定下关注气候变化这一主题，那就要考虑从哪方面减轻气候变化的影响，如何去量化成效，等等。这个目标的达成不仅依靠捐款，还依靠投资。这需要承担一定的风险，可能有的时候要扮演政府的角色，发放补助津贴、教育民众，因为这个问题很大。与此同时，影响力投资，虽不是追求经济获利，但是不拒绝经济获利。

其次是带来改变。我们要建立金融框架，把理性和慈善结合在一起。我们要研究每一个项目需要投入多少钱，其中遇到的金融风险有多大，投资回报率是多少。这个框架可能不是最好的，但是可以看出机会成本是多少。解决气候变化问题可以通过技术实现，也可以通过改变消费者的行为与政策实现。如果和企业合作，那就要列出影响力排名。这些都是很有趣的。我觉得做影响力投资的话，大家一定要关注这些细节。

我们可能从技术方面着手解决环境问题。接下来，我想讲讲人力资源的培训。

现在人们都在思索人类这个物种的潜力，我们是万物灵长，人类可以行善，也可以作恶。那怎么培养意识呢？人类在心理学、脑科学方面做了很多研究。如果人们可以明白自己的爱恨来自哪里，那我认为这有助于解决很多问题。2017 年，谷歌有一位人工智能方面的专家，他也是一位慈善家，他找我说，如果他有更多的时间，他会致力于让人们免于死亡。他觉得在未来，技术能够重造人类的每个细胞。如果能够治疗每一个细胞，就可以延长人的寿命。

在世界上，科学和技术一直呈线性发展趋势，它们使世界变得大不一样。在几十年前，我们对很多概念不太明了，但现在我们知道了金融资本的含义，了解了人工智能、机器人。如果今天我们把钱投到最需要的领域，会怎么样呢？美国现在有交通问题，未来如果有自动驾驶汽车，交通问题全部都会得到解决。针对未来的变化我们做好准备了吗？并没有。

讲到人工智能，有人说这是对世界的颠覆，会改变人们的意识，有人说其是救世者，有人认为其是终结者。在硅谷，人们已经开始问这些非常具有前瞻性的问题：未来我们怎么样去配置基金？未来技术有很大的发展潜力，可以用来行善，也可以用来作恶，希望大家可以认真考虑这个问题。谢谢大家。

薛希璞：您讲的内容非常有趣。彭敏是下一位讲者，她是湖南人，但出生在宁夏。1990 年，她独自一人来到北京，白手起家。她现在是香港荣信远东集团有限公司董事长。彭敏女士一直做房地产生意，也参与过北京的别墅开发项目。这些项目的设计非常好，为环境和生态系统做出了贡献。作为一位企业家，她竭尽所能做慈善。她也是北京一家基金会的负责人，今天她会和我们讲她三个女儿在慈善事业中的参与。这也可以看作未来开展慈善事业的范例。今天她会以自己的三个女儿为例讲一下慈善家族的下一代传承。

彭敏：非常感谢世界公益慈善论坛的邀请，我坐在这里一直忐忑不安，因为不是大的家族传承人，我听到大家的分享心里越来越踏实了。我今天的演讲很简单，也比较接地气，我发现了一件事，我的事情好像都做对了。

我想先请大家看我女儿的视频。

第一个视频里面，是我的大女儿葡萄。我是水果妈妈，二女儿是石榴。她讲她成立了自己的公益基金会，是用艺术结合公益来帮助留守儿童的，所以用她的话来讲，孩子帮助孩子的力量是最伟大的，她希望大家关注由青少年发起的公益项目。我的三女儿，小樱桃，她最喜欢的事情是画画，她的作品在公益活动中被拍卖掉，当告诉她这些钱可以帮助其他的特殊群体时，她画画是最有动力的。2019 年上半年，这个项目又筹集了 13 万元人民币，这个小学的艺术院墙刚刚做好。2019 年的 7 月份又做了第三件事情，建设艺术教室，她的项目得到了腾讯公益的支持，“99 公益日”也会看到，现在在腾讯公益上进行募捐，她的项目做了 3 年的计划。同时，孩子们学习到了这些艺术，还要回馈给社会，所有的善款再回到学校去。

我简单说了孩子们的公益活动，刚才所有嘉宾的话，对我来讲都是肯定，我很开心，我做对了事，我也希望能有机会把这个分享出去，也希望更多的机构看到目前中国有新生代的家庭在成长，希望能够有更多支持，谢谢大家!

薛希璞：谢谢彭敏的分享，您的孩子真的都非常优秀。我们进入最后一个环节，也是我们的总结环节。

龙登高：我是龙登高，来自清华大学华商研究中心。

我想谈两个方面，第一是针对我们今天的讨论所做的几点总结，第二是对于中国慈善事业的感想。

今天的讨论非常热烈，我很有收获。今天我们主要讨论了以下几点。

第一，家族财富创造与传承。这当然是慈善与公益的基础，有可持续的财富，才能够去奉献和做慈善。

第二，财富的社会分享与分配，包括慈善与公益本身。由我们今天所谈到的包括疾病治疗、养老，以及艺术和珍品拍卖，等等，可以看到慈善和公益事业涉及的范围非常广泛。另外，也表明财富创造不局限于家族，而是可以扩展到利益相关方。实际上，利益相关方体现了家族慈善、家族基金的社会责任与担当。

第三，慈善基金会本身的经营，包括怎么去投资、怎样避税等，慈善基金会通过市场运作实现增值与扩大慈善事业规模。

第四，关于慈善事业的发展趋势，这是我们今天所讨论的另外一个重点。趋势之一是，基金会从家族基金发展到了非家族基金，比如说福特。趋势之二是，慈善主体通过广泛的合作，包括跟政府的合作，或寻求合作伙伴关系来推进慈善事业。趋势之三是，慈善事业的全球化。

在慈善事业的全球化讨论中，有一位讲者谈到了中国的慈善事业，以及现代慈善事业从欧洲和北美传入中国，这点是对的，但是我想结合我的研究，谈谈中国和华人的慈善事业。

其一，中国有着深厚的慈善和公益传统，琼·克雷恩也谈到了。过去可能有一个误会，因为当代中国，各项事务大多是由政府来安排的，包括我们的慈善基金会组织等，都离不开政府。可是 1949 年以前，中国基层的公共服务大多是由民间自己安排的，基础设施是公益建造、免费使用的，比如说桥梁、义渡、道路、水利设施等。如今，这种传统却被我们忽略或者遗忘了。

其二，这种传统在中国内地很难见到了，但是在海外的华人社会仍然延续。我们今天所讨论的家族及其慈善，以及更多的公共服务在中国历史上和当今的海外华人社会随处可见。

香港华商在世界的慈善公益行动的影响力非常大。在英美许多名校，都可以看到香港华商的捐赠项目，这让我深受感动。海外华人社会和香港社会当中，体现了中华传统的延续和发扬光大。现在，它又反过来推动中国内地的慈善事业。

其三，当今中国内地的慈善公益事业，的确受到了欧美的影响，受到了香港社会和海外华人的推动。中国内地的慈善公益事业，才有一二十年的历史，因为在计划经济时期，民间都没有钱，也缺乏自主性。但是我们可以看到，中国内地的慈善公益事业发展得很快，特别是新的技术使得中国内地刚刚兴起的慈善进入了新的阶段，比如说腾讯和阿里巴巴凭借新的技术开展的慈善和公益。

这是我要谈的两个方面，谢谢。

薛希璞：您总结得非常好。接下来，我们把话筒交给曾宪章先生，让他来做最后模块的主持人。曾宪章祖籍福建，本科毕业于台湾大学电机系，之后在美国加利福尼亚大学洛杉矶分校获得计算机博士学位。他曾在美国做工业设计和项目经理，后来他回到台湾，创立全友电脑，这家公司是世界第一大扫描仪生产商，也是所在工业园区第一家公开募股的公司。在过去多年里，他一直指导学生和科技从业者，致力于促进企业教育、机构教育以及推动与本地政府的合作项目。他是不可多得的人才，他本人也是慈善家，他会对今天下午的对话做一个总结，同时我们非常高兴能够邀请到他加入我们今天下午的圆桌对话，感谢。

曾宪章：虽然我们剩下的时间不多，但是我希望大家都参与进来，今天大家能从各地飞过来，6 点了还在这里，足以看出大家的热情。我们学到了很多，今天听了许多专家的分享，我们希望提出一些想法和一些倡议，这些倡议是赠与亚洲的同事共同的智慧，有了专家的建议，我们希望大家能够集思广益，产生一些行动，我们列了 3 个行动方案给各位参考，提出来之后，欢迎在座的各位都提出建议。

第一，今天在座的每一位，都对家族传承有兴趣，多多少少也参与了公益，我们的第一个倡议是每一个人、每一个家族开始身体力行，把我们的奉献精神，把我们对社会的责任，把这些正能量传递给我们周围的朋友，我们能做多少算多少。我个人觉得，时间、精力和热情比金钱更重要，不要在乎你做多少，你今天能够资助一个学生读书，未来就能资助更多人。每一个小项目都需要大家采取行动，万丈高楼平地起，这是第一个倡议。我们希望大家开始身体力行。

第二，我们今天谈到，大家都用各种方式做慈善，我们是不是应该更有系统地把家族传承的这些经验付诸实践？成立影响力投资基金、慈善基金，这些都要可持续发展。还有一些信托，不只是财富的传承，还要加上企业社会责任，每一个企业都有基金组织，怎样承担起社会的责任？

第二个建议是，不但自己做，而且要动员自己的公司和自己的家族，使公益慈善得到传承，尤其是今天有很多年轻人，大家的思维更开放，可以用高科技的方式来助力慈善公益。

第三，独善其身还不够，中国 2020 年要实现全面扶贫，我们要进一步想到如何构建人类命运共同体，习近平总书记所提倡的人类命运共同体，有赖于国际协商合作，我们是不是也在能力范围之内，先从亚洲开始，建立一个网络，今天涵盖了 10 个国家以上，是否可以产生一个行动，这个行动是可以使大家互相学习的。在中国的乡村，这些项目会影响到很多人，这表示乡村地区很多医生都需要训练，怎么做呢？不可能将其都送到好的医学院去，时间来不及，我们想到的方式是远距离教学，我们借助企业界，把北京、上海等大都市医生的技术教到乡村里。过去讲教育不平等，但是现在有了互联网，任何偏远的地方，都可以通过互联网来学习到先进城市的教育。我们把自己的家族做好了，把中国做好了，是不是可以跨出一步，走向国际，在"一带一路"上，在南南合作上，协助这些国家，共同分享？

现在开始，我们就开放给大家发言，想发言的就可以发言。

彭倩：刚刚其实彭董事长给我们看了一个视频，那个视频讲的是摩梭人，其实那个视频没有提到关键的地方，他们还处于母系氏族社会，我回过头来联想家族慈善，家族慈善里面，女性的身影是非常多的。中国的传统文化是重男轻女，家族企业可能都是由男的继承，女的做什么呢？做慈善。

家族慈善对我来说，可以实现男女平等，或者可以使女性的角色变得更重要，它也可以让家族成员团结在一起，让所有人都在一起。中国内地的企业家，不妨拿出一小部分资金来做慈善工作，因为慈善不仅对社会好，对自己的家族也非常有帮助。

彭敏：我想补充两句。

我是一个单亲母亲，又做企业又带孩子，为什么带孩子就做到了公益方面？因为我发现和孩子一起做公益时，孩子是最好带的。因为她们很小的时候就和我成为伙伴，面对她们的疾病，面对她们很多的问题，当我没有时间，或者是我无法解答的时候，我都在公益的活动中找到了答案。我的大女儿很怕死，我们为儿童做公益的时候，她看到了得心脏病的孩子，她问我说那个小朋友会不会很快死？我让她自己去问那个孩子。她去问了那个孩子为什么每天都能这么快乐，那孩子说现在科技发达，他始终抱有希望。

从此以后，她自己都觉得没有什么可怕的。在带着她们做公益的过程中，我觉得孩子们和我一起有了对财富和生死更深的理解，也战胜了焦虑，很多家庭有很多的焦虑，我们也解决掉了这些问题。对面几位先生说的沟通、交流、教育、三观、参与、发起、家族领导力的过渡、方向感、自我认同，我和孩子在做公益的过程中全部体验了。

我想在这里说的东西是什么呢？是孩子们的自发意识，在这个过程中，它会自然而然产生。当它产生了以后，我们大人要怎么去扶持他们？我们是带着他们前进，还是慢慢让他们变成领袖，我们变成为他们打工的？我觉得这是自我的认知。我在这个过程中慢慢地退出了，我在我孩子的公益里面，慢慢变成了辅助她们的那个人，由她们做决策，我们在一起没有矛盾，青春期和更年期遇到一起也不打仗，因为坐在那里都是讨论怎么把这件事情做到最好。

我今天演讲的内容就是做公益的小孩最好带，但是为什么我改变了？因为这个场合不适合，大家都是专家，我补充这点，只是想说非常感谢这个会议，也感谢大家梳理了我的想法，谢谢大家！

邓岚：我想感谢主办方，对外友协和清华大学，最开始的发起方就是这两家，2018 年又有香港两所大学的加入，刚才曾先生讲到的倡议也是我们一直探索想要达到的境界，我们的初衷很简单，也很朴实，我们希望呼吁更多的人加入公益的大家庭，做一些我们想做、能做的事情，去改变一下世界，或者是改变一些人的命运。

感谢大家加入我们的大家庭，2018 年开始我们已经发起了一个网络，这个网络就叫人类命运共同体公益慈善协同合作网络，在论坛的开始大家也看到了视频，我们是想在这个网络之下可以有一些单独存在的、可以发展的群体，或者说是一个机构，它可以利用自己的力量、资源，能够倡导，能够行动，最终有所收获。

我觉得曾先生刚才提到的 3 点倡议非常符合论坛框架之下的理念，从我们的角度来看，我们非常支持这样的倡议，我们也非常感谢赠与亚洲和纽约梅隆银行可以举办这样的一次会议，因为对于我们来讲，能够请到一些有影响力的人物做对世界有影响力的事情，可能会产生更大的社会效应，这个倡议，如果真正能够作为我们的计划在明天的论坛上发布，将是我们此次论坛的一大亮点。

我们也希望在座的各位，或者是你们的朋友，能够看到这个倡议，看到我们的努力，加入我们的大家庭。我有一个想法，对外友协在每年的 6 月份，会邀请全球 500 强企业的 CEO 到中国来和我们的国家领导人进行交流和会谈，我觉得我们在座的家族，很多是在 500 强里面，我们是否也可以成立类似于家族善财传承委员会的机构，创造这样的机会，把我们的声音和我们想做的事情传递出去。

如果能够实现的话，我希望可以凝聚爱的力量、讲述爱的故事、播撒爱的种子、收获爱的硕果，谢谢大家!

曾宪章：谢谢邓秘书长，大家要说得言简意赅一点。

埃利奥特·唐纳利：我回应您说的两点，首先如何利用技术来为人类造福，我觉得这点非常重要。现在技术主要是服务于市场，服务于个人利益，服务于群众与政府，但在做慈善的过程中技术也非常重要。

另外我们要考虑不同的资本类型。在慈善领域，时间、精力和热情比金钱更重要，但人际关系也很重要。

王蕾蕾：之前我们也分享过，在美国，在前线工作的专业人员都知道，税务抵扣和税务优化虽然不是最重要的，但在股东家族传承事业中是非常重要的，现在中国正在进行深度的税务体制改革，我们也希望我们的专家和中国的税务工作者有更好的交流和沟通，把美国最前沿的税务思想和概念分享给中国的税务专家，使中国税务改革对家族的慈善有一定的推动，谢谢。

赵路云：谢谢，我一直关注赠与亚洲筹备的这个会议，大家都花了很多的心血，刚才的3点倡议在当下世界还比较动荡的背景下，在我们牵手开展“一带一路”项目之时，有特殊的意义。我作为《福布斯》和《理财周刊》的作者，可以通过媒体去助力我们项目的发生，我们有上海校友会，它们可能分布在10多个国家里面，我觉得我们也可以发动校友会的力量一起来支持赠与亚洲的倡议。我们有对外友协提到的善财传承，我自己也在创立一个研究中心，我们有家族联盟，有宗亲，有企业家，也有一代和二代名校的精英，如果结合曾宪章博士的倡议，我们可以把各个地区有影响力的富豪家族纳入“一带一路”项目的推动中来，谢谢。

曾宪章：有了大家的支持，我相信我们会很成功，最后，我想征询大家的意见，如果大家认为这个倡议是可行的，是大家支持的，请大家鼓掌！我们今天的会议圆满结束，明天我们会把这个稿修饰得更好一点，明天下午4点半左右，会正式发布！

九　高等教育社会捐赠的探索与实践：中国案例

主 持 人：香港浸会大学协理副校长　黄煜

清华大学法学院教授、清华大学教育基金会理事　王振民

嘉宾演讲：教育兴邦，百年树人

广东省国强公益基金会理事长　陈翀

捐赠高等教育心得分享

张荣发基金会总执行长　钟德美

中国高等教育慈善捐赠的若干思考

香港中文大学国学中心主任　邓立光

对话嘉宾：广州市东浦混凝土有限公司总经理　梁晖

深圳市政协常委、深圳市慈善会执行副会长兼秘书长　房涛

深圳市新同方投资管理有限公司董事长　刘迅

浙江大学教育基金会秘书长　沈黎勇

清华大学教育基金会秘书长　袁桅

南方科技大学教育基金会秘书长　涂蓉辉

北京大学教育基金会副秘书长　赵文莉

黄煜：各位嘉宾，各位朋友，大家早上好！我们这一场2019年世界公益慈善论坛高端圆桌分论坛现在开始！这个分论坛由两部分组成，第一部分是嘉宾演讲，第二部分是圆桌论坛讨论。期待通过这样一次圆桌论坛，大家互相交流，把我们的公益事业推向新的高度。

下面，我们有请第一位演讲嘉宾——广东省国强公益基金会理事长陈翀来给我们做演讲，他的题目是《教育兴邦，百年树人》。

教育兴邦，百年树人

广东省国强公益基金会理事长　陈　翀

非常感谢清华大学教育基金会给我们这样的机会，来分享国强公益基金会在公益方面做的一些工作。

我的题目是《教育兴邦，百年树人》。

我简单介绍一下国强公益基金会，国强公益基金会是碧桂园集团杨国强先生及联席主席杨惠妍女士创立的非公募基金会，长期以来致力于扶贫济困、兴学助教、科技创新。

基金会成立于2013年，但是杨主席做公益事业已经有20多年，在九

几年的时候就已经在做公益慈善。现在对外实际捐赠超过了 5 亿元，跟教育相关，已经覆盖了 39 所高校，我们自己也创办了基金会下属的 3 所慈善学校。

为什么杨主席要设立这样的基金会呢？他讲过，他读中学的时候，家庭贫困，国家减免了他的学费，他才能够完成学业，才能够成为对社会有用之人。

他说国家给他发了 2 块钱的补贴金，大部分人觉得 2 块钱很少，但是这对他来说很重要，他和他的同班同学分别拿着 2 块钱去了废品站，买了大量的书，两个人一起交换看，看完了之后送回废品站，又换了另外的书回来。

杨主席没有上很多年学，但是他读了很多的书，所以有了后面的事业和能力。2 块钱对于一个学生，对于一个人一生的改变影响还是很大的。

2015 年，杨主席获得了中国消除贫困奖。

PPT 上是教育在国际上各个慈善组织的捐赠中所占的比例，今天的分论坛主要是关于教育捐赠的分享。在美国，最大的是宗教的捐赠，第二个是教育，美国大学的高等教育经费来自基金会捐赠的占 30% 左右。哈佛大学 2018 年获得了 14 亿美金的捐赠，是全世界最高的高校，第二所高校是斯坦福大学。这些捐赠和教育基金会的增值接近 50 亿美金，支持了哈佛大学的整个运作。

从 100 年前到现在，各个基金会和有志于在教育方面做贡献的人，都不遗余力地为教育做贡献。这也是我们考虑在教育领域做相应工作的原因。

下面讲我们在中国的教育方面做了哪些事情。

我们的实际捐赠超过了 55 亿元，还有 20 多亿元是接下来几年的时间承诺捐赠的。教育最大的部分是扶贫问题，国家这几年对于扶贫投入了大量的精力，我们基金会也在扶贫上做了大量的工作。教育领域，也是我们最重要的一部分，我们在教育领域已经实际捐赠了 21 亿元左右，承诺的还有 20 多亿元，接下来的几年会继续捐赠。

其中在教育领域有三部分，一部分是资助学生，一部分是资助学者，一部分是支持学科发展。

我先讲资助学生的部分。

有一些嘉宾对我们比较熟悉，PPT 上是 2002 年杨主席在佛山创办的全中国唯一慈善的、免费的高中，现在已经有 3000 多名毕业生，100% 考上了大学，98% 考上了重点学校，都非常优秀。

接下来给大家放一个短片。

（播放视频）

2014 年，除了刚才的高中之外，我们又创办了一所免费的大学，这所大学现在是大专，主要培训的是职业高等教育人才。现在的毕业生已经有 1000 多人，毕业率达到 100%，入学即入职，毕业即就业。

PPT 上展示的是甘肃省在建的国强职业技术学校，甘肃省有一个特点，很多孩子读完初中就不读了，所以我们在甘肃成立了这所职业技术学校，招收初中的毕业生，学校将在 2020 年招生，每年可以招收 2000 多名学生。

PPT 上现在展示的是 1997 年设立的，现在已经 20 多年了，叫作仲明大学生助学金，运行了 10 年，都没有人知道这个助学金到底是由谁来发放，当时是由羊城晚报社来组织发放助学金，2007 年碧桂园上市之后，外界就开始知道这个助学金是由杨国强主席来资助的，已经覆盖了 1 万多名学生，每年有几百万元的捐助。

我们成立了惠（音）教育助学基金，设立了 1 亿元的助学基金，在顺德，帮助当地所有的贫困孩子。

下面讲在资助学者方面的工作。

PPT 上是我们的“国华杰出学者奖”基金，是在全国六所高校设立的助学金。我们也设立了一些教授基金，每年会从海外引进很多优秀人才，为中国的高等教育做贡献。

下面我再介绍一下学科发展。

我们设立了高校的产学研合作项目，支持了高校的学科发展。

我分享两个案例：一个是我们2018年与清华大学合作成立的国强研究院，共同致力于中国在高科技领域的发展和研究；一个是成立北京师范大学惠妍学院，为了学科有更好的发展。

我再讲讲我们在教育领域的愿景。

我们希望让社会尊重知识，让知识改变命运。我们希望能够为社会多做一些这方面的工作，能让更多人用知识改变命运。我们一方面培养学生，另一方面也设立奖金吸引更多的人才投入科研和教育中。

这是杨主席说的，感谢党和国家给他的资助，能够让他有机会帮助社会上更多有需要的人。我们也希望这项工作能够薪火相传。

最后，也谈谈我们的思考。

第一，如何构建高校捐赠和校企合作的可持续发展模式，使得多方共赢?

第二，如何传播捐赠人的慈善精神，使之薪火相传?像国家资助杨主席，杨主席再捐助更多有需要的人。

我今天的分享就到这里，谢谢大家!

黄煜：下一个是张荣发基金会总执行长钟德美女士为我们做演讲，她的题目是《捐赠高等教育心得分享》。

捐赠高等教育心得分享

张荣发基金会总执行长　钟德美

尊敬的各位领导，各位嘉宾，各位女士，各位先生，大家早上好!

今天我很荣幸能够代表台湾的张荣发基金会来参加本次论坛，除了有机会聆听各位学者、专家在公益上的真知灼见，我个人也很愿意以从业人员的角度来分享我们对高等教育捐赠的一点小心得和粗浅的看法。

张荣发基金会在大陆设立 3 项助学金，最早的是 11 年前，也就是 2008 年在清华大学设立了张荣发基金会助学金，还有北大张荣发基金会助学金，还有中国航海学会张荣发基金会助学金，2018 年底，我们总共帮助了 3000 名学子，投入的金额是 1650 万元人民币。

台湾张荣发基金会从 1985 年成立，到现在已有 34 年，我们帮助了台湾 150 所大学超过 2 万名学子，投入的金额超过 3 亿台币。

我们在美国也设立了 3 项助学金，分别在休斯敦大学、旧金山州立大学和南卡罗来纳大学。大家一定很好奇，为什么张荣发基金会要在全球统设将近 10 个助学金呢? 答案很简单，这来自本会创办人张荣发先生的初心，他生长在动乱的时代，他的家庭非常普通和平凡，他靠着半工半读完成学业，所以特别能够体会家庭贫困学子求学时的艰辛。1970 年，他刚创业没有多久，长荣海运还在亏损的状态，但他还是坚持助学。

我们都知道，世界第一所大学可以追溯到 1088 年，即意大利的博洛尼亚大学，千年以来，大学为人类文明、社会发展提供了巨大的动力，也肩负着许多的重要任务，包括知识的创新和人才的培育。

但是，对许多贫困家庭的孩子而言，大学最有可能像是高耸在他们面前的庙堂，可望而不可即。要不是有人能推他们一把，也许终其一生，他们连一小步都无法踏进去，即使他们知道，教育可能是改变他们命运的唯一机会。

张荣发创办人希望孩子们顺利求学，但是也担心有些孩子因此埋怨自己出身不好，他在台湾，在任何场合，无论是接受媒体的采访，还是基金会举办助学金的颁发典礼，他都说不要怨天、不要怨地、不要怨怼父母、不要怨恨自己的处境，这一切都要靠自己勇敢承担起来。

另外，他也鼓励同学要努力向上，改善因果。更不能忘记时刻对父母心存感恩，他相信，如果可以的话，每一个父母都希望好好照顾自己的孩子。可是，人生很多时候、很多事情，就是无可奈何。有些孩子好像听懂了他的话，听完他的演讲，他们会写信给基金会来表达他们的谢意。最让我们感动的是，张创办人在 2016 年离开了人世，当初他帮助过的很多孩子，主动来到追思会现场致敬，向他们最敬爱的张爷爷表达最深的谢意。

当然，我相信对所有教授来说，你们最能够体会“得”天下英才而教之，是人生一大乐事；对于基金会，我们也觉得能够“助”天下英才而教育之是一大乐事。我们相信每一个年轻的生命来到这个世界上，都是要受到祝福的。我们可以给年轻人一条往上攀爬的绳索，有了这一条绳索，他也许可以攀爬到集装箱船，航向人生的五湖四海；如果力量没有这么大，哪怕是一只小渔船，只要有一根小鱼竿，也可以靠捕鱼来维持生计。

大家一定想不到的是，这些孩子给我们的回馈远远比我们想象的来得快，甚至快到他们还未功成名就之时，就已经教会了我们很多的东西。因为有了这份奖学金，这些孩子更懂得惜福，他们愿意追随张荣发先生的脚步，帮助社会上需要帮助的人。最重要的是，不是等他们未来挣大钱的时候，而是此刻，就是现在，在他们正在接受别人帮助的阶段，只要有时间，他们愿意去做志愿者工作，这样的抱负和社会责任感，不是金钱能够买得到的，也不是用任何物质可以衡量的。

我们都知道，清华大学很多学生是来自各省的精英，他们都是经过苦读，从乡到县，再到一省，很多大学在倡议海外交流，如果我们能够让同学们在寒暑假到海外走走，让大家体验不同的文化背景，那也是一种学习。根据我的了解，清华大学教育基金会多年以来一直帮助同学们申请各种见习的机会，我们很高兴，就在今年暑假，我们接待了一支来自清华的学生团体。

我们帮这群孩子制订计划，让他们调研台湾的劳动教育、志愿服务和工读教育，以及在台湾大学开座谈会，我们更利用难得的机会举办了首届张荣发基金会“两岸助学生交流见面会”，让来自清华的 16 名师生和台湾 30 所大学的同学进行一次热烈的交流学习和分享，这次见面会对两岸学生来讲都是一场美丽的回忆。

另外，我们也安排了台湾农村小镇的民宿经营者来和大家讨论台湾农村如何振兴的议题，我们还特别带入了习近平总书记针对“三农”问题的谈话，那天的演讲者和同学都非常热情。

我还要分享的是，不管是在大陆，还是在台湾，张荣发基金会助学金最大的特色都是从来不设顶，不限专业。因此，我们每年都收到很多清华大学美术系的作品，无论是画画，还是其他的艺术创作，各位嘉宾有机会来台北，到我们基金会的文物厅，就可以看到这些同学的作品。

还有，2011 年，我们在清华大学特别设立了清寒学生家庭扶助金，如果家里面有紧急的状况，可以来申请。

2010 年，当时清华大学的校长带着两位副校长来拜会创办人，他们提到了清大有一些学生的家境非常困难，有些没有足够的生活费，为了节省饭票，有时候两餐当一餐吃。创办人听了很心酸，萌生了要设立家庭扶助金的念头，学校老师告诉我们说，张荣发基金会的家庭扶助金在大陆院校里面极少设立，他提到了一件事情让我们很感动，他说现在清大的毕业生，很多人感念他们求学阶段受到很多人的帮助，包括张创办人，所以，他们把就业后的第一份工作的第一份薪水捐给了学校，帮助贫困的学弟、学妹，我觉得这也是张荣发基金会在清大设立助学金最大的回响之一。

我还想补充一个小故事。

台湾基金会有访查员，有一天创办人对我说，清华大学设立了扶助金，又设立了助学金，是不是应该去同学家里面了解情况？我心里想，大陆这么大，当我们正在烦恼怎么解决这样的问题的时候，非常感谢清华大学教育基金会的老师，他们很用心地帮助我们就近安排了对在河北省的 4 位同学的家访，虽然只是在河北省，虽然只是 4 位同学，但是我们也用了四天三夜，跑了超过 1000 公里，这个距离等于是环台湾岛一周，但是我印象很深刻，我们到每一位同学家里，他们的父母都非常感谢我们的到访，有一位家长特别送了我一大包他们自己种植的棉花和土豆，还有一位同学的父亲，我们要走的时候，他爬到树上给我们摘石榴。

不管是助学金，还是家庭扶助金，我们的目的是让同学们知道，世界上还有一个角落会关心他们。

同时，我要做小小的广告。

张荣发基金会可能是全球极少数的企业型基金会，集三大文创品牌于一身，包括成立长荣交响乐团、设立长荣海事博物馆和发行免费的《道德月刊》。长荣海事博物馆提供给各级学校来参观，《道德月刊》则是负责道德教育的宣扬，谢谢北大和清大的同学常常投稿给我们。

除了刚才讲的慈善业务，我们也帮助了台湾很多的贫困家庭，我们希望能够激发孩子们的潜能。

我非常感恩上天给我这个机会，在基金会服务。

近 20 年来，我所经历过的每一个慈善公益活动，都让我深深地觉得，就像论坛说的，我们每一个人要多致力于社会服务的推广和实践。这份工作让我明白，我们何其幸运，我们只是付出免费智力，但是我们让一个人站起来往前走，特别是这股力量深深地联系着我们和扶助家庭以及孩子们，这种感觉真的不是笔墨所能形容的。

有朝一日，这些孩子终将离开校园去追寻他们的理想，但是是否成功，取决于这些孩子是否能够发挥所学，为国家、社会有所贡献，而我们只要扮演那段求学路上的陪伴角色，就心满意足了。

如果因为我们，年轻人不再感到孤单，当他们想要就学、想要拥有未来时，我们愿意为他们点燃希望。

我想，在座的嘉宾，一定和我一样，早就深刻感受到做善事所带来的快乐。美国知名的作家海伦·凯勒说过，幸福不是只让自己快乐，而是忠于一个有价值的目标。未来我们会继续忠于这一个有价值的目标，那就是继续传承张创办人的大爱精神!

谢谢大家的倾听!

黄煜: 下一位嘉宾是香港中文大学国学中心主任邓立光先生，他的演讲题目是《中国高等教育慈善捐赠的若干思考》。

中国高等教育慈善捐赠的若干思考

香港中文大学国学中心主任　邓立光

尊敬的各位领导，在座基金会的女士们、先生们，大家早上好!

今天我是代表香港的冯燊均老先生来讲话的，冯燊均老先生和他的夫人在 2008 年成立了冯燊均国学基金会，这位老人家很奇怪，他是企业家，但对国学情有独钟，而且他的家产都以捐赠给国学为目的。冯先生很低调，做了很多大好事大家都不知道，最近两年才被曝光。

2018 年，在人民大会堂，冯老先生捐赠了 1.5 亿元人民币，分为两个不同的部分，一个是捐给教育部基础教育课程教材发展中心，另一个是捐给北京大学、清华大学和北京师范大学。

为什么要这样做呢？我们的捐款跟很多基金不一样。款项捐出去，我们跟受资助的课程中心或者是其他的三所大学都会很仔细地讨论，项目具体的费用是什么，我们都有参与，如教育部的内部会议，以及三所大学的会议。

这不是不信任受资助的单位，而是一个项目的发展，我们应该协助推动。

我们所推动的国学是什么内容呢？接下来看一看。

我们现在经常说国学，“国学”是什么？

高等教育的慈善捐款该用在什么地方？用在国学的发展上，为什么？

我们讲国学，其实它有相对固定的内容。我们是以儒家为国学的代表，儒家做代表有很固定的内容。现在说文化自信，但是如果我们对自己的文化、对自己的学术不了解，那么自信无从谈起。我们推动国学特别重视在这个方面的发展。

我们的传统文化百余年来遭受了很严重的打击，整个社会、整个教育和政治都改变了，这样传统文化无法传承下去，出现了断层。这个断层如果不去填补，我们谈文化自信就只是一句口号，我们国家富强了，中国人民在政治上站起来了，然而我们的文化和我们的精神沉下去了。

我们的捐款不太多，只有 1.5 亿元，但是我们的捐款是捐给正规的学校。既然是这样的捐款，那该怎么做？

有以下两个途径。

一是自下而上的途径。

“下”是指从整个教育的层级，即幼儿园、小学、中学、大学，在基础教育里面恢复国学，由教育部的课程中心制定传统文化进入课程、进入教材、进入课堂的方案，这是最有效的做法。

二是自上而下的途径。

资助我们的大学，把款项拨过去，大学也非常尽责去满足我们的要求，我也是在大学教书，也是教中文，所以我们知道怎样和受资助的大学合作来推动这个项目。我们对一所大学有共同的支持内容，一个是奖学金，支持在国学研究方面有能力的学生，另一个是奖教金。

这样做不能保证一定能有100%的贡献，但是会有一定的贡献。由于中国传统文化方面的人才出现了断层，所以我们要尽快培养我们的国学人才。希望从基础教育方面入手，令我们的学生对国学有真心实意的爱护和支持，也希望企业发挥领头羊的作用，出资培养更多的专家和大师。

最后我想补充一点，捐赠的覆盖内容不是很多，但每一个内容我们都亲自参与，付出了很多时间。我们本来可以不参与的，即使不参与，受资助单位也会做好。我们为什么要这样做呢？就是对国家和民族的一份责任，既然要推动国学发展，我们也要参与进去，为国家出力。这就是我们不单是捐款，还要参与的原因。

最近几个月，对于湖南大学的岳麓书院，我们也支持了它，因为它培养国学人才，已经不是一般大学的做法，它培养100人，所以我们予以支持。我们的基金支持范围不宽，只是支持国学，目标是让我们的民族真真正正有文化自信。一个礼乐粲然大备的泱泱大国，必定会在我们这个时代出现，希望在座的其他基金会负责人可以参考一下我们的做法，对我们的传统国学多予支持。

20世纪80年代，我在大学读中文系，当时大家问为什么不读法律？大家都瞧不起中文，觉得读中文没有前途。此外，在大学里面，给文学院的捐款少之又少，我现在也呼吁在座基金会的负责人，如果可以的话，对传统文化的范畴可以特予支持，让我们国家能更快更多地培养文化人才。

我今天的演讲到此结束，谢谢大家！

黄煜：接下来是我们的圆桌讨论，有请清华大学法学院教授、清华大学教育基金会理事王振民来主持。讨论的嘉宾有：广州市东浦混凝土有限公司总经理梁晖；深圳市政协常委、深圳市慈善会执行副会长兼秘书长房涛；深圳市新同方投资管理有限公司董事长刘迅；浙江大学教育基金会秘书长沈黎勇；清华大学教育基金会秘书长袁桅；南方科技大学教育基金会秘书长涂蓉辉；北京大学教育基金会副秘书长赵文莉。

王振民：我们的圆桌论坛有政府慈善机构的代表，有企业家代表，也有大学基金会的代表，围绕企业、政府、社会和大学捐赠主题进行研讨。

我们每一个人对自己的孩子经常讲一句话“出门不要乱吃东西，吃坏肚子就不好了”，很少有家长说“出门不要乱学东西”，其实学错了东西、大脑坏掉了是更严重的问题，这就是教育的问题。

无论是政府、企业还是大学，我们共同的使命是教好我们的下一代。

今天我们非常荣幸邀请到 7 位杰出的代表和各位分享他们的经验。我们首先请深圳市政协常委、深圳市慈善会执行副会长房涛女士来分享。

房涛：非常感谢主办方这么好的论坛，让我有机会学习。据我理解，在中国的捐赠板块里面，我们年度捐赠基金有 300 亿元左右，每一年教育的捐赠占 30% 左右，持续这么多年在国内捐赠的第一个板块就是教育。为什么这么多人对教育进行捐赠？因为教育是最根本的公益。目前国家层面，教育的扶贫是排第一位的。

福布斯 2018 年的前 100 个慈善家，大概有 157 亿元的人民币捐赠，50% 都是教育板块的。同时，广东区域又占教育捐赠的 47%。

在中国，教育确实是捐赠的重要方向，也是企业家特别愿意去做的事情。

我观察到大学的教育里面有几方面的问题，我提出来和大家一起探讨。

第一，理科和文科的关系。

为什么这么多的捐赠愿意到理科的方向？在大学的教育中，硬件的教育更多是在学科上。理科方向的知识在产业转化上是更及时的，跟企业的优质学科和产业前端的核心竞争力的结合关系更密切。而从长期来看，大学于一个国家、一个民族、一个世界的意义在哪里？整个价值观和人文精神的意义在哪里？这可能会是短期和长期的关系。

第二，头部机构和长尾机构。

头部的捐赠人太多了，我们今天有幸来到这个会场，或者是大学的校友，或者是中国主要的经济发展捐赠人，在回报社会的过程中，头部效应促使人们一定会去找顶级的大学进行强强合作。但是大量的长尾效应如何服务？个案和系统之间的服务，怎么能够做到有一定的标准和达到一定的均衡？怎样在现有的状况下，将基金会有限的人力和时间集中到个案的优质定制服务上？这些可能是顾及不到的。

第三，公益和商业边界的问题。

我们现在大学的捐赠，哪一类纯粹？如何寻求与捐赠人诉求之间的平衡？这中间也有边界的问题。

这些问题都是大家在捐赠过程中需要思考的。我本人觉得，第一是大学基金会自己的定位到底是什么，你是依附于大学的行政管理，还是要真正回应捐赠人的需求和帮助捐赠人成长，还是要回应全国或者是世界价值观方向。不同的需求，导致了基金会不同的职能。

我相信中国捐赠的总额和比例一定是越来越大的，我也期待着有更多的社会力量对大学进行捐赠。

王振民：中国的大学这几年有一个特点，就是校友的捐赠比非校友的捐赠更加明显。我们今天请到两位清华的校友，也是非常成功的企业家，做了很多的贡献。第一位是梁晖先生，创办了广州市东浦混凝土有限公司，也是广东首屈一指的混凝土公司，近年来他和他的夫人一起做了很多的捐赠，有请梁晖先生和我们做分享。

梁晖：谢谢大家，我有一个问题想问一下，昨天我参加了世界公益慈善论坛的开幕式，今年已经是第四届，我记得第一届是在北京，第二届在上海，这一次在深圳。

我说这件事情，是说在慈善事业方面，我们国家起步还是太晚了，但是晚不要紧，因为现在国家已经发展强大了，也正是在这个时代我们开启了慈善事业的新征程，所以我觉得慈善事业大有可为。在这个大环境下，对高校的捐赠也是我们做的一件很重要的事情。我们应该把握好这个机会，把它当成我们的事业去做。

房女士讲到的捐赠比例，目前高校捐赠的比例占到 30%，和发达国家相比，这一捐赠比例如何?

房涛：中国的捐赠，每一年是 1300 亿元到 1400 亿元人民币，2018 年少一点，但是在美国是 4000 亿美金，美国的教育所占比例为 24%，但是它的绝对值比我们要大。我们也探索中国的 GDP 已经是全球第二，中国超高净值的富豪人数也已经是全球第一了，为什么我们的捐赠只占到美国捐赠的 1/24，同时占 GDP 的比重，我们大概是 0.18%，而在美国是 2.1%，绝对值之间有很大的差距。

梁晖：我也是来这里学习的，昨天参加这个会议之后，我回去思考这个问题，慈善和捐赠，首先是一种精神。

中华民族这么悠久的精神文明，慈善也是我们的一种美德。这个美德，要把它像事业一样做大做强，离不开社会的发展和国家的发展。

在物质文明发展不充分的情况下，能够大力开展慈善事业的可能性不大，但是物质文明发展到了一定的程度，像人一样，解决了基本的生存问题，精神上、价值观上得到升华之后，就会形成初步的美德。

像我自己一样，我从大学毕业之后，当时想到的是我这辈子能赚 100 万元已经非常了不起，根本没有其他的意识，但是经过自己的努力，不断把握机会，达到了目标之后，慢慢会思考更深层次的问题，这对大多数人来说是很正常的过程。

目前国家处在高质量发展期，我非常看好深圳，也看好中国未来的发展。这个时候，应该大力推进慈善事业，尤其是在高校捐赠方面。我在这里表达的意思是，未来中国 50 年的发展，我是非常看好的，所以对于慈善事业和高校的捐赠，希望在座的大家一块儿发力，争取把这个事业做到更上一层楼。

谢谢大家!

王振民：下面请刘迅先生，他是深圳市新同方投资管理有限公司的董事长兼首席投资官，有多年慈善捐赠的经验，有请刘迅先生分享。

刘迅：我是 1997 年和几位同学一起搞的投资公司，到现在做了 20 来年。一般认为，投资最关键的因素就是钱，但是按我的理解肯定是人，而不是钱。

我看到我们同期的企业积累很多，但是为什么没有做好呢? 碰到了很多的问题，这对我们的触动是非常大的。在思考这个问题的时候，我碰到了一位非常好的老师，他给了我们一些钱，让我们帮他做投资，但是在 2014 年的时候，他把 500 万元的资金拿来做助学，从那个时候起，我们明白了最重要的是钱背后的人，人怎么来用这些钱，所以人是非常关键的。

在跟随赵老师助学的过程中，我们做了差不多 15 年，现在每年有将近 2000 个受益人，捐助的初衷是雪中送炭，中国的高中生那个时候非常苦，甘肃当地高中生一天的伙食费 1 块钱，所以我们做的是高中助学。做了这么多年以后，有了一定的局限，随着国家的资助越来越多，钱是一方面，人的支持是另一方面。

我们每年去学校走访两次，和学生座谈，这是更重要的事情，他们的学习压力非常大，我们的沟通是有限的。后来我们发现，和大学合作做助学更有意义，我一进大学，有同学说终于可以松口气，大学的时间更加充裕，充裕的背后是一些价值观的形成和社会经验的积累。

大学资助有两个重要的好处。

一是大学是大师云集的地方，大学有师门，每一个大学都有几个老师的精神特别值得弘扬。

二是大学每年都有年轻人进来，这是一个持续不断的学习过程。

因为有这两个好处，所以我们可以不断地做。我们把资助分为“软”和“硬”两种，比如说场地就是硬的资助，软的资助是实践沟通。我们非常愿意支持形成力量的理念，让他们多去实践，我相信所有的支持和所有的理想，在实践中都能得到真正的检验，在实践中也会形成新的理念，帮助我们一起来建设更美好的国家。

谢谢大家！

王振民：下面的 4 位讲者来自中国知名的 4 所大学，第一位是沈黎勇先生，他现在担任浙江大学教育基金会秘书长，请他来分享。

沈黎勇：谢谢王老师，非常感谢清华大学教育基金会给我这次宝贵的机会，从昨天到今天，我收获了很多，学习了很多，今天也非常有幸和大家一起谈谈自己的思考。

我原来都是在学生一线工作，在浙江大学毕业以后，一直做学生的辅导员，后来做团委书记，这些年来，我最大的收获是每年带优秀的同学到山区去支教，我每一年都去，坚持了十几年。我曾经去离缅甸、越南、老挝只有几百公里的小县当县长，管教育，各位讲到了我的心坎上，尤其是中国的内地，有太多需要我们去帮助的孩子，也许我们伸出手就可以改变他们的未来。

我现在的工作主要是两块，一块是校友会的工作，一块是基金会的工作。我现在有一个观点，我和我们的校友、我们的企业家，以及很多未来潜在的捐赠者，不是简单地开口谈钱，而是价值的认同，这才能使我们的发展可持续。

在一个国家对大学的定位上，人才培养和科技创新肯定在第一位，我觉得还有文化的传承。比如说刚才讲的国学，我也非常赞成。中华文化五千年，源远流长，一定要传承下去。传承下去最核心的要素是人，人来自哪里？肯定是来自大学。大家关心教育，投资教育或者是专注于教育慈善，肯定是非常正确的选择。

我们这些年也在培养人才的过程中发现，大学捐赠有很多的途径和方式，有捐赠贫困生的，有捐赠交流生的，有建楼的，有捐赠学科发展的，我觉得归根到底是支持教育，支持人的发展，支持学科的进步。

我们民族的背后，就是文化。文化的传承，是我们所有人共同的目标和共同的理念。2019 年我已出差几十次，见过各类的校友和企业家，所有的校友和企业家，等到他们发展到一定程度以后，心灵都是善良的，我从顶层设计角度来看，目前中国慈善公益的法规制度制定得还不够健全和完善，我们在政策的落地上还有一些不是很顺畅的地方。

归根到底，还是文化，我们捐赠的文化还是比较多。我在校内，给书记、校长汇报的时候会指出，我们现在最大的短板不是论文和学术影响力以及科研经费，这些已经快速发展，目前最大的短板是教育经费的来源相对比较单一。

2018 年我们全校 125 亿元的支出，大部分来自国家的拨款等，我们的捐赠款非常少。但是哈佛大学一年的收益远远超出我们整年度所有的支出。浙江大学 2019 年很开心，我们 7 月份年度接受捐赠总额已经超过 30 亿元，但是我们和清华大学的差距还非常大，我们要发现自己的不足，去改变和完善自己。

王振民：第二位请南方科技大学教育基金会秘书长涂蓉辉女士分享，有请。

涂蓉辉：非常感谢主办方，本次慈善论坛在深圳召开，让我们有机会参与这个论坛，非常感谢。

刚才主持人也讲，我们南科大是非常新的大学，现在才 8 岁，和清华、北大、浙大比起来，经验非常少。但是我们南方科技大学得益于时代的发展，得益于深圳企业家创造的非常好的公益理念，虽然公益在中国刚刚起步，但是深圳还是一个发展得非常良好和快速的地区。

我们有一个捐赠人提到，深圳这座城市的发展是多么渴望一个一流的大学来做技术的支撑。有人说深圳是中国的硅谷，旧金山的斯坦福大学对那座城市的支持，是我们深圳发展的榜样和模式。市政府也高瞻远瞩，在 2011 年的时候，邀请世界先进的大学，包括港科大，筹建了南科大，深圳市的市长也担任我们的理事长，深圳市的领导班子都是我们的理事会成员，所以南科大的发展非常迅速。一个大学基金会的发展一定是依托大学的成长，大学的发展是基金会发展的基础。

我入行时间非常短，这里有清大、北大、浙大等公益组织，给了我们非常多的启发。南方科技大学也是一所公办的创新性大学，承担了教育改革的使命，我们的大额支出也是靠政府拨款，办大学需要太多资金了，但是，每笔钱要用到该用的地方。大学要创新发展，要多元发展，必须依靠基金会的力量。我们基金会主要是支持南科大的创新发展，让南科大在短时间内迅速提升，学校的发展有一些特别的需求是公办的经费难以支撑的，这也是我们工作的重点。

筹款是一部分，需要社会认知的提高，我们说捐赠是一种美德，但是需要社会的成长来给我们支撑。我觉得钱怎么用才是最重要的事情，昨天我和北大的赵老师商量，怎么用好这个钱，像国强公益基金会谈道，支持优秀的贫困学生，让他们同样有机会。因为他们走到今天特别不容易，我们要让人才均衡发展，这也是我们未来努力的方向。

南方科技大学在全国22个省（区、市）招生，有一些非常贫寒的孩子，他们到了南科大，要把自己的未来和世界一流的理工高科技的发展联系在一起，他们的压力不亚于北大、清华学生，我们招不到北大、清华这么优秀的学子，但是这些学生的努力程度和北大、清华学生差不多，这是让我们最感动的。我们的老师90%来自境外，他们对捐赠的理念非常认可，这是我们发展过程中特别有力的支持。

我们还很弱小，才起步，要向各位学习。我们中有一位捐赠人说，他当时来深圳的时候，身上只有几百块钱。但是他现在是我们培养优秀企业家的捐赠人，是我们体育场的捐赠人，他说感恩深圳最好的方式就是捐赠南科大。

谢谢大家!

王振民：下面有请清华大学教育基金会秘书长袁桅女士来分享。

袁桅：谢谢王老师，其实这是我第二次参加这个论坛。我可以说是慈善公益领域的新兵，刚到清华大学教育基金会一年，之前一直是市场化领域的人士。

我到教育基金会来的这一年，学习感受很多，我深刻地感受到了公益慈善对于整个国家教育事业的发展，包括国家的科技竞争力、优秀人才的培养以及价值观树立方面的重要作用和意义。

今天咱们的论坛是对高等教育社会捐赠的探索与实践，过去的一年多，我自己也有很多的心得和体会，父母也是大学的老师。当我到清华大学基金会的时候，我的第一个问题，可能和所有人的问题是一样的，清华大学这么有钱还会缺钱吗?

可能清华大学和很多的高校比起来，有很多的经费，如财政拨款或者其他款项等，中国有这么多所高校，清华大学是得到经费最多的，我们还缺钱吗?

我上任的时候是刚刚放暑假，那时候还没有暑假的概念，两个暑假一直在做调研，我深深地感觉到，像清华大学这样的学校，什么都不缺，就缺钱。浙大去年有100多亿元的开支，清华更多一些。我们的财政拨款只有30%，其他的经费都是靠筹款，筹款有横向的企业的和纵向的国家的，但是发达国家的高等教育，捐赠在中间越来越占到特别重要的比例。

捐赠是无偿的，一所大学要在国际上，包括在国家中发挥很重要的作用，很多东西往往是领先一步的，往往是站在学科发展、人才发展以及人类文明未来发展方向上多布局一些，这些往往是通过财政拨款和横向的合作达不到的。

从我们来以后，清华大学教育基金会的发展也得到了学校领导的高度重视，我们也专门做了改革的方案，制定了我们未来发展的“三步走”规划。

从清华大学教育基金会发展来讲，刚才发言的各位嘉宾都提到，怎么去筹款，筹款怎么支持学校，怎样促进捐赠人和大学之间的互动，除了维护捐赠资源和做好对捐赠人的服务以外，其实捐赠人和大学是相互成就、互相促进、共同发展的过程。

我也经常问，在捐赠的过程中，是捐赠人更幸福还是受捐赠的人更幸福? 我的小儿子还很小，我和他探讨，他说捐赠人更幸福。我问为什么呢?他说:“赠人玫瑰，手有余香。”

我的大儿子就说捐赠人和受捐赠人同样幸福，因为捐赠人可以通过捐赠实现自身难以实现的梦想，受捐赠的人可以心无旁骛地在他所专长的领域里面探索。

在清华大学教育基金会发展过程中，我们是慢慢地产生一些理念，要时刻把握住捐赠的公益无偿性质，尽量把资金用到一些更前端、更有创新性的领域，按照大学自身发展所需要的用途去引导。当然不同的捐赠人有不同的要求，有的捐赠人希望项目能够间接或直接地和他企业的发展有所联系。

清华大学教育基金会今年是成立 25 周年，在 25 年探索经验的历史上，我们总结出了捐赠的策略，我们其实是在五大方面开展捐赠工作的，我可以简单和大家分享一下。

第一，大师。

大师是针对所有老师的，不仅仅是针对顶级的老师，我们要从世界上引进顶级的老师来，在清华的顶级老师，财政所能给他们的收入和企业界是没有办法相比的，我们在人工智能方面的顶级教授很容易被别人挖走，我们做讲席和冠名教授来支持这些老师，包括一些院士，我们也支持一些很年轻的老师。

第二，英才。

这是针对学生的，我们又分了很多种类，比如说顶级的学生奖学金，还有英华学者项目。这个项目是所有大二选出来的顶级的学生到英国牛津大学留学一年，一年的所有费用一个学生要花 40 万元到 50 万元，通过这个奖学金来支持英华学子。学生在本科教育阶段，40% 的人能够出国交流。针对落后地区贫困学生的奖学金、助学金，清华大学已经实现全覆盖了。我们希望这些学生到了学校以后，能跟家庭条件好的学生一样，拥有出国实践和其他更多的机会，所以我们的奖学金层次非常丰富。我们希望把本科生出国实践比例提高到 60%~70%，我们的硕士和博士出国的比例已经到了 70%，希望能够实现全覆盖。

第三，求索。

过去的研发主要针对新材料、环境、人工智能等，现在我们希望把我们的研发合作，尤其是捐赠，往基础文科、基础理科以及智库型的研究，还有前沿领域的研究扩展，比如说研究人脑，研究天文，包括探索人类外太空的文明。当然也有很现实的，如燃料电池、芯片等。

第四，思源。

传统的捐赠项目是楼宇的冠名、操作的冠名，我们有成套的产品，并且逐渐规范冠名的规则，比如说一栋大楼，现在规定了一些条款，比如说达到什么样的比例，冠名以后会有什么样的展示等。

第五，公益慈善。

这方面更多是面向社会的活动。

在做这五大产品过程中，我们还会做超级筹款项目，我们把筹款项目系统性地做成产品，把产品推荐给市场上的捐赠人，让他们有选择性，根据他们的诉求来量身定做一些东西，这些其实是国际上通行的做法，我们现在推出了 2021 年“更好的清华”筹款行动。

我们感觉到，很多的捐赠人也慢慢地来和我们互动。在捐赠的过程中，我们也要做好整套的捐赠服务体系。

从教育基金会角度来讲，我们的整个工作分为筹款、用款和投资。我们现在的捐赠中，有将近一半甚至更多的是流动资金。从流动资金的增加角度来讲，中国的教育基金会产业应该正在逐渐形成，过去没有这样的产业。

我们也在探讨整个资产管理的策略模式和方法，我们的教育基金会，它不是学校的部门，它是一个生态，是一个产业，相信今后教育基金会的发展能够在中国的高等教育中发挥重要的作用，除了支持高校的发展以外，也在全社会形成一种捐赠的文化和捐赠的精神。

我们也很愿意跟同行的基金会，跟捐赠人，包括跟企业密切合作交流，大家共同探讨，谢谢。

王振民：非常感谢袁桅女士的分享。今天讲到大学筹款，赵文莉女士

1998 年就已经在北京大学教育基金会从事北大的筹款工作，她是最有发言权的，期待您的分享。

赵文莉：各位嘉宾，各位来宾，大家好！

非常高兴有机会参加这样的盛会，和各界朋友一起来探讨中国大学基金会的发展之道。刚才王老师也介绍，我在基金会从业的时间可能比几位秘书长的时间都要长。北京大学教育基金会成立于 1995 年，我非常荣幸在 1998 年 10 月北京大学 100 周年校庆之后加入了基金会。可以说，20 多年来亲身见证和参与了北京大学教育基金会的成长和变化。

借此机会，我想和大家分享两点：第一，以北京大学教育基金会为例，简单谈中国 20 多年来高校的基金会最大的变化；第二，大学的筹款工作，大家都感到很难开口，中国高校的基金会，应该怎样做好资源的拓展和筹资工作。

第一，谈谈中国高校基金会的变化。

以我个人的亲身经历而言，最大的变化是在这 20 多年来，伴随着中国经济的快速增长和中国慈善事业的迅速发展，中国高校基金会也迎来了蓬勃发展的时期，我们高校基金会的治理能力、筹资水平都有了明显的提升。

首先，说到中国高校基金会的时候，我们通常是这样说的，1994 年底，清华大学注册成立了基金会，我们把它算作中国高校第一家基金会，1995 年初，北京大学成立了北京大学教育基金会，这两家基金会的成立标志着在改革开放以后，中国高校基金会开始建立。

那么，截止到今年，绝大部分 985、211 高校和双一流建设高校有了自己的大学基金会。在 985 高校中只有一所没有成立基金会，就是长沙的国防科技大学。而双一流建设高校当中，今年的数字我没有太关注，起码在国家公布的双一流建设高校名单中，云南大学是唯一没有成立基金会的大学。我们很荣幸，今年北京大学有一位教授到那边去担任副校长，我和他说他最大的贡献应该是把云南的教育基金会成立起来。

伴随着基金会数量的增长，高校的治理能力和筹资水平也有了很大的变化。这个变化主要体现在以下几个方面。

1. 从高校的资源拓展来说，我们已经从最初的以捐赠人为导向的被动接受逐渐转变为以学校发展需求为导向的主动募集。

对于这点，我的印象非常深刻，1998 年的时候，北京大学教育基金会迎来了发展的高峰期，我们以前从来没有接受过这么多的捐赠，北京大学一些标志性的建筑都是在那个时期建立的，那个时期，我们主动募集的意识还是比较差的，我们没有这个意识，也不知道怎么样去做。我是 1998 年 10 月到基金会的，当时学校请了国内外的筹款专家对我们进行培训，我们问的最多的问题是基金会的日常工作是什么。经过 1998 年百年校庆非常繁荣的阶段之后，基金会的工作慢慢沉寂下来，我们不知道怎么做。

但是现在的情况，我觉得是截然不同了。我在基金会先做了大的筹款项目，2014 年开始负责项目管理，以前我们整个项目管理终年无休，现在大家都有很多的事情做。这个转变，给我的印象非常深刻。

2. 从具体的筹资策略和方法上来说，我们也是从单一的、零散的筹款活动开始向大规模的、有组织的筹款运动转变。北京大学去年迎来了 120 周年校庆，大规模的筹款运动转变是一个趋势。

3. 目前来说，大学受赠的形式也更加丰富。

最初的时候非常单一，但是今天不仅有现金捐赠，也有地产捐赠、股票捐赠、遗产捐赠等，捐赠的形式更加丰富。

这三个变化带来了什么样的结果？我想用一句话来说：大学基金会开始为学校的发展提供越来越全方位的支持。虽然这种支持非常有限，我们每年的经费预算都是在几百亿元，基金会真的是微不足道，但是其呈现上升的趋势，这个趋势大家要看到。

另外，具体到某一个项目、某一个领域，我们可以说基金会占据了“半壁河山”，起到了举足轻重的作用。

第二个问题，刚才王老师也说，特别是教授都感受到筹款很难开口。其实不是这样的，大学的筹款，首先要搞清楚捐赠人的理念是什么，我最深刻的感受是，捐赠人对高等教育的捐赠与对初等教育和中等教育的理念和动机是完全不同的。

比如说希望工程帮助贫穷的孩子读书，这是雪中送炭。但是对于高等教育的捐赠不是雪中送炭，不是越穷越能得到捐赠人的支持。国内外大学的校长都有非常深刻的论述，我就举两个例子。

我们大家都知道麻省理工学院，是美国非常好的大学，是筹资能力非常强的大学，在一个筹款晚会上，其院长说：这个学院绝对不会倒退，现在已经是国宝，将来会成为更珍贵的国宝，希望大家都把钱捐给我们，因为你们的捐赠将使整个美国的工业建立在更加牢固的科学研究的基础上。

香港也有一位大学校长，他说得更明确，他说大学筹款不是去讨钱，不是告诉别人自己如何穷来博得同情，要把自己最好的东西拿出来，告诉这个社会，明天社会所需要的就是今天我们所做的。

我想，从这点来说，对高等教育的捐助是为虎添翼，它紧紧围绕高等教育的使命——人才培养、科学研究、文化的传承和创新，只有在这方面做得更好，才能够得到捐助人的更多青睐。

大学和企业家的关系，绝不仅仅是受助方和施助方的关系，而是大家有共同的目的，共同完成一件事情。我们感恩捐赠人的捐赠，我们拿了钱之后，要更好地实现他们的愿望，来体现捐赠的价值。

我就简单分享到这里。

王振民：谢谢赵老师的分享。

刚才几位分享了他们的理念和做法，对我们也非常有启发。我从1994

年开始从事捐赠，其间也听到了很多的故事和见证了很多的事情。

在 2001 年，我到美国得克萨斯州的一所大学，该大学的法学院正举办一个捐赠的谢幕式，捐赠人在讲话的一开始就说："感谢母校，多次提醒我捐款。"大家工作以后都很忙，不是没有钱，而是学校没有找他。

当年新加坡大学李光耀管理学院院长找到李光耀，说学院是用了他的名字，让他帮忙筹款。李光耀问院长想找谁，院长说想找李嘉诚。李光耀说写一封信，不说要多少钱，只是把院长介绍给他，要多少钱当面和他说。后来院长拿着李光耀的信找李嘉诚，李嘉诚看到信是李光耀写的，就问要多少钱，院长说要太多了不行，不能狮子大开口，又不能要太少，想来想去说 5 个亿，李嘉诚当场就签了。

今天的讨论，我觉得非常有意义，我概括了一下有三点共识。

第一，中国经济社会发展经过 40 多年的积累，社会上确实有大量的财富。社会的捐赠和现在中国经济在世界上的地位是不相称的。美国是 4000 亿美元，我们不要 4000 亿美元，我们要 4000 亿元人民币，或者是 3000 亿元人民币都可以，中国潜力巨大，刚才企业家们也分享了他们的意愿。

第二，大学的市场巨大、潜力巨大，需求也巨大。我们在大学工作，确实感觉到国家的拨款只是维持基本的运转，大学想发展，想突出一点，想在某一个领域做突出的贡献，没有社会的捐赠根本做不到，社会对你的期望很高，但是你没有钱。随着中国教育的均衡化发展，一些顶尖大学的拨款，不会和其他的大学差得太多，现在越来越强调大学均衡。

第三，缺乏桥梁和纽带。企业捐赠者和大学之间，沟通的机会是非常少的。我在香港工作几年，香港有很多桥梁和纽带。

我觉得今天的讨论是非常有意义的，建立了企业捐赠者和大学之间的沟通平台，今天我们的讨论到此为止，我们期待将来有更多的机会与各位交流，谢谢大家!

我们今天的分论坛到此结束，谢谢大家！

十　湾区未来，儿童福利

主 持 人：论坛学术委员会委员、清华大学公共管理学院教授　刘庆龙

联合国儿童基金会驻华办事处副代表　郑道

嘉宾演讲：儿童大病救助的探索之路

中华少年儿童慈善救助基金会理事长　王林

全民教育的中国之路与国际努力

——从一个教育家的宏愿说起

中国陶行知研究会常务副会长兼秘书长　吕德雄

对话嘉宾：北京一路阳光慈善基金会创始人、理事　郭朋

凤凰网副总编辑　侯春艳

香港中文大学副校长　霍泰辉

深圳市妇女儿童发展基金会秘书长　黄文锋

救助儿童会北京代表处首席运营官　塞巴斯蒂安·库斯特

鼎昆教育集团董事长　魏巍

联合国教科文组织教育顾问　李红艳

菲律宾国际乡村建设学院主席　彼得·威廉

著名钢琴家、融合教育倡议者　萧凯恩

刘庆龙：各位早上好，在此次分论坛当中，我们主要讨论“湾区未来，儿童福利”。儿童发展、儿童健康、儿童福利都是社会非常关注的事项，很多机构在这方面做了很多的工作，而且有非常好的经验。借这次机会让大家

进行经验的交流和经验的分享，相信对于促进儿童健康事业的发展是非常好的。

请允许我介绍一下两位演讲嘉宾：中华少年儿童慈善救助基金会理事长王林；中国陶行知研究会常务副会长兼秘书长吕德雄。

首先有请王林理事长给我们做主题演讲。

儿童大病救助的探索之路

中华少年儿童慈善救助基金会理事长 王 林

尊敬的各位来宾，首先感谢大家在繁忙的会议当中来听我的汇报。我今天要讲的题目是《儿童大病救助的探索之路》。

今天我从四个方面进行分享：一、我们是谁；二、我们的探索；三、我们的发现；四、我们的展望。

第一部分：我们是谁?

我们是一家年轻的、全国性的公募基金会。我们基金会于 2010 年 1 月 12 日成立，成立至今 9 年多时间。

我们是一家全国性的公募基金会，救助的对象主要是 18 岁以下的困难儿童，现在稍微有些突破，在校大学生也在我们的救助范围之内。有五大救助形式：生存救助、医疗救助、心理救助、技能救助和成长救助。

我们是一家拥有独特办会理念的基金会，提出 12 字方针——“民间性、资助型、合作办、全透明”，9 年时间我们筹款 23 亿元，救助范围达到 32 个省（区、市），救助儿童达到 500 多万人。

为什么我们要提出民间性呢? 因为我们是全国性的公募基金会，民政部是我们的上级主管单位，但是我们提出要“去机关化”，探寻一条民间的道路，资助更多的 NGO 跟我们一起在公益的道路上并肩前行。我们共资助了 300 家左右的民间 NGO，我们和所有的合作者之间没有上下级的关系，我们在公益的道路上是合作伙伴。

全透明是指基金会财务公开透明，自基金会成立第一天开始，每一笔善款都在官网上公示，钱的流向每月会公布一次，我们坚持“全透明”的方针。

2010 年成立之初筹款 5000 万元，到 2016 年筹款突破 3 亿元，特别是 2017 年和 2018 年筹款超过了 5 个亿。2019 年可能会超过前两年，应该会达到 6 个亿。

我们是一家以公众捐款为主导的基金会，由于成立时间短，在我印象当中，只有一两家国有企业给我们捐款，而且捐款数额不多。我们更多的捐款来自公众，特别是 2015 年捐赠占比达到 79%，2017 年是 69%，2018 年是 65%，2019 年目前募集到了 3.3 亿元捐款，个人捐赠占比达到了 81%。2017 年个人捐赠达到了 4 个亿，互联网的捐赠还没有体现，高的时候是 3.6 亿元，达到 65%，现在基本上是 65% 左右。

第二部分：我们的探索。

基金会在成立之初，就在儿童五大方面即生存、医疗、心理、技能和成长救助方面全方位地展开，医疗救助在我们基金会中占有很大的比重。今天我想以其中一个名为“9958”的自主项目为例，来详细介绍基金会在医疗救助领域的探索之路，这个自主项目在基金会成立时就创建了，号称“中国儿童大病领域的 110”，主要是对儿童大病的紧急救助。

2010 年拨款 100 万元成立了“儿童的紧急救助通道”，2011 年设置了一个免费的全国救助电话 4000069958，“9958”就是谐音“救救我吧”。这个救助热线全年每天 24 小时不停，随时可以拨打救助电话求助。

2012 年“9958”先后在西安、上海、沈阳、成都和重庆等地开设救助站，并与10个地方执行团队建立合作关系。2013年“9958”设立国内最大的儿童紧急救助平台，在全国6个省级市设立中心，救助范围涵盖32个省（区、市）。

2014年紧急救助通道正式更名为“9958救助中心”，全年累计接听电话15213个，共计救助1100多名大病患儿。

2015年累计募集善款突破1亿元，全年接听求助热线34520个，并荣获第九届“中华慈善奖”。

2016年合作资源继续增加，渠道继续扩展：合作医疗专家顾问98名，合作医院125家，设立专项救助基金34个，在全国设立了25个救助站。

2017年年度筹款、接听热线数量大大提升：累计募集资金达到1.88亿元，相较于2016年提升116.8%，累计接听热线近4万个。

2018年整个“9958”的累计筹款突破5个亿，捐款人次达到3000万，救助数量超过了21000人次。

2019年将会达到6个亿的累计筹款。这是“9958”这几年成长的过程，“9958”特别得到了大病儿童家长的赞誉。

我接待过一对湖北农村的夫妻，他们的孩子出生的时候只有一斤多，看着孩子不行了，两个人到后山挖了一个坑，准备把这个小孩埋了，但是就要埋的时候孩子哭了一声，这对夫妻又把他抱回来了，因为家庭很困难，不知道怎么办，于是就拨打了“9958”的救助热线，“9958”立即启动应急机制，为他筹款，对接医院为他提供救助，这个小孩成长到现在已经三四岁了，非常好。

这仅是救助案例的其中之一，只是这个案例我接触过，特别有感触。“9958”之所以能够发展得快，能够受社会的好评，同时筹款一年能够突破2个亿，就在于它在关注民生。

关于救助的金额，截止到2019年6月，共有76个专项基金，有73个合作项目和 7 个自主项目，一共有 200 多个项目。医疗救助类型的项目在基金会中占比仅为 21%，但是筹款总量占到了基金会筹款总额的 50%。如果按照前两年 5 个多亿的标准，它也占到了一半，但是项目只占到了 20%。

救助涉及的病种比较多，截止到目前儿慈会医疗救助类项目接近 30 个，救助的病种涵盖了儿童领域里绝大部分的大病。“9958”主要救助的病种包括血液病、恶性肿瘤、重度脑瘫、儿童消化道畸形、复杂性先天性心脏病、脑神经畸形等。

“爱心家园”针对白血病、肿瘤，“微笑行动”针对唇腭裂及面部畸形，“99 心”针对先天性心脏病，“长江公益”针对脑瘫，“佑爱珑琪”针对先天性肛道闭塞、急性肝功能衰竭，主要做的是肝移植。

关于救助的地域，救助项目覆盖 32 个省、自治区、直辖市，项目实施地主要集中在“三区三洲”等国家重点扶贫地区，如云南、西藏、新疆、青海、四川、贵州、河南、吉林和广西。

救助的链条全覆盖，目前儿慈会救助类的项目已经覆盖了儿童大病救助的全链条。首先是前期干预，如“9958”的“生命绿荫”、“大病医保专项基金”、“人民友爱专项基金”和“28 天新生儿援助项目”。但是我们更多的是中期救助，比如说“9958”“99 心”，以及脊柱侧弯。还有后期康复项目“天使之家”“小水滴”，中国历来都重治疗不重康复，基金会在康复救助领域也是非常弱的。

第三部分：我们的发现。

在整个医疗救助当中我们发现儿童大病救助领域存在很多问题，有一些我们看到了，有一些没有看到但是已经感受到了。

1. 救助的病种、救助资源的分布与救助需求存在结构性失衡。实际上在老少边穷地区需求是存在的，但是救助的资源很少。举个例子，比如说四川凉山，那里没有一个儿科大夫，他们也有意识培养一个儿科大夫，但是送出去就没有回来。在500多万人口的地区没有一个儿科医生，这是很现实的情况。

2. 救助标准难以统一，救助信息无法实现共享。

3. 救助内容比较单一，都是以医疗费用的救助为主，基本上大病患儿经过专家评估之后，我们作为一个公益组织，更多提供的是救助的资金。因为救助的资源不是掌握在我们手上，所以，救助内容比较单一。对疾病心理干预服务以及对疾病研究的支持极度缺乏，一般爱心企业和捐赠人对孩子的病情比较关心，但是对疾病心理干预服务以及疾病研究等领域就不太了解了。

4. 救助时间一般是以事中救助为主，事前救助占比小。

5. 救助模式比较简单，但是项目工作人员压力很大，工作人员待遇低，工作时间比较长，一个孩子的救助可能要从始至终一直跟踪，同时他们既要救助又要筹款，压力非常大。

6. 救助要求项目的专业性强，所需资金多，但是效果存在很大的不确定性。

这些是我们目前所面临的一些问题。

第四部分：我们的展望。

作为一个社会组织，我们提出政府、商业机构与公益组织、爱心企业携手共同应对儿童大病救助，我们也希望用我们的工作来影响政府政策，希望政府能够有更多的投入。但是在目前的情况下，对于儿童大病的救助，我们希望获得政府政策支持，商业机构引入保险机制，公益组织和爱心企业开展后期的救助。

接下来我再介绍一个关于儿童大病保险的项目：中华儿慈会大病医保专项基金。这个项目已经做了很多年，愿景是每一个孩子能有尊严、有质量地实现病有所医。大病医保项目于2012年2月由中国知名媒体、公益人士联合中华儿慈会发起，旨在承接国家医保体系，通过大数据精算、精准测算保费，用科学的大病医疗补充保障方案，为更多乡村儿童争取医疗资金与公平的医疗机会。使命是探索少年儿童享有高质量医疗保障的可能性。目标是为试点县所有参保 / 参合的 0~16 周岁儿童免费提供一份全国范围内跨区域、不限病种、每人每年最高额度达 30 万元的大病医疗保障。这是我们从设计保障方案、购买商业保险、项目执行、效果评估、筹集善款到试点地区调研的项目循环。通过目前项目涉及的 11 个县 186 万名儿童来看，效果已经显现。大病医保介入之前，国家的医保政策报销和家庭自付的比例是 40 ∶60，现在进入医保之后个人自付 31.22%，每个家庭最多自付 1 万元。

目前大病医保累计的筹款已经有 8400 多万元人民币，试点用在 11 个县，其中湖南的古丈和河北怀来已经结项，理赔投保金额累计 7100 万元，累计投保人次超过 186 万，累计赔付金额达到 4500 多万元，累计赔付人数达到 1 万多人次。

试点 11 个县中以下 6 个县的模式有一定的区别：①鹤峰模式是由三方协作，由社会组织和保险机构以及政府三方出资给儿童上保险，而且以医保目录为主，医保目录之外给予辅助；②巴东模式是政府采购，由大病医保跟政府两方来负责；③开化模式是实时结算，跟医疗保障系统共同承担。④新晃模式是线上理赔，跟支付宝合作；⑤中阳模式是大病互助；⑥科尔沁右翼前旗模式是针对重大疾病的津贴（10 万元）。

最后，我们基金会创始人也是前任理事长说过一句话：世界上人们的信仰、使命和追求不尽一致，但慈善救助是人类共同的愿望。

希望我们的努力能让大病儿童有病可医，给因病致贫、因病返贫的家庭带去希望，谢谢大家。

刘庆龙： 王林理事长给我们做了一个精彩的报告，就我们的主题从宏观到中观再到微观以及具体案例进行了分析，引起了各位的关注，我们有请各位专家到台上，我们就共同关注的儿童福利问题一起讨论。

确实机会难得，刚才王林理事长给我们展现了中华儿慈会的经典案例，实际上是把近些年他们工作的进程给我们进行了充分的展示。

这里面实际上有一个重大的关联，就是政府、NGO 和病儿之间的关联，我们都知道在国家的迅速发展，特别是经济的腾飞过程中，也伴随着一些社会问题，其中病儿的问题确实需要我们从各个方面给予充分关注，学术团体、社会机构都做了很多的研究，我们也希望在这样的一个平台上，借这样一个机会大家有非常好的分享。

现在先有请香港中文大学副校长给大家做一个分享。

霍泰辉： 谢谢主持人，谢谢王先生做的非常精彩的报告。我讲广东话可以讲得很好，可是用普通话做报告还是不行，所以请允许我用英文。

非常感谢有这样的机会，也非常感谢王理事长关于中华少年儿童慈善救助基金会事宜的演讲。刚刚王先生讲到他们的基金会直接为儿童提供救助，我自己也是一名儿科的医师，在我的职业生涯中也致力于照顾生病的儿童。

但是在接下来的几分钟我会从直接的儿童救助者角色中脱离出来，从另外的角度谈一下对于儿童的救助。因为我想探讨的是儿童健康问题的根源在于贫穷。

大家都知道联合国在 2015 年 10 月的一次峰会上，确立了 17 条可持续发展目标（SDGs），目的是照顾好儿童、对抗贫困以及保障健康教育。其中第 3 条跟儿童是直接相关的，是确保所有人群的健康和福祉，而其中一个主要对象就是儿童。

我们再看一下可持续发展目标的第 3 条，在 2030 年要显著降低母婴的死亡率，以及降低 5 岁儿童和新生儿的死亡率。这是非常重要的目标。

如果我们思考一下 2019 年的可持续发展报告，就会发现联合国的这项目标显然已经有了很大的改善。在过去几年，儿童死亡率显著下降，但并非全球都有此进展。

看一下一些贫困的发展中国家以及地区，比如说撒哈拉地区，母婴死亡率大概是其他发达国家和地区的 20 倍，新生儿的死亡率也维持在 75‰，有时会达到 100‰，这意味着出生的 10 名婴儿里，有一个会夭折。在香港，新生儿的死亡率只有撒哈拉以南地区的 1%。

今天我们探讨的主题是大湾区的儿童健康和救助，我刚刚提的贫困国家和地区跟大湾区有什么关系呢? 我们必须理解，哪怕是富足的社会，仍然存在贫富差距，社会的财产分配是不均匀的，贫困现象依然是存在的。

我想以美国为例，美国是全球最富裕的国家。2016 年，有一个报告分析了美国的贫困和儿童健康问题，指出在美国有 21% 的 18 岁以下儿童处于非常不良的健康状态当中，如果包含非常接近于贫困的家庭或者是低收入的家庭，这个比重就会提高到 42%~49%，也就是说哪怕是在富裕的美国也有很多儿童生长于贫困家庭当中。

该报告还指出，这会对社会产生消极影响。比如有一些国家的新生儿出生率较低，而死亡率较高，儿童的发展受阻，没有办法建立自己的社交关系等，以及一系列的衍生问题。

而其中最令人警惕的信息是，儿童的健康问题与贯穿其一生的贫困问题息息相关。鉴于贫困对于儿童健康所造成的影响，我认为直接进行儿童救助是很重要的，这也是最基础的一项事业，无论是对于公益慈善基金组织还是政府来说都是非常重要的举措。

大湾区面临的可能不是贫困问题，而是贫富差距问题，我认为这是非常重要的一点。我就发言到这里。

刘庆龙： 谢谢霍校长，他给了我们一个非常开阔的视野，从全球的角度谈儿童的健康问题，先是贫困地区和发达国家，然后回归大湾区。特别是在大湾区的儿童福利当中，霍校长提出非常值得重视的问题就是贫富差距，如何面对贫富差距的现实制定更好的政策，有更好的 NGO 协调发展，使湾区儿童的救助能够做得更好，也给我们提供了很好的思路。谢谢霍校长。

下面有请北京一路阳光慈善基金会郭朋先生给我们分享。

郭朋：刚才王林理事长在他的演讲分享中讲道，在儿童大病救助领域以事中救助为主，事前及事后康复的干预救助占比相对较小。在一路阳光慈善基金会设立之前，我们在 2015 年 8 月跟中华少年儿童慈善救助基金会合作设立了一个专项基金，叫祝福宝贝成长基金，这个基金其实就是在尝试把更多的精力放在事前救助上。

一般是联合“北上广深”等大城市当中比较有权威的三甲医院，依靠它们有资质的医生来组建专家团队深入一些偏远、贫困、欠发达地区，尤其是医疗资源比较缺乏的地区，以这种方式给孩子做一些大病的筛查以及疾病预防知识的宣传教育。我们希望把事中的大病救助领域和事中救助前置到提前发现、提前预防的模式。

我们从 2015 年 8 月到 2019 年 8 月，筹款 2000 万余元，已经为青海、云南、湖北、湖南、山西等欠发达地区的 520 余所学校的近 20 万名在校青少年进行了大病的筛查以及疾病预防知识的宣传教育。我们一共筛查出脊柱侧弯、先天性心脏病等 2884 例，后续在充分尊重家属意愿的前提下为他们对接医疗资源，为贫困的家庭提供后续治疗资金上的资助。

同时，在北京、上海各成立了一个“祝福宝贝之家”，让他们到大城市治疗疾病，尤其是在他们等待就医或者是阶段康复的过程当中，给他们提供一个暂时的居住之处，使他们切实减轻负担。

在大病筛查的过程当中，主要成本是从大城市组建医疗团队做筛查，主要是差旅费。我们就开始探索进行了医师培训项目，把大城市的医疗资源尤其是相关病种的专家请到地方医院做培训，这样为大病筛查的初筛过程积累了很多的医生资源，大大降低了筛查成本，同时在某种程度上提高了医生的诊疗水平。

也就是说，我们从祝福宝贝专项基金开始就已经在探索从前端筛查到后端住院，包括后续贫困家庭康复的关爱的全链条救助模式。

2019 年 8 月 31 日在北京市民政局注册成立了北京一路阳光慈善基金会，跟祝福宝贝专项基金不同，祝福宝贝专项基金和儿慈会合作，依靠儿慈会公募的机制，我们的善款来源是在互联网的募资。北京一路阳光慈善基金会在筹备之初就是希望搭建能够体现企业社会责任的平台。因为企业和企业家在资金方面、技术方面甚至在人脉方面有很多优势，我们希望在这个平台上能够实现更多的跨界合作。

作为一路阳光发起人之一的华夏保险人寿公司除了深入参与大病筛查和大病初的两个项目，还将探索为贫困地区的孩子们提供更长久的保障，主要是探索大病医疗保障等公益性的保险产品。这样切实维护了脱贫攻坚的模式，减轻了贫困家庭的医疗负担。同时，依靠生命科技类的企业，依靠它们的高科技，比如说基因筛查之类的技术，让大病筛查更精准、更及时。

根据这 7 年在大病救助里面的经验，我觉得儿童大病需要企业、社会组织、政府各方面的介入，如救助、后面的保险以及康复关爱和心理疏导关爱等方面，需要大家共同努力，探索一种大病儿童的救助模式，实现政府和儿童无缝对接，给孩子们尤其是给身处大病困境的孩子们提供保障，谢谢大家。

刘庆龙：谢谢郭朋，“一路阳光”，这个名字听起来就非常好。

郭朋的介绍跟王林理事长的介绍相互关联，我特别注意到儿童的大病筛查，2015 年 8 月到 2019 年 8 月筹集到足够的款项，进行了若干的儿童大病筛查，确实把我们的救助工作又提前到了早期的发现、早期的干预阶段。而且在早期发现、早期干预当中，干预人的素质和能力确实也是重要的变量，他在这里特别谈到医师的培训，筛查出一些病以及如何进行诊断和医治是医学资源才能解决的问题，如何使社会组织跟特定的儿童救助资源有效地结合，确实也给了我们一些好的启发。

下面有请凤凰网的副总编辑侯春艳女士给我们分享。

侯春艳：各位来宾、各位专家下午好，很高兴有这样一个机会和大家分享凤凰网这么多年在公益这条道路上的实践和体会。

刚才主持人谈到今天这个话题涉及几个关键因素，有患儿、社会机构、NGO 和政府。我今天代表凤凰网过来跟大家分享，这么多年做下来，我个人认为媒体是一个比较特殊又比较重要的元素。

举个简单的例子，在今天这样的公益大论坛场合，现场就只有几千人的交流和行业内的交流，但是媒体是一个放大器。我们能够很好地把先进的理念和社会关注的东西放在媒体上传播，媒体是一个放大器和加速器，可以突破现场人数的限制，让更多人知晓。

凤凰网是凤凰卫视的子公司，也是一个独立拆分在纽交所上市的上市公司。从 2007 年开始，我们对自己履行企业社会责任这块非常重视，因此成立了自己的“美丽童行”公益项目，我们不是一个公益组织也不是公益机构，我们是一个商业公司，跟其他企业是一样的，只不过我们是一个媒体。

最初我们只能将项目立起来，从 2007 年到现在就没停过。最初我们的力量也是在探索，作为一个互联网公司在这个领域没有成熟的经验，依靠网友的力量，关注哪些地方有灾情，发动网友捐款捐物，开始只能用这样的方式积极地参与到救助当中。

做了几年之后慢慢积累了经验，当时还专门做过边远教师的评选和致敬之类的活动，更多还是利用媒体平台的优势，让社会上的人更重视，发挥每个人的作用，在慈善和公益领域做出贡献。

到了 2011 年，我们也在不断地成长和积累经验，如果我们能够去做好募款的事情，就真的能够让很多孩子实实在在地获得更多的帮助。

媒体是一个平台，可以连接很多方面，如企业界或者是个人，每一个用户都是我们可以直接面对的。同时，还有商界、政界、明星，这时候还是在利用平台效应，我们从 2011 年开始就一直致力于做慈善筹款，坚持下来到现在一共做了 19 场慈善晚宴，募集了 2 亿元资金，跟全国 10 家以上的基金会都有不同项目的合作，受惠的 67 万名儿童分布在全国所有省（区、市）。

2016 年我们甚至“走出去”，到了美国、欧洲，今年 9 月份马上在加拿大做一场募款，这部分的款项绝大部分会回到中国来，救助中国的困境儿童。同时，我们带去了理念，也把国外先进的经验带回来。

2016 年在儿慈会上成立了凤凰网的公益专项基金，开始做益童计划和护童计划。跟郭总那边比较近似，也是做前期儿童大病筛查，我们也和三甲医院的医生建立了健康档案。

护童计划是针对孤儿的大病救助，我们有媒体影响力，林志玲很有兴趣，联合发起了志玲姐姐“护童计划”。

我们作为媒体还不断地思索一些创新方式，去年北京场的筹款晚宴就不光可以筹钱，也可以筹资源，有技术可以捐技术，有设备可以捐设备。去年一个晚上就筹到了 12 个小时志愿者的时间，还有各种各样的资源。由于时间的关系我就先简单地介绍凤凰网做的跨界工作，让大家的力量结合在一起，让每一个普通的人都有机会投身于公益，让更多的普通人可以参与进来，改变孩子的命运。因此，我简单地做一下大面上的介绍，细节部分在对话的环节中跟大家展开，谢谢。

刘庆龙：谢谢侯女士给我们讲了一个美好的故事，叫“美丽童行”，67 万名儿童，这是一个多大的工作量，需要有多大的爱心和多大的热心来投入和推动这件事情。由于时间关系，她没有具体展开，后面还有对话环节跟侯女士探讨。

接下来有请深圳市妇女儿童发展基金会黄文锋秘书长给我们分享。

黄文锋：我们是深圳一个关注妇女儿童的基金会，刚开始更多是从深圳的角度考虑，但是看到儿童医疗救助这块，这么多年来也出现了不同的模式，无论是基金会自己筹款设立项目还是跟地方政府、商业机构合作，哪怕是建设一些慈善医院，以及近些年慢慢兴起的网络方式，都有很多的模式介入领域当中。

对于我们来说，医疗救助这块是整个社会福利体制当中覆盖的，在现阶段如果无法更好地覆盖就由商业机构附加的保险来覆盖。在此基础上才是社会组织、企业、公民以什么方式更好地介入，我们自己更多是探索一些小模式，通过资源整合的方式帮助患儿及其家庭来推进医疗政策。

举个比较小的例子，关于患苯丙酮尿症的孩子。当时有一群家长反映，我开始介入，于是在网上有了一些筹款。在做的过程当中，一方面是针对患儿，另一方面是针对家庭，是相对系统的支持。

同时，我们借助媒体的力量，刚才侯总也提到了媒体，还有政协委员的提案和人大代表的议案。因此，我们的项目在 2016 年底开始做，2017 年底就通过提案的方式推动深圳公共政策的改变。一方面是针对患儿的政策，另一方面是针对家庭的政策，因为这个病种的日常开支很大，而且这些开支是无法纳入医保里的。因此在这个过程中，会通过小的项目进行尝试，探索模式，再分享到其他地方。

我们在做的过程当中确实发现了一些问题，特别是公众自己发起的医疗救助往往会出现一些问题，案例不用具体讲了，比如说公开筹款方式，这种情况下，我们如何更好地做预防？

包括媒体，媒体在发挥放大器作用的同时也要发挥显微镜的作用，媒体主要是监督的功能，很多问题要通过媒体的方式约束，不好的东西要报道出来。

另外一个是行业里的标准，特别是刚才讲的病种发现、救助的流程，王理事长由于时间关系没有讲得非常细，但是他做了这么大的体量肯定有很多经验，希望我们能够学习到这些经验，这样我们可能会做得更好。时间关系，我就讲到这里。

刘庆龙：谢谢黄秘书长，黄秘书长简短的发言为我们提供了很多信息，其中一个重要信息就是社会组织如何来影响政府的公共政策。这确实是我们需要探索的非常重要的路径，社会快速发展，社会问题又非常多，在社会组织发挥作用的同时，政府也是非常重要的力量。要影响到政府公共政策的制定，让政府和社会组织有机地结合在一起，这样社会问题的解决效率会更高一些。如何考虑这些政策及其影响的路径，包括如何来跟媒体合作，黄秘书长为我们提供了一些重要的思路。

我们的话题还有很多，下面有请塞巴斯蒂安·库斯特先生，他有很多的话题跟我们进行讨论，特别是与儿童相关的目标和挑战，这个机构如何与合作伙伴共同推进和儿童健康领域可持续发展相关的问题的解决以及它们的经验，都跟大家做一个分享，下面有请塞巴斯蒂安·库斯特先生给大家演讲。

塞巴斯蒂安·库斯特：大家早上好，非常感谢有这样的机会来参加本次论坛。

救助儿童会成立于1919年，已经有100年救助儿童的经验，我们这个组织的成立也是为了确保儿童能够存活和得到保护。我们的一个愿景即实现2015年通过的联合国可持续发展目标，希望降低或消除5岁以下儿童的病发率和死亡率。当然现在全世界在这方面有了一些进展，也有一些与卫生和营养相关的问题，我们也希望在全世界提供宏观性的支持。

在中国，我们致力于解决5岁以下儿童较高的死亡率和病发率问题，比如说在中国我们已经做了很多的努力来降低5岁以下儿童的死亡率以及加大对于母婴健康关注的力度。我们也看到 5 岁以下的儿童死亡率达到了 15%，这个比例是非常高的。

我们目前实现联合国的发展目标所面临的挑战是不同地域之间的差距，比如不同国家之间的经济发展水平、卫生医疗水平的差距以及贫困地区和富裕地区的差距。中国有非常偏远的山区，这些地方的儿童死亡率比发达地区高 10 倍，这些地区很难靠自身实现联合国的发展目标。

而且有一些家庭收入比较低，有一些地方的基础设施比较差，医护资源也相对贫乏。我们所做的便是支持教育当地的医护人员，培养他们的能力，而且培养这些医护人员必须依照国际标准，并采取本地方法。我们完成培训之后也会跟本地的医院和卫生部门合作，来确保医院的工作人员能够和我们的组织更好地合作，然后整合这些流程。

我们工作的一个核心元素就是为直接的医疗救助提供支持，支持基于社区的医疗救助。我们不但希望直接救助病人，也希望跟病人的家属和家庭建立联系，帮助其建立一个互助的社区，提高其健康卫生意识，也会介绍一些适应本地文化和语境的经验和方法，还会为社区和家庭提供指导，举办一些相关活动，等等。

我们以这样的途径和方式开展项目，是为了确保获得长期的效果，保障儿童的福祉，我们也支持可持续发展。我们在其他国家也和政府开展紧密合作，跟中央政府和中央卫生部门合作，希望确保可持续性。我们也在云南、四川的医院试验一些先行的合作项目，比如开展新生儿或者是幼儿的健康改善项目，以及早期哺乳方面的改善项目。

做了这些项目之后，我们也希望推广成功经验，推行一些预防性项目，并做一个国家性的指南和指导。这个指南会提供具体的细则和引导，相关医护人员和从业者从而能更好地执行与母婴健康相关的流程，并且对其他人进行科普。这个指南将在明年颁布。这是我讲的案例，即如何实现可持续性的儿童健康发展。

刘庆龙：谢谢塞巴斯蒂安·库斯特先生进行了简单的发言，却提供了足够大的信息量。首先他们的儿童基金会叫作救助儿童会北京代表处，他们对于儿童的定义是5岁以下。而且在救助工作当中是以儿童为基点，整合医疗资源，使他们有更好的素质和能力进行救助。

特别需要注意的一个经验是能够同时跟社区和相关的儿童家庭结合起来，因为儿童的救助问题不单单是医疗机构和患者的问题，它也是一个社区、一个家庭的问题，我们要思考如何使它们有机结合在一起。这项工作的经验确实也是值得我们学习和借鉴的。

下面还有一位嘉宾，我们把时间交给鼎昆教育集团的魏巍董事长，请他跟我们进行交流。

魏巍：过去十几年我主要从行业角度做了很多捐赠和捐赠管理工作，我从行业观察趋势出发跟大家分享一些我目前看到的问题，就姑且将其作为一个引子引出大家的讨论。

作为大病救助，这些年无论是技术上还是服务上，第一个问题是我们如何使更有效的方式从探索阶段发展到验证阶段，再到最后的大规模商业化运用或者是接近商业化运用。我们一般是用主流的技术，做公募的产品和公募计划，募集很多资金，用主流方法做事，但是如何让我们做的事更有效，将成本降低？

第一个问题，比如说先天性心脏病，我们都是大规模地用主流化的方式，但是其实更好的救助方式，一旦可以大规模地应用，可以极大地提高救助效率，降低成本。

第二个问题，单个的救助成本相对较低，风险较小，结果可控。救助成本比较高，结果并不是特别可控，有一定风险的病种获得的资源就比较有限了。这对于其他病种的救助而言不是特别良性的发展。

第三个问题，瞄准问题。我们以为我们救助的患儿是贫困患儿，但是他是不是最贫困的？是不是最需要我们救助的？不一定。

还是拿先天性心脏病来说，大量的先天性心脏病患者的确诊工作是在医院完成的，如果不在农村筛查的话，就是等着家庭跟患儿到医院救治。这种方式相当于我们筛到了一大批家里特别贫困，连路费都付不起的患儿。孩子的救治目标是上移的，因为我们产品的设计，没有对这些目标患儿进行救治。

第四个问题，康复。如何为患儿提供康复服务？目前救治仅仅停留在疾病救治之上，但是真正关注一个孩子康复后的发展以及康复后所获得的服务是非常重要的，而行业里大量的资源都用在救治本身上。

在这种情况之下，这些问题出现的原因还是过去的资金来源比较单一，大量救助的资源可能有几个类型的资金来源，诉求比较统一。

这些年下来，我们运营资金的类型和资源类型有了很大的多元化改变，之前的项目资金主要来自政府和公募，现在慢慢地企业资金进来了，还有私人投资者以及银行债券等不同的资源进来。这些资源进来之后如何解决行业的问题？对于大规模的救治，公募跟政府资源因为有量，优势是最明显的。家族基金会进来以后，做的事也是一样的，是不是更多地解决怎样把更好的技术从实验往商用这个规模做，怎样能够把行业的效率提升？家族基金会进来以后，同样的是应考虑通过何种技术或实践提高行业的效率，而不是简单地扩大救助规模。这可能是我们要真正考虑的事情，只有这样做蛋糕才会越做越大，成本相应也会变低。谢谢各位。

刘庆龙：刚才魏董事长提出了一些很宏大的问题，由于时间有限，相信各位还有很多问题想跟嘉宾讨论，接下来把时间给在座的嘉宾。

现场提问：各位老师好，我是做儿童心理健康的，目前也发起了一个活动，就是关注留守儿童的心理健康问题，围绕孩子福智和福稚的发展。刚才郭朋先生提到康复阶段对于儿童心理健康的关怀，总体来说，目前人们还是主要考虑孩子的生理健康方面，对儿童心理健康方面的考虑不足。想问一下各个基金会对于这方面在未来是否有深入的考量？

刘庆龙：看看哪位嘉宾来回应一下这个问题？

郭朋：我们北京一路阳光慈善基金会成立之后，从 9 月份开始就到江西省吉安打算用 2~3 年的时间，为江西省吉安在校 90 万名未成年学生进行大病筛查以及筛查出来之后的大病救助。

同时还有心理健康的辅导问题，我们大概是 3 年计划投 3000 万元，先是培养辅导老师，通过培养辅导老师来构建地方的工作站，通过工作站的形式针对在校学生的心理问题进行疏导和辅导。

魏巍：我简单说一下，我接触过很多做儿童医院游戏的项目，主要围绕术前的准备和术后康复。这种项目做好之后可以大大减少患儿在医院治疗过程中的痛苦、缩短住院时间，甚至可以降低医疗成本，我们有详细的指标能够做出评估。但是这只是在住院期间，我没有做过康复之后这方面项目的资助，未来有机会可以尝试。

刘庆龙：其实心理的辅导也是很突出的问题。但是我想慈善机构跟当地的社会组织如何有效结合，恐怕是社会发展面临的非常具体的问题，比如说地方社工的机构，社工人员如果能够接应心理辅导，跟慈善机构更好地结合，可以更好地节省资源，目前香港已经做得非常好了。

观众提问：我非常认同魏巍董事长提到的新方法需要得到验证，以提高救助的效率，我想问一下基金会和慈善同人，在工作当中除了实际的救助项目之外，会花多少精力和资金做研究，也就是跟踪和评估自己的项目？投入产出比以及成功之处如何体现出来？或者是跟慈善公益研究院的合作体现在哪里？我比较想了解一下这方面目前的情况以及你们今后的计划。无论是政策还是项目都需要循证，这样才能让好的项目得到扩展，也可以避免一些浪费。

侯春艳：我简单说一下，正好我前面说的益童计划，也是为偏远地区从未做过健康档案、大病筛查、体检档案的孩子提供这方面的服务。

我们是一家企业，当然我们也成立了基金会，王林理事长这边也有专业的指引。正是因为我们是一家企业，魏董事长刚才也提到了我们反而有灵活性，不会形成惯性思维。我们也会不定向救助某一类病患者，根据孩子需求来，只要是符合条件、需要救助的，后面就会对接救助。但是这是有一个过程的，刚开始作为媒体没有这么大的能力筹集到这么多基金。

我们作为媒体是希望让更多的人看到有这样的问题，帮他们筛出病种，做了一段时间也有固定的募款的来源。做了一段时间之后就发现不行，我们带着所有的医生去筛出来了，筛出来了之后，医生也很着急，发现了病不去救助，这件事情的意义是什么？但是那时候资金是有限的，于是就开始复盘，开始跟儿慈会对接，因为它有“9958”，有很多资金可以对接来帮助这些孩子，可以进行打通。

我们拿着现有的这些钱，我们不是NGO，就是一家企业，所有的事情都是我们的员工联合医生做的。我们能走的场次非常有限，做了有限的几场就要把这几场做到位。原先是派医生下去，主要是给孩子做筛查，因为医生去当地筛查只需要路费和住宿费，会有剩余的钱，我们就询问这些钱能不能放在救助儿童的路费上。部分的医疗费用是否可以从这笔资金里面出？我们想把项目设计得更为合理，真正去解决问题。这是我们的一个自验和自检的过程，现在做的跟我们刚开始不一样了。如果未来能够跟慈善公益研究院形成可推广的经验，让更多人从中受益，还是具有非常现实和积极的意义的。

刘庆龙：各位来宾，好像我们的讨论刚刚把话题打开，刚刚进入对话的高潮，可是必须就此打住，因为要把会场让给下一个议题。有点遗憾，但也还好各位来宾都有联系方式，可以做会下的讨论。

各位，今天我们讨论的问题应该说是非常重要、非常突出、非常有价值的话题。

儿童是什么？儿童是社会的未来、国家的未来，关注儿童实际上就是关注社会、关注整个国家。我们利用这次机会对儿童关爱问题和儿童福利问题，从一个侧面做了相应的讨论，与其说我们把经验、做法、思考、认识在会场上做了一个展示，不如说我们共同来面对新的挑战、解决新的问题。因为社会迅速发展，儿童方面也会不断有新问题出现，如何来解决这些新问题、应对新挑战？我们的工作恐怕还是要紧锣密鼓地往前推进，希望在各位同人的共同努力下，儿童福利能够更好地落实，也希望我们会找到更完善的解决方案。谢谢各位嘉宾、各位来宾的分享，谢谢。

郑道：大家早上好，今天非常高兴来到这里，作为我们关于教育平行论坛的主持人。我的中文名字叫郑道，我是联合国儿童基金会驻华办事处的副代表，感谢主办方，也非常感谢中国人民对外友好协会会长。

我还记得我的孩子曾经从学校回来说，今天他们学到的是联合国的可持续发展目标，那时候我还非常吃惊，但是现在很多孩子了解到了这一点。

联合国发布了2030年可持续发展目标，所有成员国都在这个发展目标的框架之下。我们做了未来的发展蓝图，关于减贫、促进平等，等等。2030年可持续发展议程提出了17个可持续发展目标，这不仅面向发达国家，还面向发展中国家。

在本次讨论环节之中，我们将对儿童教育的目标进行讨论，也就是为所有儿童提供高质量教育，为所有人提供终身学习的机会。这个目标是很重要的，因为尽管在过去几年里，我们已经有了很大进步，但全球还是有许多儿童辍学，还是有许多青少年并不具有读写、计算等基本能力。我们需要加倍努力，为弱势群体等提供接受高质量教育的机会。

不仅是在课堂上面学习，我们还需要让他们获得高质量的教育。预计有 6 亿名儿童在适读年龄没有真正接触合适和高质量的教育，50% 的初中生还未达到语言读写和计算的熟练水准，66% 的儿童尽管上了学，但最终会辍学。

可持续发展目标致力于解决这些问题，我们应努力在 2030 年实现这些目标。如果我们向这些目标努力，我们还会有一些问题，比如 2 亿名儿童还是会辍学，40% 的儿童会止步于中等教育。还会有其他问题，比如说这会拉大差距。

我希望我们能在中国甚至世界范围内进行合作，努力实现联合国可持续发展目标，让所有人都可以接受同样高质量的教育。这样在 2030 年才可以完全实现可持续发展目标，让所有人有学可上。

接下来请演讲嘉宾上台，他是吕德雄先生，是中国陶行知研究会常务副会长兼秘书长。

全民教育的中国之路与国际努力

——从一个教育家的宏愿说起

中国陶行知研究会常务副会长兼秘书长　吕德雄

各位嘉宾，大家早上好，非常感谢主持人的介绍，前面对于儿童福利、儿童救助、儿童医疗的阐述非常好，接下来涉及儿童教育。

我今天演讲的题目叫《全民教育的中国之路与国际努力——从一个教育家的宏愿说起》。

1917 年秋，一位毕业于哥伦比亚大学的青年才俊，站在回国的轮船船头上，怀着“要使全中国人民都接受教育”这样一个宏愿，回到了苦难的祖国。他，就是后来被毛泽东主席称为“伟大的人民教育家”、被联合国教科文组织选为“影响世界的十大教育家”之一的陶行知。

回国之后的陶行知担任南京高等师范学校的教务主任，他提出改良课程、开放女禁、推行平民教育等主张。他了解到当时中国人口总数的 85% 在农村，提出“要把我们整个的心献给我们三万万四千万的农民。我们要向着农民‘烧心香’”。为此，他换下西装革履，穿上了布衣草鞋，舍弃高官厚禄，先后创办晓庄学校、山海工学团、育才学校、社会大学等，接收平民子弟就学，成为中国现代教育改革的先驱。

然而，在外敌入侵、内战不断的旧中国，陶行知的这一宏愿怎能实现？下面让我们看一组数字吧。新中国成立初期，中国有 5.4 亿人口，文盲率达 80%，其中 70% 是妇女。在园幼儿为 14 万人，毛入园率为 0.4%；小学在校生为 2439 万人，毛入学率为 20%；初中在校生为 95 万人，毛入学率为 3.1%；高中在校生为 32 万人，毛入学率为 1.1%；高等教育在校生为 11.7 万人，毛入学率为 0.26%。国家财政性教育经费占 GDP 比重为 1.32%。在中华人民共和国成立时，不是“所有儿童”，而是“绝大多数儿童”没有享受受教育的权利。

2018 年，中国教育得到了惊人的发展。在园幼儿为 4656 万人，毛入园率为 81.7%；小学在校生为 10339 万人，毛入学率为 99.95%，初中在校生为 4653 万人，毛入学率为 100.9%，九年义务教育巩固率为 94.2%；高中在校生为 3935 万人，毛入学率为 88.8%；高等教育在校生为 3833 万人，毛入学率为 48.1%。

陶行知先生具有先进的教育思想、“人民至上”的教育理念，且有众多同人、学生及其追随者与他一起实验、呼喊、推广，但历时 30 余年收效甚微。而在新中国成立后经过 70 年的努力奋斗，中国有了世界上最大规模的教育，城乡义务教育全面实施，尽管还存在幼教发展不充分、不平衡，教育体制改革、教学质量管理体系有待进一步改善，义务教育的优质均衡不够等短板，但总体上来说，在陶行知先生许出宏愿百年之际，“全中国人民都接受教育”的愿望基本实现，主要在于：

第一，国家重视是根本。

新中国成立伊始，毛泽东主席就指出：“恢复和发展人民教育是当前重要任务之一。”1951 年 10 月 1 日，中央人民政府政务院颁布《关于改革学制的规定》并开展大规模的扫盲教育。10 年间近 1 亿名青壮年文盲脱盲，文盲率迅速下降至 38.1%。改革开放以来，国家陆续提出优先发展教育，科教兴国、人才强国和创新驱动发展战略。1993 年，《中国教育改革和发展纲要》正式将“基本普及九年义务教育和基本扫除青壮年文盲”作为新的奋斗目标。党的十八大开启了以人民为中心发展教育的新征程，习近平总书记提出“努力发展全民教育、终身教育，建设学习型社会，努力让每个孩子享有受教育的机会”以后，国家先后颁布一系列重要文件，明确提出“普及有质量的学前教育、实现优质均衡的义务教育、全面普及高中阶段教育……残疾儿童少年享有适合的教育”。财政性教育经费投入占国家财政支出的比重连续 7 年保持在 4% 以上。

第二，法律规定是保障。

1986 年 4 月 12 日，第六届全国人民代表大会第四次会议通过了《中华人民共和国义务教育法》，以后又经全国人大会议多次修订。《义务教育法》规定，所有儿童依法享有平等接受义务教育的权利，并履行接受义务教育的义务。同时规定，政府、父母或其他法定监护人、学校、社会组织及个人的相应职责，规定了 22 种违法行为应承担的责任。据报道，这几年湖南、云南、青海都有家长因为拒绝送子女入学受到了处罚。与此同时，以《高等教育法》《教师法》《职业教育法》为代表的中国特色社会主义教育法律体系逐步形成。

第三，政策支持是关键。

依据教育事业发展的现实情况，国家有关部门相继制定有关政策，如确保流动儿童平等接受义务教育，保障残疾儿童接受义务教育，明确留守儿童、问题学生监护人和学校责任，兴办公益性、普惠性的幼儿教育等。尤其是鉴于区域之间、城乡之间、学校之间实际存在的教育差距，国家推进教育精准扶贫，重点帮助欠发达地区青壮年和贫困人口子女接受教育，阻断贫困代际传递。国家开展贫困地区义务教育薄弱学校基本办学条件专项督导。限期“改薄”，定期公布义务教育发展基本均衡县（市、区）名单等。举教育公平之旗，走均衡发展之路，抓督查、补短板、兜底线，为办好每一所学校，让每一个孩子享有公平而有质量的教育推出关键之举。

第四，慈善爱心是平台。

大善若水，泽及万物；慈心为人，善举济世。让社会充满慈善精神、使弱者得到帮助已成为一种风尚。许多公益组织或通过购买政府服务，或发动爱心人士帮扶支教。我所在的中国陶行知研究会作为国家一级社团，秉承陶行知先生爱满天下、无私奉献的伟大情操，支持公益教育。2016 年，启动针对贵州毕节提升教育软实力的三年共建行动，发动 10 多个省份的 200 多所学校结对帮扶，连续为其免费培训校长、老师。2018 年又签订新的三年资助行动协议。我们针对新疆、内蒙古、河北开展未来教育家助推计划，数千名幼儿教师受益。

儿童是世界的未来，为所有儿童提供教育的机会是世界性的话题，1990 年 3 月《世界全民教育宣言》发布，标志着为所有儿童提供普遍教育机会的理念形成。此后的一系列重要国家会议，都围绕这一主题展开。如 1989 年 11 月 20 日联合国大会通过的《儿童权利公约》，是第一部有关保障儿童权利且具有法律约束力的国际性约定。接着召开的世界儿童问题首脑会议，提出“一切为了儿童”。1996 年世界儿童基金会成立。眼下，世界多数国家认同教育机会均等观念，包括：

1. 优先，儿童优先主张，一切为了儿童。为所有儿童的生存和正常发展提供基本保护，儿童的基本需求应得到高度优先考虑。

2. 平等，教育公平是社会公平的基础或者重要方面。儿童依法享有相同的学习和发展机会。

3. 适合，要适合儿童需要的个性化、多样化、主体性学习，儿童教育质量的好坏关键在于是否适合。

4. 有效，能够实现儿童有预期的学习目标。中国目前提出在中国儿童公平教育的基础上，建设高质量的教育；丹麦提出公平与质量并行。中外在全民教育的国际合作及参与方面做出了共同努力，前面提到的《儿童权利公约》，中国全国人大常委会于 1991 年已经正式批准，中国政府和社会积极配合联合国教科文组织、联合国儿童基金会和救助儿童会，刚才救助儿童会也讲了在中国的 10 多个省份有项目落地。

中国提出在为所有儿童提供接受教育的机会的基础上，让儿童公平享有接受优质教育的机会；英国提出为所有儿童提供有效的学习课程、教育项目及质量监测体系；丹麦提出公平与质量并行，实现卓越的全民教育等。

中外在全民教育国际合作、借鉴、参与方面做出了共同的努力。1989 年 11 月联合国大会通过《儿童权利公约》后，中国全国人大常委会即于 1991 年 12 月正式批准，积极配合联合国教科文组织，以及联合国儿童基金会、救助儿童会的项目在中国落地。在首届全球全民教育会议上，与会各国代表对中国在推进全民教育方面的成就表示充分肯定，并高度赞扬中国政府对全球发展中国家教育事业发展的大力支持与贡献。鉴于非洲国家辍学者多、文盲多，以及贫困、战争导致基础教育落后的状态，中国伸出了援助之手，成立了中国 - 联合国教科文组织援非信托基金会，在中非合作论坛 2015 年峰会上，习近平表示中方将着力支持非洲破解基础设施滞后、人才不足、资金短缺三大发展瓶颈。中国教育部发布《推进共建“一带一路”教育行动》，加大对共建“一带一路”国家教育的援助力度，重点投资于人、援助于人、惠及于人。英国教育部2016年斥资4100万英镑，引进上海“掌握教学模式”，让英格兰8000所（近半数）中小学参与学习上海数学教育经验，等等。

在全民教育的发展上，中外都做出了巨大的努力，也要看到，在宏观政策、法律规定为所有儿童提供教育机会的同时，还要关注微观、局部、个体及社会协同机制。

为了让所有“儿童享有公平的教育机会，还需要许多配套措施，需要合力监护、相伴成长”，形成社会扶持机制。如微观政策、制度，须确保不至于影响儿童就学机会，家长教育需跟上，明确对孩子教育权维护的职责，社会各界、爱心人士应伸出帮扶之手，让阳光普照所有孩子。

为所有的儿童提供教育机会，让孩子共享同一片蓝天，让教育带给所有人希望，希冀成为所有人的共识与行动。谢谢大家。

郑道：非常感谢吕秘书长的主旨演讲。您分享了中国在教育方面的成就以及平等教育和普遍教育的重要性。您刚才提到了在农村的留守儿童以及特殊儿童需要得到照顾和需要得到入学的机会。

非常感谢您刚刚的介绍，接下来将邀请圆桌嘉宾上台进行讨论，首先邀请吕德雄先生作为圆桌嘉宾；李红艳是联合国教科文组织教育顾问；彼得·威廉是菲律宾国际乡村建设学院主席；塞巴斯蒂安·库斯特是救助儿童会北京代表处首席运营官；萧凯恩是著名钢琴家、融合教育倡议者。有请大家上台。

首先用掌声对圆桌嘉宾致敬。先从第一个问题开始，关于为所有儿童提供教育机会这个问题，想听一下各位嘉宾的想法。

彼得·威廉：非常感谢主办方邀请我们来到这里，我代表非营利性组织——菲律宾国际乡村建设学院回答刚刚这个问题。首先我介绍一下我们的组织以及我们的组织对于教育的观点。

我们的组织在60年间致力于解决乡村地区特殊儿童群体的教育需求问题，我想这是很重要的。因为一些大型机构或者是多边组织都在强调城市教育的重要性。我们也发现确实有很多证据显示，乡村地区的一些挑战被忽视了，问题没有得到解决。所以我们的组织一直致力于解决偏远地区的教育问题，以填补教育的缺口。

我们会考察农村社区，并与各个地方的社区和机构开展合作，包括亚洲、非洲以及全球其他地区。我们也遭遇过令人沮丧的情况，我们也了解到世界的城镇化进程越来越快，这在非洲和亚洲是非常明显的趋势。在城镇化的过程当中有一些微妙之处，比如说非洲或蒙古的某一些地方，一些乡村地区是以游牧的方式生活，他们需要经常迁徙，这可能是因为庄稼的生长季节或者是牲畜需要，这些地区可能几百年来都以这样的方式生活。我们的组织优先解决他们的教育问题。我们也了解到这些地区有2500万到4000万名儿童无法获得教育机会。

我们知道城市面临很多教育方面的挑战，在乡村地区这些情况更加严重，对于游牧民族而言，满足这部分儿童的教育需求需要比较灵活的课程设置。我们要想让这些社区的孩子接受这些课程，还需要告诉家庭和学生，只有让孩子接受教育才能让这个地区有更好的生态。我们每天在不同的地区开展10种不同的课程，可能会根据季节和他们的迁徙情况来进行调整。我们基本上就是迁徙中的教师，跟牧民一起迁徙，有时候可能会迁徙10英里甚至是几百英里这样的距离。

我们要开展行动，必须要找到牧民团体，用创新的方式帮助他们去解决问题。

郑道：非常感谢您，我把话筒给到李红艳，想请教一下联合国教科文组织是如何做的？如何缩小缺口？

李红艳：我在教科文组织工作。教科文组织是联合国系统当中非常特殊的教育组织，我们也发展出了世界的教科文教育议程。我们把 2030 年可持续发展目标当中的第 4 个目标叫作 SDG4。我们也将时刻关注这些目标在 2030 年的实现进展。在开始时，郑道先生说了很多关于第 4 个目标当中所取得的成绩，但是目前做得并不是特别好。我们有些偏离轨道了。

联合国今年的全球可持续发展报告指出，必须要让现在的一些国家可以继续地在这个轨道当中前行，实现第 4 个可持续发展目标，实际上我们已经偏离了，希望在 2030 年真的可以达到这个目标。如果继续按照这个方向走，到 2030 年可能只有 60% 的学生可以完成高中学业。这是我们现在面临的情况，我们目前完全偏离了轨道，无法完成 SDG4 的目标。我们需要思考策略加速现在的进程，这样在未来我们才能真正达成目标。

教科文组织是一个政府间组织，我们是在上游活动。我们组织国家、国际组织和国际平台进行交流。我们希望政府和民营企业可以一起想一下如何实现第 4 个可持续发展目标。

当我们在谈论包含性、平等、高质量的教育时，我们觉得如果没有公平的话就没有所谓的高质量教育，公平是最重要的，意思是我们需要打破壁垒，让所有儿童得到教育机会。我们发现出于一些有关公平的原因，很多需要接受教育的人无法接触到高等教育或高质量教育，因此我们的挑战还很大。有一些特殊孩子和有特别门槛的孩子有希望得到教育机会，但是仍然没有得到教育机会。比如说有一些女孩子无法受到教育，差不多有 2 亿个孩子没有接受教育，而当中 2/3 是女孩子，因此大多数文盲人口是女性。

教科文组织的数据显示，残障人接受教育的可能性较低，他们无法得到教育机会或达到最低等级的识字水平，很多残障孩子属于弱势群体。甚至在学校里的残障儿童也无法有效地学习，每天大概有 2 亿名的残障儿童受到校园欺凌，这也使他们无法高效学习。还有一些孩子有健康问题，或者有其他的问题，比如说他们无法有效地学习或者是高效地学习，因此需要相关策略帮助他们解决这些问题。

郑道：谢谢您的分享，这确实是上流层面的问题。接下来把话筒交给救助儿童会北京代表处的塞巴斯蒂安·库斯特。请问你们是如何缩小教育缺口的？

塞巴斯蒂安·库斯特：再次感谢主办方的邀请，让我成为其中一位分享嘉宾。我们第 2 个大目标和 2030 年可持续发展目标一致，希望让更多孩子接受教育。我们在中国比较注重农村领域，还有一些进城市务工人员的子女。

我们现在看到的一点是，偏远地区的学前教育和都市区域的学前教育之间是有一个缺口的，这个缺口主要是幼儿园的数量以及幼儿园所提供的教育水平。

社区对于学前教育的重视不是特别够，主要是它们没有足够受到培训的老师。我们开展了一些儿童发展项目，希望可以弥补缺口。在西安、青海，我们用了一些不同的方法去解决这个问题。比如说让社区给予更多的支持，并与家长进行沟通，提高管理水平；让更多的幼儿园进驻偏远地区，社区中有一些成员愿意到偏远地区教授学前教育课程，要主动询问他们是否愿意接受相关培训去到偏远地区。比如上海的老师是否可以去到云南，让他们在当地形成幼儿园以及相关社区，让他们有学习氛围。

另外一个缺口是在普及性教育里。有很多残障儿童是无法接受教育的，无论是在都市区域还是在偏远地区，都是如此。我们现在跟当地的学校合作，也建立了一些资源中心，提供了培训资源和材料。我们为残障人士所提供的教材是和国际接轨的，教师知道在他们的课程和课程设置当中如何更好地、更具包容性地使弱势群体的孩子融入普及的课堂。

郑道：我想问萧凯恩一个问题，刚刚听了三位组织代表的讲话，那您之前参加的项目有没有填补缺口的举措？前面讲的都是希望可以帮助残障人士，你们有没有建议？

萧凯恩：非常感谢主办方给我机会分享，我觉得普及教育当中最大的一个问题就是学习材料不足，比如说为视障的孩子或者是智障的孩子提供的特殊教育材料。另外，老师和家长应该可以给孩子提供心理辅导。比如说我上过一个课堂，老师、同学和家长之间是相互联系的。我想讲一个我自己的故事。有一次，大学的文学院为所有学生举办了一个活动，一位老师走过来对我说，我们这个活动是叫“活在贫困地区的活动”，你不要参与这个活动，因为我们可能照顾不好你。但是我过了几天问我的同学，这个活动到底是怎么做的？他们说其实就是躺在地上做实景演练，听完之后我觉得自己也可以参加这个活动。

所以老师扮演了一个很重要的角色，需要和同学、家长交流。我的一个建议是，定期在老师、家长和学生之间举行会议，这样大家就能得知彼此的担忧之处，学生也可以参与其中。在会议上，老师可以设置一些目标让学生接触、融入学校活动。我觉得其实作为弱势群体并不是说你应该参与更休闲的活动，更重要的是让孩子们，无论残障与否都可以融入社会，只有让孩子融入普通教育，日后才可以融入社会。

郑道：谢谢萧凯恩！下一个问题我想问一下吕德雄秘书长。您所在的组织都需要跟政府合作，这在全球都是这样的情况，无论是用什么样的模式或者是做什么样的项目，无论是乡村建设学院还是联合国教科文组织或者是教育基金，都提到了要和政府合作，您是否可以分享一下促进教育的案例及与政府合作成功的模式呢？

吕德雄：比如说现在政府非常提倡社会组织来购买政府服务，你申请一个项目经过政府有关部门审查、批准之后政府可以拨一定的经费，然后再根据你原来的计划进行落实。而有政府的背景，有政府批准的项目，有政府给的经费，下面有落地的学校、单位，这是获得成功的因素。

前几年我们做得相对多一些，这两年少了一点，是什么原因呢？就是政府购买项目里头，有一个要求是社会组织一定要配比相同的经费。比如说我拿了政府 100 万元，接下来我自己再拿 100 万元做，这对于社会组织而言压力非常大。政府支持的项目也需要基金会、爱心人士共同来做，这样可能会更好一些。谢谢。

郑道：谢谢您，那彼得·威廉主席，您所在的机构是如何跟政府合作使全面教育得以推广和成功的呢？包括资金上的支持。

彼得·威廉：作为一家机构，我们几十年来都在部署一些项目。我们也经常跟政府合作，政府是我们战略性的合作伙伴，我们一起促成了项目的成功落地。

同时，为了项目成功落地并得以推广，我们认为合作是非常重要的。我们经常跟偏远的地区合作，这些地区可能路途比较遥远，在这些地区推广项目是十分困难的。为了提高效率，政府必须成为其中的一部分。我们不仅要跟政府财政部门合作，还要让它们参与项目设计，不只是单纯作为利益相关方。

举个例子，我们在菲律宾跟政府合作做过一个项目。在过去 6 年间，我们也开创了很多独特的途径和方式，来推广全面教育。我们希望推广项目并且提高人民的意识：全面教育能够为我们带来什么？菲律宾的小学有 1/5 的儿童处于营养不良的状态，有证据显示，营养和教育的表现有非常明显的关系。我们跟政府合作推出了一个一体化改革方案。这个方案有三个举措。其一，我们为学生提供营养品。政府在其中扮演一个非常重要的角色，保证每天小学生都可以吃到不同的营养品。其二，营养是教育项目当中非常重要的部分，而且常常需要教育父母提供更有营养的食物给孩子，需要教育父母，营造营养环境，让父母有这样的意识，让他们认识到营养水平和学校教育的关联。其三，将农业和营养引入这个项目，也将学校周边的设施和产业接入这个项目，让多个合作伙伴共同促进项目落地。但是这也需要时间，比如让与农业相关的机构和部门为家长和教师提供培训，提供一些计划，便于教师和父母理解营养和学校表现之间的联系。一开始只有三家学校推行这个项目，后来又有几十所学校推广这个项目，目前规模逐渐扩大，现在有 3.6 万所学校推广这个项目，会集了数以万计的学生。如果没有政府的积极配合，这个项目无法落地。

郑道：谢谢彼得·威廉，再回到联合国教科文组织教育顾问李红艳女士，想到您所在的组织所从事的工作也是支持政府来实现联合国的可持续发展目标，你们是如何支持政府来实现可持续发展目标的呢？

李红艳：教科文组织的主要任务就是辅助政府来实现 SDG4 的各项指标，如何知道指标实现的程度呢？需要数据来帮助评估，我们跟政府一个特别重要的合作就是让政府提供我们所需要的数据。统计局每年针对这些指标开展相关数据的收集工作，每年会出版《全球教育检测报告》，会把每年检测到的问题通过报告反映出来。在此之前，各国政府会把国家的教育发展规划和 SDG4 紧密地联系起来，这是非常重要的也是最基础的一项工作。

作为政府间组织，还有一项重要工作就是让政府通过相关的公约，比如说《反对教育歧视公约》，这其实在很久之前就已经开始做了，但是还有国家没有签名，因此这项工作仍在持续中。

除了这些工作之外，还有一项重要工作是收集各个国家和地区提到的非常好的项目，把这些项目集中起来在更大的范围内进行推广和复制。

在残障领域以及性别领域，我们也进行了数据收集。跟中国政府合作有一个非常重要的特点，就是合作帮助不发达的国家和地区，比如说帮助非洲地区。我们授予了彭丽媛女士联合国教科文组织促进女童和妇女教育特使称号，她为性别平等教育在世界各地做了很多的宣传。

2016 年，中国政府跟我们合作，设立了一个奖项，专门奖励给世界各地涌现的女童和妇女方面的创新项目，每年都有颁奖活动。

2019 年教科文组织发动了一个大型的以“他的教育，我们的未来”为主题的活动，就是希望在全球各地动用更多政治、财政资源来支持女童和妇女的教育，实现《从享有教育机会到通过教育赋权：联合国教科文组织促进教育领域性别平等及通过教育促进性别平等战略（2019—2025）》。

关于残障群体的教育也是在 1994 年就有一个《萨拉曼宣言》，针对特殊的教育需求。在宣言通过 25 周年，也就是今年，下一周将在哥伦比亚组织一个国际大型论坛，专门讨论教育的包容和公平，这是全球性的大会，有很多国家的教育部部长会来参加。

要通过这样一个活动，更新国际社会对于教育的承诺，相信会有更多的推动。

郑道：刚刚听了您说的跟政府的不同的合作形式，从您的观点来看，您觉得政府应该如何跟非政府组织合作呢？无论是社会组织还是个人，如何来推广呢？

萧凯恩：我认为政府首先应该建立一些教师、学生和家长交流的平台，这样它才有机会关注全面教育所面临的问题，尤其是残障学生所面临的问题。

有了这个基础之后，企业也可以成立一些组织，或者是为非政府组织提供更多的资源，或者是为一些村庄学校提供更多的资源，来帮助那些残障儿童。比如说进行特殊教育帮助特殊学生追赶上普通学生，完成家庭作业，通过考试和测试。

教育对于残障学生来说很重要，因为只有接受教育他们才能更好地融入社区。政府可以在一些社区中举办研讨会或者是主题会，这样会使更多的人知道全面教育所面临的挑战，以上是我的一些建议。

郑道：谢谢萧凯恩，这是非常有意思的想法。下一个话题是关于创新的，从塞巴斯蒂安·库斯特先生开始，全球发展面临创新问题，我们有对于创新的愿景，您能否简短地发表一下自己的观点？您认为救助儿童会如何创新才能更加惠及儿童？

塞巴斯蒂安·库斯特：我举几个简单的例子，这些例子是我们组织在中国的案例，而且这些案例跟数字化有关。

有一些 ECCD 的员工会去做家访，我们给 ECCD 的员工全部都配备了平板电脑，这样可以将更好的想法和做法反馈给家庭和学生，也可以帮助他们了解目前所拜访家庭的情况，并且有利于后续的跟踪。后续的跟踪这方面是非常重要的，最后我们会把所有数据中央化，再进行项目当中的匹配。

我们 ECCD 的项目会用一些高科技的方式辅助家访，这样会有利于跟踪。

另外一个是基础性的项目。我们有一个关于社会情绪学习的项目，会先做一个先驱行动进行社会情绪学习，帮助学生获取他们需要的社会技能、数字技能。我认为这将是中国学生在未来非常需要的东西，可以让他们迅速地迈向现代化。

再一个是全面教育。我们开发了一个线上的教材包，老师也可以进行线上学习。这个教材包也可以在大学里培训教师时使用，这是我们在创新方面取得的一些进展。

郑道：谢谢塞巴斯蒂安的介绍，吕先生，在你们的组织当中有什么创新的模式和创新技术呢？

吕德雄：在让所有儿童接受教育、实现中国全纳教育的目标上，我们本身就是一个教育社团，刚才这位先生讲到的一些问题我们也在做。比如说利用现代教育网络，我们也在搞；利用国内一些项目，我们会做成新的项目使其进入学校。

我们还注重家长培训，要想让所有的孩子接受教育，家长不加入，光靠政府是不行的。既然是所有就必须要关注个体，因此我们在不同的地方设立家长学校，培育家长，家庭共育。目前比较成功的就是这两个方面。

郑道：谢谢吕先生，联合国教科文组织李红艳女士，请问你们有什么创新呢？你们如何推广新的点子？

李红艳：2019 年 5 月份我们在中国召开了特别大型的关于 AI 人工智能的会议，联系到全纳教育这个理念，我们关注到了在人的数字技能这方面有一种性别的差距。我们在做的一项工作就是研究这个现象，找出背后的原因，提出策略。

我们最近出版的一个刊物《如果我可以的话，我会脸红的》，首先 Siri 的声音都是女人的声音，比如说你发一个语音跟它说，“Siri，you are a bitch”，刚开始的回答是“I would blush，if I could”。我们发现这个现象非常有意思，因为有很强的性别因素在里面。现在其已经改成说“我不知道怎么来回答你这个问题”，大家可以回去试一下。

我们经过观察发现，性别刻板印象已经渗透在电子产品当中和科技产品当中了。AI 意味着未来，我们如何在这个时间内及时注意到并且不要在技术的发展过程中加剧性别不平等？

比如说我们有研究发现科学领域中有非常明显的性别差距，在所有大学从事这个领域研究的人只有 35% 是女士，还有一些领域只有 3% 的女大学生会选择这个领域。这是因为她在社会化过程当中会受到性别和刻板印象的影响，因为她认为这个领域就是男性的领域，不愿意去选择。

这些现象都值得我们思考，这就是我们目前在研究的，我们希望借此寻求促进性别平等的突破口。

吕德雄：性别教育是回避不了的问题，其实现在在中国歧视女性教育的问题解决得已经相当可以了。我想提出来的是也要关注男性教育，我们专门有一个机构叫女学生教育专委会，专门讨论女性教育，从国际到国内。

我原来是在一所师范大学工作，发现师范大学里男生特别少，幼儿园里男老师也很少，如果孩子从小接触的都是女老师，对孩子的成长是不利的。我曾经提出一个建议，女学生教育专委会可以适当地开一次男性教育论坛，我觉得这很有意义。

郑道：非常感谢吕先生，你们两个人都说了性别平等上的问题。彼得·威廉，你们在这段时间里研究了一些前沿的科技，你们是如何使用的？

彼得·威廉：作为一个组织，我们非常重视学习，不仅仅是学习的环境和前景，我们认为学习是可以帮助我们在自己的失败和成功当中汲取经验的，长期以来我都认为这是非常重要的。

你可以想象一下整个情景，之前已经说过了我们有很多的挑战和机会都是在一些非常偏远的地区，这是我们聚焦的地区。我们看到了这些团体，然后发现，这些团体已经开始为自己赋能，使用一些策略或者是在自身环境中不断地努力。

我可以给大家举个例子，对于我们来说，我们有一些时候想要重新定义创新。创新对于学习意味着什么？大家都知道人类发展指标，如果大家有听之前的分论坛，之前说的是儿童健康。但是在我们的组织中，我们认为儿童健康有很多创新模式和创新方式。在儿童教育这方面也融合了一些关于儿童健康的问题或者是贫困问题。实际上我们可以从创新的角度来看，健康和经济指标都应该是在我们做儿童教育时所要考虑到的因素。大家可能知道NPI，NPI是多种因素指标，我们把健康、生活水平这些指标都融合在一起后，发现这些都是和教育息息相关的。

我现在主要做的一件事情是会看一下乡村社区和个人家庭之间的联系。

我们发现 60%~70% 的在不良环境下成长的儿童或者是受教育能力差的儿童，家庭环境是非常糟糕的，家里积了很厚的灰。世界银行调查发现，如果可以让家庭勤于打扫或者是致力于减少家庭积灰，可以改善整体的健康条件，将整体的共同发展指标提高 97%。这就是用比较创新的方式做一些新发现和新改变，这些方式都是值得我们继续探索的。这是我们的组织所发现的事情。

郑道：谢谢，萧凯恩你在自己的生活当中有没有尝试过创新？

萧凯恩：我在说这个话题之前，想就性别教育进行回应。我知道之前很多女孩子少有机会接受教育，但是在我这一代出生的女孩子大多数可以接受教育，我也非常有幸可以成为她们中的一员。

说到创新模式，我想提出几种方式。

第一，让正常的学生模仿残障人士的活动，让他们感受到残障人士在日常生活当中所受的挑战。比如说在黑暗当中难以行走，用受伤的手打开矿泉水的瓶盖很困难。我们可以通过换位思考来让正常的学生体会到残障学生的艰难。

第二，在师范学校举办一些音乐会、戏剧演出。接受特殊教育的学生可以跟正常学生一起来组织一些活动或者是进行演出，这样可以展示特殊学生的才能。这样对于残障学生来说，可以得到群体的认可，也可以更好地得到同龄人的理解和帮助。对于教师来说，也可以更好地发现这部分学生的个性和才能。

实际上虽然我们是残障人士，但是我们渴望，也能够为社区做出应有的贡献。我们渴望教育，希望得到教师和父母的支持以及同龄人的理解和认可，也希望能够更好地享受学校生活。

教育是未来的关键，未来是由良好的教育体系所决定的，谢谢。

郑道：谢谢大家，刚才的圆桌会议硕果累累，我们学到了很多，也听到了联合国可持续发展目标的实现过程和诸多挑战，讨论了教育上的差距和弱势群体所面临的问题——性别、平等，以及全纳教育的现状、进展。

非常感谢诸位嘉宾跟我们分享他们的经历和视角，希望在座各位听众如果有兴趣，可以在会后和嘉宾进行交流。当然更多的是希望聆听诸位对教育经验的分享和对教育的认识、营养跟学校表现之间的关系。今天几位嘉宾分享的例子都是非常有意思的，我个人也非常感兴趣。可能一些因素是我们常常忽略的，我们没有想到营养、布满灰尘的地板跟学校表现有这么多的关联。

我们也看到了很多新颖的视角，非常感谢萧凯恩女士刚刚分享的案例，正常的学生通过换位思考，换位体验残障人士的需求和经历的困境，这些都是非常有帮助的想法。我们的圆桌会议到此结束，再次感谢今天早上的所有嘉宾，谢谢。

十一　善学明辨

主 持 人：北京师范大学法学院宪法与行政法教研中心主任　刘培峰

嘉宾演讲：中国民间社会发展指数报告

清华大学公益慈善研究院副院长　贾西津

好公益指数：亚洲慈善事业发展趋势

亚洲慈善与社会中心首席执行官　夏露萍

中国慈善行业调研报告

亚洲公益创投网络首席战略官　艾莉森·霍洛韦尔

善经济的思想与实践

善经济倡导者、慈济人文志业发展处主任　何日生

中国公益慈善人才的培养机制和项目探索

论坛学术委员会委员、香港中文大学社会工作学系教授及系主任　倪锡钦

国际公益人才培养计划：中国香港及泰国参访汇报

深圳市企业评价协会常务副会长兼秘书长　李亚平

国际公益人才培养计划：菲律宾及越南参访汇报

深圳市恒晖儿童公益基金会创始人　陈行甲

对话嘉宾： 清华大学公益慈善研究院副院长　贾西津

亚洲慈善与社会中心首席执行官　夏露萍

亚洲公益创投网络首席战略官　艾莉森·霍洛韦尔

善经济倡导者、慈济人文志业发展处主任　何日生

论坛学术委员会委员、香港中文大学社会工作学系教授及系主任　倪锡钦

深圳市企业评价协会常务副会长兼秘书长　李亚平

深圳市恒晖儿童公益基金会创始人　陈行甲

点评嘉宾： 亚洲理工学院尤努斯社会事业中心发展管理主任、塔玛萨特大学创新学院客座教授　法伊兹·沙阿

越南农村可持续发展中心常务主任　阮金恩

刘培峰： 我们今天上午有 7 位演讲嘉宾会阐述他们的观点，然后我们会有一个讨论，按照会议的安排，我们列了很多问题。一类是如何看待公益指数和如何看待社会组织对社会的贡献；怎么样把倡导组织、支持组织对社会的贡献纳入指标体系。一类是公益人才培养，因为这是目前最重要的问题，很多社会组织也做这样的工作。所以我们就这两类问题展开讨论。每位嘉宾报告 12 分钟，最后 1 分钟会提醒，请大家严格遵守时间限制，如果超出了时

间，就会缩短中间茶歇和自由讨论的时间，希望大家认真对待，谢谢。

让我们有请清华大学公益慈善研究院副院长贾西津教授，她讨论的是社会部门发展指数，有请。

中国民间社会发展指数报告

清华大学公益慈善研究院副院长　贾西津

大家早上好。今天要报告的内容，由于时间有限，我会略去比较复杂的研究过程，向大家分享我们的一个研究结果，这个结果可以用很简单的图形概括出来。

首先介绍一下研究方法。我们借鉴了由在公益领域非常著名的安海尔教授主导、由 CIVICUS 开发的一套指标体系—— CSI 指数，即民间社会发展指数，做了三轮跨 14 年的追踪研究，2005 年第一次，2012 年第二次，2019 年第三次，相当于每 7 年做了一轮。这套指标体系用四个维度评价民间社会的发展。我们知道现在有很多测度社会发展的指数，比如测度捐赠的、测度公益慈善的、测度社会部门的，萨拉蒙教授开发过几个指标，比如部门规模的指数。CSI 指数的特点在于它关注的是民间性。整个指标体系试图测度自下而上民间生长的力量是怎样的状态，侧重的是民间性。我们称社会部门，有人以为是慈善组织，所以我们把它称为民间社会，因为这套指数最终强调的是民间性，所以是民间社会发展的指数。这套指数怎么样测度民间社会的活力？它的方法是这样的，它的指标体系，最后是用 72 个指标来对每一个指标进行评分，这套方法最后评定的是每一个指标。每一个指标有了分之后，通过计算的方法得到亚维度的分数。然后再进行计算，得到维度的分数，所以最后得到的结果就是菱形图，是 CSI 菱形。这是最后的结果。

通过这个菱形我们能看到什么？首先它不是一个标准化的定量研究，就GDP而言，不管计算方法有多少，比如GDP是5%、4.2%，它都是有绝对意义的，5%比4.2%大，所以这是一个定量研究。CSI方法不是纯粹的定量研究，而是半定量，所以是定性与定量结合，因为这个社会非常复杂，我们用纯定量的方法描述的东西是特别有限的，我们用很多算法才能得出一个数，一定会忽略很多东西。而定性方法的好处是会非常的全面，但不是非常严格。所以这个菱形不是绝对的定量研究，而是模糊的概念。如果是同样的方法、同样的专家，会有量化意义，但如果不是纯定量、专家的评估有主观性，就不可以进行绝对的定量化比较。那么可以看什么呢？第一，可以看位点，由于有一套科学的设计方法，所以结构位点不会偏差太大。所以大家首先要看的是结构。第二，看位点的变化，比如我们三次做的有什么不同。第三，我们可以从国际库视角看待这个指标，看自己处于什么位阶。所有的指标和维度都是在强调它的民间性。比如结构很重视公民的参与，环境强调政治、法律、经济三部门之间的关系。价值维度是我们做了中国的调适，第一年的，我们用了CSI的指标，但是在中国有很多价值不太合适。比如侧重环保、扶贫等几个方面，但是社会正义没有纳入中国，所以我们做了微量的调整和合并，比如性别平等，我们设为平等，社会正义是我们自己加的，所以后两年的价值指标有一些变化。影响强调的是部门对于国家政策的影响、对社会问题的解决。这是整个方法。

我们的测度由专家委员会评分，所以是半定性半定量的，但这些评分不是完全的主观性，有一套基础素材的发现。CSI给出的方法是媒体回顾、事实发现、社区调研等，包括社会调查、文献。对于媒体回顾文本分析，前两年是用这个方法，2019年做了改变，我们把大规模替换为数据库，我们用了一些数据库的指标，把所有的呈现给专家，最后专家打分得出结果。2005年、2012年、2019年，专家有一些更换，但大体上专家保持了稳定，每年有一些变化，比如有人已经退休了、不在公益界了，有新人加入，尽管如此，得分还是很相似的，所以这个方法有一定的稳定性。由于它是结构化的，测度不了非常精微的变化，比如 0~1，30% 以下都叫 0，从 5 进到 20，得分没有变，所以是粗测度。表中列出了 CSI 的四个维度的得分、三轮的情况，显示为这个构图。这些年构图很相似，得分最高的地方在价值，其次是影响，得分低的在环境和结构，这是我们民间社会发展的现状。

看一下每个结构亚维度的得分（PPT 图）。第一，结构维度，公民参与的维度是收缩的，而资源组织和内部发展是偏于增长的。第二，环境维度，最为生长的是私人部门和社会的关系。第三，价值维度，我们能看到透明度是它最为增长的一个点。第四，影响维度，变化不太大，现在对社会问题的关注和满足社会需求方面有收缩。从这里面可以得到结论，能够看到中国的民间社会有一点点的调整，生长点是在内部的，二、三部门关系，以及治理的层次比如透明度的增加，这是生长中的。而目前的收缩或者挑战所在是结构维度，特别是公民参与，还有一些宏观环境的变化。这是我们三次研究得到的结果和民间社会的现状，谢谢大家。

刘培峰：谢谢贾西津教授。我们第二位报告人夏露萍到了，我利用主持人的身份对今天上午会议的发言次序做一下调整，我把艾莉森·霍洛韦尔调到第三位，因为他们讲的是关于慈善评估的研究，我把何日生先生调到第四位，因为他讲的是善的思想，方便大家整体的理解。现在有请亚洲慈善与社会中心首席执行官夏露萍女士。

好公益指数：亚洲慈善事业发展趋势

亚洲慈善与社会中心首席执行官 夏露萍

你们好，我的名字叫夏露萍，我是亚洲慈善与社会中心首席执行官。今天我要跟大家讲讲我们的慈善工作。

首先，我要跟大家讲一下我们的中心—— CAPS，我们常驻香港，同时聚焦全球 16 个国家和地区，加上中国台湾和香港。我们是一个研究咨询机构，我们做政策研究、应用研究、实际研究，还可以为客户定制研究。同时我们还服务于企业以及想要去做企业社会责任项目的私营机构。我们的使命是希望增加私有资源的数量并提高其质量，其中包括公益慈善事业、企业社会责任和影响力投资，帮助所有的企业去行善、举善。我们的一个研究指数叫作行善指数，在我讲这个指数之前，我想和大家分享一下为什么我们选择创建行善指数。我们知道亚洲普遍有信用缺失的问题，这是说，在亚洲，人们不信任非营利机构，人们不信任公司，有一些国家甚至是政府都没有公信力。所以在社会的不同方面，如果人们对这些机构缺少信任，人们不愿意做慈善方面的工作，他们怎么样为慈善尽力？那我们如何通过行善指数加强慈善公信力呢？之所以有这样的慈善赤字是因为有郭美美这样的事件发生，但大多数情况下人们愿意信任这些机构。大家说如果我们不相信慈善机构的话，我们怎么样做慈善？所以中国政府推行新的慈善法，希望通过立法的形式让慈善机构更加透明，有更好的公信力和指数。所以好公益指数是什么？怎么样帮助我们做好的公益？

好公益指数涉及四个方面，其中三个是跟政府相关的，包括财税政策、法律法规、采购，所有的这些都与政府紧密相关。生态系统方面就是人和公司的做法，我们的这个研究汇集了120个非营利和营利机构的信息，它们都是做善事工作。我们还有专家委员会，我们会吸取调研的对象和专家的意见，刚刚第一位发言人贾西津女士就是我们的行善指数在中国内地的重要合作者之一，所以感谢贾西津女士对我们的帮助。我们把所有的专家以及非营利机构的意见汇集并统计数据，然后做了最终的分析报告。

2018年1月，我们第一次发布这个指数，下一个指数将会发布在中国农历新年之后。2018年中国在好公益指数方面还是可以的，我会和大家讲为什么中国的表现是这样的。我想告诉大家，这项调查完成于2017年，当时国际的非营利机构法和中国的慈善法还是新的，很多人对慈善机构的影响和细节有许多不明了的地方。我们希望在2020年的时候发布中国的好公益指数，那时候中国的政策将更明朗、清晰，而人们对新的慈善法和国际慈善法的了解也将更清楚，比2017年收集数据的时候更清晰一点。

好公益指数并不是看人们在捐赠的时候有多大方，我们也不会有大量的公益慈善方法，我们主要看支持慈善事业中赠予和接受简单关系背后的基础设施是什么？规则是什么？有哪些机构？怎么样能够使得我们的资金源源不断地投入公益慈善？根据某些慈善指数，有些人更加慷慨，但我们不这么认为。我们想人本身是愿意帮助别人的，为什么有的国家的人并不愿意帮助别人？因为在他们的大环境里缺乏一个可信的机制，他们无法去赠予和帮助他人。所以在我们的好公益指数里，我们解决的关键问题是优化大环境，加强慈善机构公信力。

此外，我们发现，社会各界的行动领先于政府政策的制定，生态系统比剩下三方面的指数都高。虽然政府财税政策与法律法规并没有创造许多有利的条件让我们做慈善，但公司做了很多，在中国尤其如此。如果讲公益和慈善，这在中国是很火热的概念，而且中国的很多个体和公司在公益方面做了大量的工作。此外，我们觉得政府给予的税收激励和红利是非常重要的。这里有以下三种原因。其一，大家都想省钱。其二，政府发出的信号在亚洲是很重要的。一旦政府给捐赠方税收激励，它就从某种程度上引导了公众的行为，告诉公司说它希望有更多的社会责任感方面的项目。所以当时新加坡出台了一个 250% 的税收红利政策，也就是说你做相关的捐赠，可以享受政府 2.5 倍税收的减免。所以说政府发出的信号是很重要的。其三，我们发现一个国家的 GDP 水平与其在行善指数上的表现是没有关系的，有的国家说我们的 GDP 不好，所以没有办法减税。越南的税收政策比朝鲜要好。在我们的指数研究中，税收的多少和经济发达程度之间没有直接联系。这意味着什么？有人认为，美国的慈善资金应该相当于 GDP 的 2%。如果在行善指数研究的国家中，慈善和公益资金能达到 GDP 的 2%，这约合 540 亿美元 / 年，这将会是国外援助的 11 倍，联合国年度可持续发展目标的 1/3。所以如果我们每一年能将这么多资金投入慈善公益，那么可以解决更多的问题。

我讲讲中国的情况。在中国，众筹出现，新的慈善法公布，我们看到了中国的发展。我们发现有大约 29% 的人觉得中国的慈善法难以理解，56% 的人保持中立。而随着人们对这个方面越来越感兴趣，这个比例会发生变化。在慈善方面，有问责制、透明度，中国政府需要做更多有公信力的工作。对政府来说，它需要非营利机构做好的体系。在中国，慈善问责不超过 10%。我住在香港，我们的税给到慈善机构的差不多 10%，而中国内地的税收政策还不够好，尤其是给予慈善机构的支持还不够。

相关公益领域的报告中，中国的指数得分并不高，很大程度上是税收减免政策导致的。我们看到其他的国家有很多减税的措施，尤其是给捐赠方。中国的非营利组织和政府之间的关系十分密切，我们采访的组织中有 46% 都从政府方得到投资，这在亚洲国家中是最高的，这个平均值在 32%。公益慈善机构的人才缺失也是一个问题。84% 的组织认为大众都觉得非营利组织的工作人员要少赚点钱，薪水要比银行从业者和律师低。但我们不能有这样的偏见，我希望大家和我有同样的想法，在公益领域，我们拿到的工资应该是和其他的人相当的。我们有更多的机会进行不断的改进，而中国已经走在非常重要的道路上，我希望在问答环节可以和大家有更多的交流，谢谢。

刘培峰：我们下面请亚洲公益创投网络首席战略官艾莉森·霍洛韦尔女士为我们做中国慈善行业的调研报告。

中国慈善行业调研报告

亚洲公益创投网络首席战略官　艾莉森·霍洛韦尔

大家早上好，我非常高兴今天早上能够来到这里，和大家分享我们的报告。首先向大家介绍一下AVPN（亚洲公益创投网络），目前在亚洲地区，我们看到越来越多的国家面临十分复杂的社会挑战，没有单一的方法可以应对这些挑战。同时可以看到这些地区创造了大量财富，越来越多的组织和个人从经济的繁荣当中有所获益，其希望回馈社会，帮助应对社会面临的挑战，真正服务于自己的国家。但是除了我刚才提到的这些组织和个人希望用自己所获利益来解决问题，我们还缺乏人才与基础设施，而且我们不知道如何做有真正影响力的投资，这便是AVPN出现的原因。我们希望将财富、人才等资源引入亚洲的公益领域，并保证资本得到有效的部署，解决我们社会和环境中所存在的问题。到目前为止，我们已经在全球范围内拥有585个成员，成员来自各个不同的行业，包括基金会、信托公司、影响力基金、集团基金、中介和政府组织。虽然我们是一个国际组织，但所有这些成员都关注于亚洲区域的投资。我们为什么会如此独特？我们是一个平台，打破了不同的权益相关方之间的孤岛状态。在过去，大家很少看到基金与影响力机构之间相互沟通如何解决社会问题，这便是 AVPN 平台存在的意义。我们希望打破信息的孤岛状态，帮助我们的机构和个人寻找机会合作并分享经验，同时扩大影响力。我们主要通过两个方法帮助机构相互认识和了解，比如通过大型会议，像是我们在新加坡召开的会议；还有有效网上平台，像是我们的线上交易沟通平台。我们帮助机构学习、分享最佳实践经验，清楚地了解本地区的近况和市场。这是 AVPN 所做的事情，即教会成员成为行业领头羊，扩大自身影响力，进行合作，帮助解决社会问题。

有一点想和大家探讨，AVPN 提到社会投资的时候，我们谈到了几大部分，包括慈善投资、影响力投资、社会责任感投资等。这些部分有些是以影响力为主导，有些是以财富为主导。我们觉得资本产生社会影响是非常重要的。我们还有非财务的支持，包括人力资源。如果我们要建立起社会组织或建设公益行业和整个生态系统，就需要人力和大量知识投入。AVPN 非常关注的领域是希望成员的影响力能够最大化。我们有一个知识中心撰写了帮助不同行业发展的报告。我们帮助成员了解社会投资的最佳实践经验，带来更多创新的工具。我们的报告还包括很多案例分析，能够了解这个网络中其他组织的做法。我们关注行业的发展情况，帮助组织进入市场、知道它们的资本最好应该放在哪个市场。最后，我们会讨论很多的问题，包括生计、教育各个细分行业，探讨社会投资的创新如何影响这些领域。

最近我们推出了一个报告，在这个报告中，我们探讨了中国慈善生态系统及其发展，也给出了如何继续这种局面的建议。我们有 34 个非常知名的参与者，他们来自基金会、金融机构、研究机构、媒体、孵化器公司等。我们观察到了十分积极的信号，那就是中国的慈善资金总量在过去几十年翻番了，从 2010 年的 100 亿美元增长到了 2017 年的 234 亿美元，这是非常大的进步。而推动这一进步的资本大多来自公司，大约 65% 的资金来自集团，

21% 来自个人。我们也非常高兴看到中国慈善生态系统的发展以及有越来越多的人参与其中，就像和大家展示的平台一样，中国的慈善生态系统正在发展进步，孵化器公司、金融机构、研究机构、媒体、政府组织、非政府组织、智库，共同加入其中，共同关注于如何带来更大的慈善影响力。

毫无疑问，在过去一段时间，中国出现了大量基金会。到目前为止，中国的基金会数量超过 6000 个，在过去 10 年间增长了 17%。在中国 6021 个基金会当中，有不到 1% 完全出于捐款的机构，这是中国非常独特的情况。在中国有一些机会帮助建立这种基金会，包括社会组织，帮助它们建立信任，扩大自身影响力，这样它们会更加有效地利用资金创造更大的影响力。我们在中国最关注的领域是教育和脱贫。教育在亚洲地区是最受关注的问题，也是慈善事业最关注的问题，我们必须不断加强年轻人的能力，提高他们的技能。其次的领域是健康和可持续发展城市，这是非常有意思的。

我们有两个组织在关注中国的慈善发展，首先是企业捐款，2013 年捐款总量达到 132 亿美元，2016 年的捐款来自 1000 多个基金会，其中超过 75 个基金会的捐款额多于 150 万美元。但我们可以看到，这些公司和基金会所捐赠的不仅是金钱，它们还在影响社会和教育等诸多方面，它们的员工也在调动社会资源，它们正在致力于使自己对社会的影响最大化。

接下来我们看一下个人捐赠方面，这些大部分由中国的高净值人群完成，这一数值每年增长 33% 左右，这是由捐赠额最多的 100 名慈善家实现的。2017 年，捐赠额达到 330 万美元，这是 8.19 亿名捐赠者共同做出的贡献。我想主要的原因是有更多新的工具帮助我们的个人捐赠者，让他们能够做慈善。他们建立基金会、慈善信托公司进行更多的捐赠。我们可以看出这些慈善家对自己的家乡进行了捐赠。从这个报告中，我们可以看到在整个行业当中的四大趋势。第一，慈善行业越发正规和专业。特别是 2016 年《慈善法》出现之后，从政府的法律法规角度来说，组织机构会设想规划它们的未来发展和升级自己的慈善模型。第二，有越来越多的财务可持续发展模式出现。现在有一些组织得益于经济的繁荣发展，与此同时，它们也在思考如何通过经济的繁荣发展为社会带来益处。所以社会组织和财务可持续发展模式近年来在中国层出不穷。第三，对外交流。随着“一带一路”的推出和“南南合作”的进行，我们看到越来越多的慈善事业已经走出中国，变得更加国际化。比如气候变化和空气污染，这是全球存在的问题。第四，技术。公益慈善领域所用的技术也在不断改进，我们在腾讯公益的“99 公益日”中看到，2018 年其筹集了 1 亿多美元，这是来自中国 2800 万名捐赠人的捐款。技术让人们得以参与慈善事业。

最后想和大家分享我们的建议，我们呼吁在座各位参与慈善事业。第一，我们发现需要筹集资金成立基金会，这能让机构做到一个基金会无法做到的事情。第二，在慈善生态系统中建立中介机构，其会帮助社会机构和基金会联系，不断提高它们的能力，提高透明度，增强信任感，更重要的是帮助我们不断发展。这是我们目前所需的，中介机构在中间可以发挥很重要的作用。第三，不断加强合作，这也是 AVPN 致力所做的事情，我们希望大家使用我们的平台，在整个行业当中寻找更值得信赖的合作伙伴。第四，发现能够带来最大影响力的投资领域。有许多领域得到的投资是远远不够的，比如气候变化、青年发展和生态系统发展。第五，发掘人力资源，就像刚才的讲者提到的，要注重青年的培养。谢谢大家的倾听，如果大家感兴趣的话，可以扫描 PPT 上的二维码，下载我们的报告。我期待和大家有更多的沟通。

刘培峰：艾莉森·霍洛韦尔女士刚才有一个数据，我做一个补充，因为她的报告用的是中国基金会的数据，是 6000 多家，实际上截至 2019 年 8 月 31 日，中国的基金会已超过 7500 家。刚才几位是在讨论指数，接下来有请何日生先生，他要讲的是善经济的思想与实践，他是慈济大学人文社会学院教授。

善经济的思想与实践

善经济倡导者、慈济人文志业发展处主任　何日生

感恩大家今天给我这个机会分享善经济。我们的概念是怎么样把慈善中的善运用到经济社会中，从源头的动机开始就是善，实践的方法也是善，而不是制造问题以后，或者污染了环境以后再用所谓的“慈善”弥补它。

善是什么？东西方的角度不同，西方哲学的始祖柏拉图讲“至善”（summum bonum），强调真理，善就是追求至高的真理，重视理念而忽视物质，因为物质是容易改变的。西方对至高真理之追求源于柏拉图，基督教则强调唯一的真神——上帝是至高的真理，但有了至高的真理后，就形成了一种我是善、你是恶，我是对、你是错的思维，最后导致战争与冲突的善恶之斗。

亚里士多德后来修正了他的老师——柏拉图的哲学，他认为苹果的理念离不开苹果自身。心与物必须融合，物质欲望的基本满足是人的天性，也能激发人的积极动机。所以，他的思想是结合心与物，兼备理与事，走出了中道。

亚里士多德的理念接近中国善的观念。中国善的观念着重现实生活的幸福与道德的圆满生命。《礼记》讲道：“虽有至道，弗学，不知其善也。”这是孔子讲的话，虽然是至高的真理，但真理必须是善。学，即实践。真理必须通过实践，才知道其益处。善不是以真理框限每一个人，而是造福每一个人。虽有最高的真理，如果不能让人获益，这真理就不善。

所以真理必须是善，对于生命的完整性，善比真理还要究竟。中国的善就是利益万民、利益万物。所以连主张生命要复归于“无”的老子都强调：“上善若水，水善利万物而不争，处众人之所恶，故几于道。”善利万物，连恶都要去靠近、去帮助。孔子也说“博施于民而能济众”就是圣人，谁能够广博地施予众生、帮助众生，谁就是一个圣人，所以善是利他，为他人利益着想，为他人服务。

孟子也说，“可欲之谓善”，“充实之谓美”，满足人民所需要的就是善，每个百姓都拥有幸福才是美。佛教里也说慈悲喜舍，要无缘大慈，同体大悲。众生都是关照的对象，众生都是自己的一部分，用无私的大爱与万物、众生相结合，这是佛教从利他到觉悟的至高境界。彻底地利他，才能实现万物共荣。所以，从东方思想来说，善就是利他的意思。不是打击恶，而是教化恶，直到世间一切的恶都转化为善。

达尔文的进化论也认为，从进化过程中所衍生出来的是一种“利他”的精神，人类等各种物种能够生存下来的，都是互助和利他的物种，具备“利他”精神的物种是优势的物种。现代的医学科学家也发现动物身上有慈悲利他区块，称为“temporal cortex”。实验室中，当老鼠看到同类被杀害，慈悲利他区块会放大。人类也一样，看到他人布施，或他人苦难，自己的慈悲利他区块会放大。所以慈悲利他可以被激发、可以被放大。只要我们认知到，利他比起利己更有助于自我与群体的发展，人类会更积极地、更大幅度地实践利他。

互助、共荣才是人类真正强大和净化的动力。我在慈善领域工作了 18 年，在慈济服务学习，看到很多企业家做慈善以后发生了改变，他们把善的概念、爱的想法带进企业，用从公益行善到日常生活中乃至经营企业中的一切善行，从利己转变成利他的心态，来实践在经济生活中的善。

所以，善经济这个理念就是要引导我们深刻体悟“利他利己、利众利润”的企业哲学，能利他就会利己，能利众就会有利润。善行会在心灵层面、企业信誉度以及人际关系上产生良性循环的效应，自然地累积善财。所以，利他作为企业永续发展的根本，会带动企业家们在经营实践当中，以善致富。

亚里士多德是第一个提出善经济概念的人，他认为经济活动的目的是幸福而不是金钱，一味追求金钱是愚昧的，人要幸福一定要有爱的关系，参与公共事务，并且要持守道德、具备哲学的反思能力与遵循心灵的快乐，这是亚里士多德在 2000 多年前就提出来的善经济思想。

西方经济近代资本的善，不像西方近当代纯为个人享乐的极致化，也不是韦伯眼中的新教企业伦理，而是鼓励企业家在追求事功的满足中来荣耀上帝，但是，荣耀上帝是无止境的，所以追求事业的扩张也是无止境的。这是西方近当代资本主义的信仰基石。中国传统的经济观是以造福家族、造福乡里为职责，就像 15 世纪山西商人席铭所说的：“丈夫苟不能立功名于世，抑岂不能树基业于家哉！”商者树立家族的基业，跟儒者闻达于世是一样的，都在厚生利世。

“和合”，这个概念很重要，以中国古代的小农经济言之，幸福不是个人拥有多少财富，而是拥有多少爱的关系，家庭的、宗族的、社会的以及更大群体的爱的关联。中国的经济观就是人要顺天，跟天要合，自然资源是丰沛的，人要珍惜它，跟天地共融；考虑我们所爱的人之福祉，顾及全社会的福祉，创造群体社会的福祉，以国家的整体发展为前提，以地球的永续为目标，顺应天地，不违天地之道法。所以《周易》才有这句话：“夫大人者，与天地合其德，与日月合其明，与四时合其序，与鬼神合其吉凶。先天而天弗违，后天而奉天时。天且弗违，而况于人乎？”所以“和合”，是很重要的善的方法。

中国龙的图腾，就是古代中国各大民族融合、和合的一个象征。在距今

8000年的文物上，就已有蛇身鹿角的形态，蛇的部落跟鹿的部落打完仗之后谁也没有被消灭，而是相互融合了，所以蛇身上长着鹿角。再跟鱼的部落融合了，所以长着鱼鳞。再跟鸟的部落融合了，龙又长了能够飞翔的翅膀。龙，是一次次民族大融合的象征，代表一种信念与价值。只有利他、和合才能够共生共荣。

哈佛大学给阿里巴巴写过一个很好的个案，说它怎么成功，说它的缺点在哪里。事实上，阿里巴巴传承了龙的文化，它结合大、中、小企业的横向合作，结合上、中、下游企业的垂直合作，创造了世界上最大的互联网帝国。它把金融也放进来，缔造了支付宝系统。它通过整合将一切可能是对立的、阻碍的因素，变成助力与协力。这是共容、共享、共荣。这是善方法，不经由对抗，而是通过合作协力，收获自己与他人善经济的果实。

所以，善是什么？是利他，其方式则是和合。由善的动机，到善的方法，到善的结果，这三者具备以后才能够达到善经济的要求。这个概念是从慈济兴建台北医院的过程中发展出来的，创办人证严上人希望一座爱的医院必须以爱来兴建。建医院的目的是爱，建的过程中就必须有爱。慈济志工以关怀的态度，以循循善诱的方式，引导工人不抽烟、不喝酒、不吃槟榔，还乐于吃素。志工也投入清理与整洁工作，让工地随时处在干净的环境中。

爱的成果以爱的方式打造。善的结果必须出于善的动机和以善的方法获得。如今台北慈济医院规模宏大，医疗服务、人文备受称许，营业状况亦十分良好。从慈善机构的以善致善，到经济领域的以善致富，所以没有必要的恶，只有必要的善。消灭恶并不是打击恶，是扩大善。消灭贫也不是打击富有，是扩大爱。

亚当·斯密一直强调说，人是因为自利才开始从事商业，每个人都自利之后会创造更大规模的公益。在几百年资本主义的发展过程中，人们发觉自利不能创造更大规模的公益，每个商人的背后有一种利他的精神，当商人知道消费者要什么所以才创造什么的时候，最后结果也会是利他。

近代很有名的“囚徒困境”，用到经济学中也是一个很有名的理论，“囚徒困境”告诉我们两个囚徒只有互相合作才能创造更大的利益，如果各自守着自我利益，互相抵消，互相出卖，两个人都不能获益，只有互助和互利才能真正实现共赢，达到公共利益的最大值。

这也是经济学上的“帕累托最优”（Pareto Optimality）所提到的，在不减少既有任何一个人福利的前提下，设法增加某些人的福利，让经济资源分配达到可能的最理想状态。只有靠利他才能够让经济资源分配达到帕累托最优。所以善经济强调利他利己，它的前提是慈悲心跟同理心，只有利益万物人类才能免除目前这么多的冲突，地球才能免于逐渐崩解的危机。

在当代，资本主义强调生产极大化，生产是维持人类生活及幸福之前提，但是当生产和消费过度，人就会迷失在物质里，以物质的满足为幸福，这是物化了我们的生命，它恰恰与幸福的追求背道而驰。所以证严上人提出“珍惜物命”这个概念，这也是佛法的教导，众生皆有佛性，生产的善是基于万物皆有生命的立场去爱护物命，这样就不会极大化生产。

要想极大化就要标准化、要分工，所以工人就如同机械般工作，沦为机械体制框架下的生产工具。人性的尊重与创意全被抹杀。这是当代生产的危机。所以要爱惜物命、爱惜自我，欲望不要完全放在追逐物欲的需求上，不要被欲望奴役，让物质耗竭了自己的生命。所以珍惜物命、珍惜自我，是善经济很重要的一个观点，能够这样，就会达到利他为本、和合共善的理想状态。

接下来讲一下企业利他的核心概念。

乔布斯从 22 岁到 50 多岁往生，从创立苹果计算机到经营好莱坞动漫产业再到回苹果公司发展 iPhone，一个核心信念始终没有变，就是相信“以我们的热情，我们可以改变这个世界，并且使它变得更好”。这个核心信念的本质是利他。他提到产品如果跟环保抵触就不要设计，这是一种非常重要的立业精神。

马来西亚伟特集团创办人朱振荣是慈济的志工，他在加入慈济以后，把慈济的爱跟善引进企业，结果 7 年当中，企业扩大了 10 倍，目前是马来西亚第二大科技厂。他的夫人打造了人文空间，提倡爱和善的价值，这样的空间让大家有更多的互动机会。里面有书、有茶、有咖啡、有讲座、有用环保回收物制作的产品。工程师随时可以离开工作岗位，在这里沉思、做计划、讨论。朱振荣要打造一个爱的大家庭给员工。

朱振荣鼓励并带领员工做环保，保护环境，从事慈善事业，投入慈善事业。2017 年槟城遭遇大水患，他的 300 名工程师每天轮流到灾区赈灾，每天至少有 150 名员工在灾区当志工，赈灾完毕再回工厂做事，没有人要求加班费。所有人都在用爱跟善来体现企业人义，周一到周四都是素食。它是以一个信念为核心、以价值来引导、以爱来管理、以原则来治理的善企业指标，所以，我们相信投入慈善会更有助于企业的善跟经济的善。

善企业的 10 项修炼法则就是：以核心价值为理念，以价值来引导，以原则来治理，以爱来管理，以慈悲来创造，创造一个平等的圆形组织，以利他来创新，以典范来传承，与地球共生息，与万物共享共荣。我们期许建构一个善企业、善经济的时代，企业是善，物质就是善。希望善的理想能够体现在世界，也希望中国的善经济成为全球经济的典范，中国的善企业成为全球企业的标杆。

刘培峰：谢谢何日生先生善企业、善经济的分享，接下来请论坛学术委员会委员、香港中文大学社会工作学系教授及系主任倪锡钦教授演讲，谢谢。

中国公益慈善人才的培养机制和项目探索

论坛学术委员会委员、香港中文大学社会工作学系教授及系主任　倪锡钦

大家早上好，首先我想特别感谢我们的主办方给大家参与讨论的机会。我们的大会开得特别成功。在大会召开的两天里，我们也听了非常有启迪性的演讲。我希望我们今天能继续做出精彩的演讲。今天我讲讲怎么样培养慈善和公益方面的领导人，我想和大家举几个我们的例子。

我的演讲包括三个部分。第一个部分是为什么我们要培养慈善领域的领导人。第二个部分是怎么样培养慈善和公益方面的人才。第三个部分是我们对未来的展望。

从培养人才的原因上看，我想从我们的一些反思开始讲。第一，我们一直在不断地观察、了解目前非政府组织、慈善组织在人才培养方面存在的问题。通过观察，我们发现目前有很多慈善方面的培训，但是同质化程度非常的高，而且一般的培训可能只是展示想法，比如说如何招募志愿者，等等。与此同时，我们发现社会快速发展以及非慈善组织在亚洲迅速出现，很多从业者遇到了更多挑战和困难，所以需要更多的培训，比如他们如何应对技术方面带来的挑战。由于我们发现了人才培养当中的问题，所以我们在思考应该怎么样做。第二，我们收集了很多来自政府特别是中国政府的数据，我们的民政部在 2017 年发表的报告当中提到了，在中国有 900 万人在慈善基金会和公益组织等工作。当我们提到所谓的公益慈善领军人物时，20% 都是属于管理岗以上的人才，他们是主席、高级管理人员，等等。还有一个来自清华大学的研究，他们是 2018 年做的调研，由此我们发现有 40% 以上的慈善从业者有硕士及以上的学位。我们发现，我们可以为他们提供慈善教育和慈善

培训方面的学位认证。第三，有 60% 的从业者希望能够接受系统性的、结构性的培训。而有 69% 以上的学生非常想要接受短期的培训；60% 的学生觉得需要提升技能，以更好地服务于公益慈善行业。所以我们后来和政府进行了沟通。香港中文大学社会工作学系成立于 1964 年，2019 年是我们成立的第 55 周年，我们到现在培养了 7000 多名学生。我们有研究项目、硕士学位和博士学位，以及博士培养站。我们的毕业生有些进入了非政府组织，有些到社会前线工作，有些去本地或者国际院校教学，他们之中还有一些正确社会政策的分析者。

在此背景下，我们致力于对人才的培养，包括非政府组织和政府机构。我们有一个非政府组织的项目，提供多学科融合的培训和指导，这个项目是从 2015 年开始的，现在已经有 5 年的经验。这个项目是为了创造环境，让所有的参与者都能够提高管理能力，这样的话他们可以更好地了解，达成目标。这个项目也包括来自不同组织的人员，他们在此能得到媒体和社会方面的培训与指导，他们可以以团队的形式出现，相互学习、相互教育。我们这个项目是由瑞士银行（UBS）支持的，也有香港的教育从业者、媒体人的参与，他们会参与我们的导师团队。最后他们要去融资，成功的组织将会拿到奖金支持活动。UBS 包括《南华早报》是我们主要的合作者。

接下来想和大家探讨我们所带来的影响，我们只有过去 4 年的数据。如果我回学校的话，可以给大家展示更多 2019 年的数据。在过去 4 年当中，我们已经帮助了 103 个学生，这些帮助来自 87 个不同的组织。因为不同的组织服务不同的人群，我们在香港已经总计服务了超过 300 万人。

还有一个项目，我们是从香港的赛马会拿到的资金，叫赛马会“衡坊”培训计划。我们希望通过这样有资质的培训项目，让很多导师参与进来，这些导师是来自本地和海外的专家，我们的项目通过线上的知识平台帮助学生加强他们的学习体验。学习课程包括发展、监管、资源规划管理、媒体沟通、项目评估和影响力评估，所有的参与者都是非政府组织的成员。3 年来，我们有 240 个成员参与了这个项目。我们也在官网上公布了 100 种评估工具。我们和联合国教科文组织合作，帮香港特区政府、澳门特区政府和中国内地做了大量的项目。我们有不同层级的评估工具来评估社会影响力。同时我们提供了视频培训、导师培训，在学员毕业之后，他们需要回到自己的组织和同事进行分享。

2019 年 5~7 月，我们招募了 120 多名参与者。我们的培训包括两个部分，2019 年一个部分，2020 年一个部分，一直到 2021 年。最后我们会有专门的国际大会，包括媒体大会，宣传进一步的进展。

第一个大会将是华人社会工作教育论坛，我们会招募 30 多名慈善从业者开展华人社会工作教育合作。在 2018 年的 12 月份，我们在香港举办了一个峰会，聚焦于慈善领域的问题。在那次的论坛上，我们探讨了很多行业问题，比如社会工作中博士水平的人才培训，同时我们有创新的社会工作教学法的实践，我们也希望对非营利组织负责人产生影响。华人社会工作行业的联系网络遍布中国台湾、澳门，新加坡，美国，包括其他的地区和国家。

最后一个部分，我们要做的是设立社会服务管理的硕士学位点，这是我们和清华大学合作的，是一个硕士学位项目，主要关注社会服务管理，清华大学的老师负责教学。清华大学的教学团队将教授 7 门课程、10 个单元。我们的团队会负责 5 门课程、15 个单元的教学。最后学生会拿到香港中文大学社会服务管理（北京）文学硕士证书，同时学生可以申请到清华大学的结业证书。我们希望未来在中国有更多的社会工作领域的管理人出现，因为现在市场需要这样的人才。

接下来该怎么做？我们将会很快举办另外的会议。2018 年在香港，2019 年我们会在澳门召开华人社会工作大会。我们也会带来更多的机会，我们和瑞士银行沟通过，其也希望有更多的针对社会组织和非政府组织领导人的培训。最后，我们希望尽可能地在中国内地做一个关于提供社会服务管理的博士学位的项目。谢谢，这是我的基本演讲。

刘培峰：谢谢。现在请李亚平女士演讲。

国际公益人才培养计划：中国香港及泰国参访汇报

深圳市企业评价协会常务副会长兼秘书长 李亚平

首先我非常感谢主办方，我也觉得非常荣幸，因为我将代表第一期的同学在这里向大家做汇报。我们进行的是对中国香港和泰国的参访，现在我将针对整个公益慈善领域的参观学习做一个汇报。

我们当时第一站走访了港中大，其从理论的层面告诉我们，国际上慈善组织有怎样的理论架构，它们的项目管理和品牌推广如何进行。后面对所有的公益慈善领域非常重要的人才培养项目进行了详细的介绍。马教授向我们介绍了做非营利机构领袖项目计划的起源，包括全程跟踪的评估、成效的展示对推动公益慈善工作的重要性。内地在这个事情上很困惑，做的方式方法不是很恰当、成效不是很明显，这一点我也会做一个详细的介绍。我们也参访了香港红十字会——具有国际体系影响力的机构。还有一个就是香港民爱机构。我们还到泰国看了联合国开发计划署的工作坊，详细的工作内容我后面再介绍，这是我们之前没有想到的成效。洛克菲勒基金会是一个家族企业的基金会，在世界上布局的网络有非常健全的体系。至于其给我们带来的借鉴是什么，后面我也会说一下。

首先我想介绍一下非营利机构领袖项目计划三方合作模式。其实是瑞银提出的需求，然后港中大进行人才的培养，但我们的基金会做一些项目的时候，不知道哪些机构可以帮它们实施。于是它们觉得需要建立一个体系培养这些人才，后面我们跟港中大理论加实务型的教授组成团队，和瑞银一起建立培育计划的体系。需求方是清晰的，人才培养的体系框架也是清晰的，在培养的过程中，最后会对项目成效进行评估。在课程的教学方面，包括和项目的结合落实非常实，这和内地所实施的培养计划是不太一样的。很重要的一点是做到知行合一，我们学到的理论知识一步一步指导实践，在这个过程中，整个项目的创新和实践的结合是非常明晰的。最后马教授跟我们分享了一些数据，我看了之后非常惊讶，因为做了 4 年，有 103 名成员，成立了 87 个机构，300 万人有收益。在这个过程中，有 87 个创新项目，组织能力的提升是非常清晰的。这里也提到有 4 个项目赢得了 360 万港币的支持。总之，对于香港中文大学的参与者和非营利机构的合作研究，层次是非常清晰的。

在这个过程中集合了不同的社会资源，有 40 个培训师、31 位导师，还有不同的参与者形成了互助学习的社群，展示的时候我感到非常惊讶。从项目设计到项目实施，所有社会资源的参与和融入、最后结果的展示、社会相关群体的规模，以及项目实施领域都非常清晰。对内地人才培养方面有非常强的借鉴意义。

介绍人才培养体系的项目，我们思考了一下，应注意以下几点。第一，我们要了解需求，把真实的诉求挖出来。从项目执行体系上讲，在哪些阶段满足它。第二，相关的咨询。做这件事哪些群体可以参与进来，我们用哪些方式把这些信息发出来。第三，加入的方式。在项目执行的参与度上，他以怎样的身份在这个平台上有收获。第四，高校有很强的理论体系支撑，在项目执行过程中发挥了非常重要的作用。但是院校的人才理论体系给这个项目的支撑是怎样的？从行动力上讲，这种支撑是给人才自己的，在实施的过程中，会为人才提供理论的指导和支持。第五，人才创新项目能够落地，产成一定的成果，这是很重要的。马教授介绍的时候说，每年的 9 月份，他会为这一年的创新项目举办成果大赛，通过开放的方式，让社会了解这个项目是怎样的，同时会邀请社会机构，包括政府部门，对成果的落地进行持续性展示，得到各方的检验。第六，在这个过程中，一次一次进行资源的叠加，进行多元资源的配合。

我们考察了香港明爱的服务体系，它有一个比较完善的义工体系为机构运营提供长期支持。深圳也是一个志愿城市，做得比较早，也建立了不同的体系，但是我们是通过义工联进行管理。对于深圳义工联自己的机构，能够吸引和维系 1 万名义工，长期在项目中提供实际行动的支持，对我们来说则需要思考很多。义工怎么样获得个人的成长或者是资源的叠加？这个机构的义工会影响自己身边的亲人，不断作为传播者，为这个机构吸引更多的义工。此外，香港有 256 个服务单位，服务点超过 152 个，在不同的地方为市民提供服务，这对我们来说，一个机构很难有这么大的网络体系做这么多的点。而且它有资金来源，有政府部门的，有企业的，有不同社团的，还有经营主体的。一个机构的资金来源具有多样性，那么在相关信息的匹配上，它应如何和主体进行交织，获得更多的资源？明爱的服务领域主要包括：教育、医疗、筹款活动。

去泰国的时候，洛克菲勒的设计也是让我们比较惊讶的。在联合国开发计划署的时候我们经历了一个奇妙的创作过程，泰国联合机构，包括参访的同学，共同探讨了“一带一路”倡议下公益组织发展机遇和挑战。就是说每个机构在同一主题下，视角是非常多元的，最后形成的结果也是非常多元的。在这个体系下，每个组织、每种视角如何按照自己的功能或者需求融入这件事？最后给我们一些启发，我们如何融入“一带一路”和粤港澳大湾区的发展？在革新创新上和学习相关经验方面，我们的收获非常丰富，看到香港社会组织所做的工作非常到位。去了泰国之后，我们开始思考不同的基金会和社会服务机构应该如何形成公益生态圈。我今天的分享到这里，谢谢。

刘培峰：谢谢。我们请深圳市恒晖儿童公益基金会创始人陈行甲先生发言。

国际公益人才培养计划：菲律宾及越南参访汇报

深圳市恒晖儿童公益基金会创始人　陈行甲

谢谢主持人，谢谢大家，非常感谢主办方给我这样一个机会，向大家报告我参加国际公益人才培养计划的学习体会。刚才李亚平汇报了其参加第一期国际公益人才培养计划的学习收获，我参加的是第二期，总体来说，参加完国际公益人才培养计划后，我有非常大的收获。我们通过这一次学习，学到了很多国际上先进的公益组织的管理和运营经验，也带去了中国公益组织的经验和做法，同时向菲律宾和越南的公益组织传递了中国社会对国际社会的接纳、包容和虚心学习的态度。

我是代表深圳的公益组织出行，一行有 10 多个人，我是一个人从深圳出发的，其他人从北京出发。他们从北京出发的时候，在机场进行民主选举，就是选谁为团长，后来北京的同事选举我当团长。团长的任务是走在最前面，听课坐最前排，吃饭坐最中间，每一次讲课、每一次课程的总结和现场发言都是团长做的，所以这个活并不轻松，但是也让我在学习过程中全神贯注。

我按照学习脉络和过程汇报一下我们的学习收获。我们和菲律宾的乐视会（音）进行了深入的交流，让我对这个优秀的国际慈善组织的理念，有了非常具象的认识和了解，也近距离学习了国际慈善组织的运营经验，体验了它们的文化，感受到春风化雨的力量。这次的学习让我了解到乐视会在世界各地的布局，了解到它务实及创新的方法，看到了它在改善生活、持续发展、积极回应人道危机、提供救援、协助恢复生计、推行公众教育运动等方面的努力。我们也近距离感受到了，这样一个在公益界长盛不衰的组织得以发展的原因。我们和菲律宾的气候变化公益组织逐一交流，也学习了解了菲律宾公益组织参与解决社会问题的广度和深度，以及公益组织与地方政府的良性互动。我们也请来了一位市长，讲述菲律宾政府与公益组织如何合作推动一些社会问题的解决。

我讲一下作为团长在菲律宾的奇遇，我讲奇遇之前问大家一个问题，有多少人知道晏阳初先生？他是一位非常伟大的历史人物。晏阳初出生于四川的巴中，是世界知名的贫民教育家，也是我的人生偶像。我在基层当过官，当过中国百强县的县长，也当过国家级贫困县的县委书记。我在担任国家级贫困县县委书记期间，受到了中共中央的表彰，受到习近平总书记的亲切接见。我可能是中国第一个被提拔之后辞职的政府工作人员，为什么？我从县委书记任上辞职之后来到深圳，创办了一个公益组织，因为我有一个梦想，希望做这个时代的“晏阳初”。因此大家可以知道我跟这样的历史伟人的缘分，我惊奇地发现，晏阳初的墓地居然就在菲律宾国际乡村建设研究院，我在这个地方待了一整天，感受晏阳初为人类奉献的崇高精神。这一天的学习总结，我改变了形式，我在现场写了一首歌——《先生，我从你的故国来看你了》。课程总结的时候，我用英文把这首诗念给菲律宾的朋友。那天在现场，菲律宾国际乡村建设研究院的院长很有感触，所以他把我的诗分享给了晏阳初当年创建国际乡村建设研究院时该院的老理事长，现在的理事长是当年老理事长的孙子，他叫乔治。特别荣幸的是在世界公益慈善论坛期间，乔治单独接见了我两个半小时，我们一起讨论晏阳初先生的人类精神。我特别荣幸地告诉大家，世界著名的慈善家就在我们会场，让我们给乔治掌声。这是我参访期间非常特别的缘分。我们也拜访了越南友好组织协会，还拜访了其他的公益组织，学习它们的经验，也传递了中国民间组织对于越南的善意，沟通了和越南合作的可能性。

下面我和大家汇报一下学习代表团的感想。爱是人类最共通的秉性，是人类最美好的品质和最朴素的情感，所以公益慈善是天然的、最好的民间外交语言。我们响应中国的“一带一路”倡议，我们公益组织应在其中发挥更重要的作用。现在对于“一带一路”倡议，国际上有些国家有些微词，认为我们搞势力扩张，在这种背景下，我们通过公益组织和民间交流，广泛地在民间增进友好和互信，这是一种低成本、高收益的民间外交。最后我想说的是，深圳市把400多家公益基金会联合起来，成立深圳市基金会发展促进会。我很荣幸在一周前当选为深圳市基金会发展促进会的首任执行会长。我们这个组织成立了3个专门委员会为大家服务，一个是学术支持委员会，一个是投资顾问委员会，一个是国际交流合作委员会。我们希望通过公益组织的国际交流合作，提升整个深圳的公益组织的治理水平，我们的眼界、我们的视野能够促进我们整个国家和社会的和谐建设。这就是我给大家报告的学习体会，再一次感谢大家，谢谢。

刘培峰：谢谢陈行甲，他给我们讲了很多有趣的故事，谢谢。按照会议的安排，我们有两位评议人，他们是法伊兹·沙阿博士和阮金恩女士。

阮金恩：非常感谢大家提到了越南。大家早上好。我很高兴代表越南农村可持续发展中心参与世界公益慈善论坛，我本人在越南农村可持续发展中心担任常务主任。我访问过世界各地的和本地的非政府组织，我想和大家分享几个实例。在越南有两种非政府组织：国际非政府组织和当地非政府组织。国际非政府组织由国外提供资金支持，由外国人运营，而当地非政府组织由越南人运营，运营资金来自国内和国外。当地非政府组织是非营利组织，通过自我管理生存，在越南有越来越多这样的组织。当地非政府组织关注诸如气候变化、性别平等和农业发展方面的问题。在越南，非政府组织的网络中有两条线：一是气候变化网络，一是政府网络。我们和 130 多个非政府组织合作，主要关注农业、宜居等问题，我们也非常关注行业政策、性别平等等问题。作为一个当地非政府组织，我们和社区紧密合作。在过去 13 年的运营过程中，我们一直在和农村地区的人群打交道，我们已经有 2 万多名直接的受益人。我们也不断改善他们的生活状况和条件，我们也进行教育和项目教研。我们现在是越南领先的非政府组织，得到了越南政府的支持。越南现在有越来越多的非政府组织，它们希望获得更多的资金和支持，以帮助穷人和残疾人群。谢谢。

法伊兹·沙阿：首先谢谢主办方邀请我进行点评。用 5 分钟总结今天各位演讲人提到的精彩之处是不可能的，我想说一下我自己的想法，以及曼谷慈善事业的发展。我们提到了孟加拉国在过去一段时间将慈善事业转换成了带来回报的社会产业。大家提到了世界诺贝尔奖的得主，他认为人们希望向别人展示善意，给予别人更多的好处，人们辛勤工作并将所学所得和他人分享，人们感谢善意和给予。我们可以看到随着中国社会愈加富裕，这一点展现在了中国。现在的人们特别希望能够去提升公益组织的公信力，并且更多地赋能给我们的公益和慈善。如果大家感兴趣的话，可以给需要的人 1 美元，但是这还不够，我们可以把慈善资金投入社会组织，然后由社会组织做影响力投资。这样的话，我们就能够更好地推行我们的想法。虽然可以从慈善家那里拿钱，创立企业，但这不是为了赚钱，而是为了解决社会问题，所以很多社会组织可以帮助解决社会问题。我们可以通过创建企业的形式帮助解决社会问题，而不只是用钱解决问题，比如儿童教育、女性教育，这样的情况下我们可以创建社会企业来解决这个问题。我们知道世界上现在有 50 多家社会组织在市场中进行竞争，它们不享有免税待遇，它们自己赚钱，而且帮助解决问题，如交通、卫生安全问题，这是我们现在在智慧城市建设中面临的问题。因为我们的社会组织可以帮助我们解决问题，所以大家可以把钱捐赠给社会组织，然后通过企业运营的形式提供服务，而政府也可以给这些企业减税以减轻负担。此外，我们希望建立学习机制，有一些国家正在做这种项目。我们形成了包含 79 个大学的联盟，有 5 所是中国的大学。我们叫作慈善公益组织和高校联盟，我们总是时不时地碰面，更好地促进信息的交流、研究和合作。如果各位有兴趣的话，可以加入我们。我们的联盟会议将于 2020 年 11 月在柏林举行，我希望有更多人可以加入我们。我们现在需要建立学习机制。我们怎么样完善这个慈善组织，提高公信力？这是需要思考的。一个好的点子背后必须要有充足的资金支持，如果没有资金支持，即使有好的点子也不会成功。所以我们要给好的点子以资金，让它们更好地成长。我们需要建立这些渠道，我们也希望在第四届世界公益慈善论坛中交更多的朋友，打造善的经济。同时我们了解到学界和高校的合作，比如如何将项目推进，让我们更好地释放出社会组织的价值。我就讲这么多，谢谢。

刘培峰：谢谢法伊兹·沙阿先生。我们将进入休息时间。

刘培峰：请各位入座。欢迎各位，也感谢各位对我的支持，因为我知道台上有专家、学者和非营利组织的负责人，没有办法把你们每一个人请上台，我代表会议的主办方对大家表示歉意。我们现在开始讨论，主要是两个问题。第一，如何看待公益指数？我们越来越关注社会组织的就业、社会组织为社会提供了多少服务、怎么样吸引高净值的人群作为最重要的指标，我们的问题是如何看待这些指标。在这些指标里，对社会有着最重要贡献的倡导组织、维权组织如何？如果我们关注了高净值人群，对普通人的服务被放到这个体系中我们应如何看待？我还想和大家讨论，我们的导向是世界在变还是自己在变？因为非政府组织在推动民主力量中的贡献是很大的，而我们现在关注它对社会服务的贡献。第二，我们如何看待公益人才培养模式？因为公益人才培养是大家共同关注的话题。刚才各位讲了国外的情况，国内我们有清华大学公益慈善研究院、深圳国际公益学院，它们都做专业的人才培养，业界也做了大量的培训。但是我们会看到一些问题，因为职业培训特别像传销。我们怎么样把这个东西做得更加符合现在的需要，我要听各位的高见。我希望每一个人讲的时候讲自己最亮的点，时间短一些，给后面的人一些发言的机会。现在请夏露萍女士回答。

夏露萍：您刚才提到的第一个问题是如何评估所谓的影响。我本人遇到过很多亚洲的高净值人群。非营利组织会问一个问题：您的组织是否能够帮助我们在中国内地、香港地区和国际上募资？我的回答一般是一样的。我觉得非营利组织要把自己的故事讲给其他人听，我发现组织需要将自己得到的资金和使用资金的方法在官网上展现出来。我发现这样透明的组织会吸引到更多资源，因为公司觉得这些组织的资金管理非常到位，所以愿意为这些非营利组织募资。第二个问题是我们如何引进、培训人才。因为现在亚洲地区的财富累计达到了历史高值，这是新趋势。我来到中国的时候是 1984 年，当时的中国和现在完全不同，过去近 40 年，中国的财富累计非常惊人。如果你来自贫困的家庭，你会想要成为律师、银行家或公务员，现在最大的区别在于年轻人有了更多的选择，因为他们不一定要去关注自己收入的底线。很多的年轻人选择回报社会，进入社会服务领域，一部分年轻人建立社会企业和社会组织。现在整个慈善业已经成为一个行业，因为有慈善服务和社会服务的需求，这是一个非常好的信号。

贾西津：我回应第一个问题，因为我介绍的是民间研究指数。我自己参与过相关的指数研究，除了我自己参与的之外，还可以看到同道们做的各种指数，这是非常多的，所以我一开始说，这样的指数非常多，它们相互之间的意义在哪儿？如何看待这些指数？刘培峰提出的问题很核心，这些指数最重要的是关注的目的，我们到底要通过一个指数评什么？不同目的带来不同的关注点，比如在中国，在社会发展比较初期的时候，不管是指数还是研究者，大家关注的都是结构性的东西，所以研究指数非常热，特别是 20 世纪 90 年代末到 2000 年中期。但是这些年，我们看到中国有越来越多的科学化的研究，越来越多的人才加入。大家的关注点会转向慈善领域，或者是服务领域，所以它的点会变得更小。之间的关系有点像社会分工和社会学想实现的宏观图景，这种社会分工要具体化才能研究得细，但是也要宏观图景，我们走向专业化，有更多具体的指数可以用来衡量是非常有意义的事情。比如非营利部门占 GDP 的多少，比如富人捐赠的特点和难点。但是仅仅有分工的时候，我们需要想一下我们的结构，每一个发生的现象、每一个公益人的参与、每个人的行为，最后的目标在哪里，我们想要实现什么。我们不是为了社工而做社工，我们不是为了给予而给予，而是背后有意义的。CSI 的方法并不是那么完善和科学，为什么我们愿意每 7 年做一次，我想它的角度非常值得我们思考，会提醒我们整个社会发展的结构是怎样的，所以不仅仅是给予，不仅仅是捐赠，所有的是点，但这样的现象背后，我们要看到社会的架构。我们的结果也发现，社会部门越来越大、人才越来越多，我们做的事越来越精密化、科学化，提供的服务更加多了。但是从社会本身治理的概念上讲，作为一个治理的主体，意味着一种进步，是自生自发的秩序，是社会的结构所在。自发的社会和被管理的社会是不一样的，这种结构的意义是更大了还是更小了？从我们来看，这是值得思考的问题，而从业人员也要回溯，到底参与是为了什么？

刘培峰：谢谢。我们请艾莉森·霍洛韦尔女士发言。

艾莉森·霍洛韦尔：第一，在您提到的怎么样衡量影响力方面，我们要有一些框架，我们需要有一些大家都认可的框架用来衡量我们的影响力。因为很多慈善机构说，我们有捐赠人，所以我们有不同的考核标准给到捐赠人，告诉他们我们做了什么，看一下我们的影响力。所以要有捐赠人共同确认的框架，AVPN 也有衡量影响力的项目。我们也用了最多的指标去衡量我们项目的影响力，也希望带到亚洲，让合作伙伴更好地适用衡量的标准。第二，我们必须拿到对社会组织的反馈。大家都觉得反馈很重要，我们希望知道捐赠方的想法，同时在现实情况下，我们并不是很自然地给反馈，所以我们和美国的一个基金会一起合作做一个反馈项目。我们希望做一个项目可以跟几个比较大的基金会合作，我们几个基金会共同资助了一个项目，叫作向上倾听。我们采访慈善机构的捐赠方，比如去到银行捐赠的人，我们会问他，你捐赠的时候的感受是怎样的？你受帮助的时候有没有感觉尊严受到伤害？有没有被真正帮助到？我们希望听到双向的反馈，然后看一下我们的项目到底怎么样。因为我们认为影响力的平衡是非常重要的，它可以使我们把工作做得更好，所以这些针对我们未来影响力的报告是很重要的。第三，人才的开发和准备。现在有 35% 的亚洲财富会在接下来的 5~7 年传替到下一代的手里，很多财富家族认识到，在让年轻一代掌握财富的时候，要更好地利用财富工具影响慈善，所以我们也希望更好地引导新财富继承者的花钱之道，帮助他们更好地促进慈善和公益。我们希望动用所有成员的力量，我们有 585 个成员，他们都有自己的案例和实践，我们现在做了在线的平台，叫作 AVPN 学术，这是一个自学习的平台，在这个平台上，我们会提交大家的想法，帮助各个慈善机构做人才开发。这是我们和成员探讨的，也希望大家关注我们的项目。

刘培峰：下面请何日生先生发言。

何日生：谢谢。在中国的智慧里，老子讲“反者道之动”，任何一种大道在进行一个反作用力时，在一个正向里都可以看到抵消的力量。所谓的与天斗，黑格尔讲了一个辩证法，最后是希望和，达到更高的理想目标。最后归于一个善的概念。面对恶的看法，中国是靠近恶、挽救恶，并不是把恶消灭，其实是要教化恶，这样大慈悲的概念才能真正地整合。从这个角度来看，我们是扩大善、扩大爱，而不是打击恶、打击富有。把善扩大，这是典范。在你倡议一个事情的时候，你要有典范的建立，一切还没有开始的时候，典范是少数，典范建立以后，很多人愿意跟随。我们会有信息流，然后让社会慢慢接受你。所以你要赋予和赋能，一开始要建立典范。所以不是你要求他，而是让他感动然后跟随你，所以建立典范，达到一个程度后赋能给他，让更多人加入这个行列。但也要有信念，不然所有的创新会对这个社会产生负面的影响。刘教授提出非常好的问题，就是善和恶之间怎么样对待，没有一个是永恒的，我们能够在不同的时代提出不同的观点，一个新的东西总是有反对的力量，接纳反对的力量才能让结果更圆满，谢谢。

刘培峰：谢谢。我们请倪锡钦教授发言。

倪锡钦：我想回答第二个问题，就是对公益慈善人才的培养。在我们和清华大学开展合作项目期间，我们花了很多时间了解并评估它的影响力和具体的方法论，我们希望这个人才项目对公益慈善行业有益。我想从项目的内容和架构方面分享经验。我们要打造一种文化，去促进大家的分享。今天我们讲到非政府组织或者是社会企业或者是人才开发的时候，我们总会改变一个视角，不是说我知道所有的知识，而是我经历过你的困难，所以我们的讲师团队具有多视角、多背景。所以培训的导师必须融合做过慈善的人，也包括媒体的人，同时有在银行工作的人，他们知道怎么样去培养和教练别人。这样的话他们也能够教会我们的人才讲好故事，让他们知道尽可能提高故事的渲染力和影响力。更为重要的是，非营利组织和政府组织要解决社会问题，真正赋能给我们的学生，帮助他们了解社会所存在的问题。但是对于我们的学生而言，我们希望为他们带来批判性的思维，知道相关的知识，也要讲好故事。从多方面的视角切入，这样能够不断提升他们的能力，为社会带来变革。从软实力的角度来说或者从文化的角度来说，我们要真正了解参与者的能力，所以同学之间的相互交流是非常重要的。我们有越来越多方面的学习，对于教授来说，我们要谦虚一点，因为在学生身上也能学习，这样可以携手，比较谨慎地、一步一步地推进社会工作。现在我们有了科技、互相学习等，可以帮助进行人才培养。刚才提到的几点非常重要。此外，关于影响力的问题。第一个和第二个问题是具有关联性的，我们影响人才要有批判性的思维，然后打下基础，在大学对影响力进行评估。这很重要，因为我们培训社会工作者的原因是让他们为社会服务。这是我想讲的两个问题，谢谢。

刘培峰：谢谢。下面请李亚平讲一下。

李亚平：第一，我觉得要跟世界对话的语言体系有一致性，刚才的专家提到，无论是讲故事还是把咨询告诉世界，要知道对话的体系是什么。回到组织上讲，我们如何对咨询信息进行逻辑性、严谨性分析之后形成故事组团，然后告诉利益相关方，或者是社会公众，给到他们一些价值？在这个点上，我们在参访学习的时候，有学习 17 个发展目标，大家虽然知道 17 个目标，但是不知道具体的目标是什么。我们相关的信息要怎么样跟世界讲、和群体讲？第二，我们要形成一个机制，这个机制对于区域的组织来讲，或者是对于独立组织体系来讲，在红十字会参访的时候的感觉就是有很清晰的故事体系，能够通过这些机制和不相关的机构进行关联。作为公益指数或者作为机构和社会发展的推动价值能够连接起来，我们自己对于社会发展的经验与经济发展的贡献是相关的。紧密相连是每一个公益组织都有的特点，但是大家都是注重埋头做事，没有把信息分享出来。

陈行甲：我说两个感受，我自己有将近 3 年时间的公益实践，我创办的公益组织做到现在，有 10 名全职员工，但是都没有学过相关的公益经验，所以我想这里有巨大的培训需求。我在菲律宾国际乡村建设研究院学习的时候，有一个特别的感受，我看到了一种差距，我觉得公益人才的培养是干中学。我在国际乡村建设研究院学习时，那里有田野、有服务项目、有实践的场地、有教学的场地，到那里去感觉是接地气的、舒适的、可以体验学习的乐趣的，我感觉特别受启发。我非常期待香港中文大学和清华大学联合做可授予学位的公益人才的培养班，我们国际公益学院做的是没有学历、学位的，清华大学公益慈善研究院以研究为主，但是港中大是基于实践人才的培养，我特别期待。推动干中学这种踏实的、系统的公益人才教学方式，是公益人的使命。

阮金恩：确实，前面提到了越南当地非政府组织及其工作，包括慈善的教育和培训，我们必须要找到合适的培训群体对他们进行能力培养。对我们来说，我们有大量的慈善活动，我们希望有相关的培训，甚至对培训师再次培训。我们做了大量关于慈善工作的研究，会收集到很多的方法，通过这样的方法不断改善贫困人民的生存条件。我们也会对系统进行培训，我们的社区和政府愿意向其他的示范地区学习。

法伊兹·沙阿：我有几点响应一下大家的点评。第一，我们如何衡量影响和评估影响？我们知道全球范围内有大量的框架帮助我们进行评估，但我认为一个好的框架必须要有一定的数据来源才能帮助实现全球的部署。与此同时，需要一定层级的模块化，比如根据每个国家实际的情况挑选合适的模块进行评估，要因地制宜。我们可以一直对这些模块进行升级。我们有大量的影响力模型生成，但没有任何一个成熟的模型生成。这种跨界合作要加上对国情的思考才能得出适合的模型。我非常同意各位讲者的说法。第二，如何培养人？今天是我加入这个行业 40 年的日子，在 1999 年的时候，我还是一个教授。我们做的是 NGO 的管理项目，当时解决的问题与现在是非常相似的。年轻人想要进入非营利社会组织，但是没有办法拿到大学的学位，这是 1994 年的情况，现在这种情况依然存在。可能 20 世纪 90 年代中期，我们没有所谓的私人捐款，当时主要是政府拨款和基金会拨款，没有个人基金会或者家族基金会。随着社会的发展，现在发生了很大变化，人们在不断学习的过程中，我们要思考这个世界已经发生变化，为什么我们的学习需求没有变化？为什么以学位制为主的教育不存在？我们希望找到根本的原因所在。最近一段时间，我们推出了全球社会企业和硕士项目。我们建立我们的大学，是为了连接更多的信息孤岛，在学术研究上我们没有办法跟上社会发展的潮流。我们学校的教学法是和学生共创知识，不是老师知识的传授，而是老师和学生思想的交汇。我们希望做很多实习和在线的平台，希望有老师和学生共创的空间，我觉得这是很好的环境。如果这个行业能有相应的硕士学位，我们必须要做线上平台，然后我们还要做公益践行者板块。我们再一起进行商学院的传统学习，大家在家里就可以有上学的感觉。你只有通过一个部分的学习才能进入下一个部分的学习，只有经过实践的人才可以去往线上平台。这样的话，大家可以一层一层去做，我们现在正在做这样的创新。期末考试就是，如果你的项目通过了，你就会获得资金支持，如果你的项目不成功，被评委接受也可以毕业。但是如果评委觉得你的项目没有办法获得资金支持，你需要重新学习。

我们前面讲到的学习是很重要的，因为我们传统的学习模式并没有组织太多的学生提问和交叉式的学习。但是在一些短期项目里，一般情况下，两年的时间可能没有那么多的机会做实践，这样就没有办法真正地获得两年项目全部的价值，所以不希望大家做短期的项目。很多人上过大学，但是他可能并不能够代表所在群体的最佳的情况，比如在亚洲的文化里，一般人会让孩子去上大学，上了大学之后，他在课堂上学的东西和家庭里接受的东西是断层的，所以我们要做很多项目，让他们有沉浸式的体验，让他们把社区的知识融合进去，所以我们用古老的社会学习来取代学生完全依赖电脑的学习，我们把它叫作参与式学习。这个项目采用传统的方式，我们的学习必须要回应学习的人，也就是学生自身的需求和痛点，所以我们必须要让他本人有这种需求去学习。尤其是创立社会企业的需要，社会企业的点子非常好，但是和传统的学习非常不一样，所以我们怎么样用创新的方法促进发展呢？

这涉及方法论的问题，怎么样打造学习的文化，这是很重要的。方法论对于怎样打造学习的文化是很重要的。只有建立学习型组织，我们才能保持事业的长青，谢谢。

刘培峰：下面进入观众提问环节。

观众提问：我听陈行甲先生特别崇拜晏阳初先生，我也一样，我们是做乡村和古村的志愿者组织，我们也服务了1000多个村子。我今天想提的问题是，随着深圳建设中国特色社会主义先行示范区，社会主义和资本主义的分歧和概念重新进入我们的视野。在慈善领域，我发现资本主义慈善和社会主义慈善有很大的不同，社会主义慈善强调大家的公平、互助，更多的社会团结、更多的法治。想请各位对这些做一些甄别，社会主义慈善和资本主义慈善该往哪个方向发展？

观众提问：各位老师好，这是我的好朋友。我是做人才管理的，世界上的公益人才制度比我们成熟。我参加了“一带一路”国际公益人才交流计划，我看到国际组织的人才结构很健全。我发现从事公益慈善的主要有以下三类人。第一，毕业生或者学生，主要是应届毕业生。第二，成功人士。做让自己的内心更幸福的事情。第三，大体是商界或者在自己的领域比较失意的人，他在这个领域找到了幸福感、价值和认同感，在其他的领域没有得到认同，在公益慈善领域他的价值得以发现。所以我们在人才培养过程中要思考人才来源，我们有没有能力撬动整个社会的人才，包括从其他领域奔涌到这个领域的人才。我想说的是，我们对于人才有太多的事情要做，任重而道远，我也想加入这个团体，贡献自己的一点力量，谢谢。

刘培峰：每人做最后一句总结。

艾莉森·霍洛韦尔：我能够理解各位。我想我们正是朝着正确的方向前进。我们需要更好地回馈社会，传播给予的文化，更有策略性地一起合作，实现影响力最大化。

何日生：我们在做慈善教育时要避免过度专业化，信念和使命是整个慈善的灵魂，有这个能创造很多不同的专业，实际是整合科技，不是单一的。我们在做慈善教育的时候要注意这一点。

阮金恩：我想慈善对我们来讲是意义重大的，我们这样的学习和交流机会特别好。

李亚平：希望公益慈善领域的人才培养注意专业化、职业化、社会化的结合。

夏露萍：我们谈了很多中国慈善方面的内容。很多志愿者不够专业，这很正确。但是中国有传承几千年的慈善文化，也有善的文化渊源，包括帮助自己的家庭、自己的乡亲、自己的村落，所以我们需要把专业的东西带给人才。我们也应该真正地鼓舞和发扬中国的人文和善的精神。

贾西津：对国际公益人才的培养，除了技术和人才，我们需要对观念进行培育和讨论，因为我发现这里面有大量的误区和误解，特别是漫长的对国际慈善理解的历史。

倪锡钦：我同意，我们有非常值得人尊敬的善文化，我们也称之为善心。对于我们来说，我们应该让中国的人群加入慈善，这样的话可以看到有越来越多人加入慈善和公益行业。同时我们应该带来比较适宜的培训项目，不是照搬西方的模式，而是加强对本土善文化的使用，建立起中国慈善发展的模式，这是因地制宜的方式。我们希望吸引人们参与这个进程，与此同时，我们要真正地培训组织的领导者，只有领导者有愿景，才能带来影响和变化。我们要和外界相连，一边学一边发展，甚至分享中国的做法。研究是非常重要的，我们的慈善行业相对来说是比较浪漫的行业，之前大家都同意这一点，但是从现在开始，我们要与行业的可持续性相结合，自我批判，不断评估做出的努力，这样才能改善和改进。

法伊兹·沙阿：中国的发展特别快，之前是西方的文化输入中国。但是现在一段时间，西方有些盲目，没有发现中国的优秀实践。我本人非常关注跨国的文化交流，不管知识来自哪个体系和社会，知识本身就是知识。知识不会只教会你一两点知识，知识会教会我们如何构建体系，所以我觉得我们不能简单地说西方知识、印度知识、中国知识或日本知识，所有的知识都是超越国界的，能够帮助我们实现有效框架的打造和设计。但是对于我们来说，我们也不是盲目从其他国家引入一些模式，因为在中国已经有悠久的善文化，很多人看到了这一点。特别是中国慈善行业的工作者、社会行业的工作者，应该要真正了解善文化。比如医生，他们会有同理心，通过自己的行为帮助患者。但是把医生放到医学院他们就会学会同理心吗？不一定。人是非常复杂的，人具有非常复杂的属性，所以教育不能解决所有的问题。而中国目前有大量的评估工具和不同的课程设置，还有从西方引入的方法。但是要加强和中国本土的相关性，这个东西非常重要。不这么做的话，很多存在的问题是解决不了的，学习知识很有意思，知识本身是赋能的过程，知识赋能的过程也可以加入知识积累的过程，中国对于知识的赋能是从吸收者发展到建设者。所以我非常感谢大家，我会将我今天听到的知识，带回本国，和同事、和相关参与者进行分享，所以我觉得会谈的精神所在是相互学习。

陈行甲：因为爱是人类最共通的秉性，这决定了公益慈善是这个世界的统一语言。对于看到的资本主义慈善和社会主义慈善，我们可以研究它，研究的目的是团结，更加踏实地推动整个社会的进步。

刘培峰：谢谢。我作为主持人非常感谢各位发言人和评议人的奉献，谢谢大家。我也感谢参与讨论和倾听的诸位，这个场合是大家的，我们在共同推进这个事业，谢谢。

十二 “一带一路”公益慈善合作

主 持 人： 中国第十三届全国人大代表、香港新界社团联会理事长、香港民主建港协进联盟副主席　陈勇

对话嘉宾： 世界大区联合组织秘书长　卡洛斯·列朗

中国浙江省社会组织总会会长　梁星心

慈济基金会副总执行长　林碧玉

中国深圳市社会组织管理局局长　凌冲

李希奎： 各位嘉宾，女士们，先生们，大家下午好！今天下午的论坛设置有五个环节，分别是议题讨论、主题演讲、论坛闭幕致辞、颁发证书和论坛合作计划发布。

我们首先进行议题讨论环节，第一个专题是“‘一带一路’公益慈善合作”，下面有请议题的主持人兼对话嘉宾，中国第十三届全国人大代表、香港新界社团联会理事长、香港民主建港协进联盟副主席陈勇先生。

陈勇： 各位嘉宾下午好，我们这一节是“‘一带一路’公益慈善合作”专题。我感觉“一带一路”有两条线，北边是陆路，南边是海路。了解是爱的开始，所以这一节我们重点讨论公益和慈善，我们首先请其他几位嘉宾和我们一起对话，一起去探讨公益和慈善。我们请：

世界大区联合组织秘书长　卡洛斯·列朗先生

中国浙江省社会组织总会会长　梁星心先生

慈济基金会副总执行长　林碧玉女士

中国深圳市社会组织管理局局长　凌冲先生

有请几位。

现在台上的对话嘉宾，每人有 4 分钟的时间演讲，接下来以互动的方式互相交流。首先请卡洛斯·列朗秘书长为我们讲 4 分钟。

卡洛斯·列朗：各位来自中国人民对外友好协会的朋友，亲爱的女士们、先生们，我看到组织数量在世界范围内呈现增长趋势，我必须在这里重申这一点。我们可以看到在过去几年里——从 1997 年到 2003 年，中国的社会组织数量在急速增长，中国政府也进行了机构改革，而且将权力下放到地方政府，所以地方政府有了更多的权力进行社会治理，这是一项重要的举措。我们曾在世界各地多次讨论这个问题，包括在拉丁美洲、欧洲和非洲都进行过大量讨论，因为一国的机制改革可以为其他国家和地区提供借鉴。

在中国，我们看到你们怎么样逐渐实现国家的发展目标，包括去中心化推动国家发展等。我们认可中国是去中心化的最佳范例，必须要说这和中国在 21 世纪发起的“一带一路”倡议紧密相关。毫无疑问，这将有利于共同发展，让商业流动，创造工作岗位和财富。我们认为中国富有远见的倡议一定会得到很好的实施，它会带来巨大的就业机会和财富机会。同时，世界大区联合组织作为粮食安全的支持者，也认可“一带一路”倡议将为减少粮食不安全现象提供保障。我们确信，“一带一路”倡议会把健康带到所及之处。我们也认为“一带一路”倡议是以绿色为背景，有助于应对气候变化带来的挑战。我相信“一带一路”倡议会促进文化交流，在亚非欧三大洲之间建立起友好的联系。旧机制拘泥于某一国，聚焦于自己国家的市场，而从一开始，“一带一路”便是一个打破旧机制的倡议。“一带一路”倡议超越国界。作为地区主义和去中心化的支持者，我们必须指明这一特点。“一带一路”倡议必须考虑所有地区，推动全世界的发展。城市必须是发展的核心，应加强服务和基础设施建设。因此，从这个角度讲，我们必须从中国各省份获取经验，因为它们共同实现了去中心化，也因为这是发展。我们必须借鉴中国的经验，因为你们提出了这一个支持全球发展而非某个国家发展的倡议。这一倡议也可以是最佳观点流动的线路，我们想去中心化的主意将会是一个很好的出发点。我们诚邀中国各省份加入我们的全球地区网络。并且，我们想让中国所有的政治和社会组织参与我们和联合国共同举办的论坛，就这些议题发起讨论。我们确信该论坛将会聚集对“一带一路”倡议感兴趣的组织。在这个分享全球地区发展经验的论坛中，我想您若加入其中，会感到非常有意思。谢谢大家！

陈勇：谢谢。接下来请梁星心会长讲一讲“一带一路”倡议里与公益慈善相关的内容。

梁星心：大家好，“‘一带一路’公益慈善合作”是一个非常美好，也很有意义的话题，我想借助两个成语谈我的看法。第一个成语，珠联璧合，美好的事物结合在一起。“一带一路”倡议是国家的顶层设计，而公益慈善是全球美好的事业。它们有两个共同点：第一，都是中国改革开放的产物和象征；第二，“一带一路”倡议和公益慈善都能够超越国界、超越意识形态。就像习近平总书记所说的，“一带一路”不是某一方的私家小路，而是大家携手前进的阳光大道。我想“一带一路”倡议有公益慈善相助，必定会阳光灿烂。第二个成语，如虎添翼。“一带一路”倡议要推行，民心相通，路路畅通，民心不通，一路不通，而欲使民心相通，社会组织就需要拿出看家本领，以公益慈善相助，使“一带一路”倡议如虎添翼。社会组织和公益慈善有一个显著的特点，它们源自民间，最贴近民心，也最能够凝聚民心，所以我坚信中国有多大，中国的社会组织就有多大。中国有多强，中国的社会组织就有多强。

最后提四点建议。第一，培育好。社会组织这么重要，民心相通这么重要，一定要把社会组织培育好。让社会组织发展壮大，担当起历史的重任。第二，多交往。社团之间、社会组织之间、公民之间要多交往，才能有利于合作，合作才能共赢。第三，抓项目。通过文化类的、经济类的链接达成共识，形成决议互动，促进合作。第四，众长远。“一带一路”倡议是百年大计，不可能一蹴而就，社会组织在中国的历史并不长，如果从正式更名算起只有十几年的时间，历史的责任摆在我们面前，按照国家的部署，我们社会组织要发挥应有的力量。谢谢。

陈勇：谢谢。接下来请林碧玉女士为我们分享。

林碧玉：各位嘉宾，大家下午好，首先非常感恩有这个机会在这里向大家做一个关于“一带一路”项目合作的分享。慈济基金会关注慈善、治疗、环境保护等，我们最关注的是气候变迁和环保问题，因为气候变迁，2018 年有 8000 万人受到影响，2019 年则受到更大的影响。1991 年，因为华东水患，我们来到了江苏，在华东地区赈灾，为灾民盖房子，做了很多帮移民迁村的工作。5·12 地震时也帮助盖了 13 所学校。全球 99 个国家有我们的足迹。我们兴建的房屋，在 2018 年所帮助的对象超过 3000 万人。从“一带一路”来看，我们走访了 24 个国家，尤其是在莫桑比克受到水患的影响，我们开展了救灾工作。我们的工作受到了联合国的肯定，比如菲律宾水灾期间，协助那里的人民重建家园，创造经济力。在这期间，我们用了种种方式，比如护理。遇到水患，我们提供简便的工具，让那里的人们自己盖房子。

PPT 上是我们为他们做的很多工作，请大家浏览一下，现在工作正如火如荼地进行。针对环境保护，包括在全球，我们用很简单的十字口诀，带动大家做环保。毛毯和衣服都是塑料品拿来做的，塑料品还可以做地砖、做建材。我们也在各个地方做义诊，每年有 5 万多人受惠。我们也关注缺水的问题、难民的问题，比如在土耳其，我们为难民的孩子解决教育的问题、医疗的问题。

我们在联合国倡议，为了健康，每个礼拜要有一餐吃素食。我们在联合国发展了 17 个项目。我们愿意在“一带一路”倡议上与大家合作，共同参与解决非洲的传染病、环境保护、水资源短缺、医疗等问题，尤其是中医进入非洲，解决心理问题，感恩大家，感谢大家。

陈勇：谢谢。下面请深圳市社会组织管理局局长凌冲先生发言。

凌冲：感谢组委会把世界公益慈善论坛放到深圳举行，我们特别骄傲。深圳不仅是经济高速发展的城市，也不仅是高科技产业非常突出的城市，还是一个充满爱心的城市。我是来自政府部门的，中央给深圳发了一个文件，给了深圳新的定位，叫作中国特色社会主义先行示范区。站在我这个部门的角度，我要做什么？经济部门应打造全世界最好的营商环境，我来自民政部门，就要打造全世界最好的崇善环境，吸引更多的慈善组织、慈善家等慈善资源，这是我的工作职责。此外，我们也非常鼓励深圳的慈善资源走出国门，走向共建“一带一路”国家。过去深圳的救灾组织深入尼泊尔抗震救灾，还有一些慈善组织到斯里兰卡开展儿童的白内障手术。我们应该沿着“一带一路”为世界做更大的贡献，这是政府部门需要推动的。我们也利用深圳的区位优势，和大湾区的组织联合起来，在制度的建设、政策的制定、机制的建设、平台的建设、人才的培养等方面共同推动深圳的慈善组织实现更好的发展。同时“走出去”，为共建“一带一路”国家提供更多的服务，共同构建人类命运共同体，谢谢。

陈勇：谢谢凌冲局长。我也讲一下“一带一路”倡议中大家很关心的一点，就是安老，“一带一路”倡议还强调医保。长者很有智慧，人生阅历丰富，也有很多储蓄，现在越年轻越是不存钱，在大家选择地方养老的时候，当地的产业如果透过网络带动的话，民意更容易相通，要引进一个地方的成功经验和资源网络。我认识香港的一位教授，他退休之后年富力强，所以有10年的时间可以休息。他去到“一带一路”沿线任何一个地方，都能够带给当地很多智慧网络并推动当地发展，这一点需要大家推动更多的安老产业在“一带一路”沿线发展。

接下来是一个互动环节，建议大家简单直接。我们女士优先，我想问林碧玉女士，您刚才讲了帮助非洲的朋友，您做了这么多慈善公益工作，也认为民心相通和公益慈善是最大的困难，那您认为最需要解决的是哪几个方面的问题？

林碧玉：首先谢谢主持人。在“一带一路”沿线有很多的困难，包括交通问题，因为要救灾就要输送物资。不仅需要长距离输送，更重要的是当地交通的落后。不过，好在任何的困难都可以克服。医疗问题对其很重要，我们现在发现中医到这些落后国家是可以及时解决它们的医疗问题的，因为中医不需要很大的设备，而且中医是中国的国粹，所以中医可以做这件事。此外，在东南亚地区，水的问题很严重。非洲地区有水资源的问题，在东南亚地区，水中的盐分也是很高的，怎么样淡化是我们需要思考的。还有越南的落叶剂问题，所以我们想邀请大家一起来探讨。我刚才提出问题是希望大家可以一起解决这些困境。中华文化提倡爱和包容。我们如何把中华文化传播出去？未来的种种问题都是新的，如果把中华文化的爱和包容带到其他国家，可以扭转大家的观念。大家谈到慈善人才，其实对他们而言最重要的是使命感和信念，相信未来我们不只在共建“一带一路”国家，还可以在更多的国家看到中华文化浓浓的爱，这可以融化所有人的心。因为这样可以引导人类重视环境保护，真正地抢救地球，没有地球，就没有人类。

陈勇：对。以善以爱为保，可以融化人心，如果能够融化冰川，我们的水源也可以多一些。我想问卡洛斯·列朗先生，在您的经验里，怎么样可以减少大家对“一带一路”倡议的疑虑？“一带一路”倡议推动过程中，有哪些重大问题可以解决？

卡洛斯·列朗：我也不知道我是不是完全理解了您的问题。我想说，如果您问我目前全球范围内什么问题最突出，我们应该如何利用这个倡议解决这些问题的话，我会做如下回答。首先在中国。中国已经处于非常独特的状态当中，国家的发展速度非常快，而且经济的增速也非常喜人。这几天我和参会者也讨论了这个问题。刚才的林碧玉女士向大家介绍了慈济基金会的工作。但是大家没有注意到一点，世界上其他地区存在很多大问题，比如移民、气候变化、难民，这是其他国家和其他地区面临的大问题。昨天匈牙利的前总理说过，中国承担起非常重要的责任，这一点很重要。中国有非常重要的责任，而且对中国来说，在承担责任的同时也可以意识到其他国家所产生的问题。我的一个同事经常和我说，我们要有深入的民心相通，但现在更为重要的是，我们要能够建立起这种心灵的桥梁，各国之间要加强交往和互通，不要树立壁垒，要实现民心的互通，共同解决我们面临的问题。未来不再有疆界，因为爱是跨越国界的。对于我们来说，我们要建立全球范围内的友好合作，这是大家要完成的共同使命。

陈勇：谢谢。接下来问一下梁星心会长，您来自浙江省，您了解浙江省，可不可以讲一下在公益慈善方面，怎么样让共建“一带一路”国家的人民了解我们提出的倡议。

梁星心：讲金先讲心，浙江是经济文化，地盘很小，人也不算多，但是历史是比较独特的，在中国历史上具有浓墨重彩的一笔。中国正逐步强大起来，就该担当起历史的责任、社会的责任。我觉得“一带一路”倡议之所以是伟大创举在于它对人类的贡献，它把共建“一带一路”国家的事当作分内的事。而且浙江人很有特点，遍布全世界，走出去的多为商人。浙江有独特的优势和经验，在全世界所有的国家和地区，只要有中国商会的，大多数是浙江商会，或者是温州商会，它们促进了当地经济、社会、文化的发展，促进了中国和国外的交往。我到一些国家的小餐馆，发现我们国家的领导人也去过，这是想象不到的。民心相通以及国家的知识和国家的倡议能够深入人心，变成自觉的行动，我觉得非常的重要。所以浙江会继续发挥作用，谢谢。

陈勇：谢谢梁星心会长。刚才大家从宏观上讲了怎么样用爱和善意做好，为什么做好，大家了解了。针对怎么样做到，我问一下凌冲局长，如果大家想把公益慈善这个平台做好，如果想使它落地深圳的话应该怎么样做？

凌冲：如果是港澳台地区或者国外的慈善组织想进入深圳参与社会服务，现在有路径，可以向境内的公安管理部门申请境外非政府组织在大陆（内地）进行活动。今天上午，我们民政局在开会，商讨如何利用先行示范区这个契机向国家争取更多特殊的政策扶持以促进深圳公益慈善事业的发展。我只能说一些设想，还不是现实。可以开放一些特定的领域，比如养老、社工服务行业，这些授权可以方便境外的组织进来，帮助我们一起成长。另外，探讨如何放宽境外人士担任在深圳登记的慈善组织的负责人。这些工作是现行的，有一些是争取努力的。我们最希望的是能够营造对标世界的一流的崇善环境，实现政府职能的方便、高效，为大家服务。

陈勇：谢谢。我们用爱和善把握机遇，在国家的政策和中华民族的优良传统方面可以有更多的交流。好的方向、好的策略、好的理想要坚守好，还要把握好，最关键的是把握好时机，机不可失，时不再来。希望大家可以认识台上几位重量级的领袖嘉宾，之后有更深层次的交流，因为“一带一路”和公益慈善永远讲不完，只会越做越多，越做越好。让我们以热烈的掌声感谢台上的嘉宾。

十三　湾区发展，善商之道

主 持 人：论坛学术委员会委员、香港中文大学工商管理学院院长　陈家乐

对话嘉宾：华钻创投董事长　黄学思

盖达尔·阿利耶夫基金会国际关系部负责人 索尔坦·玛姆玛多夫

中国第十三届全国人大代表、国际潮青联合会执行会长 张俊勇

嘉宾演讲：善心改变世界

全国工商联原副主席、天津市人大常委会原副主任、中华红丝带基金理事长 张元龙

李希奎：刚才讲了很多，国之交在于民相亲，民相亲在于心相通，谢谢各位。下面进入第二个议题，请论坛学术委员会委员、香港中文大学工商管理学院院长陈家乐先生主持议题讨论。

陈家乐：女士们，先生们，大家下午好。非常荣幸，能够担任分论坛的主持人。我们这个分论坛的主题是“湾区发展，善商之道”。这个环节我们会探讨商业在整个慈善事业发展中扮演的角色。毫无疑问，商业合作在慈善事业中扮演着重要的角色。同时，在整个大湾区，在过去这些年，我们也看见了越来越多的成功企业家，他们立足湾区，打造出了非常成功的企业组织。此外，我们也看到了越来越多的人，他们努力为社会创造福祉。毫无疑问，我们必须要更好地去配置我们的资源，包括人力资源和财力资源，这样的话，不光会为股东带来价值，为我们的投资者带来回报，同时能够创造巨大的社会价值。回顾过去，我们看到越来越多的范例。我们有一些顶尖的企业家，他们看到了社会上的一些问题，包括环境恶化、收入差距等，这些企业家利用自己的财富，或者是公司的资源，帮助解决一些亟待解决的社会问题。

我们也看到了一些企业家的积极参与，帮助我们打造更加可持续的社会，同时让所有的利益相关方真正地享受企业带来的福祉和红利。

所以我觉得“湾区发展，善商之道”是很重要的话题，它能够帮助我们打造更加可持续的社会，当然也能够为我们的企业带来长青，为个体带来更

好的帮助。在这个环节里，我们有幸邀请到了几位非常杰出的嘉宾，他们来自全球各地不同的背景，他们会和我们分享他们各自的经验、见解与想法。他们会和我们分享企业如何为社会福祉做出贡献。

首先我要介绍一下这个环节的主题演讲嘉宾，全国工商联原副主席、天津市人大常委会原副主任、中华红丝带基金理事长张元龙先生，他演讲的题目是《善心改变世界》。

善心改变世界

全国工商联原副主席、天津市人大常委会原副主任、中华红丝带基金理事长　张元龙

各位来宾，各位朋友，大家下午好！作为中华红丝带基金的代表，我很高兴参加今天的论坛。中华红丝带基金是全国工商联和20多家会员企业共同建立的防控艾滋病的全国性公益组织。我们在2005年成立，14年来，在全国工商联黄孟复主席的带领下、在全国工商联各位企业家的支持下，投入超过1.9亿元，开展救助扶持、援建设施、宣传倡导等三大类多个公益项目，直接受益人达150万，取得了一定的成绩，也两度获得“中华慈善奖”。今天我和大家分享一下我做公益慈善工作的几点体会。

我们大家在努力奋斗的同时，其实都在思考一个问题：我们追求的理想社会是什么样的？中国追求的理想社会是社会主义社会。邓小平同志对社会主义有着比较有意思的描述。他说，社会主义是发展生产力、解放生产力，是消灭剥削，提高人民生活水平，消除两极分化，实现共同富裕。他还提出了什么不是社会主义：贫穷不是社会主义，发展慢也不是社会主义。我们把这两句话融合一下，那么，社会主义就是效率和公平的高度统一。我们看到

世界各个国家也在寻求这个统一，效率和公平是人类的共同追求。

那么，如何评判一个社会的公平和效率？其实公平和效率的内涵极为丰富，如果我们不考虑政治、社会、文化的影响，仅从经济的角度观察：效率对一个单位来说，就是劳动生产率；对一个国家来说，就是人均 GDP。中国的人均 GDP 接近 1 万美元，而美国是 6.26 万美元，日本是 3.93 万美元，印度是 0.2 万美元。我们的人均效率还有很大的提升空间。公平是看什么？世界上最简单的标准是基尼系数。基尼系数有几种统计方式：按财富统计，按收入统计，按消费统计。法国经济学家皮凯蒂在他的《21 世纪资本论》中提出，美国的收入差距大于财富差距，而英国的财富差距大于收入差距。这是因为英国是老牌的资本主义国家，财富积累的时间很长，美国则主要是依靠华尔街的高收入拉开差距。中国现在没有明确的官方基尼系数，我们在 2016 年以后就不再对外发布了，所以现在的基尼系数都是来自以考量收入为主的民间统计。最近世界基尼系数在 0.3 左右的国家和地区有韩国和中国台湾，美国是 0.45，中国内地的民间统计数字是 0.55，而中国香港在 0.5 左右，最高的是南非，达到 0.6 以上。最近还有一组数字可以表现我们中国的收入差距：将 14 亿人分成 5 组，20% 的人口算一组，也就是 2 亿 8000 万人，最低的一组人均年收入是 6400 元人民币，最高的一组是 7 万多元人民币，相差约 10 倍。这是按照以 20% 为一组计算，如果以 10% 为一组计算，我们的差距可能会更大。但我觉得还有很多数据没有统计进去，比如说国家的福利、企业家的捐赠，应该把这部分也平均地算入大家的收入。我们按 20% 的人口为一组来计算，最高的那组假若捐赠了收入的 10%，那么，就可以把这 10% 分到各组中，最终 10 倍的差距就可以缩小到 7.6 倍。以美国为例，美国慈善机构总资产占 GDP 的 10%，2018 年 GDP 是 20 万亿美元，那么慈善机构总资产大约是 2 万亿美元。美国的分配率在 80% 以上，收入大约是 16 万亿美元，他们每年拿出 5000 亿美元用来捐赠，大概占百分之三点几。也就是说，计入这部分收入，可能对基尼系数有比较大的影响，这是大家应该关注的。

中国2018年的实际捐赠数是754.2亿元人民币（参看《2018中国慈善捐赠发展蓝皮书》），我们的收入分配率大约为43.9%，也就是说，我们的GDP有43.9%是分给大家的，大约40万亿元人民币，我们的捐赠数占总收入的0.2%，是比较少的。

但是，我们可以得到一个结论：公益捐赠，特别是高收入者的捐赠，可以改变贫富的差距。

还有一点要注意的是分配。我们对财富的分配有以下三个层次。第一次分配是工资和利润。第二次是税收，由政府作为公共事业管理主体进行分配，这应该叫作福利。政府做的事情应该叫作福利，不应该叫作慈善。我认为，慈善不等于公益，慈善是短期的、救急的，公益是长期的、战略的，我们民间应该做公益。那么，政府在第二次分配上要把这件事做好，因为大量的财富要在这里分配。中国政府的扶贫减贫工作就体现了二次分配的力量。因此，财税用于公益的比例非常重要。第三次分配是社会捐赠。在三次分配中，每一次分配都应做好自己应该做的事，比如：一次分配就讲效率；二次分配时政府要争取做到公平，福利要做得非常到位，公共设施要做好，不必要的开支要减少；三次分配要以社会公益事业为目标。这样效率与公平的矛盾就会减小，收入的差距也会缩小了。

因此，我们得到的第二个结论就是：应在三次分配之后计算基尼系数，尤其是消费的基尼系数。

皮凯蒂的书出来之后，经济学家陈志武认为这本书有一个问题。他说芝加哥大学通过研究收入得出一个结论：美国近年的收入差从5.3倍涨到了6.4倍，而消费差从4.2倍降到了3.9倍。消费的不平等状况在改善，主要原因是社保和公益在起作用，使得消费差距实际上在缩小。比如说，咱们现在的企业家天天忙碌，哪有时间消费呢？最多是儿子在消费，企业家可能还不如员工消费得多。如果把这个计算进来，消费差距并不会有渲染的那么大。19 世纪中国的消费收入差远低于瑞典、比利时和意大利，它们的收入差要比我们国家大，但是那些国家的宗教和社会救助力量强于我们，特别是在教育和医疗上的资助。而在中国主要是宗族的救助，官方是开仓赈粮，这也许就是中国历史上农民起义比较频繁的原因。

我们应该再得到一个结论，就是：一次分配讲效率，二次分配讲公平，三次分配讲善心。善心的捐赠，尤其是在教育和医疗上，可以大幅缩小消费的差距，保证效率和公平的平衡。

再说说善心是如何产生的。我的祖父是南开大学的第一任校长，南开大学的办学经费全是靠捐赠，因此他是一位劝捐的高手，劝捐、募捐也是我的家传，所以我讲几种我在全国工商联观察到的捐赠心理。

第一种是逼捐。我们见到很多有非常纯粹的慈善心的人被逼捐，募集的款项用得不到位，成效非常不好。在全国工商联工作的时候，我们曾经有一个经验，就是把维权、公益、慈善交由一个人管。我们有句话叫：真诚的奉献来自公正的维权。现在想想，这也有逼捐的味道。

第二种是所谓的“买道儿”。很多企业为了讨好领导而捐赠，为此获得一些交换物。

第三种是通过公益慈善活动，提升和改善个人和企业的形象。

这三种都是在压力下形成的，但都需要认真对待。中国的传统慈善理念，特别体现在《聊斋志异》里的《考城隍》。阎王爷给宋姓书生提了一个问题：一人二人，有心无心。书生回答：“有心为善，虽善不赏；无心为恶，虽恶不罚。”受到满堂喝彩。这是中国非常传统的慈善心理，叫作动机和效果的统一。然而实际上很多事做得不太统一，我认为有目的地行善不给予奖励，这是有问题的。我们应该逢善必赏，所谓的赏，就是社会对善的肯定。

第四种是恻隐之心。人的同理心是道德的根基，所有的道德来自同理心，有了同理心就有了帮助别人的情怀。有一个世界捐助指数，它是以近期是否帮助过陌生人、是否捐过款、是否做过义工这三项为指标，对 146 个国家进行排名。近 5 年平均成绩第一的是缅甸，2019 年是印尼。这体现了宗教的影响，缅甸大多数民众信仰佛教，乐善好施。同样，美国的捐赠动力也是以宗教为主。在这个指数中，中国排名第 145，虽然是倒数第 2 名，但绝对值很大，24% 帮助过陌生人，相当于 3 亿人；8% 捐过款，就是 1 亿人；4% 做过义工，差不多 5000 万人。缅甸 2018 年的人均 GDP 是 1325.95 美元，其有 52% 的人帮助过他人、90% 捐过款、48% 当过义工。美国的数字则分别是 75%、62%、43%。中国已经是世界第二大经济体，不能只跟过去比，我们的目标应该是争做世界最前列的国家。实际上，全社会捐赠指标的比较，体现的是善的氛围。有了善的氛围，会让捐赠者从心里觉得做慈善顺理成章。

第五种是英雄情怀。比如洛克菲勒，建立基金会，“尽其所能获得，倾其所有给予”，发挥了自己的作用。其中很重要的是，要有一个好的项目，可以让捐赠的人认识到一生获得财富的目的就是要去帮助有需要的人。当大家知道，某个贫寒孩子的人生、某种正在肆虐的传染病，或即将影响全人类的环境污染，都会因为自己的善心援手而改变，就会有一种英雄情怀。

第六种就是体现人生价值。我们怎样看人的能力？能赚钱只能证明能力的一半，会花钱才是完整能力的体现。我们家有一个家训：“私立非私有，留德不留财。”这描述的就是一个社会企业的特征。公立必须公有，公立不能私有，公立更不能非公有；私立必须私有，私立不能公有，但私立可以非私有。孟子时代有一个人叫杨朱，他说“拔一毛而利天下，不为也”。杨朱的话有点狠，但是有一定的道理。就是说，我身上的毛是我的，要拔这根毛必须得我自己拔，别人不能拔。所以我们说，私立不能公有。但私立可以非私有。很多人有了钱之后，喜欢自己设立基金会，以体现社会价值。所以“私立非私有”这句话在当下也有着重要的意义。包括“留德不留财”，它的意思是给子孙留下钱财，未见得是好事儿，在社会中留下德行，可使后代受用无穷，这些都是我们关于劝捐的非常好的理念。

我们探讨了几种捐赠心理，我觉得最重要的，就是要有一个“善有善报，恶有恶报”的社会。我们往往重视恶有恶报，对善有善报的探讨还不够。行善应该被鼓励，只要有善的行为，我们就应该鼓励它，不让行善有压力。不论动机如何，善心是可以改变人性的。只有善有善报，这个社会才会有善心，才会有慈善的共识。社会共识就是恒理，有了恒理才有恒法，有了恒法，比如宪法、物权法、慈善法，才会受法的保护，才会有恒产。孟子说，有恒产者有恒心。我说恒产不仅仅是你的财产，还有你在社会中的权利和义务。把这个逻辑串起来就是，有了恒理才有恒产，有了恒产才有恒心，有了恒心才会有善心，那善心一定是来自社会的共识。如果整个社会有“善有善报，恶有恶报”的共识，那么在这个充满善的社会里，人的善心才能被培养、才能长存。

时间关系，我就讲以上几点体会。关于如何建立善恶有报的社会，以后有机会再和大家交流，谢谢大家！

陈家乐：非常感谢张元龙理事长精彩的演讲。我们现在邀请这个环节其他的讨论嘉宾：

华钻创投董事长　黄学思先生

盖达尔·阿利耶夫基金会国际关系部负责人　索尔坦·玛姆玛多夫先生

中国第十三届全国人大代表、国际潮青联合会执行会长　张俊勇先生

我们请其他的嘉宾发言 5 分钟，首先请黄学思董事长发言。

黄学思：女士们，先生们，大家下午好！我是来自硅谷的黄学思，今天我跟大家分享一下怎么样实现商业目标。

张元龙理事长刚刚提到如何向人们提供短期、即刻的帮助，也提到公益

是一个长期的目标，我今天想和大家谈一下中期的事情。我把这个图片放下来，因为美国证券委员会需要我们给人们做前瞻性的说明。我今天跟大家讲讲影响力投资，影响力投资是指对企业或基金进行投资，以实现产生社会或环境影响并带来金融回报的目标。10 年前，我在斯坦福大学上工商管理课，当时有一组年轻人提交了一个非常复杂的解决方案，这个方案是为非洲无法得到电力供应的人设计的。现在全世界有 20 亿人无法得到电力供应，通过配置高质量的太阳能产品，该项目实现为 9500 万人口供电，减少了 2200 万吨的二氧化碳排放量。这是一项大工程。日本京都曾通过了减少二氧化碳排放量的公约，在座各位都曾种树，但若是减少二氧化碳排放呢？在印度和非洲，一些人用不上电，所以用的是煤油灯，煤油是像汽油一样高度可燃的液体。他们只能使用煤油灯和火炉。我记得小时候，有人拿火柴去给炉子生火，当拿着火柴靠近炉子的时候，炉子会发出“砰”的一声，如果不小心站在炉子前面，你的眉毛和头发也许会被烧掉，有些不幸的人甚至因此把脸烧坏。通过配置高质量的太阳能产品，也可以减少二氧化碳排放量。我们正在提供可信赖的、价格实惠的、清洁的能源产品，为所有人开创更美好的未来，让他们过上高质量的生活。如果我们能为这些人提供太阳能的解决方案，我们就能点亮他们的未来。《福布斯》杂志评论道，这些由斯坦福商学院提供的光与电资源筹集了 100 万美元，已经影响了 100 万条生命。

这是真正商业上的成功，其来自成功的商业管理团队的经验、焦点战略和实施方法。我和一些科技公司就在做这样的事。我们为什么要关注早期阶段呢？因为回报率。“买低卖高”是一项投资策略，梅隆银行也用此策略。我们怎样才能实现此策略呢？企业家筹资的时候很辛苦，可能好几个月都没有办法筹集到资金。当我们说会用一些钱来购买他们的股票时，他们会加以考虑，或者可以在次级市场上进行购买。如果想购买独角兽公司的股票，可以去硅谷，那里有很多。那里是一个很好的地方，可以做到以低价购买股票。谢谢!

陈家乐：谢谢。有请下一位演讲人和我们分享一下，他是索尔坦·玛姆玛多夫先生。

索尔坦·玛姆玛多夫：亲爱的各位朋友，尊敬的嘉宾，女士们，先生们，首先我想特别感谢大会的主办方，感谢你们邀请我参加世界公益慈善论坛。我来自阿塞拜疆盖达尔·阿利耶夫基金会这个慈善机构，阿塞拜疆共有 1000 万人，是东西方的接口，并与俄罗斯、伊朗、土耳其和格鲁吉亚等国接壤。盖达尔·阿利耶夫基金会于 2004 年开始慈善活动，我们关注社会、经济发展，解决包括教育、公众健康、环境保护、文化与科学等方面的问题。此外，我们还投入文化传承与国家沟通等。我们与政府、非营利组织和慈善机构合作，希望为所有的捐赠者和合作伙伴带来经济福祉，提高基金会管理水平，完善基金会结构。在过去这么多年，大家对企业社会责任进行了分析，就是可持续发展、教育、环境、医疗，以及怎么样为最不幸的人提供教育和医疗的机会。我们还希望通过我们的基金会，能够为社会的各个方面创造福祉，这些是我们的工作。

在国家的社会项目里，我们目前为劳工家庭提供免费住房，希望帮助无家可归的人有更好的家居环境。我们在匈牙利也做类似的项目，如果有一些家庭是低收入群体，他们能够获得政府免费的救济房。我们还在其他的国家帮助身体残疾的小孩。在伊拉克，我们也做了一些工作，为当地的难民提供居住的条件。在教育和科学方面，我们在阿塞拜疆为小孩子打造了“儿童之家”。我们盖了 400 多个小学和幼儿园。我们在法国当地开办语言和文化学校，为少数民族的孩子提供教育。2018 年，我们在越南盖了很多小学。在俄罗斯，我们也盖了很多学校。健康问题一直是我们非常关注的一点，我们在国内关注患有糖尿病的儿童，我们也为患有心脏病的儿童做了一些项目。在巴基斯坦，我们也提供乙肝疫苗，创新了输血技术，同时建立了针对低收入家庭的诊所，为残疾儿童带来了包括轮椅在内的大量辅助设施。在吉布提，我们也专门捐赠了医疗设施，帮助本地实现发展。

文化也是很重要的方面。在阿塞拜疆，我们建立了展览馆、艺术社区、图书馆、音乐学校，举办了专门的阿塞拜疆文化瑰宝的展览。在意大利，我们也专门做了文化艺术展览，展示了伊斯兰教的文艺品。我们和中国人民对外友好协会的合作就是一个很好的例子，现在我们有一些项目在阿塞拜疆和中国进行。我们也投入全球慈善活动，比如联合国的文化和文明发展论坛，包括不同的展会、世博会等。我们所做的工作，都是希望能够不断地推广我们的文化和展示我们的文化瑰宝，这一点希望加强文化多样性，这是我们得到了阿塞拜疆政府的支持的原因，谢谢大家。

陈家乐：谢谢索尔坦·玛姆玛多夫先生，接下来有请张俊勇先生。

张俊勇：大家下午好，非常感谢大家与我一起分享怎么样建设更美好的湾区。下一步的工作怎么样做、怎么样使我们的生活和企业方面的活动结合。我有一些想法和大家分享一下。

关于我们的“9+2”城市群以后的发展，众所周知，我们搭建的湾区，按照我们的理解，这个湾区是国际大湾区，是由全球的人民一起来共商共建共赢。在打造这个湾区的过程中，会有很多新的模式，比如制度模式的创新、经营模式的创新，会在湾区里发生。同一时间，香港、澳门一直践行“一国两制”的理念。湾区将会有很多新的经济模式，如人工智能、数字经济、共享经济、互联网、物联网，新打造的可能都会推动制度上的创新。企业在这种环境里经营，我们也要考虑怎么样为股东创造利润，同时，承担社会的责任。所以在打造美好生活环境的过程中，我们要把一些元素放在湾区里。

我们会处于怎样的环境？很多东西经过人工智能、经过万物互联有很多新的改变，我们过去的社会模式都会改变。改变的话，我们可以让每一个人去选择，工作之余，他们有什么想做的，可以为下一代人做其他的事，这些都可以放在新的体制里。我相信未来的湾区，会促进世界的发展，在教育方面会有很多的沟通，比如人工智能，经过一些平台，自动化地产生交易。在这个过程中，比如供应商定它的规矩，交易完成以后，可以有一个比例，假设一个交易完成以后，有 0.03% 的比例可以用来做慈善，那么可以用它来治疗白内障，或者治疗其他的疾病，或者专门支持山区的小朋友读书。以后可以在经济的环境里考虑，把一些善行的元素放在里边。

我搭建了潮州人的平台，我是这个平台的会长。还有一个是在互联网里，用区块链的技术、人工智能的技术，把人们联系起来，建立一个新的社区，它可以把全世界分布在不同地方的人联系起来。因为现在有互联网，通过网络可以把很多人联系起来，然后做交易，如果他们有需求，比如印尼的同学想到深圳读书，他可以问群体里的人，群体里的人利用人工智能寻找方案。中间的过程要给一些费用，但是要获得一个通证，中间提供服务的会拿到这个通证，这个过程中会有一个差价，差价出现以后，会维持运转。

我推动这些平台，希望可以用新的手段，把全世界不同地方的人联系起来，为他们服务，去发挥一种联系起来的作用。通过不同的活动产生不同的价值，然后通过平台，再分配给有需要的人，这种类型的工作会越来越多。总的来说，下一步，我们应该要去努力推动。因为我们在这个时间点上会有很多机会创造新的经济平台，我觉得旧的方式方法、公益慈善的平台，其实我们是需要的，但可以用新的方式、新的模式创造更多新的舞台，让我们的工作、每一个人的生活，跟我们的企业运作联系起来。整个方式方法和过去是有很大不一样的，因为它会更快速，根据每一个公司的情况自动参与，让大家生活得很好。我觉得这一天很快会来临，谢谢大家。

陈家乐：感谢张俊勇先生的演讲，四位讲者从不同的角度跟我们做了分享。张元龙理事长做了非常详细的介绍，关于国内公益事业的发展。黄学思先生为我们介绍了影响力投资的概念。针对他们的分享我问他们一个问题，我首先问张元龙理事长，您刚刚讲到公益的发展，政府通过财富分配，改善一些人的生活状况，而关于社会保障的基金，包括养老的基金，特别是随着人口老龄化的加快，我们对其有一种期望。我想问，在公益的环节方面，有什么事情可以做?

张元龙：您问了一个非常重要的问题，中国的老龄化问题非常严重，65岁的人口将近2亿人，国家建立养老基金比较晚，全国也没有统一，有可能会捉襟见肘。一方面要靠政府加大投入力度，特别是我们的国有企业，要将自己的利润不断补充到养老基金上，这样的话，能够体现国有企业全民化。另一方面要靠自己，而且现在的老龄化，并不是指人真正老了，而是我们退出了工作岗位，实际上这些人还能为社会工作。养老方面，我们非常看重的是健康，身体要健康，我们每年的医疗费用将近4万亿元，但我们花在体育上的很少。人均体育面积2.2平方米，和日本差十几倍，所以我们还有潜力可挖。这是非常巨大的话题，谢谢。

陈家乐：谢谢。我下一个问题是问黄学思先生的，您讲了影响力投资，您也觉得现在越来越多的人在做影响力投资，在中国却没有那么多人做影响力投资。您能不能和我们分享一下影响力的发展趋势，以及它在亚洲的发展、未来怎么样推广影响力投资，让人家不仅关注投资回报，同时关注投资背后的价值和影响。

黄学思：我不知道中国的影响力投资的市场是怎样的，一般美国的影响力投资不仅带来投资回报，还产生对社会有益的成效，无论是在环境还是在社会上都是如此。我觉得中国可以做一些，我们要看最终目的，如果是希望减少二氧化碳，可以建立很好的绿化项目，比如建造很多娱乐公园。实际上，你们已经在用影响力投资的模式了。我也希望有时间到深圳市场看一下影响力发展的情况。

陈家乐：接下来的问题是给索尔坦·玛姆玛多夫先生的，您刚才介绍了盖达尔·阿利耶夫基金会，你们在欧洲等地做了一些项目，那么在中国呢？我想问的是，假设您在中国没有项目的话，未来有没有打算在中国做项目？如果做的话，对哪些领域比较感兴趣？

索尔坦·玛姆玛多夫：在我的演讲结尾，我提到和中国人民对外友好协会做的一些工作，我们在两年前签了一个谅解备忘录，在这个备忘录下我们已经在中国和阿塞拜疆做了一些项目。讲到基金会的工作重点，我们希望能够搭建起文化的桥梁，即横跨不同国家、不同民族、不同人民的桥梁。我也非常乐意强调和中国人民对外友好协会签署的谅解备忘录，我们已经在2018年做过几个计划，也创想了2020年要做的计划，比如说促进中国和阿塞拜疆慈善项目的发展。我们也希望关注中塞两国之间的工作，所以我们的基金会很愿意和中国人民对外友好协会一起打破文化隔阂。在过去一年，我们的项目推进得非常顺利，在未来几年的时间，我们能够把我们和中国人民对外友好协会的合作关系当成范例拿到别的国家推广。

陈家乐：讲到大湾区的发展，它是“9+2”的融合，包括人流、资金流、物流，我想问人才融合方面的问题。我想问张俊勇先生，从您的角度，有什么事情可以做，让香港的人才进入大湾区其他城市？

张俊勇：把香港的人才甚至是全世界的人才吸引到大湾区其他城市，是我们必须要做的。每个城市有不同的项目在推动，去吸引所需要的高端人才。很多城市如果有技术团队进去，会给他们奖金补贴，比香港很多地方都高。我们就是用资金去吸引优秀人才，这个工作在大湾区做得最多。怎么样把其他的人才请过去，让更多的人愿意去发展他们的工作、生意、家庭等？其实很多人是从文化上入手，就是要做好文化协同工作。我在人大里一直想推动的是在“一国两制”的情况下，把大湾区各地的制度，包括法律制度联合起来。法律的认同方面、社会的价值观和语言方面，这些东西可以不断地被整合。做完以后，香港更多的人愿意回来生活。在融合的过程中，还是要使湾区改变，我心目中的湾区是实践“一国两制”最好的地方。我们未来的湾区跟现在的湾区相比应该是更加包容和人性化的，是更加制度化的湾区。这种制度和内地其他城市不一样。香港有一些习惯，比如陪审员，此前在内地的法院没有陪审员的概念，现在内地有了。很多的价值观、方式方法实现了整合，在这些整合完成的时候、慢慢丰富的时候，我相信更多的人会愿意进来。中国梦不只是中国人的中国梦，还是全人类的中国梦。所以我觉得湾区应该是能吸引人才的地方。

陈家乐：谢谢。好的，现在我有一些问题想要和大家分享、交流，大家提到了慈善，包括其在过去一段时间的发展。我们看到，包括从商业合作的角度来说，从企业的角度来说，越来越多的企业拥抱慈善，所以我想问一个问题，我们可以从哪个方面做更多的工作鼓励企业做慈善，包括社会企业责任感，包括社会和环境可持续发展，我们如何让我们的企业做得更多，是劝服还是法律法规的形式?

黄学思：我一直深信，当你要建立新的创新城市或者创新大学时，新公司自己能够做出成为新兴企业的选择，可以将 10% 的股权给到共同基金、政府等。这些基金可以由商界共同使用。我们可以做到利润共享。两种方法都是共赢，如果人们得到经验教训，他们会不断地创业再创业。所以要想获得成功要更多地强调资源分配。

索尔坦・玛姆玛多夫：我们是一个基金会，我们生产的产品想要卖给投资人。但是过去 10 年，我们清楚地发现，气候变化和健康都是基于案例。有些时候慈善并不能够解决这些问题，我们必须系统性解决每个问题，这需要该项目有可持续发展的潜力，获得政府和企业的支持。我们投进去的钱必须能使企业自身获得发展，所以我们进行了更多的以项目为主的投资，尽可能地带来可持续性的投资，或者可持续性的考量。对于我们的企业来说，如果可以看到可持续性发展的项目就可以获得捐赠了。

张俊勇：这个世界通过人工智能等将大家联系在一起，当然有新的系统和机制要渐次建立，能够帮助我们应对发生的如此多的变革。刚刚黄学思提到的股权是很好的方法，但是新技术时代，新的技术包括人工智能、物联网、区块链等，一切会走向数字化。在数字化的世界当中，相对来说非常容易建立规则和规矩，比如鼓励企业和机构把它们盈利的 3%~5% 拿来做捐赠。自然而然地，这个账面上一部分净利润可以进入基金会，支持某一特殊社会问题的解决。我一直都相信，在过去或者现在，捐赠是一个比较大的任务，因为要做很多前期工作。在全新的社会当中，我们可能会有新的、系统的激励政策，鼓励公司和机构将它们利润的一部分拿出来进行捐赠。这是一种人的行为和机构的行为的改变，要让它们慢慢地适应这个改变。我们可以做到这一点。

陈家乐：我有一个问题想问张元龙理事长，我国政府可以有什么政策推动公益的发展？

张元龙：我觉得政府的责任很清楚，就是营造法治环境，一定要有“善有善报，恶有恶报”的社会氛围，只要有了这个氛围，很多人会乐意捐钱。对于企业来说，就是赚钱，赚钱就交税，政府拿税做一些福利事业。我觉得最高的境界，应该是社会企业，社会企业交税，交税之后再捐款。比较典型的是扎克伯格，企业赚钱再交给基金会，这时候企业的责任非常清楚，就是赚钱，赚钱交税，把员工养好。尤其是产品，我们现在有很多的产品，最后都是垃圾，我们处理垃圾要花钱，我们做产品的时候要想到这个东西以后怎么样处理，这是我们对未来环境非常重要的贡献。

陈家乐：张元龙先生会怎么样和企业说？

张元龙：尽其所能获得，倾其所有给予。

张俊勇：我非常同意张元龙理事长的话，企业尽其所能承担责任，然后做捐赠，让社会有更好的未来。

陈家乐：非常感谢所有的讲者，我们希望进一步推动企业和慈善工作有所进展，非常感谢，今天我从大家身上学到了很多东西。由于时间有限，感谢各位，谢谢各位讲者，与此同时，非常感谢张元龙理事长，感谢黄学思先生，感谢索尔坦·玛姆玛多夫先生，感谢张俊勇先生，谢谢。

十四　闭幕式

主 持 人：中国人民对外友好协会秘书长、中国友好和平发展基金会理事长　李希奎

嘉宾演讲：公益无国界，以理性精神推动全球公益可持续发展

腾讯集团主要创始人、腾讯公益慈善基金会发起人兼荣誉理事长　陈一丹

闭幕致辞

意大利前总理　马西莫·达莱马

李希奎：感谢主持人和各位对话嘉宾，接下来进行以《公益无国界，以理性精神推动全球公益可持续发展》为题的演讲。有请腾讯集团主要创始人、腾讯公益慈善基金会发起人兼荣誉理事长、“一丹奖”创办人陈一丹先生。

公益无国界，以理性精神推动全球公益可持续发展

腾讯集团主要创始人、腾讯公益慈善基金会发起人兼

荣誉理事长 陈一丹

尊敬的各位嘉宾，女士们，先生们，下午好，很高兴参加第四届世界公益慈善论坛，这两天，来自世界各地的公益伙伴、专家、学者齐聚深圳，共同探讨新的时代背景下，如何推动公益慈善事业更健康地发展，更好地帮助构建美好的社会，这里有许多好的经验值得细细回味，也有许多观点激发广泛共鸣。在我看来，全球公益事业的发展壮大，需要借助世界各地各种慈善理念和行动，不断交流和融通。当我们以国际视野审视全球化背景下的差异化、多元化发展样态的时候，彼此借鉴经验，我们将共同探索一条跨越国界、跨越种族，让公益慈善可以持续发展的普惠之路。

中国的慈善文化是源远流长的，从学者的考证可知，中国是世界上最早畅行慈善的国家之一，早在西周时期就设有慈善机构，而中国的慈善思想，无论是儒家讲的仁爱、佛家讲的慈悲、道家讲的慈善，还是其他诸子百家的表述，都在阐述福利社群的理念。可以说以儒、佛、道为主的中国传统文化各信仰，既是中国慈善文化的思想渊源，也是社会乐善好施风俗得以形成的基础，它们共同构成了中国慈善文化的核心。长久以来，中国的民众在善文化的氛围下成长、生活。而当代中国的慈善立法，则是在 2005 年发起研究的，到 2015 年启动审议，经历了 10 年的酝酿，于 2016 年颁布了首部《慈善法》。西方国家的公益发展呈现不同的历史和文化印记，尤其是近现代以来，伴随工业革命引发的生产力和生产关系的变化，慈善公益的理念、模式、运作方式、监督机制都发生了深刻的变革。以英国为例，英国的公益慈善事

业，最初是出于基督教的博爱精神，但它的发展离不开政府的支持。英国在17世纪初就颁布了《济贫法》，通过强制征税的方式，建立了从纳税人到受助人的体系，体现了政府在其中的强监督的作用。而美国在把英国的慈善思想和事业带到新大陆的同时，也做了明显的整合创新，尤其表现为民间自发性的互帮互助，所以它的公益文化延续博爱精神。另一个是民众参与公共事务的慈善的精神。自19世纪30年代起，各种民众慈善组织自发性大量涌现，慈善活动从个人走向团体，最终推动了美国现代公益生态的形成。可以说过去百年，美国公益的发展离不开一系列优惠措施的支持，尤其是税收减免、制度保障和制度鼓励。不难看出，公益慈善在不同国家、不同的文化环境中有着不同的理念、框架模式和方法，并且随着社会的发展而得到改良。然而公益的本质追求是相同的，即为广泛的社会群体谋福利。公益，对公有益，而在悠久的历史发展过程中，各国慈善文化借助文化交流、科技发展，彼此借鉴，相互交融，在透明、便捷的制度建设方面，也越发显得具有共性。同时在各自的文化社会背景下各具特色，共同推动全球公益慈善事业的发展和繁荣。

让我们感到自豪的是，最近十几年来，中国互联网企业越来越深入公益领域，当代的科技和公益的结合发生了令人惊喜的化学反应，各种互联网募捐信息平台不断涌现，并将公益性社会组织、企业、公众、政府有效地联结在一起，推动中国公益呈现全民参与的蓬勃发展态势。当代公益事业的形态和发展模式，可以说在互联网等科技的助力下，在中国已经焕然一新。

2007年，中国互联网行业的第一家公益慈善基金会——腾讯公益慈善基金会成立，成为中国互联网公益发展的标志性事件之一。而目前腾讯公益也成为全球最大的互联网公益筹款平台。在这个平台上，有上万家公益机构，7万多个公益项目。该平台获得了2.47亿人次的捐赠、57亿人的善款。因为科技的力量，依托互联网社交的扩散效应和产品创意，中国互联网公益像雪球一样越滚越大。正是科技的力量，把中国传统文化中的善语言与当代信息化的载体有机融合，形成独特的互联网公益发展的中国样本，这一切发展只有 10 余年的时间。

而互联网在为公益带来便捷的同时，也带来新的挑战，更流通的通信条件、更智能的硬件设备，都让公益行为越来越简单。如何在一时或者一件事的激情过后，让捐赠者真心认同自己从公益行为中获得的情感共鸣？如何让一次性的行为转化为行为习惯？如何让互联网用户和慈善机构保持信任的长期性？这些问题与互联网技术能否真正帮助全球公益慈善事业实现健康而长久的发展关系重大。我认为答案的关键在理性公益。理性公益，首先来自思考，捐赠应该是慎重思考后的捐赠，捐多捐少也受制于捐赠者的经济条件。但对公益项目的权衡选择，以及捐赠之后对项目进程和落地的关注，这些额外的时间和精力付出，可能比单纯的资金投入更重要。而理性公益也要求社会组织和互联网公益平台做好制度建设，尤其是公益组织的内部管理、信息透明等规则的制定，要一起推进。理性公益还要求在有限的条件和道德的高尚要求中找到平衡。真正的理性公益是参与方理解和尊重，公益事业的本质发展让善意结出善果。

互联网技术让人们更便捷地触达世界，让地球村成为现实，而全球公益生态的发展也已经呈现新的变化和特点。世界不同地区的人们，命运从未像今天这样，臭氧层破洞引发全球关注和探讨，亚马孙森林大火，“地球之肺”在燃烧。活在同一个地球上的人们，需要超越国界，共同关注全球的事情、关注全人类的事情。在全球这些议题上，没有一个国家可以独善其身，也不是一个国家能够独立解决的，人们真切地感受到，今天亚马孙河流域热带雨林的蝴蝶偶尔扇动翅膀，已经真实地影响到彼此的生活。

1820 年，世界上 94% 的人口，生活在极端贫困之中，1990 年，这个数字是 34%，2016 年到 9.6%，更多富裕人口和更少的贫困人口，意味着我们有更多的资源可集中用于慈善公益，意味着我们将有更多的可能性全球性地探索新的公益方式。

社会的痛点是公益的起点，归根溯源，中国传统医学上有“善功治胃病”的哲学，同样可以启发我们。就是说社会根源和希望皆在于未来，未来的教育、未来的人。在教育问题上，同样需要全球的合作，好的教育模式、好的教育研究成果、好的教育实践可以全人类共享。教育及公益的结合、教育和科技的结合，不仅仅是补救人间的疾苦，更多的是播种，实现长久的繁荣。而创新是全球教育发展的核心，我们可以看到模式的创新为教育发展带来新的面貌。比如南美洲，在那里，教育短缺反而催生了教育公平模式的创新。2017 年“一丹奖”“教育发展奖”的获得者，创立了一种模式，主张以学生为中心，倡导自主学习，在这里学生是主人，老师是学习的引领者，没有教材，只有学习指南。所以新学校的模式是应对哥伦比亚教育资源紧缺而产生的，但不妨碍它追求更高水平的教育，它是低成本、可持续的创新典范，也是自主学习和协作型学习的创新典范。也就是说发达城市追求的个性化教育已经实现了，正是因为如此，新学校的模式得以走出哥伦比亚的乡村，得到国际社会的关注和支持。联合国儿童基金会、世界银行给予研究支持，世界的教育峰会给予肯定。这些模式推广到三大洲的 16 个国家，而科技的创新也使教育的发展呈现新的面貌。

今天运用互联网科技平台，将优质的教育资源连接到任何地方，已经是非常成功的探索。2018 年“一丹奖”教育实践者的获得者阿南特教授，它创立了一个非营利的在线学习平台，6 年来，改变了世界各地超过 2000 万人的生活。其自由开放的课程，被中国、法国、俄罗斯等超过 70 个国家采用，全球 130 多家教育机构与其合作，成为其教育伙伴。知识无疆，学习无边，科技帮助我们实现这一美好的教育理想。

在腾讯公益的平台上，我们也可以看到教育和公益跨界创新的实现、众多国内教育项目落地的经验，也开启了对于国际合作的探讨，中国公益机构和联合国难民署合作，希望为非洲因为战争而流离失所的女孩重新提供新的教育机会。一个中国互联网用户，可以通过自己捐出的步数帮助一个非洲的战地女孩重新回到学校；还能在自己的朋友圈号召更多的朋友一起行善，让公益融入生产。这些生动的故事和场景让我们看到，当互联网拉近了人与人之间距离的时候，公益当中的公的含义和外延，比我们传统理解的公益扩展了很多。公益已经不局限于某一地、某一国，也不局限于某一种形式，而是跨国界、多方式，具有追求全人类普惠之意，目的是让暖流和善意送到世界每一个人的心中。

中国当代的公益慈善事业，伴随着国家的发展而兴起。我们不能忘记全球各国、各地的华人，对中国内地的无私帮助，当面对灾难时我们众志成城、血脉相连。同时公益和教育紧密相连，从南洋华侨领袖陈嘉庚先生归国办学，海内外的侨胞支持希望工程，托起亿万个孩子的梦想，到中国有大学的地方就有逸夫楼，都在激励人心、激励后人。对此，我们感怀于心、感恩于心，而今天，中国的发展日新月异，海内外华夏儿女携手做公益，为回馈全球社会贡献中国样板、中国智慧、中国力量，相信这是我们共同的心愿。

放眼这个高度全球化的时代，我们会有未解决的矛盾，也会有发展引发的问题，但人类同呼吸、共命运，全球合作，全球创新的趋势仍未改变，我们要关注未来。尤其是在当下人工智能、生物技术等科技蓬勃而出的历史阶段，从东方到西方，不同国家以各自的方式，利用互联网等在改造和创新着公益，创新着事业。在新一轮信息革命的浪潮之下，我们要去不断调整和重塑社会，公益慈善在这个过程中发挥着越来越重要的作用。我们期望以理性的精神，共同推动全球公益慈善事业实现可持续发展，使之成为全人类追求更美好世界的推动力。

在座的各位，愿我们共同努力，以公益、以科技、以教育，留下属于我们这个时代的文明印记，谢谢大家！

李希奎： 陈一丹先生告诉我们，互联网为公益插上腾飞的翅膀，科技为慈善提供了推动力、装上了更好的引擎。更重要的是，我们要有真正的理性精神，谢谢陈一丹先生。

各位嘉宾，各位代表，时间过得非常快，第四届世界公益慈善论坛即将落下帷幕，延续往届论坛在持续关注人才教育、青年发展、儿童健康等主题的同时，论坛增设善财、善商等新议题，增加学术报告的产出与发布，倡导企业与个人积极参与慈善事业。既注重务实合作，又着力平台建设，实现了信息互通、资源共享。同声相应，同气相求，各位与会嘉宾都是为了公益慈善相聚于此。

两天里，政、商、学、社各界人士就多项议题开展了富有建设性的对话和研讨，实现了公益慈善领域思想火花的碰撞，为推动公益慈善事业向前发展注入了新的活力。

汇聚众智，融合力量。将公益慈善扩展至各个领域，推动构建人类命运共同体，是我们对公益慈善事业未来的期许。我们邀请到意大利前总理担任论坛的顾问，其对论坛和慈善事业的发展给予了宝贵指导，现在我们以热烈的掌声欢迎马西莫·达莱马阁下做闭幕致辞。

闭幕致辞

意大利前总理　马西莫·达莱马

女士们，先生们，大家下午好！我非常荣幸能够在深圳见到各位，深圳是一个年轻又开放的城市，我也非常高兴参与第四届世界公益慈善论坛，作为论坛的顾问，非常感谢。每次来到深圳都能感受到其蓬勃发展的活力，同时看到整个中国的发展，中国是一个广大的市场，还有继续发展的空间，以及非常光明的未来。从我个人来看，中国的发展，首先是中国改革开放巨大成就带来的发展。其次是中国加强国际合作带来的发展。最后是“一带一路”倡议带来的政策推广。目前在贸易的发展之下，中国和世界各地建立了强有力的合作伙伴关系，我相信“一带一路”倡议不仅可以帮助中国和世界各地开展更多的合作，而且能够复制到共建“一带一路”国家，同时帮助我们不断推动人类文化的进步。作为意大利人，我自己对“一带一路”倡议深有感触，意大利和中国都是古代丝绸之路国家，我们的祖先秉承非常美好的理念，希望追求美好的生活。所以把丝绸之路作为贸易的一个沟通桥梁和走廊，能够不断地推动当时文明的发展，正是丝绸之路，将多个国家和地区紧密联系在一起。2013 年中国推出“一带一路”倡议，包括 21 世纪海上丝绸之路，我们希望能够重振古代的丝绸之路。为什么全球化是不可逆转的趋势？所谓的贸易主义和贸易壁垒无法阻挡全球化的发展。现在贸易保护主义成为全球非常关心的问题，我在读《金融时报》时，看到美国由于贸易冲突，出现了非常明显的股市下跌的情况，这是非常令人惊奇的。世界的经济，包括美国的经济深受重创，是贸易保护主义引起的，所以我们要回归理性，理性的意思就是加强合作。就像城市联盟的负责人说的，“一带一路”倡议恰逢其时，它能够帮助我们不断加强全球合作，不断扩展经济合作，不断促进经济融合，能够不断推动全球的发展。而且能够不断加强各国之间的经济交流，搭建一个全新的合作平台，同时能够提供更多的各国之间民间交流的可能性和机会。

慈善，毫无疑问，也是我们全球发展新展望当中非常重要的一个部分。也就是说我们要去减少不平等，尽可能摒除贫困，让人有尊严地生活下去。

世界的发展带来了大量的机会，但是我们不应该让任何人被抛下，全球化是以人为主的全球化。慈善是我们文化当中的一个部分，也是我们宗教当中的重要部分。在中国和意大利，我们建立了慈善机构，同时不断推动民间交流和民间沟通。在“一带一路”倡议提出和推广之下，意大利和中国进行了广泛的交流和合作。在意大利签署了谅解备忘录，中国还建立了相关的大学、慈善机构，加强双方的合作。后来我们达成了加强意大利和中国双向慈善合作的共识，在世界公益慈善论坛、中国相关的公益活动中加强双方的信任，包括交流和互相了解，这样的话才能建立起真正和平的地球村。

世界公益慈善论坛希望能够不断地推动有益的发展、全球的交流、人员的培训，包括政策的互相分享、经验的互换，第四届世界公益慈善论坛提到了慈善遇到的挑战和新趋势，包括财富的分配和公益慈善之间的关系。我们也非常高兴世界各地的嘉宾与我们一起探讨，帮助我们设想慈善发展的未来。这样非常优秀的论坛作为一个平台，我们所有的参与者非常积极地探讨了经验及看法，包括慈善在各自国家发展的经验和想法。我相信世界的公益慈善之路将会在各位的参与之下呈现更加光明的发展前景。如果我们回顾过去，可以看到越来越多公益慈善的专家和学者已经加入教育领域帮助我们强化人才培训，以及实现更好的合作，包括推动大湾区的发展，这些对我们来说是新鲜的议题。我相信世界公益慈善论坛是卓有成效的，为了实现更好的发展，我提出以下的建议。第一，继续加强世界公益慈善人才的交流和交换，不断提高慈善从业者的素质和能力。同时激励他们相互分享经验、相互学习，帮助我们不断加强世界公益慈善本身的专业性。第二，我们应该共同探讨如何建立双方或者多方公益慈善合作的框架。同时，我们要不断提高论坛的影响力，尽可能让慈善的研究者获得地区政府的支持。第三，我们应该建立起世界公益慈善论坛的机制，在这个机制上，加强共建“一带一路”国家在公益慈善领域的合作，帮助我们吸引更多的国家加入“一带一路”公益慈善的机制当中，鼓励更多的国家不断加强民间交流，包括文化交流。我相信通过我们的一致努力，世界公益慈善论坛将会成为一个非常优秀的平台，不断加强民间交往，增进民间友谊，帮助我们加深了解和信任，同时真正形成一个共享的愿景，帮助我们实现人类社会的和平和繁荣。

第四届世界公益慈善论坛是在国际慈善日举办的，论坛的主要目标是让人们加深对慈善的了解、对非政府组织的了解，同时促使全球各地的利益相关方采取行动，包括激励志愿者参与活动。作为本次世界公益慈善论坛的顾问，我也希望所有人能够携手解决全球化带来的问题，一起发展公益事业、慈善事业，为人类造福。我也期待 2020 年第五届世界公益慈善论坛的开办，谢谢大家。

李希奎：非常感谢马西莫 · 达莱马先生。马西莫 · 达莱马先生对“一带一路”与公益慈善关系完美详尽的阐述，让我们感觉到马西莫 · 达莱马先生对“一带一路”如此认同和了解。借助公益慈善的力量，推动“一带一路”建设，一直是我们论坛的目标之一。

第三部分

十五 成果发布、证书颁发

主持人：中国人民对外友好协会秘书长、中国友好和平发展基金会理事长 李希奎

李希奎：滴水能穿石，世界公益慈善论坛的成功举办，没有各方单位和人事的支持，就没有如今的收获和成果。接下来让我们有请匈牙利前总理彼得·麦杰西颁发论坛合作证书，请深圳市基金会发展促进会（Shenzhen Commonweal Fund Federation）、创行（Enactus）、TCL公益基金会（TCL Charity Foundation）和赠与亚洲（Give2Asia）四家单位代表上台。

（颁发证书环节）

李希奎：感谢彼得·麦杰西先生，下面有请意大利前总理马西莫·达莱马先生为五家论坛支持单位颁发证书。

请山西省公益事业促进会、上海市华侨事业发展基金会、浙江省社会组织总会、中华少年儿童慈善救助基金会、福建省慈善基金会代表上台。

（颁发证书环节）

李希奎：感谢马西莫·达莱马先生，也感谢相关支持单位对本次论坛的支持。

李希奎：女士们，先生们！本次论坛我们顺利开展，并完成关于公共健康、人才培养、社会创新等议题的讨论，就高等教育、儿童福利、国际合作等方面开展高端对话，诸多来自各界的权威人士发表主题演讲，为今后世界公益慈善事业的发展建言献策，成果颇丰。接下来我们将启动多项合作计划，马上进入本届论坛最后的成果发布环节。

首先请卡洛斯·列朗先生启动地方政府慈善促进合作计划，并请他与中国友好和平发展基金会副秘书长邓岚女士交换备忘录。

（启动环节）

卡洛斯·列朗： 尊敬的各位嘉宾，亲爱的朋友们，我从摩洛哥来，大家都知道，我们一起参与公益事业，让整个地区变得更加可持续发展，所以我代表我们的机构分享一下，我们机构有 600 个成员。我们很高兴和中国人民对外友好协会一起合作，做一个本地的扶贫公益项目，我们也希望能够把这个项目当成世界公益慈善论坛的成果向大家发布，谢谢大家。

李希奎： 下面赠与亚洲理事曾宪章先生、赠与亚洲总裁兼首席执行官比格尔·斯坦普德尔、赠与亚洲理事长薛希璞、纽约梅隆银行财富管理副总裁马洁芝，将共同启动善财传承计划。

（启动环节）

曾宪章： 各位嘉宾，大家下午好，现在宣布善财传承计划，发起单位：美国赠与亚洲基金会，董事长薛先生，总裁比格尔先生，第二个单位是美国纽约梅隆银行，是由马副总裁代表。昨天下午，我们开了闭门圆桌论坛，有 50 多位代表参加，达成了一致的共识，由我宣布三个行动计划。第一个行动计划，身体力行，投身公益慈善事业。希望大家能够将慈善的奉献精神和责任感视为己任，积极投入。将财富的正向精神和价值观融入社会建设和发展。第二个行动计划，建立永续的善财传承机制，包括企业社会责任基金、慈善信托、永续的慈善基金。第三个行动计划，建立国际协商合作的行动网络，包括亚洲共建“一带一路”国家、“南南合作”国家相关地区的公益慈善事业。涵盖的领域，包括妇女、儿童权益的保护，包括乡村振兴与发展，包括公共卫生与教育公平等。最后我借用乔布斯的一句名言作为结束语“我们的激情可以改变世界，让世界更为美好”，谢谢各位。

李希奎： 下面请中国友好和平发展基金会副秘书长邓岚女士启动善创未

来全球青年社会创新大赛计划。

邓岚：大家下午好，很高兴代表世界公益慈善论坛宣布善创未来全球青年社会创新大赛计划。世界公益慈善论坛将启动这个大赛，联合青年成就组织等国际组织，以及来自国内外的机构、企业和知名学府，为全球的青年提供一个交流、思考、创造的平台，鼓励和启发他们用善的初心进行创新、用创新的思维推动公益实践，为社会发展和人类进步贡献他们的智慧和方案，我们期待可以用善心汇聚善力、用善力支持善创、用善创收获善果，谢谢大家。

李希奎：下面请论坛学术委员会委员、香港中文大学社会工作学系主任倪锡钦教授和论坛学术委员会委员、清华大学公共管理学院教授刘庆龙启动社会服务领军人才培养计划，并交换硕士学位教育项目合作协议。

倪锡钦：时间过得真快，我记得 2018 年我们和大家共同分享了我们在人才培养方面的合作计划，现在我和大家共同分享我们的进展，2018 年和大家提到，要专门做一个香港社会服务的研讨会，我们这个研讨会非常成功地举办了。现在我们在社会服务方面有 30 多位专家参与，包括来自美国和新加坡的专家，中国台湾和大陆的专家。2018 年我们举办了非常成功的论坛，包括未来合作的几个部分，首先是社会服务的博士学位，能够寻找具有创新性的社会教育和方法。此外，希望加大对非营利组织人才的培养力度。我们将继续合作，同时希望研讨会在澳门举办，我们的会议将由澳门城市大学和澳门理工大学举办。另外的合作也是我们想和大家分享的，就是目前我们关于社会服务领军人才培养的工作，这是由清华大学和香港中文大学共同完成的研究，在我们的项目中，由来自清华大学的老师和香港中文大学的老师任教，学生完成学业，将会获得社会服务领军人才香港中文大学和清华大学的学士学位。此外，希望这样联合人才计划的做法，能够为我们带来中国慈善领军人才，只有这样的方法，才能带来创新服务的领军者，提高社会服务的效率，同时帮助我们更好地适应这个社会的发展。我们的课程主要是在北京进行，所以我们现在正在准备招收第一批学生。而它会是两年的项目，我们所有的学生拿到录取通知书之后将会入学。我们也会继续向大家通报我们后续在人才培养方面的进展，谢谢。

李希奎：下面请论坛筹备组召集人、清华大学公益慈善研究院副院长黄真平和深圳市基金会发展促进会代表启动基金会国际友好合作计划。

深圳市基金会发展促进会代表：很高兴代表深圳市基金会发展促进会和世界公益慈善论坛，一起宣布国际友好合作计划的启动。深圳市基金会发展促进会将和世界公益慈善论坛合力建设深圳市基金会发展促进会国际交流合作委员会。我们将推动深圳市 400 多家公益基金会“走出去”，和粤港澳大湾区、共建“一带一路”国家，以及欧美国家优秀的基金会进行行业交流、项目合作、资源对接。我们也将把上述国家、地区的优秀基金会请进来，一起交流合作。我们深圳市基金会发展促进会将和世界公益慈善论坛一起打造公益慈善行业的深圳力量、深圳形象、深圳示范，谢谢大家！

李希奎：以上五项合作计划，不仅是所有与会嘉宾的智慧结晶，也是所有人努力的方向。随着计划的发布，第四届世界公益慈善论坛将圆满落下帷幕，下面请大家欣赏论坛花絮视频。

（视频播放）

本书编写组

本书编写组由世界公益慈善论坛主办方中国人民对外友好协会、清华大学、香港大学、香港中文大学委托论坛筹备组负责组成。编写组成员包括论坛筹备组主要负责人、议题拟定建议者和论坛工作人员，既强调论坛精神的把握，也负责论坛内容编写质量。在本书编写中各位参与人的发言均做了审核，领导人致辞、重要嘉宾发言也均经过其本人确认。

编写组具体成员包括：

黄真平，世界公益慈善论坛筹备组负责人。

邓岚，中国人民对外友好协会民间外交战略研究中心主任。

李勇，清华大学公益慈善研究院院长助理，公益社创实验室主任。

赵静雅，清华大学公益慈善研究院研究人员。

李倩颖，清华大学公益慈善研究院研究人员。

王倩赟，清华大学公益慈善研究院研究人员。

朱盈盈，世界公益慈善论坛专职人员。

魏菡昱，世界公益慈善论坛专职人员。

PHILANTHROPY IN THE BAY AREA FOR BETTER LIFE

THE FOURTH WORLD PHILANTHROPY FORUM

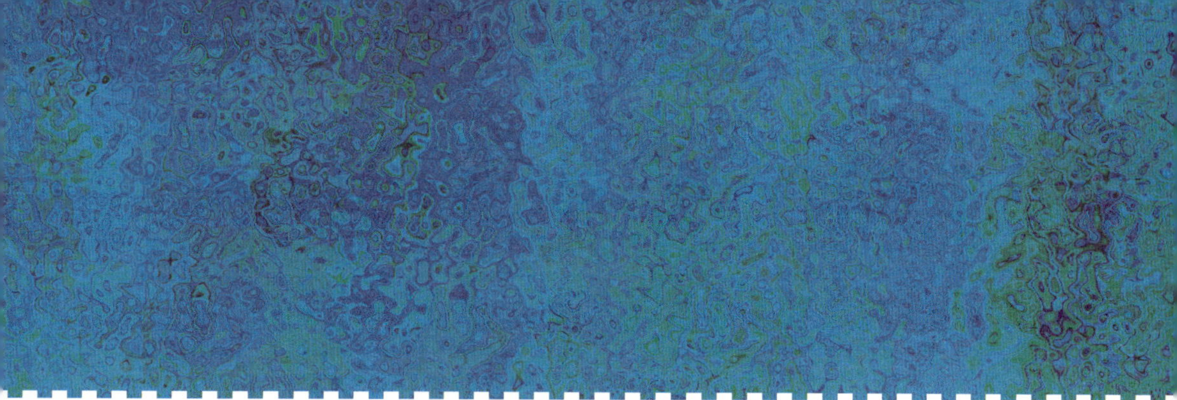

PHILANTHROPY

IN THE BAY AREA FOR BETTER LIFE

THE FOURTH WORLD PHILANTHROPY FORUM

（下册）

Chinese-English

EDITORIAL TEAM

社会科学文献出版社
SOCIAL SCIENCES ACADEMIC PRESS (CHINA)

第四届世界公益慈善论坛部分与会人员合影
Photo of Participants of the Fourth World Philanthropy Forum (WPF)

第四届世界公益慈善论坛部分与会人员闭幕式合影
Photo of Participants of the Fourth World Philanthropy Forum at the Closing Ceremony

中国第十三届全国政协副主席李斌发言

Speech by Li Bin, Vice-Chairperson of the 13th National Committee of the Chinese People's Political Consultative Conference

第四届世界公益慈善论坛会见（左起：卡洛斯·列朗、彼得·麦杰西、李斌、李小林）

Meetings of Leaders (From Left: Carles Llorens, Péter Medgyessy, Li Bin, Li Xiaolin)

论坛联合主席、中国人民对外友好协会会长李小林主持
Host of Officiating Speech, Li Xiaolin, Co-chair of the World Philanthropy Forum, President of the Chinese People's Association for Friendship with Foreign Countries

论坛联合主席、清华大学校务委员会主任陈旭致辞
Speech by Chen Xu, Co-chair of the World Philanthropy Forum, Chairperson of Tsinghua University Council

论坛联合主席、香港中文大学校长段崇智致辞

Speech by Rocky S. Tuan, Co-chair of the World Philanthropy Forum,
Vice Chancellor and President of the Chinese University of Hong Kong

香港大学副校长区洁芳致辞

（论坛联合主席、香港大学校长张翔视频致辞，香港大学副校长区洁芳代为现场致辞）

Speech by Terry Au, Vice-President and Pro-Vice-Chancellor of The University of Hong Kong
(On behalf of Professor Zhang Xiang, Co-Chair of the World Philanthropy Forum,
President and Vice-Chancellor of University of Hong Kong. Professor Zhang Xiang gave a speech via video.)

论坛顾问、匈牙利前总理彼得·麦杰西发言
Speech by Péter Medgyessy, WPF Advisor, Former Prime Minister of Hungary

论坛顾问、意大利前总理马西莫·达莱马致辞
Speech by Massimo D’ Alema, WPF Advisor, Former Prime Minister of Hungary

第四届世界公益慈善论坛开幕式会议现场

Meeting Venue of the Fourth World Philanthropy Forum Opening Ceremony

第四届世界公益慈善论坛联合主办方代表、深圳市副市长艾学峰致辞

Speech by Ai Xuefeng, Representative of co-host of the Fourth World Philanthropy Forum, Vice Mayer of Shenzhen Municipal People's Government

论坛顾问、中国民政部副部长王爱文演讲

Speech by Wang Aiwen, WPF Advisor, Vice Minister of Ministry of Civil Affairs of the People's Republic of China,

中国中央人民政府驻香港特别行政区联络办公室副主任谭铁牛致辞

Speech by Tan Tieniu, Deputy Director of the Liaison Office of the Central People's Government in the Hong Kong S.A.R

香港赛马会主席周永健演讲

Speech by Dr. Chow Wing-kin, Anthony, Chairman of the Hong Kong Jockey Club

联合国儿童基金会私人筹款和伙伴关系部总监加里·斯塔尔演讲

Speech by Gary Stahl, Director of Division of Private Fundraising and Partnerships of UNICEF

慈善湾区与人才培养专题（左起：张亮、王淑英、肖海鹏、楚明伟）

Philanthropy in the Greater Bay Area and Talent Nurturing

(From Left: Cheung Leong, Wong Suk-ying, Xiao Haipeng, Christopher Tremewan)

21世纪公共健康与慈善专题

（左起：阿尼尔·卡普尔、加斯普·布兰德佳德、刘斯奇、罗乐宣、林大庆）

Public Health and Philanthropy in the 21st Century

(From Left: Anil Kapur, Jesper Brandgaard, Liu Siqi, Luo Lexuan, Lam Tai-hing)

青年与湾区社会创新和社会企业专题（左起：何永昌、查尔斯·埃斯利、吴学明）
Youths, Community Innovation & Social Enterprise in the Greater Bay Area
(From Left: Ho Wing-cheong, Charles Eesley, Wu Xueming)

体育人慈善路专题（左起：莫滕·汉森、李娜、李希奎、胡里奥·冈萨雷斯·隆科、张强强）
Sports and Philanthropy
(From Left: Morten Mølholm Hansen, Li Na, Li Xikui, Julio Ronco Gonzalez, Zhang Qiangqiang)

高等教育社会捐赠的探索与实践——中国案例专题

（左起：涂蓉辉、赵文莉、梁晖、房涛、刘迅、沈黎勇、袁桅、王振民）

Philanthropy & Fundraising in Higher Education – China's Practice

(From Left: Tu Ronghui, Zhao Wenli, Liang Hui, Fang Tao, Liu Xun, Shen Liyong, Yuan Wei, Wang Zhenmin)

善财传承专题

Wealth and Philanthropy

赠与亚洲理事长薛希璞（左上）主持善财传承圆桌专题

珀杜家族与喜来登家族代表米齐·珀杜（右上）、清华大学华商研究中心主任龙登高（左下）

与中欧商学院教授及中欧家族传承研究中心联合主任芮萌（右下）进行专题演讲

Moderator: George SyCip, Board Chairman of Give2Asia (Upper Left)

Speakers: Mitzi Perdue, on behalf of Perdue & Sheraton Family (Upper Right).

Long Denggao, Director of Center for Chinese Entrepreneur Studies, Tsinghua University (Lower Left).

Rui Meng, Professor of China Europe International Business School,

Co-Director of CEIBS Centre for Family Heritage (Lower Right)

湾区未来，儿童福利专题——儿童健康与福祉

（左起：刘庆龙、郭朋、黄文锋、魏巍、侯春艳、塞巴斯蒂安·库斯特、霍泰辉、王林）

Future Visions for Children's Wellbeing: Children's health and welfare

(From Left: Liu Qinglong, Guo Peng, Huang Wenfeng, Wei Wei, Hou Chunyan, Sebastien Kuster, Fok Tai-fai, Wang Lin)

湾区未来，儿童福利专题——为所有儿童提供教育的机会

（左起：郑道、彼得·威廉、萧凯恩、李红艳、塞巴斯蒂安·库斯特、吕德雄）

Future Visions for Children's Wellbeing: Providing All Children with a chance of education

(From Left: Douglas Noble, Peter Williams, Siu Hoi Yan, Li Hongyan, Sebastien Kuster, Lyu Dexiong)

善学明辨专题

Education and Philanthropy

“一带一路”公益慈善合作专题（左起：卡洛斯·列朗、梁星心、林碧玉、凌冲、陈勇）

Philanthropic Cooperation with Countries along the “Belt and Road Initiative”
(From Left: Carles Llorens, Liang Xingxin, Lin Biyu, Ling Chong, Chan Yung)

全国工商联原副主席、天津市人大常委会原副主任，中华红丝带基金理事长张元龙演讲

Speech by Zhang Yuanlong, Former Vice Chairman of All-China Federation of Industry and Commerce, Former Deputy Director of the Standing Committee of Tianjin Municipal People's Congress, and Chairman of the China Red Ribbon Foundation

湾区发展，善商之道专题（左起：张俊勇、索尔坦·玛姆玛多夫、黄学思、张元龙、陈家乐）

How to Develop a Good Business Path in the Greater Bay Area

(From Left: Thomas Cheung Tsun-Yung, Soltan Mammadov, Wong H. Henry, Zhang Yuanlong, Kalok Chan)

腾讯集团主要创始人、腾讯公益慈善基金会发起人兼荣誉理事长陈一丹演讲

Speech by Chen Yidan, Co-Founder of Tencent Group, Initiator and Honorary Chairman of Tencent Charity Foundation

论坛联合主席、中国人民对外友好协会会长李小林为匈牙利前总理彼得·麦杰西颁发第四届世界公益慈善论坛顾问证书

WPF Advisor Certificate Presentation（From Left: Li Xiaolin, Péter Medgyessy）

论坛联合主席、中国人民对外友好协会会长李小林与意大利前总理马西莫·达莱马
举行会见并颁发第四届世界公益慈善论坛顾问证书
Meetings of Leaders and WPF Advisor Certificate Presentation
（From Left: Massimo D’ Alema , Li Xiaolin）

论坛联合主席、中国人民对外友好协会会长李小林为
第四届世界公益慈善论坛合作伙伴颁发证书
WPF Partner Certificate Presentation

论坛顾问、匈牙利前总理彼得・麦杰西
为第四届世界公益慈善论坛战略合作伙伴及合作伙伴颁发证书
WPF Strategic Partners and Partners Certificate Presentation

论坛顾问、意大利前总理马西莫・达莱马为第四届世界公益慈善论坛支持单位颁发证书
WPF Supporting Units Certificate Presentation

世界公益慈善论坛·地方政府慈善促进合作计划启动
（左起：卡洛斯·列朗、阿尼尔·卡普尔、邓岚）
Launch of Regional and Local Governments Philanthropy Promotion Cooperation Plan
(From Left: Carles Llorens, Anil Kapur, Deng Lan)

世界公益慈善论坛·善财传承计划启动
（左起：曾宪章、薛希璞、马洁芝、比格尔·斯坦德伯格）
Launch of Philanthropy and Wealth Inheritance Plan
(From Left: Carter Tseng, George SyCip, Jennifer Ma, Birger Stamperdahl)

世界公益慈善论坛·社会服务领军人才培养计划发布

（左起：倪锡钦、刘庆龙）

Announcement of Social Services Leading Talents Training Plan

(From Left: Ngai Sek-yum, Liu Qinglong)

世界公益慈善论坛·基金会国际友好合作计划启动

（左起：黄真平、陈行甲）

Launch of Foundation's International Friendship and Cooperation Program

(From Left: Huang Zhenping, Chen Xingjia)

国际公益人才培养计划代表团在泰国参加联合国开发计划署（UNDP）
社会组织国际合作培训工作坊

International Philanthropic Talent Development Plan Delegation attended the UNDP's training workshop on the international cooperation of social organizations in Thailand

国际公益人才培养计划代表团在越南与越南友好组织联合会主席阮芳娥女士（中）合影

International Philanthropic Talent Development Plan Delegation with Ms. Nguyen Phuong Nga (Center), President of Vietnam Union of Friendship Organizations in Vietnam

国际公益人才培养计划代表团在菲律宾出席“中菲气候变化研讨会”
International Philanthropic Talent Development Plan Delegation attended the "China-Philippines Seminar on Climate Change" in the Philippines

国际公益人才培养计划代表团在中国香港参加香港中文大学国际慈善项目管理培训工作坊
International Philanthropic Talent Development Plan Delegation attended the training workshop of The Chinese University of Hong Kong on the Management of International Philanthropic Projects

世界公益慈善论坛2019年华人社会工作协同合作年会会议现场

Meeting Venue of the WPF 2019 Annual Meeting of Collaboration Mechanism for Chinese Social Work

世界公益慈善论坛2019年华人社会工作协同合作年会部分与会嘉宾合影

Group Photo of WPF 2019 Annual Meeting of Collaboration Mechanism for Chinese Social Work

世界公益慈善论坛2018年华人社会工作协同合作年会部分与会嘉宾合影

Group Photo of the WPF 2018 Annual Meeting of Collaboration Mechanism for Chinese Social Work

世界公益慈善论坛2018年华人社会工作协同合作年会部分与会嘉宾于会场合影

Group Photo of the WPF 2018 Annual Meeting of Collaboration Mechanism for Chinese Social Work of at the Meeting Venue

Contents

Part I Keynote Speeches

Part II Thematic Sessions

Part I

Keynote Speeches

I LAUNCHING SPEECHES

Moderator: Li Xiaolin, President of the CPAFFC, Co-Chair of WPF
Speakers: Li Bin, Vice-Chairperson of the 13th National Committee of the Chinese People's Political Consultative Conference
Péter Medgyessy, Former Prime Minister of Hungary

Write a New Chapter of Philanthropy

Li Bin, Vice-Chairperson of the 13th National Committee of the Chinese People's Political Consultative Conference

Honorable Mr. Péter Medgyessy,
Distinguished guests,
Ladies and Gentlemen,

Good Morning. It's my pleasure to join you in the Fourth World Philanthropy Forum in this beautiful, open and prosperous city, Shenzhen. Today marks the anniversary of the International Day of Charity as well as China Charity Day. It is of special significance for guests from all sectors, both Chinese and foreign, who are dedicated to the development of philanthropy and gather in such a big event. I would like to extend my warm welcome to all of you here.

The world today is undergoing rapid development, profound changes and major transformation. As the international situation becomes more complicate, multipolarity and economic globalization keep deepening, breakthroughs have been made in various technologies, social informatization make a greater impact, and international communities have become increasingly interconnected and interdependent. Peace, development, cooperation and mutual benefit are now the most desirable goals all around the globe. Chinese people have always valued friendship, responsibility, faith and peace. The seek for peace and harmony has been deeply rooted in our minds. China has been and will always be a builder to world peace, a contributor to global development and a proponent for the international order. We will continue to unswervingly pursue the path of peaceful development and contribute to building a community of shared future for mankind. We will continue to strengthen mutual integration and support with countries around the world under the principle of consultation and sharing. We will share the fruits and opportunities of our own development with the rest of the world and contribute our wisdom, solutions and expertise to the achievement of common development.

Within such a new historical context, philanthropy has been playing an important role. General Secretary Xi Jinping has repeatedly stressed the need to raise the awareness of philanthropy and put more efforts into this sector. Philanthropy is a symbol of benevolence, wealth and kindness, a way to express our fundamental human emotions and our love towards others. It is also instrumental in improving people's livelihood. The continuous development of philanthropy is one of the important criteria for the progress of social civilization. We need to take practical measures to promote respect and friendship among different nations. In this way, we could build a more harmonious community and a long-lasting civilization.

Recent years have seen rapid growth in China's philanthropy sector. By the end of 2018, in China, the social donation has totalled RMB 112.8 billion, and the number of social organizations has reached over 806,000, with 2.197 billion hours of volunteer services and a contribution value of RMB 82.3 billion. Supporting regulations and policies for the Charity Law has been issued, such as those regarding the administration of social organizations, and the transparency of philanthropic organizations, providing a more robust legal system for philanthropic work. As a result of such rapid development in philanthropy, we have launched this World Philanthropy Forum in China, to promote academic exchanges, policy discussions, experience sharing and talent development among philanthropic organizations globally. We aim to engage more philanthropic organizations to contribute to society, provide a vital platform for philanthropic organizations of different countries to share more resources and contribute to the philanthropic development around the globe. This year, our forum is held in Shenzhen, an important city in Guangdong-Hong Kong-Macao Greater Bay Area, with the theme of "Philanthropy in the Bay Area for Better Life". We will exchange views and experience on a wide range of topics, including talent development, youth innovation, health, education, the " Belt and Road

Initiative", all centred around philanthropy, the development of Greater Bay Area and livelihood improvement, to establish mutually beneficial cooperation. We hope that this forum could make good contributions to the development of philanthropy in the world.

Ladies and Gentlemen, Dear friends,

As the Chinese saying goes, "The highest form of goodness is like water", philanthropy will gradually benefit all the society like water moistens the soil. I hope that all of you are presenting here, in this philanthropy community, do not forget your original aspirations, innovate to make the forum more valuable and provide insights for the future.

For this purpose, I have three points to make. Firstly, we should improve the operation of the forum and strengthen cooperation. The World Philanthropy Forum, as an important communication platform, is established to strengthen trust and support among philanthropic organizations so that more resources and information could be shared. It is also a place to share and discuss the achievements of charity, philanthropy and social work. I suggest that social service organizations establish long-term relationships with companies to increase the impact of this platform and gain additional support, cooperation in philanthropic activities in public service areas such as health care and child protection to be promoted both at home and abroad, and international philanthropic initiatives to be implemented for the benefit of all people. Secondly, we should strengthen research in various fields and promote academic exchanges. The World Philanthropy Forum has attracted numerous renowned philanthropists, philanthropic organizations, social service agencies and philanthropic service providers ever since its launch. So far, we have established an academic committee and launched a philanthropic organization. In the future, we should keep improving the construction of the academic committee, and exert the influence of the forum as an academic platform, to attract well-known academicians, experts and professionals to join the research team. This will help us to build a think tank full of philanthropic expertise. With the support of the team, we could conduct philanthropy index research to provide insights for its commercial and professional development. Thirdly, we should join hands to create a wonderful world. Philanthropy represents our most sincere emotions. It is a noble cause that could alleviate the humanitarian crisis and benefit all humankind. Philanthropy transcends nationality, race and culture. In every country, you could see philanthropic groups helping the poor and aiding the needed. The development of philanthropy is a symbol for the advancement of civilization. It calls for the participation of every citizen and the support of more social enterprises. Everyone can do some good deeds. We encourage more enterprises to engage in philanthropic activities, to do our part for the world, to make a difference through our deeds. In this way, we could build a community of shared future for mankind, and create a world that is prosperous, open, inclusive, clean and beautiful.

Ladies and gentlemen, dear friends, philanthropy is the most sincere and direct way to express love. Let's remain our original aspirations, join hands to write a new chapter of philanthropy and create a better future.

Finally, I wish a complete success of the forum. Thank you!

Take Advantage of Financial Power to Promote a Better Society: Hungarian Model of Economic Recovery

Péter Medgyessy, Former Prime Minister of Hungary

Dear Ms. Li Bin, Ms. Li Xiaolin,
Ladies and Gentlemen,

Good morning. First of all, thank you for having me to join this important forum. I'd like to extend my congratulations for the successful opening of this event, and a special thanks to the host for the hard work you have done and will do in the next couple of days. My topic today is How the "Hungarian Model of Economic Recovery" Contributes to Community Inclusion and Shared Prosperity. It is a relatively complex topic. I would like to talk on three aspects. First, I will introduce the Hungarian model. Then, I will share my thoughts on the new forms of finance and philanthropy around the globe. Finally, I will talk about immigration, one of the most challenging issues in the world.

Now, let's move to the first part of my speech. The humanitarian crisis mentioned by Ms. Li Bin just now is very serious in today's world, and also a huge challenge. Hungary has always been at the center of reform in the region and an open economy, even during the cold war period. We have joined international financial organizations such as IMF, World Bank, OECD, WTO, among others. We have tried to conduct the reform within the socialist framework and thought patterns. However, the reform was meant for a transition to the market economy. We hope we can add some market economy elements into our system selectively, not completely. Back in 2002, Hungary became the first country in the Middle and East Europe to open to China market. We were the pioneer at that time. Moreover, I am delighted for this move.

Despite our previous reform efforts, Hungary was still impacted by the 2008-2009 financial crisis. So, we decided to take another important economic reform. We made a tough but strong decision in 2009 to take a critical step towards financial balance. In 2002, we started a new fiscal and monetary policy to maintain economic balance. From 2015 until 2019, Hungary's economic growth rate remained at 4% to 5%, a significant achievement for European countries. It made us one of the fastest-growing economies in the EU region. Our fiscal deficit was about 2%, relatively low. Our inflation rate kept at an acceptable level of 2% to 3%. Furthermore, our unemployment rate was as low as 3% to 4%. These facts were what we were all proud of. Yet, we did have weaknesses in the labor force and certain labour activities. In 2004, Hungary joined the EU, and I also participated in signing the agreement. At that time, we gained strong support from the EU, with about €5-7 billion per year. Nevertheless, our cooperation was not limited within the EU; we also had very good relations with China. Since 2002, Hungary's diplomatic relations with China have been strengthened year by year. I am proud to say that this is the consensus of Hungarian political decision-makers. Of course, in a democratic country, the consensus is always hard to reach, as there are often different arguments and concerns. However, we have managed to reach this consensus to build a good relationship with China and keep strengthening our friendship. At the same time, we also have very good relations with the United States, India and Russia. This is because our foreign policy is based on pragmatism. It is a good way for us to welcome direct investment from abroad as we develop. The total investment by foreign companies in the stock exchange is about $100 billion, which is a very sizable number for a small country like Hungary. But, we haven't solved the problems we face, such as the widening income gap between different social groups, and poverty still existing in Hungary. In order to further contribute to the stable and peaceful development of Hungary, we must narrow the gap between the rich and the poor. Such social problems may be well addressed by the rise of the middle class, which however needs a long time to take shape. And, that's where philanthropy comes in. There are also problems with the current Hungarian education system. Although we have made great strides with well-known Hungarian universities, there is still a long way to go. Meanwhile, our health care system also needs to be improved. I think this is a problem facing many countries around the world. For me and the leaders of my country, we have to take this responsibility. We have to improve and optimize our health care system. Moreover, reform is the only solution. To make these happen, or to support what I said earlier, we have great philanthropic programs as a result of our economic opportunities. Good GDP is the basis for philanthropy, as its success requires not only a sound and well-developed economy but also a group of people who are willing to remain committed to this noble cause. Philanthropy is about belief, but also about money. In Hungary, philanthropy exists and operates in the form of foundations, and the number of foundations is growing. We have very important children's foundations, private foundations, as well as foundations that help disadvantaged people stay healthy. We also have funds to support the arts and culture. Overall, we have made great progress successfully, but we also need further growth for philanthropy. We need to raise philanthropic awareness, call for citizens to fulfil their natural duties and obligations. I am not very satisfied with our current status, but I believe it is a good start.

Secondly, the first World Philanthropy Forum in 2016 and the years in between have witnessed economic, culture and globalization development, as well as the progress made in philanthropy globally. This important conclusion tells something about where we are now in terms of economic development, philanthropy achievements and financial system. To elaborate on my point, I'd like to give two examples. Let's look at the United Nations first. UN attaches great importance to philanthropy. It appoints a dedicated adviser to promote its innovation and development and sets up a new department reporting directly to the Secretary-General. All of their work is philanthropy oriented. The Deputy Secretary-General directly led the implementation of this initiative at that time.

By the way, the former France finance minister has also contributed much to the development of philanthropic ideas and practices. The group has proposed several mechanisms ranging from government policies to public-private partnerships to sponsorship mechanisms, as well as broader issues of public concern, such as environmental protection. Several institutions and organizations, such as AMC and the Market Promotion Association, have come up with innovative solutions that give a strong boost to the pharmaceutical and philanthropic industries, especially for poorer countries. It will be a very long list if I mention all the organizations here. We also see advances being made in various philanthropic activities and the whole philanthropic work in the world. We hope that with our concerted efforts, we could further raise awareness and change the way people think about philanthropy. Now, let's look at my second example. The former Prime Minister of Haiti set up an institution dedicated to encouraging the formation of joint ventures and provides them with government financial support for innovation. It is not an easy decision. Now, a large amount of philanthropic money has poured into education to support its development. They have raised money around the world for this purpose. I think the approach of Haiti is a good idea. We should all think about it and promote it in the rest of the world. The funding model of philanthropy has constantly been changing and improving. As new organizations and individuals join such initiatives, the system is getting more funds. We know very well that philanthropy won't work without philanthropic awareness and money.

Finally, I would like to talk about a special but huge issue - immigration. When it comes to immigration, I think the essence of philanthropy here is to love the whole human beings. Immigration is about global mobility, which also means national mobility. Sometimes, there are conflicts as to how to handle such mobility of people from different countries. Governments have to resolve such disputes. Ever since 2000, the world has seen massive migration waves. Some government's responses are understandable to me. They want to shut down the borders or build walls to deny the entry of illegal immigration. However, is it really necessary? We shall find a long-term solution to curb unusual emigration. Emigration also has something to do with environmental changes. It may imply that some countries are suffering from water shortage, food shortage or drought. Their local education issues can also cause emigrants and refugees. If we don't take emigrants and refugees seriously, then what we are doing now should never be called philanthropy. In my opinion, we must analyze the deep causes of the formation of refugees and migrants from a humanitarian and philanthropic point of view and find a long-term solution. Speaking of long-term solutions, we have to tackle education and water supply issues, we also need to think about how to help them achieve better development, and create more jobs in certain regions. But first and foremost, we need to address the issue of regional conflicts. We can awaken people's desire for peace in those areas. We also need to create as more conditions as necessary to achieve that goal, so that people there can live and work in peace. Closing the borders may be necessary, but it is not enough to solve the existing problems.

Ladies and Gentlemen, As I have already explained, philanthropy covers a wide range of areas. It requires us to take responsibility and think broadly. What I have suggested are also limited compared to what this forum can do. We all live in this community with a shared future. Thanks again for your listening. I wish a full success of the forum in the next couple of days. Thank you!

II GUEST SPEECHES

Moderator: Li Xikui, Secretary-General of the CPAFFC, Chairman of the CFFPD

Speakers: Professor Tan Tieniu, Deputy Director of the Liaison Office of the Central People's Government in the Hong Kong Special Administrative Region

Chen Xu, Chairperson of the Tsinghua University Council, Co-Chair of the WPF

Professor. Terry Kit-Fong Au, Pro-Vice-Chancellor of the University of Hong Kong

Zhang Xiang, President and Vice-Chancellor of the University of Hong Kong (HKU), Co-Chair of the WPF

Professor Sung Chi Rocky Tuan, Vice-Chancellor and President of the Chinese University of Hong Kong (CUHK), Co-Chair of the WPF

Ai Xuefeng, Deputy Mayer of the Shenzhen Municipal People's Government

Speech by Professor Tan Tieniu

Tan Tieniu, Deputy Director of the Liaison Office of the Central People's Government in the Hong Kong Special Administrative Region

Dear Ms. Li Bin, Mr. Péter Medgyessy,
Mr. Wang Aiwen,
Ms. Li Xiaolin,
Ms. Chen Xu,
Professor Tuan Rocky S.,
Professor Au, Terry Kit-Fong,

It is truly a privilege to join the annual World Philanthropy Forum in Shenzhen on this special day. I would like to thank Ms. Li Bin, Mr. Péter Medgyessy, and other distinguished guests for taking your time to attend this forum. Your presence has reflected the broad appeal and influence of this event. On behalf of the Liaison Office of the Central People's Government in the Hong Kong Special Administrative Region, I wish to extend my congratulations on the convening of this forum and a warm welcome to all of the friends travelling from afar to join us. My respect also goes to CPAFFC, Tsinghua University, HKU, CUHK and Shenzhen Municipal People's Government.

In 2016, in order to promote the development of world philanthropy and strengthen international exchanges and cooperation, CPAFFC and Tsinghua University, etc. co-launched the World Philanthropy Forum, which attracted friends from all over the world and began to garner greater influence within the community. I am excited to see that HKU and CUHK have become co-organizers of this important forum starting from 2018. I believe this initiative is of great significance in facilitating exchanges and building trust between Hong Kong and the Chinese mainland, especially in the cooperation of philanthropy, education and scientific research. In particular, the choice of Shenzhen in the Greater Bay Area for the 2019 Forum is even more significant. We all know that the development plan for Guangdong-Hong Kong-Macao Greater Bay Area is a major strategic initiative launched by the Chinese government. It is hailed not only as a new attempt to break new ground in pursuing opening up on all fronts in a new era, but also a further step in taking forward the practice of "one country, two systems." I am aware that the forum has a theme every year. The theme of this year is "Philanthropy in the Bay Area for Better Life". It is also what we pursue for in the construction of the Greater Bay Area. Furthermore, a better life can never be realized without the support of higher education and technology innovation. Today's forum is co-hosted by Hong Kong's leading universities, Tsinghua University and CPAFFC. Their rich knowledge and expertise will be supplementary and complementary to each other. Many of you may be very concerned about the situation in Hong Kong. It has grabbed global attention. I have to say that Hong Kong is in a difficult time right now, perhaps the most difficult since its return in 1997. However, we have reasons to believe that the Chief Executive and the SAR Government are capable of leading us out of the current predicament. We will firmly support their effective governance and law enforcement by the Hong Kong Police Force. We believe that the future will be even better and that the Pearl of the Orient will continue to shine. Hong Kong has a long history and fine tradition in philanthropy. I can list a lot of philanthropic organizations and institutions in Hong Kong, such as the Tung Wah Group of Hospitals (TWGHs), established in 1870, Hong Kong's largest and most influential philanthropic organization. In Hong Kong, many successful and caring people contribute generously to the promotion of philanthropy. A lot of buildings and research facilities in universities, including those in the Chinese mainland, are named after its Hong Kong donors.

I sincerely hope that we can use the World Philanthropy Forum as a platform to strengthen exchanges and cooperation between the Chinese mainland and Hong Kong, as well as cooperation between China and the international community, so that we can work together to create a better life and a better home, and build a community of shared future for mankind. I also sincerely hope that this forum will be held in Hong Kong one day in the near future. Finally, I wish a full success of the forum. Thank you!

Speech by Chen Xu

Chen Xu, Chairperson of the Tsinghua University Council, Co-Chair of the WPF

Dear Ms. Li Bin,
Mr. Péter Medgyessy,
Ms. Li Xiaolin,
Mr.Wang Aiwen,
Professor Tuan Rocky S.,
Distinguished guests,
Ladies and Gentlemen,

Good Morning! It's my pleasure to join you in Shenzhen for the FourthWorld Philanthropy Forum on the occasion of the 4th Charity Day of China. On behalf of Tsinghua University, I would like to extend a warm welcome and thanks to all of you for your presence.

Since its establishment four years ago, the World Philanthropy Forum has been committed to promoting the healthy development of global philanthropy. We have held our forums in different cities, from Beijing to Shanghai to Shenzhen.

During this process, we have broadened our views, and learned to see things from different perspectives, and attracted more people from the philanthropic community. With the concerted efforts of kindred spirits from all walks of life, the World Philanthropy Forum has become a comprehensive exchange platform for philanthropy to conduct cross-discipline research and initiatives, playing an increasingly important role for building a community of shared future for mankind as well as the peace and development of the world.

2019 marks the 70th anniversary of the founding of the People's Republic of China and the 20th anniversary of the return of Macau to China. At this important historical point, the Party Central Committee and the State Council have issued The Development Plan for the Guangdong-Hong Kong-Macao Greater Bay Area and the Opinions on Supporting Shenzhen in Building a Pioneering Demonstration Zone for Socialism with Chinese Characteristics. This initiative fully demonstrates the firm confidence and strong determination of the Party and the State to make new ground in pursuing opening up on all fronts, to practice further "one country, two systems", and to fulfil the Chinese Dream of national rejuvenation. During the meeting with the delegation from Hong Kong and Macao to celebrate the 40th anniversary of China's reform and opening up, President Xi Jinping fully affirmed the six major roles played by compatriots from Hong Kong and Macao and people from all walks of life in the course of reform and opening up. These roles include the leading role in investment and industry prosperity, the demonstration of the market economy, the booster for institutional reform, the bridge of two-way opening-up, the pilot place for a first try, and the reference of urban management. He also highly appreciated the enthusiastic contribution of compatriots from Hong Kong and Macao to the philanthropy of education and poverty alleviation in the Chinese mainland. For a long time, a group of Hong Kong and Macao entrepreneurs have been donating funds to build schools in the Chinese mainland to support the development of education because they love this country and know how important education can be. Tsinghua University is also one of the beneficiaries. Today, our many teaching buildings and research facilities and some of our important education and scientific research foundations come from the generous donation of our compatriots from Hong Kong and Macao. These donations have provided valuable support for the reform and development of Tsinghua University. Their brotherly love deeply moves us.

As China is making new ground in pursuing opening up on all fronts, Shenzhen, as an important window of China's reform and opening-up and an early demonstration area of socialism with Chinese characteristics, will play a more significant role in implementing the important strategy to construct Guangdong-Hong Kong-Macao Greater Bay Area. Shenzhen is not only an important leverage to boost the development of the Greater Bay Area, but also a higher starting point to pursue reform and opening up in the new era. It also serves as a key node for China to go globally and connect with the world.

Tsinghua University has a long-established and fruitful relationship with Shenzhen. Over the past 20 years of long-term cooperation, we have witnessed the vibrant development of Shenzhen and also the pioneering spirit of the SAR. The theme for this forum held in Shenzhen - Philanthropy in the Bay Area for Better Life - conveys a profound message. As a key component in constructing socialism with Chinese characteristics, philanthropy is a moral practice that appeals to a large group of ordinary people, covers a wide range of areas, takes many forms, and engages diversified participants. Therefore, it plays an important role in promoting economic and social development, safeguarding and improving people's livelihoods, and promoting socialist core values. We hope to take this forum as an opportunity to promote the traditional Chinese virtue of pursuing goodness, to mobilize the broadest philanthropic forces and enhance exchanges with the best practices in the world. Let's face up to the challenges ahead, be confident and work together to promote the development and construction of Greater Bay Area and the pilot demonstration area of socialism with Chinese characteristics. Let the prosperity of our motherland and the bright future of the Greater Bay Area be shared by generations to come. Let the community share the historic responsibility of national rejuvenation and the spirit of philanthropy.

"Youth is the future of a nation and the future of our world." With the motto of "Self-Discipline and Social Commitment", Tsinghua University attaches great importance to cultivating philanthropic awareness, social responsibility, the love for the country and human beings of young students, in the hope that they can become great talents of our time. Meanwhile, Tsinghua University is also an active player in philanthropic research. We have established a national think tank - Institute for Philanthropy Tsinghua University - to provide insights and academic support for the development of philanthropy through high-level research. Education carries the most in-depth expectations of the country and the people, and receives the most care from all sectors of society. Cultivating more outstanding talents with the spirit of responsibility and dedication is the best way for education to give back to our country and our people. In the future, Tsinghua University will hold on to the principle of "Cultivating People of

Moral Character", and promote philanthropic education and research. We will join hands with all parties to build a better Greater Bay Area, and make our due contribution to the development of the country, the happiness of the people and the progress of human civilization.

I would like to thank CPAFFC, HKU, CUHK, Shenzhen Municipal People's Government and friends from all walks of life for your strong support of the forum! I believe this forum will generate more wisdom and actions about how to leverage the strength of philanthropy for the construction of the Greater Bay Area and to write a wonderful chapter for a better tomorrow.

Finally, I wish the forum a great success!

Thank you.

Speech by Professor Terry Kit-Fong Au

Terry Kit-Fong Au, Vice-President and Pro-Vice-Chancellor of the University of Hong Kong (HKU)

Distinguished Guests,
Dear friends,

Good morning. I am proud to join this forum on behalf of HKU. In the past four years, WPF has been actively promoted the global development of philanthropy and social work. It's an honour for HKU to co-host this forum, which is also a huge responsibility and a long-term mission for us. Our President and Vice-Chancellor, Professor Zhang Xiang, who thinks very highly of this forum, could not make it here. That's why he has sent his best wishes via this video. Let's take a look. Thank you.

Video Speech by Professor Zhang Xiang

Zhang Xiang, President and Vice-Chancellor of the
HKU and the Co-Chair of the WPF

Distinguished Guests,
Ladies and Gentlemen,

Welcome to the fourth WPF. I am sorry that I couldn't meet you in Shenzhen to witness the opening of the forum due to a schedule conflict. I would like to extend my thanks to the team members for your hard work and to the guests for your active participation. The forum would not be held without your efforts. I also wish the forum a great success.

The forum has earned support and trust from various parties in the past three years. Now it has grown into an important exchange platform for all the academicians, experts and professionals around the globe to discuss the future of world philanthropy. I think it is a significant move for the forum to take place in Shenzhen this year. Ever since the issue of the Outline of the Development Plan for the Guangdong-Hong Kong-Macao Greater Bay Area, it has welcomed increasing business and trade cooperation as well as cross-sector exchanges. While we enjoy a rapidly developing economy, the demand for public services such as education and medical care are also on the rise. This presents new opportunities and challenges for philanthropy work in the Bay Area, requiring united and shared experience, strength and wisdom among all sectors.

As the oldest higher education institute in Hong Kong, HKU has been dedicated to cultivating future leaders and talents, and encourage students to serve the society with what they have learned. For this purpose, we have committed to improving the capability of our philanthropy and non-profit departments.

In the future, we will continue to foster knowledge exchange and use our knowledge for the benefit of the society, culture and environments under the support of the governments and the public. We hope to discuss and share with friends old and new in this forum to provide insights for the future development of philanthropy in the Greater Bay Area. Universities should perform as the engine for innovation to turn this area into a world technology and social innovation hub. With your concerted efforts, I believe this forum will bring out fruitful results. Thank you.

Speech by Professor Sung Chi Rocky Tuan

Sung Chi Rocky Tuan, Vice-Chancellor and President of the Chinese University of Hong Kong (CUHK)

Distinguished Leaders and Guests,
Dear Colleagues,

Welcome to the WPF 2019. It is an honour for CUHK to co-host this forum with CPAFFC and Tsinghua University since last year. Furthermore, it takes great efforts for all of us to gather in Shenzhen today.

Launched in 2016, the WPF has united leaders and outstanding talent from various fields to promote global philanthropy, social services, academic exchanges and talent development based on their expertise and experience in philanthropy. Since its inception, CUHK has been committed to sustaining a culturally diverse environment in which the discovery, accumulation and application of knowledge is deemed as a way to fulfil our responsibility of improving people's life, addressing global challenges and meeting urgent social needs, with the ultimate aim to benefit Hong Kong, China and the world at large.

Finally, I'd like to extend my thanks to the other organizers, especially Shenzhen Municipal People's Government, various ministries that have given their support to the forum, as well as our distinguished speakers, university partners and institutions that have actively participated in the forum. In the next two days, all of us will share our views on the future development of philanthropy in the Bay Area. I wish a complete success of this forum. Thank you.

Speech by Ai Xuefeng

Ai Xuefeng, Deputy Mayer of the Shenzhen Municipal People's Government

Distinguished Mr. Péter Medgyessy,
Ms. Li Bin,
Ms. Li Xiaolin,
Dear Guests,
Ladies and Gentlemen,

Good morning!

On the occasion of the fourth "China Charity Day", we are pleased to gather in this beautiful city of Shenzhen to hold the fourth WPF. On behalf of the Shenzhen Municipal People's Government, I would like to extend a warm welcome to all the leaders and guests who have come from afar, and express my thanks to all the people across various sectors at home and abroad for your attention and support to the development of charity in Shenzhen.

As an important window of China's reform and opening-up, Shenzhen has made remarkable achievements in various fields and has become an international city full of charm, vitality and innovation. With the support of the Ministry of Civil Affairs and the Guangdong Provincial Government, Shenzhen Municipal People's Government has made great efforts to improve people's well-being, cultivate public awareness of philanthropy, and optimize related policies. Ultimately, we have established a modern philanthropy ecosystem, guaranteed by a sound system, the rule of law, good management, as well as a healthy and orderly environment. In recent years, Shenzhen has pioneered a number of new achievements in China's philanthropic field. We have reshaped the institution for community foundations and established the first public foundation initiated by the private sector. We launched the "99 Charity Day" internet event with the largest number of participants in China. We also filed the first domestic charitable trust plan. Besides, Shenzhen has co-organized various Chinese philanthropy program exchanges and exhibitions in the last seven years, and have ranked among the best of China City Philanthropy Index in terms of comprehensive strength for several consecutive years.

On the occasion of welcoming the 70th anniversary of the founding of the new China, we are gathering in Shenzhen to hold the fourth WPF. Our guests will discuss extensively on the topic of "Philanthropy in the Bay Area for Better Life", offering a feast of ideas. I hope that all of you could offer valuable insights for the philanthropy and social development of Shenzhen. I believe the fruitful results of this forum will certainly have an important impact on the development of philanthropy in China, especially in the Guangdong-Hong Kong-Macao Greater Bay Area.

After 40 years of development, Shenzhen has stood at the critical node for the construction of an early demonstration zone of socialism with Chinese characteristics. We will implement the strategy of being a "model of urban civilization" and a "benchmark for people's well-being", shoulder the responsibilities of the Special Economic Zone, strive to hand over a satisfactory answer for philanthropy in the new era, and make a greater contribution to the promotion of innovation and development of philanthropy in China and the rest of the world.

Finally, I wish this forum a great success!

III KEYNOTE SPEECHES

Speakers: Wang Aiwen, Vice Minister of the Ministry of Civil Affairs
Dr. Anthony Chow Wing-kin, Chairman of the Hong Kong Jockey Club (HKJC)
Gary Stahl, Director of Division of Private Fundraising and Partnerships of UNICEF

Construct a More Prosperous Greater Bay Area and a Better World with the Power and Spirit of Philanthropy

Wang Aiwen, Vice Minister of the Ministry of Civil Affairs

Distinguished Guests,
Ladies and Gentlemen,

It's a pleasure for me to attend the fourth WPF. On behalf of the Ministry of Civil Affairs of the People's Republic of China, I would like to extend my warmest congratulations on the convening of the forum.

Today marks the fourth "China Charity Day", which is celebrated every year on September 5 according to the Charity Law promulgated in 2016, to spread the culture, philosophy and spirit of philanthropy. Not long ago, the Ministry of Civil Affairs also announced a special logo for "China Charity Day" to further raise public awareness of the charity. At a time when China has successively issued a strategic decision to support the development of the Guangdong-Hong Kong-Macao Greater Bay Area and the construction of an early demonstration zone of socialism with Chinese characteristics in Shenzhen, the forum co-hosted by CPAFFC, Tsinghua University, HKU and CUHK will play a catalytic role in summing up the experience in the development of philanthropy at home and abroad, promoting the accelerated development of philanthropy in the Greater Bay Area, and leveraging philanthropic forces to contribute to the historical process of building a strong and modernized socialist country with Chinese characteristics and a community with a shared future.

Promoting the development of the Greater Bay Area is a major decision made by the Party Central Committee with Comrade Xi Jinping at its core. On July 1, 2017, the *Framework Agreement on Deepening Cooperation among Guangdong, Hong Kong and Macao to Promote the Development of the Greater Bay Area was signed. Later, the issue of developing the Greater Bay Area* has been included in the report to the 19th National Congress. After that, the CPC Central Committee and the State Council released the *Outline Development Plan for the Guangdong-Hong Kong-Macao Greater Bay Area and the Opinions on Supporting Shenzhen in Building a Pioneering Demonstration Zone for Socialism with Chinese Characteristics* respectively in February and August of 2019. The above important initiatives not only draw a new blueprint for the economic and social development of the Greater Bay Area, but also set new goals for the development of its philanthropy work.

Since the reform and opening up, China's philanthropic endeavours have made gratifying achievements, with outstanding contributions from Guangdong, Hong Kong and Macao.

China's philanthropy has expanded rapidly, showing great potential for further development. With the issuance of *Law on Donations for Public Welfare, Regulations for the Management of Foundations*, and *the Charity* Law, the legal system of philanthropy is becoming more robust. Internet philanthropy is flourishing and developing rapidly, gaining widespread social attention and participation. From the foot of the Lion Rock to the Source of Three Rivers, charitable activities are carried out everywhere, sending warmth to the needy, passing on care among urban and rural communities, creating a better society and more harmonious relationships.

The Guangdong-Hong Kong-Macao Greater Bay Area, as a forerunner of reform and opening up, is not only the most economically vibrant and open region in China, but also a pioneer in social development and cultural cultivation, providing a material and spiritual foundation for the development of philanthropy in the region, and a fertile ground for nurturing modern philanthropy in China since the reform and opening up. There are more than 900 charitable organizations in Guangdong, ranking second in the country in terms of number and total net assets. In addition to serving the local community and working at the grassroots level, they are also actively involved in poverty alleviation, rural revitalization, and the development of science, education, culture, health and sports in other parts of the country, and some have even gone abroad. Guangdong has become a highland for exporting philanthropic talent and ideas. Hong Kong and Macao have profound charitable traditions. Doing good has become a habit for people here and they know how to do it right. Such qualities and expertise have vigorously promoted the culture and development of philanthropy work in this region. For a long time, charitable organizations in Hong Kong and Macao have served as important providers of local social welfare, providing a large number of services to improve the livelihood of the elderly, children and the disabled. They also have long been active in supporting the development of the Mainland, and have provided selfless assistance in major natural disasters, For example, in the 2008 Wenchuan earthquake, the total disaster relief funds allocated by the Hong Kong Government and donated by its people reached HK$23 billion. Numerous primary and secondary schools have been built across the cities and villages of the Mainland with the donations of our compatriots in Hong Kong and Macao. This fraternal love has been deeply cherished by the people in the Mainland.

China has embarked on a new journey to build a modern socialist country in all respects, bringing significant historical opportunities for the development of philanthropy. It’s important for Guangdong, Hong Kong and Macao to ride the wave.

The new momentum also will unleash a bigger and brighter future for philanthropy as the realization of the Chinese Dream of the great rejuvenation of the Chinese nation requires greater and broader support from the philanthropic community. While the understanding of philanthropy varies somewhat from culture to culture, the power of philanthropy can transcend countries and regions, systems and cultures, and even connects history and future. While the scope of philanthropy varies greatly in different legal systems, it reflects a universal human ethic and is an important cornerstone in building a modern society. In terms of material form, philanthropy is a redistribution of social resources, transforming social donations and volunteer participation into services that can meet social needs and solve social problems. In terms of value, philanthropy is the conveyance of greater love, reshaping the society with ethics and moral beliefs, connecting people and enabling them to support each other. In building a community of shared future, philanthropy could serve as a bridge and an important foundation.

The Greater Bay Area is one of the most economically and socially developed regions in China and an important window for China to open up to the world. We expect you to be not only the leader of economic development and technology innovation, but also the pioneer in social development and philanthropy. We are pleased to see that Guangdong, including Shenzhen, has in recent years attached great importance to the cultivation of charitable organizations and charitable forces. As a result, philanthropy has played an effective role in galvanizing social innovation. The resilience of philanthropy in bridging differences and integrating diversity has been brought into play. Furthermore, the importance of philanthropy to social harmony and the progress of civilization has been fully demonstrated. Taking this power of philanthropy further into play to promote the integrated development of the Guangdong-Hong Kong-Macao Greater Bay Area will be an important social practice to help reform and opening up, as well as an important initiative to build an early demonstration zone of socialism with Chinese characteristics.

China's philanthropy works is still in progress and have great potential for the future. It could be better utilized to meet people's needs for a better life. New ways need to be explored to engage broader social forces and provide more charitable services. More measures need to be taken in moral guidance and values cultivation. Generally, a greater contribution has yet to be made to a more harmonious and civilized society. Compared with other regions in China, the Guangdong, Hong Kong and Macao region is already taking the lead in philanthropic development. With the advancement of the Shenzhen Pilot Demonstration Zone and the construction of the Greater Bay Area, philanthropy in the Greater Bay Area will have even better prospects. We hope that the Greater Bay Area, by exploring new ways to cultivate philanthropic forces and accumulate effective experience, and drawing on both China's outstanding philanthropic culture and modern philanthropic concepts, will take a pioneering step to develop philanthropy with Chinese characteristics for the new era to provide a reference for other regions.

I'd like to make five proposals to speed up philanthropy in the Greater Bay Area. Firstly, the region could give full play to its pioneering and exemplary status, call for charity communities to provide quality service to improve child-care, education, elderly care, medical care and the livelihood of the disabled. It may also address differentiated and diversified needs through philanthropy activities and volunteering services, thereby increasing the people's sense of well-being and gain. Secondly, the region could take advantage of technological innovations such as "Internet +" and smart technology to boost philanthropy. Thirdly, the region could give full play to its comprehensive leading advantages and effectively guide the flow of philanthropic talent and ideas to poor regions, to contribute more to poverty alleviation and east-west regional cooperation and achieve mutual win-win results. Fourthly, the region could utilize the advantages of regional cooperation to promote the integrated development of philanthropy in the Greater Bay Area, and explore new practices of philanthropy in implementing "one country, two systems". Finally, the region could build on its international strength, making the Greater Bay Area a frontier for integrating Chinese and Western cultures and cultivating a socialist mode, culture and theory of philanthropy with Chinese characteristics.

Ladies and Gentlemen,

As the functional department in charge of philanthropy, the Ministry of Civil Affairs pays great attention to and supports the holding of the WPF. We are a regular participant of this forum every year. In recent years, China's philanthropic undertakings have accumulated a wealth of experience and played an important role in helping to alleviate poverty and promote the development of people's livelihoods and social progress. We hope that by continuing to hold this high-level forum, we will continue to share our experience and practices in poverty alleviation and other areas, and provide the philanthropy community with more Chinese wisdom and solutions. All the guests are welcomed to speak freely to reach consensus so that the forum will continue to bear fruitful results. We are willing to support the WPF to expand its influence and role further to become a symbol and an important platform for international exchanges in the field of philanthropy. Let's work together to connect our hearts and build consensus through philanthropy endeavours. Let's enrich our resources to benefit more people around the globe.

Finally, I wish the forum a complete success and all the best. Thank you.

Philanthropy Cooperation for a Better Society: Experience of the Hong Kong Jockey Club

Anthony Chow Wing-Kin, Chairman of the HKJC

Dear Ms. Li Bin,
Dear Mr. Péter Medgyessy,
Distinguished Leaders and Guests,

Good morning. I would like to give this speech in Mandarin so that I could deliver the message to as many people as possible. It's a real challenge for me because my Mandarin may not be as fluent as Cantonese.

First of all, it's an honour for me to share, on behalf of the Jockey Club, how our unique operation model has created economic and social value for Hong Kong. Some of you may not be familiar with our Club. So I would like to make a brief introduction before talking about what we do and how we do it.

The Jockey Club was founded in 1894, aiming at promoting horse racing and equestrian sports through membership. Now, it has grown into a world-class racing club and the only authorized operator of horse race betting in Hong Kong. Our betting mechanism supports the government's efforts to crack down illegal gambling while meeting the market demand for betting. And all of the revenue generated by betting has been used to fund social development and philanthropy work in Hong Kong. We have two major contributions to society, one of which is the tax we have paid. The Jockey Club is the largest single taxpayer in Hong Kong. According to our financial results announced at the end of August 2019, we paid HK$23.3 billion of taxes to the Hong Kong SAR Government in 2018-2019, accounting for 6.8% of the revenue of the Inland Revenue Department. The second major contribution is our donations. Dedicated donations approved in 2018 reached a record high of HK$4.3 billion, supporting 294 social programs. The Club can trace its long tradition of donating to charitable causes back to at least 1915. And the focus of our charity work has been closely aligned with the development of society. In the 1940s to 1950s, when Hong Kong struggled to cope with post-war reconstruction and a massive influx of immigrants, our donations mainly went into education, medical facilities and other social sectors. By the 1970s, we shifted our focus to build sports and recreational facilities such as the Ocean Park to respond to increasing demand for physical exercise and recreation. Furthermore, we also pay attention to specialized education. The funding of the Hong Kong University of Science and Technology (HKUST) pays testament to this. In 2019, to respond to social concerns regarding the operation of philanthropy, we changed the way we approve dedicated funds, reaching out to different social forces for solutions.

Here, I'd like to share with you two essential points for the operation of the Jockey Club. Firstly, while meeting social needs, our Club has always been investing in the development of the young people, the care for the elderly, and the development of arts, to name but a few. Our funding is primarily used to deepen our understanding of the root causes of social problems. We also use other platforms to reach out to partners such as governments, NGOs and businesses to respond to the needs of society and to develop solutions to improves people's livelihood. The Jockey Club also encourages service innovation and focuses on how to make good use of money. For example, Hong Kong now is faced with ageing problems. It is estimated that by 2020, one-third of the population will be people above 65 years old. Therefore, we have conducted several programs to tackle this issue. Since 2015, we have cooperated with the SAR government to launch a staged project of "Jockey Club Age-friendly City" in 18 districts. We have adopted a bottom-up and district-based approach and cooperated with local gerontology research institutes. We aim to promote a friendly atmosphere that respects the elderly, to improve their well-being and construct a society of common prosperity. Secondly, it's important to improve working standards and join hands with social service agencies and NGOs. Most of our charitable donation projects involve not only donations to agencies and NGOs who have applied for the first time, but also professional training to teachers, social workers, etc. We have projects for teachers and social workers to train relevant talents. In years, the Jockey Club has been committed to building a better society through the Charities Trust. We have seen great improvement in our performance, which enables us to make more donations to the charitable community. We are now one of the world's top ten charity donors. The Club's substantial donations to the community are made possible by its unique integrated business model, which create social value through responsible sports wagering such as horse racing.

We believe that a single force could solve no problem. Philanthropy has played an important role in urban development. In recent years, due to social development and the issuance of the Charity Law, philanthropy sector in the

Chinese mainland is thriving. As globalization picks up pace, new philanthropy models have emerged. A new era for philanthropy is approaching.

We look forward to communicating with peers from the Mainland and international community to discuss and address social issues. The Jockey Club launched an international "Philanthropy for Better Cities Forum" in 2016. We have invited philanthropists, entrepreneurs, and NGOs in Greater China to communicate and share experience, expand cooperation and establish long-term partnerships, to build better cities. The second forum was organized in 2018, which attracted representatives from 1400 districts. The next forum will be held in September 2020. We welcome all of you to attend. In the Outline Development Plan for the Guangdong-Hong Kong-Macao Greater Bay Area issued in February 2019, the CPC Central Committee and the State Council points out that Hong Kong and Macao should strengthen cooperation with the Mainland. As a part of the Bay Area, I am looking forward to our future communication and cooperation.

Finally, I'd like to thank the Central Government, Shenzhen Municipal People's Government and the organizers - CPAFFC, Tsinghua University, HKU and CUHK - for arranging this precious opportunity for exchanges. I wish the forum a complete success. Thank you.

Contribute to Social Development and a Brighter Future for Children with Philanthropy

Gary Stahl, Director of Division of Private Fundraising and Partnerships of the UNICEF

Distinguished Ms. Li Bin,
Ms. Li Xiaolin,
Mr. Péter Medgyessy,
Mr. Wang Aiwen,
Mr. Ai Xuefeng,
Hosts and Co-Organizers,

Good morning. I am honoured and pleased to speak here on behalf of the executive director Ms. Henrietta Fore from UNICEF, and send her best regards to all of you. During her one-and-a-half-year tenure, she has visited China three times to make good on her commitment to building a partnership with China. This is not only to support the Chinese government in addressing child-related challenges at home, but also to work with China to improve the lives of children in the world.

UNICEF is committed to strengthening cooperation between the two parties. It has provided support to China's 271 million children in the areas of hygiene, nutrition, health, child protection, education and social policy. We have developed a new plan for 2021-2025, which has taken into account the views of the Chinese government. We are implementing existing programs while keeping developing new ones. New programs will focus on adolescents, gender responsiveness, the unmet needs of urban children, children in poor areas and children with disabilities. The Executive Director of the UNICEF had signed a contract at the recent the "Belt and Road Initiative" Forum with China's National Development and Reform Commission recognizing China's cooperation with UNICEF aimed at providing central and public services for children, young people and their families. This paves the way for UNICEF and the Chinese government to work together in China and globally.

To date, we have worked together on projects such as the International Syrian Refugee Project in Lebanon and the nutrition project in Somalia, and are about to start a hurricane relief project and an African health project in South Africa. The challenges for the international community to achieve the Sustainable Development Goals (SDGs) are enormous. In this process, China will play a significant role. The 2030 United Nations SDGs include 17 goals that will address the social, economic and environmental dimensions of sustainable development. UNICEF is working with more than 190 countries to achieve these goals. Globally, UNICEF handles an average of 300 sudden-onset incidents per year. We have raised more than $3.9 billion to provide humanitarian assistance to 410 million children in 59 countries. At present, it is difficult for philanthropists to make the most effective contribution, given the complexity of the development situation and the urgent challenges we face.

Bill Gates often says that the resources in his foundation are a mere drop in the bucket. According to data estimates, we need $2.5 trillion a year to reach our development goals. It is abundantly clear that philanthropy alone cannot fill this huge funding gap. We must have innovative ways to bring charities, the UN, governments and businesses together to drive sustained changes. Let me give you two examples of how the United Nations achieve development goals through the path of philanthropy and sustained activities.

The first example took place in India. UNICEF partnered with a family foundation to launch the first comprehensive Indian household nutrition analysis program, providing national data on micronutrient levels, parasites and nutritional risk factors for disease in children and adolescents. Thanks to the initial philanthropic investment, the national Government and local actors now have the data needed to carry out projects to improve children's nutritional levels.

In the second example in South Africa, we are working on youth access to rights, with funding from long-standing philanthropic partners. This includes a community-based childcare model in which selected, trained and supervised child-care and youth-care workers provide basic support and care services in areas of extreme poverty plagued by AIDS. Such support includes accompanying children to school, clinic or hospital, helping them access important documents and services, doing laundry and cooking with them, and helping them understand how to take care of themselves. The results we have achieved are twofold. Young people have received vital support and community members have gained income and an economic base for development. The four-year experiment was so successful that the model is to be replicated in the whole country by the South African Government.

These examples show the different ways in which philanthropists are investing and working with UNICEF to bring about lasting change. These actions have allowed support from foundations, wealthy individuals and philanthropic groups to grow from $150 million in 2012 to $400 million in 2017. Now, each year we have up to 5 million supporters worldwide. We benefited 400 million people in 2017 and 500 million in 2018, and we want more people to join us.

UNICEF has developed successful partnerships with the private sector and philanthropists in China. For example, we've partnered with Tencent on an Internet child protection program and with Johnson & Johnson on a Healthy Families for Pregnant Women program. We also collaborate with other partners, such as working with Haier, to support social-emotional research with school children. Our Champions for Children program allows philanthropists to partner with us on Barefoot Social Workers Project.

I believe these projects also have the support of some of the people in this room. We thank you for your effort in improving the lives of children in China, the countries along with the "Belt and Road Initiative" and the rest of the world. At present, there are many opportunities to collaborate and build partnerships. I hope you will consider partnering with us in our efforts to benefit the children of China and the world. If, like us, you want the children of the world to have a bright future, to grow up healthy and educated in a safe environment, then please don't be embarrassed to talk about how to make things better for the children of China and the world. Thank you again.

Part II

Thematic Sessions

IV PHILANTHROPY IN THE GREATER BAY AREA AND TALENT NURTURING

Moderator: Christopher Tremewan, Secretary-General of the Association of Pacific Rim Universities (APRU)

Speakers: Xiao Haipeng, Vice-President of the Sun Yat-Sen University (SYSU)

Wong Suk-Ying, Professor in the Department of Sociology, Associate Vice-President of the CUHK

Cheung Leong, Executive Director of Community & Charities at the HKJC

Christopher Tremewan: Welcome to the thematic session of Philanthropy in the Greater Bay Area and Talent Nurturing. Hello, I am Christopher Tremewan, Secretary-General of the APRU. Founded in 1997, APRU is a consortium of leading research universities in the Pacific Rim. We now have 50 members, 11 of which are top universities from the Mainland, and 3 of which are universities from the Hong Kong SAR. The Secretariat is currently based in Hong Kong. We very much hope that we can strengthen the research and innovation ecosystem in Hong Kong and the Greater Bay Area. The current chair of the APRU is the Chancellor of UCLA. There are three presidents from Chinese universities on our Steering Committee. They are Sung Chi Rocky Tuan, Vice-Chancellor and President of the CUHK, Wei Shyy, President of the HKUST, and Xu Ningsheng, President of Fudan University. We hope to strengthen the cooperation in research within the Greater Bay Area, and improve our capabilities in education and innovation field to address challenges posed by international policy changes. We are also committed to achieving the UN's SDGs, combating climate change, and improving global health. It is to this end that we have been working with non-profit social organizations, government agencies, and businesses. So it is a great honour for me to be the moderator of the session this afternoon. Now, let me introduce to you our first speaker, Mr. Xiao Haipeng. He will talk about the potential collaboration opportunities in higher education, and health sciences within the Greater Bay Area. Mr. Xiao Haipeng is a professor of pharmacy at SYSU and a senior specialist in endocrinology at the First Affiliated Hospital of the Sun Yat-Sen University, a very famous hospital in Guangdong Province. He is also a health care consultant to the central government and chairman of several medical education consortia and medical school unions. He is currently the Vice President of SYSU.

Let's welcome Mr. Xiao Haipeng.

Mr. Xiao Haipeng: Thanks for your introduction. Distinguished Mr. Wang, ladies and gentlemen, it is truly a privilege to be invited to give a speech at the WPF. I am very grateful to the organizers for this opportunity to introduce the Greater Bay Area to the world. I'd like to take this opportunity to share with you the health sciences in higher education in this region. *Outline Development Plan for the Guangdong-Hong Kong-Macao Greater Bay Area* released by the CPC Central Committee and the State Council on February 18th, 2019 marked the establishment of the fourth Bay Area in the world. The Greater Bay Area consists of Hong Kong, Macao and nine cities in the Pearl River Delta region of Guangdong, including Guangzhou and Shenzhen. As the most open and economically vibrant region in China, the Greater Bay Area will become a global axis dedicated to technological innovation and development and a showcase for in-depth cooperation between the Mainland, Hong Kong and Macao. It is also a typical example of how China implements science & technology innovation and development, as well as the "Belt and Road Initiative". We have quite renowned universities and higher education institutes in this region. Let me show you some numbers.

The Greater Bay Area covers a total area of 56,000 square kilometres with a population of about 70 million people. In terms of higher education, the Greater Bay Area is one of the strongest and most dynamic regions in China. The Greater Bay Area is home to four of the world's top 100 universities from Hong Kong, one of the world's top 500 universities from Macao, and one of the world's top 300 universities from Guangdong Province——Sun Yat-Sen University. However, our higher education is inadequate when compared with the other three Bay Areas. We also have fewer PhD students than the rest of the world. This means that we can have a huge potential for growth in the areas of health and higher education. To promote higher education cooperation in the Greater Bay Area, we established the Guangdong-Hong Kong-Macao University Alliance in 2016 to build our strengths and resources in this region. As one of the founders and board members of the Alliance, SYSU is dedicated to achieving the development goals of the Greater Bay Area. Founded in 1924 by Dr. Sun Yat-Sen, "Father of the Republic of China", SYSU is now one of the top 10 universities in China. It now has five campuses located in Guangzhou, Zhuhai and Shenzhen, which are very important cities in the Greater Bay Area. The Guangzhou campus specializes in medicine, art, science and engineering, the Zhuhai campus focuses on in-depth studies of the ocean, the universe, soil and atomic bomb engineering, while the Shenzhen campus, which will soon open, will include a medical school and a new science academy. We have more than 56,000 full-time students and over 17,000 faculty members. We have 63 departments and 10 affiliated hospitals. 19 academic disciplines——the second-highest number in China——are ranked among the top 1% (ESI) in the world. Besides, we have established partnerships with 230 schools around the world. Medicine is the cornerstone of our university. Zhongshan School of Medicine was founded by Dr. Sun Yat-sen in 1866, and inscribed by Mr. Deng Xiaoping, the former leader of China. The motto "Heal people's body and soul in addition to treating illness" underlines the spirit of the medical school. In the past 100 years, Zhongshan School of Medicine has produced many renowned medical experts who have a great influence on the Chinese medical community.

Many of the "firsts" in Chinese medicine took place here, such as the first gallstone removal surgery and the first anaesthesia surgery. Medicine is among the most competitive disciplines in SYSU, especially basic medicine and clinical medicine, which are recognized as "Double First-Class" disciplines. It is one of the four universities in China that have "Double First-Class" basic medicine and clinical medicine majors. Over the past eight years, the pass rate for graduates of Zhongshan School of Medicine on the National Medical Licensing Examination in China is among the top 3. Furthermore, they are also prize winners in the National Clinical Skills Competition organized by the Ministry of Education and the National Health Commission from 2011 to 2014. Currently, Zhongshan School of Medicine has the second to the best health care system in China, with 10 affiliated hospitals, seven in Guangzhou, one in Zhuhai, and two in Shenzhen. Among them, the largest and most technologically advanced one is the First Affiliated Hospital of Sun Yat-sen University, which is now based in Shenzhen and has branched out in Huizhou and the Greater Bay Area. Located in Nansha district, the centre of the Greater Bay Area, the First Affiliated Hospital of Sun Yat-Sen University (Nansha) has 5 state key disciplines and the technical qualification recognized by the National Health Commission. It has been improving its health care services to the public as well as its professional development.

Numerous achievements have been made in areas of liver transplantation, human decellularized nerve transplantation, and peritoneal dialysis system——the largest in the Asia Pacific region. The Lancet also regards us as the world's largest medical system in the world. We have been focusing on scientific and technological research, and are committed to advancing the development of science and medicine in China. Our precision medicine has also gained attention in the world. Now, in order to promote scientific and technological research, we have established a precision medicine organization in the hospital, which contains five closely related elements, namely basic research, testing, clinical care, big data, biobanks, etc. This is where precision medicine is heading for and has been applied to our fields of oncology, diabetes, gastroenterology, neurology, public health, and more. We are looking forward to the application of precision medicine in the Greater Bay Area. We also make use of international resources. We have established partnerships with many other medical institutions in the world, such as Joslin Diabetes Center, Brown University, University of Birmingham, the University of Melbourne, who are also the partners in Medical Union initiative. In the next three years, we will continue with our medical plans.

We have already established the International Hospital in Nansha district, which is located in the centre of the Greater Bay Area, and will be twice as large as the First Affiliated Hospital of Sun Yat-Sen University. It is half an hour's drive from Hong Kong and Macao. The Nansha District is a trial zone for deeper research into the Greater Bay Area. As a free trade zone, Nansha has very close free trade relations with Hong Kong and Macao. The Nansha International Hospital will be completed by 2021. With an area of 20,000 m2, it will be the largest hospital in China. Our hospital is now exploring the possibility of co-building a hospital with the University of Birmingham. Other well-known universities in the UK are also seeking opportunities to build hospitals in China. The Greater Bay Area is a place with enormous opportunities and unlimited possibilities. We have the support of government policy and a fervent aspiration for higher education. I'd like to take this opportunity to invite all of you to contribute your wisdom to a better Greater Bay Area. Thank you.

Christopher Tremewan: Thank you Dr. Xiao Haipeng, for your excellent speech. Our second speaker is Dr. Wong Suk-Ying from the CUHK. She is not only an active member in the APRU, but also a professor in the Department of Sociology, Director of Student Financial Assistance Agency and Associate Vice-President of the CUHK. She has been a visiting lecturer to Beijing Normal University and Nankai University while pursuing her PhD at Stanford University. Prior to joining the CUHK in 1997, she had taught in both the United States and Japan, where she won several awards. Let's give the floor to Dr. Wong Suk-Ying.

Wong Suk-Ying: Distinguished leaders, ladies and gentlemen, good afternoon. It is quite a challenge for me to speak here today, because I am here to step in for our Vice-Chancellor and President Professor Sung Chi Rocky Tuan, who has to go back to Hong Kong immediately for something urgent. In Hong Kong, I would be called a substitute worker. Yet this seemingly easy task can be challenging at times. I'll try my best and your tolerance will be much appreciated.

My topic today is about the Guangdong-Hong Kong-Macao Greater Bay Area. As you all know, the CPC Central Committee and the State Council released the *Outline Development Plan for the Guangdong-Hong Kong-Macao Greater Bay Area* in February 2019. It takes me a long time to go through this important outline. I think we all should understand it better as it has outlined several key focal points. We need to think about whether higher education could ride the tide and deepen the integration of industry, academia and research. I'll first introduce the strategy, position and development goal for the Greater Bay Area. Then, we will look at the timetable against its goals, to see how we could contribute to Hong Kong, to China, and the larger world through this national strategy.

We can see from this chart that the Guangdong-Hong Kong-Macao Greater Bay Area covers a wide range. There are four-bay areas in the world, among which, the Greater Bay Area and the New York Bay Area are the largest. The total GDP of the Greater Bay Area has surpassed that of the San Francisco Bay Area. Speaking of bay areas, I have invited a professor to talk in details about the uniqueness of the San Francisco Bay Area. In General, our GDP has already surpassed that of the San Francisco Bay Area and come very close to that of the New York Bay Area.

The *Outline Development Plan for the Guangdong-Hong Kong-Macao Greater Bay Area* is very detailed and elaborate. I'll talk about the five strategic positions here. 1. a vibrant world-class city cluster; 2. a globally influential international innovation and technology hub; 3.an important support pillar for the "Belt and Road Initiative", which is an imperative strategy for China. 4. a showcase for in-depth cooperation between the Chinese Mainland, Hong Kong and Macao. Such a demonstration zone will exert great influence on the development of the world. 5. a quality living circle for living, working and travelling. These are also the key objective of our forum.

By 2022, the framework to build an international first-class bay area with a pleasant ecological environment by 2035 should essentially be formed. That is to say, sixteen years from now, we will see full and comprehensive development throughout the Bay Area.

The Greater Bay Area consists of 2 SARs and 9 nine Pearl River Delta (PRD) municipalities. Four of them are referred to as core cities, namely Hong Kong, Shenzhen, Guangzhou and Macau, while six of them are key node cities, namely Zhuhai, Zhongshan, Foshan, Jiangmen, Huizhou, Zhaoqing and Dongguan. It also outlined six important and systematic development directions for the area. 1. To strengthen the cooperation in technology innovation. Technology innovation is a major area for the development of the Greater Bay Area. 2. To enhance the in-depth integration of industries, academia and research. 3. To deepen the reform of the innovation system in the Greater Bay Area. The infrastructures are relatively easy to build, and it's clear that the central government wants to make thorough reforms in the existing economic mechanisms. 4. To promote the transformation of scientific and technological achievements. This transformation is very important. It also provides opportunities to the young people in the Greater Bay Area. We hope that such opportunities will further increase as the transformation takes place. 5. To boost cooperation in education. Some initiatives have already been in place. 6. The overall guidance is to strengthen new industries, including information technology, biotechnology, high-end equipment manufacturing and new materials. Regarding the development policies of the HKSAR, the outline mentions several key points, such as education, medical industry, financial services, environmental protection and sustainable development, and youth development.

In her last policy address, Hong Kong Chief Executive Carrie Lam Cheng Yuet-Ngor proposed to allocate HK$40 billion as research fund to encourage the all-round development of Hong Kong's universities.

One of Hong Kong's future priorities is to build an international innovation platform for science and technology, especially to promote the mobility of research factors, as further improvements need to be made in this area. From the perspective of talent training, the Greater Bay Area has a high mobility of high-end talent, but it is still necessary to strengthen technological research and to support research infrastructure. In general, Hong Kong needs to do well in four areas through the development of industry, academia and research.

For example, CUHK already has a branch within the Greater Bay Area, namely the CUHK-Shenzhen.

A lack of talent is the major challenge for the development of the Greater Bay Area. The difference in cultures and systems, hardware and supporting measures, as well as stakeholders' views also add to the difficulty. Vice-Chancellor and President Professor Tuan Rocky S. asks me to deliver this message for him: Our close neighbours are our best friends. We should work more closely together with other cities. That's all for my presentation. Thank you.

Christopher Tremewan: Thanks for your speech, Dr. Wong Suk-Ying. Our third speaker is Mr. Cheung Leong, Executive Director of Community & Charities at the HKJC. He joined the HKJC in 2014, and is also a member in the United Nations Sustainable Development Solutions Network (SDSN) in Hong Kong. Prior to joining the Jockey Club, he was a partner at Bain Capital, Managing Director of Global Sourcing and Supply Chain Management at Esquel Group, Founder and CEO of an educational Internet start-up, and Senior Consultant at the Boston Consulting Group (BCG). He is also the CEO and consultant of several social enterprises in Hong Kong. He is currently a member of the Elderly Commission and the Community Care Fund Task Force of the Government of the Hong Kong SAR, and a director of the Hong Kong Mortgage Corporation Limited (HKMC). Mr. Cheung Leong holds an MBA from Harvard University and BA from CUHK, where he is now a visiting professor. Now, Let's welcome Mr. Cheung Leong to give us a speech.

Cheung Leong: Distinguished leaders, respected professionals, dear friends, it's an honour for me to share with you the management experience of our Charity Trust, my view of Hong Kong as a part of the Greater Bay Area, and talent development from the perspective of charity foundations.

You may have known from our Chairman Dr. Anthony Chow Wing-Kin about the operation model of the HKJC. The Club is a non-profit organization in Hong Kong. We don't have any shareholders. All the money comes from betting and from the citizens. We are the largest single taxpayer in Hong Kong, accounting for 6-7% of the Hong Kong government's tax revenue. What does this mean? Let me make it clearer by giving you an example. Many of you here are from higher education. The annual grant from the University Grants Committee (UGC) of Hong Kong is around HK$18 billion, while we could pay HK$20 billion tax each year. So, the Club is a very important source of tax revenue for Hong Kong. In addition to tax, we have established the Charity Trust, with an annual donation of HK$4 billion. Back in 2009, the donation was only just over a billion Hong Kong Dollars.

Our Board discussed how to do charity several years ago. And we identified several key areas, including ageing, youth, sports, arts and culture, and child-care. We wanted to see the challenges more clearly and find a solution. We need to think about what kind of talent we want from the philanthropy perspective, rather than from the higher education perspective; think about how to lead the participants in philanthropy, including social workers and foundation operators, and think about how to improve our ability and expand our network. I'll just leave it here.

Now, I want to talk about my views on education. In years, we have been doing three things for higher educations. Let's take a look at the chart. The left side refers to infrastructure construction, which is very easy to understand. Back in the 1990s, when the Club has reached a significant size, we donated about HK$2 billion for the founding of HKU. We also funded the Hong Kong Academy for Performing Arts (HKAPA). Higher education institutions themselves have a strong capacity for research and influence on social policy. By joining forces with social service agencies, they can develop innovative collaborations around different topics that can provide some of the more helpful references for our policies.

We also made many efforts in knowledge transfer. We have thought deeply about our talent development initiatives, including the provision of scholarships, so that the recipients will not just receive money to complete their studies, but will become empathetic individuals in the future, which is very important.

In terms of basic education, we believe that innovation is a very important factor. In order to keep up with the times, citizens must constantly innovate themselves. The following are what we have mainly done in the past years: 1. The exchange and discussion of values on various platforms. 2. Innovation abilities cultivation. We have different charity projects, some for individuals, others for institutions. We are looking forward to seeing the innovation spirit in the education community. 3. The adoption of alternative teaching concepts. Considering the strict rules in primary and secondary schools, we are introducing psychology into schools to help reduce stress on students. 4.The development of new courses. In terms of scientific courses, we have developed a programming course with the Hong Kong Polytechnic University (PolyU) to a great effect. 5.The support for integrated education. In general, education innovations require explorations. Our focus is to bridge the gap with science, technology and education.

The last example is the JC A-Connect: Jockey Club Autism Support Network program for children with ASD. We have 8000 children with ASD in Hong Kong covered by the program. What could we do to help them integrate into classroom teaching and mainstream schools? How to help alleviate the pressure on their parents? This program has run for 4 years until now. Over 500 schools are included in this project, covering 60% of students with ASD. Moreover, we hope that more children could be benefited. It is a very fruitful project. The Hong Kong SAR Government is now considering developing a policy based on the practice. However, that doesn't mean we will withdraw from it. When this validated method becomes a policy, we could fund other innovation projects. Thank you.

Christopher Tremewan: Thank you, Mr. Cheung Leong. Just now, we heard three great presentations on higher education, health care, and the opportunities and challenges facing the Guangdong-Hong Kong-Macao Greater Bay Area. We learned that we need upgraded models, strategic positions and innovative approaches to build an ecosystem in this area. Our time for discussion will be limited since our speakers have offered us so many valuable insights. But still, I have a question for the three of you. My institution is well aware that the challenges facing the Pacific Rim are not confined to any one country or region, meaning that addressing them requires different countries and regions to find new ways of cooperation——not just across borders, but across disciplines and institutions. The construction of the Greater Bay Area is to bring many challenges, which could be classified into three types. The first challenge is about cooperation. What kind of cooperation model should be promoted? To be more specific, what kind of cooperation model between different universities, between universities and charity organizations, and between NGOs and governments could better boost the development of the Greater Bay Area both as a concept and as a reality? As our overriding goal is to promote the well-being of society, we need to define the way we measure success. To start with, we can first talk about cooperation, well-being and the criteria of success. Now, let's move on to the topic of a new cooperation model for the Greater Bay Area. Mr. Xiao Haipeng, could you please answer this question first?

Xiao Haipeng: We are all expecting a new cooperation model. I believe, with the support of charity organizations, we will get enough funds for talent training, faculty training, and student exchange programs. Furthermore, our hospital is now building a laboratory, which will be accessible for the whole Greater Bay Area.

Christopher Tremewan: Thank you. Let's hear from Dr. Wong Suk-Ying.

Wong Suk-Ying: From a university perspective, we definitely need closer collaboration between the government, industries and research institutions. For example, we don't know how to raise funds for start-ups. Angel funding may be a choice. I think this can be solved in the foreseeable future by collaboration between companies, industries and universities. We have two solutions for this. First, we can learn from the development experience of the Tokyo Bay Area in Japan to establish a good interface mechanism between industry, academia and research. In contrast, we now rely too much on individual network and experience. Second, we need active collaboration and participation from SMEs. In 2017, only 1% of SMEs in the Greater Bay Area had the technical competence required by international standards, so I think there is great potential for growth in this area as well.

Christopher Tremewan: So, what's your idea, Mr. Cheung Leong?

Cheung Leong: "Cooperation" is a great word that encompasses both conflict and consensus. What you have said about our ultimate goal is wonderful. We hope to generate social influence. However, "social influence" is not always persuasive enough to get others into cooperation. For me, motivation is also critical. We have taken the lead in the UNSDSN in Hong Kong. There is this initiative to unite all universities in Hong Kong and promote sustainable development on campus. HKJC is also willing to fund such a good initiative. It is very intriguing. But it will take a long time for the universities to co-establish such a mechanism. For me, cooperation is a good thing, but it depends on motivation and effective funding.

Christopher Tremewan: Thank you very much. I couldn't agree more with what you said; it does take some time and money to identify common interests. The first thematic session is very fruitful. Thank you all.

V Public Health and Philanthropy in the 21st Century

Moderator: Professor Lam Tai-Hing, Sir Robert Kotewall Professorship in Public Health, the Chair Professor of Community Medicine, HKU Li Ka Shing Faculty of Medicine

Speakers: Anil Kapur, Chairman of the Board, World Diabetes Foundation (WDF)

Jesper Brandgaard, President of the Novo Nordisk Haemophilia Foundation Council (NNHF)

Liu Siqi, Co-Founder and Supervisor of the BGI Group, Chief of Supervisor of the Shenzhen Mammoth Foundation

Luo Lexuan, Director General of Health Commission of Shenzhen Municipality

Lam Tai-Hing: Good afternoon. Now, let's move on to our second thematic session. I am Lam Tai-Hing from the HKU. The theme of this session is Public Health and Philanthropy in the 21st Century. We have four speakers, each with 10 minutes to speak. We hope there will be some time left for free discussions. Now, let me give the floor to our first speaker Mr. Anil Kapur, Chairman of the Board, WDF.

Anil Kapur: Ladies and Gentlemen, first of all, I would like to thank the organizers for inviting me to the forum. My appreciation also goes to the CPAFFC and the three host universities. We all know that health is the cornerstone for human development, but we sometimes don't pay enough attention to it. As health is closely linked to the environment, education and economy, it is also the biggest challenge to sustainable human and social development in the 21st century. Considering that the main challenges we are facing now are some non-communicable diseases, we have established the WDF in 2002 dedicated to preventing and treating diabetes in developing countries. We aim to alleviate human suffering related to diabetes and its complications and address the most urgent needs of people in developing countries. Diabetes is a very big challenge right now, and many people are not aware of its danger. In the next 20 years, it will afflict nearly one billion people on the planet. 629 million people will suffer from diabetes, and 532 million people will be hospitalized because of the disease. It literally threatens the life and health safety of half of the planet's population, but many people are helpless to do anything about it.

Untreated diabetes can cause serious complications and even lead to premature death. I'm going to give you some details later. However, I would like to remind you that diabetes also presents the biggest opportunity to establish an integrated health care system in the 21st Century because it could lead to many other diseases that we face in the modern world. WDF was established in 2002 with a generous donation from Novo Nordisk company and was intended to address the issue of AIDS in South Africa. The next speaker of this session is the former Chief Finance Officer of the Novo Nordisk company, Jesper Brandgaard. He is now the President of NNHF, and has decided to shift the focus on diabetes in China. As the Chairman of the Board of WDF, It's my honour to see that our managers are also experts in the field of diabetes.

WDF has more than 100 partners in towns and cities all over the world. We support demand-driven projects, which are generated local projects that are integrated into established ones. We have always respected our partners and beneficiaries. We meet them locally on a regular basis to strengthen dialogues and better understand their needs. WDF is served as a catalyst. Every penny we put into the projects will come out twice as much. Compared to the scarce donations received in the past years, we have exerted much greater influence with a contribution of $150 million contributions. We aim to benefit the local communities through our projects even after the projects expire.

We allow partners to seek other funds to scale the activities. We value links that may have been forgotten. For example, we are the first institution to mention the connection between diabetes and tuberculosis, and we are also concerned about the relationship between maternal health and chronic non-communicable diseases. In the future, we will also see connections between diabetes and chronic non-communicable diseases. We can talk about that today if we have time. As of now, we have funded 558 projects with a total contribution of nearly $150 million. Except that, we also have supported several projects on diabetes in developing countries. We have the following two focal points. First, we aim to make free medical care available to more people, such as teaching patients and their families about non-communicable diseases, building clinics and improving their professionalism, and establishing mentoring systems. Second, we have strengthened the prevention of diabetes. We have been promoting maternal health through our projects by providing health protection courses. We start diabetes protection as early as when the baby is born. Even before that, we protect the mother to ensure the delivery of a healthy baby. In China, for example, 1 in 5 women gives birth to a child at risk of developing gestational diabetes, which can affect the health of both mother and child during pregnancy and in the future. These are the problems that we aim to solve in cooperation with institutions and organizations. To give more support, we hold summits, sessions and stakeholder meetings with the hope to sow the seed of change in the long run. Over the past 17 years, 8.4 million patients have been treated and 11.4 million have been medically examined through our programs. We have helped train 412,000 professionals and improved the capacity of 13,858 clinics to treat diseases. But these treatments are not limited to diabetes; they also include diseases such as hypertension.

What have we learned from these years of experience? Since we intend to solve local problems, the project applicant should identify local needs first. Furthermore, the projects should be controlled entirely and implemented at the local level. We should start with small projects, build trust before expanding the scale. We should encourage people to come up with innovative and viable, replicable solutions that could address the needs and meet the demand. We should preserve the local environment and health systems and refrain from unsustainable actions. We should adapt our perspectives to the local environment. We should ensure that the entire project is aligned to national health standards, goals and action plans. We have reinforced existing projects and integrated them with new projects to improve the health system and our capabilities. We also need to ensure that projects are targeted at vulnerable populations. We have provided our partners with technical support, interactive learning, and local networks. Moreover, we have been working together with more stakeholders and decision-makers to capture, promote and share successful solutions to the projects. One of the things that we have done is to strengthen South-South cooperation. We make Nigerians know that things which could be done in India could also be done in Nigeria. It is totally unnecessary to bring equipment and manpower all the way to Europe. So, building South-South exchange networks is very important for us, which means we can transfer what we learn across borders to our neighbours. I could talk a lot more about what the Foundation has done, but the time is running out. That's all for my presentation. Thank you very much.

Lam Tai-Hing: Now, let's welcome Jesper Brandgaard, President of the NNHF to give his speech.

Jesper Brandgaard: Thank you. It's my honour to participate in the WPF on behalf of the NNHF. Our foundation is dedicated to the prevention and treatment of haemophilia and diabetes. Today, as the President of the NNHF, I'm going to give you two practical examples of what the foundation is all about. Our principles are very similar to those of the WDF, which Dr. Kapur has just described. When the NNHF was founded in Switzerland in 2005, we realized that Novo Nordisk could actually contribute to the world rather than just being a company producing drugs. The foundation was set up to bring more care to the world, which is why we have the WDF, and three years later, we have the NNHF. We want to go with global experts and local people to improve expertise, provide more diagnosis and registration, enhance education and empower the world. We have done 274 projects in 73 countries, which is probably a small share compared to the diabetes project that Mr. Anil Kapur was talking about.

What have we done in China? Haemophilia is a lesser-known condition in China. When we started working in China 10 years ago, only 7,000 haemophiliacs were diagnosed. Now 30,000 haemophiliacs have been treated, and there are probably hundreds of thousands of haemophiliacs in China. We conducted 10 projects on haemophilia in China, through which we diagnosed more than 4,000 haemophiliacs and upgraded 113 laboratories in China. We also have several web channels for patient registration. We've trained 1,500 health care practitioners and built a technology center in China. We also have developed a close relationship with patients and communities. That's what we have been doing in the past 10 years. The first project I would like to discuss is in Panama, which is one of our classic projects. It's about raising health awareness through the construction of science and technology centres. This project is very similar to the one we are currently running in Shandong province. It worked so well that it was one of our most successful projects in 2018.

Now, I would like to talk about our project in Panama. In 2007, Panama had very limited health care resources, with only one primary care centre in the city. In one hospital, we discovered the local need to establish more primary care centres. We found that many of the local haemophiliacs lived in the countryside. They were in a very bad situation and was unable to travel to the city for treatment. So, the first step in undertaking this project was to find a partner to build the care centre together. We found a renowned doctor to work with us on building the centre, not only to train the medical staff but also to teach the patients and their families about it. In the second step, we established six centres and we provided in-depth training to six doctors, six nurses, and six social workers, and we also provided financial assistance to haemophiliacs in need. In this way, we were able to reduce the travel costs for patients to receive treatment by 76%. This is a great achievement. This classic example shows how we foster sustainable health care capacity in developing countries.

The second example is in Uganda. In 2015, only 42 out of 3,600 people were diagnosed with haemophilia. The capital, Kampala, had very limited medical resources. It lacked the infrastructure to diagnose haemophilia. The first step in our project was to conduct a public awareness campaign in Uganda. We set up laboratories and trained local technicians. Some trainers volunteered to go to Uganda. 49 more haemophiliacs were diagnosed and 140 people participated in the project. We hoped to extend this initiative to the whole country, both in terms of awareness, training in the prevention of haemophilia and early detection of patients. Two years after the initiation of the project, we have diagnosed an additional 200 patients. Finally, we worked with patient organizations to come up with a policy agreed by the Parliament on how to treat haemophilia in Uganda. As a charity organization, it is important to work with patient organizations, as this is the gateway to information about local government policies on disease treatment.

The above two projects are examples of what we've done around the world. Thank you for listening.

Lam Tai-Hing: Next, let's invite Mr. Liu Siqi, Co-Founder and Supervisor of the BGI Group, to the stage.

Liu Siqi: Thanks for your introduction. Distinguished guests, ladies and gentlemen, good afternoon, I am very pleased to be here to present my experience in the field of public health.

BGI Group is an atypical local company in Shenzhen. Over the past 20 years, we have been dedicated to the integration of industry, education, and research. It is atypical in that we have always focused on the research of public health. Thanks to the great opportunity of China's reform and opening up, although the journey has been difficult, we are still able to become the world's largest genomic research centre and the world's largest genomic industrial base.

Today I'm sharing with you BGI Group's thoughts on public health, an idea that focuses on newborn health. There are 7,000 genetic diseases in China, and roughly 30 million families have to accept a child born with a congenital disability every year, at the expense of 30 billion yuan. As physicians, our primary concern is being able to find a way to prevent certain birth defects, which must be something that occurs frequently and can be improved within our means. Our main focus has been on Down syndrome, which was discovered in the West 150 years ago. In 1959, we learned that it was caused by chromosomes and identified the underlying clinical symptoms. Apart from delayed intellectual development which causes the patients to end up with a mental level of someone aged seven or eight, there are two additional characteristics: orbital hypertelorism and three copies of chromosome 21. This has been going on for over 150 years, and there's not much people can do to prevent it, even though the biological identification is clear. Traditionally, there are three methods: 1. blood tests, but the results do not appear until a very late stage and the false positive rate is extremely high; 2. ultrasound, which also does not reveal anything until a late stage; 3. amniocentesis, which is very accurate but not widespread and has a high false-positive rate. It also can cause miscarriages and accidents. All of this slowed down the study of Down syndrome. Until in 1997 there was a very important discovery at the CUHK that pregnant mothers may have trace amounts of DNA, some of which could be detected using PCR at the time, which greatly encouraged the early detection of Down syndrome features. However, the lack of signal from the genomic sequence was highly likely to cause false positives. Furthermore, the operation was very time-consuming and not suitable for large-scale clinical testing. Therefore, clinical tests were performed on people who are more familiar with the procedure, such as older women. So, routine testing technologies generally acceptable for the mass were not available at that time.

The BGI Group noticed this technology in 1999. At that time, we were thinking about two things. 1. Given the sensitivity of the technology, is it possible to achieve a large-scale test? 2. In alignment with the bigger goal of creating a healthy China, we aimed to collaborate with the government to seek a way to benefit China and the world at large. During this process, the BGI Group has done quite a lot of work. In 2007, the BGI Group adopted the most advanced technology at that time, namely the next-generation sequencing technology, which was deterministic for the use of future genome technology in clinical testing. The most notable feature of this technology was that it had outstripped the Moore's law in terms of scale, speed and cost. The emergence of this technology made it possible to improve the accuracy and prevalence of the experiment with a lower cost. We introduced the high-throughput sequencing technology at the beginning of 2006 and released the result in 2010 followed by a series of papers. About 200 million people were spot-tested, the BGI Group tested 400 of which. Our test discovered 18,000 Down syndrome patients, making a huge contribution to Shenzhen. From 2009 to 2017, with the support of the government, we have reduced the overall testing cost to CNY800, which is expected to be further lowered in the future. We have made two major contributions. One is that, due to our efforts, approximately 70% women now have access to the test for Down syndrome in Shenzhen. In the 8 years, the birthrate of newborns with Down syndrome has been reduced from 3.49 in 10,000 to 0.8 in 10,000. More importantly, we have pioneered a model in Shenzhen that is possible to benefit all Chinese people. So, we brought the model to Changsha, which followed Shenzhen to have made it available to all citizens. By 2019, all pregnant women in Shijiazhuang, Hebei province were able to receive the test through the project. The project has been implemented in 18 provinces and municipalities. We are also running projects regarding the defection of patients, and tumours, utilizing our genome technology to improve the livelihood.

Lam Tai-Hing: Thank you. Next, let's welcome Mr. Luo Lexuan, Director General of the Health Commission of Shenzhen Municipality to give us a speech.

Luo Lexuan: Distinguished guests, dear experts, ladies and gentlemen, good afternoon. Thanks for having me here today to talk about health along with the other three speakers. I will take this opportunity to introduce the public health status in Shenzhen. The Healthy China Initiative has become a national strategy. In the strive for a relatively comfortable life, the Party and our State has attached great importance to the health issue. General Secretary Xi Jinping has stressed on the Health Conference that a well-off society could not be realized without good public health. Public health is equally important as economic development. The people's sense of gain, happiness and security are all inseparable from their health, so health has become a national strategic plan and an important symbol of national prosperity. In such a context, the State has adopted a series of strategic initiatives, including the medical reform in 2009, which aimed to establish fundamental medical and health care systems that provide fair access and improved convenience for the people. Focusing on the establishment of the medical and health care systems, we have put in place four guarantee systems——the public health service system, the medical care system, the medical security system and the pharmaceutical supply system. For the implementation of the above four systems, eight key measures need to be taken. Built on the medical and health care reform, we have come up with an overall design during the 13th Five-Year Plan. In order to build a basic health care think tank, it is important to improve several systems——accelerating a graded diagnosis and treatment system; deepening the comprehensive reform of public hospitals; improving the universal basic health insurance system; guaranteeing pharmaceutical supply; and strengthening the regulation of the health care system after its reform and opening up.

On the 2016 National Health Conference, China has put forward the Healthy China Strategy and issued the Outline for Healthy China 2030 along with a dedicated plan and outline for medical reform. Based on these plans, China issued the Healthy China Action Plan in 2019. The Action Plan proposed 15 special campaigns to "intervene in health influencing factors, protect full-life-cycle health and prevent and control five major diseases." There are six influencing factors for intervention, the fundamental of which is the full access for health education, while the key is improving health literacy. The World Health Organization (WHO) guidelines emphasize four cornerstones, from sensible diets, fitness for all, wellness programs to mental health. There are four stages for full-life-cycle health——the health care for the pregnant women and infants, for primary and secondary school adolescents, for adults with the main focus on occupational health issues, and for the elderly—— covering the full cycle from fetus to death. The five major diseases are cardiovascular disease, diabetes, chronic disease and tumour.

Shenzhen is also in the process of implementing the national strategy, with the main lines of work being to remedy shortcomings, raise the level of primary medical care, build up leading advantages and promote public health. Firstly, Shenzhen did not start to develop rapidly until 40 years ago. The lack of resources is our biggest problem. There is still a huge gap between our health care capacity and the needs of 20 million people. The number of doctors in Shenzhen only accounts for a small portion of the total number of Guangdong province, and China. Secondly, we are planning to establish a graded diagnose and treatment system. Thirdly, we are striving to improve our overall medical capacity. Fourthly, we will implement the "Healthy China" strategy with the priority to improve people's health. Specific measures have been in place in the above four areas, including building more hospital facilities. Our goal is to have 603,000 beds by 2020, with 4.3 beds per 1,000 people and 3.8 doctors per 1,000 people. We have introduced the Three Prestigious program, namely introducing advantageous resources from home and abroad, including prestigious hospitals, prestigious doctors, and prestigious clinics. All hospitals except those under construction are handed over to renowned hospitals for operation, for example, the HKU Shenzhen Hospital, which is by nature a public hospital run by HKU, with all daily maintenance costs subsidized as per the standard of public hospitals. We have promoted the establishment of national oncology hospitals and medical departments in Shenzhen. For example, the Third People's Hospital of Shenzhen was approved as a national clinical research centre for infectious diseases. In terms of improving public health, we have comprehensively promoted the construction of a healthy Shenzhen, with specific actions to improve health literacy and medical service, among others.

We also undertook 17 national health reform tasks, including the area of food safety. The reform has led to a significant improvement in the efficiency of resource allocation, with the proportion of personal health expenditure lowered to less than 20%.

Upon the promulgation of the *Opinions of the CPC Central Committee and the State Council on Supporting Shenzhen in Building a Pioneering Demonstration Zone for Socialism with Chinese Characteristics*, we have formulated ten key tasks in promoting health——push for health-related legislation at the local People's Congress level, a pioneer in three areas, and achieve key breakthroughs in six areas. We have set three milestones with the ultimate goal of building a world-class medical hub. Thank you all.

Lam Tai-Hing: The above speeches are very informative, leaving only a few minutes for questions and answers. Do you have anything to ask the guests? Now I will leave the time to our audience. However, I'd like to raise the first question here. How is Shenzhen contributing to the development of the Greater Bay Area?

Luo Lexuan: Thank you for your question. The development of the Greater Bay Area is also a national strategy. It consists of 9 cities in the Guandong province and 2 SARs, namely Hong Kong and Macao. Regarding its development, the State has set five goals, the core of which is to build a global technology and innovation centre. The Greater Bay Area takes Guangzhou, Shenzhen and Hong Kong as its core engines, with emphasis on Hong Kong's status as the international innovation hub. In my view, in order to achieve these goals, the core engine cities must realize the convergence of rules and the interconnection of systems, especially the integration in the flow of people, logistics and information, which is the key to the development of this area. It's important that we go forward hand in hand.

Lam Tai-Hing: I think Shenzhen has done an excellent job compared to other regions in China.

Luo Lexuan: Shenzhen Municipal People's Congress is the first to enact public health-related law. But we still have many problems in terms of enforcement. However, I do feel the public awareness are increased. Our top priority now is to implement the 15 major health campaigns.

Lam Tai-Hing: I have a question for Dr. Liu Siqi. You mentioned gene in your speech. How does it relate to philanthropy?

Liu Siqi: Our foundation is intended to empower philanthropic organizations to leverage the power of technology. We mainly offer help to the poverty-stricken areas in two ways. Besides, we want to make the concept of the genome more scientifically appealing, after all it is too difficult to understand. However, when we integrate it with other popular science, it becomes more acceptable for the public. This is really helpful. China has seen dramatic changes in the last 20 years. Our idea of doing genome research back then was opposed by mainstream scientists. The vast majority of scientists don't agree with our idea, but by now, the Human Genome Project we created has been written into elementary school textbooks. We can see that there a strong drive to make science more popular and the development of science is really fast.

Lam Tai-Hing: The fruit of genomic research is usually the privilege of the rich. I'm very impressed that you have made it available to ordinary people. Both of you come from foundations. Why do you emphasize on the sustainable model instead of providing direct financial aid to local people?

Jesper Brandgaard: For both the World Diabetes Foundation and the NNHF, simply providing medication services to patients would put us in a moral dilemma. We aim to help patients to treat the diseases which might accompany them for a lifetime. If we only help them financially, it would only work for a while. Instead, collaborating with governments, establishing capacity centres would allow us to help them in the long term. We're working with some of the poorer provinces in China right now. We will monitor the performance of the projects and expand them to other places, to optimize related policies and build a sustainable and long-term system.

Anil Kapur: I totally agree with you. Sustainability is vital, especially in terms of prevention, which is more forward-looking than treatment. We don't think diabetes is expensive to treat, but it could be extremely costly if we do nothing in prevention and treatment. So, what we're doing is helping to build local capacity and address issues such as the inadequate supply of clinics. We provide education and training opportunities so that people have equal access to services. That's how we make it sustainable. If we simply distribute the medications to patients, the local environment would never change. As a foundation, we can't solve the diabetes problem alone. We need to work with local governments and communities and build partnerships to optimize local systems. In any region of the world, treating diabetes and providing medications does not need much money. What is important is to bring attention to the problem, increase understanding and build capacity. Let me give an example of preventive treatment of diabetes. I would like to share how we have changed our model in this case. Our foundation had this idea to work with the Chinese Center for Disease Control and Prevention (China CDC) and the Chinese Center for Diabetes Control and Prevention. We have run our programs in six cities, including Shenzhen, Xiamen, Xi'an, Shanghai, Beijing and Qingdao. In the beginning, we were engaging and collaborating with the community health centres. Nevertheless, we did not pay enough attention to the diabetes communities. We simply acted in accordance to our standard procedures. As a result, our programs had gained little local support. But in Qingdao, we launched large-scale campaigns with Qingdao Municipal Health Commission and managed to get 1.2 million people screened for diabetes. It would not be possible without collaboration with the local government. Simply providing medications could not enable us to establish a sustainable system.

Lam Tai-Hing: Sure, if we could get 1.2 million people to be screened in each city. In a few years, a lot of people would benefit from this program.

Liu Siqi: Concerning the treatment of the diseases we talk about, it's great to reduce costs and allow more people to enjoy the dividends of technology. However, there is not as much data available in China, and the incidence of certain diseases is on the rise. More education and training are needed to raise people's awareness of disease prevention and treatment.

Jesper Brandgaard: In my previous experience as a CFO, the most basic aspects of treating the disease are changing behaviour, losing weight and doing more exercise.

Anil Kapur: I think it is a fundamental treatment for diabetes and other diseases. This program started in Europe. Data from China, including the famine of the 1960s, showed that children born then we're vulnerable to diabetes and cardiovascular disease. So why are we developing economy in such a rush? There are some lessons to be learned. Education will address health and nutrition issues in the long run, but very few people are aware of this. I also mentioned tuberculosis, which is very prevalent in China. But now China is more concerned about AIDS, a disease that only has limited impact. Instead, tuberculosis and diabetes affect a very large base of people, and diabetes is the main threat factor in spreading tuberculosis. Our programs have been successful in both China and India, where we double screened for the two diseases. We inform those patients with diabetes that they might also have tuberculosis. We urge them to change their lifestyle.

Lam Tai-Hing: Now that there is no further question from the audience, let's conclude the second thematic session. We wish the Greater Bay Area to become an area of health and joy, and be embraced by the whole world. Thanks for the presentations and opinions of our guests. And thank you all for your participation.

VI Youths, Community Innovation & Social Enterprise in the Greater Bay Area

Moderator: Wu Xueming, Chairman and Executive Chairman of the Youth Association of the Greater Bay Area

Speakers: Professor Charles Eesley, Associate Professor and W.M. Keck Foundation Faculty Scholar, Department of Management Science and Engineering, Stanford University

Andy Ho Wing-Cheong, Executive Director, the Hong Kong Federation of Youth Groups (HKFYG)

Wu Xueming: Hello, everyone. I am the chairman and executive chairman of the Youth Association of the Greater Bay Area, and the moderator for this session. Now, let's welcome Mr. Charles Eesley, the Associate Professor and W.M. Keck Foundation Faculty Scholar, Department of Management Science and Engineering of Stanford University to the stage.

Charles Eesley: Thanks for inviting me to this forum. Today, I am very happy to have this opportunity to discuss these meaningful topics with so many people in Shenzhen.

The project was a joint effort between me and William Miller, another professor at Stanford University. Throughout my career, I've focused half on research and half on start-ups. When it comes to research and education, my focus is on entrepreneurship, especially in developing economies.

Stanford is a world-renowned university that does a great job in entrepreneurship and innovation. Many alumni run for-profit businesses, but what is less well known is that our students, alumni, and faculty are also very active in creating non-profits and social enterprises. In addition to these well-known for-profit companies shown on the slides, we have many alumni who have created non-profit companies, such as the Acumen Fund.

The person to the right of this picture is one of my students. She was talking about the framework of knowledge we teach that can be applied to for-profit businesses as well as non-profit social enterprises. She took my class——"Tech Entrepreneurship"——and has worked on projects while learning the course. After graduation, she was approached by her childhood friend from Pakistan and eventually the two of them decided to promote female education in Pakistan. She turned down a well-paying job at a London consulting firm to start a foundation with her partner. The Foundation provided financial support for projects to promote female education in Pakistan and India. Now she has also created a venture capital fund company dedicated to fostering female entrepreneurship in the Middle East. This girl is one of the proudest students I have ever taught because of the impact she has had on the world.

Here is another example. There is a Stanford University company called Embrace, which provides incubators for newborns. The company was originated from a course called "Affordable Limit Design". Let me tell you what this course is about. In developing economies such as those in Africa, incubators are essential. In the United States, incubators are used in hospitals and are very expensive, costing $20,000 for one. In this project, the students wanted to solve this problem for the poor by making cheaper incubators that are warm and waterproof at a price of for $25. It was a technological innovation in engineering.

One more example is a project that you will hear from one of my colleagues, Huang Xueshi from Silicon Valley, at 3:00 p.m. tomorrow. So, I won't talk too much here. The project focuses on villages in African countries, where some children may get burned by the use of kerosene lamps. It provides solar lighting for those that use kerosene lamps at night, providing safe and inexpensive lighting for the 500 million people in South Africa who do not have access to electricity.

Over the years, these projects and activities on social entrepreneurship have had a defined model. And special organizations for educating the next generation and developing non-profit institutions have been established. The Stanford King Center on Global Development, funded by the King family, is sponsoring students this summer to work in Thailand to foster social entrepreneurship and economic development. Stanford Seed is another project focused on innovation to reduce poverty and promote economic development.

I'm primarily responsible for collecting data on start-ups. We surveyed Stanford alumni that looked at 140,000 or so alumni who graduated from seven departments between the 1930s and 2011. That's a very wide spectrum. We received 27,000 responses. Professor Wang has collected the GDP data for the Greater Bay Area. We also collected data on start-ups by Stanford alumni, and turn their revenue into GDP. If we regard what has been created by our alumni as a city, it would be the world's tenth-largest economy in terms of GDP. If we look at the contribution of Stanford University to the development of the Silicon Valley, we will find the most important one is that it has attracted a lot of talents. A large number of students comes from California, and a very high portion of elites have decided to stay in California after graduation, and commit themselves to the economic development of the San Francisco Bay Area, either through start-ups or through working for high-tech companies. So, Stanford University is a magnet for talent. It has fed the Silicon Valley and the Bay Area with numerous elites. This is an important example. We once asked one of our alumni: Do you come to Stanford because of its reputation for social entrepreneurship or something else? And we see more and more alumni choose Stanford for its reputation in social entrepreneurship.

As I just mentioned, there are not only alumni who create for-profit companies, but also alumni who create non-profits. Let's take a look at the data. Some alumni create angel funds, some become early employees, and some become board members. We can see that there is a certain link between for-profits and non-profits. The former is used to create economic value, while the latter is used to distribute value. We also researched the sectors in which non-profits operate, including education, economic development, global health and consumer advocacy. We can also see which faculties the non-profit founders came from. The majority of alumni comes from the Law School, followed by the College of Education and the Business School. What I want to emphasize is that we can collect this data on social entrepreneurship and non-profits for scientific research to discover what exactly contributes to entrepreneurial success. What kinds of technologies and educational experiences allow students to become more influential and more successful in building social institutions? That the kind of research we have done.

In the early years, it is increasing trendy for graduates to create non-profits, with more and more graduates getting involved. However, this trend has slowed down in the past 10 years as it takes rich life experience for them to judge whether they can create a non-profit organization with sufficient resources. One of the things that is very encouraging to me is the growing interest in creating for-profit organizations among graduates from 2000-2017, including recent Stanford graduates.

Many have founded non-profits after for-profits, showing a transition of mind in the process of economic value creation and wealth accumulation. Their revenues from for-profits companies become the funding source for their non-profit organizations, thus giving back to the community and society with their wealth.

Finally, I'd like to mention the Stanford Center for Social Innovation that supports student entrepreneurial activities, one of which has been around for some years called the Stanford Social Entrepreneurship Hub. The centre has been helping students to pursue careers in the non-profit sector starting from 1990s. The Taproot Foundation is another organization, established by the Business School. This institute provides consulting services to non-profits, and students can help non-profits solve problems they encounter in information technology and human resources. The Haas Center for Public Service is another agency established in the 1980s to support students to get internships in non-profit organizations and provide them with training materials. Fusion is the institution that brings together future social innovators and entrepreneurs. The Center for Philanthropy and Civil Society is a recently established institution that focuses on teaching and social entrepreneurship with a more scientific orientation, which means that these students will analyze data, trends, or look for success factors. So the centre may need to do research based on evidence.

That's all for my presentation. Thank you very much for listening, and I'm very much looking forward to the Q&A session later. Thank you.

Wu Xueming: Thanks for the wonderful speech given by Charles Eesley. Now, let's welcome Mr. Andy Ho Wing-cheong, Executive Director of HKFYG, to the stage.

Andy Ho Wing-Cheong: Thank you very much. Good afternoon. I am very glad to have this opportunity to share with you the experience of HKFYG. I will make the presentation in English. And later, I will discuss with you in Mandarin. Charles Eesley has shared with us his experience in the university. And what I am going to talk about is youth service.

This part is about young people as a force to change. I'll share my insights into why young people are involved in the process of social innovation. Young people have their advantages in four areas. First, young people are more motivated and are willing to chase their dreams and goals, rather than just making money. Second, they are more innovative and less bounded by traditional models. Third, young people of this era are used to multitasking. They enjoy doing meaningful work and also value the balance of work and life. Fourth, social innovation can teach young people how to do it better. There is no better coach than social innovation, through which young people can develop their skills and gain more profound understandings about certain social issues.

I'd like to share why I commit myself to this area. In 2005, many people were aware of the news that the United Nations and the International Labor Organization (ILO) had put forward four core strategies to tackle youth unemployment: creating jobs, promoting entrepreneurship, enhancing employability and offering fair opportunities. We need to give more considerations to these aspects. Meanwhile, we have launched a new program——Youth Business Hong Kong. It is a micro-financing project aiming at training young people's entrepreneurial skills so that they can have a better development.

This is a very important project. Here I'd like to share with you the road map for the Youth Business Hong Kong, and how we are going to implement it. In 2002, we made our first foray into programs that support youth entrepreneurship, cultivating youth entrepreneurship and entrepreneurial mindset, which is different from what the original employment service offered. In 2005, we launched the Hong Kong Youth Entrepreneurship Program to support the Youth Business International, our first "one-stop" service for local young entrepreneurs in Hong Kong, which has filled the gap in the youth start-ups sector. In 2014, we had the Qianhai Shenzhen-Hong Kong Youth Innovation and Entrepreneur Hub (E-Hub), a project that opened in December of that year in Qianhai, Shenzhen. The E-Hub is a tripartite initiative by the Qianhai Authority, Shenzhen Youth Federation and HKFYG, and therefore has a strategic partnership with the latter two federations. Since the successful introduction of dozens of youth enterprises in the E-Hub, we have established a new project, the Hong Kong Federation of Youth Groups Jockey Club Social Innovation Center, which was established in 2015 to support young people to create and execute their own entrepreneurial plans and create sustainable development programs.

It takes us 17 years of experience and wisdom to make remarkable achievements in youth entrepreneurship, such as more useful service models and multiple service programs that allow young people to start businesses quickly and effectively and integrate into social innovation programs in a short period of time. In 2020, we will have a new project in Chengdu, Sichuan province, which is a major step for us to disseminate our experience to our partners in the Mainland widely.

What kind of support could be an offer to the young people? We serve young people aged 18-40, providing them with innovation services, including start-up training. We can provide them with the start-up knowledge they need as start-up entrepreneurs, such as more knowledge about market expansion and marketing. We also offer initial start-up funds ranging from HK$20,000 to HK$200,000 for young people to create their businesses with the guidance of our alliance. Apart from that, we have arranged various events to support their development, such as the Global Entrepreneurship Alliance Forum. Let me share with you what we have learned from our experience.

First, social impact and sustainable development is vital. The majority of young entrepreneurs in Hong Kong has good creativity and the entrepreneurial mindset, enabling them to solve problems with science and technologies. However, sometimes they simply give little consideration to the sustainability of the projects. That means they only come up with a program yet fail to think about how to execute it sustainably.

I'll give you a successful example. A young man initiated an ecological program that provides a solution for environmental protection. He disposes of leftover coffee grounds to raise awareness of food waste recycling in the community——a marketable concept with the possibility of generating products. That's why his program can achieve sustainable development.

Second, what is required is not technology, but experience and passion. Sometimes we ask young people why they start the company. They may simply say that because the company could use AI technology. They did not aim at solving any problem. They started the company because they think developing AI technology is a good idea. That's what we want to figure out when we decided whether or not to support youth start-ups. I also asked an interior designer the same question. He said he started a small team of interior designers to make up for the fact that his father died a few years ago and never lived in a comfortable home in his lifetime. His team has been expanding continuously starting from 15 members. This is a very good example of entrepreneurial spirit. Running an enterprise is never easy but becoming an entrepreneur is even more difficult.

Finally, I'd like to talk about the gaps we have in the social innovation ecosystem where we need support. First, we are not sowing enough seeds because fostering entrepreneurship is not an easy task. We must educate young people about this as early as possible. Second, we lack the cross-sector association. Hong Kong is actually very supportive of entrepreneurship, but most of its supporters are fighting alone. So this brings about a huge problem for young people——once they join a program, they have to go over some procedures all over again in order to get financial support. Third, social entrepreneurs have not received customized support. In the future, there should be synergies in Hong Kong or the Mainland to work together to provide customized support to social entrepreneurs, which I think will be very much needed by young people. That's all I want to share today. I am looking forward to furthering discussions with you. Thank you.

Wu Xueming: Let's move to the Q&A session. I'll spend one minute to introduce myself. I graduated from Harvard University, and gained rich experience in the EMS market. After that, I went to graduate school at MIT. Now, I am the chairman and executive chairman of the Youth Association of the Greater Bay Area. With regard to the current problems in Hong Kong, all we want is peace instead of violence. We believe that all demands should be expressed through peaceful means. My first question is for Mr. Charles Eesley. As you know, there are four-bay areas in the world. Two of them are in the US——the San Francisco Bay Area and New York Bay Area. The third one is in Japan, namely, the Tokyo Bay Area. And the fourth one is the Guangdong-Hong Kong-Macao Greater Bay Area in China, which is our topic today. What do you think we can learn from the other three Bay Areas? Or what Stanford University has to offer for the Greater Bay Area? Does the Greater Bay Area in China have the potential to catch up with the San Francisco Bay Area, and become the second Silicon Valley? Is it possible for Shenzhen to do so?

Charles Eesley: This is an interesting question, I had also heard about the Guangdong-Hong Kong-Macao Greater Bay Area initiative before I came here and I didn't think at the time that the Bay Area has an agenda to promote start-ups and technology development. Seriously speaking, I think it's catching up, but there are still some gaps. I saw some data a while ago. We know that Beijing has the largest number of venture capital firms and start-ups, followed by Shanghai and Hangzhou, with the Greater Bay Area in the third place. In terms of the growth rate of Chinese venture capital, China is among the top, probably the highest in the world, especially in the past year when the total amount of Chinese venture capital funds surpassed the US for the first time with a ratio of 93 billion to 91 billion. However, different economies have respective periods of ups and downs. Considering valuations and capital flows, and the next waves of fluctuation are yet to be known.

Wu Xueming: Thank you. My next question goes to Professor Andy Ho Wing-Cheong. We know that there are very successful start-ups in Qianhai. Since I am also in the technology sector, do you have any advice for me? For example, how could we sustain the development of incubators? How to continuously invest in successful start-ups? How could we avoid homogeneity? There are already over 700 incubators in Shenzhen's Nanshan District, are there really that many people starting a business? How do you think of it?

Andy Ho Wing-Cheong: The E-Hub is an excellent beginning. It is a very good experience from Hong Kong and Qianhai. But how can we make this project better? Whether starting a business in Qianhai, or in the larger Greater Bay Area, I believe the biggest difficulty for young entrepreneurs is that they are unfamiliar with the local conditions, which is a huge obstacle for their work. In this regard, I think we could help young people to gain a better understanding of the different regions so that they can develop more smoothly. The Bay Area does have a lot of incubators, which gives rise to the issue of homogeneity. However, each incubator has its own characteristics. Many of the different incubators today are actually intended to encourage diversity of interest among youth. For example, we all know that Huaqiang Road is a good place for youth start-ups, but other places can also offer different advantages. From this perspective, homogeneity is not a problem. Such differentiated advantaged, when used properly, could also promote youth entrepreneurship, allowing different incubators to play to their strengths.

Wu Xueming: Thank you very much, Mr. Ho. I have another question for Dr. Charles Eesley. You've just given us a lot of insights on how to develop the Greater Bay Area. We are very interested in non-profits and philanthropy. In your view, what else could attract and retain talent besides financial support? Many of them are doing volunteer work without pay. For example, we have 200 members in our association. Only 2 of them are paid, while the rest are all volunteers. How can we give these volunteers a sense of purpose and motivation to work for free? They are all graduate students and will be starting full-time jobs after graduation. So I've been thinking about it lately. Could you give us some advice? I'm sure many young people will face this problem.

Charles Eesley: This is an important issue as talent is an essential factor. It is not easy to retain talent even for for-profit organizations and even more so for non-profits. So, challenges do exist. As society becomes wealthier, we see a phenomenon in Silicon Valley where the most talented people, after they have accumulated a certain amount of money, often want to work to make a difference in the world rather than only to make a living. It also holds true for companies in Silicon Valley. They may also struggle with hiring if they can't convince engineers and managers that what they do are benefiting tens of millions of people and even changing the world. I have a friend who was shot in the head by the Taliban.

After a miraculous recovery, did she give up on her campaign to encourage women's entrepreneurship in Pakistan, or did she no longer have the courage to give public speeches? The answer is no. She believes that women need to be better educated, especially young women. And she wants to inspire more people to take the program forward. Then she will tell others this story. These are very good examples.

Wu Xueming: Thank you. What you have shared is fabulous. I have a question for Mr. Ho Wing-cheong, Andy. Since youth are the primary source for social entrepreneurship, how to get young people to start businesses in the Greater Bay Area? My second question is we know that many people are willing to make donations to Stanford University, but how do people finance a non-profit organization? How do we convince people to donate? Other than raising money from our loved ones or family, what other ways are there to finance our business?

Andy Ho Wing-Cheong: We surveyed to find why young people in Hong Kong did not start a business in China. It turned out the most important reason is that they know nothing about China. So, they lost interest. So, if we want to attract them, we need to give them a sense of empathy. Empathy is vital for young people to develop their careers or start a business in a certain place.

Wu Xueming: My second question is about fundraising for non-profits, and it is for both of you. We know non-profits have very noble goals, but how could we convince donors?

Charles Eesley: I have personally raised money for Stanford University and charitable foundations, and my wife, who has also raised money for the American Diabetes Foundation, has a lot of experience in fundraising. Though a bit intimidated at first, we know this is a skill we have to master and keep practising. Since we intend to engage with people who want to get involved in charity, we have to overcome that fear. When we manage to do that, we are able to build very close relationships.

Andy Ho Wing-Cheong: My answer is simple: we can get more support if we can get people to think about the social impact of the project. You just brought up a great question about social innovation. I think it will help a lot if we can get them to consider that this kind of business can solve social problems. That will bring more support.

Wu Xueming: Thank you both for sharing your experience and having such an enlightening dialogue with us. Thank you very much. This shall conclude our thematic session.

VII Sports and Philanthropy

Moderator: Zhang Qiangqiang, General Manager, Beijing Sports University Industrial Management Group

Speakers: Julio Gonzalez Ronco, General manager, Real Madrid Foundation (RMF)

Li Na, Chinese tennis player, Asia's first Grand Slam Singles Champion

Li Xikui, Secretary-General of the CPAFFC, Chairman of CFFPD

Morten Mølholm Hansen, Chief Executive Officer & Secretary-General of Denmark National Olympic Committee (NOC)

Zhang Qiangqiang: Dear friends, this is the last session for today. It is a tiring day. I can even hear stomachs rumbling with hunger. Some are louder than others as if there is a competition going on here.

I am very glad that sports have been included in this forum, as it has been endowed with different meanings nowadays. Our great leader Mao Zedong once said: "One should be mentally gentle and physically strong." General Secretary Xi Jinping also said: "Sports carry the dream of national strength and revitalization. It takes strong sports to make a strong China." Sports have become a national development strategy nowadays. In today's session, we are honoured to have prominent sports figures to share with us. Let's welcome Mr. Julio Gonzalez Ronco, the General manager of RMF.

Julio Gonzalez Ronco: Good afternoon. Thank you for giving me this opportunity to talk about what the RMF has done in philanthropy.

This is a new perspective for us to learn what kind of charity we could do in the world.

Nelson Mandela once said: "Sport has the power to change the world. It has the power to unite people in a way that little else does. Sport can create hope where once there was only despair." This idea echoes another person who said that sports are a national pastime. It's not just a game. It has a unique educational value and requires a spirit of cooperation. So we can see that there are actually many different activities of the RMF, which was founded in 1997 as a non-profit organization. This is how the Real Madrid CF engages with society. In 2008, we were recognized as a development agency by the Spanish Agency for International Cooperation and Development (AECID). The framework of our work is based on the *UN Convention on the Rights of the Child*, so that's why we have a lot of Real Madrid players involved in training programs with children. Sports can help children grow physically, intellectually and emotionally. Sport is also a tool that can help us promote peace, an element of social cohesion, and a better way to kill some time.

These are different sports programs in various places. They are the major channels for Real Madrid CF to build a better image and achieve its humanistic objectives. Our goal is to develop humanism, not to build the strongest team. We target young people aged 6-17 in our country, and we also go into shelters, hospitals, etc., to help the disabled and elderly. At the international level, we have socio-sports schools for young people aged 6 to 17, which will also cover different continents and gradually spread to countries around the globe. There will be a great deal of sporting activity in all countries.

Our activities, mainly basketball or football-related, could adapt to situations in specific countries. Students are not discriminated against in any way. Most importantly, this is a social football school and is not affiliated with Real Madrid CF in any way and is not recruiting students for it. We value respect, equality, friendship, autonomy and tolerance. Football is a team sport, so tolerance is very important. Equality, friendship and autonomy are virtues that every country promotes, which are also demonstrated in India and Russia. Our goal now is to support cultural studies and vocational training in parallel with sports activities. We hope that, through our efforts, we could encourage self-respect, eliminate social barriers and achieve equality in sports. When you do a sports showcase, you will realize it's a small community and the two teams need some cooperation to meet the challenge. The RMF is the fulcrum of the project. However, it requires partnerships with institutions. That's why we work together with local authorities or sponsors in order to unite the public and private sectors within one framework.

These are the activities we have done in Cambodia.

Moreover, we did contribute to society in certain ways. We have special training. We tell coaches what they can use to improve the way their students learn. Since we are not just nurturing their vocational skills, but also cultivating their characters to make them good citizens of society, we need personalized coordination, program media outreach, etc. For the RMF, social sport is a lifelong commitment. We will be professional and efficient, and above all, encourage children to see education as an important path to a brighter future.

These are some photos of our activities. The material we plan and organize is geared towards different sports, such as football or basketball, but we will incorporate very basic subject knowledge. Furthermore, we've assembled great people to compile these materials. We believe that true education is about nurturing one's character and improving oneself. True education should give equal importance to both character building and sports, where personal development and sports training go hand in hand. And we will see to it that there will be a trainer specialist to follow up on everyone's training to ensure consistency.

We may be training a particular program in one part of the world while providing support in another. But we will help schools run and grow, wherever it may be. We will provide them with more supervisory coaches and more support for their work.

We also have some international programs participated by sports stars, who are very important to our foundation.

This is the distribution of our projects in June 2013 (PPT chart).

This is the distribution of projects in 2019 (PPT chart), and we have launched such activities in over 77 countries.

This is the data of our international programs.

That's all for my presentation. Thank you. We hope to work with non-profits in the future. We think non-profits are all about love——to make our communities and the larger world a better place. For me, this is our ultimate mission. Thank you.

Zhang Qiangqiang: Thanks for the wonderful speech by Mr. Julio Ronco Gonzalez. In his speech, he quoted Mr. Nelson Mandela's words: Sport has the power to change the world. Mr. Mandela also said if there are more stadiums, there will be fewer prisons. Sports could play an irreplaceable role in the growth of teenagers. Now let's welcome Ms. Li Na, the Chinese tennis player, Asia's first Grand Slam singles champion.

Li Na: Distinguished guests, good afternoon, I am Li Na. I am glad to share with you my thoughts on philanthropy here in Shenzhen. As a former professional player, becoming a world champion is my childhood dream. I guess it is also a dream shared by all players engaged in sports. During the journey, I have encountered numerous difficulties. Luckily, with the support of my family and friends, my professional coach and teammates, my dream finally came true. Without their care, support and love, I could never be what I am today. Seeing so many people in the world giving up their dreams due to poverty, natural disasters or unexpected circumstances, I feel it is my duty to help them. That's why I have been dedicated to philanthropy in the first place.

For all these years, I've seen children in charity organizations around the country. Some of them are survivors from the Yushu Earthquake. Some are from Wuhan Children's Welfare Institute. I've also been to a school offering education to homeless children, a school for the blinded and a kindergarten located in the deep mountain of Yunnan province. Although their living and learning environment may not be as good as most of their peers, and they have to carry heavy burdens at such a young age, I always see their smiling faces when I play sports and games with them, which is very touching. As a mother of two children, I have become more concerned and passionate about maternal and child care and charity.

No one knows the power of sports better than I do. Sports really can change the world and change a person's life. It not only makes our body stronger, but also improve our personality. It helps us gain strong willpower, cultivates our spirit of cooperation, allowing us to explores more possibilities for life. Throughout my years of playing sports, I have enjoyed the happiness, confidence, and the courage to embrace any challenges. It may not be as visible as my trophies, but it is a treasure that I will cherish for the rest of my life. So after retiring, I have found a new start. I hope to share what I have gained from my professional sports career with more people, especially women and children, so that they could be inspired by sportsmanship and be brave enough to pursue their dreams and conquer more seemingly impossible tasks.

In June 2019, I went to a rural kindergarten in Dali, Yunnan province, where a children's preschool education and care program was underway. Before that, the kindergarten had no playground but a pitch of land full of weeds. By the time of my visit, a playground had been constructed, with swings, pools and other entertainment facilities, where children could run about, play various balls and toys. It is a great place for them to explore the unknown, challenge themselves, learn and grow. The teacher there told me that most of the kids are left alone by their parents. Some of them even come from single-parent families. They have faced many difficulties in life. Ever since the implementation of the project, children started to change dramatically. They have become better at sports, making friends, learning and creating. When they invited me to play with them, I was so overwhelmed with happiness. It made me have this strong feeling that I was doing the right thing.

It's a great time for Chinese athletes and Chinese philanthropists alike. Every athlete has the hope of getting better results on the field of play because we have more resources now. We could also interact with people via social media to extend our influence. Besides, as shown at the fourth WPF, China's philanthropy is developing rapidly, with an increasing number of people participating in and supporting philanthropy. More quality projects and professional philanthropy institutions are emerging. Cross-sector cooperation in philanthropy has even become a trend. So here I am calling for more athletes to join the charity sector and pass on our understanding of sportsmanship to the public, especially to help children and women achieve healthy development. Charity should not be limited to a single sector; rather, it should be a common mission for all of us. Thank you.

Zhang Qiangqiang: Thank you, Li Na. In our words, our champions are the heroes of the nation and the strength of the country. They shape the country's position in the world with their good image of resilience and hard work. Our heart is filled with excitement and pride every time the national flag is hoisted. Now let's give the floor to Mr. Li Xikui, Secretary-General of CPAFFC, and Chairman of CFFPD.

Li Xikui: Good afternoon. When preparing for the meeting, I told the moderator that three of the four speakers in this session are sports professionals. I'm the only exception. So today I'm going to talk about my experience as a non-professional.

I always believe that the power of sports is immense, so is the influence and appeal of athletes as the spirit of sportsmanship is beyond the limit. It seems to me that, as a human social activity, sports may take the form of competition and rivalry, but if we look deeper, it is all about cooperation and communication. This is something we can feel when watching sporting events. Sports transcend borders, languages, and races. The session of this forum is part of our efforts to combine sports and philanthropy. This is also what the CPAFFC and the CFFPD have long been trying to do. In fact, some of such programs have already been designed. For example, last month, we have co-launched several charity activities with Yao Ming Foundation, including sporting activities like basketball and football games. In March 2019, we watched an event featuring special athletes. So I think the special appeal of sport when combined with the influence of charity, will certainly make a huge difference. Like what Mr. Mandela has said, as quoted by the General Manager of RMF, sport has the power to change the world. We also have a good example of this in China. Everyone is familiar with the Ping-pong diplomacy between China and the United States 40 years ago, when a small ping-pong ball takes the world forward and led to a handshake between China and the US. So what can we do to combine sports and philanthropy? 1. We need to develop good methods for such integration. 2. We need to have great design abilities for sporting activities, programs and events. In August 2019, our foundation used to organize the Youth Football Invitational Tournament of Sister Cities in Hebei province where I saw how kids are transcending languages, borders, and races on the sports field. It has been very effective in terms of integration. So, we need to design better programs and activities. 3. We need to spread the culture and spirit of sportsmanship. Earlier, I spoke with Li Na about the US Open that is currently being held. Some Chinese athletes are also playing the game. I told Li Na that she outplayed them not only in terms of techniques. More importantly, she has this strong spirit that is rarely seen in those athletes. That is why, in carrying out our projects and organizing our activities, we must spread the culture and spirit of sport. It is not a spirit and culture that only professionals can have, but one that should be possessed by all of us. So we have set up this session to promote sportsmanship and philanthropy belief, with hope to combine the two better. Thank you.

Zhang Qiangqiang: The CPAFFC has organized many cases where sports are used as a vehicle to promote international exchanges. We thank Mr. Li Xikui for his hard work. Now let's welcome Morten Mølholm Hansen, Chief Executive Officer & Secretary-General of NOC.

Morten Mølholm Hansen: Thank you. Today it's my honour to have the opportunity to speak to you about the progress of sports and sporting events in Denmark. As a football and tennis fan, I am more than happy to sit here with the head of the top football club and a famous tennis player.

First of all, who are we? We are the NOC, with 62 national sports federations, 2 million active members, and 470,000 volunteers. It may seem to be a relatively small number compared to China, but considering that the total population of Denmark is just over 5 million people, we could see it is a remarkable achievement for the sports sector in Denmark. We want to win a medal at the Olympic Games, so we are very keen to promote more actions to be taken by Danish people in this regard. We hope to make the whole event more inclusive and open, and to make the world more open and inclusive.

To be a member of a sports club in Denmark means that you have to be able to play not only football but also cricket. Although the clubs are sports-related, more importantly, they could offer you the opportunity to meet people from different social backgrounds.

We have this additional thought that we want Denmark to be the most active country in sports by 2025. In our vision, by 2025, at least 50% of the Danish population should be members of sports clubs and at least 75% of our people should become passionate about sports. So we need to drive a number of people from inactive to active. Although it may not be easy to encourage non-sports lovers to engage in sporting activities, this is what our government has decided to do. We find that many people are dying from smoking while sports keep people healthy. We have also established many partnerships in Denmark, such as the Sports Promotion Board and various levels of governments and officials. If we want to succeed, we have to rethink ourselves and reinvent our sports events. Previously, family members seldom play sports together, which may be due to a lack of time. So we must focus on social sports. We hope that there will be different suitable sporting activities throughout one's lifetime. Furthermore, we want our sporting activities to be more accessible. For example, we could play soft football on a small field. The next video will show you how this activity works.

(Video)

We also have programs on how to cooperate with schools to promote the Olympic games. The Olympic games in schools are not for picking elite athletes. It would be participated by students in the class.

(Video)

How could we turn non-sports lovers into active participants? We have a running event launched by the Danish royal family, which is broadcast a live on national television every year. In 2019, 80,000 people participated in the event and we want everyone to be a part of it. We can also provide training to show how to start with short distance running.

Thanks for your patience.

Zhang Qiangqiang: Denmark is really the land of beauty and wealth. We all know about the Danish mermaids, and only after hearing this presentation did we realize that they put a lot of effort into fitness for all. Now let's move to the discussion session.

We all know that although Spain has a population of only 50 million people, it is recognized as a world sporting powerhouse, having achieved great success in basketball, football, tennis and cycling. In addition to the support of the state, the development of sports cannot be separated from the efforts of the social sports sector. I'll invite Dr. Julio Ronco Gonzalez to introduce the operation model of Real Madrid CF.

Julio Gonzalez Ronco: When it comes to Real Madrid CF, I think the most important thing is that we have very good traditions as football is a very competitive event in Spain. For years, there are also other events competing with football, which is actually a good thing. However, football remains a healing sport, allowing us to earn respect, value and unity through fighting together. We have to collaborate in order to win. We also have set up other organizations in Spain as well as partnering with public authorities and sponsors. In 2018, we worked together with various agencies to cultivate synergistic abilities, enabling a better development for football and sports at large. What's more, people are now aware that playing football is a good way to educate the next generation.

Zhang Qiangqiang: Thank you very much. Real Madrid CF has set the standard for football games. We hope that Chinese football will continue to work hard and learn from the experience of the best clubs to bring glories to our nation. I have a question for Mr. Li Xikui. Just now, you have elaborated on your overall plan on sports. You also mentioned the Ping-pong Diplomacy in 1971 between China and the US. So what are the projects you want to promote in the future?

Li Xikui: We have three priorities in the future. One is that we will continue to promote international communication through sports programs as it could transcend nationality and language to bring us closer. The second priority is to cultivate the culture of sports. I think it is important to raise the cultural awareness among the public. For example, Mr. Deng Xiaoping used to say that football needs to be trained at childhood. So the CFFPD has a football foundation for young children starting from kindergarten. We hope that such programs could help them to learn the culture of sports at an early age. Our third priority is to integrate sports with philanthropy. More efforts will be put in this area.

Zhang Qiangqiang: Thank you. I also have a case to share with you. The Beijing Sport University has given rise to the first Tibetan champion wrestler in the world. This is an example of how sports could change one's life and the life of one's entire family. It helps him integrate into society and become a role model in the world and a leading light in the society. My next question will go to Li Na. I once had a chance to talk with your first coach. I asked her to coach me as if I were you. And I gave up after 15 minutes. She mentioned how tenacious you were.

Li Na: I had no choice at that time.

Zhang Qiangqiang: My question is, what is the temperament and quality of a champion?

Li Na: I was so lucky to meet my Argentina coach in the last two years of my career. During our cooperation, we often have a short conversation after the competition. He used to ask me this question: What do you think is the difference between a winner and a champion? I spent a whole night thinking about it and gave him my answer in the next morning: To be a winner, all you have to do is to win the competition. However, if you want to be a champion, you have to live like a champion. I used to have a few bad habits during the contest, such as throwing my racket angrily to the floor. One day I suddenly realized that if I couldn't treat my racket well, then I wouldn't get a good experience with it. And when I vented my anger, I didn't consider how the 10,000 audiences in the stadium and more people in front of the TV would feel. Passing this bad habit on to the people watching the game isn't just bad for me, it's bad for the program. I won't let others touch my racket except for my team members. The racket is the weapon of a tennis player. We need it to conquer our competitors. This is something I learn as I get more mature. I want to be a champion in life, not just a winner in court. That's my responsibility.

Zhang Qiangqiang: Thank you. Li Na. We used to be called the "Sick man of East Asia", which is really humiliating to a country of a large population and vast land. Physical and mental weakness is the major reasons for modern Chinese to be bullied by the Western powers in modern history. I would love to promote Li Na's championship spirit among our youth to make them stronger. Thanks again to Li Na. We all know that Denmark, a country with only about 40,000 square kilometres and a population of more than 5 million people, has achieved unparalleled success in the world of sports. The world media have named it as one of the "eight most powerful and amazing countries in the world of sports". Mr. Morten Mølholm Hansen, what lessons do you think we can learn from your practice in term of promoting a combination of sports competitions and fitness for all?

Morten Mølholm Hansen: I think one of the reasons for our success is that we have a system. We have players from clubs who pass that culture on to their parents and other people around them, so 90% of the children are exposed to that culture and engage in some kind of sport. Some children are actually athletically gifted and we have a follow-up system to support their development on the field. Children in Denmark are voluntary and very active in sports. With more than 10,000 sports clubs in the country, there really is a culture of sports for all, which is very important.

Zhang Qiangqiang: Thank you. 10,000 is an impressive number. We really need to learn from Denmark as it has so many good social organizations as a small country. This is the last session for the forum. Do you have any questions to ask our guests?

Audience: Hello, ladies and gentlemen, I am from Hong Kong. A few years ago, my friends and I founded an organization called the InspiringHK Sports Foundation, which aims to enhance the resilience of young people in Hong Kong and help them achieve better growth through sports, especially students from low-income families. We served over 1,000 children, but only 30% were girls. We try to persuade parents to participate in activities. However, many parents would say no. Moreover, it's even more challenging to engage girls. So I have a question for Li Na. You know we are so proud of you. How will you encourage girls to play sports, for example, football?

Li Na: Thanks for your question. That is not going to happen in my family. I always encourage my son and daughter to play sports. I think sports are particularly good for socializing and you can learn teamwork through sports. It is not about being a champion; it is about being a little stronger tomorrow than you are today. That's the essence of sports. And that's why so many people in the world are engaged in sports. But there may be a cultural difference between the East and the West. In fact, in more than 80% of Western families, parents will ask their children to do exercise along with them. It takes time to change, especially in how people think. For example, some girls are particularly athletic, but in their adolescence, they gave up their dreams and didn't do what they wanted to do in order to fit in. Many girls may have given up their dreams due to external factors. What I'd like to tell our female friends is that we should hold on to our dreams. It may not be realized in the end, but at least we have tried.

Zhang Qiangqiang: Time for the last question.

Audience: I have a question for Mr. Julio Gonzalez Ronco. I come from a foundation. I see you have done many things and developed many programs in schools. We want to provide training in schools. And we have already been partnering with a school in a foreign country. Could we introduce some of your programs into our activities?

Julio Gonzalez Ronco: I think the all-round development of a child needs not only the support of the community, but also the cooperation of the parents and the school. Sports is good because it helps us find a way to recognize that children need much exercise; it's not just about getting them to go to some sporting event.

Audience: Do you think there a chance for the two foundations to work together? For example, could we cooperate at the school level?

Julio Gonzalez Ronco: We could have a little talk over it later. We have signed agreements with many organizations hope to offer many programs to schools. Many of our programs are launched with non-profits who also provide similar projects to schools. We have to ensure the sustainability of our projects. Some organizations are non-profits. But I am not saying non-profits are bad. It's just because we need some financial support, resources and help. We need to make the project sustainable so that it can operate for the long term. Like we have said, sports doesn't just make a difference to one single person, it makes a difference to the community and the future.

Zhang Qiangqiang: Our organizers hold such a forum with the hope that in this way, countries and organizations around the world can join hands to empower philanthropy. Sports could change our life, and make the world a better place. That's all for today. Thank you.

VIII Wealth and Philanthropy

Moderators: George Sycip, Board Chairman, Give2Asia
Carter Tseng, Board Member, Give2Asia

Speakers: Rui Meng, Member of WPF Academic Committee, Professor of the China Europe International Business School (CEIBS), Co-Director of theCEIBS Centre for Family Heritage
Mitzi Perdue, from Perdue & Sheraton Family
Fan Yong, President, Asia Institute of Art & Finance (AIAF)
Birger Stamperdahl, President & CEO, Give2Asia
Elizabeth Deppen Knup, the Ford Foundation Representative to Beijing, China
Justin Miller, Wealth Strategist for the BNY Mellon
Joan Crain, Senior Director for the BNY Mellon
Winnie Peng Qian, Director of Tanoto Center for Asian Family Business and Entrepreneurship Studies, Director of Thompson Center for Business Case Studies, Hong Kong University of Science and Technology (HKUST)
Laurence Lien, Chairman of Lien Foundation; Founder of the Asia Philanthropy Circle (APC)
Sirkka Korpela, Director of the UNDP business partnerships division
Elliott Donnelley, Founding General Partner of the Chicago-based White Sand Investor Group, LP.
Peng Min, Chairman of the Board, Faith Winner (Far East)
Long Denggao, Member of the WPF Academic Committee, Director of Center for Chinese Entrepreneur Studies, Tsinghua University (CCES)

George Sycip: Distinguished leaders, ladies and gentlemen, good afternoon. Thank you all for joining us this afternoon. I'm also pleased to see representatives from all walks of life: government, philanthropy sector, universities, research institutions, family offices, and wealth inheritance advisers, bankers, and lawyers. Each one of us here today comes from a unique sector which makes us truly diversified.

Before my presentation, I'd like to give some remarks.

As I don't speak Chinese, I would like to talk about how I looked up the Chinese and English meaning of the word "philanthropy". I did some research with Google Translate, but I think there is a difference between philanthropy and charity. So I decided to call our forum today "World Philanthropy and Charity Forum".

You know, charity and philanthropy is not the same same, which I hope you could pay special attention to. What's the meaning for charity and philanthropy?

Charity is meant to provide short-term help. It has something to do with compassion. In comparison, philanthropy is a long-term and strategic process. I am not saying that charity is not good. Charity and philanthropy are both meant to solve problems.

Some say that charity is to meet short-term needs while philanthropy seeks to fulfil long-term needs. So, digging a well in a village suffering from water shortage is charity. But helping the village to find a solution to be self-sufficient is philanthropy.

We also want to make a distinction between the term "philanthropy" and "charity", which differ in that philanthropy is generally about giving, not taking, whereas charity focuses on the needs of more individuals.

Next, let's think about how philanthropy has developed in the Western world.

I did some research and I found that the word "philanthropy" first appeared in the West in the 16th century, with its roots in the Latin word meaning "to love and do good to others". In the 1620s, our immigrants began to use the word in literature. Charity or philanthropy actually coincides with the Eastern mindset of helping people.

In Chinese, we use the concept of goodness. So what is the difference between goodness and philanthropy? One of our guests here mentioned the concept of goodness, and we will talk about it later. Goodness is even more profound.

Let's look at philanthropy on the other hand.

In the West, the word philanthropy is derived from two words: "phil" means to love and care, while "anthrop" means mankind. So when we put the two words together, it means to love and help people.

As human history evolves, so is the word philanthropy, which now no longer refer only to people, but also to animals and plants, as well as to the soil we live in and the water resources around us. Now you can see that our new generation has given philanthropy and charity a richer meaning, because they have realized that the soil is the basis of our existence. So now charity and philanthropy also concern with environmental protection.

Philanthropy, though a word from the West, actually coincides with Feng Shui in the East, especially in the Chinese book *The Book of Changes* (Yijing) which mentions the "Five Elements" or the symbolic meaning of the number "1". Recent research on quantum physics also points out that everything in the world is particles and waves. They collide and intertwine at the same time within the concept of time and space. There are many books in the West about quantum physics and quantum mechanics.

Today I'm just pointing out that when looking at the theme of this forum, there are different interpretations in the East and West towards philanthropy and charity concerning the subject of the good deeds.

The theme for this afternoon's session is "Wealth and Philanthropy". What does this mean? If we look " 善财 " up in Google Translate, it will come up with "Good fortune", which makes no sense in English. The official translation should be how to transmit and provide family wealth, namely, how could we put the legacy to good use?

What does good mean in this context? Good usage and transmission are all about how wealth should be inherited or used? You may also ask how such good usage is related to charity and philanthropy. In 771 BCC, people discussed about what is goodness. 2,500 years ago, another discussion was made about whether human nature is inherently evil or inherently good. As a result, the Confucians believed that human nature was good, while the Legalists believed that it was evil. Today, we will not debate over human goodness and evil. What we want to do is to bring out the good in humanity.

What does goodness mean? It is virtuousness, kindness, loyalty, filial piety, etc. For the inheritors of Confucianism, goodness is the concrete practices at the operational level, such as doing good deeds and thinking positively. From a philosophical point of view, such a concept of doing good deeds and being a good person is taken by Confucianism as the golden rule.

Confucius used to say, "[A man of Ren] helps others become established if he desires to establish himself, and helps others reach their goals if he desires to reach his." What does this mean? If you want to stand up for yourself, you must help others stand up, and if you want to achieve something, you must first help them to achieve their dreams. More than 2,000 years have passed, Confucianism has become the golden rule of Chinese culture. Similarly, the West also promotes "Do unto others as you would have them do unto you." as taught in *the Bible.*

Why am I telling this story? Because I want to tell you that this is the reason for me to do charity at the first place.

We also talked about this concept yesterday. My grandfather believed in this Golden Rule. When I was six or seven years old, he gave me a card that had this Golden Rule written on it. I was very young at the time and I didn't know what they were talking about. So I asked my parents why my grandfather would show me this card and the Golden Rule. It was March 1957 when my parents told me that my grandfather had been in prison during World War II and that he had to do some self-reflection. At the time he was imprisoned by the Japanese, who kept him alone. He was meant to be executed, but he later managed to survive. He had hired Japanese drivers and butlers before the war, and got on well with them. At the time when Pearl Harbor was bombed, his gardener and housekeeper were working as spies for the Japanese. After my grandfather was captured, the Japanese were very nice to him because he did a lot of good deeds in his spare time. It was these good deeds that ultimately saved his life, as he lived the motto "Do unto others as you would have them do unto you".

In the 1950s, he launched the Freedom and Clean campaign. It provides clean water to areas that do not have access to good water sources, particularly in the Philippines, for health and nutritional considerations. The Philippines issued a number of stamps in the 1950s to commemorate the campaign. He co-launched the campaign with someone from Sichuan province and has a doctor's degree. The campaign is actually very transformative. The Philippine government has even issued coins to commemorate these activities. We can also see other philanthropists being transformational thinkers like Einstein, including the founder of Disney.

They started another campaign to teach farmers how to read and write. The doctor I mentioned comes from a remote village in Sichuan province. Maybe some of us here are from his hometown too. Together they went on to have launched the International Campaign for Rural Reconstruction in the 1960s. If you look at the relevant history, you will see that this campaign has lasted about 60 years.

It has exerted great influence and will become even more impactful in the local region and the world.

Let me now introduce the schedule for this afternoon. It comprises of three themes and a summary speech. The first theme is about how we can give back to society through wealth management. The second one is about how we can get the most out of our philanthropic structure. The third one is about innovation in philanthropic management and related trends. Each of these topics will last approximately one hour. Furthermore, there will be a short recap after the last speech. For each theme, we will have a Q&A session. And additional time will be left for further summaries and Q&As in the end.

Let's move on to the first theme. We will have three speakers. The first speaker is Mr. Rui Meng, who has a PhD in accounting and finance, and is now a member of the WPF Academic Committee, and a professor of CEIBS. He also held key positions in financial institutions such as the Hong Kong Stock Exchange, where he was responsible for some of the internal training for China Mobile, China Construction Bank and others. In the meantime, he has published a number of high-quality papers, one of which named "The Influence and Utility of Family Governance" is of great help to today's session. In his paper, he talked about the Three Circles Model instead of the Two Circles Model utilized by non-traditional non-family corporations. If you have questions about it, you may ask him later.

Rui Meng has been engaged in China's philanthropy sector for quite a long time. Let's welcome Dr. Rui Meng to share with us his experience on how to manage multi-generation wealth better and give back to the society.

Rui Meng: Thank you for your introduction, Mr. George Sycip. I'm delighted to join you today to share my insights on philanthropy, especially my insights on the work in China. Our organization was founded five years ago with a focus on a family legacy, financial planning, and of course philanthropy. We have also published a report on this. In particular, we will release a report on wealth management and philanthropy of Chinese listed families in November 2019.

We also offered a course on "Family Office" four years ago. I'm going to share with you the first lesson with my students. Since I prepared my slides in Chinese, I will make the presentation in Chinese.

The first point I want to make is to let's change the world with wealth.

We are at a very critical juncture today. I would like to speak about the impact of global population growth on the sustainable development of all humankind.

Let's look at this slide. The first time the global population reached 1 billion was in 1804, and it took 123 years to add another billion people to the world. But since then, the world has grown by 1 billion people every decade or so. According to the projections of global demographers, there will be nearly 9 billion people in the world by 2048. Is this a number that our planet is capable of handling? This is something our generation needs to consider.

Then my students are guided to think about what their ultimate goal is in creating wealth.

The book, *The Folding Society*, reveals that human civilization has made great strides in the past, such as lifting 1.5 billion people off the poverty line in the past 25 years, but there are still many imperfections. For example, of today's 7 billion people, 50% are unbanked, 4 billion still live below the $3.50 poverty line, and 1.4 billion have no access to electricity.

Although people around us in this city are doing fine, there is still a large population living in poverty. The United Nations has created the *2030 Agenda for Sustainable Development*, which calls for us to achieve 17 goals. According to the projections of United Nations experts, the investment needed every year is almost $4 trillion. However, only less than $1.5 trillion is being invested today, leaving a shortfall of $2.5 trillion. So how are we going to address this $2.5 trillion gap?

Let's look at how global wealth is distributed. Every year there is a global financial distribution report. This is the adults over the age of 18 worldwide. At the very bottom of this wealth pyramid, there are almost 3.3 billion people, or 71% of the adult population. How much wealth does this 71 per cent of the population possess? Less than 4%.

Nevertheless, at the top of the wealth pyramid, 0.7 percent of the population owns more than 40 percent of the wealth. If you add up the top of the pyramid, that's almost 8% of the population, who owns 85% of the wealth. So, the solution to global issues depends on what the people at the top of the pyramid do in the first place.

The most significant difference between family and non-family businesses is that the former ones have multiple goals. For families, there are other goals besides wealth creation, including social impact, family well-being, and the sustainability of the foundation. Family businesses have to strike a balance between multiple goals. This requires a tool to help them, the best of which is charity and philanthropy.

I tell my students that the family business is not only a vehicle for accumulating wealth and pursuing personal enjoyment, but also a vehicle for promoting spirit, values, love and responsibility.

Why is that?

Scholars have found differences between family and non-family firms in that socio-emotional factors impact the former. It can be represented by five letters—— "F" stands for family influence, "I" stands for the identity of family members;

"B" stands for their bond with the society, "E" stands for emotional attachment between family members; and "R" stands for their relations.

The biggest difference between family firms and non-family firms is that they pursue not only material wealth, but also spiritual wealth, namely the socio-emotional factors.

After listening to the lesson, many of the students felt an aspiration for this.

Then I went on to share my views with them. There is a saying that China is the "new money" and foreign countries are "old money". The experience of the "old money" has told us that charity and philanthropy are the most important codes for family continuity. The CEIBS has done a lot of research, including research on Asia. They interviewed more than 200 Asian families engaged in philanthropy. One of the questions asked was what motivates families to give back to the community actively and to help those in need through philanthropy. More than half of the families interviewed responded that they wanted to form a lasting family legacy through family philanthropy. So, philanthropy is the best tool.

When we talk about legacy, we not only refer it to the legacy of wealth but more importantly, the legacy of family values. This allows the next generation to understand the true meaning of wealth. It also provides a platform to bring the family together so that they could be educated to become better individuals.

The long-term systematic family philanthropic investment reflects the wealthy family's sense of social responsibility. Giving back to the society will also win social recognition and respect for the family, which endows them with a sense of belonging and social capital. Social capital, or trust, is a term that has become very popular in academia in recent years.

What China's entrepreneurs today generally lack is a sense of security or social identification. The charity can play a role in helping them develop a family culture of engaging in the charity that is passed down from generation to generation. So I give them the conclusion that the glory of a family does not depend, or at least not in the long run, on the amount of wealth, but on the attitude of each member of the family towards wealth.

I showed them that the major philanthropic foundations around the world come from families. Such personal motivation, or positive energy in Chinese, could lead to greater happiness and longevity according to numerous psychological and medical research. This is a nine-year-long study with more than 7,000 samples done by Yale University and the University of California, Los Angeles, to see how social relationships affect mortality and life expectancy.

This nine-year follow-up found that people who were happy to help others had significantly better health and life expectancy than those who were reluctant to help others. The two schools looked at different races, classes and their habits, but came to the same conclusion. In fact, doing good or promoting positive energy also means a lot to the individual.

So what's so good about it? The Chinese have a saying: "Wealth does not pass three generations." This has been a curse to family businesses. What you have earned will likely to lose in less than five generations. This is the original version of the "Three generation rule".We also have a saying that: "A family could last for ten generations if its legacy is a virtue, shorter if the skills of reading and farming, less short if knowledge, and as short as three generations if wealth." We can see that if you could inherit the values and spiritual wealth generation by generation, chances are your family is going to last for a long time.

At the end of my course, I told them that the purpose for them to study in CEIBS and to set up a family office should be enabling wealth to do what it is supposed to do, that is to change the world.

We are neither the slaves of wealth nor its owner.

I told the story of the Hermès family members, who say that "Hermès is not something I have inherited from my parents, but something I have borrowed from my children." I'm going to modify that a little bit: Your wealth today is also borrowed from society, for which you're just a temporary steward. You should put that wealth to good use so that it can be leveraged to solve the common sustainability problems that human society faces today, as I talked about on my third slide.

That's the first lesson I taught to the students of our CEIBS Family Office because I wanted my students to have the right values. Making wealth truly benefit the individual, the family, and even society is not just something that only families need to do; schools and the professionals here also have a role to play.

Thank you.

George Sycip: Professor Rui Meng used to be our teacher. His speech is so attractive that I want to go back to university to attend his class again.

The next speaker is Ms. Mitzi Perdue, who represents two Family Offices. Her husband has written a book in French that was once ranked NO.5 in Amazon's business reviews, and I hope everyone will read it. She carried on the family business after her husband passed away.

Before she married Mr. Perdue, she joked that rice and chicken wings went well together just like the two of them. Her father co-founded the Sheraton Hotels during the Great Depression, in the 1930s. By the 1940s, Sheraton became the first five-star hotel to be listed on the New York Stock Exchange and opened more than 100 hotels around the world. In 1985, Sheraton was also the first overseas hotel group to open a new hotel in China, called the Great Wall Sheraton Hotel Beijing. The family members were living in California at the time. Now the hotel is no longer part of Sheraton Group.

When it comes to rice, the family had a very large business. The American Women's Association had a lot of members there, and most of the women in the membership worked in jobs related to the production and cultivation and sale of rice.

A graduate of Harvard University herself, she is an avid reader and is familiar with a wide range of topics. She is a columnist and currently writes a column for *Women's Health* magazine. She has also written columns on technology, biotechnology, and genetic sequencing in the past. Apart from writing articles, she is also a world-renowned TV series writer, and a host of over 100 episodes of television shows and interviews. It is a pleasure to have you here to share your family's history.

Mitzi Perdue: Thank you for your introduction. Professor Rui Meng has delivered a wonderful speech. Our thoughts happen to be very similar. I've been exposed to two family businesses and our approach to family wealth inheritance solutions is exactly the same as what you've just told us, so I kept nodding my head as you gave your presentation.

I want to share with you today a company that produces chicken legs, which is the Perdue family. The Perdue family started the business 99 years ago. It is one in a thousand families that have flourished for nearly 100 years. In the US and even globally, only 30% of families make it through to the next generation. However, family businesses are not always run by family members. We are involved in real estate, have a tire business in Germany, and a number of other businesses.

My father and my uncle have both done these businesses. Nevertheless, what keeps the family going to this day? I think Professor Rui Meng has already told us the answer. But I would also like to tell you about a study done by an American professor.

The professor has been studying family businesses that have emerged over the past 100 years. He said the difference between the families that fulfill their legacy and those that fail to do so is charity. In the third and fourth generation, if the family hasn't discovered the importance of philanthropy and giving back, the wealth won't be passed on. I think that the results of these researchers' experiments coincide with our reality.

I'll share a little more about the Perdue and Henderson families' experiences with you, as we have a large size economically and have both been passed down for a long time. So why could the two families last for such a long time? The primary reason is charity. Charity brings family members together, gives us a sense of identity, and brings us pride and dignity.

Yet, the Perdue family and the Sheraton family do charity differently. There are two effective ways I want to share.

In the Perdue family, my husband had a lot of considerations whenever he set up a foundation. We know that in the poultry farming industry, farmers as income earners live mainly in rural areas, where they are less densely populated and less wealthy. I had previously come across a case where one of the communities approached us and said that they were now in great need of thermal imaging cameras that would allow them to see an image of a woman holding a dog. A man in town approached us at the time and said that big city residents could easily buy one of these thermal imaging cameras, but $20,000 was too much for them to afford.

So, Perdue's foundation helped them buy these cameras. A few months later, there was a fire in that area. It was all smoky. People can breathe, but their vision is unclear, which can affect the rescue. But with a thermal imaging camera, you can see the people in the smoke and give them a helping hand. It's good to know that what you donate can benefit people.

In addition to financial assistance, we also offer a number of programs for Perdue family workers and their families. You may not be able to see clearly what this photo is about. I can tell you that you are looking at oysters or oyster shells. This is a large oyster producing area where many oysters will produce new oysters inside these shells. We put those shells back into the sea. We have about 22,000 employees and they are all involved. There once was a big storm after which all the employees and their families helped each other rebuild their homes.

The Henderson family adopts a different approach. The Perdue family will work with several foundations funded by the community. But things are totally different with the Henderson family. The Henderson family has five branches, each choosing the foundation they support. If you look at the back of this little flyer of Give2Asia, you'll see the donation percentage printed on it, which is very similar to the Henderson family. Some people may choose to donate in health care, education, disaster relief, for example, for 100 times in each area but with very limited amounts. In this regard, we are very different.

Let me give you some more details.

Among the five branches, the branch I am involved in pays special attention to charity and philanthropy. Four months ago, on April 11, 2019, I heard a speech in the Cayman Islands about how the United Nations would eliminate human trafficking, especially sex trafficking, by 2030. It is a situation unknown to many Americans. According to the United Nations, more than 40 million people are now victims of human trafficking, most of whom are girls. 8 million of them end up in sex slavery and are between the ages of 4 and 12. They may be assaulted eight or nine times a night, and they live only seven years after that, either due to overdose, suicide, or die of other diseases.

I was very touched when I heard the speech. I think it's horrible and I want to do everything I can to help them.

However, if I write a check for an enormous amount of money to help these people out of their misery, it means I'm going to cut the funds that would have gone to other foundations. Some of the foundations where I serve on the board may not get enough support. How should I make my choice? I suddenly thought of an idea. I own some very valuable items in my treasure chest that are about 400-500 years old and are family heirlooms. I know they are historical artifacts, they are very valuable and I love them very much. If I put them up for auction, it would certainly get a lot of attention.

It just occurred to me that maybe I could turn things into money. Then I went around asking people if they were interested. As a result, we set up the Global Anti-Trafficking Auction. It is an online auction platform based in the US. I hope there will be such an auction in China too. The idea is to put something up for auction and use the money to aid those who have been trafficked. This is how we contribute to fulfilling the UN SDGs.

This image shows something possessed by Alexander II in 1825. We plan to conduct a global auction for it in January 2021. In addition to its financing role, we hope the auction will raise awareness and charitable outreach.

That's what we do as a charity branch under the Henderson family. You could also see the things that Dr. Rui Meng has said in the practice of my family. Thank you.

George Sycip: Thank you, Ms. Mitzi Perdue. Ms. Li Bin also mentioned children and women protection in her speech this morning. I am very glad to hear that. The protection of children and women really needs to be strengthened. I also saw in your speech the efforts of your foundation in this regard.

The next speaker is Professor Fan Yong. His work is closely related to what you have said. Mr. Fan Yong is the Founder and President of Asia Institute of

Art & Finance (AIAF), the Honorary Dean of School of Management, Fudan University, and the Honorary Dean of School of Management, Shanghai University. He is also a visiting scholar for Chinese culture inheritance in Nanyang Technological University (NTU), and a banker interested in culture and arts. Today, we are honoured to have him on the same stage with our guest from the Perdue family.

The charity has always supported arts, but can it be the other way around? Let's take a look at how family philanthropy and the arts could support each other with Professor Fan Yong.

Fan Yong: Thanks for your introduction and the invitation to this forum. It's my honour to make a presentation in front of the scholars, experts and professionals here. My research mainly focuses on the segment of the role art has been playing in social development.

Today, my topic is more specific. I will talk about how art will become a new trend in the future of family inheritance in China.

I will analyze this trend from two aspects: first, what role art plays in the process of family succession in both East and West; second, how people in Chinese history, from the emperor down to the common people, pass on value through art.

First of all, I'd like to share with you four keywords for the role of artwork in family heritage. The first word is "glory", which is yearned by almost any family. We could say this is what they strive for. The second word is "education", which is also highly valued in terms of both family education and school education. The third word is value "preservation" as we all want our wealth to preserve its value eternally over time. The fourth word is "taxation", which is a very important tool for adjusting the distribution of wealth in society. So, how can we promote our charitable and philanthropic efforts through art to serve society and to distribute our wealth more effectively?

We also see in the West, especially in its modern history, more families and even the entire society have attached great importance to the preservation of historical and cultural heritage. Many wealthy families are collecting cultural artifacts and think highly of their value.

I will tell you a few stories of several famous families.

I'm sure we are all familiar with the Medici family. Without the Medici family, the Renaissance would not necessarily have been like what we know today. The contribution made by the Duke of Medici was significant as some of the famous works of the Renaissance were done with the financial support of his family and himself. Now we see one of the ten largest art museums in the world and some famous arts and architectures. We may find them familiar because we see them so often in museums. We also see an interesting person from the United States, Paul Getty. He is a rich but stingy man, yet surprisingly generous in protecting culture and art. He made a great decision on his deathbed to set up a trust fund to invest in art and culture. As a result, he has become known around the world as the founder of an institution that has made a significant contribution to the preservation and inheritance of art. These people we see are the ones that have made great contributions to society and have served as role models for us.

There are many other families in the USS and we have just been honored to hear from one of its representatives, who seats next to me, to share what her family has done.

Above are the contributions Western families have made. Now let's take a look at how China treats culture and art.

How culture and art is preserved and developed by families as society evolves?

China is the focus of our research. There have been five art and culture collecting booms in China's history. Culture and art collecting in a benign sense is a way to take custody of social wealth in the form of private wealth, and a fulfilment for our obligations and responsibilities to society. One of the prime time for collecting was the Song Dynasty in China with the royal family took the lead. There was an emperor who was so fond of art that he became a great artist himself. The picture you see is some of his paintings and calligraphy. With the emperor leading the way, the scholar-officials and the nobility started to collect cultural and artistic works in pursuit of social wealth and culture and art.

By the Ming Dynasty, the literati played an increasingly important role in collecting culture and art. Most of them chose to become officials. Not only did they enjoy culture and art, they also created their own works. Given their status, economic power and the transmission of value, they became role models for society. The Ming Dynasty was also the era when Chinese capitalism was born, and systematic theoretical knowledge of how to collect culture and art took shape. It also published two books, which could help us to study the collection of art. They were categorized, systematic and historical, enabling us to understand better the social values represented by art and what positive effects it has on human society and on sentiment enrichment of individuals.

In the Qing dynasty, there was also a great emperor who did something very important in the art collection. Out of his passion for collecting art, he compiled a book based on his collection of valuable cultural artworks from all the dynasties.

The book is like the encyclopedia of cultural and artistic heritage. To this day, we must look up this book if we want to understand what important cultural artifacts are in our history. We see that many large families tend to use it as a guidebook when it comes to collecting.

In the turbulent period of the Republic of China, there were four famous young men, all of whom came from political or wealthy families. One of them was named Zhang Boju. When the Eight-Nation Alliance invaded Beijing, a piece of cultural relics of the Qin Dynasty fell into private hands. In order to protect it, he sold all his family assets in exchange for the painting, preserved it and later donated it to the Palace Museum.

There was also a man named Wang Shixiang, who, in a time of economic deprivation, collected many precious Chinese relics based on his preference with great perseverance. Some were donated to the Palace Museum while others were given to charity through public auction.

From emperors to ordinary people, everyone loves art and culture. Why? It is because of the recognition of beliefs and values. Art becomes something accessible to everyone, and naturally becomes an important vehicle for family heritage.

Here, there is a family that has lasted for three generations. We have just said that "Wealth does not pass three generations.", but are there some exceptions in terms of cultural continuity? Here is an example. In the Qing Dynasty, there was a scholar, historian and collector named Wu Dacheng, his son Wu Hufan was also a great writer, artist and connoisseur. He not only inherited the family's wealth, but more importantly, the family's culture, which has been passed down to the third-generation offspring Wu Yishen, who was born in the 1990s.

After hearing the stories of the West and ancient China, let's look at the present. Since the reform and opening up, we have focused on economic construction and material consumption, and now we are turning to spiritual consumption. So our attention will naturally shift to artworks. We hope our future generations, who are well educated and possess a stronger sense of responsibility and mission, will find their interest in history and culture.

This is a Hong Kong family that has been passed down to the third generation engaged in the art industry. Its third-generation offspring had studied English and American literature abroad and was an entrepreneur with humanistic spirit. When he inherited the family business, he proposed to use culture and art to improve the business so that it can endure longer.

The essence of my presentation is how to pass on our material and spiritual wealth. I think art is a very good vehicle. Thank you. And your support is very much appreciated.

George Sycip: Thank you for your wonderful speech. Though we may start the Q&A session right now, I think it would be better to wait till the second topic ends.

So, if you have questions, please hold them. Let's move on to the second topic, which is closely related to the first speech. It's about how wealth could contribute to philanthropy.

Our first speaker for this topic is Birger Stamperdahl, the President & CEO of Give2Asia. He has been pushing the advancement of the Give2Asia organization and has been a leader in Asian philanthropy. Give2Asia's footprint spans 25 countries, including China. It works with families, companies and foundations to help groups and communities that are in dire need of help. It also works with more than 2,000 non-governmental organizations (NGOs) with members from all sectors of society. Give2Asia provides them with financial assistance, health support, help for children and women, and the help of lifting poor areas out of poverty. Let's welcome Birger Stamperdahl to share with us.

Birger Stamperdahl: Thank you. First of all, I'd like to thank the CPAFFC, Tsinghua University and other co-hosts to organize this forum. I just want to briefly share with you today my own experience and what Give2Asia has done over the past years.

Some of the previous guests have talked about family philanthropy and how to pass on family wealth from an individual perspective, as well as their personalized decisions. And I would like to share with you the work that Give2Asia does, our perspectives and viewpoints.

First of all, I would like to tell you about our background. Give2Asia wants to help family members make better decisions, support their projects, and provide guidance on execution. The work we do is very practical. We also focus on the impact of these family projects and work with families beyond our borders. We think the philanthropic family can be based in a location while their projects take place elsewhere.

We will also provide some financial support for charitable projects, including education, health, disaster relief and environmental protection projects. China is one of the regions that we focus on the most. Next, I'd like to give you an overview of the global landscape of philanthropy.

Our main focus is on families with an international outlook. The efforts of Give2Asia can be found in different regions, including the United States, Australia, Canada, and Europe. Currently, Asia is our foothold and focus of attention. We are also looking at cross-border projects. We want our philanthropy to be sustainable and long-lasting. We will take root in Asia and consider the concerns of our donor family, as well as the project itself.

When we consider international projects, it's important that we also pay attention to local partners. Projects that are sustainable and long-lasting usually take root in the local community and are very familiar with the local conditions.

Besides, we also have to consider the financing situation, where local partners can build a local donation network. They know the local areas better, so we feel that we need to consider local partners as well in terms of charity financing. This is what we have done in China, Singapore, Australia, and the UK, but our focus is still in the Asia Pacific region aiming to involve philanthropic families in different projects.

Next, I'd like to talk about these families that we engaged. Why are they involved in charity? What are their motivations and considerations for choosing a project? I would also like to talk about the international flow of funds.

Sometimes, family members are trying to invest money in a specific area. Some of the Chinese Americans we work with, for example, want to donate to their native land, or are particularly concerned about a particular issue, such as health, the environment, education and health care, or focus on a particular group, such as victims of human trafficking. Overall, we want a more prosperous and richer society.

In this process, in addition to financing, we could also leverage the network of these donor families to address their concerns. We have to consider what the family's priority concerns are. We've approached a wide variety of families. I am not saying some of them are good and others are not. What I mean is they have different preferences. Some are donating to one program at a time and their interest is focused on one region and one program, while others prefer synergistic giving, they want to work with other donors, such as for-profit businesses and governments to gain broader community impact.

I would like to say that the projects Give2Asia are involved with are very diverse. Some of these projects have a regional impact, while others have an international one. We have to consider the interests of the donor families themselves and their motivations. Do they want to do a local project, a national project, a regional project or an international project? Sometimes they may prefer local projects, and sometimes they want an international perspective. Next, I want to talk about three specific cases, two of which I've gotten permission from the donors to mention their names.

The first case is a large international project initiated by the philanthropist Margaret, a member of a large philanthropic family in the United States. The family's first area of philanthropy was disaster relief and mitigation. This was a top priority when Margaret established the foundation's goals. And her geographical focus was largely limited to the United States. But now the next generation of her family is involved in the management of the foundation. They are concerned about the new environment and also know what resources are available for disaster relief and mitigation, and how to help people become more prepared. They undertake preparedness activities because they recognize the importance of disaster prevention. They work with a number of other donors and they would like more donors to join them in supporting the project. Local communities and institutions may be more concerned about the situation in their own region. So the project is regional, mainly in Nepal, Myanmar or other parts of South-East Asia. The above is how the foundation involved in philanthropy. Such foundations may also choose to partner with governments to expand their programs. We also work with international NGOs, IRRR, and with local governments. This is an example of how a multi-generational family constantly adjusting and positioning the intent of their family foundation.

Another example is a foundation based in Silicon Valley, which was also one of the first Give2Asia donors. Unlike the previous example, this foundation has a broader focus that goes beyond several regions like China. But The foundation has a special focus on China where it has set up a scholarship program. Now the foundation is run by the second generation of family members. The family members have different roles in different functions throughout the program. Some, for example, are concerned with our finances, while others are concerned with other aspects of the program. Every year, they visit the beneficiaries of these scholarship programs because they want to bond with them on a personal level. They now offer more than 100 scholarships a year in China so that students from low-income families who cannot afford tuition can receive their scholarships. They now offer scholarships to five schools. This program also is participated by multiple generations of the family.

The last project was an anonymous one involving a Chinese-American. He has no geographical focus or preference, but he is very interested in developing local leadership in a number of ways. For every project he donates to, he would go to the field for closer observation. In addition, he is very willing to share his life experiences and what he has learned, which is a hallmark of multi-generational philanthropy, passing the experience on to the next generation of family members or philanthropists outside the family, thus expanding the impact of the entire event.

I believe the three cases I've presented echo what several speakers have just said. How to unite different families under the same theme? Disaster relief and mitigation, for example, could be a theme that foundations can rally around.

Finally, I want to share ways to encourage cross-generational philanthropy. We feel that members of the philanthropic family want to see that the charity they are doing is really effective. They want to see those effects, so they come to the project site themselves. Sometimes they want to see what the goals of the family or the project as a whole are, whether the project has made some achievements or not. If these philanthropists in the family are very aware of the success and progress of the project, they will be more enthusiastically involved.

That's why we engage more with family members in the decision-making process. One generation doing charity may encourage the next generation to get involved as consultants. Bringing members of the next generation into the project can have many benefits.

The last point I would like to make is about the obstacles that charity faces in moving forward—the lack of trust.

When it comes to charity, people very often want to know if our funds are going where they are supposed to go and if it is transparent in term of how they are spent. There is a lack of trust in this area. It's important to build trust with people that we are putting the funds to good use. We need to convince everyone that we are moving towards the same goal.

We need to take further measures in terms of increasing trust. As an institution, we need to consider how we can increase trust in the charitable sector. In the case of an NGO, it may receive funds that can be used to boost the confidence and trust of donors.

I hope the above examples will give you some insights into how to make cross-generational philanthropy work better.

George Syicp: Thank you for your presentation, Mr. Birger Stamperdahl. Speaking of examples, Give2Asia itself is also a good example. Today, we are honoured to have Elizabeth Knup from the Ford Foundation to join us. Compared to Give2Aisa which was founded in 2001, the Ford Foundation is like a big sister. We've been working together very well, and have wonderful cooperation in other countries. I'd like to thank the Ford Foundation for its collaboration. I know that Elizabeth Knup will leave early today, I think we should give her a chance to speak.

This morning, the representative of the HKJC mentioned that their foundation is already the fifth largest in the world in terms of private giving. Although Give2Asia is relatively small in comparison, it is still a very valuable example.

Elizabeth Deppen Knup will leave here soon. Let's give her the floor.

Elizabeth Deppen Knup: I would like to thank the forum organizers for inviting me to participate in today's WPF.

What I am going to talk about are some interesting examples. The Ford Foundation was also a family foundation at the beginning, but it is no longer a pure family foundation now. I will share with you the process behind this change and answer some of the questions mentioned earlier.

Everyone knows that Henry Ford founded the Ford Company and his son started the Ford Foundation in 1936 with just $20,000. Before his death, Henry Ford's son put his stock in the Ford Company into the Ford Foundation. In its early days, the Ford Foundation was a family foundation, run primarily by the resources of the Ford family. At that time, Ford's headquarters was located in Michigan, USA, which was also the headquarter for the Ford Foundation. The Foundation's programs were also primarily based there and focused on the local community, its employees and projects, especially those related to the Ford Company and the Ford family.

Then, in the late 1940s, the Ford Foundation became the largest philanthropic organization in the world.

But things have changed now. The second-generation of Mr. Henry Ford thought now that the Ford Foundation had become the largest foundation; it was time to consider what kind of role it should play as a leader. Should they continue to keep their eyes on Michigan, or should they put their attention to the entire world? So, they hired several consultants to give them a report.

The report mapped out the future of the Ford Foundation. It proposed the Ford Foundation to become an international foundation, shifting its focus from areas that are good for Ford family members to industries that are good for the world. The report, which came up at the end of World War II, recommended that the foundation focus on areas related to democracy, poverty reduction and human dignity.

Then the Ford Foundation transitioned to a larger, more internationally oriented foundation. We began to grow outside the United States, opening a second office in India in 1952 and a third in Egypt in 1953, which are still in operation. Eventually, we have 20 offices around the world, which have been reduced to around 10. We are still a foundation with an international focus. The second generation, Mr. Ford, served as our Trustee and Chairman of the Board until his retirement in 1976. Since that time, no member of the Ford family has served on the Ford Foundation Board of Trustees or made decisions about the use of funds.

The Ford Foundation thus has become a dedicated, independent foundation. We have our board of directors who choose the members and chair, who manages the entire foundation and reports to the board. Besides, the board members all have grant-making responsibilities. Originally we were no longer associated with the original Ford family, but in 2019 our President went to Detroit to meet with the Ford family and confirmed that the third generation of Henry Ford would be our board member. The Ford family is now back at the Ford Foundation, but it's not because he's a Ford family member, but because he himself is interested in public service and philanthropy in Detroit and Michigan. He joined the Foundation as a professional.

The Ford Foundation's transition from a family foundation to a non-family foundation is interesting. But we still have to keep our roots in mind. Now we're also focusing on philanthropy in Michigan and Detroit. That's the family transition story I want to share with you.

Ms. Mitzi Perdue just gave us a very good presentation. Like you, we're also wondering how to make better use of art as an important vehicle for philanthropy. The president of our Ford Foundation has proposed a project: Art for Social Justice. He said that he hopes that people who collect art like you can sell and auction art. And we would like to help you with your charity efforts in the United States.

We also want the money from these charitable artworks to be used for charity. And we want to work with people like you to discover the charitable value of artwork and address issues like human trafficking or mass incarceration in the United States. These artworks have value in their own right, but can be exploited for other values as well. We want to turn the value of these artworks into other philanthropic projects that we're interested in. So I wanted to say to Ms. Mitzi Perdue that we have similar thoughts. I think it's an innovative way to fully mobilize and leverage resources and funds so that they can really help us address the social issues that we care about.

Furthermore, I think that all of us here today would agree that the challenges of human trafficking, mass incarceration, education and health cannot be solved by one single foundation, person or entrepreneur through their acts or corporate philanthropy. They are challenges that we all need to face together.

As the first guest said, there is no way for a single foundation or government to achieve the United Nations sustainable development goals. We are one of the largest foundations in the world. However, from our perspective, we do not have the means to meet so many challenges either. So you are welcome to work with us.

Collecting and selling for good is an area that you can explore in the future. That's all I have to say, thank you all!

George Sycip: Since we are all interested in this area, we have Justin Miller and Joan Crain to share their experiences.

Let's start with Justin Miller. What is your current approach to art, wealth preservation and philanthropy? Particularly for the passing of wealth from one generation to the next, what wealth plans do your children and grandchildren have?

Justin Miller is a Wealth Strategist for the BNY Mellon. He will speak to us today about taxes and family governance. He's also a law professor and has spoken at many industry conferences as well. He's also a member of the New York Bar Association, just got his PhD from the University of California, Berkeley, and his degree from New York University School of Law. The family's wealth needs management just as the country needs planning. For business executives and family owners, how should they do their estate planning, probate planning, wealth planning, and tax planning? These are common issues faced by the richest families in the world. Since the tax is a very important topic in their own right, and what he's talking about today is of great interest to most members of family office management, so I'm going to turn the microphone over to Justin Miller.

Justin Miller: People always want to know the secret of passing on family wealth. Why do some families always have a way to pass on their wealth to the second, third and fourth generation? Why can these families survive the time? BNY Mellon has a great team of employees, project experience and schools, but we learn from our clients. BNY Mellon is the oldest privately held bank, the first banking group to be listed on the New York Stock Exchange, and the first trust company. Today, BNY Mellon is also one of the largest investment banks in the world. At the same time, we have the longest history. Even after seven generations, some of our clients are still around. I'd like to talk about four characteristics that these clients have in common. When you talk about a successful family, it will share at least one of these four characteristics.

First, let me give you some background knowledge. When we talk about passing on wealth, what exactly does it mean? Wealth is passed down from one generation to the next. When many people hear about wealth, they think it is financial capital and money. So they take for granted that the legacy of wealth is first and foremost about money. Money is important, and although some say it is not the most important thing in life, it is nearly equivalent to the oxygen of the earth. We know that money is essential, but successful families don't just accumulate wealth or financial capital, they also try to pass on four other different kinds of assets.

Across all disciplines, we have human capital, talent capital, social capital, and other kinds of capital. The four types of wealth I'll talk about below are what our clients want to pass on beyond their capital.

The first one is the individual capital. They want each family member to be successful, well-educated and live independently. The second one is collective capital, where they want the family members to come together so that the family is more like a community. The third one is that they want to keep a community fund. No family lives in a vacuum and that's why they will bring actual support to the community. It would be the first place for charity to take shape. The fourth is spiritual wealth. The family members will give respect to whatever religion or creed. There is a relationship between the material legacy and the spiritual legacy in that the money of successful families will help them increase other types of wealth. This is also the experience of successful families.

What problems do you typically encounter in the process of building a successful family? Many people say, "Wealth does not pass three generations" and there are similar views in China and the United States. Why is that? Because it is a normal phenomenon that the first generation earns money, the second generation spends money and the third generation runs out of money. Interestingly, all countries, regardless of culture, economic status, religious beliefs or tax policies, have a similar proverb to express this perspective. It is a matter of human nature. Such a phenomenon exists in all countries.

In the U.S., many related studies have found that extended families have a 70% failure rate by the third generation. Let's take a look at this. A professor at the Massachusetts Institute of Technology began related research in 1983, and another professor conducted a further analysis in 1987. According to these similar studies, the failure rate of large families may reach 90% by the fourth generation.

The first generation is our customers who accumulate wealth from scratch. They may be very successful CEOs, real estate developers, or entrepreneurs. Many of the second generations are professionals, such as doctors and lawyers, who have inherited the wealth of the previous generation and are very well educated. What professions do the third generation usually work in? They may be actors, artists, musicians, or even surf instructors, among others. Many families, having accumulated wealth over several generations, will allow their offspring to do whatever they want without being enslaved by money. Some of these offspring are actors, musicians, teachers and social workers. I'm not saying that these professions are bad. I'm just saying that we want these people to have a job instead of being addicted to drugs, gambling, etc., something that the family wants to avoid.

Now let's look at how to achieve future wealth preservation.

Firstly, we've found that successful families don't plan their legacies themselves. Instead, they outsource to a team of professionals with investment bankers, accountants, lawyers, and executives to help them with the plan. They will focus on legal documents, tax laws, etc., as well as the family itself. Those on the left are concerned with making money available to the family members, while those on the right are concerned with helping family members to make money. This team not only focuses on tax law and finance, which of course we know is very important for financial success and tax avoidance, but also on family unity, such as how to keep the family together.

Secondly, what do successful families need to do? First, they have to think about how the family money should be invested. Should they now head their businesses, sell them out or hire good investment managers? The challenge is that people are psychologically bad at investing. If you're a member of a family business or a real estate developer, you're more likely to make passive investments like stocks and bonds.

The first decline of the S&P in 2018 caused panic in public. Why did the numbers dip? Because you cannot expect the market to change all the time linearly. What happened in 2018? There are major news and headlines around the world that cover the daily happenings, but they rarely talk about positive things. Most of them are negative news, which is more eye-catching. It would be very frustrating to watch such news every day. But if you stay away from the noise and just look at the stock market dynamics, you'll find it's like an ECG for a heart attack victim. However, investing is not the only concern of the team.

Thirdly, we need to pay attention to our taxes. How can we better avoid taxes? You should definitely hire a tax advisor. I am a tax attorney myself. In the U.S., we have all kinds of taxes and legal countermeasures to avoid them. For a multinational corporation, it may be the case that you're in Asia and your kids are in the United States. You have to think about these multinational structures, and this is a process where charity may come into play. It's the most tax-efficient way to do charity work.

Fourthly, successful families are wary of failure. Many families have good advisors to help them handle their investments and taxes well. Beyond that, what is their fourth magic bullet? That is to focus on the family itself, that is, on family management, family dynamics and family relationships. It's a difficult question to ask, for example, how much money do I need to leave to my children? Beyond which point it would be too much? Sometimes we need to figure out the critical point below which the money is not enough, and above which the money would be too much. That's what Warren Buffett said in an interview with Fortune magazine. All these banks also have done all kinds of research to tell us how much is the right amount of money to give. Let's look at what we should do with cross-generation wealth transfer. Of course, your children will live a well-off life with your money. However, let's say you leave him $6 million; it will shrink over time. Our research finds that we do have an answer for this. But the answer to this question is yet another question, instead of a particular amount of money. Here, we are going to answer one question with another, which is normally not something we will teach our students to do at school. Yet it does make some sense in this scenario. The question is what you have done to prepare your child and are they ready? Some kids may have hundreds of thousands of dollars in their 20's, but it can ruin their life for they could use the money doing drugs or end up divorced. It indicates that too much money has been transferred to them. Some families leave a lot of money to their children but bring out great results such as enabling them to engage in charity, among others. So, how do we prepare our children for this? There are five measures.

1. Ensure better education for family members.

2. Communicate with their family members.

3. Establish the right family values.

4. Get them engaged in charity earlier. In many cases, the second generation of a wealthy family does not get involved in charity work until after the death of the first generation, which is not right.

5. Enable a smooth transition of family leadership. I am not saying that the second generation should just take over control. But there needs to be a good succession plan.

These are some of the questions we need to answer about family management. Who is in charge, where, when, and how? If your family can answer these questions well, then your family will be bound to have an enduring business.

What can charity do for the family? The role of charity is reflected in three aspects: the first is tax cuts, which is the key reason why the U.S. GDP is doing well; the second is social identity, which people care a lot about; and the third is that participating in charity can enhance people's happiness from a psychological perspective. Charity and happiness are positively correlated; it's what you give and donate that makes you happy.

But how could we achieve this goal? Please welcome my colleague Joan Crain to share her views.

Thank you.

George Sycip: Thanks for the presentation of Justin Miller. You may have heard of a Broadway musical about a U.S. Secretary of State who is also the founder of the Bank of New York. I don't know if there's a connection here, but our next speaker is also a top music student, who perhaps helped create the success of this musical. Joan Crain is an executive at the BNY Mellon who has worked with a number of cross-generational families over the past 25 years, focusing on family governance and success, cross-border planning, among others. We really appreciate the work of her team.

As we know, the BNY Mellon is recognized by Fortune magazine as an outstanding team in family wealth management. Today Joan will give us an overview of some of the innovations and trends in philanthropic families and how to manage family wealth effectively.

Joan Crain: I'm going to say something a little off-topic. My colleague just mentioned engaging the second-generation to do charity earlier with their parents. A lot of times, family clients come to us and say they don't know how to get started. They don't know how to get their kids involved and take over their work. So I think at the beginning I want to talk about something more specific about the family, children of different ages and how to make the family grow.

The first question is at what point do I involve my children in family governance? Some people asked why Buffett wanted to prepare his children for this. He said, "You see the tree is growing so big because someone prepared it ahead of time. Families also need to prepare their children at an early age."

We've also surveyed some groups and clients about when to start philanthropy. The answer is the sooner the better. And what does that mean? Is it after high school, college, or university graduation? Some people say simply wait until they're ready. If so, others argue that you have to keep waiting until they're ready. That could take forever because they will never be ready unless you push them.

So the most important thing is to make sure that children learn from their parents as role models during their most precious learning time, say at age 3, 4, or 5. That's the best way to get kids ready. I think Carter and his daughter are doing just fine. Carter is one of the world's greatest philanthropists and his daughter learns firsthand about philanthropy from an early age. But it's not at all enough for a child to learn from a role model, and we have to have something else to prepare for.

Our client also taught us a trick. If someone gives your child some money, be it the Lucky Money or pocket money, he may spend it right away because he feels that he has earned it; thus he's perfectly justified to spend it. However, before he spends it, the parents can prepare three jars for him and ask him to save some money in the first jar, then put the same amount in the second jar and donate it to an organization or individual who needs the money. The money in the third jar would be what he can spend after he saves and donates the money.

Another way is to take advantage of the holidays. The best opportunity to give the benefits back to others is Thanksgiving, which falls on a Thursday and 99% of us in the U.S. don't go to work on that Friday. We can use Thanksgiving as an opportunity to talk to our kids about how we can do some charity projects. As our kids grow up, maybe into middle and high school, they can also get involved in projects where they can make small investments and donations.

Some of our clients have started the plan to pass on the family wealth to the fourth and even fifth generation. They feel that charity is very important to them. They put their children on board for one to two years with the non-voting right. After two years the board would give that slot to a younger child. This process is very important. Occasionally some parents also allow their children to have voting rights so that their children can feel the joy of being philanthropic and have the autonomy to make decisions. It is also a way for them to discover leadership skills among children. As in the example of the Ford family earlier, it is highly likely that in the third or fourth generation, there would be a child who particularly wanted to be a philanthropist. So the larger family could discover the best successor through small activities.

We also have a phenomenon called "the elephant in the room", which is our potential risk. When we talk about family philanthropy, we would always look at the role of the spouse. One day, the children of the family will marry someone outside of the family. Will we include their spouses into the board? The answer may be yes and maybe no, depending on specific situations.

There was once a family that was going to hold its board meeting. Everything had been scheduled in advance and I had spoken to its members prior to the event. But before I left for the venue, I was called by a client who had five children. He said his brother's spouse was coming to the meeting as well. I said he hadn't told me that before. He then told me that he wouldn't be there should his brother's wife come. Of course, his other sister didn't want the family member to bring the spouse to the family event either.

My advice to family members, in general, is that maybe you don't want your family member's spouse to be involved in the decision to pass on the trust wealth, but if it's a philanthropic endeavour, it's best to include them as well. Since your children have decided to spend the rest of their lives with this person, you'd better incorporate them into the charitable program as well. And the more you can get them involved, the better.

You can also play the card game. Mitzi has also mentioned it, where someone writes on a card what they think is most important. There could be "giving" on one card and "health" on another. We also use many such cards and prioritize them. Parents will also invite their children to the game and tell them all the cards will be different. However, every time I do an experiment with my clients, I find that for many families, there will be three or four cards with similar contents. If you find within the family that the child is very interested in certain issues, such as climate change or sea-level rise, then you can set up projects that relate to these issues. In this way, the children will be more interested.

Communication is also important as it facilitates co-decisions. However, what if family members don't live together? Today with modern technology, we have more opportunities. In one of the families we serve, there was a 14-year-old boy who wasn't at all interested in attending charity meetings. So we suggested that he could create an online platform for family members to communicate. As a result, the boy did a great job. He created an online platform that enabled family members around the globe to have weekly discussions online. He also had to ensure that face-to-face communication could take place once a year, not just meeting on the phone via video, but that the whole family could find a time to have a meal together and chat about their work.

For a successful family, it is not difficult to do philanthropic projects as long as there is good communication between the family members. For some philanthropic and wealthy families, their members may not want to be identified as the offspring of a wealthy family, but rather as the creators of their children's wealth and philanthropic projects. New technologies are now available to help us communicate better.

Some family members not only want to be seen as family heirs, but also as trailblazers in the eyes of future generations. As we all know, technology helps with philanthropy and can also help children with giving. One example of this is Tencent's "99 Charity Day". It is an important program that allows many people to donate to various charity projects from their mobile phones or computers. If you are concerned about the transparency of these projects, you can also track them. Tencent has already established an online platform for this. Alipay and WeChat Pay also have similar projects to help poor areas of China, such as to plant trees in certain areas. In the case of Alipay, if you use it, you will receive green energy to water and plant trees. These are all technological innovations.

As we've said before, there are many problems with global philanthropy as well. We were surprised to find through our research that philanthropic concerns are the same around the world, yet each country has its unique practices. How can we use foundations in the U.S., UK and Canada to better handle taxes? If one wants to give or gift one's wealth to others, it is not allowed in Singapore because foreign gifts are not allowed there. Suppose someone wants to pass on their family wealth as a gift, what should they do? It requires a good structure to make it happen, like setting up a private foundation. In this case, we would choose the largest donor who would be most benefited based on tax residence. In this way, we will better help the founder of this foundation.

We can set up a subsidiary under the foundation, which can be located in another country, so that other people can benefit from some tax reduction. We also need to consider the location of the family's primary business when setting up the foundation and what the relationship is between the two locations. Donations can be made directly or indirectly. Philanthropy in Asia is generally through direct giving projects, such as funding a school or providing financial support, or making portable drinking water available for Cambodia. Through such projects, we can provide some direct financial support to a local or foreign charity organization. If you want to know the details of the project, please feel free to ask me.

I also want to talk about trust and will. We could build wealth through good deeds. So what's your best advice when it comes to charity?

For example, how much tax has been settled in the process and how much positive feedback has been received for the business as a whole? My advice is to establish simple structures. Also, family foundations are passed down from generation to generation, and the new generation always expects quick impact, such as setting quantitative goals for projects. In philanthropy, the most important things are trust and transparency, because people want to see positive change triggered by philanthropy. They are also very interested in investment and access to finance, all of which are topics that the other guests will talk about. Impact and environmental investments are also very important.

I am also a member of the Community Foundation Board. We want to know how to better promote social control and environmental excellence through investment. We want to teach people how to fish as it is more important than just giving them fish. When you want to do something, if you get too anxious at the beginning, you won't be able to begin, probably because there is too much information. Voltaire said earlier, "The best is the enemy of the good." It's hard to take the first step if you're trying to be perfect in the beginning. So we need to get started at the first place.

George Sycip: Now we have several minutes for questions and answers. Today we have heard a lot of great contents. Do you have any questions?

Peng Qian: Thank you. It was a wonderful speech. I have a question for Ms. Mitzi Perdue. I'm a professor at the Hong Kong University of Science and Technology, and my area of research is family foundations and family philanthropy. In my classroom, I often divide family philanthropy into two categories: traditional philanthropy and strategic philanthropy. Based on my observations and case studies, I have found that many families in Hong Kong are focusing on strategic philanthropy, which is like a bonding agent that brings the family members closer together. This is because traditional philanthropy is mainly through writing cheques and therefore is a one-time event, while strategic philanthropy requires more involvement from family members. So, I would like to ask the Perdue family, you just mentioned in your PowerPoint that philanthropy allows family members to connect, how exactly do you choose strategic philanthropy projects? How do family members make decisions together?

Mitzi Perdue: We may get 20 or 30 charity requests, which I could talk to you in details when we have time. We have a donation club comprises of kids between the ages of 12 and 18. They have $20,000 to spend based on mutual agreement. The club allows the kids to be part of the decision making. Even spouses and non-blood relatives could take part in. The club has been operated effectively. In this way, we can make the spouse feel more involved and give them a sense of belonging.

Some of my friends, and other people I know, have this experience that young people are very innovative and have new ideas for charities. We believe that charity should not be just a short-term benefit. I want students to think about how they can use innovative technology to bring new ideas and thoughts to charity. Thank you.

Justin Miller: I want to add that writing a cheque isn't family philanthropy. Instead, it's just a donation. Family philanthropy would engage siblings and cousins. A 12-year old family member may have equal voting power with a 60-

year old member. It's a process of gaming and negotiation. It' an effective way to help us choose which projects we want to support and decide how much money to spend.

Why is this approach effective? Let me give you an analysis from the perspective of organizational theory, which is applied in family management. The success of family philanthropy lies in horizontal operation, that is, siblings and cousins in the same generation make decisions together. If, in a family, the father tells the child what to do, then it is vertical management which usually proves to be not very good. In comparison, the horizontal way is better. As we know, in horizontal management, decisions are made by kids of the same generation. It is a very meaningful experience to engage young kids between 12 to 18 in philanthropy decisions.

George Sycip: The club composed of members between 12 and 18 years of age is an interesting case. Do you have any other questions? If so, you may ask in private. Now, let's take a break for 5 minutes before coming back to the last two sessions.

George Sycip: In the next session, we will discuss some of the innovations and trends for the future, especially those related to family philanthropy. Our first speaker is Mr. Laurence Lien, a supporter and leader in the non-profit sector in Singapore, the third and first generation of the Lien family. He is the Chairman of the Lien Foundation, President of the National Volunteer & Philanthropy Centre (NVPC), Chairman of the Community Foundation of Singapore (CFS), Deputy Chairman of Caritas Singapore, Vice-President of the Centre for Non-Profit Leadership (CNL), Founder of the Asian Philanthropy Circle (APC), and a former Member of Parliament for Singapore, focusing on civil society issues. With a primary focus on the non-profit sector, Mr. Lien also holds a number of public offices in Singapore and holds degrees from several schools including the National University of Singapore, Oxford University and Harvard University's Kennedy School of Government. In 2010, Mr. Lien was awarded the Eisenhower Fellowship. The Lien Foundation was established by Mr. Laurence Lien's grandfather, Lien Ying Chow. It focuses on using innovative ideas to address social issues, such as children's education, elderly care, and environmental sustainability. Next, please join me in welcoming Mr. Laurence Lien to introduce what innovations and trends in family philanthropy are on the horizon.

Laurence Lien: Thanks for the introduction of the moderator. But the information is a little bit out of date. I no longer hold some of the posts. Now, I am the Chairman of the Lien Foundation; and Founder of APC. I have resigned from

NVPC.

I did not start in the family business. Instead, I have worked for the Singapore government for 14 years. I then realized that I could play a role in civil society and create a philanthropic ecosystem because not many people were doing that. My personal experience in philanthropy is inseparable from the Lien Foundation. My grandfather was not very good at communicating, developing visions and making succession plans. I joined the Foundation's board in 2002 when my grandfather was 96. He passed away two years later. There wasn't a strategic plan in place at that time to grow the Foundation on a step-by-step basis.

We wanted to do charity innovatively. But we soon found that more time was needed for people to take it in. We looked at what a philanthropic foundation could do and found that it could increase impact, raise money, and solve social problems. I think this is not only the footprint of the Lien Foundation, but also the overall trend of philanthropy in the world.

We have long term plans to build a 10-year or 20-year funding relationships because we have a lot of partners who can provide a lot of good and new solutions. They could make good use of our donations. The Lien Foundation works with leading people in this field who already have a lot of insights and experience in this area.

We want to be more strategic in our charity work, covering as wide a range as possible, while the focus on specific projects. It will be both detailed and broad. Moreover, of course, the decision-making process needs to change from a "rule by the voice of one man alone", "the big bosses make the decisions" approach to a more democratic and broad-based approach. It should be a horizontal structure instead of a vertical one, which is still at the stage of exploration.

We also focus on philanthropic projects in traditional areas, such as water, health and the environment, which are popular in other parts of the world, as well as exploratory, high-risk projects.

What I've just shared is a current trend in the philanthropic world that may not yet be the mainstream. Because mainstream philanthropic projects are traditionally created and controlled by the first generation of family members. Whereas traditional charity is about individual heritages and individual interests, we now need more of a democratic, intelligent approach.

We now see that there are people who do charity that goes far beyond foundations. I would like to mention a colleague of mine from APC who was supposed to be here today as a speaker, but unfortunately, his father has just passed away and he could not travel here. He was born in Hong Kong and settled in

Singapore, has an extraordinary foundation, and he hopes to explore new models for retirement and elderly care.

It's a relatively new field. More than 20 years ago, when Singapore's ageing problem wasn't so serious, he and his partners developed a new senior care program that would provide primary senior care first and then personalized care. Our government has always been able to learn from their experience and incorporate it into government programs. They are doing so well in elderly care that their foundation is deemed as the most important organization for elderly-care training in Singapore. They have been fighting at the forefront of elderly care with remarkable achievements. They are leveraging government and public resources with funds from their family charitable foundation.

We see some people in APC who in the past have been using corporate money as a starter fund for family philanthropy. There are several reasons for doing so. First, it used to be that the eldest family member was in charge of the discretionary affairs because he was the origin of power for the family charity. However, as time went by when more and more family members in the second and third generation become involved, the company was no longer able to take full responsibility for the operation and management of the family charity. The family felt that the foundation set up by the company was essentially related to the company's business and social responsibility. As a result, the foundation members did not have a lot of autonomy and was very hard to decide on large projects. So they established another family foundation, transitioning from the old model of a corporate foundation to family philanthropy. They work with the city government, including with the Department of Health, to focus on children's health and girls' education. In the Philippines, they also promote project collaboration in the public sector. The transition has been very successful. They're now doing very well in infants, women and children health care. And they're not led by one person like they used to be. Instead, everyone is engaged in impact investing. The above is what I would like to say about the strategic business partnership.

We created APC so that we can learn from each other. It would be great if we could promote and apply some very effective models. People usually say that "1+1>2". We also hope that our members could join together to solve huge problems that no individual organization can do, such as environmental issues. We also recently had a foundation dedicated to peace initiatives, which are in high demand in war-torn areas of the world.

Hopefully, our philanthropy will be more strategic and synergistic, which is the change I see in APC. And I believe it must be the trend in the future.

George Sycip: Thank you for your wonderful presentation, Mr. Laurence Lien. Our second speaker is Sirkka Korpela who comes from Finland. She used to work in Germany. After many years' experience in the oil and gas field, she joined the United Nations, focusing on UNDP projects in South America. Later, she moved to New York as Director of the UNDP business partnerships division. She is also an adjunct professor at Columbia University's School of International and Public Affairs, where she serves as a trustee of the International Institute of Rural Reconstruction. She is now helping her children take care of her grandchildren. They are studying Chinese together. She has lived in Beijing for four years and has also been providing analysis for CCTV. Today she will talk to us about public-private partnerships.

Sirkka Korpela: Thanks for the invitation of the organizers, especially Give2Asia. Thanks for having me here. I am glad to come back to Asia, in particular China.

The topics people are talking about today really make me excited. Philanthropy to me means acting with a passionate heart. The current innovations and trends in philanthropy make me think about the role of partnerships. I think it's about how we can improve our results, and increase our impact and scale, especially how to advance philanthropy better and obtain results.

At the Business Roundtable held in the U.S. a few weeks ago, it was said that shareholder wealth accumulation is now not the only goal of companies. I think it means that companies need to take other stakeholders into account as well. In philanthropy, I think every stakeholder plays an important role, and one of the ways to move philanthropy forward is through partnership. But who should people partner with to upgrade their philanthropic efforts and keep them rooted in the philanthropic sector?

I think it would be best to form alliances with other foundations. If you align with these foundations, you can work together, interact, exchange, share or promote experiences, and synergize your resources. That way, the start-up fund for the project will be more abundant.

You can also work with NGOs, as well as with small NGOs based on project practice, such as the World Wide Fund for Nature (WWF). All of these can be important links in the process of moving your project forward. These small NGOs are also important, and working with them is vital if you want your charity project to have a lasting impact.

Who else can you work with? When you implement a specific project or event, as it becomes larger and more complex, it is important to bring in more partners who may become your enablers. Maybe there will be a huge difference in backgrounds, cultures, and even the personalities of the person who heads the foundation, so there needs to be someone who brings all the people together to facilitate discussions, understandings and collaborations.

We also need some very important partners, namely government agencies, even high-level ones. For your project to have the maximum impact possible, it is important to engage government agencies during project planning and strategy development phase, so that they would take into account your project when developing policies.

Other partners include UN agencies. I used to work for UNDP business partnerships division. Many UN agencies also act as enablers and intermediaries to help us dialogue and collaborate with more NGOs, businesses, governments, and foundations. We also promote projects at the regional level and collaborate with other agencies as well.

How do we manage a partnership after it was made? The exact management model will depend on the nature and scope of the project. There are times when people are pursuing similar goals. As we talked about earlier, you need to find a very appropriate marketer. A couple of years ago, an organization called RED did a great job of promoting a program that focused on the fight against AIDS, and we could sign an agreement with each other to define our respective rights, responsibilities and optimize our professional knowledge. I think in the fight against malaria and in the face of global challenges, our alliances could be more loosely structured. And we can also form partnerships based on specific contracts.

Parties can come together to set several clear and measurable goals, with definite timelines. Why are partnerships necessary? The main reason is that we can pool the wisdom of all parties involved to have a greater impact and scale up the project. Besides, we can enjoy greater predictability.

Quality will be monitored and ensured when all parties are involved in the project and can communicate with each other. Sometimes, the more difficult and complex the problems are, the more differentiated resources need to be involved. So, the main purpose is to bring all the parties together. So, what are the advantages of working with governments? First and foremost, we can align our solutions with outside donor requirements and government policies.

And then we have to consider the working style of the government, as well as bureaucracy, election season and the number of years a politician has worked. Public-private partnerships are very much encouraged in the United States. It seems that the U.S. government is cutting budgets and putting more pressure on the private sector, so we have to think about the very complex implications of working with the government. It's also important that we give considerations to local governments as well.

We are all people with passion. We need to collaborate with others to turn passion into concrete actions. Thank you.

George Sycip: Thanks for the great presentation of Sirkka Korpela. Our next speaker is Mr. Elliott Donnelley. He has a long resume, perhaps because he is the tallest man in the room. He's the founding general partner of the Chicago-based White Sand Investor Group, LP. and a fifth-generation member of the Chicago based RR Donnelley family. He has also founded a number of companies in Silicon Valley and other areas. Elliott lived in Beijing from 1981-1991 teaching in schools. He is on the advisory board of Stanford's Global Project Center, where he focuses on world infrastructure projects. He also serves on the board of trustees of the Philanthropy Workshop and is a major funder of the World Education Network, which was originally founded by the Rockefeller Foundation. This network has 450 members in 46 countries. He is also a board member of LGT Venture Philanthropy Foundation. His frequent publications include papers on strategic philanthropy, family foundations, legacy, and innovations in philanthropy. As a dance teacher, Elliott Donnelly is also a very good dancer. Today, he will share best practices in impact investing and philanthropy with us. Thank you for your attendance.

Elliott Donnelley: Thanks for the introduction of the moderator and the precious opportunity offered by the organizers. My appreciation also goes to the CPAFFC, Tsinghua University, HKU, CUHK, and the Shenzhen Municipal People's Government for establishing such a platform to bring us together. Today, I would like to talk about the innovation and development trend in philanthropy.

I'll start with a story about love, war, dancing classes, and more. My great-great-grandfather, an Irish immigrant, fell in love with the daughter of one of the wealthiest families in Canada. He went to propose to the father, who would not allow his daughter to marry a poor boy. So he persuaded the girl to elope with him. To prove himself to his father-in-law, he went to Chicago in 1864 and established a printing company, which, over the past 150 years, has become the largest printing company in the world. In the process, he practised the family management philosophy mentioned by the previous speakers.

My parents' love story is also very touching. My father was sent off to Vietnam to fight in the war, while my mother lived in Chicago with other family members. She found that the values of the company had changed and the next generation was somewhat lost. After my father returned home, my mother said she wanted him to stay in California, saying that he might have a good future if he went to Chicago, but that it would be better for the children if he stayed in California. My father agreed to that decision and went to Berkeley in 1969 where he became an entrepreneur and received good education. At that time, I was surrounded by friends who did not come from very wealthy families, but most of their parents were college professors and engineers, among others. It was only later when I was 13 that my father told me the history of the family when I discovered that the Donnellys shared my last name. I didn't grow up in the family, but that made me a member of the "first generation".

Then I went to Yale University where I joined the rowing team and began to study Chinese. In 1981, I went to Beijing to teach aeronautics at Beijing University of Aeronautics and Astronautics. My grandmother wanted to bring the family together before she passed away, so the family members from all over the world were gathered. I slowly became involved in the family's philanthropic work and also learned about finance and accounting. At that time, I was inspired by the family business. I learned a lot at Yale as well as in the family business. I decided to follow the path of finance, wealth, and philanthropy. I'll also talk more in detail about dancing I mentioned earlier.

In 2003, I met a man in China who mentioned a Philanthropy Workshop program. I decided to join it. Later I also joined the Rockefeller Foundation's program and became more deeply involved in philanthropic work, which has continued to this day. I am now very passionate about philanthropy and I believe that we can create some very meaningful programs to change our world through philanthropy and finance.

Next, I will talk about three things: impact investing, impact investing in philanthropy, and the connection between human potential & financial growth and technology, and how they are reshaping the human society and our future. In 2007, Rockefeller Center coined the term "impact investing," which makes people aware of the impact of the arts on philanthropy and the role they play in the investment and philanthropic process. This stems from the strong support to American philanthropy made by actors. Organizations like the Rockefeller Foundation are very influential, but most of the time these foundations only donate about 5% of their assets. So what happens to the remaining 95%? I think it's a question worth exploring.

Some of our colleagues have made many wonderful promises. We need to consider how to live up to them. People get very excited when they hear about investing, but a lot of times they don't know the meaning and impact behind it. We see that philanthropy has a big impact on investments, but a lot of people don't really understand what those impacts are.

The market may favour or disfavour the cause of humanity. It is meant to benefit the stakeholders, which is its sole purpose of existence. Impact investing, however, is about what will not happen. Moreover, the definition of impact investing is to deliver beneficial social, ecological, and environmental impacts along with economic benefits. But impact investing is also constrained by the marketplace, because in order to make a financial gain, an organization has to compete with other institutions in the marketplace and at the same time ensures that it makes a beneficial impact. We will also discuss the market rate of return.

I used to teach students at a finance university in South Africa. What I did was I provided a philanthropic grant and I had to think about whether I could solve the problem in a way that created higher value. A lot of people are confused about impact investing. People are probably very happy to hear us talking about it. The total amount of impact investing by insurance companies, family funds, and private funds can total trillions of dollars.

The total charitable funding in the United States is $74 billion, while the total global funding has reached trillions of dollars. One would think that it would be nice if all those funds could be used for good. But here is one thing that people don't notice: Do these funds really do what they were originally intended to do? Currently, our corporate structure only spends 5% of our earnings on philanthropy, so we need to think about new ways and new structures to enable impact investing. We also have to think about taxes because we get a tax benefit for making impact investments, but is that benefit doing good or evil? There are also grants. As an impact investment, each family has to put in some money. How do we address the issues that really need to be addressed? The answer is innovation.

The family decides to dedicate 10% of their funds to a specific project. Now the allocation of funds is important. We should first identify the areas of concern, i.e. the most desired impact it wants to create. For example, if climate change is identified as a concern, then it is important to consider how to mitigate the effects of climate change, how to quantify the effects, etc. Achieving this goal depends not only on donations but also on investments. This requires a certain amount of risk-taking and may sometimes involve playing the role of a government, providing subsidies and educating people, as this is a big issue. At the same time, impact investing does not seek economic profit, but it would not turn it down either.

The second thing is to bring about change. We need to create financial frameworks that combine rationality and philanthropy. We need to look at how much money is needed for each project, how much financial risk is involved, as well as ROI. This framework may not need to be the best, but it needs to show the opportunity cost. Addressing climate change can be achieved through technology, or through changing consumer behaviour and policy. If you work with companies, then you need to list the impact rankings. These are all very interesting things. I think it's important for people to pay attention to these details if they're doing impact investing.

We may start with the technical aspects of environmental issues. Next, I would like to talk about human resources training.

People are now contemplating the potential of the human species. We are the most advanced animals who can do both good and evil. So how do we develop awareness? Humans have done a lot of research in psychology and brain science. If we can understand where our love and hate come from, that will help solve a lot of problems. In 2017, Google had an expert in artificial intelligence, who was also a philanthropist, came to me and said that if he had more time, he would work on saving people from death. He felt that in the future, technology would be able to recreate every cell of the human race. If it were possible to treat every cell, our life span would be extended.

Science and technology have been trending linearly, which makes the world a totally different place. A few decades ago, we didn't understand many of the concepts, but now we know what financial capital means and what artificial intelligence and robotics are. What if today we invested our money in the areas that need it most? The United States has traffic problems now, and in the future, if there are autonomous cars, all traffic problems will be solved. Are we prepared for the changes that lie ahead? Not really.

When it comes to artificial intelligence, some say it's disruptive to the world and will change people's consciousness, and some say it's a saviour, while others call it the terminator. In Silicon Valley, people are already asking these very forward-looking questions: How are we going to allocate funds in the future? There is great potential for future technology which could be used for good as well as evil. I hope you will think about this issue seriously. Thank you all.

George Sycip: That was an interesting presentation. The next speaker is Peng Min, a Hunanese born in Ning Xia. In 1990, she moved to Beijing on her own and started from scratch. She is now the chairman of the Hong Kong Faith

Winner (Far East). Ms. Peng Min has been in the real estate business and involved in villa development projects in Beijing. The projects are well designed and eco-friendly. As an entrepreneur, she does her best to do charity. She is also the head of a foundation in Beijing. Today she will talk to us about her three daughters' involvement in philanthropy. This can also be seen as an example for future philanthropy. Today she will talk about the legacy tradition of philanthropy family, using her three daughters as an example.

Peng Min: Thank you so much for the invitation to the WPF. I've been a little bit nervous sitting here because I'm not from a big family. But after hearing what you all shared, I feel reassured. My presentation today is very simple, nothing preachy. I have discovered that I am doing the right thing.

I would like to invite you to watch several videos of my daughters.

The first video features my oldest daughter, Grape. I'm the mom of "fruits", my second daughter's name is Pomegranate and my third daughter's name is Cherry. This is Grape talking about setting up her charity foundation to help left-behind children by combining art with charity. In her words, the power of children helping children is the greatest. She wants people to pay attention to charity projects initiated by teenagers. My third daughter's hobby is painting. Her artwork is auctioned off at charity events. She was particularly motivated to paint when told that the money would help other special groups. In the first half of 2019, the project has raised another 130,000 RMB. This elementary school's art-wall has just been finished. In July 2019, she did another project—building art classrooms. Tencent Charity Foundation supported her project. It was displayed on Tencent's "99 Charity Day" and is now raising money on the Tencent charity platform. Her project is planned to last three years. Through this project, the children will learn about art and all the artworks they create would contribute to society. That means all the donations collected through the artworks will be given back to the school.

This is a brief introduction to the philanthropic activities that my children have undertaken. All of the words of the guests are so kind to me. I am also happy that I am doing the right thing. I hope that I can have the opportunity to share these experiences with others. I hope more organizations will see that there is a new generation of families growing up in China now. And I hope to gain more support. Thank you all!

George Sycip: Thanks for your presentation, Ms. Peng Min. You have three excellent children. Now, let's move to the last session. Our speaker will give a summary of the previous presentations.

Long Denggao: Hello, everyone. I am Long Denggao from the CCES, Tsinghua University.

My presentation will be divided into two parts: a summary of today's discussion and my thoughts on philanthropy in China.

Today's discussion was very lively and beneficial to me. We mainly discussed the following points:

The first point is about family wealth creation and transmission, which is the foundation of charity and philanthropy as it is only with sustainable wealth that one can give and do charity.

The second point concerns the social sharing and distribution of wealth, including philanthropy. From what we have discussed today, such as disease treatment, elderly care, arts and treasure auctions, among others, we can see that philanthropy covers a wide range of areas.

It was also pointed out that wealth creation was not limited to the family, but could be extended to stakeholders. In fact, stakeholders are the embodiment of social responsibility and commitment of family philanthropy and family foundations.

The third point relates to the operation of the charitable foundation itself, including how to invest and how to avoid taxes. Charitable foundations increase value and scale up charity work through market operations.

The fourth point relates to trends in philanthropy, which is one of the main focuses of our discussion today. To summarize, there are three trends. The first is the evolution of foundations from family foundations to non-family foundations, for example, the Ford Family. The second is that philanthropic entities are advancing philanthropy through a wide range of collaborations and partnerships, including with government agencies. The third trend is the globalization of philanthropy.

In the discussion of the globalization of philanthropy, one of the speakers talked about Chinese philanthropy and said that modern philanthropy came to China from Europe and North America. There is nothing wrong with this statement, but I would like to talk about the philanthropy of Chinese and overseas Chinese in light of my research.

Firstly, China has a strong tradition of philanthropy, which was also mentioned by Joan Crain. As we know, in contemporary China, most philanthropy activities are arranged by the government, including charitable foundation organizations, which cannot exist without the support of the government. But before 1949, most of the public services at the grassroots level in China were arranged by the private sector itself, such as philanthropic infrastructure, including bridges, ports, roads, and irrigation facilities, all offered free of charge. This tradition was ignored or forgotten by us, which led to a certain misunderstanding.

Secondly, although this tradition is rarely seen in the Chinese mainland, it continues to exist in overseas Chinese societies. The family and its philanthropic efforts, as well as other public services that we have discussed today, can be found throughout China's history and in overseas Chinese societies today.

The influence of Hong Kong Chinese businessmen in global philanthropy is enormous. I am deeply touched by the fact that many prestigious schools in the U.K. and the U.S. have received donations from Hong Kong Chinese businessmen. The overseas Chinese community and the Hong Kong community are not only continuing and promoting Chinese traditions, but now feeding back to philanthropy in the Chinese mainland.

Thirdly, today's philanthropy in the Chinese mainland is indeed influenced by Europe and America and promoted by Hong Kong society and overseas Chinese. The philanthropy in the Chinese mainland, however, has only a decade or two of history, as the private sector had no money or autonomy during the planned economy. However, we can see that philanthropy in the Chinese mainland is developing rapidly, especially as new technologies have enabled the emerging philanthropy in the Chinese mainland to enter a new phase, such as the philanthropy carried out by Tencent and Alibaba with new technologies.

That's all for my presentation. Thank you.

George Sycip: That's a great summary. Now let's give the floor to Mr. Carter Tseng, who will be the moderator for the last two sessions. Originally from Fujian province, Tseng graduated from National Taiwan University with a bachelor's degree in Electrical Engineering and received his PhD in Computer Science from the University of California, Los Angeles. He worked as an industrial designer and project manager in the United States before returning to Taiwan and founded Microtek, the world's largest scanner manufacturer and the first listed company in the industrial park. For many years, he has been mentoring students and technology professionals, promoting corporate and institutional education, and fostering collaborative projects with local governments. A rare talent and philanthropist, Tseng will wrap up this afternoon's conversation. We're also delighted to have him join us for this afternoon's roundtable conversation. Thank you.

Carter Tseng: We don't have much time left, but I'm calling on everyone to get involved. The fact that you flew in from all over the world and stayed until 18:00 today is a testament to your enthusiasm. It's been a fruitful day. Having heard from 10 experts, we have learned a few ideas and initiatives out of the collective wisdom of our colleagues in Give2Asia. With these proposals from professionals, we hope that we can generate some actions. We have listed three courses of action for you to consider, and we look forward to your feedback.

Everyone here today is interested in family legacy and is more or less involved in philanthropy. Our first initiative is that every person and every family starts to practice what we've preached, passes on our dedication, our responsibility to society, our positive energy to our friends around us, as much as possible. I personally feel that time, energy and passion are more important than money. It doesn't matter how much money you have donated. Even if you could only sponsor one student at this time, with continued efforts, you will be able to sponsor more students. The most important thing is to take actions, no matter how small the projects are. As the saying goes, the loftiest towers are built from the ground up.

Secondly, today we have discussed different approaches to philanthropy. Shouldn't we put these family legacy lessons into practice more systematically? We can set up sustainable impact investment funds, charitable funds and trusts to pass on wealth and fulfil our corporate social responsibility. Every business has foundations, but how are they going to take on their social responsibility? That's something we need to consider.

So my second suggestion is to not only do it yourself, but to mobilize your own company and your own family so that philanthropy becomes part of the legacy. There are many young people today who are more open-minded and can use high technology as an enabler for philanthropy.

Thirdly, going it alone is not enough. Both China's goal of eradicating poverty for all by 2020 and building a community of shared human destiny advocated by General Secretary Xi Jinping is dependent on international consultation and cooperation. I have a suggestion that maybe we could build a network that covers more than 10 countries within our capacity, starting with Asia. We could generate an action that facilitates people to learn from each other. In rural China, these projects will affect a lot of people, because many doctors in rural areas need training, but how? It's impossible to send them all to a good medical school, which would be too time-consuming. So we came up with the idea of distance teaching. We teach the skills of doctors in big cities like Beijing and Shanghai to doctors in villages with the help of the business community. Educational inequality used to be an issue, but now with the Internet, you can learn from advanced cities no matter how remotely located you are. My suggestion is that we could implement this in our family first and then in China, before going global to share such practice with countries along with the "Belt and Road Initiative" and those involved in South-South Cooperation.

Now, it's time for open discussion. Everyone is free to voice his or her opinions.

Peng Qian: Just now Ms. Peng Min showed us a video about the Mosuo people, who still live in a matrilineal society, a key message the video did not mention. It reminds me of family philanthropy, where women are very much in the picture. Traditional Chinese culture favours men over women, and family businesses may all be inherited by men. So what will women do? The answer is philanthropy.

For me, family philanthropy could drive gender equality, or highlight the role of women. It can also bring the family together and unite the strength of all. I suggest that entrepreneurs in Chinese mainland allocate a small portion of their funds to charity work, as charity is not only good for society, but also very helpful to their own families.

Peng Min: I'll add a few words here.

I'm a single mother taking care of both my business and my children on my own. So what makes me engage my children in my philanthropic efforts? Partly because I've found it is a good way to raise them. They become partners with me at a very young age. Sometimes, they may have a lot of questions about diseases and others, which I don't have time to answer or simply don't have an answer. However, these questions would later find their answers in charity work. My oldest daughter is very afraid of death. When we were working on a children's project, she met a child who had a heart attack. She asked me if that child was dying. I told her to ask that child herself. She went and asked the boy why he was so happy every day despite his serious illness. The boy told her that the development of technology had given him the hope of being cured some day.

Since then, she feels there is nothing to fear any more. In practicing philanthropy, I feel that my children and I have developed a deeper understanding of wealth, life and death, and have overcome a lot of anxieties that are common to many families. We have gone through all the experiences, including communication, exchange, education, values, involvement, initiation, family leadership transition, sense of direction, and self-identity that a few gentlemen across the table spoke of.

So what's my point here? I want to say that philanthropy is a spontaneous awareness that arises naturally in the mind of children. When it arises, how are we, as adults, going to support them? Do we take them forward, or do we gradually allow them to become leaders? Personally, I think it should be the latter. In practicing philanthropy along with my children, I have become an assistant and they have become decision-makers. There was none of the conflict between us that adolescent girls and menopausal moms often encounter. When we sit together, we would be discussing how to make this work better.

My presentation today is about how doing charity work with children is a great way to raise them. As for the reasons for my change, I am afraid it is not appropriate to mention on this occasion. Thank you so much for this conference and for helping me clarify my thoughts, thank you all!

Deng Lan: I would like to thank the organizers, CPAFFC and Tsinghua University, the two earliest founders, as well as the two universities in Hong Kong that joined us last year. The initiative that Mr. Tseng has just mentioned is also what we aim to implement. Our original intention is very simple and down-to-earth, that is, to call on more people to join the philanthropy family and do what we are allowed to, what we wish for, and what we are capable of, to change the world or change the fate of certain people.

Thank you for joining our family. Since 2018, we have launched a network called the Community of Human Destiny: Collaborative Network of Philanthropy and Social Services, which was introduced in the video at the beginning of the forum. We are trying to form a group of individuals, or an institution under this network, which can use their power, resources and platforms to advocate, take actions, and ultimately make a difference.

I think the three initiatives that Mr. Tseng just mentioned are very much in line with the concept under the framework of the forum. We will strongly support such initiatives. Our appreciation also goes to Give2Asia and BNY Mellon for hosting such a conference, because having so many influencers discussing things that will change the world will certainly enlarge our social impact. These initiatives, if indeed launched as a plan tomorrow, will be one of the highlights of our forum.

We also hope that all of you, or your friends, will join our family after seeing these initiatives and our efforts. I have an idea that every year in June, CPAFFC may invite CEOs of Fortune 500 companies to come to China to talk with our national leaders. I wonder if our families here, many of whom are in the Fortune

500, could also set up organizations like Philanthropy and Family Wealth Legacy Committee to create such an opportunity to pass on our voices and ideas.

If it were to happen, I hope that we could see more people devoted to the philanthropy world, hear their stories of how they sow the seeds of love and bring benefits to society. Thank you all!

Carter Tseng: Thank you, Ms. Deng Lan. Let's be concise and brief.

Elliott Donnelley: I have two points to make in response to what you have said earlier. One is how to use technology to benefit human beings. I think it is very important. Now, technology primarily serves the market, individual interests, the public and the government, but it can also play an important role in philanthropy.

My second point is that we need to consider different kinds of capitals. In philanthropy, time, energy and passion can be more important than money, so does the interpersonal relationship.

Wang Leilei: As we've shared before, professionals working on the front lines in the U.S. know that tax deductions and tax optimization, while may not be the most important, play a critical role in a shareholder's family legacy business. Now that China is undergoing a deep tax system reform, we also hope that our experts and Chinese tax professionals will have better communication and exchanges over the most cutting-edge tax ideas and concepts of the U.S. so that Chinese tax reform will be a boost to family philanthropy. Thank you.

Zhao Luyun: Thank you. I have been following how Give2Asia prepares for this conference. Clearly, we have all put a lot of effort into it. As we work jointly on the "Belt and Road Initiative " in such a turbulent world, the three initiatives just mentioned have special significance. As the author of Forbes and Money Week, I suggest that we can help the project through the media. We also have the Shanghai Alumni Association, which has a presence in more than 10 countries, and can be used to support the initiatives of Give2Asia. We have the Philanthropy and Wealth Legacy Program mentioned by CPAFFC, and I am also creating a research centre. We can also call on wealthy families around the world to establish family alliances. In this way, we have family alliances, relatives, entrepreneurs, Generation-one and Generation-two elite university graduates, who could all contribute together to the promotion the "Belt and Road Initiative ". Moreover, inspired by Dr. Tseng's initiatives, we can also include influential wealthy families from various regions too. Thank you.

Carter Tseng: With your support, I am confident we will succeed in the end. Finally, I would like to ask for your opinions. If you think these initiatives are feasible and you are willing to support them, please applaud! Thank you. We have a successful meeting today. Later, we will make a few revisions and improvement to the draft of initiatives. It will be officially released tomorrow at 16:30.

IX PHILANTHROPY & FUNDRAISING IN HIGHER EDUCATION: CHINA'S PRACTICE

Moderator: Professor Huang Yu, Associate Vice-President of the Hong Kong Baptist University (HKBU)

Wang Zhenmin, Professor of the Tsinghua University School of Law, Secretary-General of the Tsinghua University Education Foundation (TUEF)

Guest Speeches: Chen Chong, Chairman of the Guangdong Guoqiang Public Welfare Foundation

Zhong Demei, Chief Executive Officer of the Zhang Rongfa Foundation

Dr. Tang Lap Kwong, Director of the Centre for Chinese Classical Learning, the CUHK

Speakers: Liang Hui, General Manager of the Guangzhou Dongpu Concrete Co., Ltd.

Fang Tao, Member of the Standing Committee of the Shenzhen Municipal Committee of the Chinese people's political consultative conference, executive vice president and secretary-general of Shenzhen Charity association

Liu Xun, Chairman of the Shenzhen Xintongfang Investment Management Co., Ltd.

Shen Liyong, Secretary-General of the Zhejiang University Education Foundation (ZUEF)

Yuan Wei, Secretary General of the Tsinghua University Education Foundation (TUEF)

Tu Ronghui, Secretary-General of the Southern University of Science and Technology (SUSTech) Education Foundation

Zhao Wenli, Deputy Secretary-General of the Peking University Education Foundation (PKUEF)

Huang Yu: Distinguished guests, dear friends, good morning. Now, I declare the opening of the high-level roundtable breakout session of the WPF 2019. It consists of two parts: guest speeches and roundtable discussions. We hope that this roundtable will allow us to interact with each other and take our philanthropy to new heights.

Now, let's welcome our first speaker Mr. Chen Chong, Chairman of Guangdong Guoqiang Public Welfare Foundation. The title of his speech is *Education is Essential for Both Talent Development and a Nation's Rejuvenation.*

Education is Essential for Both Talent Development and a Nation's Rejuvenation

Chen Chong, Chairman of the Guangdong Guoqiang
Public Welfare Foundation

I would like to thank TUEF for giving me this opportunity to share some of the philanthropy work that Guoqiang Public Welfare Foundation has been doing.

The title of my speech is *Education is Essential for Both Talent Development and a Nation's Rejuvenation.*

Guoqiang Public Welfare Foundation is a non-public foundation founded by Mr. Yeung Kwok Keung, Chairman of Country Garden Group, and its Co-Chair Ms. Yang Huiyan. The foundation has long been committed to poverty alleviation, education and technology innovation.

Although the foundation was not established until 2013, Mr. Yeung's history of philanthropy can be traced back to the 1990s. That was some 20 years ago. Up to now, the foundation has donated more than 5.5 billion yuan to the society, including education donations to 39 universities. Besides, we have established three charity schools under the foundation.

Why did Mr. Yeung establish such a foundation? He said that when he was in secondary school, he was exempted from tuition by the government due to low-income family conditions. If not so, he would never have completed his study and done something useful to society.

He also received a subsidy of 2 yuan from the government. For many people, it was only a small amount of money. Yet for him, it was particularly helpful. At that time, a classmate of his also received the same subsidy. They often went to the waste stations together where they could buy tons of used books with the money. They then read all the books they bought together and resold them to the waste station in exchange for more books.

Mr. Yeung did not study long in school, but he read a lot of books, which was very helpful to his career and success. From his story, we can see that 2-yuan could also make a difference to a student and his entire life.

In 2015, Mr. Yeung received the "China Poverty Eradication Award".

This shows the percentage of education donation, which is our theme for this breakout session, against the total donations made by global international organizations. In the U.S., education accounts for the second-largest donations next to religious donations. About 30% of educational funds for American universities comes from foundations. Harvard University received a $1.4 billion endowment last year, which was the largest donation ever to a single educational institution in the world, and the second largest one went to Stanford University. The value of donations and education funds has increased to $5 billion, which are used to support the entire operation of Harvard University.

From 100 years ago to the present, foundations and dedicated individuals have gone out of their way to contribute to education, inspiring us to engage in philanthropic work in this special field.

Now, I'll talk about what we have done for China's education community.

As I said earlier, our actual donations exceeded 5.5 billion yuan. Poverty alleviation is an important part of our charitable work. We have done quite a lot in this area as it is also the focus of the Chinese government in recent years. Education is another key area where we have already donated about 2.1 billion yuan, with more than 2 billion yuan committed and to be donated in the next few years.

Our donations to the education sector could be classified into three categories: financial support for students, for scholars and disciplines.

Let me first talk about financial aid to students.

Some guests may have heard of it. This is the only free high school in China, founded by Mr. Yeung in Foshan in 2002. The school now has more than 3,000 graduates, 100% of whom have gone on to universities. More importantly, 98% of them went to national key universities. They are really great.

Now, I'll show you a short video.

(video)

In addition to the high school I just mentioned, we have established a free junior college in 2014, to provide vocational training. Now it has produced over 1000 graduates, with a 100% graduation rate, all employed upon graduation.

This is our Linxia Guoqiang Vocational - Technical School in Gansu province, where it is common for students to give up study after secondary school. So, we founded this school to enrol secondary school graduates. The enrollment will start from next year, with a capacity for 2,000 students per year.

This program is called Zhongming University Student Scholarship, which has run for more than 20 years ever since 1997. Interestingly, in the first 10 years, the grants were distributed by Yangcheng Evening News, so no one knew who was the real funder. It wasn't until 2007, when Country Garden went public, that people began to know Mr. Yeung Kwok Keung funded it. At that time, the scholarship has supported 10,000 students with millions of grants per year.

We established the Huiyan Education Fund with initial funding of 100 million yuan to aid economically disadvantaged kids in Shunde city.

Next, I'll introduce what we have done to support scholars.

This is the Guohua Eminent Scholar Fellowship established to support scholars in six higher education institutions in the country. We also set up several foundations for professors. They have helped in attracting and retaining an array of oversea talents each year, which is a great contribution to China's higher education.

Now, let's move to our support for discipline development.

We have established industry-academia-research collaboration programs at universities to support the development of academic disciplines. Let me share two examples. One is the Guoqiang Research Institute, which we set up last year with Tsinghua University to focus on China's development and research in the high-tech sector, and the other is the establishment of the Huiyin Academy at Beijing Normal University to promote academic development.

Now, I'll talk about our vision for the education sector.

We hope to build a society which respects knowledge and allows people to change their life with knowledge. We hope our efforts in this regard could empower more people to change their destiny. So, apart from providing financial support to students, we have also established funds to attract more talents to devote themselves to science, research and education.

Mr. Yeung said that he was very grateful for the personal support he received from our Party and government, without which, he would not have the ability to help more people in needs. We hope our endeavour could be passed on.

Finally, I'd like to share some of our thoughts.

First, how to build a sustainable development model of university donations and university-enterprise cooperation to create a win-win situation?

Second, how do we spread the spirit of donor philanthropy so that it can be passed on? For example, in our case, Mr. Yeung's philanthropy donation is motivated by the grant he received from the country.

That's all for my presentation. Thank you.

Huang Yu: Our next speaker is Ms. Zhong Demei, CEO of Chang Yung-Fa Foundation. The title of her speech is *Experience Sharing in Donations to Higher Education.*

Experience Sharing in Donations to Higher Education

Zhong Demei, CEO of the Chang Yung-Fa Foundation

Distinguished Leaders,
Dear Guests,
Ladies and Gentlemen,
Good morning.

Today I am honoured to represent the Taiwan Chang Yung-Fa Foundation to participate in this forum, and to have the opportunity to listen to the insights of the scholars and experts on philanthropy. Personally, I am more than happy to share my views on donations to higher education from a practitioner's perspective.

The Chang Yung-Fa Foundation established 3 bursaries in the Chinese mainland. The earliest one was established 11 years ago, in 2008, at Tsinghua University. The other two were established at Peking University and the China Maritime Society. By the end of 2018, we have helped a total of 3,000 students with 16.5 million yuan.

Established 34 years ago in 1985, the Taiwan Chang Yung-Fa Foundation has helped 20,000 students in 150 universities in Taiwan, with an investment of NT$ 300 million.

We have also established 3 bursaries in the United States, at the University of Houston, San Francisco State University and the University of South Carolina. You must be wondering why the Chang Yung-Fa Foundation has set up nearly 10 bursaries worldwide. The answer is very simple. Mr. Chang Yung-Fa has done this out of his wish. Born to an ordinary family and grown up in a time of turmoil, he relied on part-time jobs to complete his education, so he was particularly aware of the hardships of students from low-income families in pursuing their study. Even in 1970, not long after he started his business when Evergreen Marine was still losing money, he still didn't give up sponsoring students.

As we know, the first university in the world was the University of Bologna in Italy, dating back to 1088. For a thousand years, universities have provided a great impetus for the development of civilized society and have been entrusted with many important tasks, including the innovation of knowledge and the nurturing of talent.

However, for many children from low-income families, the university is most likely to be a beautiful destination that is visible but never accessible. Without outside help, they may never get a step closer, even though they know that education may be their only chance to change their lives.

As the founder, Mr. Chang Yung-Fa hopes that children could pursue their study smoothly. However, he is somewhat worried that students may complain about their families. So in every occasion in Taiwan, be in an interview with Media, or a granting ceremony held by the foundation, he would always encourage them to accept the reality and strive for a better life instead of complaining about the poor conditions provided by their parents or the injustice of fate.

In addition, he always encourages students to work harder and change their lives, reminds them to stay grateful to their parents. He believes that all parents in the world are doing their best to take care of their children. It's just sometimes, and things are beyond their reach. Some of the children seemed to understand what he said. After listening to his speech, they would write to the foundation to express their gratitude. What touched us the most was that when Mr. Chang passed away in 2016, many of the children he had helped come to the memorial venue to pay their respects and express their deepest gratitude to their beloved Grandpa Chang.

Of course, I believe that for all of the professors, it is the greatest joy in life to be able to "gain" the talent of the world and to teach them; for the foundation, we also find it a great joy to be able to "help" the talent of the world to pursue education. We believe that every young life on this earth is to be blessed. We can give young people a rope to climb up, with which, he may be able to climb to the container ship and sail to all corners of the world; if he is not strong enough and only makes it to a small fishing boat, as long as there is a small fishing rod, he can also make a living by fishing.

What you won't believe is that these kids are giving back to us much faster than I could have ever imagined. They have already taught us a lot of things before they have achieved success. Because of the bursaries, these children know how to appreciate their good fortune even more. They are willing to follow in the footsteps of Mr. Chang Yung-Fa and help those in need in the community. Most importantly, right now, when they are at the stage of receiving help from others, they are willing to do volunteer work as long as they have time, rather than waiting until they earn big money in the future. Such ambition and social responsibility cannot be bought with money or measured in any material form.

As we know, many students at Tsinghua University are the cream of the crop in each province, having studied hard to compete at the village, county and provincial levels. Many universities are taking initiatives to exchange experiences overseas. Allowing students to travel overseas during their summer and winter vacations to experience different cultural backgrounds is another way of learning compared with classroom study. As far as I am concerned, the TUEF has been helping students apply for various internship opportunities for many years. We were delighted to host a group of students from Tsinghua University this summer.

We made plans for these children to research labour education, volunteerism and work-study education in Taiwan, and to hold seminars at National Taiwan University. We also used this rare opportunity to hold the first "Chang Yung-fa Foundation Cross-Strait Student Meetup", where 16 students and teachers from Tsinghua University and students from 30 universities in Taiwan shared their experiences. The meeting has left beautiful memories for students on both sides of the Taiwan Strait.

In addition, we invited B&B operators from small towns in Taiwan to discuss with us how to revitalize the rural economy. We also discussed, in particular, the talk of General Secretary Xi Jinping on the "Three Rural Issues", namely agriculture, rural areas and rural people. The speakers and students were very enthusiastic that day.

Whether in Chinese mainland or Taiwan, the most distinctive feature of the Chang Yung-Fa Foundation bursary is that it is never capped and there is no limit to majors. As a result, we receive many works of art from Tsinghua University every year, including paintings and other artistic creations. If you have the opportunity to come to Taipei, please come to our foundation's Heritage Hall to see these students' works on display.

In addition, we set up a Family Support Fund for Poor Students in 2011, which could be applied in the event of a family crisis.

In 2010, the then president of Tsinghua University brought two vice-presidents to pay a visit to Mr. Chang. They mentioned that there were some Tsinghua University students from very difficult families, who did not have enough money for daily living that they had cut back on meals. Mr. Chang was very saddened to hear this and came up with the idea of setting up a family support fund, which according to the teacher of Tsinghua University, is very rare in the Chinese mainland. The teachers also told us that many graduates of Tsinghua University, out of the gratitude for those who helped them with their studies, including Mr. Chang, donated their first salary to the school to help younger students. It's quite touching. I think this is also one of the biggest rewards for the Chang Yung-fa Foundation of Tsinghua University.

I'd like to tell you a story.

At our Foundation in Taiwan, we have people responsible for checking the status of the grantee. One day Mr. Chang said to me, since we had set up support funds and grants at Tsinghua University, should we not go to the homes of our students to find out what is going on? Given the vast area of the Chinese mainland, we didn't have a clue about how to arrange the trip. Luckily, the teachers from TUEF helped us to make careful arrangements for a home visit to four students from Hebei Province, which is relatively close in the distance. Even though we only visited four students from one province, we spent four days and three nights travelling more than 1,000 kilometres, a distance equivalent to travelling around the island of Taiwan for a week. I was very impressed by the visits. The parents were very grateful to us. One parent gave me a big bag of cotton and potatoes that they had grown themselves, and another student's father climbed up a tree to pick pomegranates for us as we were leaving.

Be it a bursary or a family support fund, and our purpose is to let the students know that there are people in the world who care about them.

At the same time, I'd like to take this opportunity to make us known to as many people as possible.

The Chang Yung-Fa Foundation is probably one of the few corporate foundations in the world. We have three major cultural and creative brands, including the Evergreen Symphony Orchestra, the Evergreen Maritime Museum and our free monthly magazine, *Moral Monthly*. The Evergreen Maritime Museum is open to schools of all levels, while the Moral Monthly is responsible for promoting moral education. We are also grateful to students from Peking University and Tsinghua University for their frequent contributions to our newsletter.

In addition to the philanthropy work we just talked about, we have also helped many low-income families in Taiwan, hoping to inspire them to tap their potential.

I am very grateful to have this opportunity to serve at the foundation.

Every philanthropic effort I've experienced in the last 20 years has made me feel deeply that, as the forum says, each of us needs to be more committed to the promotion and practice of social service. This work has made me realize how fortunate we are that we can give people the power to move forward simply by using our intelligence. Moreover, this power deeply connects us to the families and children we are helping, giving us a feeling that goes beyond description.

Someday, these children will leave school to pursue their dreams. Their success depends on whether or not they are able to use what they have learned to contribute to their country and society. We are content to accompany them during their school life.

We hope that, because of us, young people will no longer feel alone. We are willing to give them hope when they want to learn and strive for the future.

I'm sure that the guests here, like me, have long felt deeply the happiness that comes from doing good deeds. Helen Keller, a famous American writer, once said that "True happiness... is not attained through self-gratification, but through fidelity to a worthy purpose." In the future, we will continue to stay true to our worthy goal, which is to inherit the spirit of universal love of Mr. Chang!

Thanks for listening.

Huang Yu: Our next speaker is Dr. Tang Lap-kwong, Director of the Centre for Chinese Classical Learning, CUHK. The title of his speech is *Thoughts on Charity Donations to China's Higher Education.*

Thoughts on Charity Donations to China's Higher Education

Dr. Tang Lap-kwong, Director of the Centre for Chinese Classical Learning, CUHK

Distinguished Leaders,
Ladies and Gentlemen,

Good morning,

Today, I am speaking on behalf of Mr. Fung Sun Kwan, who established the

Fung Sun Kwan Chinese Arts Foundation with his wife in 2008. Mr. Fung is an entrepreneur, yet extremely interested in traditional Chinese culture. Most of his wealth goes to this area. He has kept a low profile, so many good deeds he has done have only come to light in the last two years.

In 2018, Mr. Fung donated 150 million yuan at the Great Hall of the People, which was mainly divided into two portions, with one portion goes to the MOE's Center of Curriculum for Basic Education and the other goes to Peking University, Tsinghua University and Beijing Normal University.

Why is that? Unlike many foundations, we will discuss the cost of the project in detail with the donee after donations. This means that we will be involved in the implementation of the project, for example, by attending internal meetings of MOE or the three universities.

This is not a lack of trust in the funded entities, but rather a belief that we should assist with the project.

So what kind of traditional Chinese cultures we are sponsoring?

What is traditional Chinese culture?

How should the charity donations to higher education be used? We think it should be used to promote traditional Chinese culture.

What we call traditional Chinese culture is represented by Confucianism, the meaning of which is relatively fixed. We often talk about building cultural confidence. However, if we don't understand our own culture and doctrines, then there is no way to talk about self-confidence. So, when we promote traditional Chinese culture, we pay special attention to the development in this area.

Our traditional culture has suffered a serious blow for more than a century. With radical changes in society, education and politics, the transmission of traditional culture has come to an abrupt halt. Without concrete measures, cultural self-confidence is just a slogan. We are economically richer and politically more powerful, yet our culture and our spirit are in the doldrums.

150 million yuan is not that much. As it is donated to formal schools, how should we achieve our goal with this money?

There are two approaches.

The first is the bottom-up approach.

In this case, the "bottom" refers to all levels of basic education institutions, including kindergarten, primary school and secondary school. MOE's Center of Curriculum for Basic Education will make sure that traditional culture should be incorporated into textbooks and be taught in class in the basic education level. This is the most effective practice.

The second is the "top-down" approach.

The "top" refers to universities, who after receiving our donation will try their best to meet our requirements. I myself teach Chinese at a university, so we know how to work with the sponsored university to promote this project. We have two types of funding for universities; one is for students while the other is for teachers to support their research in traditional Chinese cultures.

The above two approaches may not guarantee 100% effectiveness, but it will certainly make a difference. As there is a gap in the talent pool in traditional Chinese culture, we need to train our students as soon as possible. We hope to start with basic education so that our students will have a genuine love and support for traditional Chinese culture. We also hope that companies will play a leading role in funding the training of more experts and masters.

Finally, I have one more point to make. Our donations do not have wide coverage, but we are involved in every project we sponsored and have devoted a lot of time. We could have stayed out of it because the grantee would also do a good job without our participation. So why did we get involved? It is out of a sense of duty to the country and the nation. Since we want to promote the development of traditional Chinese culture, we have to do our part.

In recent months, we have also sponsored Hunan University's Yuelu Academy, as it is quite different from other universities. This time, they intend to train another 100 students. Instead of getting involved in multiple fields, our fund focuses only on supporting traditional Chinese culture, intending to make our nation truly culturally confident. We believe a great country with great music and rituals will be about to reappear in our time. We hope that other foundation leaders here can refer to our practice and support our traditional Chinese culture.

In the 1980s, I was studying Chinese in college. At that time, people asked me why I didn't study law, because they all looked down upon the major of Chinese and thought there was no future in it. Moreover, the Faculty of Arts seldom received donations. We now appeal to the heads of the foundations present here to support traditional culture as much as you can, so that our country can train more cultural talent sooner. That's all for my presentation. Thank you.

Huang Yu: Now it's time for roundtable discussions. It will be held by Mr. Wang Zhenmin, Professor of Tsinghua University School of Law, Secretary-General of TUEF. Speakers for this session include: Mr. Liang Hui, General Manager of Guangzhou Dongpu Concrete Co., Ltd., Ms. Fang Tao, Member of Shenzhen Municipal Standing Committee of CPPCC, Vice President and

Secretary-General of Shenzhen Charity Federation, Mr. Liu Xun, Chairman of Shenzhen New Top-Funder Investment Management Co., Ltd., Mr. Shen Liyong, Secretary-General of ZUEF Ms. Yuan Wei, Secretary-General of TUEF, Ms. Tu Ronghui, Secretary-General of SUSTech Education Foundation, and Ms. Zhao Wenli, Deputy Secretary-General of PKUEF.

Wang Zhenmin: This roundtable session is attended by representatives from government charities, entrepreneurs and university foundations, who will discuss the themes of corporate, government, social and university donations. We often tell our children, "Don't eat unhygienic food when you go out, it's not good for your stomach", but few parents would say, "Don't learn something bad when you go out". In fact, this could be more serious because if you learn something bad, it's not good for your mind. This is where the importance of education lies.

Whether it's government, business or universities, our common mission is how to teach our next generation.

Today we are honoured to have seven distinguished representatives to share their experiences with you. We would first like to invite Ms. Fang Tao, Member of Shenzhen Municipal Standing Committee of CPPCC, Vice President and Secretary-General of Shenzhen Charity Federation, to share with us.

Fang Tao: Thank you very much for hosting such a wonderful forum which gives me a precious opportunity to learn from others. I would like to make a few points. One is that, as I understand it, the size of China's annual endowment fund has reached 130 billion yuan, with education donations accounting for about 30% of it every year, which over the years has continued to maintain a leading position in domestic donations. Why do so many people donate to education? Because education is the most fundamental sector where philanthropy should pay attention to. Now, poverty alleviation in education is currently the number one priority for our country.

The top 100 Chinese philanthropists for 2018 released by Forbes roughly donated a total of 15.7 billion yuan, with 50% going into the education sector. Among them, the Guangdong region accounted for 47%.

In China, education is really an important destination for donations. It is also something that entrepreneurs are particularly willing to do.

Based on my observations, there are several aspects of university education that I propose to discuss with you.

1.Science vs. Liberal Arts.

Why do so many educational donations favour science? In university education, in the short term, scientific knowledge can be more timely applied in commercial production and more closely integrated with quality business disciplines and the core competitiveness of the front end of the industry. However, we also have to think in the long run. What is the significance of university to the country, the nation and even the world? What is the significance of values and humanism? This is a short-term vs long-term choice.

2. Head vs Tail Institutions.

Those fortunate enough to be here today includes university alumni as well as major donors from Chinese economic sector. In giving back to the community, the head effect drives people to seek out top universities for strong collaborations. But what about a large number of tail institutions? How could we strike a balance between serving individuals and serving institutions, while meeting certain criteria? How to focus the foundation's limited manpower and time on quality customized services on a case-by-case basis. Currently, this may be quite challenging.

3. The Boundary of Philanthropy and Business

Of our current giving to universities, how much endowments are without any potential intentions? How do you balance the needs of the donee with the demands of the donor? It also has something to do with boundary identification.

These are all questions that you need to think about during donations. In my personal opinion, you first need to determine the positioning of the university foundation. Are you attached to the administration of the university, or do you want to truly respond to the needs of donors and help them grow, or do you want to respond to national or world values? Different needs will lead to different functions of the foundation.

I believe that China's total donations and the proportion of education donations will continue to grow. I also look forward to more social forces donating to universities.

Wang Zhenmin: One of the characteristics of Chinese universities in recent years is that alumni donate more than non-alumni. Today we have two Tsinghua alumni who are also very successful entrepreneurs and have made a lot of contributions. The first one is Mr. Liang Hui, the founder of Guangzhou Dongpu Concrete Co., Ltd., which is a premier concrete company in Guangdong province. In recent years, he and his wife have made many donations together. Let's welcome Mr. Liang Hui to share with us.

Liang Hui: Thank you. Yesterday I attended the opening ceremony of the fourth WPF. As I remember, the first and second WPF was held in Beijing and Shanghai respectively. This time, it is Shenzhen.

In this respect, our country's philanthropy can be said to have started very late. But even so, embarking on a new journey of philanthropy in this era when China is gaining momentum could promise us a bright future. Against this backdrop, donations to higher education institutions are of great significance. We should seize this opportunity and devote ourselves to it wholeheartedly.

I have a question for Ms. Fang. You mentioned that now 30% of our annual donations go to the education sector. How does it compare with that of developed countries?

Fang Tao: China's annual social giving is between 130 billion and 140 billion yuan. In 2018, the number is slightly less. In the U.S., education donation accounts for 24% of the total amount, which is $400 billion. So it is much larger than us in absolute terms. We can't help thinking now that China's GDP is already the second-largest in the world, and the number of ultra-high nets worth individuals in China is at the top, how come our amount of donations is only 1/24th of that of the U.S.? Calculated as a percentage of GDP, the China-U.S. ratio is 0.18% to 2.1%, and there is a large gap between absolute values.

Liang Hui: It's also a learning opportunity for me to be here. After attending this conference yesterday, I did some thinking on charity and giving, and drew a conclusion that it is first a spiritual pursuit.

The Chinese nation has a long history of spiritual civilization, among which charity is one of our long-cherished virtues. The systematic promotion of this virtue could not be possible without the development of society and the country.

Large scale philanthropy is unlikely in economically backward situations. But when material civilization evolves to a certain degree where there is no need to worry about survival, people would have a loftier spiritual pursuit, and ultimately develop the virtue of charity.

In my case, for example, after I graduated from college, all I thought about was that it would be amazing for me to make a million yuan in my lifetime, and I had no other thoughts at all. But after working hard on my own and constantly taking opportunities to reach my goal, I would gradually think about some deeper issues. This is a very normal process for most people.

The country is still in a period of rapid development. I am very optimistic about Shenzhen and the future of China. This is a great opportunity to vigorously promote philanthropy, especially in terms of higher education donations. What I want to say is that I am very optimistic about China's development in the next 50 years, I hope that everyone here can work together to drive charity and higher education donations to a higher level.

Thank you.

Wang Zhenmin: Now, let's welcome Mr. Liu Xun, Chairman and Chief Investment Officer of Shenzhen New Top-Funder Investment Management Co., Ltd., to share with us.

Liu Xun: I started my investment company in 1997 with a few classmates. It's been over 20 years now. It is generally believed that the most critical factor in investing is money, but in my opinion, the key is people instead of money.

I have witnessed the failure of many businesses that were started at the same time as ours due to various problems in their operation, despite that they have accumulated a lot of wealth. These cases made me think. Then I came across someone who not only gave us some money to invest for him, but also spent 5 million yuan to aid students in 2014. From then on, I realized that what really matters is how people make use of money. People are the key.

We have been funding students along with Ms. Zhao for about 15 years with 2000 recipients each year. Our original intention is to provide timely help to high school students in China, who was at that time struggling to meet basic needs. Take students in Gansu province, for example. They only have 1 yuan to spend on meals every day. That's the reason we decided to provide financial aid to these high school students. After so many years, we find there is a certain limit in this approach. On the one hand, the government has been increasing subsidies. On the other hand, it's hard to find supporters.

We visited the schools twice each year to talk with students. Given the tremendous academic pressure, such kind of communication was not that helpful. Then we found out that collaborating with universities is a more meaningful way to support students. University students are less stressed. They have more spare time, allowing them to cultivate their values and accumulate social experiences.

There are two advantages to support university students:

First of all, the university is a place where great teachers to be found. Almost in every university, there would be several respectable teachers whose spirit is worthy of promotion.

Secondly, each year there will be new students entering universities. This is an ongoing process.

Because of these two advantages, we would continue our efforts. Our financial support is classified into two categories: the construction of infrastructure and opportunity for social practice. We want them to engage with society, which we believe is the real testbed for their aspirations. We hope that students will find their beliefs during their course of serving society and help us build a better country.

Thank you.

Wang Zhenmin: The following four speakers come from four famous universities in China. The first one is Mr. Shen Liyong, Secretary-General of ZUEF. Welcome.

Shen Liyong: Thank you, Mr. Wang. I would like to thank TUEF to give me this precious opportunity. I have learned a lot from yesterday to now. It's my honour to share my thoughts with you.

My work has always been dealing directly with students. After graduating from Zhejiang University, I worked as a tutor for students and later as the secretary of the Youth League Committee. Over the years, I am proud of the fact that I have been taking outstanding students to attend teaching programs in the mountain areas every year for more than a decade. I used to be the county head in charge of education for a small county only a few hundred kilometres from Burma, Vietnam and Laos. I totally agree with what you have said. There are too many children in the Chinese mainland who need our help, and our small efforts may be able to change their future.

I now mainly work with the Alumni Association and the ZUEF. I believe that in order to be sustainable, it's important that our alumni, entrepreneurs, and many potential future donors must not just negotiate how much money to donate, but recognize the value of the donation.

As for the positioning of the university, cultivating talent and technological innovation definitely come first, and then there is the cultural heritage. In this respect, I totally agree with what you said about supporting traditional Chinese culture. We have a splendid culture for 5,000 years. We have the responsibility to pass it on. For culture transmission, talent is the key. Universities are where such talent come from. All of our attention, investment and philanthropy efforts in the education sector are the right choice to make.

Over the years, in the process of cultivating talent, we have found that there are many ways of donating to the university, including support for poor students, exchange students, buildings, and academic disciplines, which are all efforts supporting education, human development, and academic advancement.

Culture is what sustains the development of our nation. Cultural continuity is our common goal and belief. I have travelled dozens of times in 2019 and met all kinds of alumni and entrepreneurs, all of whom are very kind after achieving a certain level of success. From the perspective of top design, I think the laws and regulations for philanthropy work in China is not robust enough, and there are also problems with policy implementation.

Everything boils down to culture issues. We have donated a large share of our money into culture heritage. When reporting to the Secretary of the Party Committee and the president of our university, I pointed out that, our biggest shortcoming was not the number of high-quality papers, academic impacts or research funds, which have been progressed rapidly, rather, it was the relative homogeneity of educational funding.

In 2018 Zhejiang University's annual expenditures amounted to 12.5 billion yuan, most of which came from state grants, etc. The amount of donations we received was minimal. In contrast, Harvard's annual receipts far exceeded our annual expenditures. The good news is that as of July 2019, we have received more than 3 billion yuan in total annual gifts, but there is still a huge gap between Tsinghua University and us. We need to identify our shortcomings so that we could enhance our situation.

Wang Zhenmin: The second speaker is Ms. Tu Ronghui, Secretary-General of SUSTech Education Foundation. Welcome.

Tu Ronghui: I would like to thank the co-organizers of this forum, including the Tsinghua University to host this year's WPF in Shenzhen so that we all have the opportunity to be here. Thank you.

As the moderator mentioned, SUSTech is a young university established only 8 years ago. Compared with Tsinghua University, Peking University and Zhejiang University, we have relatively little experience. However, we are still benefiting from the advancement of this era, from philanthropy beliefs nurtured by Shenzhen Entrepreneurs. Though philanthropy is just taking off in China, Shenzhen is an area where it has achieved rapid progress.

One of our donors once said how desperate the city of Shenzhen was for a top-notch university to provide technical support for its development. Some people refer to Shenzhen as the Silicon Valley of China. The support of Stanford University in San Francisco for that city is deemed as an example and model for us to follow. In 2011, The Shenzhen Municipal Government invited the world's leading universities, including HKUST, to participate in the preparations for the establishment of SUSTech. With the mayor of Shenzhen serving as the chairman of the school's board of trustees, and the leadership of city government serving as board members, SUSTech has undergone rapid development, which has laid a solid foundation for the development of our Education Foundation.

I am new to this sector and have learned a lot from the practice of other philanthropy organizations in Tsinghua University, Peking University and Zhejiang University. SUSTech is also a public, innovative university with the mission of promoting education reform. Our money also comes from government grants. Running a university could be extremely costly, and we have to ensure every penny goes to where it should be. The university must rely on the power of the foundation to innovate and achieve diversified development. Our foundation is mainly to support and expedite the innovative development of SUSTech. So we mainly focus on some special needs that could not be met with public funding.

Fundraising is one aspect, but more importantly, there is a need to raise social awareness, which is the only way to really turn our often-talked about virtue into actual support. I think how the money is used the most important thing. Yesterday I discussed with Ms. Zhao from Peking University how to use the money to support outstanding poor students, as the Guoqiang Foundation talked about, so that they can have the same opportunity, because it's not easy for them to get to where they are today. Moreover, we need to make sure that our talent could develop in a balanced way, and that's the direction of our future efforts.

SUSTech's enrollment is open to 22 provinces, autonomous regions and municipalities across the country. Some of our students are very poor. When they come into SUSTech, they are connecting their future with the development of the world's leading science and technology institution. Though our students may not be as good as those from Peking University and Tsinghua University, they are working equally hard, which makes us particularly touched. Ninety percent of our teachers are from outside of the Chinese mainland. They totally embrace the idea of donation, which offers great support to our development.

Small and weak as we are now, we are ready to learn from all of you. One of our donors said that when he first came to Shenzhen, there were only hundreds of yuan in his pocket. Now, he is the donor of our entrepreneur training program, and our stadium. According to him, donating to SUSTech is the best way to give back to Shenzhen.

Thank you.

Wang Zhenmin: Now, let's welcome Ms. Yuan Wei, Secretary-General of the TUEF, to share with us.

Yuan Wei: Thank you, Mr. Wang. This is my second time to join the WPF. I came to TUEF only a year ago, which makes me a newcomer in the philanthropy sector. Before that, I am a marketing professional.

In the past year, I have gained a lot. I have deeply felt the important role and significance of philanthropy to the development of the entire national education, including the country's scientific and technological competitiveness, the training of outstanding talent and the establishment of values.

The theme of today's session is philanthropy and fundraising in higher education, which I have been thinking about for the past year. What's more, my parents are also university teachers. So, when I first joined the TUEF, I couldn't help wondering why Tsinghua University is still lack of money, as I had the impression that it is a well-funded university.

As far as I know, compared with other higher education institutions, Tsinghua University is abundant with monetary support including financial allocation from the government and other funds. Is it probably the most subsidized university in China? How come we still need more money?

However, upon taking the job last summer, I started my research on its financial status. Now, two summers have passed, I became to realize that money is among the most needed stuff for Tsinghua University and alike. We've heard just now that the annual expense for Zhejiang University last year was more than 10 billion yuan. I am going to tell you that Tsinghua University spends even more. Yet only 30% of our expenditures comes from the financial allocation, the rest of it all relying on fundraising, including seeking support from companies and government. In contrast, for higher education in developed countries, an increasing percentage of money comes from donations.

Donations are for free. For a university to play an important role in the international arena or the country, it should stand in the leading position, in discipline development, talent cultivation, or the vision for the future development of human civilization. These goals usually could not be achieved through financial allocation or collaboration with companies.

Since we joined the TUEF, it has gained high attention from the university leadership. We have drafted a reform scheme with a "three-step" plan for our future development.

As the speakers just discussed—how to raise funds, how to use the funds raised to support the development of the university, how to promote the interaction between the donor and the university, how to maintain the donated resources and how to serve the donor better—these are all areas of work of the TUEF. In fact, the donor and the university could realize mutual achievement, mutual promotion and common development.

I often think of this question: Who is happier? The donor or the donee? My youngest son is still very little. One day I asked his opinion, he said that the donor was happier. I asked him why. He quoted the saying that "The roses in her hand, the flavour in mine."

My older son has a different view. He thinks the donor is just as happy as the donee, because the donor could achieve his dream through donating, while the done could concentrate on exploring his speciality.

During our development, we have realized that it's important to cater for the needs of the university and try to use the donations in more front-line oriented and innovative areas. However, despite the no-compensation nature of donations, donors may have different requirements on how to use the funds, for example, to have some direct or indirect connections with the development of their businesses.

This year marks the 25th anniversary of TUEF. For the past 25 years, our use of donations could be reduced to five strategies.

Firstly, we use donations to attract and retain teachers.

We would like to attract top teachers from around the world. As we know, teachers' salary in Tsinghua University mainly comes from the financial allocation, completely incomparable to the business world, making it difficult to retain them, for example, our top professors in Artificial Intelligence. So we hire those elite professors who have taken positions in the business world as well as some fellows of the academy as Chair Professorship or Endowed Professor. We also use donations to support young teachers.

Secondly, we use donations to support our students.

Such funds could be further classified into many categories, such as scholarship for top students, and "Yinghua Scholars" program, through which, we would pick the top sophomore students to study in Oxford University in the U.K. for a year. The entire expenditure for one student is about 400,000 to 500,000 yuan, all funded by the scholarship. During the undergraduate years, 40% of students have the opportunity to go abroad for exchanges. We have also set up scholarships and bursaries for all economically disadvantaged students from poverty-stricken areas. We hope that these students could have the same opportunities to go abroad and engage in other activities just as other students. So we have various levels of scholarship. We hope that 60%~70% of our undergraduates could have the opportunity to go abroad. The ratio for our masters and doctors has reached 70%. We expect it to be 100%.

Thirdly, we use the donations for R&D.

In the past, our R&D has focused on new materials, the environment, and artificial intelligence. However, now we hope to expand our research, especially those funded by donations, to include basic liberal arts, basic science, and think tank research, as well as frontier areas such as research on the human brain, astronomy, civilization in outer space, and more practical areas such as fuel cells and chips.

Fourthly, we will help increase the donor's brand awareness.

Traditionally, buildings or operations will be named after the donor. Now, we have a full set of products and rules for naming. For example, in constructing a building, what is the threshold for the building to name after a certain donor, and how is it going to be displayed.

Fifthly, we use the donations for philanthropy.

We mainly carry out community-oriented philanthropic activities.

Apart from the five strategies, we have also initiated fundraising programs, where we turn them into products and recommend the products to donors. In this way, they could choose something customized for their needs. This is actually a common practice in the world. Now, we have launched a fundraising program called "A Better Tsinghua".

It seems that many donors are trying to interact with us. During donations, we will also make sure to offer a complete set of services.

The entire workflow of the TUEF could be divided into three parts: fundraising, spending and investing. Now the percentage of working capitals has risen to more than half of the total funds. In this sense, China's emerging education foundation sector is gradually taking shape.

We are also exploring the whole strategic model and method of asset management. Our education foundation is not a department of the university, but ecology and an industry. We believe that the future development of the education foundation can play an important role in China's higher education, not only supporting the development of universities, but also creating a culture of giving in the whole society.

We are also happy to work closely with our fellow foundations, donors, businesses and parties for further discussions. Thank you.

Wang Zhenmin: Thanks for the presentation of Ms. Yuan Wei. Speaking of fundraising, Ms. Zhao Wenli has been worked with PKUEF, responsible for the fundraising of Peking University from 1998. She is an expert on this. We are looking forward to your presentation, Ms. Zhao.

Zhao Wenli: Dear guests, good morning.

I am very glad to join such a grand event and discuss the development model of university foundations in China. Just as what Mr. Wang has said, my career in the foundation sector may be longer than any of the above speakers. PKUEF was founded in 1995, and I joined it in October 1998 after the 100th anniversary of Peking University. I can say that I have personally witnessed and participated in the growth and changes of PKUEF over the past 20 years.

I would like to take this opportunity to share my experience with you. My presentation consists of two parts. First, I will talk about the biggest change in university foundations in the last 20 years, with PKUEF as an example. Secondly, I will talk about how to enrich resources and raise funds, as fundraising has always been a headache for university foundations.

First of all, I would like to talk about the changes in China's university foundations.

From my personal experience, the biggest change is that over the past 20 years, China's university foundations have ushered in a period of vigorous development thanks to the rapid development of China's economy and philanthropy sector. The governance capacity and fundraising level of our university foundations have been significantly improved.

To begin with, let's review the history of China's university foundations. At the end of 1994, Tsinghua University registered its foundation, the first university founded in China, followed by PKUEF in early 1995. The establishment of these two foundations marked the beginning of the establishment of university foundations in China after the reform and opening up.

As of this year, the vast majority of Project 985 and Project 211 universities and double first-class universities have their foundations. The only exception to Project 985 universities in the National University of Defense Technology in Changsha. And among the list of double first-class universities, Yunnan University is the only university that does not have a foundation. This year, a professor from Peking University will be its vice president. It's an honour for us, of course. I told him that it would be a great contribution if he could set up an education foundation for Yunnan University.

As the number of foundations increases, there have been significant changes in the governance capacity and funding levels of universities, which are mainly reflected in the following aspects:

1. In terms of enriching resources, we have gradually shifted from passively accepting what the donors had to offer, to actively seeking funds from donors to cater to the needs of the university.

Back in 1998, the Peking University Education Foundation hit its peak of growth, and we received an unprecedented amount of donations. Some of the iconic buildings of Peking University were built at that time. We barely had any idea of active fundraising and did not have a clue as to how to raise funds. After I joined the Foundation in October 1998, the university invited fundraising experts from home and abroad to instruct us. I remember the most frequently asked question during the training was "What's the daily work of the foundation?". That was because after the centennial celebrations in 1998, and there was not too much work to do for the foundation. More importantly, we didn't know what to do.

But now, things have been totally different. I participated in a big fundraising project before taking the leading role in 2014. We have so many things to do every day. This is a very impressive transition for me.

2. In terms of specific fundraising strategies and methods, we are also shifting from single, sporadic campaigns to large-scale, organized operations and maintenance. In light of Peking University's 120th-anniversary ceremony last year, this shift has become a trend.

3. The forms of donations to universities become more diversified.

Compared to the original single form, donations are now available not only in cash, but also in real estates, stocks, and legacy.

So what are the results of these three changes? I would like to put it in one sentence: University foundations are beginning to provide more comprehensive support for the university. Although the support provided by foundations is really insignificant compared to our annual budget of tens of billions of RMB, it is on an upward trend, which I wish all of you could see.

That being said, our foundation has actually played a crucial role in specific projects or areas.

As Mr. Wang has said, professors often feel embarrassed to "ask for money". This is what I am going to talk about in the second part of my speech. Actually, I think there is nothing to be embarrassed about. The most important thing for fundraising in universities is to know the intention of the donors. The motivation for a donor to support higher education could be totally different from his or her donation to primary schools or secondary schools.

For example, Project Hope is intended to help those children who could not afford to study. This kind of donation is to help those in urgent needs. But it is not the case in donations to higher education. You don't have to be very poor to get a donation. Many university presidents at home and abroad have made profound statements on this. Let me give you two examples.

We all know that MIT is a very good university in the United States with a very strong fundraising capability. At a fundraising gala, their president said something like, and this institute will never go backwards. Instead, it is a national treasure now and will become an even more precious one. I'm calling all of you to donate to us, because your donations will put the entire American industry on a stronger foundation of scientific research.

There was also a university president in Hong Kong who made it even clearer when he said that university fundraising is not about begging for money and telling people how poor they are to get sympathy, but about showing your strength and telling the community that what tomorrow's society needs is what we do today.

I think, in that sense, the contribution to higher education is like reinforcing its strength. It focuses on the mission of higher education, human resource development, scientific research, cultural heritage and innovation. The better we do, the more likely we are preferred by our donors.

The relationship between a university and an entrepreneur is never just a relationship between a recipient and a giver. It's more like both parties working together to accomplish something with a common purpose. We appreciate the donor's gift, and because of that, we must use that money to fulfil their wishes better and demonstrate the value of such donations.

That's all for my presentation.

Wang Zhenmin: Thank you. Ms. Zhao.

The ideas and practices that you have just shared are very inspiring. I have been involved in donor management since 1994, and I have heard many stories and witnessed many events.

In 2001, I went to a university in Texas, the United States, where I attended an endowment curtain call at their law school. I heard the donor begin his speech by saying, "I want to thank my alma mater for reminding me many times to donate." It tells us that everyone is busy at work. If they didn't donate, it was likely not for lack of money, but because the school didn't come to him.

Back then, the Dean of the Lee Kuan Yew School of Public Policy at the University of Singapore approached Mr. Lee Kuan Yew and said that since the school was named after him, it would be kind if he could help with fundraising. Mr. Lee Kuan Yew asked the Dean, "Who is your targeted donor? The dean said he wanted to see Sir Ka-Shing Li. So, Lee Kuan Yew said he would write a letter, not mentioning the amount of money, but introducing the dean to him. The Dean needs to talk to Sir Ka-Shing Li in person about the amount of the donation. The Dean later visited Sir Li Ka-Shing, with Lee Kuan Yew's letter. Sir Li Ka-Shing read the letter and asked how much money did the Dean need. After careful consideration, he finally put forward the idea of raising 500 million yuan. To his surprise, Sir Li Ka-Shing signed the donation agreement on the spot.

I think today's discussion is very meaningful. In summary, we have reached three consensuses:

First, after 40 years of economic and social development in China, there is indeed a huge accumulation of wealth in society. The society's donation is not commensurate with the current status of China's economy in the world. The total annual donations in the United States reached 400 billion U.S. dollars, but our target need not be so high. We can set it at 400 billion yuan, or 300 billion yuan. Given that entrepreneurs have just expressed their willingness to donate, we can say that the potential is enormous.

Second, the market for university endowments is huge, so do its potential and demand. Working in universities, we do feel that state funding is just enough to keep the basics running. Universities cannot grow and make outstanding contributions in a particular field without donations from the community. The society has high expectations for universities, which takes a lot of money to accomplish. With the trend of a balanced education in China, state funding for some top universities won't be much higher than that of others.

Third, there is a lack of communication between corporate donors and universities. From my several years' work experience in Hong Kong, people there are doing much better.

Today's discussion bears a significant meaning as it has established such a communication platform between the two parties. We look forward to more opportunities to connect with you in the future. Thank you!

That's all for this breakout session. Thank you!

X FUTURE VISIONS FOR CHILDREN'S WELLBEING

Moderator: Liu Qinglong, Member of the Academic Committee of the WPF and Dean, Professor of the School of Public Policy and Management, Tsinghua University

Dr. Douglas Noble, Deputy Representative of the UNICEF China Office

Guest Speech: Wang Lin, Chairman and Secretary-General of the China Charities Aid Foundation for Children (CCAFC)

Lyu Dexiong, Executive Vice President & Secretary-General of the Chinese Society for Taoxingzhi Studies

Speakers: Guo Peng, Founder and Board Member of the Beijing Sunshine All the Way Charity Foundation

Hou Chunyan, Deputy Editor-in-Chief of Ifeng.com

Fok Tai-Fai, Pro-Vice-Chancellor of the CUHK
Huang Wenfeng, Secretary-General of the Shenzhen Women and Children's Development Foundation
Sebastien Kuster, Chief Operating Officer of Save the Children China, Beijing Office
Wei Wei, Chairman of the Dingkun Education Group
Li Hongyan, Educational Consultant of the UNESCO
Peter Williams, President of the International Institute of Rural Reconstruction (IIRR)
Michelle Siu Hoi Yan, Michelle, Pianist, Integrated Education Advocator

Liu Qinglong: Good morning, everyone. Our theme for this breakout session is "Future Visions for Children's Wellbeing". The development, health, and welfare of children are all matters of great concern to society, and many institutes have very rich experience in this area. I believe this is an excellent opportunity for everyone to exchange and share experience, to promote the development of children's health.

First of all, please allow me to introduce the two speakers: Wang Lin, Chairman and Secretary-General of CCAFC; and Lyu Dexiong, Executive Vice President & Secretary-General of Chinese Society for Taoxingzhi Studies.

First of all, please welcome Mr. Wang Lin to give us a keynote speech.

Exploration of Children's Serious Illness Relief

Wang Lin, Chairman and Secretary-General of the CCAFC

Distinguished guests, first of all, thank you for taking the time to listen to my report. The topic of my speech today is *Exploration of Children's Major Illness Relief*.

I'd like to share with you today from four aspects: 1. who are we; 2. our exploration; 3. our discovery; and 4. our outlook.

Part I: Who are we?

We are a young and national public-raising foundation established on January 12, 2010, and has been operating for more than 9 years.

As a national public-raising foundation, our main targets of assistance are needy children under the age of 18, now has expanded to cover college students. Our assistance is intended to provide support at five levels: to meet their basic living needs, offer necessary medical treatment, promote their psychological health, teach them skills and help them grow.

As a foundation that mainly provides monetary assistance, we have established the philosophy to cooperate with private organizations and run with full transparency. In the past 9 years, we have raised 2.3 billion yuan, and assisted more than 5 million children from 32 provinces, autonomous regions and municipalities.

Why do we value private organizations? Actually, we are a national public-raising foundation reporting to the Ministry of Civil Affairs. However, instead of being labelled as a public institution, we prefer to integrate with private sectors, and fund more NGOs to join us on the road of philanthropy. We have funded about 300 NGOs in total, and there is no hierarchical management structure because we regard them as our partners.

Full transparency refers to the openness and transparency of the foundation's finances. Since the first day of the foundation, every donation has been publicized on the official website, and the flow of money will be announced once a month.

This is the fundraising situation of our foundation from 2010 to 2018.

Our annual fundraising capability continues to rise, from 50 million yuan in 2010 when the foundation was established, to more than 300 million yuan in 2016. It even surpassed 500 million yuan in 2017 and 2018, and is expected to reach 600 million yuan in 2019.

We are a foundation mainly funded by public donations. As we were established not long ago, as far as I can recall, only one or two state-owned enterprises have donated to us with little amount. More of our donations have come from the public, which in particular accounted for 79% in 2015, 69% in 2017, and 65% in 2018. So far, in 2019, we have raised 330 million yuan, 81% of which was donated by individuals. In 2017, individual donations reached 400 million yuan. Online donations were not included at that time, which reached 360 million yuan at the peak, accounting for about 65% as of now.

Part II: Our Exploration.

Ever since its establishment, the foundation started to provide comprehensive assistance to children at five levels: to meet their basic living needs, offer necessary medical treatment, promote their psychological health, teach them skills and help them grow. Among them, Medical assistance takes up a large proportion. Today, I would like to take one of the independent projects named "9958" as an example to introduce in detail how we explored in the field of medical assistance. This independent project known as the "911" for children with serious illnesses in

China, was established as soon as the foundation was founded. It mainly aimed at providing emergency assistance for children with serious illnesses.

In 2010, we allocated 1 million yuan to set up the "Emergency Assistance Channel for Children". In 2011, we set up a free national assistance helpline of 4000069958, and "9958" is a homophone for "help me" (Jiu Jiu Wo Ba). The helpline is available around the clock.

In 2012, "9958" successively opened assistance stations in Xi'an, Shanghai, Shenyang, Chengdu and Chongqing, and established cooperative relationships with 10 local executive teams. In 2013, "9958" established the largest children's emergency assistance platform in China, and set up centres in six provincial-level cities across the country, covering 32 provinces, autonomous regions and municipalities.

In 2014, the emergency assistance channel was officially renamed as "9958 Assistance Center", and a total of 15,213 calls were answered throughout the year, assisting more than 1,100 children with serious illnesses.

In 2015, the accumulated fundraised exceeded 100 million yuan, and 34,520 helplines were answered throughout the year, and we were awarded with "the 9th China Charity Award".

In 2016, our cooperation resources continued to increase and channels continued to expand: there were 98 cooperative medical expert consultants and 125 cooperative hospitals, and 34 special funds for assistance and 25 assistance stations nationwide were established.

The amount of fundraising and helpline answered in 2017 was greatly increased: the accumulated funds raised reached 188 million yuan, which was an increase of 116.8% compared to that of 2016, and the total amount of helpline answered was nearly 40,000.

In 2018, the entire accumulated fundraising of the "9958" exceeded 500 million yuan, the number of donators reached 30 million, and the number of people receiving assistance exceeded 21,000.

So far, the accumulated fundraising has exceeded 600 million yuan, and fundraising of this year is expected to exceed 200 million yuan. This is the growth process of "9958" in recent years. It has received wide recognition among the parents.

I once received a couple from the rural area of Hubei Province. Their newborn was only about 0.5 kilogram in weight, showing nearly no sign of life. Luckily, when the parents were burying the baby in the nearby hill, they caught a faint cry. The baby was still alive. So the couple took him back home. Yet, given to their poor economic conditions, there was little they could do about it, so they called the "9958" helpline, who immediately started the emergency mechanism to raise funds for the baby and contacted a hospital to provide treatment. The great news is that the child has grown up to be three or four years old now.

This is just one such example, which is particularly impressive because of my participation. The reason for The platform 9958 to develop rapidly, be well received by society, and raise more than 200 million yuan a year, is that it cares for people.

As of June 2019, there are a total of more than 200 projects, including 76 special funds, 73 cooperative projects and 7 independent projects. The number of medical assistance projects accounts for only 21% of the foundation, but the total fundraising accounts for 50% of that of the foundation. The percentage also holds true if calculated against the annual fundraising of 500 million yuan per year in the previous two years

The assistance covers a wide range of illnesses. Up to now, there are nearly 30 medical assistance projects launched by CCAFC, covering most of the serious illnesses of children. The platform 9958 mainly deals with the assistance for blood diseases, malignant tumours, severe cerebral palsy, digestive malformation of children, complex congenital heart disease, and cranial nerve malformation, etc.

"Loving Home" (www.yigong.net) is for leukaemia and tumour; "Operation Smile" is for cleft lip and palate, and facial deformity; "99 Hearts" is for congenital heart disease; "Changjiang Public Welfare" is for cerebral palsy; and "Youai Longqi" is for congenital anorectal occlusion and acute liver failure, which are mainly treated by liver transplantation.

These assistance projects cover 32 provinces, autonomous regions, and municipalities in China. The projects are mainly implemented in the "three regions and three prefectures" and other key national poverty alleviation areas, such as Yunnan, Tibet, Xinjiang, Qinghai, Sichuan, Guizhou, Henan, Jilin and Guangxi.

The assistance chain is fully covered. At present, the assistance projects of CCAFC have covered the whole chain of assisting children with serious illnesses. The first thing to do is the early intervention, such as the project of "Green Shade of Life" by Children's Emergency Center, "Special Fund for Critical Illness Medical Insurance", "Special Fund for People's Friendship" and "28-day Newborn Assistance Project". However, we are more engaged in the mid-term assistance, such as "9958", "99 Hearts" Project, and the assistance project for scoliosis. We also carry out the post-rehabilitation projects, including "Angel Home" and "Little Water Drop". Since people have always been emphasizing treatment rather than rehabilitation in China, the foundation is also fragile in rehabilitation assistance.

Part III: Our Development.

In the entire medical assistance, we have found that there are many problems in the assistance for children with serious illnesses, some of which are more obvious, while others have been detected but are still more subtle.

1. There is a structural imbalance among the types of illnesses that requires assistance, the distribution of assistance resources and the demands for assistance. In fact, there is demand in the old revolutionary base areas, areas with concentrations of ethnic minorities, border areas and areas with relatively high incidences of poverty, but there are few resources for assistance, for example, in Liangshan areas of Sichuan Province, where there is no pediatric doctor. People are aware of the necessity of training a pediatric doctor, but not a single trained candidate return. As a result, there is no paediatrician in an area of more than 5 million people.

2. The assistance standards are difficult to be unified, and assistance information cannot be shared.

3. The assistance mainly take the homogenous form of medical expenses. Which means, we would simply provide funds as a public welfare organization after experts have assessed the seriously ill children. This is because we don't own medical resources. Besides, there is an extreme lack of support for psychological intervention services and research on illnesses. Generally, individual and enterprise donors are more concerned about the health condition of children, but they know little about the psychological intervention services for illnesses and research on illnesses.

4. Generally, the assistance mainly happens during the incident, and it is rare to take action prior to the incident.

5. The assistance mode is relatively simple, but the project staff is under great pressure with low pay and relatively long working hours. To assist a child, staff may have to follow from the beginning to the end, and they have to be responsible for both assistance and fundraising, which is very stressful.

6. The assistance requires that high professionalism of the project and a large amount of funds, but the effect is very uncertain.

These are some of the problems we are facing right now.

Part IV: Our Outlook.

As a social organization, we propose that the government, commercial institutions, public welfare organizations, and enterprise donors work together to help children with serious illnesses. We also hope that our work can influence government policies so that the government can make more investment. However, under the current circumstances, for the assistance of children with serious illnesses, we hope to get support from the government policy, the introduction of insurance mechanisms from commercial institutions, and later assistance from public welfare organizations and caring enterprises.

Next, I would like to introduce another project about insurance for children's serious illnesses: the Special Fund for Critical Illness Medical Insurance of CCAFC. This project has been done for many years with the vision that every child can be treated with dignity and quality. The Critical Illness Medical Insurance Project was initiated in February 2012 by well-known Chinese media and public welfare individuals in conjunction with CCAFC. It aims to undertake the national medical insurance system, and achieve medical funds and fair medical opportunities for more rural children through big data actuarial calculation, accurate calculation of premiums, and scientific supplementary medical insurance plan for serious illnesses. Its mission is to explore the possibility of children enjoying high-quality medical protection, and its goal is to provide all children from 0 to 16 years of age who have participated in or are qualified to participate in the pilot counties in China with a free cross-regional critical illness medical insurance under no limitation of illness types but a maximum annual limit of 300,000 yuan per person. Our project cycle is from guarantee plan design, commercial insurance purchasing, project implementation, effect evaluation, fundraising to research in pilot areas. With 1.86 million children in 11 counties covered by the current project, its effect is becoming apparent. Before the intervention of critical illness medical insurance, the ratio of reimbursement of national medical insurance policy and family self-pay payment was 40 to 60. Now, after entering medical insurance, the self-pay payment of an individual is 31.22%, and each family should pay 10,000 yuan at most.

At present, the accumulated fundraising for critical illness insurance has reached more than 84 million yuan, and has been piloted in 11 counties, among which Guzhang County in Hunan Province and Huailai County in Hebei Province have completed the settlement. The total amount of insured claims is 71 million yuan, and the total number of insured persons exceeds 1.86 million. The total amount of compensation has reached more than 45 million yuan, and the total number of people getting compensation has reached more than 10,000.

There are some differences in the models of the following 6 counties among the 11 pilot counties: 1. Hefeng adopts the model of tripartite collaboration, in which social organizations, insurance institutions and the government provide funds for children's insurance mainly based on the medical insurance catalogue, and the assistance is provided for illnesses outside the catalogue. 2. Badong adopts the model of government procurement, which is undertaken by both the critical illnesses insurance and the government. 3. Kaihua adopts the model of real-time settlement, which is jointly undertaken with the medical security system. 4. Xinhuang adopts the model of settling claims online and cooperating with Alipay. 5. Zhongyang adopts the model of mutual assistance in critical illnesses. 6. The Horqin Right Front Banner adopts the model of providing an allowance for major illnesses (100,000 yuan).

Finally, the founder of our foundation, who is also the former chairman of the board once said, "People in the world have different beliefs, missions and pursuits, but philanthropic assistance is the common aspiration of mankind".

We hope that our efforts can make children with serious illnesses be treated and bring hope to families that are reduced to poverty due to illness. Thank you.

Liu Qinglong: Chairman Wang Lin gave us a wonderful report, and analyzed specific cases from the macro and the mid-scale to the micro views bases on our theme, which attracted everyone's attention. Let's invite experts to the stage and discuss together on children's welfare issues of common concern.

There is indeed a rare opportunity. Just now, Chairman Wang Lin showed us the classic cases of CCAFC. In fact, he fully demonstrated the progress of their work in recent years.

There is actually a significant connection among the government, NGOs and sick children. We all know that the rapid development of the country, especially the economic take-off, is also accompanied by some social problems, including those of sick children that really need us to give full attention to from all aspects. Academic groups and social institutions have done a lot of research, and we also hope to take this opportunity to make a good sharing on such a platform.

Now, I would like to invite the Pro-Vice-Chancellor of CUHK to share with us.

Fok Tai-Fai: Thank you, moderator. Thank you, Mr. Wang, for your excellent presentation. Though I can speak Cantonese very well, I can't deliver this presentation fluently in Mandarin, so please allow me to use English.

Thank you very much for this opportunity, and I am also very grateful to Mr. Wang for his speech on CCAFC. Mr. Wang just mentioned that their foundation directly assists children. I am also a paediatrician myself, and I have also devoted myself to caring for sick children in my career.

But in the next few minutes, I will step out of the role of a direct child assistant, and talk about the assistant of children from another perspective. Because what I want to talk about is that the root cause of children's health problems is poverty.

As you all know, 17 SDGs were established at a summit of United Nations held in October 2015. These goals are to take care of children, fight poverty and guarantee health education. Among them, Article 3 is directly related to children, which is to ensure the health and wellbeing of all children and all people, and one of the main targets is children.

Let's take a look at the goal of Article 3. By 2030, the mortality of mothers and infants will have been significantly reduced, including the mortality of 5-year-old children and newborns. This is a very important goal.

If we think about the Sustainable Development Report of 2019, it is clear that we have seen big improvements in achieving this goal. In the past few years, child mortality has dropped significantly, but not globally.

Let's take a look at some poor developing countries and regions, such as the Sahara. The maternal and infant mortality rate is about 20 times that of other developed countries and regions. The neonatal mortality rate is also maintained at 75‰, sometimes reaching 100‰. This means one out of every 10 babies born will die. In Hong Kong, the neonatal mortality rate is only 1% of that in sub-Saharan regions.

Today we are discussing the topic of children's health and assistance in the Greater Bay Area. What is the relationship between the developing countries and regions I just mentioned and the Greater Bay Area? We must understand that even in an affluent society, there is still a gap between the rich and the poor. The distribution of social property is uneven, and poverty still exists.

Take the United States, the richest region in the world, as an example. In 2016, there was a report of the poverty and children's health problems in the United States, which pointed out that 21% of children under the age of 18 in the United States were in a very bad state of health, and if families that were very close to poverty or of low-income were included, this proportion would increase to 42% - 49%. That is to say, even in a country as rich as the United States, there are a lot of children growing up in low-income families, too.

The report also pointed out that this would have a negative impact on society. For example, in some countries, there is the low birth rate and high death rate of newborns, the hindrance of development of children, inability to establish their social relationships, etc., and a series of derivative problems.

The most alarming thing is that children's health problems are closely related to the poverty problem throughout their lives. In view of the impact of poverty on children's health, I think it is very important to directly assist children, which is also the most basic undertaking. It is a very important measure for both public welfare and philanthropic foundations and the government.

What the Greater Bay Area may face is not poverty, but the gap between the rich and the poor, which is worth considering. That's all for my speech.

Liu Qinglong: Thanks to Chancellor Fok. He gave us a very broad vision to talk about children's health from a global perspective. He first analyzed situations in the poverty-stricken areas and developed countries, and then returned to that of the Greater Bay Area. Especially in the children's welfare of the Greater Bay Area, Chancellor Fok pointed out that the issue of great importance is the gap between the rich and the poor. He also provided us with good ideas about how to make better policies for dealing with the reality of the gap between the rich and the poor, how to realize better-coordinated development of NGOs, and how to do a better job in the children's assistance in the Great Bay Area. Thank you, Chancellor Fok.

Next, let's welcome Mr. Guo Peng from Beijing Sunshine All the Way Charity Foundation to share with us.

Guo Peng: Just now, Chairman Wang Lin shared in his speech that assistance for children with serious illnesses mainly happens during the incident, and the proportion of intervention assistance prior to the incident or after rehabilitation is relatively small. Before the establishment of Beijing Sunshine All the Way Charity Foundation, we set up a Special Fund for Blessed Baby in cooperation with CCAFC in August 2015. In fact, we have been trying to put more energy into assistance prior to the incident through this fund.

Generally, we would cooperate with the relatively authoritative tertiary hospitals in big cities such as Beijing, Shanghai, Guangzhou and Shenzhen, and organize expert teams with their senior doctors to go to some remote, poor and underdeveloped areas, especially areas that relatively lack medical resources, to provide children with screening for serious illnesses and publicity and education on illness prevention. We hope to advance the assistance of serious illnesses and assistance during the incident to the mode of early detection and early prevention.

From August 2015 to August 2019, we have raised more than 20 million yuan. We have provided the screening for serious illnesses and the publicity and education on illness prevention to nearly 200,000 teenagers in more than 520 schools in underdeveloped areas in Qinghai, Yunnan, Hubei, Hunan, Shanxi and other cities and provinces. We have screened a total of 2,884 cases of ophthalmic disease, orthopaedic disease, scoliosis, and congenital heart disease. On the premise of fully respecting the willingness of family members, we provided low-income families with medical resources and financial support for follow-up treatment.

At the same time, the "Blessed Baby Home" was set up in Beijing and Shanghai respectively to allow them to treat their illnesses in big cities, especially when they were waiting for medical treatment or in the stage of recovery. We provided them with a temporary place to live, and effectively reduced their burden.

In the process of screening for serious illnesses, the main cost came from travelling expenses of medical teams from big cities to the local places for screening. So, we started to carry out doctor training programs, through which, we introduced medical resources into local hospitals, including experts of related illnesses to train local doctors. In this way, we have trained a lot of doctors capable for the preliminary screening process of serious illnesses, which greatly reduced the screening cost and improved the diagnosis and treatment capabilities of doctors to some extent.

In other words, since the Special Fund for Blessed Baby was established, we have been exploring the whole chain of assistance model from front-end screening to back-end resident doctors, including follow-up rehabilitation of low-income families.

Beijing Sunshine All the Way Charity Foundation, a fund different from the Special Fund for Blessed Baby, was registered and established in the Beijing Municipal Bureau of Civil Affairs on August 31, 2019. The Special Fund for Blessed Baby cooperates with the CCAFC and relies on its mechanism of public fundraising, and our donation source is fundraising on the Internet. Meanwhile, from the beginning of its preparation, the foundation has been longing for building a platform that can embody enterprise social responsibility. We hope to achieve more cross-border cooperation on this platform since enterprises and entrepreneurs have many advantages in terms of capital, technology and even connections.

As one of the initiators of the Sunshine All the Way Charity Foundation, Hua Life Insurance Co., Ltd., in addition to participating in the two projects of screening for serious illnesses and initial stage of serious illnesses, will also explore the longer-term protection for children in the poverty-stricken areas, mainly exploring insurance products of public welfare such as the medical insurance for serious illnesses. In this way, the model of poverty alleviation has been effectively maintained and the medical burden of low-income families has been reduced. At the same time, it also relies on the life science and technology enterprises for their high-tech technologies, such as gene screening technology, which will be used in the screening for serious illnesses to make it more accurate and timely.

Based on these 7 years of experience in assisting to serious illnesses, I think that children's serious illnesses require the intervention of enterprises, social organizations and the government, by providing services such as assistance, subsequent insurance, rehabilitation care, and psychological counselling care. It requires everyone to work together to explore the assistance mode for children with serious illnesses, realize the seamless connection between the government and children, and provide protection for children, especially those who are suffering from serious illnesses. Thank you.

Liu Qinglong: Thank you, Guo Peng. "Sunshine All the Way" is a great name.

Guo Peng's presentation is interrelated with that of Mr. Wang Lin. I have paid special attention to the screening of children's serious illnesses. From August 2015 to August 2019, sufficient funds have been raised to carry out a number of screening for serious illnesses for children, which has indeed advanced our assistance work to the stage of early detection and early intervention. Moreover, in early detection and early intervention, the quality and ability of the intervening person is indeed an important variable. He specifically talks about the training of doctors, screening for some illnesses, how to diagnose and treat the illnesses that can only be solved by medical resources, and how to make effective integration of social organizations with specific assistance resources for children, which do give us some good inspiration.

Now, let's welcome Ms. Hou Chunyan, Deputy Editor-in-Chief of Ifeng.com, to share with us.

Hou Chunyan: Good afternoon, distinguished guests and experts. Im glad to have this opportunity to share with you the practice and experience of Ifeng.com in philanthropy for so many years.

Just now our moderator mentioned that today's topic involves several key factors, including children with illnesses, social institutions, NGOs and the government. Today, on behalf of Ifeng.com, I will share with you about my personal idea after so many years' engagement in this industry that the media is a relatively special and important element.

Today's WPF is only exchanges among several thousand people and communication within the industry, but the media is an amplifier. We are able to disseminate advanced concepts and social concerns through the media, which will be served as an amplifier and accelerator to reach far more people beyond the audience here.

Ifeng.com, a subsidiary of Phoenix TV, is also a separate company listed on the New York Stock Exchange. Since 2007, we have attached great importance to fulfilling our enterprise social responsibility, so we set up our public welfare project of "Forever Happiness". We are neither a public welfare organization nor a public welfare institution, but a commercial company, just like other enterprises. The only difference is that we are media. In the beginning, we were wading across the river by feeling for the stones. All we could do is to set up the project first, which has been running since 2007. As an Internet company with no mature experience in this field, we relied on the power of netizens to focus on where disasters occurred and mobilized them to donate money and materials. At first, we could only participate in assistance in this way.

After several years, we gradually accumulated some experience. At that time, we held, in particular, the activities such as the paying tribute to the most respectable teachers in remote areas. What's more, we made use of the advantages of the media platform to attract people's attention and give play to everyone's role in charity and philanthropy.

It wasn't until 2011, after a period of experience and growth, that we began to think that if we could do a better job of fundraising, we could tangibly help a lot of kids.

Media is a platform that could be reaching every user, as well as the business, politics and the entertainment world. Since 2011, we have been committed to philanthropic fundraising, taking advantage of the platform effect. Up to now, we have organized 19 charity dinners and raised 200 million yuan. We have cooperated with more than 10 foundations across the country in different projects, benefiting 670,000 children in all provinces, autonomous regions and municipalities.

In 2016, we even went out to the United States and Europe. We will hold a fundraising event in Canada in September this year, and most of the money will be sent back to China to help children in need. We took our philanthropy belief abroad and brought home with us the advanced foreign experience.

In 2016, we set up the Special Charity Fund of Ifeng.com in CCAFC, and started to do the children's benefiting plan and the children's protection plan. Similar to Mr. Guo's situation, we also conducted early screening for children's serious illnesses, and also established health records with doctors in tertiary hospitals.

The children's protection plan was to help orphans with serious illnesses, and we made use of the influence of media. The celebrity Lin Chi-ling was very interested in it, so she jointly launched the sister Chi-ling Children's Protection Plan.

As a media, we are constantly exploring new ways of philanthropy. Last year's fundraising dinner in Beijing was not only about raising money, but also about raising resources, including technologies and equipment. As a result, we collected 12 hours of volunteer time and various resources in just one single night. Due to the time limit, I will briefly introduce the cross-border work done by Ifeng.com to combine everyone's strength, and allow every ordinary person to participate in philanthropy and changing the destiny of children. More details will be discussed with you in the session of dialogue. Thank you.

Liu Qinglong: Thank you, Ms. Hou, for telling us a wonderful story called "Forever Happiness". It must be a lot of work to do in assisting 670,000 children, and a great deal of love and enthusiasm to be devoted to promoting this project. Due to the limited time, she did not elaborate, but there will be a dialogue session to discuss with Ms. Hou later.

Next, please welcome Huang Wenfeng, Secretary-General of Shenzhen Women and Children's Development Foundation to share with us.

Huang Wenfeng: We are a foundation in Shenzhen that focuses on women and children. At the beginning, we considered more from the perspective of Shenzhen. However, in the area of children's medical assistance, we have developed different modes over the years, including setting up projects through fundraising, cooperating with local governments and commercial organizations, constructing charity hospitals, and the online method that has slowly emerged in recent years, among others.

Currently, medical assistance is covered by the social welfare system and supplemented by commercial insurance. If the two combined still could not meet the need of patients, social organizations, enterprises and citizens will think of a better way to step in. We are exploring to take some measures to help promote medical policies for children with illnesses and their families through resource integration.

Here's a little story about a child suffering from phenylketonuria. Upon receiving the request for help from a group of parents, I held several fundraisings online, which aimed at providing comprehensive supporting for both the children and their family.

At the same time, we used the power of the media mentioned by Ms. Hou, as well as the proposals or motions of the members of CPPCC and deputy to the NPC. Therefore, we started the project at the end of 2016 and pushed for the change of public policy in Shenzhen by raising proposals at the end of 2017. These changes are meant to support better the sick children, as well as their families as the daily expenses of this disease, are extremely high, which could not be covered in medical insurance. Therefore, in this process, we have implemented some small projects, exploring how to make then work and then promoted them in other areas.

We did discover some problems in this process, especially for the medical assistance initiated by ordinary people through public fundraising, for example. I won't go any further into this case. But how can we better prevent the problems?

Media should not only serve as an amplifier but also a microscope to oversee problems, some of which should be restrained by the power of media, while others should be disclosed.

Lack of industry-standard is another problem, especially the standard for the process of disease discovery and assistance I just mentioned. Mr. Wang did not elaborate it for lack of time, but his great effort in this filed is very inspiring for us. I hope we can share and learn from these experiences, so that we may do better. The time is up, and this is the end of my speech.

Liu Qinglong: Thank you, Secretary-General Huang. His brief speech has provided us with a lot of information. One of the important information is how social organizations influence the government's public policies, which is indeed a very important path that we need to explore. With rapid social development and numerous social problems, the government is also a very important force while social organizations play their roles. Secretary-general Huang has provided some important ideas on about how to influence the formulation of the government's public policies, so that the government and social organizations can organically combine together to make the social problems solved more efficiently, and how to consider these policies and the path of influence, including how to work with the media.

We still have a lot of topics. Let's invite Mr. Sebastian Kuster. He has a lot of topics to discuss with us, especially the goals and challenges related to children, and how this organization works with its partners to advance the issues related to the sustainable development of children's health, and he will share their experience. Next, please welcome Mr. Sebastian Kuster to give a speech to everyone.

Sebastian Kuster: Good morning, everyone. I am grateful for this opportunity to participate in this forum.

Save the Children was founded in 1919 and have more than 100 years of experience in helping children. Our organization was founded to ensure that children can survive and be protected. One of our aspirations is the United Nations Sustainable Development Goal adopted in 2015, which is to reduce or eliminate morbidity and mortality among children under five years of age. Now, of course, there's been some progress in this area both globally and in China, but there are also issues related to health and nutrition, so we hope to provide macro and overall support around the world.

In China, we are committed to solving the problem of higher mortality and morbidity for children under 5 years of age and newborns. For example, in China, we have made a lot of efforts to reduce the mortality rate of children under 5 years of age and increase the attention to maternal and child health. We have also seen that the mortality rate of children under 5 years of age has reached 15%, which is very high.

The challenge we are currently facing to achieve the development goals of the United Nations is the gap among different regions, such as the level of economic development and health care between different countries, as well as the gap between poor and rich regions. China has very remote mountainous areas, where the child mortality rate is 10 times higher than that in urban and developed areas, and it is difficult for these areas to achieve the development goals of United Nations on their own.

Moreover, some families have relatively low incomes, and some places have relatively poor infrastructure and medical care resources. What we do is to support the education of local medical staff and develop their abilities, and the training of these medical staff must follow international standards and adopt local methods. After completing the training, we will also cooperate with local hospitals and health departments to ensure that hospital staff can better cooperate with our organization, and then integrate these processes.

A core element of our work is to provide support for direct medical assistance and support community-based medical assistance. We hope to not only help children and patients directly, but also to establish contacts with patients' relatives and families, help them build a mutual-aid community, improve their health awareness, and introduce some experiences and methods about how to adapt to the local culture and context. Besides, we will provide guidance for communities and families to organize some related activities, and so on.

We carry out projects in this way and in order to ensure the long-term effect and protect the wellbeing of children, and we also support sustainable development. We are also working closely with the governments in other countries, and cooperating with the central government and the central health department to ensure sustainability. We are also experimenting with some pioneering cooperation projects in hospitals in Yunnan and Sichuan, such as the health improvement projects for newborns or young children, and the improvement projects for early lactation.

After doing these projects, we also hope to promote successful experience, implement some preventive projects, and make a national guide. This guide will provide specific rules and guidance for relevant medical staff and practitioners to implement better the processes related to maternal and child health, and to inform about relevant knowledge to other people. This guide will be issued next year. This is the case that I want to talk about, namely, how to achieve sustainable health development of children.

Liu Qinglong: I would like to thank Mr. Sebastian Kuster, who just gave a simple but very informative speech. First of all, their children's fund is called Save the Children China, Beijing Office, and their definition of children is those who are under 5 years of age. Moreover, they focus on children while implementing the assistance work, and integrate medical resources, so that they have better quality and ability to carry out assistance.

One experience that requires our special attention is that they can combine with the community and related children's families at the same time, because the children's assistance is not only an issue of medical treatment and patients, but an issue of a community and a family, and we must think about how to make them organically combined together. This work is indeed worthy of our study and reference.

We have another guest next. Let's welcome Wei Wei, Chairman of Dingkun Education Group, to share with us.

Wei Wei: In the past decade or so, since I work in this industry, I have done a lot of donation and donation management work. From the perspective of industry observations, I will share with you some of the problems I have found now, which could be used as the starting points for your further discussions.

As of the assistance of serious illnesses, the most important thing in recent years, whether in technology or service, is how we can develop a more effective way to advance from the exploration stage to the verification stage, and to the stage of final large-scale commercialization or something close to commercialization. We generally use mainstream technology to make products and plans of public fundraising, raise a lot of funds, and adopt mainstream methods, but how do we finish our work more effective and reduce costs?

The first problem, for example, for congenital heart disease, we all use the mainstreaming method on a large scale. But in fact, if there is a better method for assistance, it can greatly improve the assistance efficiency and reduce the costs once it can be applied on a large scale.

The second problem is that single assistance has relatively low cost, small risk, and controllable result. However, for those illnesses with high assistance costs, not particularly controllable results and certain risks, the available resources are relatively limited, which makes the assistance for other illnesses unable to develop in a particularly benign way.

The third problem is about targeting. Do we think that the child we assist is a poor child with illnesses, but is he the poorest? Is he the one that needs our assistance the most? Not exactly so.

Take congenital heart disease as an example. A large number of patients with congenital heart disease are diagnosed in hospitals. If the screening is not done in rural areas, we must wait for families and children to come to the hospital for treatment. With this method, it is unlikely that we screen and find out a large number of children whose families are extremely poor and cannot even afford the travelling expenses. The target for children's treatment has been moving upward because the design of our products is not for the treatment of these target children.

The fourth problem is rehabilitation. How to provide rehabilitation services for children? At present, our assistance only focuses on the treatment of illnesses, but it is very important to really pay attention to the development and the services obtained of a child after rehabilitation. Nevertheless, a large number of resources in this industry are spent on the treatment itself.

Under this circumstance, the reason for these problems is that the source of funds was less diversified. That means a large number of aid resources came from just several types of sources, showing that the demands are somewhat concentrated.

Over the years, the types of our operating funds and resource have undergone great diversification. The previous project funds mainly came from government and public fundraising, but now the enterprise funds are slowly coming in, as well as those from private investors, bank bonds and other different resources. How to solve the problems of the industry after these resources come in? For large-scale treatment, public fundraising and government resources have the most obvious advantages due to their quantity. After the family foundations came in, the tasks to do were not changed. Is there a need for more solutions on how to transform better technology from experiment to commercial scale, and how to improve the efficiency of the industry? After the family foundations came in, it is also important to consider what technologies or practices could be used to make the industry more efficient, rather than simply increasing the size of assistance. This may be something we should really consider. Only in this way will the industry develop better and the cost is reduced accordingly. Thank you.

Liu Qinglong: Chairman Wei pointed out some huge problems just now. Due to the limited time, I believe you still have many questions to discuss with the other guests. I will give the time to the guests here today.

On-site Question: Hello, everyone. My work is related to the mental health of children. Now I have launched a campaign to focus on the mental health of left-behind children and the development of their wisdom and personality. Just now, Mr. Guo Peng mentioned the care for children's mental health in the rehabilitation stage. Generally speaking, at present, people mainly care about the physical health of children but pay less attention to their mental health. So I would like to ask, have foundations given further consideration to this aspect in the future?

Liu Qinglong: Who would like to answer this question?

Guo Peng: After the foundation of Sunshine All the Way Charity Foundation, we have been in Ji'an, Jiangxi Province since September, and we plan to use 2-3 years to screen 900,000 underage students there for serious illnesses and carried out the assistance of serious illnesses after screening.

At the same time, we will also address the problem of mental health counselling. We plan to invest 30 million yuan in three years to train tutors first, build local workstations after, and provide instruction and counselling on mental problems for students in the workstations.

Wei Wei: I would like to give a brief answer. I have been exposed to a lot of projects about children's hospital games, which mainly focus on preoperative preparation and postoperative rehabilitation. After this kind of project is done, it can greatly reduce the pain of children in the hospital treatment process, shorten the length of hospitalization, and even reduce medical costs. We have detailed indicators to make an assessment. However, this only concerns the hospitalization period. I have not funded projects after rehabilitation, so I would like to have a try if I have the chance in the future.

Liu Qinglong: Indeed, mental counselling is also a particular problem, but I think how to integrate philanthropic institutions with local social organizations effectively is probably a very specific problem faced by the social development. For example, if social workers in local social work organizations can carry out mental counselling and better integrate with philanthropic institutions, it can help better save resources. Hong Kong has done a very good job in this part now.

Audience's Question: I strongly agree with what's mentioned by Chairman Wei Wei that the new method needs to be verified in order to improve the efficiency of assistance. I would like to ask the foundations and colleagues in philanthropy that, in addition to actual projects of assistance, how much effort and money do you spend on research, that is, to track and evaluate your projects? How to reflect the ratio of inputs to outputs and how to measure the success? Or what's your cooperation with the Institute for Philanthropy Tsinghua University? I would like to know more about the current situation in this regard and your future plans, because both policies and projects need to be evidence-based so that that good projects can be expanded and unnecessary waste can be avoided.

Hou Chunyan: I would like to briefly talk about the children's benefiting plan I mentioned earlier. It also provides services for children in remote areas who have never had health records, serious disease screening or physical examination records.

We are an enterprise, and of course, we have also established a foundation. Chairman Wang Lin also has provided professional guidance in this regard. As an enterprise, we are more flexible and less susceptible to habitual thinking as Chairman Wei just mentioned. We will also provide non-targeted assistance to certain patients according to their needs. That means as long as they meet the conditions, we will help them receive assistance. However, it takes time to do this, and as a media, we didn't have the capacity to raise so much money at the beginning.

As a media, we hoped that more people could see such problems, and in order to help them screen out the illnesses, we would have fixed sources of fundraising after a period of time. However, it turned out to be unfeasible. We took all the doctors to screen out the illnesses, but after that, the doctors were very anxious. Although we had found the illnesses, we didn't make any assistance, so what was the meaning of doing this? But at that time, funds were limited, so we restarted and connected with CCAFC for its helpline of "9958" could bring a lot of funds to help these children, and help us get through.

We make use of the money that we have, because we are not a non-government organization but an enterprise, and everything is done by our staff working together with doctors. The number of activities we can participate in is very limited, and we have to strive for getting the best results from them. In the past, we mainly sent doctors to screen children. Since we only needed to pay for the travelling and accommodation for doctors to screen children locally, there would be some money left. We wondered if the money could be used for the travel expenses of saving children. Can part of the medical expenses be paid out of this fund? We want to design the project more rationally to really solve the problems, and this is a process of our self-inspection and self- verification. What we do now is different from what we did in the beginning. It will be very realistic and positive if we can form experience that can be promoted with Institute for Philanthropy Tsinghua University in the future to benefit more people.

Liu Qinglong: Distinguished guests, it seems that our discussion has just opened the topic and just entered the climax of the dialogue, but we must stop there because we have to move to the next topic. It's a pity, but fortunately, all the guests have shared the contact information and we can discuss off the conference.

Ladies and gentlemen, what we are discussing today should be a very important, outstanding, and valuable topic.

What's the significance of children? Children are the future of a country and society. Caring for children is actually caring about the society and the whole country. We took this opportunity to discuss the issues of caring for children and welfare of children indirectly. Instead of only showing our experience, practice, thinking, and understanding on the spot, we can say we are facing the new challenges and solving new problems together. With the rapid development of society, there will be new problems for children. How to solve these new problems and deal with new challenges? I'm afraid we still have to push our work forward intensively. I hope that with the joint efforts of all of you, the welfare of children can be better implemented, and we can find a perfect solution. Thank you for your sharing.

Dr. Douglas Noble: Good morning, everyone. I am very happy to be here today as the moderator of our Parallel Education Forum. My Chinese name is Zheng Dao, and I am UNICEF Deputy Representative to China. I would like to thank the organizers and the chairman of the CPAFFC.

I still remember that my child once came back from school and said that what they learned that day was the United Nations SDGs, which made me rather surprised. But now many children are getting what it is.

The United Nations has issued the SDGs by 2030, and all member states are under the framework of this development goal. We have made a blueprint for future development, about poverty reduction, promotion of equality, and so on. The 2030 Agenda for Sustainable Development puts forward 17 sustainable development goals, which are not only for developed countries but also for developing countries.

In this discussion session, we will discuss the goals of education for children, that is, to provide high-quality education for all children and provide life-long learning opportunities for all. This goal is very important because although we have made great progress in the past few years, there are still many children who drop out of school around the world, and there are still many young people who do not have basic abilities such as reading, writing and calculation. We need to redouble our efforts to provide disadvantaged groups and women with access to high-quality education.

Not only make them study in the classroom but also need we give them access to high-quality education. It is estimated that 600 million children have no real access to appropriate and high-quality education at the schooling age, and that 50% of secondary school students have not yet reached the proficiency level of language reading, writing and calculation. Although 66% of children go to school, they will eventually drop out.

The Sustainable Development Goals are committed to solving these problems, and we should strive to achieve them by 2030. If we work hard for achieving these goals, we will have some problems to be solved. For example, 200 million children will still drop out of school, and 40% of children will quit at secondary education. As a result, there will be other problems, such as the gap further widening.

I hope we can cooperate, both in China and around the world, to achieve the United Nations SDGs so that all people have access to the same quality of education. Only in this way can the SDGs be fully achieved by 2030, and everyone can receive an education.

Our next speaker is Mr. Lyu Dexiong, Executive Vice President and Secretary-General of the Chinese Society for Taoxingzhi Studies. Let's welcome him to the stage.

The Chinese and International Efforts of Education for All: An Educator's Vision

Lyu Dexiong, Executive Vice President and Secretary-General of the Chinese Society for Taoxingzhi Studies

Distinguished guests, good morning. I would like to thank our moderator for the introduction. The previous speakers have made excellent points on welfare, assistance and medical treatment for children. Now let's get to the children's education.

The title of my speech today is *The Chinese and International Efforts of Education for All- an Educator's Vision.*

In the autumn of 1917, standing on the bow of a ship returning home, a young talent who graduated from Columbia University returned to his distressed motherland with the great ambition of "enabling all Chinese people to receive education". He was Tao Xingzhi, who was later called "the Great Educator for People" by Chairman Mao Zedong and was elected as one of the "Top Ten Educators influencing the world" by UNESCO.

After returning to China, Tao Xingzhi served as the Director of Academic Affairs of Nanjing Higher Normal School. He proposed to improve the curriculum, end the education bans on female, and promote civilian education. He learned that 85% of China's total population was in rural areas at that time, so he proposed that "we must dedicate ourselves to our 340 million peasants, and we must think about their benefits". To this end, he took off his suit and leather shoes, put on cloth coats and straw sandals, gave up high post with abundant salary, and successively founded Xiaozhuang School, Shanhai Studying Group for Workers, Yucai School and Social University, receiving civilian children to study and becoming a pioneer in China's modern education reform.

However, in old China with foreign invasion and constant civil wars, how could Tao Xingzhi realize his ambition? Now let's look at a set of numbers. In the early days after the founding of the People's Republic of China, it had a population of 540 million, with an illiteracy rate of 80%, of which 70% were women. There were 140,000 children in the kindergarten, with a gross enrollment rate of 0.4%. The number of primary school students was 24.39 million, with a gross enrollment rate of 20%. The number of junior middle school students was 950,000, with a gross enrollment rate of 3.1%. The number of high school students was 320,000, with a gross enrollment rate of 1.1%. There were 117,000 students in higher education, with a gross enrollment rate of 0.26%. The proportion of government expenditure on education in GDP was 1.32%. When the People's Republic of China was founded, not "all children", but "the vast majority of children" did not enjoy the right to education.

In 2018, China's education achieved amazing development. There are 46.56 million children in kindergartens, with a gross enrollment rate of 81.7%; 103.39 million students in elementary school, with a gross enrollment rate of 99.95%,

46.53 million students in junior high schools, with a gross enrollment rate of 100.9%, and the consolidation rate for nine-year compulsory education of 94.2%; 39.35 million students in high school, with a gross enrollment rate of 88.8%; and 38.33 million students in higher education, with a gross enrollment rate of 48.1%.

The advanced educational thoughts and educational philosophy of "people first" of Mr. Tao Xingzhi, which though was experimented, supported and promoted by many of his colleagues, students and followers, achieved the little effect in more than 30 years. However, thanks to the hard work of Chinese people in the last 70 years after the founding of the People's Republic of China, we have enjoyed the largest scale of education in the world, with compulsory education fully implemented in urban and rural areas. Although there are still shortcomings such as insufficient and unbalanced development of early childhood education, inadequate reform of the education system and quality management system of teaching, unbalanced distribution of high-quality compulsory education, the vision Mr. Tao Xingzhi made 100 years ago — all Chinese people to receive an education — has been basically realized. Why is that? The reasons for the rapid education development are mainly as follows.

First, it has been given high priority by the state.

At the beginning of the founding of New China, Chairman Mao Zedong pointed out, "Recovering and developing people's education is one of the important tasks at present." On October 1, 1951, the Government Administration Council of Central People's Government promulgated the *Regulations on Reforming the Schooling System* and launched a large-scale literacy education. In 10 years, nearly 100 million young and middle-aged illiterates became literate, and the illiteracy rate dropped rapidly to 38.1%. Since the reform and opening up, the state has developed strategies of giving priority to education, rejuvenating the country through science and education, strengthening the country through talent, and driving development through innovation. In 1993, *the Program for China's Education Reform and Development* officially set "basically universalizing nine-year compulsory education and basically eliminating illiteracy among young and middle-aged people" as a new goal. The 18th National Congress of the Communist Party of China started a new journey of developing education with the people as the centre. After General-Secretary Xi Jinping proposed to "strive to develop education for all and lifelong education, build a learning society, and strive to let every child have the opportunity to receive education", a series of important documents have been promulgated by the state, clearly proposing "to popularize high-quality preschool education, to achieve high-quality and balanced compulsory education, and to fully popularize high school education...children and adolescents with disabilities enjoy suitable education." The share of fiscal expenditures on education in national fiscal expenditures has remained above 4% for seven consecutive years.

Second, it has been written into laws.

On April 12, 1986, the Fourth Session of the Sixth National People's Congress passed the *Compulsory Education Law of the People's Republic of China*, which has been amended many times by the National People's Congress since then. *The Compulsory Education Law* stipulates that all children have the equal right to receive compulsory education according to law and fulfil their obligation to receive compulsory education. At the same time, it stipulates the corresponding duties of the government, parents or other legal guardians, schools, social organizations and individuals and their responsibilities for 22 kinds of illegal acts. According to reports, in recent years, parents in Hunan, Yunnan, and Qinghai have been punished for refusing to send their children to school. At the same time, the legal system of socialist education with Chinese characteristics represented by the *Higher Education Law*, *Teacher's Law* and *Vocational Education Law* has gradually formed.

Third, it has been implemented across the country through various policies.

Based on the actual development of education, relevant state departments have successively formulated relevant policies, such as ensuring that migrant children receive equal compulsory education, ensuring that children with disabilities receive compulsory education, clarifying the responsibilities of guardians and schools for left-behind children and trouble-making students, and establishing public welfare and inclusive early childhood education. In particular, in view of the actual educational gaps between regions, between urban and rural areas, and between schools, the state promotes targeted poverty alleviation through education, focusing on helping young adults and children of low-income families in underdeveloped areas receive education and blocking the intergenerational transmission of poverty. The state also conducts special supervision on the basic conditions for running compulsory schools in poverty-stricken areas, demands for improvement within a certain period of time and regularly releases the list of counties (cities and districts) with a basically balanced development of compulsory education. In conclusion, our government has upheld the banner of equity in education, followed the path of balanced development, focused on supervision and inspection, improved the weak links of social security and provided social assistance to people in extreme poverty, and launched key measures to ensure that every school runs well and every child enjoys equal and quality education.

Fourth, it has been supported by society through philanthropy.

Kindness is like water, benefiting all within its reach. Those who are benevolent are willing to make the world a better place through their philanthropic efforts. Promoting charity spirit and helping the weak has become a fashion in society nowadays. Many philanthropy organizations have supported education through purchasing government services or encouraging volunteer teaching in underdeveloped areas. As a national first-class association, Chinese Society for Taoxingzhi Studies, which I serve for, have also supported China's education through philanthropy with the legacy of Mr. Tao Xingzhi's great sentiment of love to the world and selfless dedication. In 2016, we launched a three-year initiative to improve the soft power of education in Bijie, Guizhou, and organized more than 200 schools from more than 10 provinces to provide free training for principals and teachers. In 2018, a new three-year funding action agreement was signed. Thousands of preschool teachers have benefited from our future educator booster program in Xinjiang, Inner Mongolia and Hebei.

Children are the future of the world, and providing educational opportunities for all children is a worldwide topic. The release of the *World Declaration on Education for All* in March 1990 marked the formation of the concept of providing universal educational opportunities for all children. Since then, a series of important national conferences have been launched around this theme. For example, the *Convention on the Rights of the Child*, adopted by the United Nations General Assembly on November 20, 1989, was the first legally binding international agreement to protect children's rights. The World Summit for Children, which was held next to that, declared "All for children". The World Children's Fund was founded in 1996. At present, most countries in the world agree with the concept of equal educational opportunities. Such beliefs include:

1. We should adhere to the "children-first" principle. All things we do should be for the benefit of children. We should provide basic protection for the survival and normal development of all children. The basic needs of children should be given high priority.

2. Education equity is an important aspect, if not the foundation of social equity. Children enjoy the same learning and development opportunities in accordance with the law.

3. We need individualized, diversified, and subjective learning that meets the needs of children. The key to the quality of children's education lies in suitability.

4. We need to ensure that our education can effectively meet the expected

goals. China proposes that on the basis of providing all children with the opportunity to receive education, children should be given equal opportunities to receive high-quality educations; the United Kingdom proposes to provide all children with effective learning courses, education programs and quality monitoring systems; Denmark proposes that equity and quality should go hand in hand to achieve the excellent education for all.

China and foreign countries have made joint efforts in international cooperation and participation in education for all. After the *United Nations General Assembly adopted the Convention on the Rights of the Child* in November 1989, the Standing Committee of the National People's Congress of China formally approved it in December 1991, and actively cooperated with the projects of UNESCO, UNICEF and Save the Children for their implementation in China. As Save the Children has mentioned, there are projects carried out in more than 10 provinces in China.

At the first global conference on education for all, representatives from the participating countries fully affirmed China's achievements in promoting education for all and highly commended the Chinese government for its strong support and contribution to the development of education in developing countries around the world. In view of the high number of dropouts and illiteracy in African countries, and the backwardness of basic education caused by poverty and war, China has extended a helping hand and established the China-UNESCO trust fund to help Africa. At the Forum on China-Africa Cooperation in 2015, President Xi Jinping stated that China would work hard to support Africa in breaking through the three major development bottlenecks of lagging infrastructure, insufficient talent, and shortage of funds. The Ministry of Education of China issued the *Promoting the Joint Construction of the "Belt and Road Initiative" Education Action* to increase assistance for the joint construction of the "Belt and Road Initiative" national education, focusing on investing in, assisting and benefiting people. The British Ministry of Education spent £41 million in 2016 to introduce Shanghai's "teaching model of mastery", allowing 8,000 (nearly half) primary and secondary schools in England to participate in the learning of Shanghai's mathematics education experience, and so on.

Great efforts have been made both at home and abroad in the development of education for all. It should be noted that while macro policies and laws provide educational opportunities for all children, micro, local, individual and social coordination mechanisms should also be paid attention to.

In order to ensure "all children to enjoy equal educational opportunities, many supporting measures are needed, including joint supervision and accompanying growth", and formation of the social support mechanism. For example, micro-policies and systems must ensure that they do not affect children's school opportunities. Parents should keep up with them in education and make clear their responsibility to safeguard children's right to education. People from all walks of life and caring people should give a helping hand so that all children can be benefited.

We hope that it can become the consensus and action of all people to provide educational opportunities for all children, let children share the same blue sky, and let education bring hope to all people. Thank you.

Dr. Douglas Noble: Thank you very much, Mr. Lyu, for your keynote speech about China's achievements in education and the importance of equal education and universal education, and how left-behind children and special children in rural areas need to be taken care of and given access to education.

Next, we will invite the roundtable guests to the stage for the discussion. First, we will have Mr. Lyu Dexiong; Ms. Li Hongyan, Educational Consultant of UNESCO; Mr. Peter William, Chairman of IIRR; Mr. Sebastian Kuster, COO of Save the Children China, Beijing Office; and Miss Siu Hoi Yan, Michelle, Famous Pianist and Advocate of Integrated Education. Please come on the stage.

First of all, let's give a round of applause to the roundtable guests. Let's start with the first question. On the issue of providing educational opportunities for all children, I would like to know your opinions.

Peter William: I would like to thank our organizers for inviting us here. I will answer this question on behalf of the non-profit organization, IIRR. First, let me introduce our organization and its views on education.

Our organization has been committed to solving the educational needs of special groups of children in rural areas for 60 years. I think this is very important because some large institutions or multilateral organizations are only emphasizing the importance of urban education. Indeed, we have found a lot of evidence that some challenges in rural areas have been ignored and the problems have not been resolved. Therefore, our organization has been committed to solving education problems in remote areas to fill the gaps in education.

We would visit rural communities and cooperate with communities and institutions in various places, including Asia, Africa and other parts of the world. Likewise, we have encountered frustrating situations and learned that the world's urbanization process is getting faster and faster, which is a very obvious trend in Africa and Asia. There are some subtleties in the process of urbanization. For example, in some parts of Africa or Mongolia, people in some rural areas live in a nomadic way, and they need to migrate frequently, which may be caused by the growing season of crops or the needs of livestock. People in these areas have probably been living this way for hundreds of years, so our organization gives priority to solving their educational problems. We have also learned that 25-40 million children in these areas have no access to education.

We know that cities face many educational challenges, and these situations are even more serious in rural areas. For nomads, meeting the educational needs of children requires more flexible curriculum settings. If we want children in these communities to accept these courses, we also need to tell families and students that only by allowing children to receive an education can this area have a better ecology. We give 10 kinds of different courses in different regions every day, which may be adjusted according to the season and their migration. We are basically teachers who follow their migration and travel with the nomads, and sometimes we may migrate as far as ten miles or even hundreds of miles.

We must take action, and find nomadic groups to help them solve problems in innovative ways.

Dr. Douglas Noble: Thank you very much. I will give the microphone to Li Hongyan. I would like to ask, how does the UNESCO solve it? How to narrow the gap?

Li Hongyan: I work at the UNESCO, which is a very special educational organization within the United Nations system, and we have developed the world's educational, scientific and cultural agenda. We call the fourth goal of the SDGs by 2030 the SDG4. We are also constantly keeping an eye on the progress towards achieving these goals by 2030. In the beginning, Dr. Douglas Noble said a lot about the achievements in the SDG4, but it is not working very well at present. We are a little off track.

The United Nations' report of Global Sustainable Development this year pointed out that some countries must continue to move forward on this track to achieve the SDG4. In fact, we have already deviated from this goal and hope to achieve it in 2030. If we continue in this direction, only 60% of our students may finish high school by 2030. This is the situation we are facing now. We are completely off track at the moment and fail in achieving the SDG4. We need to think about strategies to accelerate progress now so that we can truly achieve our goals in the future.

The UNESCO is an intergovernmental organization, and we are working in the upper reaches. We organize exchanges among countries, international organizations and international platforms. We hope that the government and private enterprises can think about how to achieve the SDG4.

When we are talking about gender, equality, and high-quality education, we feel that if there is no equity, there will be no so-called high-quality education. Equity is the most important thing, which means that we need to break down barriers and allow all children to have educational opportunities. We have found that for some equity reasons, many people in need of education have no access to higher education or high-quality education, so we still face a great challenge. There are some special children and children with special conditions who hope to get educational opportunities, but they get no access. For example, some girls cannot receive an education. Almost 200 million children are not educated, and two-thirds of them are girls. Therefore, most of the illiterate population are women.

Data from UNESCO show that people with disabilities are less likely to receive an education. They cannot get educational opportunities or reach the lowest level of literacy, and many children with disabilities are also in the disadvantaged groups. Even children with disabilities in school are unable to learn effectively. About 200 million children with disabilities are bullied in school every day, which prevents them from learning effectively, too. Some children have problems in health or other aspects, for example, they cannot learn effectively or learn efficiently, so they need relevant strategies to help them solve these problems.

Dr. Douglas Noble: Thank you for sharing. This is indeed something that needs to be addressed at a higher level. Next, let's hand over the microphone to Sebastian Kuster from Save the Children China, Beijing Office. How did you narrow the education gap?

Sebastian Kuster: Thanks again to our organizers for inviting me to share with you. Our second major goal is in line with the SDGs by 2030, which aims to make more children receive an education. In China, we pay more attention to the rural areas, and some children of migrant workers in cities as well.

What we have seen now is that there is a gap between preschool education in remote areas and that in urban areas. This gap is mainly due to the number of kindergartens and the level of education provided by kindergartens.

Communities do not pay enough attention to preschool education, mainly because they do not have enough teachers who have been trained. We have carried out some child development projects, hoping to fill the gap. In Xi'an and Qinghai, we have tried different ways to solve this problem. For example, we ask for more support from the communities and communicate with parents to improve the management level; we let more kindergartens settle in remote areas, and as some members of the communities are willing to teach preschool educational courses in remote areas, we can actively ask them if they are willing to receive relevant training for teaching in the remote areas. Also, we can ask whether teachers in Shanghai can go to Yunnan to form kindergartens and related communities there, so that they can have a learning atmosphere.

Another gap is in universal education. Many disabled children cannot receive education in both urban areas and remote areas. We are now cooperating with local schools and have also established some resource centres to provide training resources and materials. The teaching materials we provide for people with disabilities are in line with international standards. Teachers know how to better and more inclusively integrate children from disadvantaged groups into universal classrooms in their courses and curriculum.

Dr. Douglas Noble: I would like to ask Miss Siu Hoi Yan, Michelle a question. We just listened to the speeches of three representatives of their organizations. Have the projects you participated in before done anything to fill the gap? They talked about their hope to help the disabled, so do you have any suggestions?

Michelle Siu Hoi Yan: I feel very grateful to the organizers for allowing me to share. I think one of the biggest problems in universal education is the lack of learning materials, such as special education materials for children with visual impairment or intellectual impairment. Also, teachers and parents should be able to provide mental counselling to their children. For example, I used to attend a class where teachers, classmates and parents were in contact with one another. I want to tell a story of my own. Once, the College of Liberal Arts organized an activity for all students. A teacher came over and said to me, "Our activity is called 'living in the poverty-stricken areas', so you should not participate in it because we may not be able to take good care of you." However, after a few days, when I asked my classmates how this activity was carried out, they said that they just lay on the ground for the live-action rehearsal, which made me think that I could do it, too.

Therefore, the teacher plays a very important role and needs to communicate with classmates and parents. One of my suggestions is to hold regular meetings between teachers, parents and students so that everyone can learn about each other' s concerns, and students can participate in. In the meeting, teachers can set some goals for students, and involve them in school activities. I think that being a disadvantaged group does not mean that you should participate in less physically demanding activities. What is more important is to allow children, whether disabled or not, to integrate into society. Only by involving children into general education can they integrate into society in the future.

Dr. Douglas Noble: Thank you, Miss Siu Hoi Yan, Michelle! Next question, I would like to ask Secretary-General Lyu Dexiong. Your organization needs to cooperate with the government, and this is the case all over the world, no matter as a kind of model or a project, for IIRR, UNESCO or an education fund. Speaking of cooperating with the government, can you share the case of promoting education and the successful model of cooperating with the government?

Lyu Dexiong: For example, the government now advocates social organizations to purchase government services. After you apply for a project that has been reviewed and approved by relevant government departments, the government can allocate a certain amount of funds, and then implement it according to your original plan. To be successful, the project needs to have a government-related background, approved and funded by the government and to be carried out by schools or other organizations.

We did a little more a few years ago than in the past two years. What's the reason? In the government purchase project, there is a requirement that social organizations' expenses must match the same funds provided by the government. For example, if I take 1 million yuan from the government, I must take another 1 million yuan from myself, which can be very stressful for social organizations. It may be better if government-supported projects also invite foundations and caring people to do together. Thank you.

Dr. Douglas Noble: Thank you. Chairman Peter William, how does your organization cooperate with the government, including financial support, to promote and make the comprehensive education a success?

Peter Williams: As an institution, we've been deploying projects for decades. We also cooperate regularly with the government, which is our strategic partner, and together we have contributed to the successful implementation of projects.

At the same time, in order for the project to be successfully implemented and promoted, we believe that cooperation is very important. We often work with remote areas that may be far away and it is very difficult to promote projects in these areas. In order to improve efficiency, the government must be part of it. We must not only cooperate with the finance department of government, but also involve them in project design, not just as stakeholders.

For example, we worked on a project in the Philippines in cooperation with the government. Over the past 6 years, we have also created many unique ways and methods to promote comprehensive education. We hope to promote the project and raise the awareness of the people: what can comprehensive education bring us?

One-fifth of the children in primary schools in the Philippines are undernourished. There is evidence that nutrition and educational performance are strongly related. We cooperated with the government to launch an integrated reform plan, and there are three initiatives in it. First, we provide nutrition for students. The government plays a very important role in it to ensure that pupils can eat different nutrients every day. Second, nutrition is a very important part of education programs, and it is often necessary to educate parents to provide more nutritious food to their children. We should educate parents to create a nutritional environment and have such awareness, and let them realize the relation between nutrition levels and school education. The third is to introduce agriculture and nutrition into this project, and also integrate facilities and industries around the school into it, allowing multiple partners to promote the implementation of the project jointly. However, it also takes time. For example, parents and teachers of agricultural-related institutions and departments can provide training and some plans to help teachers and parents understand the relationship between nutrition and school performance. At the beginning, only three schools implemented this project. Later, it was promoted by dozens of schools, and as the scale is gradually expanding, now 36,000 schools are promoting this project, gathering tens of thousands of students. Without the active cooperation of the government, this project cannot be implemented.

Dr. Douglas Noble: Thank you, Mr. Peter William. Let's get back to Ms. Li Hongyan, Education Consultant of UNESCO. I think that the work of your organization is to support the government to achieve the SDGs of the United Nations. How do you support the government to achieve the SDGs?

Li Hongyan: The main task of UNESCO is to assist the government to achieve the various indicators of SDG4. How do we know the extent to which the indicators have been achieved? We need data to help with the assessment, and one of the most important cooperation we have with the government is to get the government to provide the data we need. The Bureau of Statistics collects relevant data for these indicators every year, annually publishes the *Global Education Monitoring Report*, and reflects the problems monitored every year through the report. Before this, governments of various countries will closely link national education development plans with SDG4, which is a very important and most basic task.

As an intergovernmental organization, another important task is to get governments to adopt relevant conventions, such as the *Convention against Discrimination in Education*. This has been done for a long time, but there are still countries that have not signed it, so this work is still ongoing.

In addition to these efforts, we also have an important task to collect good projects mentioned by various countries and regions, and bring these projects together for promotion and replication on a larger scale.

We also conduct data collection in the field of disability and gender. A very important feature of cooperation with the Chinese government is to help underdeveloped countries and regions, such as Africa. Ms. Peng Liyuan was named as the UNESCO Special Envoy for Girls' and Women's Education, and she has done a lot of publicity for gender equality education around the world.

In 2016, the Chinese government cooperated with us to set up an award especially for innovative projects of girls and women emerging from all over the world, with the awarding ceremony annually held.

In 2019, UNESCO launched a large-scale event themed, hoping to use more political and financial resources around the world to support girls' and women' s education, and to realize *From Enjoying Education Opportunities to Empowerment through Education: UNESCO's Strategy to Promote Gender Equality in and through Education (2019-2025).*

Regarding the education for disabled groups, there was also *The Salamanca Statement* in 1994 to meet special educational needs. On the 25th anniversary of the adoption of the Statement, that is, this year, a large international forum will be organized in Colombia next week to discuss the inclusion and equity of education. This is a global conference, and ministers of education from many countries will attend.

To renew the international community's commitment to education through such an event, I believe there will be more promotion.

Dr. Douglas Noble: I just heard what you said about the different forms of cooperation with the government. In your opinion, how do you think the government should cooperate with NGOs? Whether it is a social organization or an individual, how to promote it?

Michelle Siu Hoi Yan: I think the government should first establish some communication platforms for teachers, students and parents, so there will be an opportunity to pay attention to the problems faced by comprehensive education, especially the problems faced by students with disabilities.

With this foundation, enterprises can also set up some organizations, provide more resources to NGOs, or provide more resources to some village schools to help the children with disabilities. For example, special education helps special students catch up with ordinary students, complete homework, and pass exams and tests.

Education is very important for students with disabilities, because only by receiving an education can they better integrate into the community. The government can hold seminars or theme meetings in some communities, so that more people will know the challenges for comprehensive education. These are some of my suggestions.

Dr. Douglas Noble: Thank you, Miss Siu Hoi Yan, Michelle. It is a very interesting idea. The next topic is about innovation. Let's start with Mr. Sebastian Kuster. Innovation has become a problem for global development. About the vision we have for innovation, can you briefly express your opinions? How do you think Save the Children can innovate to benefit children more?

Sebastian Kuster: I would like to give a few simple examples, which are the cases of our organization in China, and these cases are related to digitization.

Some employees of ECCD will make home visits. We equip all employees of ECCD with tablet computers, which enable them to better provide ideas and methods to families and students, and also help them monitor and understand the current situation of the families they visit and facilitate the follow-up tracking. Follow-up tracking is very important in this regard, and finally, we will centralize all data before matching it in the project.

Our ECCD project will use some high-tech methods to assist home visits, which will facilitate the tracking.

The other is a fundamental project. We have a project on social-emotional learning that starts with a pioneering action on social-emotional learning to help students acquire the social and digital skills they need. I think this is something that Chinese students will urgently need to help them move quickly towards modernization.

The other is a comprehensive education. We have developed an online package of teaching materials, and teachers can also learn online. This teaching package can also be used to train teachers in universities. This is some progress we have made in innovation.

Dr. Douglas Noble: Thank you, Mr. Sebastian Kuster, for your introduction. Mr. Lyu, what are the innovative models and technologies in your organization?

Lyu Dexiong: We are an educational society in terms of the goals to let all children receive education and realize the inclusive education in China. We are also working on some of the issues that this gentleman mentioned earlier. For example, we are also engaged in the use of modern education network, and we will make new projects to get children into schools through some domestic projects.

We also pay attention to parent training. If we want all children to receive education, we cannot rely on the government alone unless parents join us. Since what we want is all, we must pay attention to individuals, so we set up parent schools in different places to train parents and educate children together with families. These have been the two successful areas so far.

Dr. Douglas Noble: Thank you, Mr. Lyu. Ms. Li Hongyan of UNESCO, what innovation have you done? How do you promote new ideas?

Li Hongyan: In May 2019, we held a very large conference on AI in China. In connection with the concept of inclusive education, we noticed a gender gap in human digital skills. What we are doing right now is to study this phenomenon, find out the reasons behind it, and come up with strategies.

We recently published a journal, which is *I would Blush, if I could*. First of all, Siri's voice has been a woman's voice. For example, if you say, "Siri, you are a bitch", the initial response should be "I would blush, if I could". We found this phenomenon very interesting because of a strong gender factor in it. Now it has changed to "I don't know how to answer your question.". You may have a try later.

We have discovered through observation that gender stereotypes have penetrated into electronic and technology products. AI means the future, but how can we notice it in time to avoid aggravating gender inequality in the development of technology?

For example, our research has found that there is a very obvious gender gap in the field of science. Only 35% of the people engaged in research in this field in all universities are women, and in some fields only 3% of female college students would choose science. This is because she will be affected by gender and stereotypes in the process of socialization, and because she thinks this field is the field of men, so she is unwilling to choose it.

These phenomena are worthy of our consideration. This is what we are studying right now, and we hope to seek a breakthrough in promoting gender equality.

Lyu Dexiong: Gender education is an unavoidable issue. In fact, the problem of discrimination against women in education in China has been solved quite well. What I want to mention is that we should also pay attention to male education. We have an organization called the Female Student Education Committee, which focuses on female education from international to the domestic level.

I used to work at a normal university and found that there were very few boys in the normal university, and very few male teachers in the kindergarten. It would be bad for children's growth if they are only exposed to female teachers from an early age. I once put forward a suggestion that the Female Student Education Committee can properly hold a male education forum. I think this is very meaningful.

Dr. Douglas Noble: Thank you very much, Mr. Lyu, both of you talked about the issue of gender equality. Mr. Peter William, you have been studying some cutting-edge technologies during this time, how do you use them?

Peter William: As an organization, we attach great importance to learning, not just the environment and prospects of learning. We believe that learning can help us learn from our own failures and successes. For a long time, I have been attaching importance to it.

You can imagine the whole situation. As I said before, we have a lot of challenges and opportunities in some very remote areas, which are the places that we're focusing on. We found out these groups, and then discovered that they had begun to empower themselves by using some strategies or continuing to working hard.

I can give you an example. For us, we sometimes want to redefine innovation. What does innovation mean for learning? You would know about the human development indicators. If you participated in the previous breakout session about children's health. As far as our organization is concerned, we believe that there are many innovative models and methods for children's health. In the aspect of children's education, there are also some issues related to children's health or poverty. In fact, if we look at them from the perspective of innovation, both health and economic indicators should be factors that we consider when we work on children's education. You probably know that there is a kind of NPI, the multi-factor indicator, and after we integrated the indicators of health, education, and living standards, we found that these are closely related to education.

One of the main things I'm doing right now is looking at the connections between rural communities and individual families. We have found that 60% to 70% of children who grew up in a bad environment or children with poor learning ability have a very bad family environment and a lot of dust accumulated at home. A World Bank study has found that if families can do cleaning more frequently or devote themselves in reducing household ash accumulation, the overall health conditions can be improved, and the overall common development index can be increased by 97%. This is to make some new discoveries and changes in more innovative methods, which are worthy of our continued exploration, and this is what our organization has discovered.

Dr. Douglas Noble: Thank you, Miss Siu Hoi Yan, Michelle. Have you ever tried to be innovative in your life?

Michelle Siu Hoi Yan: Before I talk about it, I want to respond to gender education. I know that many girls had few opportunities to receive education before, but most of the girls born in my generation can receive education, and I am very fortunate to be one of them.

Speaking of innovation models, I would like to suggest several methods.

First, let normal students imitate the activities of people with disabilities, so that they can feel the challenges that people with disabilities face in their daily lives. For example, it is difficult to walk in the dark, and it is difficult to open the bottle of mineral water with an injured hand. We can let normal students experience the difficulties of disabled students through empathy.

Second, hold some concerts and drama performances in the normal schools. Students receiving special education can organize some activities or give performances together with normal students, to show their talents. In this way, students with disabilities can be recognized by the group, and can also be better understood and helped by their peers. For teachers, they can also better discover the personalities and talents of these students.

In fact, although we are people with disabilities, we are eager and able to make due contributions to the community. We are eager for education, we hope to get the support of teachers and parents and the understanding and recognition of our peers, and we also hope to enjoy school life better.

Education is the key to the future, and a good education system determines the future. Thank you.

Dr. Douglas Noble: Thank you. The roundtable has been very fruitful. We have learned a lot and heard about the process and challenges of achieving the SDGs of the United Nations and discussed the education gap, the problems of gender and equality faced by disadvantaged groups, and the current status and progress of inclusive education.

Thank you very much for sharing your experiences and perspectives with us. I hope our audience can communicate with the guests after the meeting if interested. Of course, I hope to hear more from you about the sharing of education experience and the relationship between education awareness, nutrition and school performance. The examples that you have shared today are very interesting, and I'm personally interested in them. Maybe there are some factors that we often overlook. We didn't expect nutrition and dusty floors to be so much related to school performance.

We have also seen many novel perspectives. Thanks very much for the case that Miss Siu Hoi Yan, Michelle has just shared. It's very helpful for normal students to empathize and experience the needs and difficulties of people with disabilities. That's the end of our roundtable. Thanks again to all the guests this morning. Thank you.

XI EDUCATION AND PHILANTHROPY

Moderator: Liu Peifeng, Director of the Center of Constitution and Administrative Law, Law School, Beijing Normal University

Guest Speech: Jia Xijin, Deputy Dean of Institute for Philanthropy, Tsinghua University

Dr. Ruth A. Shapiro, Chief Executive, CAPS

Allison Hollowell, Chief Strategy Officer of the AVPN

Her Rey-Sheng, Director of the Tzu Chi Culture & Communication Foundation Development Office, "Economy of Goodness" Advocator

Professor Steven Sek-yum Ngai, Member of the Academic Committee of the WPF, Chairman and Professor of Social Work Department, the CUHK

Li Yaping, Executive Vice President and Secretary-General of the SZEEA

Chen Xingjia, Founder of the (Shenzhen) Henghui Children's Charity Foundation

Speakers: Jia Xijin, Deputy Dean of Institute for Philanthropy, Tsinghua University

Dr. Ruth A. Shapiro, Chief Executive of the CAPS

Allison Hollowell, Chief Strategy Officer of the AVPN

Her Rey-Sheng, Director of the Tzu Chi Culture & Communication Foundation Development Office, the "Economy of Goodness" Advocator

Steven Sek-yum Ngai, Member of the Academic Committee of the WPF, Chairman and Professor of Social Work Department, CUHK

Li Yaping, Executive Vice President and Secretary-General of the SZEEA

Chen Xingjia, Founder of the Henghui Children's Charity Foundation

Commented by: Dr. Faiz Shah, Director of Development Management, Center for Science and Technology, Asian Institute of Technology, Visiting Professor of Institute of Innovation, Thammasat University

Nguyen Kim Ngan, Managing Director of Centre for Sustainable Rural Development (SRD)

Liu Peifeng: We have 7 speakers who will elaborate their views this morning, and then we will have a discussion. According to the arrangement of the meeting, we have listed many questions, one category of which is how to view the public welfare index and the contribution of social organizations to society; how to include the contributions of advocacy organizations and support organizations to society in the index system. Another category is the training of philanthropic talent, because this is the most important issue at present, and many social organizations do such work, too. Thus, we shall discuss these two categories of issues. All guests should finish the report within 12 minutes, and you will be reminded in the last minute. Please strictly abide by the time limit. The excess of time will shorten the interval for the tea break and the time for free discussion, so I hope everyone can take it seriously. Thank you.

Let's invite Professor Jia Xijin, Deputy Dean of Institute for Philanthropy, Tsinghua University. She will talk about the social sector index. Welcome!

The Following up Research of China CSI

Jia Xijin, Deputy Dean of Institute for Philanthropy, Tsinghua University

Good morning, everyone. Due to the limited time, I will skip the relatively complicated research process in the report, and share with you a research result that can be summarized in a very simple diagram.

First, I would like to introduce the research methods. We have drawn on the Civil Society Index or CSI index developed from CIVICUS by Professor Anheier, who is very famous in the philanthropic field. We have conducted three rounds of follow-up studies over 14 years, the first one is in the 2005, the second is 2012, and the third is 2019, which means we have done a round of research every 7 years. This index system evaluates the development of civil society in four dimensions. We know that there are many indexes to measure social development, such as those for donations, for philanthropy and social sectors. Professor Salamon has developed several indicators, such as the index of sector size. The characteristic of the CSI index is its focus on civil forces. The entire index system tries to measure the vitality of such forces. We used to call them social sectors, which were mistaken by the public as philanthropic organizations.

So, we decide to call them civil society. Then what's the method used for such measurement? The CSI indicator system consists of 72 indicators, each of which is rated with a corresponding score. Individual indicator scores are aggregated to sub-dimensional scores, which in turn yield dimensional scores, resulting in a CSI diamond.

What can we see from this diamond? First of all, it is not a standardized quantitative index like GDP, where 5% is absolutely greater than 4.2%. Instead, the CSI is a combination of qualitative and quantitative research methods. Given the complexity of society, the elements described by a purely quantitative approach are certainly limited, and scores may not reflect the full picture. In contrast, qualitative methods have the advantage of being comprehensive, but they are not rigorous enough. So this diamond is not the result of an absolute quantitative study or a qualitative one, but something in between. If the same experts make the quantitative assessment following the same methodology, then the significance can be seen in the results themselves. However, since CSI is not a purely quantitative assessment and the expert's evaluation is subjective, then the final results cannot be compared quantitatively. So how is one to interpret the assessment results? First, we can look at the structure. Due to a set of scientific design, the structural site will not deviate too much. Second, we can look at the changes in the site, such as the difference between the results of our three studies. Third, we can compare this indicator against the international database to see what is our current level. All indicators and dimensions emphasize the involvement of civil forces.

In its four dimensions, the "structural" dimension emphasizes citizen participation, while the environmental dimension emphasizes the relationship among the political, legal and economic sectors; for the value dimension, we used the CSI indicators directly in the first year, and found that many of the indicators did not apply to China, for example, CSI focuses on environmental protection and poverty alleviation but does not include social justice. So we made a slight adjustment and consolidation, changing the indicator “gender equality” to “equality” and adding the indicator “social justice” that in the second and third years of the survey, there have been some changes in the value indicators for the sector. The "impact" dimension emphasizes the sector's influence on national policies and solutions to social problems. This is a description of our survey methodology.

An expert committee scores our indicators, so this is a mix of qualitative and quantitative measurement. The scoring is not completely subjective as it is based on a set of findings. The methods given by CSI are media review, fact discovery, community research, etc., and include social investigation and literature analysis. The method of text analysis on media review was used in the first two years, but in 2019, we made a change and replaced the large scale with the database. We presented all database indicators to the experts for them to score the results. In 2005, 2012 and 2019, the expert committee remained stable with minor changes every year, for example, some people were retired or no longer in the philanthropic field, or there were new joiners. Despite this, the scores were very similar, so this method is relatively reliable. Since it is structured, it cannot measure very subtle changes. For example, from 0 to 1, and below 30% are regarded as 0, and from 5 to 20, the scores have not changed, so it is a rough measure. The table lists the scores in four dimensions of CSI and the situation of three rounds, which are shown as this composition. The compositions of these years are very similar. The highest scores lie in the "value" dimension, followed by "influence", and the low scores are in the "environment" and "structure" dimension. This is the current situation of the development of our civil society.

Let's look at the score of each sub-dimension of the structure (PPT chart). Firstly, in the "dimension of structure", citizen participation is shrinking, while resource organization and internal development tend to grow. Secondly, in the dimension of the environment, the relationship between the private sector and society grows most. Thirdly, in the dimension of value, we can see that transparency is rising the fastest. Finally, the dimension of influence has not changed much, and now there is a shrinkage in focus on social issues and the satisfaction of social needs. It can be concluded from this that there is some evolvement in China's civil society driven by internal factors. The relationship between the second sector and third sector as well as the capacity for governance is improving, such as transparency. The current shrinkage or the challenge lies in the "structure dimension", especially the civic participation, and some changes in the macro-environment. These are what we have found in three studies, showing the current status of civil society. Thank you.

Liu Peifeng: Thank you, Professor Jia Xijin. Our second speaker, Dr. Ruth A. Shapiro, has arrived. As the moderator, I would like to rearrange the speakers' order for the meeting this morning. For your better understanding of the overall speeches, I'll make Ms. Allison Hollowell the third one because she and the speaker before her will talk about research on philanthropic evaluation. Mr. Her

Rey-Sheng will be the fourth speaker because he is going to talk about thoughts of goodness. Now let's welcome Dr. Ruth A. Shapiro, CEO of CAPS.

Doing Good Index: Development Trend of Asian Philanthropy

Dr. Ruth A. Shapiro, Chief Executive of the CAPS

Hi! My name is Ruth A. Shapiro and I am the CEO of the CAPS. Today I am going to talk about our philanthropic work.

First of all, I would like to talk about our centre, CAPS. Based in Hong Kong, we focus on 16 countries and regions around the world, including Taiwan and Hong Kong. As a research and consultation organization, we do policy research, applied research and practical research, and we can customize the research for customers as well. At the same time, we also serve enterprises and private organizations that want to engage in programs of corporate social responsibility. Our mission is to increase the quantity and quality of private resources, including philanthropy, corporate social responsibility, and impact investment, to help all enterprises work on philanthropic issues. One of our research indexes is called the Doing Good Index, and before I talk about it, I want to share with you why we chose to create it. We know that there is a general lack of credibility in Asia, which means that in Asia, people don't trust non-profits or companies, and some countries and even governments don't have credibility. So in different aspects of society, if people don't have much trust in these institutions and don't want to do philanthropic work, how can they do their best for philanthropy? So how can we strengthen the credibility of philanthropy through the Doing Good Index? Scandals like Guo Meimei once caused such a philanthropic deficit, but in most cases people are willing to trust these institutions. People would ask if we don't trust philanthropic institutions, how can we do philanthropic work? Therefore, the Chinese government has introduced a new charity law, hoping to make philanthropic institutions more transparent and have better credibility and index through legislation. So what's Doing Good Index? How does it help us engage in good philanthropy?

Doing Good Index involves four aspects, among which, fiscal and taxation policies, laws and regulations, and procurement are closely related to the government.

The forth aspect is the ecosystem, which involves the practice of individuals and companies. The study collects information from 120 non-profit and for-profit organizations that are engaged in philanthropy. We also have an expert committee, and we will hear from our research participants and the experts. Ms. Jia Xijin, who just gave the first speech, is one of the important collaborators of our Doing Good Index in the Chinese mainland. We would like to thank her for her help. And that is why we have gathered all the opinions of experts and non-profit organizations, statistically analyzed the data, and then made a final analysis report.

In January 2018, we released this index for the first time, and the next index will be released after the Chinese Lunar New Year. In 2018, China did well in Doing Good Index. I would like to tell you why China can have such a performance. I want to tell you that this survey was completed in 2017, when the law of international non-profit organizations and China's charity law were still new, and only a few people had a clear understanding of the influences and details of philanthropic institutions. We hope to release China's Doing Good Index in 2020, when Chinese policies can be more certain, and people will have a clearer understanding of the new charity law and international charity law than they did when the data were collected in 2017.

The Doing Good Index is not about how generous people are when they donate, and we do not have a lot of ways to engage in philanthropy. We mainly focus on: What the infrastructure is behind the simple relationship of giving and receiving in support of philanthropy? What are the rules? What institutions are there? How can we make our funds continuously invested in philanthropy? According to some philanthropic indexes, some people are more generous, but we don't think so. We think that people themselves are willing to help others, but why are people in some countries unwilling to help others? Because of the lack of a credible mechanism in their society, they are unable to donate or help others without concerns. Therefore, in our Doing Good Index, the key problem we solve is to optimize the overall environment and strengthen the credibility of philanthropic institutions.

Besides, we have found that the actions of all sectors of society are ahead of government policy formulation, and the ecosystem index is higher than those of the other three. Although government fiscal and tax policies and laws and regulations have not created many favourable conditions for us in the philanthropy, the companies have done a lot, especially in China. Philanthropy is a very popular concept in China, and many individuals and companies in China have done a lot of work in this field. Besides, we feel that tax incentives and dividends from the government are very important, and there are three reasons as follows. Firstly, we all want to save money. Secondly, the signals sent by the governments are critical in Asia. Once the government provides tax incentives to donors, it guides the public behaviour to some extent, telling companies that it wants more socially responsible programs. So at that time, Singapore introduced a 250% tax dividend policy, which means that you could get 2.5 times the tax deduction from the government by making relevant donations. Hence the signals that the governments send are important. Thirdly, we find that there is no correlation between a country's GDP level and its performance reflected by the Doing Good Index. Some countries say that our GDP is not good, so there is no way to reduce taxes. Vietnam's tax policy is better than North Korea's. In our index study, there is no direct correlation between tax revenues and economic development. What does this mean? Some people think that philanthropic funds of the United States should be equivalent to 2% of its GDP. If the philanthropic funds can reach 2% of GDP in the 15 countries studied by the Doing Good Index, which is about US$ 54 billion per year, this will be 11 times that of foreign aid, and one-third of the UN's annual sustainable development goals. So if we can invest this amount of money in philanthropy every year, we can solve more problems.

Now let's get to the situation in China. We witnessed the development of China through the emergence of crowd-funding and the promulgation of new charity law in this country. Nevertheless, we have found that about 29% of people find China's charity law difficult to understand, and 56% of them remain neutral. As people become more interested in this area, this ratio will change. In terms of philanthropy, there is accountability and transparency, and the Chinese government needs to make more effort to strengthen its credibility. For the government, it needs a system that has been well-managed by non-profit institutions. Philanthropic accountability is no more than 10% in China. I live in Hong Kong, and almost 10% of our tax is given to philanthropic institutions, whereas the tax policies in the Chinese mainland are not good enough, especially in terms of the support given to philanthropic institutions.

The score of China's index is not high in reports related to the philanthropic field, which is mainly caused by tax relief policies. We have seen that other countries have a lot of tax reduction measures, especially for donors. China's non-profit organizations have a close relationship with the government. 46% of the organizations we interviewed received investment from the government, which is the highest among Asian countries where the average value is 32%. The lack of talent is also a problem for philanthropic organizations. According to 84%

of organizations, the general public thinks that non-profit organization staff should earn less, with lower salaries than those of bank practitioners and lawyers. However, we cannot have such prejudice. I hope everyone agrees with me on this. In the philanthropic field, we should get comparable salaries as other people do. We have more opportunities for continuous improvement, and China is already on the right path. I hope to talk with you more in the Q&A session. Thank you.

Liu Peifeng: Let's invite Ms. Allison Hollowell, Chief Strategy Officer of AVPN, to give us a talk on China's philanthropic industry.

Research Report on Philanthropy in China

Allison Hollowell, Chief Strategy Officer of the AVPN

Good morning, everyone. I am very happy to be here this morning to share our report with you. First, I would like to introduce the AVPN. At present, we see that more and more countries in Asia are facing very complex social challenges, and there is no single way to deal with them. At the same time, we can see that a lot of wealth has been created in these regions, and more and more organizations and individuals have benefited from the economic prosperity. They hope to give back to society, help the society cope with the challenges, and truly serve their own country. However, in addition to the fore-mentioned organizations and individuals who want to use their benefits to solve problems, we still lack talent and infrastructure, and we don't know how to make truly influential investments, which is why the AVPN came into being.

We hope to introduce wealth, talent and other resources into the philanthropic field in Asia, and ensure that capital is effectively deployed to solve the problems in our society and environment. So far, we have had 585 members worldwide from a variety of industries, including foundations, trust companies, impact funds, group funds, intermediaries and government organizations. Although we are an international organization, all these members focus on investment in Asia. What's unique about us? In the past, people rarely saw how funds and impact organizations communicated with each other to solve social problems; this is where the AVPN came in, breaking isolation among different stakeholders. We want to help our organizations and individuals find opportunities to cooperate and share experiences while expanding impact. We mainly help organizations understand each other through two methods. One is through large conferences, such as the ones we held in Singapore; the other is through effective online platforms, such as our online transaction and communication platform. We help organizations learn to share best practice experience and get a clear picture of what is happening and what the markets are doing in their regions. This is what the AVPN does—to teach members to become leaders in the industry and expand their impact, cooperate and help solve social problems.

One thing I want to discuss with you is that when talking about social investment, we talked about four parts, including philanthropic investment, impact investment, socially responsible investment, etc. Some of these are dominated by impact, and some by wealth. We think it's important that capital has a social impact. We also have non-financial support, including human resources. If we want to build social organizations or build the philanthropic industry and the whole ecosystem, we need human resources and a lot of knowledge input. One area that the AVPN concerns much about is the maximization of the impact of its members. We have a knowledge centre that writes reports to help different industries develop. We help members understand the best practices in social investment and bring more innovative tools. Our report also includes a number of case studies to help understand the practices of other organizations in this network. We pay attention to the development of the industry, help organizations get into the market and know which market their capital should be best placed in. As of last, we will discuss many issues, including livelihood, education and other sub-sectors, and explore how innovation in social investment affects these areas.

We recently launched a report, the *Philanthropy in China Report*. In this report, we discussed China's philanthropic ecosystem and its development, and also gave suggestions on how to continue this trend. We have 34 well-known participants from foundations, financial institutions, research institutions, media, and incubator companies, etc. We have observed a very positive signal that China's total philanthropic funding has doubled in the past few decades, from US$10 billion in 2010 to US$23.4 billion in 2017, which is a huge step forward. Most of the capital that promotes this progress comes from companies, of which 65% comes from group companies and 21% from independent companies. We are also very pleased to see the development of China's philanthropic ecosystem and more and more people are involved in it. Just like what has been shown on the platform, China's philanthropic ecosystem is growing, in which incubator companies, financial institutions, research institutions, media, government organizations, non-governmental organizations, and think tanks are joining together to focus on how to make a greater philanthropic influence.

There is no doubt that in the past period of time, a large number of foundations have emerged in China. So far, there are more than 6,000 foundations in China, which means an increase of 17% in the past 10 years. Less than 1% of the 6,021 foundations in China are completely donated by institutions, which is how foundations work in China. There are some opportunities in China to help establish such foundations, including grassroots organizations and social organizations, who help them build trust and expand their influence so that they will use funds more effectively to create greater influence. The areas we are most concerned about in China are education and poverty alleviation. Education is the most concerning issue in Asia, and that in the field of philanthropy. We must constantly strengthen the capabilities and skills of young people. The second area we are most concerned about is the health and sustainable cities, which is very interesting.

We have two organizations focusing on the development of philanthropy in China. The first is corporate donations, which totalled US$13.2 billion in 2013. In 2016, the donations came from more than 1,000 foundations, of which more than 75 foundations donated more than US$1.5 million. However, we can see that not only do these companies and foundations donate money, but they also have an influence on society, education, and many other aspects and their employees are mobilizing social resources to maximize their impact on society.

Next, let's take a look at individual donations, most of which are done by high-net-worth individuals in China. Thanks to the top 100 philanthropists, its value increases by about 33% every year. In 2017, the donation amounted to US$3.3 million, which came from 819 million donors. I think the main reason is that there are more new tools to help our individual donors and enable them to be engaged in philanthropy. They set up foundations and philanthropic trust companies to make more donations, and we can see that these philanthropists have donated to their hometowns. From this report, we can see the four major trends in the entire industry. First, the philanthropic industry is becoming more formal and professional. In particular, after the promulgation of the *Charity Law* in 2016, from the perspective of government laws and regulations, organizations begin to envisage and plan their future development and upgrade their philanthropic models. Second, there are more and more financial sustainable development models. Some organizations are now benefiting from the economic boom, and at the same time, they are also thinking about how to benefit society through the boom. Therefore, social organizations and financially sustainable development models have been emerging in China in recent years. Third, the external exchange. With the launch of the "Belt and Road Initiative" and the South-South Cooperation, we have seen more and more philanthropic works go global aiming at solving such global issues as climate change and air pollution. Fourth, technology. The technology used in philanthropy is also constantly improving. We saw on Tencent Charity's "99 Giving Day

Finally, I'd like to share with you our suggestions, and we call on all of you to get involved in philanthropy. First, we have found that we need to raise funds to establish a foundation, which allows the organization to do things that a foundation cannot do. Second, the establishment of intermediaries in the philanthropic ecosystem will help connect social institutions with foundations to continually improve their capabilities, transparency and trust, and more importantly, help us constantly develop. This is what we need now, and intermediaries can play a very important role among parties. Third, we need to continuously strengthen cooperation, which is what the AVPN is committed to. We hope you will use our platform to find more reliable cooperative partners in the entire industry. Fourth, we want to discover the investment areas of the greatest influence. There are many areas with extremely insufficient investment, such as climate change, youth development and ecosystem development. Fifth, we need to explore human resources, and as our speaker just mentioned, we should focus on the training of youth. Thank you for listening. If you are interested, you can scan the QR code on the PPT to download the *Philanthropy in China Report*. I look forward to more communication with you.

Liu Peifeng: Ms. Allison Hollowell told us the number of foundations in China was over 6,000, based on the data from the China Foundation. In fact, as of August 31, 2019, there were more than 7,500 foundations in China. The previous speakers were talking about the index. Now, let's welcome Mr. Her Rey-Sheng, Professor of College of Humanities and Social Sciences, Tzu Chi University, and he will talk about the idea and practice of the Economy of Goodness.

Thoughts and Practice of Charity Economy

Her Rey-Sheng, Director of the Tzu Chi Culture & Communication Foundation Development Office, "Economy of Goodness" Advocator

Thank you for giving me this opportunity to share the Economy of Goodness today. Our concept is how to apply the goodness in philanthropy to the economy and society, which means the original motive as well as the method of practise should be good, rather than making up problems or pollutions through the so-called "philanthropy".

What is goodness? The perspectives of the East and the West are different. The concept of "summum bonum" proposed by Plato, the ancestor of Western philosophy, emphasized truth. According to him, goodness is the pursuit of the supreme truth, which values minds over matters because the latter are subject to change. As a result, Plato's idea becomes the origin for Westerners to pursuit supreme truth. Christianity emphasizes that God is the supreme truth. However, the belief in supreme truth gives rise to good and evil, right and wrong, leading to wars and conflicts.

Aristotle later revised the philosophy of his teacher Plato. He believed that the concept of an apple was inseparable from the apple itself. Mind and matter must be integrated, and it is human nature to basically satisfy the material desires, which can also stimulate positive motivations. Therefore, his theory is a balanced mix of mind and matter, nature and phenomenon,

Aristotle's idea is close to the Chinese idea of goodness, which focuses on the happiness of real-life and the perfection of morality. It was written in *The Book of Rites* that "Although there is the supreme truth, if you don't learn it, you won't know how good it is." This was said by Confucius. Goodness is for the benefit of everyone instead of setting restrictions. You could not call something the highest truth if it is not for the benefit of all people.

Therefore, the standard for truth is goodness, which is more important than truth itself when considering the integrity of life. In Chinese philosophy, goodness is to benefit all people and all things. Therefore, even Lao Tzu, who advocated that life should return to "nothing," emphasized that "The supreme good is like water, which nourishes all things without trying to. It is content with the low places that people disdain. Thus it is like the Tao." That is to say Goodness benefits all things, and even approaches and helps the evil. Confucius also said that a saint is one who can "extensively benefit people, and be able to assist all". So, goodness means considering the benefits of others and serve others.

Mencius also said that "A man who commands our liking is what is called a good man." and "He whose goodness has been filled up is what is called beautiful man.". According to him, to satisfy people's needs is goodness; to make other fulfilled is beautiful, Buddhism pays great attention to compassion, mercy, joy, and abandon, and require us to treat everything equally, and feel pity for all beings.

All beings are objects that need to be taken care of, and all beings are part of ourselves. The combination of selfless love with all substances and all beings is the highest state from altruism to enlightenment in Buddhism. Only through thorough altruism can we achieve common prosperity. Therefore, in Eastern thought, good means altruism. It is not about fighting evil, but about edification to turn all evil into good.

Darwin's theory of evolution also believes that what has been derived from the evolution process is a kind of "altruistic" spirit. The various species that can survive, such as human beings, are mutually supportive and altruistic, and those with an "altruistic" spirit are superior. Modern medical scientists have also discovered that there are compassionate and altruistic blocks in animals called "temporal cortex". In the laboratory, when the mouse saw other mouse being killed, the compassionate and altruistic blocks would be activated. The same happens to human beings. Seeing others giving or suffering, their compassionate and altruistic blocks would amplify. Therefore, compassion and altruism can be inspired and amplified. As long as we realize that altruism is more conducive to the development of self and group than self-benefit, human beings will practise altruism more actively and substantially.

Mutual assistance and common prosperity are the truly powerful and purifying motivator of mankind. I have been working in the philanthropic field for 18 years, and as I serve and learn at Tzu Chi, I see that many entrepreneurs have changed after doing philanthropic work. They have brought the concept of good and the idea of love into enterprises, and when they do good in philanthropic work, in daily life, and even in operating enterprises, their focus on self-benefit has changed to the altruistic mindset, so as to practice good in economic life.

Therefore, the concept of the Economy of Goodness is to guide us to understand profoundly the corporate philosophy of "altruism is self-benefit, and the profit for all". If one can be altruistic, he/she will benefit himself/herself; and if one can benefit for the mass, it will be profitable. Good deeds will have a virtuous circle effect on the spiritual level, corporate credibility and interpersonal relationships, which will naturally accumulate good wealth. Therefore, altruism, as the foundation of the sustainable development of enterprises, will encourage entrepreneurs to get wealthy through good deeds.

Aristotle was the first person to put forward the concept of the Economy of Goodness. He believed that the purpose of economic activities is happiness rather than money, and it is foolish to pursue money blindly. To be happy, people must have loving relationships, participate in public affairs, keep moral, have the ability to reflect philosophically, and follow the spiritual joy. This was the idea of the Economy of Goodness that Aristotle put forward more than 2000 years ago.

The good of modern capitalism in the Western economy is not like the modern and contemporary Western acme of pure personal enjoyment, nor is the same as Weber's Protestant work ethic, but encourages entrepreneurs to glorify God in the pursuit of career satisfaction. However, there is no end to glorifying God, so there is no end to the pursuit of career expansion. This is the cornerstone of faith in modern and contemporary Western capitalism. The traditional Chinese economic view is based on the responsibility of benefiting the family and the hometown. Xi Ming, a Shanxi businessman in the 15th century, said that "Creating a family business is just as important as academic honour and official rank. For merchants, it's important to benefit the community during the growth of the business, just like intellectuals should exert their influence."

The concept of "harmony" is very important. As for the small-scale peasant economy in ancient China, happiness was not about how much wealth an individual had, but about how much loving relationship one maintains, no matter with the family, clan, society or larger groups. China's economic view was that people should follow heaven and harmonize with heaven. Natural resources were abundant, but people should cherish them and be in harmony with heaven and earth. We should consider the well-being of our loved ones and the whole society, create the well-being for the community, take the overall development of the country as the premise, take the sustainability of the earth as the goal, conform to and never violate the law of the heaven and the earth. Therefore, it was said in *The Book of Changes* that "The great man is he who is in harmony, in his attributes, with heaven and earth; in his brightness, with the sun and moon; in his orderly procedure, with the four seasons; and in his relation to what is fortunate and what is calamitous, in harmony with the spirit-like operations (of Providence). He may precede Heaven, and Heaven will not act in opposition to him; he may follow Heaven, but will act (only) as Heaven at the time would do. If Heaven will not act in opposition to him, how much less will men! how much less will the spirit-like operation (of Providence)! " So "harmony" is an important carrier of goodness.

The totem of the Chinese dragon is a symbol of the integration and harmony of various ethnic groups in ancient China. Both deer horns and snake body can be found on the cultural relics dating back to 8000 years ago. According to legend, after the battle between the snake tribe and the deer tribe, none of them was destroyed. Instead, they merged with each other, so the snakes had deer horns on their bodies. Then they merged with the fish tribe, so the relics had fish scales;

then they merged with the bird tribe, so the dragon had wings to fly. The dragon is a symbol of great national integration, and represents a kind of belief and value. Only through altruism and harmony can different ethnic groups coexist and prosper together.

Harvard University wrote a good case analysis about Alibaba about how it succeeded and what its shortcomings were. In fact, Alibaba has inherited the dragon culture by combining the horizontal cooperation among large, medium and small enterprises and the vertical cooperation among upper, middle and downstream enterprises to create the world's largest Internet Empire. It also brought in finance and created the Alipay system. It transformed everything that might be in opposition or hindrance into helping and collaborative forces through integration. This is mutual tolerance, sharing and common prosperity. It is the method of good, not through confrontation, but through cooperation and collaboration, to reap the fruits of the Economy of Goodness for ourselves and others.

So what is good? It is altruism achieved by harmony. The economy of Goodness could only be achieved when one has the motivation and methods to do good deeds, which brings about a good result. This concept was developed from the process of constructing the Taipei Tzu Chi Hospital. The founder Master Cheng Yen wanted to the hospital to built for love and with love. Guided by Tzu Chi volunteers in a caring and patient manner, the workers no longer smoke, drink or eat betel nuts, but are willing to have vegan food. Volunteers are also engaged in clean-up and tidy work, so that the construction site always has a clean environment.

The hospital is the fruit of love and has been built with love. A good result must come from a good motivation through good means. Today, the Taipei Tzu Chi Hospital is a large-scale hospital with highly praised medical services and humanistic culture, and good business performance. Those helped by philanthropic institutions tend to help others. Those businesses engaged in philanthropy tends to gain more economic benefits. It can be concluded that there is no need to be evil, but there is certainly necessary to be good. Just like the way to eliminate evil is not fighting it, but spreading good, the way to eliminate poverty is not fighting wealth, but spreading love.

Adam Smith always emphasized that people only start their businesses out of self-benefit, and greater-scaled public welfare can be created when everyone achieves self-benefit. However, in the development of capitalism for hundreds of years, people have found that self-benefit cannot create greater-scaled public welfare. There is a spirit of altruism behind every business person. They create things wanted by consumers, which is also a kind of altruism.

The famous "prisoner's dilemma" in modern times is also a well-known theory if applied in economics. It tells us that two prisoners can only create greater benefits by cooperating with each other. If they both stick to their benefits, offset and sell each other out, neither of them can benefit. Only by mutual assistance and benefit can a win-win situation and the maximum value of public benefit be truly achieved.

This is also mentioned in the "Pareto Optimality" of economics, which tries to increase the welfare of some people on the premise of not reducing the welfare of any individual person, so that the allocation of economic resources can reach the most ideal state. Only by altruism can the allocation of economic resources reach the Pareto Optimality. Therefore, the Economy of Goodness emphasizes altruism and self-benefit, and its premise is compassion and empathy. Only by benefiting all substances can human beings avoid so many conflicts at present, and the earth can avoid the crisis of gradual disintegration.

In the contemporary era, capitalism emphasizes the maximization of production, which is the premise to maintain human life and happiness. However, when production and consumption are excessive, people will get lost in the materials and take material satisfaction as happiness. This is the materialization of our lives, which is the complete opposite of the pursuit of happiness. Therefore, Master Cheng Yen put forward the concept of "cherishing substance", which is also the Buddha's teaching. All living beings have Buddha-nature, and the good of production is based on the standpoint that everything has life to cherish substance. In this way, production will not be maximized.

Standardization and division of labour are necessary for maximization, so workers work like machines and are reduced to production tools under the framework of the mechanical system. The respect and creativity of human nature are completely obliterated, and this is a crisis of contemporary production. Therefore, we should cherish substance and ourselves, and we should not place our desire completely on the pursuit of materials, be enslaved by desire, or let the materials exhaust our life. So cherishing life and ourselves is a very important viewpoint of the Economy of Goodness. In this way, the ideal state of altruistic oriented harmony and universal good can be achieved.

Next, let's talk about the core concept of corporate altruism.

From Steve Job's 22 years old to his death at the 50s, from founding Apple to running the Hollywood animation industry and to developing the iPhone back in Apple, one of his beliefs remained the same, which was "with our passion, we can change the world and make it better." The essence of this core belief is altruism. He mentioned that products should not be designed if they are against the environment, and this is a very important business spirit.

Chu Jenn Weng, the founder of ViTrox Corp Bhd in Malaysia, is a volunteer of Tzu Chi. After joining us, he introduced Tzu Chi's love and good into the enterprise. As a result, the enterprise has expanded tenfold in 7 years and is currently the second-largest technology factory in Malaysia. His wife has created a humanistic space that advocates the value of love and good, and this space allows people to have more opportunities for interaction. There are books, tea, coffee, lectures, and products made from recycled and environmentally friendly materials. Engineers can have a break from their jobs at any time to meditate, plan, and discuss here. Chu Jenn Weng wants to build a big loving family for employees.

Chu Jenn Weng encourages and leads employees to protect the environment and devote themselves in philanthropy. When floods hit Penang in 2017, his 300 engineers took turns to the disaster area every day for the relief work. At least 150 employees worked as volunteers in the disaster area every day, and they returned to the factory to work thereafter without asking for overtime pay. Everyone is showing corporate' s humanistic culture with love and good, while they are vegetarian from Monday to Thursday. It is a caring enterprise with belief at its core, guided by value, managed by love, and governed by principles. Therefore, we believe that being engaged in philanthropy is more beneficial to the good of the enterprise and the economy.

The ten cultivation principles of the Caring Enterprise are: taking core values as the concept, guiding with values, governing with principles, managing with love, creating with compassion, creating an equal circular organization, innovating with altruism, inheriting with an example, coexisting with the earth, and sharing common prosperity with all beings. We hope to build an era of caring enterprises and the Economy of Goodness. If the enterprises are good, the substances are good. I hope that the ideal of good can be reflected in the world, and I also hope China's Economy of Goodness can become a model of the global economy, and Chinese caring enterprises can become the benchmark for global enterprises.

Liu Peifeng: Thank you, Mr. Her Rey-Sheng, for your sharing of the Caring Enterprises and the Economy of Goodness. Next, let's welcome Professor Ngai Sek-yum, Member of the Academic Committee of WPF, Chairman and Professor of Social Work Department, CUHK to give us a speech. Thank you.

The Training Mechanism and Project Exploration of Chinese Philanthropic Talent

Steven Sek-Yum Ngai, Member of the Academic Committee of the WPF, Chairman and Professor of Social Work Department, the CUHK

Good morning, everyone. First of all, I would like to thank our organizers for giving us the opportunity to participate in the discussion. Our meeting has been particularly successful, and during these two days, we have also heard very enlightening speeches. I hope we can continue to make wonderful speeches today. Today, I will talk about how to cultivate leaders in philanthropy, and I want to give you a few examples of what we're doing.

My speech consists of three parts. The first part is why we should cultivate leaders in the philanthropic field. The second part is how to train talent in philanthropy. The third part is our outlook for the future.

In terms of the reasons for training talent, I would like to start with some of our reflections. First, we have constantly been observing and understanding the current problems of non-governmental organizations and philanthropic organizations in talent training. Through observation, we have found that there is much training in philanthropy, but they are highly homogeneous, and the general training may just show ideas, such as how to recruit volunteers, etc. At the same time, we have found that with the rapid development of society and the rapid emergence of non-philanthropic organizations in Asia, many practitioners face more challenges and difficulties, so they need more training, such as how to deal with the challenges brought by technology. Since we have found problems in talent training, we are thinking about what we should do. Second, we have collected a lot of data from the government, especially the Chinese government. Our Ministry of Civil Affairs reported in 2017 that 9 million people were working in social organizations, philanthropic foundations and non-profit organizations in China. When we talk about so-called leaders in philanthropy, 20% are people with management positions and above, such as chairmen, senior managers, etc. Another study conducted in 2018 by Tsinghua University found that more than 40% of philanthropic workers had a master's degree or above. So we found that we could offer them degree certification in philanthropic education and philanthropic training. Third, 60% of practitioners hope to receive systematic and structured training. More than 69% of students are eager to receive short-term training; 60% of students feel that they need to upgrade their skills to better serve in the philanthropic industry. So we communicated with the government later. The Department of Social Work of CUHK was established in 1964, and 2019 will be the 55th anniversary. We have trained more than 7000 students so far, and we have research projects, master's and doctoral degrees, and doctoral training stations. Some of our graduates join non-governmental organizations, some work at the frontline of society, some teach at local or international institutions, and some are analysts of correct social policies.

In this context, we are committed to the training of talent, including a talent for non-governmental organizations and government agencies. We have a non-governmental organization program that provides multidisciplinary training and guidance. This program started in 2015, so we have 5 years of experience by now. This program aims to create an environment where all participants can improve their management skills so that they can better understand and achieve their goals. This program also includes people from different organizations, and they can receive here training and guidance from the media and society. They can form teams, learn from and educate each other. Our program is supported by the Union Bank of Switzerland (UBS), and also involves people in the education and media industries in Hong Kong, who will participate in our mentor team. In the end they are going to finance, and successful organizations will get bonuses to support their activities. UBS and *South China Morning Post* are our main collaborators.

Next, I want to discuss with you the impact we have made, but we only have data for the past 4 years. If I go back to school, I can show you more data for 2019. In the past 4 years, we have helped 103 students with assistance from 87 different organizations. In total, we have served more than 3 million people in Hong Kong because different organizations serve different populations.

There was another program called the Jockey Club MEL Institute Project, and we received funds from the HKJC through it. Through such a qualified training project, we hope to involve many mentors who are experts from both local and overseas. Our project helps students enhance their learning experience through an online knowledge platform. Courses to be learned include development, supervision, resource planning and management, media communication, project evaluation and impact evaluation. All participants are members of NGOs. Over the past three years, we've had 240 members in this project. We also published

100 evaluation tools on our website. Cooperating with UNESCO, we have helped the Hong Kong SAR government, the Macao SAR government and the Chinese mainland with a number of projects. We have different levels of evaluation tools for social impact. At the same time, we provide video training and mentor training. After graduation, students need to go back to their organizations to share with colleagues.

From May to July 2019, we recruited more than 120 participants. Our training consists of two parts, one in 2019 and the other in 2020, and the training will end in 2021. Finally, we will have dedicated international conferences, including media conferences to promote further progress.

The first conference will be the Chinese Social Work Education Forum, where we will recruit more than 30 philanthropic practitioners to carry out Chinese social work education cooperation. In December 2018, we hosted a summit in Hong Kong that focused on issues in the philanthropic filed. At that forum, we discussed a number of industry issues, such as the training of doctoral talent in social work. At the same time, we had the practice of innovative social work teaching methods, and we hoped to have an impact on the heads of non-profit organizations. The Chinese social work industry has a network of contacts throughout Taiwan, Macao, Singapore, the United States, and other regions and countries.

And finally, what we're going to do is set up our Master's degree in social service management, which is a master's degree program that we cooperate with Tsinghua University. It focuses on social service management, and teachers of Tsinghua University teach its courses. The teaching team at Tsinghua University will teach 7 courses and 10 units, while our team will be responsible for teaching 5 courses and 15 units. At last, the students will get the degree certificate of Master of Arts in Social Service Management (Beijing) granted by CUHK. At the same time, students can apply for the course-completion certificate of Tsinghua University. We hope there will be more managers in the social work field in China because the market needs such talent now.

What should be done next? We will hold another meeting soon. The meeting was in Hong Kong in 2018, and in 2019 we will hold a Chinese social work conference in Macao. We will also bring more opportunities. We communicated with Swiss Bank, and they also hope to have more training for leaders of social organizations and NGOs. Finally, we hope to try our best to launch a doctorate program in social services and management in the mainland of China. That's all for my speech. Thank you.

Liu Peifeng: Thank you. Now, let's welcome Ms. Li Yaping to give us a speech.

International Philanthropic Talent Development Plan: Visit Report in Hong Kong and Thailand

Li Yaping, Executive Vice President and Secretary-General of the SZEEA

First of all, I would like to thank the organizers for hosting this event. I am also much honoured as well because I will report to you here on behalf of the first-phase students. We paid the visits to Hong Kong and Thailand. Now I will make a report on the visit and study of the entire philanthropic field.

We chose CUHK as our first destination, where we learned from a theoretical level the theoretical frameworks of international philanthropic organizations, and the methods of their project management and brand communication. In the following part, we have introduced in detail a very important talent training project for all philanthropic fields. Professor Ma talked about the origins of the project plan for the leadership of non-profit organizations, including the evaluation of the whole process, the display of results, and the importance of promoting philanthropic work. The mainland is very confused on this matter, and since its methods are not very appropriate, the effect is not very obvious, of which I will also make a detailed introduction. We also visited the Hong Kong Red Cross, an institution with influence in the international system, and Caritas Hong Kong as well. We also went to Thailand to see the workshop of UNDP. I will introduce the detailed work content later, which brought us an unexpected result. The Rockefeller Foundation is a family business that has a very sound network around the world. As for what it brings to us, I will talk about it later, too.

First of all, I would like to introduce the tripartite cooperation model of the leader project plan for non-profit organizations. In fact, it was proposed by UBS, and CUHK carried out the training of talent. Nevertheless, when our foundation was working on some programs, we did not know which institutions could assist in the implementation. Therefore, they felt that they needed to establish a system to train these talents. Later, we formed a team with theoretical and practical professors from CUHK and set up a system of training plan together with UBS.

The demand side was clear, and the system framework for talent training was also clear. During the training process, the final project effectiveness would be evaluated. The course teaching, including the integration and implementation of the project, was very practical, which is different from the training plan implemented in the mainland. It was very important to achieve the unity of knowledge and action, and let the theoretical knowledge we had learned guide the practice step by step. In this process, the combination of innovation and practice of the entire project was very clear. In the end, Professor Ma shared some data with us, which made me very surprised, because after 4 years, there were 103 members, 87 organizations established, and 3 million people are making profits. In this process, there were 87 innovative projects, and it was very clear that the organizational capability had been improved. It is also mentioned here that 4 projects have received financial support of HK $3.6 million. In short, the levels of collaborative research between participants and non-profit organizations of CUHK were very clear.

In this process, different social resources were assembled, and there were 40 trainers, 31 mentors, and different participants to form a community of mutual learning. I was very surprised by their presentations. From design to implementation of the program, the participation and integration of all social resources, the display of final results, the scale of relevant social groups, and the field of program implementation were all very clear, which has lessons for the mainland.

For the talent training system, there are several major points we should pay attention to: First, we need to understand and dig out the real demand and figure out it should be met in which stages in terms of the project execution system. Second, relevant consultation. We have to know what groups can be involved in doing this, and in what ways we can send these messages out. Third, the method of participation, which includes the involvement in project execution, and in what identity one is benefited from this platform. Fourth, with the support of the strong theoretical system, the colleges and universities play a very important role in the project. However, how does the theoretical system for the talent of the universities support this project? In terms of action, such support is for talent themselves. In the process of implementation, theoretical guidance and support will be provided for talent. Fifth, it is very important for talent innovation projects to be implemented and produce certain results. Professor Ma told us that in September each year, he would hold an achievement contest for this year's innovation project to let the society know about the project in an open way. At the same time, he would invite social institutions, including government departments, to continually display the results of the achievements and receive inspections by all parties. Sixth, in this process, resources are superimposed one after another and multiple resources are coordinated.

We visited the service system of Caritas Hong Kong, which has a relatively complete volunteer system to provide long-term support for the operation of the organization. Shenzhen is also a voluntary city. The volunteer organization there started early and has established different systems, but we manage it through the volunteer association. Shenzhen Volunteer Association itself can attract and maintain 10,000 volunteers and provide practical support in the program for a long time, but for us, we need to think a lot. How can volunteers gain personal growth or superimposition of resources? Volunteers in this organization will affect their close relatives and continue to serve as communicators to attract more volunteers for this organization. In addition, there are 256 service units in Hong Kong, with over 152 service points to serve the public in different places. For us, it is difficult for an organization to have such a large network system and cover so many points. Moreover, it has sources of funds, including those from government departments, enterprises, different associations, and business entities. If an organization has diverse funding sources, how should it interweave with the subjects to obtain more resources in matching relevant information? The main service areas of Caritas Hong Kong include education, health care, social services and fund-raising activities.

We were also surprised to see Rockefeller's designs when we went to Thailand. When we were at the UNDP, we experienced a wonderful creative process. We discussed the development opportunities and challenges of philanthropic organizations under the "Belt and Road Initiative " with the joint agencies of Thailand, including the students who visited there. In other words, under the same theme, different organizations had very diverse perspectives, and the final results were also very diverse. Under this system, how could each organization and every perspective integrate into the same issue with its function or need? Finally, we were given some inspiration. How can we integrate into the development of the "Belt and Road Initiative" and the Guangdong-Hong Kong-Macao Greater Bay Area? In terms of innovation and learning from relevant experience, we have gained a lot. We saw the excellent work done by Hong Kong social organizations, and after we went to Thailand, we started to think about how different foundations and social service organizations could form a philanthropic ecosystem. That's all for today. Thank you.

Liu Peifeng: Thank you. Now let's welcome Mr. Chen Xingjia, Founder of Henghui Charity Foundation, to give us a speech.

International Philanthropic Talent Development Plan: Visit Report in Philippines and Vietnam

Chen Xingjia, Founder of the Henghui Charity Foundation

Thanks for our moderator, and thanks for all of you. I am very grateful to our organizers for giving me such an opportunity to report my learning experience from the participation in the International Philanthropic Talent Development Plan. Just now, Mr. Li Yaping reported on the gains from his participation in the first phase of the program, and I participated in the second phase. Generally speaking, I have gained a lot. Through this study, we have learned a lot about the management and operation experience of international advanced public welfare organizations, brought there the experience and practices of Chinese philanthropic organizations, and conveyed to the counterparts in the Philippines and Vietnam the attitudes of acceptance, tolerance and modestly-learning of the Chinese society towards the international community.

I travelled on behalf of the philanthropic organizations in Shenzhen, and there were more than 10 people in our delegation. I set out from Shenzhen alone, while the others set out from Beijing. When they departed from Beijing, they held a democratic election at the airport to elect the head of the delegation. As of last, my colleagues in Beijing elected me. As the head, I must be at the forefront, including sitting in the front of the class, sitting in the middle when having the meals, and giving summaries and on-site speeches for all lectures and courses. Therefore, it was not an easy task, but it also allowed me to concentrate on the learning process.

I will report our gains according to the context and process of study. We had an in-depth exchange with Oxfam in the Philippines, which gave me a very concrete understanding of the ideas of this excellent international philanthropic organization. I closely learned its operational experience and experienced their culture and the stimulating influence of education. From this study, I learned about Oxfam's global deployment, its pragmatic and innovative approaches, and its efforts in life improvement, sustainable development, active response to humanitarian crises, emergency rescue, assistance in the restoration of livelihoods, and promotion of public education campaigns. We also got a closer look at why this enduring organization in the philanthropic field can develop. We communicated with the philanthropic organizations on climate change in the Philippines one by one. We learned about the breadth and depth of the Philippines philanthropic organizations' involvement in solving social issues, as well as the positive interaction between them and local governments. We also invited a mayor to talk about how the Philippines government and philanthropic organizations cooperate to promote the resolution of some social issues.

Let me talk about my adventures in the Philippines as the head of the delegation. But before I start, I would like to ask you a question: How many of you know Mr. Yan Yangchu? He was a great historical figure. Born in Bazhong, Sichuan, he was a world-renowned educator for the poor, and also an idol of mine. I once worked as an official at the grassroots level, as a head of one of China's top 100 counties, and as a secretary of the County Committee in a national-level poverty-stricken county. During my tenure as the party secretary, I was honoured by the Central Committee of the Communist Party of China and received a cordial reception by General Secretary Xi Jinping. I might be the first government worker in China to resign after being promoted. Why? After resigning from the post of secretary of the County Committee, I came to Shenzhen and founded a philanthropic organization because of my dream to be the "Yan Yangchu" of this era. Therefore, you can see my predestined relationship with such a great historical figure. I was surprised to find that Yan Yangchu's cemetery was actually at the International Institute of Rural Reconstruction in the Philippines. I spent a whole day there and felt the noble spirit of Yan Yangchu's dedication to mankind. For the study summary of that day, I changed the form and wrote a poem on the spot, which was called *Sir, I Come to See You from Your Homeland*. During the course conclusion, I read the poem in English to friends in the Philippines. The President of the International Institute of Rural Reconstruction was very impressed that day, so he shared my poem with the former president of the council of the institute when Yan Yangchu founded it, and his grandson George is the current president of the council. It was especially fortunate for me that George met me individually for two and a half hours during the WPF, and we discussed Mr. Yan's humanitarian spirit. It is my privilege to tell you that this world-renowned philanthropist is at our venue. Let's applaud for George. This was a very special adventure of predestined relationship during my visit. We also visited the Vietnam Union of Friendship Organizations and other philanthropic organizations to learn from their experience, convey the goodwill of Chinese non-governmental organizations towards Vietnam and communicated about the possibility of cooperation with their country.

Now let me share with you my feelings of participating in the study delegation. Love is the most common human nature, and the most beautiful quality as well as the simplest emotion of human beings, so philanthropy is the natural and the best language for people-to-people diplomacy. In response to China's the "Belt and Road Initiative", as the philanthropic organizations, we should play a more important role. Some countries in the world complain about the "Belt and Road Initiative", saying that China is expanding its power. Under this background, we have widely promoted friendship and mutual trust among the people through philanthropic organizations and non-governmental exchanges, which is a kind of low-cost and high-yielding people-to-people diplomacy. Last but not least, Shenzhen has joined more than 400 philanthropic foundations to establish the Shenzhen Commonweal Fund Federation, and I was honoured to be elected as its first executive president a week ago. Our organization has established three special committees to serve everyone, including the Academic Support Committee, the Investment Advisory Committee, and the International Exchange and Cooperation Committee. We hope that through the international exchange and cooperation of philanthropic organizations, we can improve the governance level of philanthropic organizations in Shenzhen. Our vision can promote the harmonious construction of our entire country and society. This is the experience I want to share with you. Once again, thank you.

Liu Peifeng: Thank you, Mr. Chen Xingjia. You just told us many interesting stories. Thank you very much. As scheduled, we have two commentators, Dr. Faiz Shah and Ms. Nguyen Kim Ngan.

Nguyen Kim Ngan: Thank you very much for talking about Vietnam. Good morning, everyone. I am very pleased to participate in the WPF on behalf of SRD, where I serve as the Executive Director. I have visited NGOs around the world and local NGOs, and I'd like to share a few examples with you. There are two types of NGOs in Vietnam: international NGOs and local NGOs. International NGOs are funded by foreign countries and operated by foreigners, while local NGOs are operated by Vietnamese with funding from both domestic and foreign sources. Local NGOs are non-profit organizations that survive through self-management, and such organizations are increasing in Vietnam. There are two NGO networks, the network of climate change and the network of government, and local NGOs are concerned with issues such as climate change, gender equality and agricultural development. We work with more than 130 NGOs, and we mainly focus on agriculture, livability and other issues. We also pay close attention to issues like industry policies and gender equality. As a local NGO, we work closely with the communities. In the past 13 years, we have been dealing with people in rural areas, and we have more than 20,000 direct beneficiaries. We continuously improve their living conditions, and we also carry out education and project teaching and research. We are now the leading NGO in Vietnam backed up by the Vietnamese government. There is an increasing number of NGOs now, and they hope to obtain more funds and support to help the poor and the disabled. Thank you.

Dr. Faiz Shah: First of all, I would like to thank our organizers for inviting me to comment. It is impossible to summarize the highlights in the speeches you have given today in 5 minutes, so I want to talk about my thoughts and the development of philanthropy in Bangkok. We mentioned that Bangladesh had transformed philanthropy into a rewarding social industry in the past years, and the winner of the Nobel Prize who believes that people want to show kindness to others and give out more benefits. In other words, People work hard and share what they have learned with others, and people appreciate kindness and giving. We can also see this in China as its society becomes richer. People now especially hope to enhance the credibility of philanthropic organizations and energize our philanthropic work. People concern about others can give the US $1 to those who need it, but this is not enough. We can invest philanthropic funds in social organizations to enable them to make impact investments. In this way, we can better promote our ideas. Although people can get money from philanthropists and start their businesses, it is not about making money, but solving social problems. Thus we can say that many social organizations can help solve social problems. We can help solve social problems by establishing enterprises, not just using money to solve the education for children and women. We know that there are now more than 50 social organizations in the world competing in the market. Since they do not enjoy tax exemption, they make money on their own to help solve problems such as transportation, health and safety, and these are the problems we face in the construction of smart cities. People can donate money to such helpful social organizations, and then social organizations can provide services in the form of operating enterprises, whose burden can be eased through the tax reduction authorized by the government. In addition, we hope to establish a learning mechanism, and some countries are doing such projects. We have formed an alliance of 79 universities, 5 of which are from China, and we are called the "Alliance of Philanthropic Organizations and Universities". We have meetings from time to time to better promote the exchange of information, research and cooperation. If you are interested, you are welcome. Our alliance meeting will be held in Berlin in November 2020, and I hope more people can join us. We now need to establish a learning mechanism, so as to think about questions like how to perfect this philanthropic organization, and how to improve our credibility. A good idea has to be backed by sufficient financial support, without which, even the best idea can't come true. So we need to fund good ideas to let them become better. We need to launch funding channels, and we hope to make more friends at the 4th WPF and build the Economy of Goodness. At the same time, we have learned about the cooperation between academia and universities, such as how to promote projects, so that we can better unlock the value of social organizations. That's all I want to share. Thank you.

Liu Peifeng: Thank you, Dr. Faiz Shah. Now let's take a break.

Liu Peifeng: Please have your seats. Welcome, and thank you for your support. On behalf of the organizers, I would like to apologize to all of you for not being able to bring each and every one of you on stage to be with the experts, scholars, and leaders of non-profit organizations. We shall now begin our discussion with two main questions. The first one is how to view the philanthropy index. We are paying more and more attention to the employment of social organizations, and we also regard how many services social organizations provide to society and how to attract high-net-worth individuals as the most important indicators. Our question is how to view these indicators, and among which, what the advocacy organizations and rights protection organizations that have the most important contributions to society are like? If we pay attention to high-net-worth individuals, how do we treat the services for ordinary people being put into the system? I also want to discuss with you whether our orientation is the changing of the world or the changing of ourselves? NGOs have made great contributions to the promotion of democratic forces, but we are now concerned about its contribution to social services.

The second question is how we view the training model of philanthropic talent. After all, the training of philanthropic talent is a common concern. The former guest speaker just mentioned about the situation abroad, and in China, we have Institute for Philanthropy Tsinghua University and the China Global Philanthropy Institute in Shenzhen. They all offer professional talent training, and our industry has done a lot of training as well. Nevertheless, we will see some problems because vocational training is particularly like the pyramid scheme.

I'd like to listen to your advice on how to make this thing more in line with current needs. I hope all of you can focus on the highlights when elaborating your opinions, and save some time to give opportunities to the following speakers. Now I would like to invite Dr. Ruth A. Shapiro.

Dr. Ruth A. Shapiro: The first question you just mentioned is how to evaluate the so-called impact. I have met many high-net-worth individuals in Asia. Non-profit organizations would ask the question that "Can your organization help us raise funds from the mainland of China, Hong Kong and all around the world?" My answer is generally the same. I think that non-profit organizations have to tell their own stories to others, and I also find that organizations need to show their funds and methods of using funds on official websites. As far as I am concerned, such transparent organizations will attract more resources because companies would think the funds are well-managed, and they are therefore willing to raise funds for these non-profit organizations. The second question is how we introduce and train talent. The wealth in Asia has now reached a record high, which is a new trend. I came to China in 1984, when this country was completely different from now. The accumulation of wealth in China over the past nearly 40 years has been staggering. If you come from a low-income family, you will want to become a lawyer, a banker or a civil servant. The biggest difference now is that young people have more choices because they don't have to worry about the bottom line of their income. Many young people choose to repay society and enter the field of social services, and some of them establish social enterprises and social organizations. Since there are needs for philanthropic and social services, now the philanthropy has become an industry, which is a very good signal.

Jia Xijin: I would like to answer the first question because my presentation is about the civil research index. I have participated in relevant index research myself. In addition to my research, I can see the various indexes that my peers have done. The numbers of indexes are enormous, just like what I said at the beginning of my presentation. What's their relationship with each other? How to deal with them? The question raised by Liu Peifeng is significant. For these indexes, the most important thing is the purpose of attention. What exactly do we evaluate through an index? Different purposes lead to different concerns.

For instance, at the early stage of social development of China, both the indexes and their researchers focused on structural things, so the research index was very popular, especially from the late 1990s to the mid-2000s. However, in recent years, there are more and more scientific research in China and more and more talent joining in. People's focus turns to philanthropy, service, social work, or donation from the rich, so the research index is going to be more specialized. The relationship between them is a bit like that between the social division of labour and the macro picture that sociology wants to achieve. This social division of labour needs to be specific before it can be studied in detail, but it also needs to be viewed from the macro picture. As we become more specialized, there are more specific indexes to measure things of great significance. For example, how much of the non-profit sector accounts for GDP, or the characteristics and difficulties of donations from the rich. Still, when there is only a division of labour, we need to think about our structure, every phenomenon that occurs, the participation of every philanthropist, everyone's behaviour, what the final goal is, and what we want to achieve. We are not doing social work for the sake of social work, nor are we giving for the sake of giving, but for the meaning behind those actions. The method of CSI is not so perfect and scientific; so why do we do it every seven years? I think its perspective is worthy of our thinking, and it will remind us of the structure of the development of the entire society. Therefore, it is not just about giving or donation, but about all those points. Our research has also found that the social sector is getting bigger and bigger, and there are more and more talent. We are doing things more precisely and scientifically and providing more services. But from the concept of social governance, being the subject of governance means a kind of progress, a spontaneous order, and the structure of society. A spontaneous society is different from a governed society. So, is the structure becomes more significant or less severe? From our point of view, it's worth thinking about, and practitioners also need to look back and think why they participated in.

Liu Peifeng: Thank you. Now, let's give the floor to Ms. Allison Hollowell.

Allison Hollowell: First, since you just mentioned about measuring the impact, we need to have some frameworks that everyone agrees on to measure our impact. Many philanthropic organizations claim to have different evaluation standards for their donors, and the donors shall know the impact of philanthropy once being told what the organizations have done. As a result, there must be frameworks that all donors agree on. AVPN also has projects to measure the impact, and we use the most indicators to measure the impact of our projects, hoping to bring them to Asia so that our partners can better apply the measurement standards. Second, we must get feedback on social organizations. Everyone agrees that feedback is important, and we want to know what donors think, but in reality, people don't give feedback naturally, so we launch a feedback project collaborating with a foundation in the United States. We hope to cooperate with several larger foundations, so several foundations, including us, have jointly funded a project called "Upward Listening". We interview donors of philanthropic institutions, such as people who make donations at the bank, and we would ask them that "How did you feel when you donated? Did you feel your disrespected when you were helped? Have you been really helped?" We want to hear two-way feedback to judge how our project is doing. We think the balance of impact is very important because it can make us do our jobs better, so the reports about our future impact are very important. Third, talent development and preparation. 35% of Asian wealth will be passed on to the next generation in the next 5 to 7 years. Many wealth families recognize that when the younger generation control wealth, they should better use wealth tools to influence philanthropy, so we also hope to guide the new heirs of wealth better to spend money and help them better promote philanthropy. We hope to gather the power of all of our 585 members who have their own cases and practices. We currently have an online platform called AVPN Academic, which is a self-learning platform where we submit members' ideas to help various philanthropic institutions with talent development. This is what we are exploring with our members, and we hope you can pay attention to our project.

Liu Peifeng: Next, let's invite Mr. Her Rey-Sheng.

Her Rey-Sheng: Thank you. In the wisdom of China, Lao Tzu mentioned "the cyclic change of motion is the movement of Tao", which means when any kind of Tao exerts a reaction force, the offsetting force can be seen in a positive direction. In terms of the so-called fighting against nature, Hegel gave a dialectics, which ended with harmony in the hope of achieving a higher ideal goal, and finally came down to a concept of good. From a Chinese perspective, evil is not something to be eliminated. Instead, one should approach evil and try to turn it into good through edification. Only in this way can the concept of great compassion be truly integrated. From this point of view, we are spreading goodness and love, rather than fighting evil and wealth. Those who spread goodness can be a role model for others. It's important to have role models at the beginning of an initiative. At first, role models may be scarce. As more people join in, others would follow. As such information reaches the larger community, the actions will be gradually accepted by society. So, it's important to endow and empower by setting up role models at the beginning. When people are moved by what you have done, they will follow you without being asked to. In this way, more people will join in. However, you must also have faith; otherwise, all innovations will have a negative impact on this society. Professor Liu raised a very good question about how to treat good and evil. Neither of them is eternal because we can put forward different views at different times. There is always opposition to new things. What we should do is the accept the existence of the opposition. Only in this way, we can see things holistically. Thank you.

Liu Peifeng: Thank you. Now let's invite Professor Ngai Sek-yum to speak.

Steven Sek-Yum Ngai: I want to answer the second question, that is, the training of philanthropic talent. During our collaboration with Tsinghua University on the project, we spent a lot of time understanding and evaluating its impact and specific methodology, and we hope this talent project will be beneficial to the philanthropic industry. I want to share my experience in terms of the content and architecture of the project. We need to build a culture that promotes sharing. Nowadays, when we talk about NGOs, social enterprises or talent development, we always change to another perspective. It's not that our lecturers know everything, but that they've experienced people's difficulties, so lecturers in our team have multiple perspectives and backgrounds. Therefore, the training instructors must integrate people who have been engaged in philanthropic work, people who work in the media, and people who work in banks, because they know how to train and coach others. In this way, they can also teach our talent to tell good stories and make them as powerful and influential as possible. More importantly, NGOs and government organizations have to solve social problems and truly empower our students to help them understand the problems in society. Meanwhile, for our students, we hope to bring them critical thinking, relevant knowledge, and the ability to tell good stories. They should have multiple perspectives to improve their abilities and bring about social change continuously. From the perspective of soft power or of culture, we need to understand the capabilities of participants truly, so mutual exchanges among students are very important. Our learning involves more and more aspects. Our professors need to be humble because we can also learn from students, so that we can work hand in hand and advance social work more carefully and step by step. Now we have such methods as technology and mutual learning to help develop talent. The points I just mentioned are very important. Besides, on the issue of impact, the first and second questions are related. We must have critical thinking in influencing talent, and then lay the foundation for evaluating impact in universities. This is important because the reason we train social workers is to let them serve society. These are the two questions I want to talk about. Thank you.

Liu Peifeng: Thank you. Let's invite Li Yaping.

Li Yaping: First, I think it is necessary to have consistency in the language system of dialogue with the world. As one expert just mentioned, we should know what the system of dialogue is, whether we are telling our stories or the consultations to the world. For the organization, how can we conduct a logical and rigorous analysis of the consulting information to form a group of stories, and then tell interested parties or the public, so that they can get some value? In this regard, we have 17 development goals when we visit and study. Although we all know there are 17 of them, we do not know what their specific contents are, so how can we tell the world and the community about our information? Second, we need to have a mechanism that has a very clear story system that can be used to connect with unrelated organizations, especially regional organizations, independent organizations, or when being visited by the Red Cross. The reason why the promoting values can be connected for philanthropy indexes or development of social and institutions is related to our own experience of social development and contribution to economic development. Being closely connected is a characteristic of every philanthropic organization, but people are too busy working silently to share information.

Chen Xingjia: I would like to share two things. I have practised in philanthropic practice for almost 3 years. There are 10 full-time employees now in the philanthropic organization founded by me. However, none of them has relevant philanthropic learning experience, so I think there is a huge demand for such training. When I was studying at the International Institute of Rural Reconstruction in the Philippines, I had a special feeling. I saw a gap, and I thought the training of philanthropic talent is like the education in secondary school. There were fields, service projects, practical venues, and teaching venues in International Institute of Rural Reconstruction. I felt down-to-earth, comfortable, happy from learning, and particularly inspired. I am looking forward to the degree-conferral training course for philanthropic talent jointly launched by CUHK and Tsinghua University. The training of our China Global Philanthropy Institute does not offer a diploma or degree, and Institute for Philanthropy Tsinghua University focuses on research. The training CUHK is for practical talent, so I am particularly looking forward to it. It is the mission of philanthropic workers to promote the pragmatic and systematic teaching for philanthropic talent in a similar way of the education in secondary school.

Nguyen Kim Ngan: Indeed. I mentioned earlier the local Vietnamese NGOs and their work, including philanthropic education and training, and we must find a suitable training group to improve their capabilities. For us, we have a lot of philanthropic activities, and we hope to have relevant training, and even the retraining for trainers. We have done a lot of research on philanthropic work to collect many methods, through which we can constantly change the living conditions of the poor. We will also conduct training within the ecosystem, and our community and government are willing to learn from other demonstration areas.

Faiz Shah: I have several points to say in response to your comments. First, how do we measure and evaluate the impact? We know that there are a lot of frameworks around the world to help us with our evaluation, but I think a good framework must have a certain data source to help achieve global deployment. At the same time, a certain level of modularity is required, such as selecting the appropriate modules for evaluation according to the actual situations of various countries, and adapting them to local conditions. We can keep upgrading these modules. We have a large number of model generations for impact, but none of them is mature. Such cross-border cooperation needs to be coupled with consideration of national conditions in order to produce appropriate models. In this regard, I couldn't agree more with the other speakers. Second, how to train people?

Today marks the 40th year of my engagement in this industry. In 1999, I was still a professor, and what we did at that time was an NGO management project to solve very similar problems. Young people wanted to enter non-profit social organizations, but there was no way to get a university degree. This was the situation in 1994, and it's still the case now. Perhaps we did not have so-called private donations in the mid-1990s. At that time, it was mainly government grants and foundation grants, and there were no individual or family foundations. With the development of society, great changes have taken place, and people are continuously learning. What we need to think about it, if the world has changed, why haven't our learning needs changed? Why there is no education based on the academic system? We want to get to the root cause. Recently, we launched a master's program of global social enterprise. We established our university to connect more isolated information islands, but we cannot keep up with the trend of social development in academic research. The teaching method of our university is to create knowledge with students, not the transfer of teachers' knowledge, but the intersection of teachers' and students' ideas. We hope to set up a lot of internships and online platforms, and hope that there will be a space where teachers and students can create together, which I think is a very good environment. If there is a corresponding master's degree in this industry, we must build an online platform as well as a public welfare practitioner section. We will also engage in learning like that in the traditional business school again so that we can feel like going to school at home. Only after the successful completion of one part of learning can you enter the next, and only those who have practised can go to the online platform. In this case, everyone can do it level by level, and this is the kind of innovation we are currently working on. In terms of the final exam, if your project passes, you will get financial support. Even though your project is unsuccessful, you can also graduate if the judges accept it. However, you need to study again if the judges feel that your project cannot be funded.

The learning we talked about earlier is important because our traditional learning model does not involve much student's questioning and cross-learning. However, in some short-term projects, there may not be so many opportunities to practice within two years under normal circumstances, so there will be no way to get the full value of the two-year project truly. Therefore, I do not want you to do short-term projects. Many people have studied in colleges, but they may not be the best representatives for the conditions of their groups. For example, in Asian culture, most children go to college as their families wish, but what they learn in the classroom is completely different from what they have been told at home, so we have a lot of projects to give them immersive experience and to let them integrate knowledge from the community. Thus instead of relying entirely on computers for learning, we use the time-honoured social learning, which we call participatory learning. This project uses traditional methods. Our learning must respond to the needs and pain points of the students, so we must let them have the needs of learning, especially the need to establish a social enterprise. The idea of social enterprise is very good, but it is very different from traditional learning, so how do we use innovative methods to promote development?

It's a question of methodology. How to build a learning culture is very important, and the methodology is important for building a culture of learning. By building a learning-oriented organization, we can keep our career alive. Thank you.

Liu Peifeng: Now let's move to the Q&A session.

Audience's question: Mr. Chen Xingjia mentioned he has a special admiration for Mr. Yan Yangchu, so do I. We are a volunteer organization in villages and ancient villages, and we have served more than 1,000 of them. My question today is that as Shenzhen builds a pilot demonstration zone of socialism with Chinese characteristics, the differences and concepts of socialism and capitalism have re-caught our attention. In the field of philanthropy, I found that capitalist philanthropy is very different from socialist philanthropy, and socialist philanthropy emphasizes fairness, mutual assistance, more social solidarity and more rule of law. I would like to know your opinions on which direction to go?

Audience's question: Hello, everyone, this is my good friend. My job is talent management, and I think the international philanthropic talent system is more mature than what we have in China. I participated in the "Belt and Road Initiative" International Philanthropic Talent Exchange Program, and I saw that the talent structure of international organizations is very sound. I've found that there are mainly three types of people engaged in philanthropy. The first type of people is graduates or students, mainly fresh graduates. The second type of pf people is successful people who want to do something that makes them feel happier. The third type of people is generally those who are not so successful in business or any other fields. They feel happy, meaningful and recognized in philanthropy, where their values have been discovered, while things are contrary for them in other fields. Therefore, we should consider the source of talent in the process of talent training. Do we have the ability to attract talent from the entire society and let them rush to philanthropy from other fields? What I want to say is that we have too many things to do with talent management. There is still a long way to go, and I also want to join this group and make my contribution. Thank you.

Liu Peifeng: Please conclude with just one sentence.

Allison Hollowell: I can understand you. I think we are heading in the right direction. We need to better give back to society, respond to the culture of giving, and work together more strategically to maximize impact.

Her Rey-Sheng: When we are doing philanthropic education, we must avoid over-specialization. The faith and mission are the souls of the entire philanthropy, with which we can create many different majors. In fact, it is an integration of technologies, instead of a single one of them. We should pay attention to this when doing philanthropic education.

Nguyen Kim Ngan: I think philanthropy is of great significance to us, and it's a great opportunity for us to learn and communicate like this.

Li Yaping: I hope the talent training in the philanthropic field can pay attention to the combination of specialization, professionalization and socialization.

Dr. Ruth A. Shapiro: We have talked a lot about Chinese philanthropy. Many people are indeed volunteers and grassroots, and they are not professional enough. However, China has a philanthropic culture that has been passed down for thousands of years, and it also has cultural origins of goodness, including helping one's own family, folks, and village, so we need to train talent to be professional.

We should also truly encourage and carry forward the spirit of humanity and goodness in China.

Jia Xijin: In addition to technology and talent, we need to develop and discuss the concepts when training international philanthropic talent, because I have found that there are a lot of mistakes and misunderstandings, especially the long history of understanding the international philanthropy.

Steven Sek-Yum Ngai: I agree with you. We have a very respectable culture of good, which is the so-called kindness. For us, we should let the Chinese people join philanthropy so that we can see more and more people join the charity and public welfare industries. At the same time, we should bring a more suitable training program, not to copy the Western model, but to strengthen the use of good local culture and establish a model of Chinese development of philanthropy, which is a way of adapting to local conditions. We hope to attract people to participate in this process, and at the same time, we must really train the leaders of the organizations, and only leaders who have a vision can bring about impact and changes. We have to connect with the outside world, develop while learning, and even export the practice of China is very important, but our philanthropy industry is relatively romantic. Everyone agreed to this before, but from now on, we have to combine with the sustainability of the industry, self-criticize, and constantly evaluate the efforts we make, so as to make improvement.

Dr. Faiz Shah: China is developing particularly fast. In the past, China imported culture from the West. Nowadays, the West sometimes has been too blind to discover China's excellent practices. I am very concerned about cross-border cultural exchanges. No matter which system and society the knowledge come from, knowledge itself is knowledge. Knowledge doesn't just teach one or two things, but teaches us how to build systems, so I don't think we can simply make the classification as Western knowledge, Indian knowledge, Chinese knowledge or Japanese knowledge, because all knowledge transcends national bounders and helps us build and design effective frameworks. However, for us, we are not blindly introducing some models from other countries, because there is already a long good culture in China, which has been recognized by many people. In particular, Chinese philanthropic workers and social workers should really understand the culture of good. For example, doctors, they will have empathy and help patients through their behaviours. But will they learn to empathize once they are in medical school? No. People are very complicated with complex attributes, so education cannot solve all the problems. China currently has a large number of evaluation tools and different curricula, as well as methods introduced from the West, but it is very important to strengthen the relevance to the local Chinese conditions. Otherwise, many existing problems cannot be solved. Learning knowledge is very interesting since knowledge itself is a process of empowerment, and the process of knowledge empowerment can also join the process of knowledge accumulation. China's empowerment of knowledge has evolved from a learner to a builder. So I am very grateful to everyone, and I will bring the knowledge I heard today back to my country and share it with colleagues and relevant participants. Hence, I think the spirit of our talks is to learn from each other.

Chen Xingjia: Love is the most common nature of mankind, and this determines that philanthropy is the universal language of this world. We can research the capitalist philanthropy and socialist philanthropy we have seen for the purpose of uniting and promoting the progress of the entire society more pragmatically.

Liu Peifeng: Thank you. It's nearly time to finish, and as the moderator, I am very grateful for the dedication of speakers and commentators. Thank you. I also want to thank everyone for your participation in the discussion. This is a great occasion for all of us to advance this cause together. Thank you.

XII Philanthropic Cooperation with Countries along with the "Belt and Road Initiative"

Moderator: Chan Yung, Representative of the 13th National People's Congress of China, Chairman of the New Territories Association of Societies (NTAS) and Vice-Chairman of the Democratic Alliance for the Betterment and Progress of Hong Kong (DAB)

Speakers: Carles Llorens, Secretary-General of the Organization of United Regions / Global Forum of the Regional Governments and Associations of Regions (ORU-Fogar)

Liang Xingxin, President of the Zhejiang Association for Non-profit Organization

Lin Biyu, Deputy Chief Executive Officer of the Tzu Chi Foundation

Ling Chong, Director of Social Organizations Administration of Shenzhen Municipality

Li Xikui: Distinguished guests, ladies and gentlemen, good afternoon! There are five sessions in the forum this afternoon, including Discussion on Issues, Keynote Speeches, Closing Speeches of the Forum, Certificate Issuance, and the Release of the Cooperation Plan.

We will first start the Discussion on Issues. The first topic is Philanthropic Cooperation with Countries along with the "Belt and Road Initiative". Now let's welcome Mr. Chan Yung, Brave, Representative of the 13th National People's Congress of China, Chairman of the New Territories Association of Societies (NTAS) and Vice-Chairman of the Democratic Alliance for the Betterment and Progress of Hong Kong (DAB).

Chan Yung: Ladies and gentlemen, good afternoon. This session is for the topic of Philanthropic Cooperation with Countries along with the "Belt and Road Initiative". I think that there are two routes in the "Belt and Road Initiative ", with the land route on the north and marine route on the south. Understanding is the beginning of love, so in this session, we will focus on public welfare and charity. Let's first invite several guests into the dialogues and discuss the grand blueprint for future philanthropic cooperation of the "Belt and Road Initiative", and they are: Mr. Carles Llorens, Secretary-General of the ORU-Fogar; Mr. Liang Xingxin, President of Zhejiang Association for Non-profit Organization; Ms. Lin Biyu, Deputy CEO of Tzu Chi Foundation; And Mr. Ling Chong, Director of Social Organizations Administration of Shenzhen Municipality.

Welcome.

Now the speakers on stage shall each have 4 minutes to speak, and then communicate in an interactive way. First, let's give the 4 minutes to Mr. Carles Llorens.

Carles Llorens: Friends from the Chinese People's Association for Friendship with Foreign Countries, ladies and gentlemen, I must reiterate that I see the number of organizations is increasing worldwide. We can see that in the past few years, from 1997 to 2003, the number of social organizations in China has grown dramatically, and the Chinese government has also carried out institutional reforms and devolved power to local governments, so local governments have more power to govern society, which is an important measure. We have discussed this issue many times around the world, including in Latin America, Europe and Africa, because institutional reform in one country can provide experience for other countries and regions.

We have witnessed how you gradually achieve the national development goals in China, including decentralization, to promote national development. We agree that China is the best example of decentralization, and we must say that this is closely related to the "Belt and Road Initiative " launched by China in the 21st century. There is no doubt that this will be conducive to common development, which promotes business and creates jobs and wealth. We believe that China's visionary initiative will be well implemented, and will bring huge employment and wealth opportunities. At the same time, as a supporter of food security, the ORU-Fogar also recognizes the "Belt and Road Initiative " as a guarantee to reduce food insecurity. We are convinced that the "Belt and Road Initiative" will bring health wherever it is implemented. We also believe that it is based on a green background and helps to cope with the challenges brought about by climate change. I believe that the "Belt and Road Initiative" will promote cultural exchanges and build friendly ties among Asia, Africa and Europe. The old mechanism was only suitable for one country and focused on its market, while from the beginning, the "Belt and Road Initiative" was an initiative to break the old mechanism and transcend national borders. As supporters of regionalism and decentralization, we must identify this feature. The "Belt and Road Initiative" must consider all regions and promote development around the world. Cities must be the core of development, so their service and infrastructure construction should be strengthened. Therefore, from this perspective, we must gain experience from China and its provinces because they have jointly achieved decentralization and also because this is development. We must learn from China's experience because China puts forward this initiative to support global development rather than the development of a certain country. This initiative can also be the route through which the best ideas flow, and we think that the idea of decentralization will be a good starting point. We sincerely invite provinces of China to join our global regional network. Moreover, we want all Chinese political and social organizations to participate in the forum jointly organized by the United Nations and us to initiate discussions on these issues. We are confident that the forum will bring together organizations interested in the "Belt and Road Initiative". I think it would be very interesting for you to join this forum to share the experience of global and regional development. Thank you!

Chan Yung: Thank you. Next, let's invite President Liang Xingxin to talk about the content related to philanthropy in the "Belt and Road Initiative".

Liang Xingxin: Hello, everyone. The "Belt and Road Initiative" philanthropic cooperation is a very nice and meaningful topic. I want to use two idioms to talk about my views. The first idiom is "putting pearls and jade together", which means we make connections for beautiful things to make a perfect match. The "Belt and Road Initiative" is the top-level design of the country, and philanthropy is a beautiful cause worldwide. They have two things in common: first, they are the products and symbols of China's reform and opening up; second, the "Belt and Road Initiative" and philanthropy can transcend national borders and ideologies. As General Secretary Xi Jinping has said, the "Belt and Road Initiative" is not a private road of a certain party, but a sunny avenue for everyone to advance hand in hand. I think the the "Belt and Road Initiative" will be surely smooth and successful with the help of philanthropy. The second idiom is "giving wings to a tiger", which means making things even better. The "Belt and Road Initiative" must be implemented for closer ties with people, so that everything will be better; if there is any blockage to the people, things may be hindered. To bring people closer, social organizations need to use the greatest strengths and make the "Belt and Road Initiative" even more powerful with the help of philanthropy. Both social organizations and philanthropy have a distinctive feature, which is, as they originate from the people, they are the closest to them, and are most capable of uniting them. Therefore, I firmly believe that China's social organizations are as powerful and strong as China is.

Finally, I want to make four suggestions. Social organizations and closer ties with people are so important that we must well develop social organizations. First, we should well develop. Let social organizations grow and take on the important tasks of history.

Second, we should have more exchanges. More exchanges between associations, social organizations and citizens can facilitate win-win cooperation. Third, we should focus on the projects. We shall reach consensus through cultural and economic links, form resolution interaction, and promote cooperation. Fourth, we shall focus on the long term. The "Belt and Road Initiative" is fundamental for centuries to come and cannot be achieved overnight. Social organizations have a short history in China. Counting from the settlement of its official name, social organizations only have more than ten years of history, and the historical responsibility lies before us. According to national deployment, our social organizations must exert our due strength. Thank you.

Chan Yung: Thank you. Next, let's invite Ms. Lin Biyu to share with us.

Lin Biyu: Distinguished guests, good afternoon. First of all, I am very grateful for this opportunity to share with you on the cooperation of the "Belt and Road Initiative". Tzu Chi Foundation focuses on philanthropy, treatment, environmental protection, etc., and our biggest concerns are climate change and environmental protection, which have affected 80 million people in 2018 and even more in 2019. In 1991, due to the flood, we went to Jiangsu to relieve the disaster in Eastern China, built houses for the victims and did a lot of work to help the migrants move to the villages. We also helped build 13 schools during the Sichuan earthquake of 2008. We have left our footprints in 99 countries around the world, and the houses we built helped more than 30 million people in 2018. From the perspective of the "Belt and Road Initiative", we have visited 24 countries, especially in Mozambique, which was affected by floods, and we carried out disaster relief work there. Our work has been recognized by the United Nations, such as helping people rebuild their homes and create economic power during the floods in the Philippines. During this period, we used various methods, such as nursing. During floods, we provided easy tools for people there to build their own houses.

These are the work we've done for them, and I'd like you to take a look. Now our work is in full swing. For environmental protection even around the world, we use a simple ten-character formula to encourage people. Blankets and clothes are made of plastic products, which could also be used as floor tiles and building materials. We run free clinics in various places, benefiting more than 50,000 people every year. We are also concerned about water shortages and refugees. For example, in Turkey, we solve the problems of education and medical care for refugee children.

We are advocating at the United Nations that for the sake of health, we must have a vegetarian meal every week. We have developed 17 projects at the United Nations, and we are willing to cooperate with you on the "Belt and Road Initiative" and jointly participate in solving the problems of infectious diseases, environmental protection, water shortage, and medical treatment in Africa, especially the introduction of traditional Chinese medicine there to solve psychological problems. Thank you very much.

Chan Yung: Thank you. Next, let's welcome Mr. Ling Chong, Director of Social Organizations Administration of Shenzhen Municipality.

Ling Chong: Thanks to the organizing committee for holding WPF in Shenzhen, which makes us particularly proud. Shenzhen is not only a city with rapid economic development, but also a city with outstanding high-tech industries, and a city full of love. I work in the government department, and the central government has issued a document to Shenzhen, which redefined Shenzhen as the Pilot Demonstration Zone of Socialism with Chinese Characteristics. From the perspective of my department, what should I do? The economic department should create the best business environment in the world. I come from the civil affairs department, so it is my duty to create the world's best environment to attract philanthropic organizations, philanthropists, and other philanthropic resources. In addition, we also strongly encourage Shenzhen's philanthropic resources to go abroad for the co-construction of countries along the route of the "Belt and Road Initiative". Disaster relief organizations from Shenzhen once went to help with the earthquake relief in Nepal, and some philanthropic organizations went to Sri Lanka to carry out cataract surgery for children. We shall make greater contributions to the world along with the "Belt and Road Initiative", which is what government departments need to promote. We shall also take advantage of Shenzhen's location advantages and teamed up with organizations in the Guangdong-Hong Kong-Macao Greater Bay Area to jointly promote Shenzhen's philanthropic organizations to achieve better development in terms of system construction, policy formulation, mechanism construction, platform construction, and talent training. At the same time, we shall "go out" and provide more services for the joint construction of countries along the route of the "Belt and Road Initiative" and jointly build a Community with a Shared Future for Mankind. Thank you.

Chan Yung: Thank you, Mr. Ling Chong. I will talk about one thing that people are very concerned about in the "Belt and Road Initiative", which is the elderly services. The "Belt and Road Initiative" attaches great importance to medical insurance. Unlike young people who seldom save money, elders are wise, rich in experience and savings. If the retirement industry is internet-driven, then it will be easier to achieve closer people-to-people ties. It's also important to introduce successful experience and resource network of other places. I know a professor in Hong Kong who retired in the prime of his life, so he has 10 years to take a rest. Wherever he goes along the route of the "Belt and Road Initiative", he can bring there a lot from the smart network and promote local development. To achieve this, it requires everyone to promote the development of more industries for elderly services along the route of the "Belt and Road Initiative".

Next, we will enter an interactive session, and I suggest everyone keeps direct and straightforward. Ladies first. I have a question for Ms. Lin Biyu. You just talked about helping African friends. You have done so much philanthropic work, and you also think that the closer ties with people and philanthropy are the biggest difficulties. What do you think are the problems that need to be solved the most?

Lin Biyu: Thank you, dear moderator. Disaster relief requires the delivery of supplies, but there are many difficulties along the route of the "Belt and Road Initiative", including transportation problems. Not only long-distance transport is difficult, more importantly, but the local transportation is also backward. Fortunately, all difficulties can be overcome. Medical problems are vital to them, and we have now found that traditional Chinese medicine can solve their medical problems in the backward countries because as the essence of China, it does not require large equipment, so it becomes a solution. Besides, in Southeast Asia, the water problem is very serious. There is a problem of water resources in Africa, and the salinity of the water is also very high in Southeast Asia, so we need to think about how to desalt it. Besides, there is an issue of defoliant in Vietnam, so we would like to invite you to discuss it together. I just raised the questions in the hope that we can solve these dilemmas together. Chinese culture advocates love and tolerance, but how do we deliver Chinese culture? All problems from the future shall be new to us. If we bring the love and tolerance of Chinese culture to other countries, we can change people's minds. Everyone talks about philanthropic talent. In fact, what is most important to them is their sense of mission and faith. I believe that in the future we will not only co-build countries along the route of the "Belt and Road Initiative", but also find the love of Chinese culture in more countries, which will make everyone's heart melt. In this way, we can guide mankind to pay attention to environmental protection and truly rescue the earth, since without the earth, there would be no human beings.

Chan Yung: Yes. Taking kindness and love as guarantees, we can melt people's hearts, just like if we can melt glaciers, we can have more water. I would like to ask Mr. Carles Llorens that, in your experience, how can you reduce people's doubts about the "Belt and Road Initiative"? In the process of promoting it, what major problems can be solved?

Carles Llorens: I don't know if I fully understood your question. I would like to say that if you ask me what problems are most prominent in the world and how should we use this initiative to solve these problems, I will answer as follows. First, China is already in a very unique state as it is developing very fast, and the economic growth rate is also very gratifying. I have also discussed this issue with other participants in the past few days. Just now, Ms. Lin Biyu introduced to us the work of Tzu Chi Foundation. However, everyone did not notice that there are many big problems faced by other countries and regions in the world, such as immigration, climate change, and refugees. Yesterday, the former Prime Minister of Hungary said that China assumes very important responsibilities, which is very important. For China, while taking these important responsibilities, it can also be aware of the problems created by other countries. A colleague of mine often says to me that we must have in-depth ties with people, but what is more important now is that we must be able to build this kind of spiritual bridge, strengthen exchanges and communication between countries instead of building barriers, realize the closer ties with people and jointly solve the problems we face. There will be no borders in the future because love crosses borders. For us, we need to establish friendly cooperation on a global scale, which is the common mission that everyone wants to accomplish.

Chan Yung: Thank you. Next, I would like to ask President Liang Xingxin, you are from Zhejiang Province, and you are familiar with it. Can you tell us about how to let the people of countries along the route of the "Belt and Road Initiative" understand our initiative in terms of philanthropy?

Liang Xingxin: Before we get to the economy, let's first talk about the cultural background. Zhejiang is a province famous for its economic culture with a small territory and relatively small population. However, its history is quite unique, which makes it remarkable in Chinese history. As China grows stronger, it should shoulder its historical and social responsibilities. In my opinion, the "Belt and Road Initiative" is a great initiative because of its contribution to mankind, and it the joint construction of the countries along the route of the "Belt and Road Initiative" as its duty. Zhejiang people are characteristic and all over the world, and most of them go abroad to do business. Zhejiang has its unique advantages and experience. In all countries and regions of the world, as long as there are Chinese chambers of commerce, they are most likely to be the Zhejiang Chamber of Commerce or the Wenzhou Chamber of Commerce. They have promoted the development of local economy, society and culture, as well as the exchanges between China and foreign countries. I went to small restaurants in some countries and found that the leaders of our country had also been there, which is unimaginable. I think it is very important to have a closer tie with people, and make national knowledge and national initiatives deeply rooted in people's hearts to become conscious actions. Therefore, Zhejiang will continue to play its role. Thank you.

Chan Yung: Thank you, President Liang Xingxin. Just now everyone talked about how to do things well with love and kindness on a macro level, and why we must do well. As for how to do well, I would like to ask Director Ling Chong, if people want to make a successful philanthropic platform landed in Shenzhen, what should we do?

Ling Chong: If a philanthropic organization from Hong Kong, Macao and Taiwan or abroad wants to enter Shenzhen to participate in social services, there is now an access to apply to the domestic public security administration for foreign NGOs to conduct activities in the Chinese Mainland (inland). This morning, our Civil Affairs Bureau had a meeting to discuss how to use the opportunity of the pilot demonstration zone to seek more special policy support from the state to promote the development of philanthropy in Shenzhen. I can only tell you about some assumptions, but they are not yet the reality. We can open up certain sectors, such as elderly services and social worker services, and these mandates can facilitate overseas organizations to come in and help us grow together. In addition, we will explore ways to make it easier for foreigners to take charge of philanthropic organizations registered in Shenzhen. These jobs are currently conducted, and some require more effort to be realized. What we hope most is to be able to create a world-competent and first-class environment that worships good, realize the convenience and efficiency of government functions, and serve everyone.

Chan Yung: Thank you. We use love and kindness to seize opportunities, and we can have more exchanges on national policies and the fine traditions of the Chinese nation. Good directions, good strategies, and good ideals must be firmly adhered to and seized. The most important thing is to seize a good opportunity because once we miss it, it may never come again. I hope you can get to know some of the key leaders and guests on the stage to have more in-depth exchanges afterwards, since the "Belt and Road Initiative" and philanthropy will never be finished, but only multiply and develop better. Let's give a big round of applause to the guests on the stage.

XIII How to Develop a Good Business Path in the Greater Bay Area

Moderator: Kalok Chan, Member of Academic Committee of the WPF, and Dean of the CUHK Business School

Speakers: Wong H. Henry, Chairman of the Diamond TechVentures

Soltan Mammadov, Head of International Relations Department, Heydar Aliyev Foundation

Thomas Cheung Tsun Yung, Deputy to the 13th NPC and Executive Chairman of the International Teochew Youth Federation

Guest speech: Zhang Yuanlong, Former Vice Chairman of All-China Federation of Industry and Commerce, Former Deputy Director of the Standing Committee of the Tianjin Municipal People's Congress, and Chairman of the China Red Ribbon Foundation

Li Xikui: We have talked about a lot just now. State-to-state relations are based on amity between the people, and amity between the people is based on closer ties mutually. Thank you. Next, let's move on to the second topic. I'd like to invite Professor Kalok Chan, Member of Academic Committee of WPF, and Dean of the CUHK Business School, to preside over the discussion.

Kalok Chan: Ladies and gentlemen, good afternoon. It is a great honour to be the moderator of the breakout session. The theme of our session is "How to Develop a Good Business Path in the Greater Bay Area". In this session, we will discuss the role of business in the overall development of philanthropy. There is no doubt that business cooperation plays an important role in philanthropy. At the same time, we have also seen more and more successful entrepreneurs throughout the Guangdong-Hong Kong-Macao Greater Bay Area in the past few years who have created very successful business organizations based on the Greater Bay Area. Besides, we are also seeing an increasing number of people who are striving to contribute to the well-being of society. There is no doubt that we must better allocate our resources, including human resources and financial resources, so that we can not only bring value to shareholders and return to our investors, but also create great social value. Looking back, we see more and more examples. We have some top entrepreneurs who have seen some social problems, including environmental degradation, income disparity, and these entrepreneurs use their wealth, or the resources of their companies, to help solve some urgent social problems.

We have also seen the active participation of some entrepreneurs who help us build a more sustainable society, and at the same time, they make all stakeholders truly enjoy the well-being and dividends brought by the enterprises.

So I think "How to Develop a Good Business Path in the Greater Bay Area" is a very important topic, which can help us build a more sustainable society, and of course, bring longevity to our enterprises and better help to individuals. In this session, we are fortunate to have invited several very distinguished guests from different backgrounds around the world. They will share their respective experiences, insights and ideas with us. They will share with us how enterprises contribute to social well-being.

First of all, I would like to introduce the keynote speakers in this session, Mr. Zhang Yuanlong, Former Vice Chairman of All-China Federation of Industry and Commerce, Former Deputy Director of the Standing Committee of the Tianjin Municipal People's Congress, and Chairman of the China Red Ribbon Foundation. The topic of his speech is "*Kindness can change the World*".

Kindness Can Change the World

Zhang Yuanlong, Former Vice Chairman of All-China Federation of Industry and Commerce, Former Deputy Director of the Standing Committee of the Tianjin Municipal People's Congress, and Chairman of the China Red Ribbon Foundation

Dear guests and friends, good afternoon! As a representative of the China Red Ribbon Foundation, I am very happy to participate in our forum today. China Red Ribbon Foundation is a national public welfare organization jointly established by the All-China Federation of Industry and Commerce and more than 20 member companies to prevent and control AIDS. We were established in 2005, and over the past 14 years, under the leadership of Chairman Huang Mengfu of the All-China Federation of Industry and Commerce. With the support of entrepreneurs from the All-China Federation of Industry and Commerce, we have invested more than 190 million yuan in carrying out philanthropic projects in three major categories, such as relief and assistance, construction support for facilities, and publicity and advocacy. As the direct beneficiaries have reached 1.5 million, we have made certain achievements, and also won the "China Charity Award" twice. Today, I would like to share with you some of my experiences in philanthropic work.

While all of us are working hard, we are actually thinking about a question: What is the ideal society we are pursuing? The ideal society China pursues is a socialist society. Comrade Deng Xiaoping had an interesting description of socialism. He said that socialism is to develop and liberate productive forces, to eliminate exploitation, improve people's living standards, eliminate polarization, and achieve common prosperity. He also proposed what is not socialism: poverty is not socialism, and slow development is not, either. Let us put these two sentences together, and thus we get that socialism is a high degree of unity of efficiency and impartiality. We see countries around the world searching for this unity. Efficiency and impartiality are the common pursuits of mankind.

So, how to judge the impartiality and efficiency of a society? In fact, their connotation is extremely rich. If we do not consider the influence of politics, society and culture, we only observe from the perspective of the economy: for a unit, efficiency is labour productivity; for a country, it's GDP per capita. China's GDP per capita is close to US$10,000, while those of the US, Japan, and India are respectively US$62,600, US$39,300, and US$2,000. There is still a lot of room for growth in our per capita efficiency. How to judge the impartiality? The simplest standard in the world is the Gini coefficient. There are several statistical methods for the Gini coefficient: statistics by wealth, statistics by income, and statistics by consumption. Piketty, a French economist, argued in his book *Capital in the Twenty-First Century* that the income gap in the United States was greater than the wealth gap, while the wealth gap in the United Kingdom was greater than the income gap. This is because the United Kingdom is an old capitalist country with a long history of wealth accumulation, while the United States is largely dependent on the high incomes of Wall Street to bridge the gap.

Currently, China does not have a clear official Gini coefficient, and we did not publish it any longer after 2016, so the current Gini coefficient is based on civil statistics based on income. Recently, countries and regions with a Gini coefficient of around 0.3 in the world include South Korea and Taiwan. It is 0.45 for the United States, 0.55 for the civil statistics of the Chinese Mainland, around 0.5 for Hong Kong, and the highest is for South Africa, which is above 0.6. Recently there is a set of figures that can show the income gap of our China: if we divide 1.4 billion people into 5 groups, while 20% of the population is counted as one, that is, 280 million people in a group, the lowest group's annual income per capita is 6400 yuan, and that of the highest group is more than 70,000 yuan, so there is a difference of nearly 10 times. This is based on a calculation of 20% as a group. If 10% is taken as a group, the gap may be greater. However, I think there are still a lot of data that are not included in the statistics. For example, the welfare of the state and the donations of entrepreneurs should also be evenly included in the income of everyone. If we counted 20% of the population as a group, and the top group donated 10% of its income, we could divide that 10% into other groups and the 10-fold gap would eventually narrow to 7.6 times. Taking the United States as an example, the total assets of philanthropic institutions in U.S. account for 10% of GDP. In 2018, its GDP was US$ 20 trillion, then the total assets of philanthropic institutions were about US$ 2 trillion. Since the distribution rate in the United States is more than 80%, its income is about US$ 16 trillion, and they take out US$ 500 billion each year for donations, which accounts for a little over three percent. In other words, if this part of income is included, it may have a relatively large impact on the Gini coefficient, which is what we should pay attention to.

China's actual donations in 2018 were 75.42 billion yuan (see *Blue Book on*

Charity Donation Development in China 2018), so our income distribution rate is about 43.9%, that is to say, 43.9% of our GDP, which is about 40 trillion yuan, is distributed to everyone. Our donations account for 0.2% of total income, which is relatively small.

However, we can draw a conclusion that philanthropic donations, especially those from people with high income, can change the gap between rich and poor.

Another thing to note is the distribution. There are three levels of distribution of wealth. The first distribution is wages and profits. The second is taxation, which is distributed by the government as the management subject of public utilities and should be called welfare. What the government does should be called welfare, not charity. I think that charity is not equal to philanthropy in that Charity is meant to meet short-term and urgent needs, while philanthropy is long-term and strategic. The civil organizations should do philanthropy. Therefore, the government should do a good job in the second distribution, because a lot of wealth will be distributed here. The poverty alleviation and reduction work of the Chinese government shows the power of secondary distribution. Therefore, the proportion of fiscal and taxation for philanthropy is very important. The third distribution is social donations. Each of these three distributions should do what it should do. For example, it requires efficiency in the first distribution; in the second distribution, the government should strive for impartiality, welfare and public facilities must be appropriately done, and unnecessary expenses should be reduced; the third distribution should aim at social public welfare undertakings. In this way, the contradiction between efficiency and impartiality will be reduced and the income gap will be narrowed.

Therefore, our second conclusion is that the Gini coefficient, especially the Gini coefficient of consumption, should be calculated after three distributions.

After Piketty's book came out, the economist Chen Zhiwu found out a problem in it. He said that the University of Chicago had got a conclusion by studying income: the income gap in the United States has increased from 5.3 to 6.4 times in recent years, while the consumption gap has dropped from 4.2 to 3.9 times. The inequality of consumption is improving, mainly because social security and public welfare are working so that the consumption gap is actually narrowing. For example, as our current entrepreneurs are busy working every day, how can they have time for consumption? Their sons are most likely to spend money, and the entrepreneurs probably spend less than their employees. If you take this into account, the consumption gap is not as large as it appears. In the 19th century, China's consumption income gap was much lower than those of Sweden, Belgium, and Italy, and their income gaps were larger than that of our country, but the religious and social assistance forces of those countries were stronger than ours, especially the financial aid in education and medical treatment. In China, it is mainly the clan to provide assistance, and the government issues food relief. This may be the reason why the peasant uprisings were relatively frequent in Chinese history.

We should come to another conclusion, that is, the first distribution focuses on efficiency, the second distribution on impartiality, and the third distribution on kindness. Donations out of kindness, especially in education and medical treatment, can greatly reduce the consumption gap and ensure a balance between efficiency and impartiality.

Let me introduce how kindness comes about. My grandfather was the first president of Nankai University, and the funding for the operation was entirely based on donations. Therefore, he was a good persuader of donation, and donation persuading and fundraising have also been my family heritage. Therefore, I would like to share with you some of the donation psychology I observed in the All-China Federation of Industry and Commerce.

The first is forced donation. We have seen a lot of people with a very pure charitable heart being forced to donate, and the funds raised were not appropriately used, resulting in very poor effect. Working at the All-China Federation of Industry and Commerce, we had a practice that we entrusted the management of rights protection, public welfare and philanthropy to one person. We had a saying that sincere dedication comes from the protection of the impartial rights. Now that I think about it, it was a more or less forced donation.

The second is the so-called "paying for the rewards". Many enterprises donate in order to please their leaders and get something as exchange.

The third is to promote and improve the image of individuals and enterprises through philanthropic activities.

All these three come into being under pressure, but they all need to be taken seriously. China's traditional philosophy of philanthropy is particularly embodied in *Strange Stories from a Lonely Studio and The Examination for the Town God.* King of Hell asked a scholar surnamed Song a question: When you are alone facing a choice between right and wrong, will you make a different choice from that you make in front of someone else? The scholar replied: "Those who do good deeds for fame and fortune are hypocrisy, so they should not be rewarded; those who do evil things unintentionally should not be punished accordingly." His answer received a lot of applause. This is a very traditional Chinese psychology of philanthropy, called the unity of motive and effect, but the reality is that a lot of things are not uniformly done. I think it is wrong if no reward is given. We should reward everything that is for good, and the so-called reward is the affirmation of kindness by society.

The fourth is empathy. Human empathy is the foundation of morality, and all morality comes from empathy. With empathy, we have the eagerness of helping others. There is a World Giving Index, which ranks 146 countries based on three indicators: recently, whether they have helped strangers, whether they have donated money, and whether they have volunteered. The country with the highest average score in the last five years is Myanmar, and in 2019 it is Indonesia. This reflects the influence of religion. Most people in Myanmar believe in Buddhism and they are happy in doing good. Similarly, the motivation for donations in the United States is mainly based on religion. In this index, China ranks 145th, the second-lowest, but with large absolute value. Among them, 24% has helped strangers, which is equivalent to 300 million people; 8% have donated money, which means 100 million people; and 4% have been volunteers, which almost 50 million people. Myanmar's GDP per capita in 2018 was US$1325.95. 52% of its people have helped others, 90% have donated money, and 48% have been volunteers. The figures in the United States were relatively 75%, 62%, and 43%. China is already the second-largest economy in the world, so we should aim at becoming the leading country in the world rather than just comparing ourselves with the past. In fact, the comparison of the giving indexes of the whole society reflects the atmosphere of kindness. With such an atmosphere, donors will feel that it makes sense to be philanthropic.

The fifth is heroic feelings. For example, Rockefeller played his role by setting up a foundation that "earns and gives as much as he can". It is important to have a good program that helps donors realize the lifetime wealth is to help those in need. When people know that the life of a poor child, a certain infectious disease that is raging, or the environmental pollution that is about to affect all of mankind, will be changed entirely because of their kind help, they will have a kind of heroic feeling.

The sixth is to reflect the value of life. How do we judge a person's ability? Making money can only prove half of it, and spending money is the manifestation of a person's overall ability. Our family has a family motto: "Privately-run is not privately-owned, and leaving virtues is better than leaving money". This describes the characteristics of a social enterprise. The assets of a publicly-run enterprise must be publicly-owned, instead of private-owned. The assets of a privately-run enterprise must not be publicly-owned, but it can be used to serve the public. In the time of Mencius, there was a man named Yang Zhu. He said, "Even if a hair plucked out from me can benefit the whole world, I will not do it". Yang Zhu's words are a bit cruel, but there is some truth in them. In other words, the hair on my body belongs to me. To pluck this hair, I must do it myself, and no one else can. That is why we say a privately-run enterprise cannot be publicly-owned but can serve the public. Many people like to set up their foundations to reflect social values after they have money. Therefore, the phrase "privately-run is not privately-owned" also has important significance at the moment. In the phrase "leaving virtues is better than leaving money", it implies to leave money for one's future generations is not necessarily a good thing. Leaving virtues in society, on the other hand, can be of great benefit to future generations, and these are very good ideas we have about persuading donations.

We have discussed several kinds of donation psychology, and I think the most important thing is to build a society where "good begets good, and evil begets evil". We often attach great importance to the idea that evil begets evil, and the discussion of good begets good is not enough. Good deeds should be encouraged, as long as there is good behaviour, we should encourage instead of putting pressure on it. Whatever the motive is, a good heart can change human nature. Only when good begets good can people in the society have kindness and consensus of philanthropy. The social consensus is an eternal truth, and only with the eternal truth can there be a constant law. Only when there are constant laws, such as the constitution, property law and charity law, will people be protected by law and have permanent property. Mencius said that those who have permanent property have perseverance. I said that permanent property is not only your property, but also your rights and obligations in society. If we follow this logic that constant laws lead to permanent property, permanent property leads to perseverance, and perseverance leads to kindness, kindness must come from the consensus of the society. If the whole society has a consensus that "good begets good, and evil begets evil", then in this society full of good, human kindness can be cultivated and can survive.

Due to the time limit, that's all I have thought about. Regarding how to build a society where good and evil have their rewards, if I have the opportunity in the future, I will exchange with you again. Thank you!

Kalok Chan: Thank you very much for the wonderful speech, Chairman Zhang Yuanlong. We now invite other guests into the dialogue of this session: Mr.

Wong H. Henry, Chairman of Diamond TechVentures; Mr. Soltan Mammadov, Head of International Relations Department, Heydar Aliyev Foundation; Mr. Cheung Chun-yung, Deputy to the 13th National People's Congress (NPC) and Executive Chairman of the International Teochew Youth Federation.

Let's invite other guests to speak for 5 minutes. First, Chairman Wong H. Henry, please.

Wong H. Henry: Good afternoon, ladies and gentlemen! I am Wong H. Henry from Silicon Valley. Today I'd like to share with you how to achieve business goals.

Chairman Zhang Yuanlong just mentioned how to provide people with short-term and immediate help, and also mentioned that philanthropy is a long-term cause. Today I want to talk to you about the medium-term. I put this picture down because the U.S. Securities and Exchange Commission wants us to give people forward-looking explanations. I'll focus on the impact of investing, which refers to investing in enterprises or funds to generate social or environmental impacts and bring financial returns. Ten years ago, when I took a business administration course at Stanford University, a group of young people submitted a very complicated solution, which was designed for people in Africa who had no access to electricity. There are now 2 billion people in the world without access to electricity. Through the deployment of high-quality solar products, the project has achieved the power supply for 95 million people and reduced 22 million tons of carbon dioxide emissions. This is a big project. Kyoto in Japan once passed a convention to reduce carbon dioxide emissions. Everyone here has planted trees, but what about reducing carbon dioxide emissions? Some people in India and Africa do not have access to electricity, so they use kerosene lamps. Kerosene is a highly flammable liquid like gasoline. They can only use kerosene lamps and stoves. I remember when I was a child, someone lit the stove with a match. When a match was held close to the stove, the stove would make a loud "bang". If you accidentally stand in front of the stove, your eyebrows and hair might be burned off, and the unfortunate people even get their faces burned. By configuring high-quality solar products, carbon dioxide emissions can also be reduced. We are providing reliable, affordable and clean energy products to create a better future for everyone and enable them to live a high-quality life. If we can provide solar solutions for these people, we can light up their future. *Forbes* commented that these optical and electrical resources provided by Stanford Graduate School of Business have raised $1 million and have already affected one million people.

This is a real business success, which comes from the experience, focus strategy and implementation methods of a successful business management team. That's what I am working on with some technology companies. Why should we pay attention to the early stages? Because of the rate of return. "Buy low and sell high" is an investment strategy, which is also used by BNY Mellon. How can we implement this strategy? Entrepreneurs are struggling to raise funds and may not be able to do so for several months. When we say that we will use some money to buy their stock, they will think about it, or they can buy it on the secondary market. If you want to buy stock from unicorns, you can go to Silicon Valley, where there are plenty of them. It is an ideal place to buy stocks at low prices. Thank you!

Kalok Chan: Thank you. I'd like to invite our next speaker, Mr. Soltan Mammadov.

Soltan Mammadov: Dear friends, distinguished guests, ladies and gentlemen, first of all, I would like to thank the organizers of the conference for inviting me to participate in the WPF. I come from the Heydar Aliyev Foundation of Azerbaijan, and our foundation is a philanthropic organization. Azerbaijan, with a total population of 10 million people, serves as the gateway between East and West and borders Russia, Iran, Turkey, and Georgia. Heydar Aliyev Foundation started its philanthropic activities in 2004. We focus on social and economic development and solve problems in education, public health, environmental protection, society, culture and science, and other issues. In addition, we invest in cultural heritage, national communication, etc. We cooperate with governments, non-profit organizations and philanthropic organizations, hoping to bring economic benefits to all donors and cooperative partners, and improve the management and structure of the foundation. Over the years, we have been analyzing enterprise social responsibilities, which are sustainability, education, environment, healthcare, and how to provide educational and healthcare opportunities to the least fortunate. At the same time, we also hope that through our foundation, we can create well-being for all aspects of society, so those are what we are doing.

In the national social project, we currently provide free housing for working-class families, hoping to help the homeless have a better living environment. We are doing similar projects in Hungary, too. If some families are low-income groups, they can get relief housing from the government for free. We also help children with physical disabilities in other countries. We have also done some work in Iraq to provide living conditions for local refugees. In terms of education and science, we have built a children's home for children in Azerbaijan. We have built more than 400 primary schools and kindergartens. We run language and culture schools in France to provide education for children from minorities. In 2018, we built many primary schools in Vietnam. We have built a lot of schools in Russia as well. Health has always been a big concern for us. We are concerned about children with diabetes in Azerbaijan, and we have also done some projects for children with heart disease. In Pakistan, we have provided hepatitis B vaccines, innovated blood transfusion technology, established clinics for low-income families, and provided a large number of assistive facilities, including wheelchairs for disabled children. In Djibouti, we have donated specialized medical facilities to help local development as well.

Culture is also a very important aspect. In Azerbaijan, we have established exhibition halls, art communities, libraries and music schools, and held a special exhibition of Azerbaijan's cultural treasures. In Italy, we specially organized cultural and art exhibitions for the cultural and artistic works of Islam. Our cooperation with the Chinese People's Association for Friendship with Foreign Countries is a good example, and now we have some projects in Azerbaijan and China. We also engage in global philanthropic activities, such as the UN Forum on Culture and Civilization Development, different exhibitions, World Expos and so on. We hope to constantly promote our culture and display our cultural treasures through our jobs, and to enhance cultural diversity, which is why we have the support of the Azerbaijan government. Thank you.

Kalok Chan: Thank you, Mr. Soltan Mammadov. Next, let's welcome Mr. Cheung Chun-yung.

Cheung Chun-Yung: Good afternoon, everyone. Thank you very much for sharing with me how to build a better Bay Area. About how to do the work in the next step and how to combine our life with corporate activities, I have some ideas to share with you.

The future development of our "9+2" urban agglomeration is well known to all. The Bay Area we built, according to our understanding, is an international Greater Bay Area where people from all over the world come together to discuss, build and realize win-win. In the process of building this Bay Area, there will be many new models, such as innovation of institutional models and business models. At the same time, Hong Kong and Macao have been practising the concept of "One Country, Two Systems". There will be many new economic models in the Bay Area, such as artificial intelligence, digital economy, sharing economy, Internet and IoT, and the newly created ones will probably promote institutional innovation. For enterprises operating in this environment, we must also consider how to make profits for shareholders, and assume social responsibilities at the same time.

Therefore, in the process of creating a better living environment, we must put some elements in the Bay Area.

What kind of environment will we have? A lot of things will undergo many new changes through artificial intelligence and the Internet of Everything, and so will our past social patterns. If that happens, we can let everyone choose what they want to do outside of work and what they want to do for the next generation. These can all be placed in the new system. I believe that the Bay Area will promote the development of the world in the future, and there will be a lot of communication in education, such as artificial intelligence, which automatically makes transactions through some platforms. In this process, for example, the suppliers shall negotiate its rules. After the transaction is completed, a certain proportion of the transaction volume, say 0.03%, can be used for philanthropy, so it can be used to treat cataracts or other diseases, or specifically support the schooling of children in mountainous areas. In the future, some elements of good deeds can be considered and put in the economic environment.

I built a platform for Chaozhou people, and I serve as its chairman. On the Internet, I also use blockchain technology and artificial intelligence technology to connect people and build a new community, which can connect people from different places around the world. Currently, we have the Internet, through which many people can be connected and then make transactions. If they have a need, for example, a student from Indonesia wants to study in Shenzhen, he can ask people in the group, and the people in the group can use AI to find solutions. It shall generate some cost during the process, and a pass must be obtained. The intermediate service provider will get the pass, so there will be a price difference in the process. When the price difference occurs, it can keep going.

I promote these platforms, hoping to use new means to connect people from different parts of the world, to serve them, and to play a connecting role. Different values are generated through different activities, and then distributed to those in need through the platforms. This type of work will increase. In general, the next step, we should put more efforts to promote. Since we have many opportunities to create new economic platforms at this time. I think the old methods, as well as philanthropic platforms are actually what we need, but we can use new methods and new models to create more new ones. Let our work and everyone's life be connected with our business operations. The whole method is very different from the past, because it will be faster, and companies will automatically participate according to their situations, so as to let everyone live a good life. I think that day will come soon. Thank you.

Kalok Chan: Thank you for your speech, Mr. Cheung Chun-yung. Four speakers have shared with us from different perspectives. Chairman Zhang Yuanlong gave a very detailed introduction on the development of domestic philanthropy undertakings, and Mr. Wong H. Henry introduced to us the concept of impact investment. In response to their sharing, I would like to ask each of them a question. My first question is for Chairman Zhang Yuanlong. You just mentioned the development of public welfare. The government uses wealth distribution to improve the living conditions of some people. With regard to social security funds, including pension funds, we have an expectation, especially as the population ages faster. So I would like to ask that, what can be done in terms of public welfare?

Zhang Yuanlong: You have asked a very important question. China's ageing problem is very serious. There are nearly 200 million people aged 65 years old. It was relatively late for China to establish the pension funds, which have not been nationally unified, so there may be too many difficulties to cope with. On the one hand, we must rely on the government to increase investment, especially our state-owned enterprises, to continuously add their profits to the pension funds, so as to reflect the nationalization of state-owned enterprises. On the other hand, we have to rely on ourselves. The current ageing does not mean that people are really old, but are out of the workforce. In fact, these people can still work for society. In terms of the elderly care, what we attach great importance to is health, and we need to be healthy. Our annual medical expenses are nearly RMB 4 trillion, and we spend very little on taking exercise. Our per capita sports area is 2.2 square meters, which is ten times less than that of Japanese, so we still have the potential to explore. This is a very huge topic. Thank you.

Kalok Chan: Thank you. My next question is for Mr. Wong H. Henry. You talked about impact investment, and you also think that more and more people are engaged in impact investment, but not so many in China. Can you share with us the development trend of impact, its development in Asia, and how to promote influence investment in the future, so that people not only pay attention to the return on investment but also pay attention to the value and impact behind the investment?

Wong H. Henry: I don't know what the impact investment market in the mainland is like. Generally, impact investment in the United States not only brings a return on investment, but also produces beneficial results both for the environment and society. I think China can do something, but we have to see the ultimate goals. If we want to reduce or remove carbon dioxide, we can build good green projects, such as building many amusement parks. In fact, you are already using the impact investment model. I also hope to take the time to visit the Shenzhen market to see the development of impact.

Kalok Chan: The next question is for Mr. Soltan Mammadov. You just introduced the Heydar Aliyev Foundation. You have done some projects in Europe and Asia, then what about China? What I want to ask is, if you have no projects in China, do you plan to do projects in China in the future? If you do, which areas are you interested in?

Soltan Mammadov: At the end of my speech, I mentioned some of the work that we have done with the Chinese People's Association for Friendship with Foreign Countries. We signed a memorandum of understanding two years ago, under which we have already done some projects in China and Azerbaijan. Speaking of the focus of our foundation, we hope to build cultural bridges across different countries, different ethnic groups and different people. I am also very glad to highlight the memorandum of understanding signed with the Chinese People's Association for Friendship with Foreign Countries. We made several plans in 2018 and have also formulated plans for 2020, such as promoting the development of philanthropic projects in China and Azerbaijan. We also want to focus on the work between these two countries, so our foundation is very willing to work with the Chinese People's Association for Friendship with Foreign Countries to break the cultural barriers. In the past year, our projects have progressed very smoothly. In the next few years, we will be able to use the cooperative relationship between us as a model to promote it in other countries.

Kalok Chan: Speaking of the development of the Greater Bay Area, it is a "9+2" integration, including the flow of talent, capital, and logistics. I would like to ask about the integration of talent. Mr. Cheung Chun-yung, I would like to ask, from your point of view, what can be done to attract Hong Kong talent to enter the Greater Bay Area?

Thomas Cheung Tsun-yung: What we must do is to attract talent from Hong Kong and the world to the Greater Bay Area. Each city has different projects being promoted to attract the high-end talent it needs. Many cities offer bonus and subsidies to introduce technical teams, higher than those in many places in Hong Kong. We use funds to attract talent, and that's what we do most in the Greater Bay Area. How to recruit other talents so that more people are willing to develop their jobs, businesses, families, etc.? In fact, many people start from the culture, that is, to do a good job in cultural collaboration. What I have always wanted to promote in the National People's Congress is the integration of the systems, including the legal systems, of the Greater Bay Area and Hong Kong under the "One Country,

Two Systems". In terms of legal identity, social values and language, these things can be continuously integrated. After that, more people in Hong Kong will be willing to come back and live here. The Bay Area must undergo changes in the process of integration. The Bay Area in my mind is the best place to practice "One Country, Two Systems", and compared with the current Bay Area; our future Bay Area should be more inclusive, humanized, and institutionalized. This system is different from that of other cities in the Mainland. There are some customs in Hong Kong, such as jurors. There was no concept of jurors in mainland courts before, but now there is. Many values and methods have been integrated, and when these integrations are completed and gradually enriched, I believe that more people will be willing to come here. It is not only Hong Kong people who are coming, but also people from all over the world. The Chinese dream is not only for the Chinese people, but also for all mankind, so I think the Bay Area should be a place that can attract talent.

Kalok Chan: Thank you. Okay, now I have a few questions that I want to share and communicate with you. You mentioned philanthropy, including its development in the past period of time. We can see that, from the perspective of business cooperation and the perspective of enterprises, more and more enterprises are embracing philanthropy, so I would like to ask, from which aspects we can do more to encourage companies to do philanthropy, including improving their sense of enterprise social responsibility, and realizing the sustainable development of society and the environment, and how can we make our enterprises do more? Through persuasion or laws and regulations?

Wong H. Henry: I have always believed that when you want to build a new innovative city or an innovative university, the new company can make a choice as a newly-rising enterprise by giving 10% of its equity to mutual funds, the government, etc. These funds can be used jointly by the business community, and we can share the profits. Both methods are win-win. If people learn from experience, they will continue to start their businesses. Therefore, to be successful, more emphasis must be placed on resource allocation.

Soltan Mammadov: We are a foundation, and we make products to sell to investors. But in the past 10 years, we have clearly discovered that climate change and health are based on cases. Sometimes it is not philanthropy that can solve these problems. We must solve each problem systematically, which requires the project to have the potential for sustainable development and obtain support from the government and enterprises. The money we invest in must enable the company to develop itself, so we have made more project-based investments, as much as possible to bring sustainable investment or sustainability considerations. For enterprises like us, if we have projects with sustainable development, we can get donations.

Cheung Chun-Yung: The world connects everyone through artificial intelligence and technology. Of course, there are new systems and mechanisms to be established over time to help us cope with so many changes that have occurred. The equity that Wong H. Henry mentioned just now is a good method, but in the era of new technology, new technologies include AI, the Internet of things, and blockchain, will all be digital. In the digital world, it is relatively easy to establish rules and regulations, such as encouraging companies and institutions to donate 3% to 5% of their profits. Naturally, part of the net profits on the bank book can go to the foundation to support the resolution of a particular social problem. I have always believed that in the past or now, the donation is a relatively large task because a lot of preliminary work has to be done. In a new society, we may have new and systematic incentive policies to encourage companies and institutions to donate part of their profits. This is a change in the behaviour of people and institutions, and they must be slowly adapted to this change. We can make it happen.

Kalok Chan: I have a question to ask Chairman Zhang Yuanlong, what policies can our government adopt to promote the development of public welfare?

Zhang Yuanlong: I think the responsibility of the government is very clear, that is, to create a legal environment. There must be a social atmosphere of "good begets good, and evil begets evil", and as long as there is, many people will be willing to donate money. For enterprises, it means making profits, and profits bring about taxes, which can be used by the government on some welfare services. I think the highest state should be becoming social enterprises, because they pay taxes, and then make donations. The typical example is Zuckerberg, whose company makes money and then gives it to the foundation. At this point, the company's responsibility is very clear, which is to make money, pay taxes, and maintain employees—especially products. We have a lot of products now, which turn out to be garbage, and we need to spend money to dispose of this garbage. Therefore, when we make products, we must think about how to deal with them in the future. This is a very important contribution to the future environment.

Kalok Chan: What will Mr. Zhang Yuanlong tell the enterprises?

Zhang Yuanlong: To earn and give as much as you can.

Cheung Chun-Yung: I agree with Mr. Zhang Yuanlong's words very much that the enterprises should do everything they can to take responsibility, and then make donations to give society a better future.

Kalok Chan: For all our speakers, thank you. We hope further to promote the progress of enterprises and philanthropic work. Thank you very much. I have learned a lot from you today. Due to the limited time, I have to thank all speakers now. Chairman Zhang Yuanlong, Mr. Wong H. Henry, Mr. Soltan Mammadov, and Mr. Cheung Chun-yung, thank you.

XIV Closing Ceremony

Moderator: Li Xikui, Secretary-General of the Chinese People's Association for Friendship with Foreign Countries and Chairman of the China Friendship Foundation for Peace and Development

Guest Speech: Chen Yidan, Co-Founder of the Tencent Group, Initiator and Honorary Chairman of the Tencent Charity Foundation

Closing Speech: Massimo D'Alema, former Prime Minister of Italy

Li Xikui: Thanks to the moderator and all the distinguished guests. Next, let's welcome Mr. Chen Yidan, Chief Founder of Tencent Group, Founder and Honorary Chairman of Tencent Foundation, and Founder of "Yidan Prize" to give us the speech of "*Contribute to the Sustainable Development of Cross-border Philanthropy with Rational Spirits*".

Contribute to the Sustainable Development of Cross-border Philanthropy with Rational Spirits

Chen Yidan, Co-Founder of the Tencent Group, Initiator and Honorary Chairman of the Tencent Foundation

Distinguished guests, ladies and gentlemen, good afternoon. I'm glad to attend the fourth WPF. In these two days, philanthropic partners, experts and scholars from all over the world have gathered in Shenzhen, to explore how to promote the healthier development of philanthropy in the new era and how to help better build a great society. There are many good experiences worthy of careful review, and many views that arouse widespread resonance. In my opinion, the development and growth of global philanthropy undertakings require constant exchanges and integration of various philanthropic ideas and actions around the world. When we look at the differentiated and diversified development patterns in the context of globalization from an international perspective, we will learn from each other's experience, and jointly explore a way that transcends national boundaries and races and enables the sustainable development of philanthropy to benefit all.

China's philanthropic culture has a long history. According to the research of scholars, China is one of the earliest countries in the world to practice philanthropy. There were philanthropic institutions as early as the Western Zhou Dynasty. Chinese philanthropic thoughts, whether it is the benevolence of Confucians, the compassion of Buddhism, beneficence of Taoist or the expressions of the hundred schools of thought, are all expounding the concept of the welfare community. It can be said that the various beliefs in Chinese traditional culture mainly based on Confucianism, Buddhism, and Taoism are not only the ideological origin of Chinese philanthropic culture, but also the basis for the formation of philanthropic customs and practices in the society, which together constitute the core of China's philanthropic culture. For a long time, Chinese people have grown and lived in an atmosphere of good culture. However, the charity legislation in contemporary China was initiated in 2005 and deliberated in 2015. After ten years' preparation, the first *Charity Law* was promulgated in 2016.

The development of philanthropy in Western countries presents different historical and cultural imprints. Especially since modern times, with the changes of the relationship between productivity and production triggered by the Industrial Revolution, the concept, mode, operation mode, and supervision mechanism of philanthropy have undergone profound changes. Take the United Kingdom as an example. The philanthropic undertakings in the UK were originally based on the philanthropic spirit of Christianity, but they could not develop without the support of the government. Britain promulgated the *Poor Law* in the early 17th century, and established a system from taxpayers to aid recipients through compulsory taxation, reflecting the strong role of the government in the supervision. While the United States brought British philanthropic thoughts and causes to the new continent, it also made obvious integration and innovation, especially in the spontaneous mutual help among the people, so its philanthropy culture reflected the fraternity spirit. The other is the philanthropic spirit for the public to participate in public affairs. Since the 1830s, various public philanthropic organizations have spontaneously sprung up, and philanthropic activities have spread from individuals to groups, which ultimately promoted the formation of a modern philanthropic ecosystem in the United States. It can be said that in the past hundred years, the development of philanthropy in the United States cannot be separated from the support of a series of preferential measures, especially tax relief, system safeguard and system encouragement. It is not hard to see that philanthropy has different concepts, framework models and methods in different countries and cultural environments, and has been improved with the development of society. However, the essential pursuit of philanthropy is the same, that is, to seek welfare for a wide range of social groups. Philanthropy is beneficial to the public. In the long history of development, philanthropic cultures in various countries have learned from and blended with each other through cultural exchanges and technological development, and they have more and more similarities in the construction of transparent and convenient systems. At the same time, they have their characteristics under their respective cultural and social backgrounds and jointly promote the development and prosperity of global philanthropy.

What makes us proud is that in the past decade or so, Chinese Internet companies have become more and more deeply involved in the field of philanthropy. The combination of contemporary science and technology and philanthropy has undergone a surprising chemical reaction. Various online information platforms for fundraising constantly emerge and philanthropic social institutions, enterprises, the general public, and government are effectively linked together to promote China's philanthropy to be flourishing with public participation. It can be said that the form and development model of contemporary philanthropic undertakings have changed completely in China with the help of the Internet and other technologies.

In 2007, Tencent Foundation, the first philanthropic foundation in the Internet industry of China, was established, becoming one of the landmark events in the development of China's Internet philanthropy. At present, Tencent Charity has also become the world's largest Internet philanthropic fundraising platform, on which there are tens of thousands of philanthropic institutions and more than 70,000 philanthropic projects. The platform has received 247 million donations from 5.7 billion donors. Owning to the power of science and technology, and relying on the proliferation effect of Internet social interaction and product creativity, China's Internet philanthropy has been growing like a snowball. It is the power of science and technology that organically integrates the language of good in traditional Chinese culture with the carrier of contemporary information technology to form a unique Chinese sample of the development of Internet philanthropy, and all these developments only take more than 10 years.

While the Internet brings convenience to philanthropy, it also brings new challenges. Better communication conditions and smarter hardware devices make philanthropic activities easier and easier. How to make donors truly agree with the emotional resonance they have gained from philanthropic activities after the passion of a moment or one event has gone? How to turn one-off behaviours into the behavioural habit? How can Internet users and philanthropic institutions maintain trust for the long term? These issues have a great bearing on whether Internet technology can truly help global philanthropy to achieve sound and long-term development. I think the key to the answer lies in rational philanthropy, which first comes from thinking. Donation should be made after careful consideration, and it is also subject to the financial conditions of the donor. However, the extra time and energy expenditure such as the weighing and selection of philanthropic projects and the attention to the progress and implementation of the project after donation, maybe more important than pure capital investment. Rational philanthropy also requires social organizations and Internet philanthropy platforms to do a good job in institutional construction, and the formulation of internal management, information transparency and other rules for philanthropy organizations should be especially promoted. Rational philanthropy also demands a balance between the limited conditions and the noble demands of morality. The true rational philanthropy is the understanding and respect of the participants, and the essential development of philanthropy causes kindness to produce good results.

Internet technology makes it easier for people to reach the world and makes the global village a reality. Meanwhile, the development of global philanthropy ecology has also taken on new changes and characteristics. The fate of people in different parts of the world has never been as it is today, when the hole in the ozone layer has aroused global concern and discussion and the Amazon forest fire is burning the "lung of the earth". People living on the same earth need to transcend the national boundaries and pay attention to the global and mankind issues. No country can detach itself from these global issues, nor can it solve them on its own. People actually feel that the occasional fluttering of butterflies in the Amazon rainforest today has a real impact on each other's lives.

In 1820, 94% of the world's population lived in extreme poverty. In 1990, this figure was 34%, and in 2016 it was 9.6%. There are more rich people and fewer poor people, which means that we have more resources can be concentrated on philanthropy, and we will have more possibilities to explore new ways of philanthropy globally.

The pain points of society are the starting points of philanthropy. Tracing back to the history, the philosophy of "treating stomach diseases with good deeds" in traditional Chinese medicine can also inspire us. It means that both the roots and hopes of society lie in the future, future education and future people. In terms of education, global cooperation is also needed. All mankind can share good educational models, good educational research results, and good educational practices. The combination of education and philanthropy, and the combination of education and technology are not only to remedy human suffering but also to sow seeds and achieve long-term prosperity. Innovation is the core of global education development, and we can see that model innovation brings a new look to education development. In South America, for example, education shortages have encouraged innovation in educational equity models. Winners of the 2017 "Yidan Prize" and "Education Development Award" created a model that advocates student-centred and self-directed learning, where students are the masters and teachers are the leaders of learning, and there are no textbooks for teaching, but only study guides. Therefore, the new school model was created in response to the shortage of educational resources in Colombia, but it does not prevent it from pursuing a higher level of education. It is a low-cost, sustainable model of innovation, as well as a model of self-directed and collaborative learning. That is to say, the individualized education pursued by the developed cities has been realized and it is because of this that the new school model has gained international attention and support beyond the Colombian countryside. The United Nations Children's Fund (UNICEF) and the World Bank supported the research, and the World's Education Summit gave affirmation to it. These models have been extended to 16 countries on three continents, and technological innovation has also given a new look to the development of education.

Today, it has been a very successful exploration to connect high-quality educational resources to any place via Internet technology platforms. Professor Anant, the winner of the "Yidan Prize" for education practitioner in 2018, founded a non-profit online learning platform that has changed the lives of more than 20 million people around the world in the past six years. Its free and open curriculum has been adopted by more than 70 countries, including China, France and Russia, and more than 130 educational institutions around the world have cooperated with it as the educational partners. As knowledge and learning is boundless, science and technology can help us realize this beautiful educational ideal.

On the platform of Tencent Foundation, we can also see the realization of cross-border innovations in education and philanthropy, the implementation experience of many domestic education projects, and the discussion on international cooperation. Chinese philanthropy institutions cooperate with United Nations High Commissioner for Refugees (UNHCR), hoping to provide new educational opportunities for African girls who were displaced by the war. A Chinese Internet user can help a girl suffering from the African war go back to school by the number of steps he/she donates on WeChat; at the same time, he/she can call on more friends via Moments (a function of WeChat) to do good deeds together and integrate philanthropy into production. These touching stories and scenes let us see that when the Internet shortens the distance between people, the meaning and extension of philanthropy in philanthropy have expanded a lot than how we understood it conventionally. Philanthropy is no longer confined to a certain place, country, or form, but is trans-boundary and multi-method. It aims at pursuing the universal benefit of all mankind, with the purpose of bringing warmth and goodwill to the hearts of everyone in the world.

Contemporary philanthropy in China is rising with the development of the country. We should not forget the selfless help of Chinese people from all over the world to the Chinese mainland. When facing disasters, we are united as one and related by blood. At the same time, philanthropy and education are closely linked. There have been Mr. Tan Kah Kee, the leader of overseas Chinese in Southeast Asia who returned home and ran schools, overseas Chinese at home and abroad supporting the Hope Project to realize the dreams of hundreds of millions of children, and Yifu Buildings in every university, all of which are an encouragement to people and future generations, making us feel touched and grateful. Today, China is advancing rapidly. Chinese people at home and abroad are striving together for the philanthropy and contributing to the global society with Chinese model, Chinese wisdom and Chinese strength. I believe this is our common aspiration.

In this era of high globalization, we may face unresolved conflicts and problems arising from development. However, the trend of co-development of mankind and global cooperation and innovation remains unchanged, and we need to focus on the future. Especially at the current historical stage when AI, biotechnology and other technologies are booming, and different countries from the East to the West are transforming and innovating philanthropy and undertakings by making use of the Internet and technology in their ways. In the new wave of the information revolution, we have to adjust and reshape the society constantly, and philanthropy is playing an increasingly important role in this process. We hope that with a rational spirit, we will jointly promote the sustainable development of global philanthropy, and make it a driving force for all mankind to pursue a better world.

All of you here, I hope we can work together to write the mark of the civilization of our time with philanthropy, technology and education. Thank you!

Li Xikui: Mr. Chen Yidan told us that the Internet had given wings to philanthropy and technology has provided a driving force and a better engine for philanthropy. More importantly, we should have a real rational spirit. Thank you, Mr. Chen Yidan.

Distinguished guests and delegates, time is passing too fast. The fourth WPF is about to come to an end. While continuing the themes of talent education, youth development and children's health of previous forums, the forum has added new topics such as the caring finance and the caring business, increased the output and release of academic reports, and advocated the active participation of enterprises and individuals in philanthropic undertakings. It not only pays attention to pragmatic cooperation but also focuses on platform construction, realizing information exchange and resource sharing. Like-minded people respond to each other and bond naturally, and all our guests meet here for philanthropy.

Over the past two days, people from the political, business, academic and social sectors have engaged in constructive dialogues and discussions on a number of issues, achieving the collision of ideas in the philanthropic field and injecting new vitality into the development of philanthropy.

We should gather all wisdom and strength. Extending philanthropy to various fields and promoting the building of a Community with a Shared Future for Mankind is our aspiration for future philanthropy. We have invited the former Prime Minister of Italy to serve as a consultant for WPF, who has provided valuable guidance on the development of WPF and philanthropy. Now let's give a warm round of applause to welcome His Excellency Massimo D'Alema to give a closing speech.

Closing speech by Massimo D'Alema

Massimo D'Alema, Former Prime Minister of Italy

Ladies and gentlemen, good afternoon! It is a great pleasure for me to meet all of you here in Shenzhen, a young and open city. I am very happy to participate in the fourth WPF, and I want to thank you for inviting me to be the consultant of the forum. Every time I come to Shenzhen, I can feel its vigorous development and see the development of China. China is a huge market with potential for further development and a very bright future. In my opinion, China's development is, above all, the result of its tremendous achievements in reform and opening up. Secondly, China's strengthening in international cooperation has brought development. Finally, the "Belt and Road Initiative" has promoted the policies. At present, with the development of trade, China has established a strong partnership with other countries of the world. I believe that the "Belt and Road Initiative" will not only help China and other countries of the world to carry out more cooperation, but also can be copied for the co-building of the countries along the route of the "Belt and Road Initiative", and help us continuously promote the progress of human culture as well. As an Italian, I am deeply impressed by the "Belt and Road Initiative" Initiative. Both Italy and China are countries along the ancient Silk Road. Our ancestors adhered to a very beautiful ideal and hoped to pursue a better life. Therefore, using the Silk Road as a communication bridge and corridor for trade can continuously promote the development of civilization at that time. It was the Silk Road that closely linked the entire world.

China put forward the "Belt and Road Initiative" in 2013, including the Maritime Silk Road in the 21st Century, hoping to revitalize the ancient Silk Road. Why is globalization an irreversible trend? The so-called trade protectionism and trade barriers cannot stop the development of globalization. Now trade protectionism has become an issue of great concern to the world. When I was reading the *Financial Times*, I was surprised to see that the U.S. had a very obvious stock market decline due to the trade conflicts. The world economy, including that of the United States, has been hit hard by trade protectionism, so we need to return to rationality, which means we should strengthen our cooperation. As the director of Cities Alliance has said, the "Belt and Road Initiative" is proposed at the right time to help us continue to strengthen global cooperation, expand economic cooperation, and promote economic integration and global development. Moreover, it can continuously strengthen economic exchanges among countries, and provide more possibilities and opportunities for people-to-people exchanges among countries by building a new cooperation platform.

Philanthropy is undoubtedly also a very important part of our new vision for global development. In other words, we should reduce inequality, eliminate poverty as much as possible, and let people live with dignity. The development of the world brings many opportunities, but we should not let anyone be left behind since globalization is human-oriented. Philanthropy is a part of our culture and an important part of our religion. We have founded philanthropic institutions in China and Italy, and at the same time continue to promote people-to-people exchanges and communication. Under the "Belt and Road Initiative", Italy and China have conducted extensive exchanges and cooperation. A memorandum of understanding was signed in Italy, and relevant universities and philanthropic institutions have also been established in China to strengthen the bilateral cooperation. Later, we reached the consensus on strengthening bilateral cooperation in philanthropy between Italy and China, and strengthening mutual trust, including exchanges and mutual understanding in the WPF and China-related philanthropy activities, so as to build a truly peaceful global village.

The WPF hopes to continuously promote beneficial development, global exchanges, and personnel training, including mutual policy sharing and experience exchange. It has been mentioned in our fourth WPF the challenges and new trends encountered by philanthropy, including the relationship between the distribution of wealth and philanthropy. We are also very pleased to have distinguished guests from all over the world to join the discussion and help us envision the future of philanthropy. This excellent forum serves as a platform, and all our participants have been actively discussing their experiences and perspectives, including the experience and ideas of the development of philanthropy in their respective countries. I believe that philanthropy in the world will have a more promising prospect with your participation. If we look back, we can see that more and more philanthropic experts and scholars have joined the education field to help us strengthen talent training and achieve better cooperation, including promoting the development of the Greater Bay Area. These are new topics for us. I believe that the WPF is fruitful, and in order to achieve better development, I would like to propose the following suggestions. First, we shall continue to strengthen the interaction and exchange of philanthropic talent in the world, and continuously improve the quality and ability of practitioners in philanthropy. At the same time, we shall encourage them to share their experiences and learn from each other, and help us in return to continuously strengthen the professionalism of the world's philanthropy. Second, we should jointly explore how to establish a framework for bilateral or multi-party philanthropic cooperation.

Meanwhile, we must continue to increase the influence of WPF so that that philanthropic researchers can gain support from local governments as much as possible. Third, we should establish a mechanism for the WPF. On this mechanism, we should strengthen cooperation among countries along the route of the "Belt and Road Initiative" in the field of philanthropy to help us attract more countries to join the "Belt and Road Initiative" philanthropic mechanism, and encourage more countries to strengthen people-to-people exchanges, including cultural exchanges continuously. I believe that through our concerted efforts, WPF will become an excellent platform to continuously strengthen people-to-people exchanges, enhance people-to-people friendship, help us deepen understanding and trust, and truly form a shared vision to help us achieve peace and prosperity of human society.

The fourth WPF held on the International Day of Charity, mainly aims to deepen people's understanding of philanthropy and NGOs, and at the same time encourage stakeholders around the world, including motivating volunteers, to take action and participate in the activities. As a consultant of this WPF, I also hope that everyone can work together to solve the problems caused by globalization, and develop philanthropy together for the benefit of mankind. I also look forward to the opening of the 5th WPF in 2020. Thank you.

Li Xikui: Thank you very much, Mr. Massimo D'Alema. He just gave perfect and detailed elaboration of the relationship between the "Belt and Road Initiative" and philanthropy, and we can tell Mr. Massimo D'Alema recognizes and understands the "Belt and Road Initiative" very well. It has always been one of the goals of WPF to promote the construction of the "Belt and Road Initiative" with the power of philanthropy.

Part III

XV Release of Outcomes and Issuance of Certificates

Moderator: Li Xikui, Secretary-General of the CPAFFC and Chairman of the CFFPD

Li Xikui: Constant dripping water can wear stones. The WPF would not be successfully held or have produced such constructive outcomes today without the support of all parties. Next, let's invite Mr. Péter Medgyessy, Former Prime Minister of Hungary to issue certificates for the partners of WPF. Let's welcome the four delegates of the Shenzhen Commonweal Fund Federation, Enactus, TCL Charity Foundation and Give2Asia to the stage.

(Certificates Issuance)

Li Xikui: Thank you, Mr. Péter Medgyessy. Next, I would like to invite Mr. Massimo D'Alema, former Prime Minister of Italy, to issue certificates to the five support units of WPF.

Let's invite delegates from Shanxi Public Welfare Promotion Association, Shanghai Overseas Chinese Foundation, Zhejiang Association for Non-profit Organization, CCAFC, and Fujian Province Charity Federation to the stage.

(Certificates Issuance)

Li Xikui: Thank you, Mr. Massimo D'Alema, and also thank the relevant units for their support of this forum.

Li Xikui: Ladies and gentlemen! We have successfully carried out this forum and completed discussions on public health, talent training, social innovation and other topics, and we have conducted high-end dialogues on higher education, children welfare, international cooperation, etc. Many authoritative figures from various circles have delivered keynote speeches, offering advice and suggestions for the future development of the world's philanthropic undertakings, and achieving fruitful results. Next, we will launch a number of cooperation plans and immediately enter the link of the final result presentation of this forum.

First of all, let's invite Mr. Carles Llorens to launch the Regional and

Local Governments Philanthropy Promotion Cooperation Plan, and exchange memorandums with Ms. Deng Lan, Deputy Secretary-General of the China Friendship Foundation for Peace and Development.

(Startup Link)

Carles Llorens: Distinguished guests, dear friends, I am from Morocco. As you all know, we participate in public welfare undertakings and make the whole region more sustainable, and I will share it on behalf of our organization. There are 600 members in our organization. We are very happy to work with the Chinese People's Association for Friendship with Foreign Countries on a local philanthropic project of poverty alleviation. We also hope to present this project as the result of the WPF. Thank you.

Li Xikui: Next, Tseng Carter, Board Member of Give2Asia, Birger Stamperdahl, President & CEO of Give2Asia, George SyCip, Board Chairman of Give2Asia, and Ma Jiezhi Jennifer , Vice-President of BNY Mellon Wealth Management, will jointly launch the Philanthropy and Wealth Inheritance Plan.

(Initiation)

Carter Tseng: Distinguished guests, ladies and gentlemen, good afternoon. Now we announce the launch of Philanthropy and Wealth Inheritance Plan. Sponsors for this plan include Give2Asia, delegated by Chairman SyCip and President Birger, and BNY Mellon, delegated by Vice President Ma. Yesterday afternoon, we held a closed-door roundtable forum attended by more than 50 delegates. According to what has agreed yesterday, I will announce three action plans. The first action plan is to commit ourselves to philanthropy. I hope you can take the dedication and responsibility of philanthropy as your responsibility with active participation. The positive spirit and values of wealth shall be integrated into social construction and development. The second action plan is to establish a perpetual mechanism for the inheritance of good wealth, including corporate social responsibility funds, philanthropic trust and perpetual philanthropic funds. The third action plan is to establish an action network for international consultation and cooperation, including the co-construction of countries along the route of the "Belt and Road Initiative" in Asia and philanthropy in relevant areas of the countries under "South-South Cooperation". The areas covered include protection of the rights and interests of women and children, rural revitalization and development, public health and education equity, etc. Finally, I'd like to conclude with a quote from Steve Jobs: "People with passion can change the world for the better" Thank you.

Li Xikui: Next, I would like to invite Ms. Deng Lan, Deputy Secretary-

General of the CFFPD, to launch the Philanthropy for Future Competition Plan.

Deng Lan: Good afternoon, everyone. On behalf of the WPF, I am very pleased to announce the plan for the Philanthropy for Future Competition. The WPF will launch this competition by uniting international organizations such as Junior Achievement (JA), as well as institutions, enterprises and well-known universities from home and abroad, to provide youths around the world with a platform for communication, thinking, and creation. The platform will encourage and inspire the youth to use their original intention of good to innovate, use innovative thinking to promote public welfare practices, and contribute their wisdom and solutions to social development and human progress. We expect kindness could bring about forces for good, which support innovations that produce good results. Thank you.

Li Xikui: Next, let's invite Professor Ngai Sek-yum, Member of the Academic Committee of WPF, Chairman and Professor of Social Work Department, CUHK, and Professor Liu Qinglong, Member of the Academic Committee of WPF and Professor of School of Public Policy and Management, Tsinghua University, to launch the Social Services Leading Talents Training and exchange the Cooperation Agreements on the Master's Degree Education Program.

Steven Sek-Yum Ngai: How time flies. I remember that in 2018, we shared our cooperation plan in talent training with you. Now I would like to share our progress. In 2018, I mentioned to you that we should hold a seminar on social services in Hong Kong. Now, this seminar has been successfully held. Currently, we have more than 30 experts participating in social services, including experts from the United States, Singapore, Taiwan Area and Chinese mainland. In 2018, we held a very successful forum, including several parts of future cooperation that started with a doctorate in social service, aiming to find innovative social education and methods. In addition, we hoped to increase the training of talent for non-profit organizations. We will continue to cooperate and hope that the seminar can be held in Macao. Our meeting will be hosted by the City University of Macao and Macao Polytechnic University. Another cooperation we want to share with you is the training for leading talent in social services that we are currently working on. This is a program jointly completed by Tsinghua University and the CUHK. Teachers from these two universities teach the program, and students who complete their studies will receive bachelor's degree of the Leading Talent in Social Service from the CUHK and Tsinghua University. Moreover, I hope that such a jointly launched talent program can bring us leading talent in China's philanthropy. Only in this way can we introduce leading talent into innovative services, improve the efficiency of social services, and help us better adapt to the development of this society. Our courses are mainly conducted in Beijing, and we are now preparing to recruit the first batch of students. It will be a two-year program, and all our students will be enrolled once they receive their admission letters. We will continue to inform you of our follow-up progress in talent training. Thank you.

Li Xikui: Next, Let's welcome Huang Zhenping, Convener of the Forum Preparation Team and Deputy Dean of Institute for Philanthropy Tsinghua University, and the representative of the Shenzhen Commonweal Fund Federation to launch the Foundation's International Friendly Cooperation.

The representative of the Shenzhen Commonweal Fund Federation: I am very pleased to announce the launch of the Foundation's International Friendly Cooperation on behalf of the Shenzhen Commonweal Fund Federation and the WPF. Shenzhen Commonweal Fund Federation will join hands with WPF to build the International Exchange and Cooperation Committee of Shenzhen Commonweal Fund Federation. We will promote more than 400 public welfare foundations in Shenzhen to "go global" and conduct industry exchanges, project cooperation, and resource interfacing with the Guangdong-Hong Kong-Macao Greater Bay Area, countries along the route of the "Belt and Road Initiative", and outstanding foundations in Europe and the United States. We will also invite outstanding foundations from the countries as mentioned above and regions for exchange and cooperation. Our Shenzhen Commonweal Fund Federation and the WPF will build the strength of Shenzhen, the image of Shenzhen, and the demonstration of Shenzhen of the philanthropic industry. Thank you!

Li Xikui: The above five cooperation programs are not only the wisdom of all the guests present, but also what we strive for. With the release of the plan, the fourth WPF will come to a successful conclusion. Please enjoy the forum highlights video.

(Video)

图书在版编目(CIP)数据

慈善湾区 美好生活：第四届世界公益慈善论坛：上下册：汉英对照／《慈善湾区 美好生活：第四届世界公益慈善论坛》编写组编. -- 北京：社会科学文献出版社，2020.10

ISBN 978-7-5201-7044-4

Ⅰ.①慈… Ⅱ.①慈… Ⅲ.①慈善事业-世界-文集-汉、英 Ⅳ.①D57-53

中国版本图书馆CIP数据核字（2020）第144418号

慈善湾区 美好生活（上下册）

——第四届世界公益慈善论坛

编　　者／本书编写组

出 版 人／谢寿光
组稿编辑／刘骁军
责任编辑／姚　敏　柴　宁
文稿编辑／王　娇

出　　版／社会科学文献出版社·集刊分社（010）59367161
地址：北京市北三环中路甲29号院华龙大厦　邮编：100029
网址：www.ssap.com.cn
发　　行／市场营销中心（010）59367081　59367083
印　　装／三河市龙林印务有限公司

规　　格／开　本：787mm×1092mm　1/16
印　张：37.25　插　页：3.5　字　数：583千字
版　　次／2020年10月第1版　2020年10月第1次印刷
书　　号／ISBN 978-7-5201-7044-4
定　　价／190.00元（上下册）